Coveted lands and seas of the Mauritian

Mauritius lost the Chagos and Tromelin islands to the big powers coveting its territories and seas, the United Kingdom and France, respectively, and now wants them back (See inside for latest developments). The maps on the back cover of the book and the one below of the shared continental plateau (Jint Marine Area) between Mauritius and the Seychelles, show that Mauritius, although a small island-state, Mauritius has one of the largest Exclusive Economic Zones (EEZ) in the world covering a total area of 1.9 million square kilometers. The JMA area is the joint maritime area shared by Mauritius and the Seychelles.

The back cover map is contained in a document of the Government of Mauritius, *"From The Ocean Economy"*, Prime Minister's Office, Government of Mauritius, December 2013. The one below was jointly submitted by Mauritius and Seychelles to the UN Commission on the Limits of the Continental Shelf in 2008 and was approved.

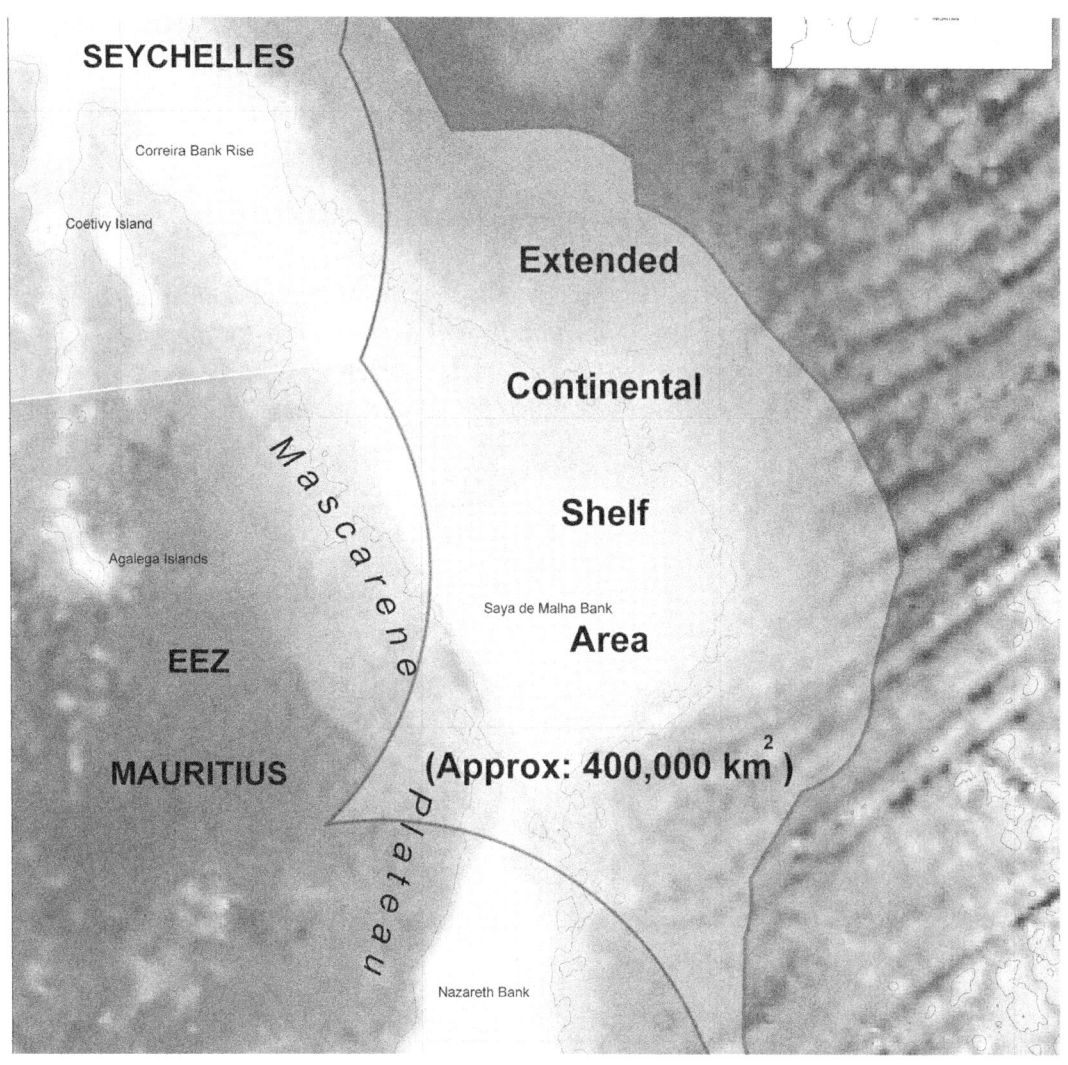

Printed by:

All rights reserved. No part of this publication may be reproduced or transmitted, in any form or by any means, without permission.

SYDNEY SELVON
A NEW COMPREHENSIVE HISTORY OF MAURITIUS

Volume 2: From British Mauritius to the 21st Century - 2nd Edition

"No person should have to fight inch by inch for equal rights, equal education, and equal political representation...Today... in a spirit of reconciliation, Mauritians in Mauritius (should) ensure that those Mauritians who have emigrated, and continue to do so for family and professional reasons, are not branded as 'traitors' – a sad term used during a Diaspora convention a few years ago... the Mauritian people must recognise the fact that all communities have made a vital contribution to our history, irrespective of their origins."

(From the Report of the Truth and Justice Commission on the descendants of slaves and indentured labour, submitted to the President of the Republic of Mauritius in 2011.)

"If there is no struggle, there is no progress. Those who profess to prefer freedom and yet depreciate agitation, are people who want crops without ploughing the ground; they want rain without thunder and lightning; they want the ocean without the roar of its many waters. The struggle may be a moral one, or it may be a physical one, or it may be both. But it must be a struggle. Power concedes nothing without a demand. It never did and it never will."

(Frederick Douglass (1818-1895), escaped slave, author, editor of the North Star, and later the New National Era, abolitionist, orator, statesman and reformer. From his autobiography, *Narrative of the Life of Frederick Doughass, An American Slave*, 1845)

M.DS Editions 2017-2018. E-mail: sydneyselvon@gmail.com

© Sydney Selvon ISBN -

All rights reserved. No part of this publication may be reproduced or transmitted, in any form or by any means, without permission.

Port-Louis: the Champ de Mars from the 19th to the 21st century

Introduction to Volume 2

From the 19th century to the 20th : The way we were

This second volume of A New Comprehensive History of Mauritius leads the reader from the aftermath of the 1886 general election to the early 20th century when Mauritius had radically changed mainly on the social and economic fronts and then to 21st century. Communications had also greatly improved with the external world. But in the field of politics, prior to 1948, there had been absolutely no progress in terms of the democratic rights of the masses of workers, planters, labourers and even those of the lower bourgeoisie classes, composed of all communities, who were not rich enough to vote.

The next chapter starts with the events following the first parliamentary elections, but an incursion into the Mauritius of the early 20th century at this stage is a leap forward into time, more precisely in the early 1900s, is necessary to better understand the overall evolution of the country from one century to another. We are dealing here with the transition from Beaugeard's era to the first major popular political mobilisation of the majority of the population accomplished by Dr. Eugène Laurent, often referred to by the British at the Colonial office as an 'Indian' leader, as we will see later, probably because of his ancestry, and Gandhi's envoy to Mauritius, Manilal Maganlal Doctor.

During the three decades that elapsed, a majority of the new Indian immigrants had settled in Mauritius and a rich and prosperous bourgeoisie had emerged, composed of sugar estate owners and planters and successful traders and people of other professions. Evolving in parallel, the elite of the Coloured population also produced a prosperous bourgeoisie. Indians and Creoles of the petites bourgeoisies and working classes did not yet have the right to vote simply because they did not belong to the multiethnic club of people, including those of the Indian immigrants and prosperous Coloured people and Creoles who were rich enough to enjoy the voting right and who, in their majority, voted to the Legislative Council a majority of conservative representatives, often dubbed by adversaries as 'the landed interests' during the Legislative Council debates. A look at the voting patterns of the members of the Council and their speeches provides a good insight, as will be seen later on, into the 'status consciousness' resulting, as in all human societies, from the process of social stratification, as discussed in detail in the first volume. [1]

In the early 1900s, Mauritian society is viewed from outside in some detail in such publications as Mauritius Illustrated [2] in 1915, and the 1911 Encyclopedia Britannica. [3] We provide references to the first publication named in the two volumes, and it is worthwhile to read below some extracts from the 1911 Encyclopedia Britannica where Mauritius is depicted as a rather successful colony on the economic front, albeit without touching, like Mauritius Illustrated, on the plight of the working masses of labourers and artisans and the unemployed. Nevertheless, there are elements of the descriptions of the island that are worth reading.

Excerpts (readers will also notice the class/ethnic prejudices expressed and also that the Creoles, here, are the Whites born in the colonies as per the normal dictionary meaning):

"The inhabitants consist of two great divisions, those of European blood, chiefly French and British, together with numerous half-caste people, and those of Asiatic or African blood. The population of European blood, which calls itself Creole, is greater than that of any other tropical colony; many of the inhabitants trace their descent from ancient French families, and the higher and middle classes are distinguished for their intellectual culture. French is more commonly spoken than English. The Creole class is, however, diminishing, though slowly, and the most numerous section of the population is of Indian blood...

"...the total population in 1901 was 373,336.2 This total included 198,958 Indo-Mauritians, i.e. persons of Indian descent born in Mauritius, and 62,022 other Indians. There were 3,509 Chinese, while the remaining 108,847 included persons of European, African or mixed descent, Malagasy, Malays and Sinhalese. The Indian female population increased from 51,019 in 1861 to 115,986 in 1901. In the same period the non-Indian female population but slightly varied, being 56,070 in 1861 and 55,485 in 1901. The Indo-Mauritians are now dominant in commercial, agricultural and domestic callings, and much town and agricultural land has been transferred from the Creole planters to Indians and Chinese. The tendency to an Indian peasant proprietorship is marked. Since 1864 real property to the value of over £1,250,000 has been acquired by Asiatics. Between 1881 and 1901 the number of sugar estates decreased from 171 to 115, those sold being held in small parcels by Indians. The average death-rate for the period 1873-1901 was 32.6 per moo. The average birth-rate in the Indian community is 37 per moo; in the non-Indian community 34 per moo. Many Mauritian Creoles have emigrated to South Africa. The great increase in the population since 1851 has made Mauritius one of the most densely peopled regions of the world, having over 520 persons per square mile."

It is to be noted that there were also Malagasys, Malays and Sinhalese, who must have blended into the other communities, but the languages of those people and their cultural traditions must have been still surviving, more or less, in those days. The author of this book has always advocated the introduction in Mauritian schools of the Malagasy language, which is closely related to the Malay language (Madagascar is an Afro-Asian society due to massive population migration from Southeast Asia from about 1,000 years ago). One also notes that in Mauritius Illustrated, as already observed in the first volume, the 'Indo-Creoles' are often treated as one large entity in comparison to the others and that when the term Indo-Mauritians is used, it means Hindus, Muslims and Christian Indians.

Another aspect is communications, which had also developed considerably from the 19th century. The Encyclopedia Britannica observed:

---

[1] Volume 1, Chapter 33.
[2] Op cit. (Volume 1).
[3] < http://www.1911encyclopedia.org/Mauritius> Accessed 11 July 2012.

"There is a regular fortnightly steamship service between Marseilles and Port Louis by the Messageries Maritimes, a four-weekly service with Southampton via Cape Town by the Union Castle, and a four-weekly service with Colombo direct by the British India Co.'s boats. There is also frequent communication with Madagascar, Reunion and Natal. The average annual tonnage of ships entering Port Louis is about 750,000 of which five-sevenths is British. Cable communication with Europe, via the Seychelles, Zanzibar and Aden, was established in 1893, and the Mauritius section of the Cape-Australian cable, via Rodriguez, was completed in 1902.

"Railways connect all the principal places and sugar estates on the island, that known as the Midland line, 36 miles long, beginning at Port Louis crosses the island to Mahebourg, passing through Curepipe, where it is 1822 ft. above the sea. There are in all over 120 miles of railway, all owned and worked by the government. The first railway was opened in 1864. The roads are well kept and there is an extensive system of tramways for bringing produce from the sugar estates to the railway lines. Traction engines are also largely used. There is a complete telegraphic and telephonic service."

There is also an interesting description of the island's economy:

"The soil is suitable for the cultivation of almost all kinds of tropical produce, and it is to be regretted that the prosperity of the colony depends almost entirely on one article of production... Guano is extensively imported as a manure, and by its use the natural fertility of the soil has been increased to a wonderful extent... Of the exports, sugar amounts on an average to about 95% of the total. The quantity of sugar exported rose from 102,000 tons in 1854 to 189,164 tons in 1877... The Brussels Sugar Convention of 1902 led to an increase in production, the average annual weight of sugar exported for the three years 1904-1906 being 182,000 tons. The value of the crop was likewise seriously affected by the causes mentioned, and by various diseases which attacked the canes. Thus in 1878 the value of the sugar exported was £3,408,000; in 1888 it had sunk to £1,911,000, and in 1898 to £1,632,000. In 1900 the value was £1,922,000, and in 1905 it had risen to £2,172,000. India and the South African colonies between them take some two-thirds of the total produce. The remainder is taken chiefly by Great Britain, Canada and Hong-Kong."

Aloe fibre was another major product of Mauritius in those days:

"Next to sugar, aloe-fibre is the most important export, the average annual export for the five years ending 1906 being 1840 tons. In addition, a considerable quantity of molasses and smaller quantities of rum, vanilla and coco-nut oil are exported.

Mauritius had a deficit in her trade balance with other countries:

"The average annual value of the exports for the ten years1896-1905 was £ 2,153,159; the average annual value of the imports for the same period £1,453,089. These figures when compared with those in years before the beet and bounty-fed sugar had entered into severe competition with cane sugar, show how greatly the island had thereby suffered. In 1864 the exports were valued at £2,249,000; in 1868 at £2,339,000; in 1877 at £4,201,000 and in 1880 at £3,634,000. And in each of the years named the imports exceeded £2,000,000 in value. Nearly all the aloe-fibre exported is taken by Great Britain and France, while the molasses goes to India."

We learn also that the Chinese in Mauritius harvest the sea for some delicacies that they export to the Far East:

"Among the minor exports is that of bambara or sea-slugs, which are sent to Hong-Kong and Singapore. This industry is chiefly in Chinese hands. The great majority of the imports are from Great Britain or British possessions."

It was in that already complex social setup that the first large mass struggles of the 20st century were initiated, for the first time in the history of the island, by Dr. Eugène Laurent and Manilal Doctor.

Chapter 35, which follows, deals with the main events that occurred after the birth of Parliament."

Chapter 35

The rise and fall of the Democrats and the Liberals

The party system, which had seemed to take roots during the electoral campaign that led to the 1886 general elections, weakened subsequently during Parliamentary debates.

The conservatives of the Reform Party had the support of a multiethnic mix: the affluent classes of Whites, Coloured and Indians. The Democrats, sometimes dubbed as radicals, were on the left side of the political arena, in comparison with the Reformists, in the sense that they claimed an electoral franchise that would reach out to the lower bourgeoisie and the skilled workers, and they were supported by another multiethnic mix of similar racial and religious composition, from the middle and lower middle classes as well as the artisans of Port-Louis. In truth, they were in good position to ask for a still lower franchise and start a mass movement.

Actually, Beaugeard had begun campaigning in Parliament against a fiscal system which weighed heavily on the poor and asked the abolition of duties on basic food items, while Edgar Antelme came up with a motion in favour or an extension of the electoral franchise: the introduction of "universal suffrage."

Motion for 'universal suffrage' by Edgar Antelme

Edgar Antelme, who had been elected as a Democrat, proposed a motion on November 4, 1887, asking the Legislative Council to vote in favour of constitutional changes *"in the interests of the good working of the elective principle and the good administration of the Colony."* He then went on to attack the 1886 electoral franchise which he found *"too restricted"* and even *"a shame"* for the country. The 1886 Constitution, he said, *"has produced a very restricted list of electors, the number of whom is mere derision for a country which is so rich and populous."* [1]

Antelme went to the extent of proposing *"universal suffrage"* in his speech where, however, he did not include the Indians belonging to the working classes at the bottom of the social ladder, that is, the indentured labourers and the poorer classes generally. Arguing for that radical electoral reform, he admitted that he found it difficult for him to say that he was speaking in the name of the population of the country.

What would have been the result of Antelme's limited version of universal suffrage? First, it was, at that date, the boldest proposal regarding franchise, one that was the widest ever proposed in the country. It is worthy to note, at this stage, the following factors that influenced thinking in those days about the Indian vote: [2]

- The Indians/Indo-Mauritians were employed on temporary contracts, and, initially, a few thousands of them had been returning to India, which led many people, even the liberal-minded, to believe that they had to be left out of the political system, at least until they settled down as permanent citizens. Nevertheless, when one reads Antelme's speech, especially about his constituents, and on the basis of census data, a huge proportion of Indians had settled down permanently, many working as small planters and doing countless jobs also outside the sugar and even the agricultural sector in general. Those people needed to be better served by the State, and so they had the right to be able to democratically choose their political representatives.

- Another fact is that, anyway, Antelme's franchise proposal was revolutionary for the times as it would have considerably increased the number of Indian voters, which was only 300 in 1886, mainly rich planters, some of whom were sugar factory owners, and traders, to include additionally those immigrants who had left the sugar estates and formed with the Creole working and lower-middle classes, an extremely promising potential for a democratic mass movement. Antelme's limited version of the universal suffrage would have paved the way, in any case, and much earlier in our history (that is, much before 1948), for the extension of the franchise to more employees, workers and self-employed at the lower rungs of the social hierarchy.

Actually, Edgar Antelme was courting seriously the Indian electorate. During his interventions, he strongly pleaded in favour of a better system for providing them with clean water, as at Montagne Ory, where he described the water problem in detail and challenged a colleague to accompany him to see how carrying buckets of water from the Pailles public fountains was a painful exercise for the villagers. He used to boast of *"My Indians"* just in the same

---
1 Legislative Council. Debate, 4th November 1887.
2 Author's analysis.

way, probably, as the British liberal gentleman-politician who spoke in a paternalistic tone of his working class supporters. It appears from his speech that this Franco-Mauritian member of the Legislative Council was popular among the non-voting section of his electoral district, an emerging Indian bourgeoisie of non-sugar workers, and he wanted them to register as electors.

Antelme, however, while presenting his motion, clearly stated that he knew that it would be rejected by the Council. Nevertheless, Beaugeard's refusal to vote in favour of the motion was quite surprising and it was then that the Democratic Party split, with Antelme criticising de Coriolis and Beaugeard, both elected in Port-Louis. It must be remembered that Beaugeard had been also a candidate in Moka and had lost. He did not trust the rising Indian bourgeoisie which, as **Le Cernéen** had predicted, turned out to be, as voters, as politically conservative as the other bourgeoisies. In fact, the professional and business classes were becoming increasingly multiethnic. Beaugeard's mistake was probably confusing the petites bourgeoisies of Indians with the wealthy Indo-Mauritians who generally voted with the conservatives.

How could Antelme, a Franco-Mauritian, go to such lengths as asking for *'universal suffrage,'* at least for the petites bourgeoisies, including skilled workers, self-employed Indians and Creoles who were successful as artisans, small traders and planters? Firstly, Franco-Mauritians were never a homogenous ethnic group and like other communities were subject to social stratification. Secondly, it should be borne in mind that Antelme was speaking three years after the Reform Act of 1884 which, in Britain, had just extended, for the first time, the right to vote to the agricultural labourer. One should also take note that the previous Reform Act, which had extended the vote to the urban working classes in Britain in 1867, had been presented by the Conservatives, and Antelme, who was not a Conservative, but closely followed the political scene in the UK, has espoused the increasingly liberal views of a large fraction of the British political establishment.

In his speech, Antelme alluded to what was the order of the day in Britain. If the Liberals were to win power in Britain, he said, the franchise in Mauritius would have to be lowered. In a polemic opposing him and fellow Democrat de Coriolis during the 1884 debate, he asked the latter to read the **Pall Mall Gazette**, a prestigious British publication, to inform himself of the serious possibility of universal suffrage in Great Britain soon.

Restricted franchise causes friction in the country, he said. *"A man possessing a number of rupees can vote, whereas another man who does not have the same number of rupees cannot participate in the vote,"* he added. He also declared that he would be, henceforth, following a different political path from Beaugeard. He told Coriolis that promises made to the electorate by them should be fulfilled concerning the right to vote. Otherwise, he said, one should not be contented with just the democratic label and accept to be considered officially of an inferior parliamentary status in comparison with the official and nominated members. [1]

Beaugeard explained very briefly his stand, without refuting fully Antelme's arguments. He was probably already a broken man, uncertain about his political future. The man who had petitioned London against Pope Hennessy, the father of the Mauritius Constitution of those days, said, *"Our Constitution is a first step in the path of political liberties. It allows the country to be represented in the Legislature and to be consulted therein."* Beaugeard also said that *"employés are excellent electors,"* meaning that he was satisfied with the votes of the salaried lower middle class bourgeoisie who voted for him. He also summed up his position on the 1886 Constitution as follows: [2]

"My opinion (...) is as follows: firstly, that the census be so extended as to ensure a larger number of electors; and, secondly, that the number of elected members be such as to be numerically superior at least by one, to the number of Government Members taken together, the officials and the nominees, including the President of the Council."

Edgar Antelme was not convinced. He was himself proposing that the number of electors should be increased. The motion was then put to vote and rejected by 9 votes against 2.

Only Edgar Antelme and Dr. N.A. Edwards (elected as a Reformist in 1886) voted for, while the division of votes showed the following members as having voted against the motion: Ferguson, Arlanda, Ambrose, Fraser, Greene, Meldrum, Rouillard, Lovell, H. Leclézio, Célicourt Antelme, Coriolis, Beaugeard, and the seven government public officers who were nominated members of the Council.

Even if the motion had no chance of being approved, had the Democratic Party voted collectively and held public meetings with the masses of Creoles and Indians economically active outside the sugar estates who would have

---
1 Legislative Council. Debate, op cit.
2 Ibid.

Dr. Eugène Laurent and Manilal Mangalall Doctor

The most important political event of the beginning of the 20th was the foundation of Action Libérale by Dr. Eugène Laurent (top left), joined by Gandhi's envoy, Manilall Doctor (top right). Below, a page from the Stateman's Year Book 1921 describing Mauritius.

Prominent representatives of the 'Francos'

Members of the Legislative Council representing the 'Francos': Clockwise from top: Joseph Duclos, Henri Leclézio, Maurice Martin and Euréka, Leclézio's sumptuous villa in Moka, today an architectural and historical attraction for local and foreign visitors.

been included in an enlarged franchise as proposed by Edgar Antelme, history might perhaps changed course. The Democrats could have presented petitions to the governor and to the British government in London, and that would have given birth to a real mass movement years before the coming of Dr. Eugène Laurent's and Manilal Doctor's Action Libérale party.

One more reference to the situation in Great Britain is necessary here, as the decision-makers of Mauritius closely monitored political developments there, like reading the **Pall Mall Gazette**. The British party system also had started developing in the second half of the 19th century from two main political currents, one represented by the Carlton Club of the Tories (the Conservatives) established in 1832, and the other by the Reform Club of the Whigs, constituted in 1836.

The National Union of Conservative and Constitutional Associations formed in 1867 gave birth to the modern Conservative Party and the National Liberal Federation founded in 1877 gave birth to the Liberal Party, while the Labour Party was only created in 1906 by the Labour Representation Committee, constituted in 1900 as a coalition of the Social Democratic Federation (1881), the Fabian Society (1883) and the Independent Labour Party (1893), to which delegates of more than 60 trade unions joined their forces. The pace of political evolution in UK was gradual and slow.

After Edgar Antelme's motion, the Democratic Party faded out of existence rapidly, in spite of the common stand its members adopted the following year against the return of Pope Hennessy. Edgar Antelme, sometimes quick-tempered, fought at least two duels, one in Mauritius against a man called C. de la Roche, and one in Réunion Island against another person called Ducray. He obtained, in the Legislative Council, in 1889, the appointment of a commission of inquiry in the affairs of Rodrigues.

As for Beaugeard, he focused on his struggle for the rights of the salaried classes among whom were a number of electors who supported him in Port-Louis, especially the employees of the Railways Department at Plaine Lauzun. But he was opposed by the conservative elements of the Legislative Council on a number of issues on which he defended the interests of the salaried employees. [1]

On the question of taxation, he proposed a new system that would alleviate the burden under which the under-privileged classes were groaning. He obtained the approval of the British State Secretary in 1888 for his proposals in favour of the abolition or reduction of duties on the food of the poorer classes and the imposition of house and land taxes so as to create a new fiscal order protecting the poor and make the richer classes finance public expenses. He obtained for the salaried employees of Port-Louis the right to vote at the municipal elections.

On another important issue, he opposed new public holidays, asserting that workers who depended on daily wages would lose money. It was thus that he opposed the petition to the Legislative Council of the Muslim leaders of the colony for two religious holidays, though other members were in favour. But he also opposed the Catholic Church, then under the complete control of the richest classes of the country and applying segregation in churches, when the Bishop of Port-Louis tried to extend the English scholarships to private secondary institutions. The leading Franco-Mauritian colonists had resented the opening of the Royal College, as from 1832, to the Coloured persons. They had founded private schools where several of them sent their children for secondary education. Historian Quenette writes that as far as 1944, Raoul Rivet made remarks in the legislature about the risk of granting some favours to any institution which *"would be communal and confessional."*

When Bishop Meurin, following in Bishop Sacarisbrick's step, mobilised the conservative Catholics and a number of newspapers, and petitioned the British government about the English scholarships, Beaugeard organised a meeting and sent a counter-petition in January 1888. Edgar Antelme opposed Beaugeard on that issue. But Beaugeard obtained a rare support in the press: that of **Le Progrès Colonial** of Evenor Hitié which considered the supporters of Meurin as the enemies of democracy. The British government maintained the monopoly of the Royal College. Later Beaugeard asked in the Legislative Council whether it was advisable to send away from the country Mgr Meurin so that peace and order could be properly maintained among the population. That was refused by the government.

Beaugeard, writes his biographer R. Quenette, had well defined opinions about religious instruction in schools. He was not against religious instruction *"of any denomination"* but was opposed to making it *"the ground work upon which to erect the structure of public instruction, primary as well as secondary."* On such issues, he was strongly opposed by the conservatives who, however, sometimes recognised his political talents. They supported him when,

---

[1] Unless otherwise stated, on Beaugeard's life and actions in the Legislative Council: **Le Grand Beaugeard**, op cit; **Legislative Council Debates**.

for the first time, he obtained, by way of motion in the Legislative Council, that two elected members be appointed to sit as members of the Executive Council of the government, which, in those days, was the equivalent of today's ministerial Cabinet. [1]

Beaugeard was quite pathetic towards the end of his career. After he resigned by explaining that he had financial problems, many of the conservatives supported him in his quest for a pension for past services in the public service where he had been victim of gross injustice. When he became a nominated member of the Legislative Council, Edgar Antelme, who had begun his career in Beaugeard's Democratic Party, clashed with him with rare virulence in the Council. Finally, he abandoned active politics in 1895, after the dissolution of the Council prior to the 1896 general elections.

Before his death in 1898 at the age of 66, after distinguished services as the chief medical officer of the mental hospital at Beau Bassin, he witnessed the first steps of another brilliant medical practitioner, the still young Dr. Eugène Laurent, who was candidate, but lost the contest against the conservatives. Even R. Quenette, an admirer of Beaugeard, who was, undeniably, a great Mauritian politician and a distinguished leader of the lower middle classes of the Coloured and Creole populations, asks himself whether Beaugeard would not have been better inspired to be more "*audacious*" in his political programme in the face of the resistance put up by the upper classes of the country who had allied themselves with governor Pope Hennessy.

Anyway, Beaugeard and his Democratic Party failed in those days with regard to a crucial duty for any anti-Oligarchy party: the duty of seeking support among the under-privileged masses of former slaves and Indian immigrants for their political action. Beaugeard was already well aware, in 1887, of the importance of the Indian immigrants as they were actually settling in large numbers in the island, as he himself admitted in Council on September 20, 1887: [2]

"At one time, the Indian population of the Island consisted almost entirely of the indentured labourers; (...) The direct Indian element here has dwindled almost to nothing; we have now to deal with a class of Creole Indians."

He meant the Indians born in and so, native to Mauritius, or Indo-Mauritians, as they were also called in the past. The idea of universal suffrage could have given the Democrats a better chance
to prove their faith in real democracy and to demonstrate also that Edgar Antelme was not that eccentric politician some believed him to be, especially because of the duels he fought.

Another apparent contradiction of Beaugeard's group was their stand concerning the Civil Service Cooperative Stores, which existed in the 1880's. During a debate in Council, Coriolis said that he was in favour of the cooperative movement and that *"the principle of cooperation is one which is gaining ground daily, not only in England, but in all the great centres of Europe, and even of the world."* [3] But he and Beaugeard, nevertheless, accused the cooperative society of competing with the private trading class by selling goods to the general public and not to its shareholders only.

However, there may have been no contradiction if one also understands that the small traders must have been complaining to their elected representatives about the cooperative society selling to the general public. Later, in the 20th Century, the cooperative movement was to help save from extinction the small Indian and Creole self-employed persons in the areas of farming and animal-rearing. Extending the cooperative movement proved to be a positive mass political action in the 20th Century. [4]

All general elections after Beaugeard continued to be dominated by the conservatives, dubbed the Oligarchs. As already seen in the previous chapter, at the Colonial Office as well as in the British Parliament, there was an increasingly negative opinion among various top officials regarding the unchallenged rule of the oligarchy of Mauritius and the under-representation of the Indo-Mauritians and there was also strong suspicion that the Franco-Mauritians were not loyal to the Crown when it came to conflicting situations between Britain and France as was the case in 1898 in Madagascar. [5] This was what prompted Joseph Chamberlain, Secretary of State for the Colonies, in a correspondence with the Mauritius Governor Sir Charles Bruce, to propose the nomination of an Indo-Mauritian

---

1 The decision was obtained in 1889. In: ***Select documents on the constitutional history of the British Empire and Commonwealth***, op cit: P.P. 1890 XLVIII (5897) pp. 615-616. A footnote comment is that this development was *"almost without precedent among the Crown colonies."*
2 Legislative Council. Debate 20th September 1887.
3 Mauritius Legislative Council debates.
4 Author's analysis of the historical evolution of the cooperative movement.
5 See previous chapter.

to the Council and the lowering of the franchise to increase the Indian electorate, to which Bruce objected and proposed instead to use his power of nomination *"to include – if not members of the [Indian] community – at least a majority of members prepared to support the just and reasonable claims of the Indian community."* [1]

It was up to Dr. Eugène Laurent to try reverse the course of history. He was finally elected in Port-Louis in 1906 and, during the following year, he formed the Action Libérale. Laurent was eventually helped by Manilal Doctor, an Indian Lawyer sent by Karamchand Mohandas Gandhi, the future Mahatma Gandhi, who had visited Mauritius briefly in 1901 on his way back to India from South Africa.

Dr. Eugène Laurent unites the Indo-Creole masses

Dr. Eugène Laurent managed to do what Beaugeard had failed to accomplish: within the severe limits of an electoral franchise restricted to a handful of rich, he forged an alliance of the anti-Oligarch elements among the Coloured, Creoles, the small White bourgeois and the Indo-Mauritian small planters and workers. That coalition caused real panic, by 1911, among the affluent classes, who were afraid that they were on the way to be swept out of the monopolistic position they held on political power over the country. It was the first time that the masses entered the political scene, even though for a brief period. [2]

Like Beaugeard, Dr. Eugène Laurent had been a laureate of the English Scholarship at the Royal College in 1876. He was then 17. His biography in **Mauritius Illustrated** states that he was *"a medallist in medical jurisprudence, clinical medicine, pathology, materia medica, and therapeutics, and M.B., London University, 1881; B.S., 1883, Assistant to Dr. Holland, Soho Square Hospital, 1880; Clinical Assistant to Sir Douglas Powell, Brompton Hospital, 1881-1883; Senior Resident, Bedford Hospital, 1884-1885."* Back in Mauritius in 1885, he continued to write remarkable scientific articles in The London Medical Journal and The Lancet, *"one of these articles being reprinted in Sir Morel McKenzie's book on diseases of the throat"* where *"mention is also made of Dr. Laurent's invention for the removal of fish bones from the throat."* He contributed articles also to the **British Medical Journal** on abscesses of the liver and *"took an active part in combating the smallpox epidemics of 1890, 1905 and 1913, in Mauritius."* [3]

Beaugeard, Laurent and, later, Curé, the Lallah brothers and Seewoosagur Ramgoolam all proved that the opening of the Royal College to the non-Whites had been one of the most important developments of 19th Century Mauritius. The Royal College was considered equivalent to the best institutions of its kind in Great Britain and even in the 20th Century, it provided Mauritius with a significant number of distinguished leaders in various spheres of life. In the 19th and early 20th Centuries, the College was often the subject of debates in the Council of Government and then in the Legislative Council as it was one of the most vital institutions of Mauritius.

It was the seat of several scientific and technical exhibitions and on prize- giving days, the speech of the governor was regarded as a major political event and covered by the press. A number of famous British intellectuals taught at the College, which enjoyed great prestige in Great Britain. The English Scholarships made the institution even more important in Mauritian life. The names of the laureates were engraved for posterity and there is even a list of them in **Mauritius Illustrated** (op cit).

Laurent had entered the political arena in 1892, when he was elected to the Port-Louis municipal council. He was mayor of the capital in 1905, 1907, 1908, 1909, and 1912. During his various terms of office, there were many improvements in the town, with the council rationalising the municipal regulations, nominating a Municipal Poor Law Doctor, constructing several concrete bridges, making the fire brigade more efficient, creating a municipal laboratory, etc. He also introduced a system of progressive taxation, the tenant's tax, to finance the activities of the municipal services.

He once more tried to enter the Legislative Council in 1906, and was elected in Port-Louis. In the Legislative Council, he asked for measures to combat malaria, which, in those days, caused several deaths, especially among the poorer classes. His intervention resulted in the coming of an illustrious figure, Ronald Ross, the British scientist who was born in India in 1857, and who had won the Nobel Prize in 1902, after explaining the mechanisms of the transmission of the disease from mosquitoes to human beings and exposed the causes of epidemics.

---

[1] In **Select documents on the Constitutional History of the British Empire and Commonwealth**, op cit. Documents cited are despatches: **Chamberlain to Bruce**, 28 February 1900 and **Bruce to Chamberlain**, 25 June 1900.
[2] This situation is well reflected in **Mauritius Illustrated** (op cit) in the articles virulently hostile to the Indo-Creole masses that rallied under the political banner of Action Libérale. At one point, the popular masses are even treated as '*ignorant*' and dubbed '*the inferior classes.*'
[3] **Mauritius Illustrated**, op cit.

Gandhi, as he was when he visited Mauritius and later in life

The young Gandhi was, as he described himself in his memoirs, a firm believer in the British colonial system before, later in life, turning against it to liberate his motherland from the grips of the British colonizers. The above photo show him as he was when he came to Mauritius. The insets show him during a later phase of his life when he took up the struggle. He is one of the most respected historical figures of all times.

Like Beaugeard before him, Laurent was a member of the Board of Education and he also became Director of the Mauritius Institute. Like other members of the country's White, Creole and Indian bourgeoisie, in those days, he liked horse-racing and owned, according to M*auritius Illustrated* "*the well-known horses 'Vice', 'Lightning', 'Grand Roi', 'Stag', and 'Gyp', which won many prizes, including the Labourdonnais Cup.*" [1]

In 1907, a young Indian lawyer, Manilal Doctor, came to Mauritius, where he had been sent by one of his colleagues, Mohandas Karamchand Gandhi, who had visited Mauritius in 1901, and later went on to become the famous Mahatma Gandhi, one of the greatest Indian and world leaders of all times.

Gandhi was on his way from Natal, South Africa, to Bombay, India, on board the ship **Nowshera**, which stopped in Mauritius from October 30 to November 19, 1901. He had, as a lawyer and opinion leader, defended the Indian community of South Africa against racial prejudice and oppression by the White minority. He knew that the fate of the Indians in Mauritius was no better, especially on the sugar estates, where they were employed as coolies.

He was given a very warm welcome by the prominent members of the Indian community in Mauritius, Hindus, Muslims, Tamils, and those Indian immigrants who were already Christians in India.

A well-known Mauritian attorney-at-law, Henri Bertin, introduced him to some of their colleagues of the legal profession in the island. Governor Sir Charles Bruce, a specialist of the Sanskrit language which he had taught at King's College in London, received Gandhi, who was already famous for his action in South Africa. Like Manilal Doctor, Gandhi was still in the first phase of his political career, when he still believed that equality and justice could be sought within the British Empire and in the context of the imperial legal system. He used the Royal Proclamation of 1858, writes Uttama Bissoondoyal, "*as the Magna Carta of the British Indians*" since he considered the Indians in the British colonies as British subjects and deserving treatment and respect as such from the authorities. [2]

That Royal proclamation read thus: "*We hold ourselves bound to the Natives of our Indian territories by the same obligations of duty which bind us to all our subjects.*" Bissoondoyal writes, "*For Gandhi, racism in South Africa was perverting his dream of an Imperial brotherhood where all 'the different parts of the British Dominions' were welded 'into one beautiful unbreakable whole'. In the presence of a series of anti-Indian laws, he proposed the method of constitutional agitation, and of arousing public opinion.*"

His powerful independence message would come later. He was fighting discrimination within the system for the time being Very little could distinguish him or Manilal Doctor, in those days, concerning their considerable talent as lawyers and even the British-styled suits they wore, from other respected members of the legal profession in Britain, South Africa or Mauritius.

Uttam Bissoondoyal observes, "*...it is essential to know that up to 1901 Gandhi was a firm believer in British Rule and was not in principle against the mixture of British capital and Indian labour which gave rise to the process of Indian immigration. It is only later that he condemned it.*" He quotes Gandhi: "*It is no part of ours to look to the convenience of the Colony.*"

"*But he wanted a policy of amelioration, not one where the indentured labourers still 'remain in the state of semi-slavery and ignorance for ever'. He is beginning to see education as the key to that policy as education, ability and integrity are seen as the distinguishing traits of social advance .. He set up an Educational wing of the Indian Natal Congress.*"

However, Gandhi was endowed with a remarkable power as an orator and political thinker. The force with which he professed equality when he returned to India has rarely been equalled subsequently in the world by political leaders, except Martin Luther King or Mandela. He described himself and the Hindus of Naokhali, India, bent on communal violence, in the following terms:

"*I am a Muslim and a Hindu and a Christian and a Jew and so are all of you.*" [3]

When he came in Mauritius in 1901, his reputation had preceded him in the island. The press covered his visit. He was received at the Supreme Court. Among the Indo-Mauritians who gave him a very warm welcome, there was Ahmed Goolam Moharned, of whom he was a guest in Port-Louis. The newspapers **The Standard** and the **Journal de Maurice** described him as a distinguished Indian lawyer, and the former added that Gandhi had an excellent reputation in South Africa where he was considered as "*a real gentleman in every sense of the word, and was highly*

---

1 This part is based on Laurent, The Hon. Eugène, from Biographical Notes, Mauritius Illustrated, op cit, on the leaders of Mauritius in 1914. Page 438.
2 Bissoondoyal, U., Gandhi and Mauritius and Other Essays, Mahatma Gandhi Institute, Mauritius 1988.
3 Ibid.

esteemed by the judges and the members of the South African bar." [1]

The articles in the Mauritian newspapers about his visit indicate two attitudes. One of respect for the able barrister, another of prejudice towards Indians in general. Leoville L'Hornme, poet, librarian and leading figure of the Coloured persons, as Uttama Bissoondoyal reminds us, went to the extent of expressing *"a visceral reaction"* to the fact that Gandhi had encouraged a son of Goolam Hossen Ajam, one of his hosts, to be a candidate at elections and that he expressed the opinion that Indians in Mauritius should get involved in Mauritian politics. L'Homme wrote the following to express his reaction:

"It is possible that one of them may be elected, in a month's time, as a member of the Municipal Council, and that one will see people sitting as councillors whose hair is infested with lice and who will let fall their slippers to thrust between their toes the fingers of their hands with which, after the Council meeting, they will endeavour to shake the Mayor's hands ... If our motherland and our history must be reduced to the dimensions of a book-keeping register for the sale of ghee, or of tamarind balls..." [2]

That type of article mars the history of the Mauritian press and was current in the 19th and the first half of the 20th Centuries. Such articles depicted with the same degree of prejudice the slaves and their descendants and the Indian and Indo-Mauritian workers. History is history. Facts are facts. What was written was written. Historians must tell the truth, hoping that the country never reverts to such a social context once more, in one way or another, as anybody, White or Black or of any other ethnic or religious group can be a racist.

Of course, under all latitudes and in all human communities, prejudice caused by cultural differences does exist. Malcolm de Chazal, the famous Mauritian poet, wrote, *"This country cultivates sugar cane and prejudice."* [3] He was of Franco-Mauritian origin and a White man, but he systematically denounced racist tendencies among his own community. De Plevitz was a Frenchman settled in Mauritius, whose action in favour of the Indian immigrants in Mauritius (he was physically assaulted for that), was, in many ways, like that of Gandhi in South Africa, writes U. Bissoondoyal.

Gandhi in Mauritius, in 1901, addressed the Indians at well-attended receptions. He asked them to give priority to the education of their children, according to local press reports about his visit. *The Standard* wrote, on November 15, 1901, that *"he said that Indians should mix with politics because it was their right and their duty."* The paper comments, however, that statement in the following way, with all the prejudices of the times and an avowed desire of cultural assimilation:

"We must admit that Mr Gandhi was right in almost all he said at the dinner given to him by his countrymen. A time will surely come when distinguished Indians will come forward and take some of the first places in politics as they have done in Commerce. They are even now, among the richest people of this country; when they will be also among the most learned and the most civilised, who will object to their taking leading positions in politics? Who will object to their standing as candidates even for the legislative council? Who will have anything to say if they are elected as members of that Council?

"(...) The Coloured Creoles were once in the same position; but when they had become as learned and as civilised as their white countrymen, they were accepted by them as members of political and commercial institutions.

"There still exists much prejudice as to the social gatherings. The White and Coloured population do not mix freely at balls, concerts and private receptions. But in the present state of things it is far better that it be so, and any attempt at more intimate mixing should not be tried for several good reasons.

"The English men, the Mahomedan Indians, the Madras Indians, and the Chinamen have got different societies for themselves, it is as good that the White and Coloured Creoles should keep separate in everything that relates to social gatherings, and private life."

That newspaper extract gives an exact idea of how communities related to each other in those days. The

---

[1] *The Standard* and *Le Journal de Maurice*, various articles on Gandhi's visit during the period 30 October to 19 November 1901.
[2] Quoted in *Gandhi and Mauritius and Other Essays*, op cit, page 28.
[3] Chazal, Malcolm de, **Petrusmok: mythe**, Editions Léo Scheer, Mar 24, 2004 - 501 pages, page 9: « Ce pays cultive la canne et les préjugés. »

Governor Chancellor

Sir John Chancellor (in the middle, hand in pocket) was Governor of Mauritius from 13 September 1911 to 28 January 1916 and witnessed the post-electoral events during which a multiethnic mix of rich voters caused the defeat of the tandem Eugène Laurent/Manilall Doctor on the basis of class interests. Chancellor is seen here at a later time in Palestine, where he was High Commissioner for the UK.

The Mauritius railways in the old days

Pictured, here, is a model of a wagon of the Mauritius Railways.

colour bar law, abolished in 1829, was still working as an invisible and rigid social law.

One notes also that the direct descendants of the slaves and the estate labourers are completely left out: they are not even mentioned as the newspaper was dealing with the higher levels of the various ethnic bourgeoisies, not the labouring classes.

It was not until the second half of the 20th century that such unwritten racial laws would be eroded under the influence of the great cultural changes of the 1960's throughout the world and the radical reform of the Catholic Church at the Vatican Council II, which aimed at suppressing discriminatory practices within the church itself (like reserved seats at church on class and racial lines, for instance).

Political and religious matters in the early 20th century

The 1911 census of the population of Mauritius indicated a total of 257,700 Indians/Indo-Mauritians, of whom 202,750 Hindus, 39,120 Muslims, 14,100 Indian Christians, and 1,730 '*others*,' on a total population of nearly 369,000. [1]

As regards religion, Hinduism was already the religion of a majority of Mauritians after about a century and a half during which Christianity had been the main religion of the population. Hinduism started to undergo major reforms and modernisation with the advent of the Arya Samaj movement, established in India in 1875 by Swami Dayananda Saraswati. It was introduced in Mauritius 23 years later, in 1898, according to Pahlad Ramsurrun, by a Bengali Sepoy, Bholanath Tiwaree. That reform had far reaching consequences on Hinduism in Mauritius as leaders like Ramparsad Ooja of Castel, Meghvarna of Vacoas and Khemlall l.allah of Curepipe Road took up the challenge, the latter obtaining the support of Manilal Doctor in 1910. The movement owes much to another leader, Dr. Chiranjiv Dhardwaj, who registered the Port-Louis Arya Samaj in 1913, under the name of Arya Paropkarani Sabha. [2]

The Arya Samaj current, as compared to orthodoxy, brought about better mobilisation and united the various factions of the Hindu community. A number of conversions back to Hinduism were obtained by the movement as it worked among members of the community who had switched to other religions. To this day, the Arya Samaj is a major socioreligious movement in Mauritius.

That digression was necessary to situate the context of Gandhi's visit to Mauritius and that of Manilal Doctor's political action in the island. Gandhi's stay was too short to influence immediately Mauritian politics in those days. But he had highlighted the important question of the future political role of the Indians and this needed to be addressed.

In 1908, Cashinath Kistoe, a young Mauritian-born Indian worker of the Savanne, in the South of Mauritius, who toiled in the fields together with indentured labourers, was thrown in prison for having organised protest movements against their working and living conditions. He was going to take up successfully the challenge of giving the Indo-Mauritian workers and small planters the chance to influence the political scene: he emerged as the first endogenous leader of his community, especially at grassroots level, among the labouring classes. [3] He went on to pursue religious studies in India and came back to officiate at religious ceremonies, while also continuing his political struggle, like Reverend Jean Lebrun had done for the enfranchised slaves.

But while Kistoe started his movement in the Savanne, Manilal Doctor was leading the struggle on the legal, social and political front, together with Dr. Eugène Laurent's Liberal Democratic Party or Action Libérale. Laurent and the Indian lawyer sent by Gandhi were seeking the votes of the Indo-Mauritians to create a large Indo-Creole mass movement among the petites bourgeoisies and working classes before the advent of Dr. Curé's Mauritius Labour Party.

But the limited electoral franchise of those days gave the right to vote to only two per cent of the population. The number of Indian electors, comprising a large number of conservative voters due to common interests among the wealthy (labourers were left out), had risen from less than 400 in 1886 on a total of 4,000 electors to about 1,400 on a total of about 7,800 electors in 1906, when Laurent had been elected for the first time to the Legislative Council,

---
[1] A detailed sub-division of those figures dividing every community into ethnic sub-groups and castes, was made by Sir Henri Leclézio, a conservative member of the Council of Government, in Mauritius Illustrated (op cit, p. 141) where he stated, "Our population is, therefore, composed of a dozen elements quite different from each other by their ethnic character and by the social distinction which keep them apart."
[2] Ramsurrun, Pahlad, *Arya Samaj Movement in Mauritius*. Beau Bassin, Mauritius 1970.
[3] Peerthum, Satteeanund, **Pandit Cashinath Kistoe, pionnier du movement Arya Samaj**, op cit.

the year before Manil Doctor came to Mauritius.

The young Indian lawyer started his career in Mauritius, where he was allowed to practise, by provoking an incident which brought much attention and respect upon him from the Indo-Mauritian community. He refused, at the Supreme Court, to take off his traditional turban, arguing, contrary to the established European custom, that removing it would mean disrespect on his part. He defended Indian labourers in Court and visited them in the rural areas, including the sugar estates, campaigning against the infamous *"double cut"* of their wages. He defended the small planters and alleged that the factory owners were not giving them their fair share of sugar extracted from their canes.

His contribution to the Arya Samaj movement was decisive. The movement went on to open "**hundreds of Hindi evening schools for boys and girls throughout the island in the village baitkas,**" writes Ramsurrun. Manilal Doctor founded the newspaper *The Hindustani*, which published articles in Hindi. He encouraged education among the Indians and founded also the Young Men's Hindu Association. His action resulted in a greater awareness in India, where he kept contact with Gandhi, of the fate of the Indo-Maurltlans, and, at the same time, it aroused the interest of the latter in local politics, especially the legislative elections.

But it should also be noted that within the Indo-Mauritian community as within the Christian religions in Mauritius, there were quite serious disputes.

The Arya Samaj movement was attacked by the orthodox Hindus, and for several years, the two groups campaigned against each other across the country and, as Dr. K. Hazareesingh has recalled in his Histoire des Indiens à l'île Maurice,[1] things deteriorated to the extent that "a dispute had even to be tried by the Supreme Court." Hazareesingh adds:

"It centred around a case relating to the genealogical tree of an orthodox Hindu who claimed to be a member of the Kshattriya community. The most famous lawyers of the time were engaged in this battle. The Court decided against the plaintiff, but so far as public opinion was concerned, caste, as a 'sacred' institution that could not be tampered with, was itself on trial and was fighting its last battle."

Within the Muslim religious community also, in the two first decades of the 20th century, cases went to the Supreme Court, and even to the Privy Council in London, observes Moomtaz Emrith in his History of the Muslims in Mauritius,[2] observes, "The control of the Jummah Mosque led to a long legal battle due "to a conflict (…) between the Hallai Meiman and the Surtee Muslims on one side and the Cutchee Meiman Muslims on the other." Another dispute arose between two divergent religious currents over the Rose-Hill Mosque, he writes. The case landed in the Supreme Court.

Nevertheless, in politics, the community was gearing up to play an increasingly important role in the political arena, even though the majority of Muslims, those at the lower rungs of the economic ladder, did not yet have the right to vote. Action Libérale did play a crucial role in increasing political awareness among the Muslims also, especially within the ranks of the small planters and labourers. The latter played an important role in constituting, with the Hindus and the Creoles, those masses of 'Indo-Creoles,' as Pezzani called them in Mauritius Illustrated (op cit) that came on the political and electoral stage in the 1900s.

Within the Catholic religious community, as already stated, severe conflicts from the 19th to the 20th centuries opposed mainly White conservatives and a number of their Coloured allies to those political leaders of the Creoles who fought against the colour bar that, even after its official abolition, persisted well into the 20th century. Politicians like Eugène Laurent and Raoul Rivet tried to curb the influence of the Catholic Church on the government as it tried to maintain exclusivity for the Franco-Mauritian sugar barons in some areas of education.

Class-based political agitation for democracy on the rise

Action Libérale tried its best, under the leadership of Dr. Eugène Laurent and Manilal Doctor, to unite a majority of Indo-Mauritians (Hindus, Muslims and about 14,000 Indian Christians), lower middle-class Whites (like Edouard Nairac, for instance) and Coloured, and Creoles on a common political programme. The final objective of this political force that was essentially class-based and anti-oligarchy, was:
- To secure a majority of seats in the Legislative Council despite an electoral franchise dating from 1885 and favouring the affluent classes that voted consistently for the conservative political leaders, mainly of

---
[1] Hazareesingh, K., *Histoire des Indiens à l'île Maurice*, Librairie d'Amérique et d'Orient, Paris 1973.
[2] Op cit.

- Franco-Mauritian origin; and
    - To obtain constitutional reform so as to add to the electoral list the majority of the population where Creoles and Indo-Mauritians would constitute the bulk of the electorate: that would have ensured a major political revolution, with far-reaching consequences.

When that became clear, panic ensued among the conservatives as betrayed by the virulent tone of political comments from them in **Mauritius Illustrated** (op cit), after the 1911 general elections. They had opposed, in the first decade of the 20th century, the nomination of another Royal Commission of Inquiry which was being asked by Action Libérale as well as by the British Government who proposed such a commission as a precondition to granting a loan to the sugar magnates.

Religious and class differences within the middle, lower middle and working classes, played no role in those days, unlike today, as their leaders, Dr. Eugène Laurent, Manilal Doctor, René Mérandon, Edouard Nairac, Anatole de Boucherville, Goolam Mamode Issac campaigned to unite them under the same liberal political banner.

As in Britain, liberalism was the most important challenge to conservatism before the advent of socialism. When Edgar Antelme was defending his motion in the Legislative Council (as related above) for *"universal suffrage,"* he actually declared that liberalism would soon force Mauritius to enlarge the electoral franchise.

If we look at the career of René Mérandon du Plessis, for example, we may understand how people, who, coming from old Franco-Mauritian families, adhered, as he did, to the liberal ideology, to militate together with Manilal Doctor, Gandhi's follower, Goolam Mamode Issac and others. Mérandon, who had migrated overseas, returned to Mauritius in 1972 and, writes K. Hazareesingh, *"retained till the end his love for small men; he lived abroad for thirty years (...) and spent his last days among the tillers of the field in a small village outside Port Louis."* Hazareesingh adds: *"He died there shortly after and in accordance with his wishes was buried in the local cemetery among those for whom the bells did not toll."* [1]

He was, at the beginning of the 20th century a very promising politician who, according to Allister Macmillan, *"seems destined in the near future to become one of the foremost leaders of his dearly-loved country."* Born in 1882 *"of an old family of planters,"* says his biography in **Mauritius Illustrated**, [2] published in 1914, he attended the Royal College, then studied engineering in France and England, read for the English bar at Gray's Inn and was called in 1906. *"On his return to Mauritius, he felt the call of the land, and proved himself very successful as the owner of an aloe estate. He and his brother are owners of upwards of 2,000 acres of pasture land in Black River District, and take the deepest interest in the local breed of cattle, which they are trying to improve, as well as in country life generally."*

Macmillan also observes that in politics, he favoured the Royal Commission of Inquiry *"in the face of bitter opposition"* and *"upheld by a large number of inhabitants of the colony, he asked for the reform of the laws dealing with companies, the establishment of an agricultural bank, and the study of the irrigation problem."* Macmillan also adds: *"Only thirty-one years of age, strongly opposed to some of the financial circles, whom he accuses of taking too large a share of the planters' profits. Mérandon was destined for a brilliant political career."*

One sentence is particularly revealing in his 1914 biography: *"His long stay in England, part of which he spent in the country, has made him thoroughly acquainted with English ways and ideas."* He must have been influenced, as many successive leaders of the masses in Mauritius, by the advocacy of social policies more favourable to the downtrodden in all of Western Europe when he was there, especially in Britain and France.

Some prominent Mauritian liberal leaders like Manilal Doctor, Dr. Eugène Laurent and René Mérandon later migrated, the first named being '*disillusioned*' as Anauth Beejadhur wrote. [3] Their political movement was short-lived, suffering crushing defeat at the elections of 1911.

British liberalism, it seems, had considerable influence in those days in Mauritius. Gandhi, as Uttama Bissoondoyal asserts, was still in a phase of his life when he believed that equality and justice would be achieved within the bounds of the British Empire. He wrote, in his famous autobiography *The story of My Experiments With Truth*:

"Hardly ever have I known anybody to cherish such loyalty as I did to the British Constitution. I can see now that my love of truth was at the root of this loyalty. It has never been possible for me to simulate loyalty or, for that matter, any other virtue. The National Anthem used to be sung at every meeting that I attended in Natal. I then felt that I must also join in the singing. Not that I was unaware at the defects of British rule, but that I thought it was on the whole acceptable. In those days I believed that British rule was on the whole beneficial to the ruled.

1 Quoted in: Selvon, Sydney, L'histoire de Maurice, des origines à nos jours, Mauritius, 2003..
2 Op cit.
3 Beejadhur, Anauth, Les Indiens à l'Ile Maurice, La Typographie Mauricienne, Port-Louis 1935.

"The colour prejudice that I saw in South Africa was, I thought, quite contrary to British traditions, and I believed that it was only temporary and local. I therefore vied with Englishmen in loyalty to the throne. With careful perseverance I learnt the tune of the National Anthem and joined in the singing whenever it was sung. Whenever there was an occasion for the expression of loyalty without fuss or ostentation, I readily took part in it." [4]

That was the Gandhi who visited Mauritius in 1901. He had not yet started his great and heroic struggle for the independence of India and for decolonisation in general. Socialism had not yet gained the influence which it obtained in the following decades in Britain and, some time later, in Mauritius. There was little that, in those days, differed in the outlook of men like Dr. Eugène Laurent, Manilal Doctor and the young lawyer M.K. Gandhi who visited Mauritius in 1901: moulded by the British system of education and government, they opted for justice and equality within the bounds of the colonial system.

The Labour Party in Britain was born in 1906 from movements that gathered momentum in the 1890's. In Mauritius, it was not until the 1930's that socialism would become a decisive factor in local politics. However, it is worth noting that a workers' party called the Parti Ouvrier, created by Jean Pierry, convened, before the general elections of 1896, the two Council members of Port-Louis seeking re-election, William Newton and Dr. Virgile Rohan, the latter a democrat who had supported Beaugeard.

According to Quenette, [5] Pierry and his colleagues presented their manifesto and obtained the support of the two candidates. They asked, essentially, better protection for workers against industrial accidents, unemployment benefits and retirement pensions for workers. Newton, a conservative, and Rohan, a Democrat, were elected in Port-Louis, but Rohan's democratic colleague Edgar Vaudagne, son of the former successor of Rémy Ollier at La Sentinelle, was defeated in the same electoral district in 1896. Dr. Eugène Laurent was defeated in the Plaines Wilhems electoral district.

The working masses of the country depended on the liberal politicians to improve their condition, and some of those liberals came sometimes from wealthy families who were traditionally conservative-minded. This explains the numerous contradictions noted by historians in their outlook, especially concerning interracial relations at social level. But liberalism was a formidable positive force which paved the way for further political emancipation of the Mauritian masses, in spite of its electoral failure.

The Mauritian liberals suffered two major setbacks: no electoral reform enlarging the franchise was granted following the 1909 report of the Royal Commission and most of their candidates and the Indo-Mauritians who stood for election were defeated at the general elections two years later.

Action Libérale. Eugène Laurent and Manilal Doctor supported the nomination of a Royal Commission of Inquiry on the sugar industry, which was the main condition set down by the British government from whom the Mauritian sugar magnates had solicited a financial loan to redress their financial situation following a fall in sugar prices and the decline of annual harvests. The Mauritian conservatives, who dominated the Legislative Council and entertained bitter memories of the 1872 Royal Commission obtained by de Plevitz with the support of former governor Gordon, refused any idea of a new Royal Commission of Inquiry. Their request for a loan of 400,000 pounds sterling was turned down by the British government, who still insisted for a Commission of Inquiry on the financial situation of the country.

As the British Government was linking the loan to a Royal Commission, the sugar barons decided to backpedal. *"(…) Henri Leclezio, who had been active in supporting the demand for a loan, suddenly changed tactics, and moved in the council of government that a loan be declined. In a speech to the Chamber of agriculture he warned that a royal commission would unleash ' the Asiatic peril' (' le peril asiatique') by recommending that Mauritius could be more economically administered as a part of British India. Mauritius would then have Indian magistrates and officials at a low price ('à vil prix')."* [6]

An inquiry into the situation of the railways in the island was conducted, meanwhile, by Sir David Hunter, of the Natal Government Railways, who recommended a major overhaul of the vehicles and equipment. [7]

1st decade of the 20th C.: Intense political campaigning

---

4 Gandhi, M.K., *The Story of My Experiments With Truth*, Beacon Press, USA 1957.
5 Le grand Beaugeard, op cit.
6 *Chamber of agriculture proceedings*, 8 Apr. 1908, C0882/9/I IO, quoted in Ballhatched, op cit.
7 In: *Mauritius Railways Department, Report of the general manager on the recommendations contained in Sir David Hunter's expert enquiry and Messrs. Hawkshaw and Dobson's report thereon,* Coignet, Mauritius 1908.

After the refusal of the local conservatives of a new Royal Commission, the members of Action Libérale led a campaign across the country against the sugar magnates. They formulated several demands in addition to supporting the appointment of a Royal Commission. They asked for an extension of the franchise to democratise the political system. That political campaign forged the Indo-Creole alliance in such a way that the Oligarchs, as the conservatives were dubbed, were, for the first time, seriously challenged since the days of Beaugeard's Democratic Party in the 1880's.

That was the first time that the masses had been brought on the forefront of the Mauritian political scene. Public meetings were held in every region of the island. Laurent, Mérandon and Manilal Doctor, the latter speaking in Hindustani, had captivated their audiences with their demands.

It must also be noted that in those days, in Port-Louis and elsewhere, there were many unemployed Indians, some of them starving, according to Manilal Doctor, who confirmed the fact that, to keep down wages, the employers had abused of the British and Indian governments' facilities granted to them to import Indian labour and had brought into the country a largely excessive number of immigrant workers. Those who had completed their indenture were left aside in favour of new engagements in India at lower wages. K. Hazareesingh writes that Manilal Doctor, making fiery speeches, had the following resolutions voted by his audiences across the island:

"That an enquiry be made into the condition of the Indian Labourers, many of whom are dead or starving in the streets of Port Louis, and into the story of their being induced by false pretences to come from India and into their present helpless position after the completion of the indenture.

"That the proposal to substitute maize for rice is really to break trust with the poor indentured labourers, who have been induced to come to Mauritius by misguiding touts under false promises of making fabulous fortunes, and who, at the present day, are sometimes forced to eat uneatable rice." [8]

The appointment and definition of the mission of the Royal Commission were announced in the House of Commons by Colonel Seely, Under-Secretary of State for the Colonies in the following terms:

"The Commissioners are Sir F. A. Swettenham, the late Governor of the Straits Settlements; Sir R. L. O'Malley, formerly Chief Justice of British Guiana and Judge of the Consular Court at Constantinople; and Mr. H. B. Drysdale Woodcock, barrister-at-law. The Commissioners are directed by their Commission to make inquiry into the administrative and financial condition of the government of the Colony, particularly with a view to the introduction of economies, and to suggest such measures as may appear best calculated to restore and maintain the Colony's prosperity." [9]

The Commission arrived in Mauritius on June 18, 1909. The leaders of the liberal movement, including Dr. Laurent and Manilal Doctor, testified before the commissioners. [10] Manilal Doctor asked that Mauritius be included within the jurisdiction of the British Indian government as India was the major economic partner of the island and buying its sugar. In such a way, Mauritius would save Rs 1.5 million as a result of the abolition of the Indian import duties on Mauritian sugar and the price of sugar would decrease in India. It must be noted, here, that some Mauritian conservatives at one time favoured the idea of associating the administration in Mauritius with that of British India for economic reasons: import of cheap labour and marketing of their sugar.

Manilal Doctor also argued that the planters were not given their fair share of sugar from their canes by the sugar millers and that their canes were not properly and honestly weighed prior to milling operations. Mérandon, as already mentioned, had, during the campaign of the liberals, accused the financial sector of depriving the planters of what was due to them. Manilal Doctor encouraged Indians to testify before the commissioners, one of them being Jaypal Maraz, who was then harassed by the police, an act which was condemned by the Commission. Dr. Laurent approved the political moves by the Indo-Mauritians; de Boucherville asked for autonomy; Edouard Nairac supported the liberal programme of democratisation.

That was a great moment for the leaders of Mauritian Liberal Democratic Party, which then actively prepared itself for the electoral campaign of 1910-11.

But Action Libérale obtained no substantial political reform after the publication of the report of the Royal Commission. The franchise was not extended to the Indo-Creole masses who formed the bulk of their political support and who would, most probably, have swept from power in the Legislative Council, long before the 1948 general elections, the Oligarchs who had held sway since 1886.

8 *History of Indians in Mauritius*, op cit.
9 House of Commons, Hansard, *Mauritius (Appointment of Commission)*, HC Deb 20 May 1909 vol 5 cc562-3.
10 *Report of the Royal Commission, 1902: Minutes of proceedings and evidence,* Vol. 2. H.M.St.O..

Dr. Xavier Nalletamby, Council member appointed to represent the Indo-Mauritians, had proved, during his testimony, that he was unaware, generally, of the real conditions of the Indo-Mauritian working classes, especially on the sugar estates. As a matter of fact, the commissioners had reported that *"no Council can legitimately claim to speak authoritatively for Mauritius as a whole which does not contain a substantial proportion of members who represent that hitherto unrepresented community of Asiatic descent which plays such an important part in the life of the colony and comprises more than two-thirds of the population."*

They added, *"One of the most difficult of the problems which lie before the Mauritius Government is that of its relations with the population of Indian descent. For about three-quarters of a century it has been found possible for the Colonial Government to regard the Indian as a stranger among a people of European civilisation – a stranger who must indeed be protected from imposition and ill-treatment and secured in the exercise of his legal rights, but who has no real claim to a voice in the ordering of the affairs of the colony.*

"From what we have learnt during our enquiry, we very much doubt whether it will be possible to continue to maintain this attitude. The Indian population of the colony is easily governed and has, we believe, no natural inclination to assert itself in political matters so long as reasonable regard is paid to its desires on a few questions to which it not unreasonably attaches importance. In our opinion the fact that the first settlers in Mauritius were of French and African origin, and that as a consequence of the history of the island the legal and social system of the colony is mainly French in character, ought not to preclude the government from taking steps to relieve the Indian population from the provisions of a system which press heavily upon them and are regarded by them as a real grievance. It is no sufficient answer to their representations to say that their ancestors came to Mauritius of their own will and must accept the conditions in force here. Such an argument must be conclusive in the case of a small section of the community – such as for example the Chinese – but it loses its force when it is urged against the aspirations of British Indian subjects who outnumber the rest of the inhabitants by more than two to one and who have so important a part in the industrial life of the community."

One of the commissioners, O'Malley, reported that only two per cent of the population had the right to vote, of whom a quarter consisted of public employees.

There was no recommendation for an extension of the electoral franchise, or to grant a reform of labour legislation to improve the lot of the small planters and labourers. There was nothing of that sort save a sum of 15,000 pounds sterling to help set up credit cooperative societies, which later on were beneficial to the small planters. Nothing was granted in terms of political liberties that would have met the demands of Action Libérale and produced the constitutional reform they had been expecting. On the contrary, as the Truth and Justice Commission has pointed out,

"In fact, the Royal Commission of 1909 provided support to the plantocracy by recommending that loans should be granted for the rehabilitation of Government railways and for the improvement of cultivation, factory machinery or mechanical tractions and for a remunerative irrigation scheme. There was no recommendation for labour per se. The Royal Commission did not even try to mitigate the plentiful cheap labour policy."

As Manilal Doctor had pointed out, Indians were starving as a result of this cheap labour policy which, obviously, relied on maintaining a large army of unemployed people. Rampant unemployment was clearly an artificial creation of the multiethnic community of the richest planters of the island. They cooperated in their insatiable quest for more cheap labour, so no wonder that poverty reached the extremely high level that Manilal Doctor had observed.

Quoting the Commission's report, the Truth and Justice Commission, much like a book of historical research in 1984, *Vacoas-Phoenix. La genèse d'une ville* (op cit), underlines the class factor while commenting the report: *"There was also a class factor involved and J. F. Trotter, Protector of Immigrants, did comment on this: according to him, only the 'better class of Indians' wished to educate their children. Manilal Doctor, in his statement to the Royal Commission, stated that education was beyond the reach of poor parents, even with regard to scholarships. All the scholarships for Higher Education were awarded on the basis of qualifying examinations which needed extra learning; therefore, only the children of prosperous Indians would qualify for these scholarships, as their parents could afford private tuition for their children. Even if a poor parent wanted to send his child to a secondary school, it was most unlikely that the child would qualify for it."* [11]

A committee chaired by Lord Sanderson was then appointed in London, to report about the immigration of Indian workers to Crown colonies.

The result of that inquiry was, as Manilal Doctor had hoped – as well as the London Anti-Slavery Society which was following the affair very closely, Indian immigration of indentured labourers was abruptly suspended, provoking the fury of the Mauritian conservatives like Henri Leclézio. They protested vehemently and militated in favour of the resumption of the import of cheap indentured labour, deliberately ignoring the devastating social effects of unemployment. [12]

A decade later they would once more, together with Indo-Mauritian capitalists of the sugar industry who accompanied them in a delegation to India with two sirdars, import cheap labour from India. But after a report by Kunwar Maharajsingh, [13] the indenture system or *"new system of slavery,"* as Gandhi himself termed it, [14] would be finally abolished.

Devasting electoral defeat for the Liberals

The January 1911 general elections were preceded by intensive campaigning on party lines, opposing the Oligarchs and the Liberals. The number of registered electors had strangely declined. The two parties and their supporters had nearly clashed during the registration of the electors. The police and the military were placed in a state of alert because of the strong political and social tension which prevailed.

Most of the liberal candidates lost the elections, except for their leader who stood for re-election in his Port-Louis stronghold together with Edouard Nairac: both were elected. Manilal Doctor was deeply aggrieved by that electoral disaster. He left the island a few months later, on September 23, 1911, disillusioned by the fact that a number of very conservative Indian employers had sided with the Oligarchs led by Henri Leclézio, as had been the case during the debates over the forest and river reserves ordinances of the 1880's.

Uttama Bissoondoyal quotes Gandhi himself concerning the work of Manilal Doctor in Mauritius. Though satisfied that the latter had exerted an influence in the abolition of indenture, there were some problems. In a letter dated September 24, 1911, nine months after the general election, Gandhi, observes U. Bissoondoyal, wrote to Dr. Mehta the following comments about Manilal Doctor's action in Mauritius:

"He doesn't have capable helpers in Mauritius, how can a proper newspaper be brought out? Besides, where are the readers? (...) Now that he has been in Mauritius, done all that public work and won the people's affection, the best course for him, as I see it, would be to brave all hardships until he could earn a living." [15]

But Manilal Doctor's work in Mauritius had, nevertheless, durably influenced Mauritian politics in the sense that it inspired greatly the Indo-Mauritian community's grassroots leaders like the Bissoondoyal brothers Basdeo and Sookdeo. The latter would look for inspiration from gandhism and the Indian independence movement, especially in the 1930s and 1940s, working hand in hand with the founder of the Mauritius Labour Party, Dr. Maurice Curé.

No political history of Mauritius would be complete without an analysis of the birth of two main antagonistic political philosophies within each and every ethnic community of the island: conservatism versus liberalism. Later, as in Britain, liberalism would be superseded by more radical currents with the advent of the Labour Party in the 1930's. In Mauritius, the scourge of communalism would further embroil the political affairs of the country.

But disillusion was also deeply felt among a number of supporters of the liberal movement of Dr. Laurent, especially the small bourgeoisies of Coloured and Creoles aspiring for jobs. The 1911 defeat blocked all the avenues they had hoped for to progress socially, professionally and politically in a completely and stubbornly *"blocked"* society where race and colour were obsessive considerations. Some believed that the Indo-Mauritian electorate would remain predominantly conservative, especially as there seemed to be no way to extend the franchise to the Indians in the lower rungs of the social stratification. Maybe communalism started there and then in modern Mauritian

---
[11] **Truth and Justice Commission**, op cit, with the following citations: **Statement of J. F. Trotter, Report of Sanderson Committee**, 1910, Pt. II, p.356; Statement of Manilal Doctor, Report of Royal Committee, Part B, p.160.
[12] They continued to attack virulently the Sanderson Committee's recommendations that ended '*bluntly*' and '*abruptly*' the importation of cheap labour. See: **Mauritius Illustrated**, op cit, page 70 (in Pitot's **History of Mauritius,** op cit) and page 204 (in an article on the Mauritius Chamber of Agriculture)..
[13] See Chapter 32.
[14] Van Der Veer, Peter, **Religious Nationalism: Hindus and Muslims in India,** University of California Press, 1994, page 117.
[15] **Gandhi and Mauritius**, op cit, page 16.

politics, from the atmosphere of mutual distrust which can result from the bitterness of a crushing electoral defeat attributed to specific and wealthy ethnic lobbies.

Many members of the General Population left Mauritius, like the Indian lawyer Manilal Doctor and Dr. Laurent (eight years later), in the face of increased persecution by the dominant oligarchy. The struggle against that oligarchy, until the mid-1930's, seemed to yield no results and a feeling of despair was inevitable. Dr. Beaugeard was ruined and almost begged for a pension: the only handful of people who could pay a private doctor in the 19th century were supporters of the Oligarchy and they avoided him. In the same way, Curé would be ruined in the 1940's. Manilal Doctor, an able lawyer and journalist, was incapable of earning his living as Gandhi observed. So he left the country to the disappointment of Gandhi. Dr. Laurent left the island in 1919, his party having split after failing to force a reform of the electoral franchise which could have led to power his coalition of lower middle and working classes of Indo-Creoles.

Among the conservatives, in spite of the rejoicings that followed victory, a certain panic also spread after the 1911 elections. There was anti-Indo-Creole communalism stemming mostly from distrust and fear of mass revolt and insubordination, which found fertile ground to breed on among the affluent Franco-Mauritians, since Manilal Doctor and Dr. Eugène Laurent had, for the first time, demonstrated that the masses could be effectively mobilised to challenge them seriously.

Feelings ran high indeed before and after the general elections. When the results were proclaimed in January 1911, crowds of young Action Libérale supporters belonging to the under-privileged classes demonstrated their joy in Port-Louis where Action Libérale was victorious. They gave vent to their anger in some constituencies at seeing the victorious Oligarchs jeering their defeated rivals. There was considerable tension throughout the island and several violent incidents occurred.

Full-scale riots were barely avoided in Curepipe, but nothing could stop the furious crowds in Port-Louis, where rumour had spread that Dr. Laurent had been murdered by the pro-Oligarchs in Curepipe, from attacking Oligarch supporters and whatever, in their eyes, rightly or wrongly, symbolised Oligarch power: those newspaper offices where the Oligarchs derived support and about forty business premises like the Dauban Sawmill, the Ducasse House at La Bourdonnais Street, the Chamber of Agriculture, and so on.

The police could not control the situation and the military were called in to restore order. The Liberal leaders, especially Dr. Laurent, Goolam Mamode Issac and Edouard Nairac did their utmost to appease the crowds. Finally, order was restored and a commission of inquiry chaired by Major General Sir Ronald Macdonald instituted. Some rioters were prosecuted and convicted.

The panic that transpires in all the articles that the Oligarch leaders wrote in Mauritius Illustrated indicates clearly their state of mind, Roger Pezzani speaking of the "Indo-Creoles" who are not "meek lambs" and who, according to him and Henri Leclézio, were not fit to take part in the electoral process, being "a servile horde yet unreclaimed from heathendom and barbarism." Anti-Indian and anti-Creole racism reached new heights. The same Leclézio made such virulent racial remarks that Anatole de Boucherville relied to his article *'People and Politics'* in **Mauritius Illustrated**[16] in a publication of his own, published in 1914.[17]

However, not all Whites were rich nor were all of them racists. Also, not all rich Whites were racists. Whenever there are racist reactions,, the engine of it is fear. However, it takes a long, long time to eradicate prejudice - if it is eradicable from the complex nature of the human being.

---

16 Op cit.
17 Boucherville, Anatole de, *Pour l'autonomie, lettres à l'Hon. Leclézio... précédées et suivies des articles publiées dans "La Croix" et "La Patrie" par René Mérandon,* Ile Maurice 1914.

Chapter 36
More failures for the anti-Oligarchs

It was difficult for the working classes to remain quiet within a political-social-economic system that excluded them completely from choosing freely their representatives in the legislature. It was indeed a system, as already mentioned in Chapter 34, that engendered poverty and social exclusion to such levels that could be described as extreme among the lowest rungs of the social hierarchy. The riots of 1911 had been an expression of anger against that system and more struggles would happen to help alleviate poverty, economic inequality and ensure a profitable reorientation of the national economy.

Due to an electoral system twisted in their favour by the property-based franchise, the Oligarchs had won a massive victory except in Port-Louis where the two liberal candidates, Dr. Eugène Laurent, the leader of Action Libérale, and Edouard Nairac had been elected. Indo-Mauritian liberal candidates were defeated in the rural areas, including Boodhun Lallah in Pamplemousses and Sirkissoon Dassayne in Moka, where he had stood against the leader of the Oligarchs, Henri Leclézio. Dr. Hassen Sakir, a veteran from Beaugeard's former Democratic Party, was nominated to the Council after the elections as a representative of the Indo-Mauritian community.

It is interesting at this stage to address the role of the Tamil component of the Indo-Mauritian community. The fact that they comprised a large number of Indians who were already Christians in Mauritius from the 18th century, or in India also, and that other Tamils in general inter-married frequently with Christians and the Indian Christians and had Christian names, has tended to blur their actual role. This has been effectively explained by historian Reddi who observes about the Tamil community:

"The Merchant class also fought for Indian representation in the Council of Government and championed the cause of the Indians on a number of crucial issues. (...) coloured candidates at Municipal elections were forced to appeal to the Indian community. In 1860, the first Indian mayor of Port Louis was Eliacin Francois, a Tamil Christian and in 1885 another Indian Christian merchant, Gnanadicrayen Arlanda was appointed Indian nominee in the Council of Government.

"Although these Indians rarely spoke on behalf of the Indians; yet they paved the way for future politicians. Throughout the nineteenth century, both at Municipal and general elections, there were one or two Tamils, who stood as candidates. They were unsuccessful but they kept an interest in politics. Towards the late 19th century they were joined by one or two north Indians but the efforts of the Indians' both Tamils and north Indians proved to be sporadic,

"In 1909 the arrival of Manilal Doctor, Gandhi's emissary, to Mauritius resulted in a fresh spurt of political activity among Indians, both the Indian merchant classes and the descendants of the indentured labourers. Both the Muslim and the Tamil merchant classes made claims for representation in the Council government and disavowed the earlier government nominees, Nallethamby, a Tamil Christian, and Dr Sakir, a Muslim, who were viewed as too creolised to be representatives of Hindu and Muslim interests respectively.

"Under the influence of Manilal Doctor, they petitioned for the teaching of Indian languages, the creation of public cremation grounds and public holidays for Divali, Dussara, Holi, Maha Sivarathree and Sivmavrani . In 1909, Veerapa Padayachee of 20 Rampe Street, Port Louis, organised a meeting to thank the Secretary of State for the Royal Commission of Inquiry of 1909 and asked for its recommendations to be implemented. It was at his place that Manilal Doctor met Indians to discuss the recommendations of the Royal Commissions. Pressure from the Tamil Community resulted in the provisional appointment of K. Narainsamy to the Council of Government, and in 1911, they continued to press for a permanent appointment."
[1]

The right to vote under the 1886 Constitution still in force had been restricted to only 6,186 people in 1908,[2] on a total Mauritian population of 368,791. [3]

Prior to that, there had been 4,061 electors, as already mentioned, in 1885, on the eve of the first general election in the history of the island, out of a population that had already reached 359,874 in 1881. Six years later, at the elections of 1891 the number increased only slightly to 4,717 registered voters, of whom 4,029 voted, the total population being then 370,588, according to Governor Sir Charles Cameron Lees. [4]

In 1911, at the time of the general elections, the Indo-Mauritians plus those still classified as Indians had reached a

---
1 Reddi, Sadisivam J., The Influence of the Merchant Class on the Tamil Community in Mauritius, at Tamilnation.org.
2 *"The number of registered electors on 31st December, 1908, was 6186..."* : In: *The Dominions office and Colonial office list ...: comprising historical and statistical information respecting the overseas dominions and colonial dependencies of Great Britain*, Waterlow & Sons, London 1910; see also Madden and Darwin, op cit.
3 Mauritius Central Statistics Office, vol. 36. **Population and Vital Statistics, Table2 - Population growth in intercensal periods - Island of Mauritius,** 1851–2000.
4 *Lees to Knutsford, no. 76, 18 Feb. 1891.* CO 167/661, cited in Ballhatchet, op cit.

total of 257,697 (the Indians: 35,396; the Indo-Mauritians.: 222,301). The Creoles and Coloured *petites bourgeoisies* and working classes were also seriously underrepresented as their number was about 100,000 if the figures provided by Sir Henri Leclézio are considered: *"In 1919 Sir Henri Leclezio thought the general population included 6,000 white French, 5,000 upper-class Creoles (he called them 'gentry of colour'), and 15,000 middle-class Creoles."* [5] Those 100,000 were not represented and this was also the case for over a quarter of a million Indo-Mauritians and Indian residents most of whom were settling down in the country.

At the Colonial Office, a radical liberal politician, J. Chamberlain, the Secretary of State for the Colonies, was thinking of ways to reduce the influence of what was formally referred to as the Mauritius oligarchy of French descent over the affairs of the country by suggesting more Creole and Indian participation and appointments as K. Ballhatchet observes. [6]

Chamberlain (who was the father of future British P.M. Neville Chamberlain) minuted the following on a despatch from Mauritius Governor Sir Charles Bruce as follows (written in 'minuting' style):

"The Indians are I think in a majority of the population & it is most desirable that their interests shd. be represented. I will face the storm. When it has settled down we shall be stronger in Mauritius than we have ever been & the French oligarchy will be kept in order by the other races." [7]

The '*other races*' alluded to the lower bourgeoisies of Coloured and Creoles, not to the Coloured elite that was allied to the Oligarchy. [8]

Lutchumun Bissoondoyal, the father of Basdeo, born in 1906, and Sookdeo, born in 1908, had witnessed the events. Uttam Bissoondoyal, in his book *"Promises to Keep"* has written about the reminiscences of his grandfather, which gives the true atmosphere of hope and of a budding political awareness among the Indians as they attended the meetings of the Action Libérale:

"The dim awareness of politics was already there in the Indians and Lutchumun Bissoondoyal was no exception. He had seen Manilal Doctor ill-treated in Rivière des Anguilles when he was addressing a public meeting there (...) In 1908, he had followed a procession headed by the roulotte of the Action Libérale proclaiming assertively 'La vérité en marche.' The procession had left Port Louis at noon on 1st June and went through Nouvelle France and Grand Bois to Souillac where the meeting was held on Sunday. It was the first time he had really listened to a public meeting. He did not very much understand the main orators.

"René Mérandon and Willie Dawson were making a case for a Royal Commission.

"He was, however, more impressed by Boodhun Lallah who spoke in Hindustani (...) Edouard Nairac who was to preserve his reputation of a liberal politician and professional throughout his career appealed to the Indo-Mauritians to get themselves interested in the able importance was given to the contribution of the party of Eugène Laurent and Manilal Doctor as well as the former Democratic Party of Beaugeard to the cause of democracy in Mauritius. They lived through those difficult but exciting years and Sookdeo Bissoondoyal recalled the Port-Louis of 1913 thus:

"There was no electricity, no sewerage, no tarred roads. At night, the streets were lighted up with lanterns. Oil or candles were used. A man used a ladder to climb and light the lanterns one by one." [9]

An important economic factor was to come into play. As already mentioned, the sugar industry has been periodically going through problems of a declining labour force and dips in the prices of sugar. Those two factors were among the principal causes of an increase of '*morcellements*' by which large sugar estates sold or rented parts of their lands to obtain revenue and to address the labour shortage. C. J. Robertson writing in 1930, observes:

"Amongst economic causes the chief is the progress of 'morcellement,' the breaking-up of the estates into small holdings, which results in a scarcity of hired labour on the remaining estates. The rapid extension of this process began after 1910, under the stimulus of low prices,

---

[5] In Ballhatchet, T*he Structure of British Official Attitudes: Colonial Mauritius, 1883-1968* in *The Historical Journal*, Vol. 38, No. 4 (Dec., 1995), pp. 989-1011, Cambridge University Press, <http://www.jstor.org/stable/2640097> Accessed: 09/03/2012. The author cites *Leclézio to J. Middleton*, 21 Apr. 1919, C0167/826/34921. Leclézio's analysis of the ethnic groups is similar to the one he did at that time in *Mauritius Illustrated*, op cit.
[6] Ballhatchet, Kenneth, ibid.
[7] *J. Chamberlain, minute,* 18 Jan. [1900], CO167/724/1065 as quoted by Ballhachet, K, ibid.
[8] Ballhatchet, K. ibid.
[9] Ibid.

many of the estates selling land to former labourers on easy terms, usually on condition that the land remains under cane. In this way the proportion of cane land held by Indians increased from 30.3 per cent in 1909 to 43.1 per cent in 1917, and then more slowly to 46.2 per cent in 1922." [10]

By becoming self-employed planters, the Indo-Mauritians, albeit the fact that a majority of them were not rich, were becoming an economic community with similar interests and, therefore, a force to be increasingly reckoned with. Action Libérale had obtained the support of the majority of them, but they still did not enjoy the right to vote and would not do so until Curé's Labour Party would rock the colonial establishment and the big barons of the sugar industry and obtain the necessary constitutional reform in 1947.

Similarly, there were the lower bourgeoisies of Creole skilled workers and clerks, teachers, civil service employees and manual workers, small meat and other agricultural producers, etc. They also supported the Liberal Party of Laurent and Manilal Doctor and, later, Curé's Labour Party.

Then the First World War (1914-1918) broke out. The Mascarene Islands were barely affected by the major military operations, though in the case of the Seychelles, which had been detached from Mauritius in 1903 and depended on a significant amount of trade with Germany, the situation was different: the Seychellois suffered from a major economic and financial crisis and Mauritius granted to their administration a sum of Rs 100,000 voted by the Council of Government at the request of the British Colonial Office in London. A large number of Mauritians went to serve in the war among the British and French forces in Europe against the Germans and in Mesopotamia against the Turks. Many of them were killed in action or wounded.

On purely economic grounds, the First World War was a golden opportunity for the sugar industry, as Mauritian sugar fetched high prices in England. The trading classes, in particular the Indo-Mauritians who had trading houses in Port-Louis, increased the country's commercial links with the East, especially as regards the import of food items, mainly cereals of all sorts. Important fortunes were thus built in the island from sugar and trade, and the country prospered until the mid-1920s when the price of sugar fell abruptly. The boom reinforced the social stratification that was occurring within the Indo-Mauritian community, with the gap increasing between the top and the botton of the social hierarchy on the basis of class interests.

At the 1916 elections during the war and the economic boom, the Oligarchs, under the banner of their Parti de l'Ordre, won once more a large majority among a total electorate of about 6,000 voters, except in Port-Louis where the liberal leaders, Dr. Eugène Laurent and Edouard Nairac were re-elected. But in the following years, the ranks of the Action Libérale were deprived of several of its members and supporters who decided to support a rather unexpected and surprising political movement in favour of the retrocession of Mauritius to France.

London worried by retrocession to France and Indian 'terrorists'

The British in London and Mauritius had been seriously worried by Action Libérale's leaders Dr. Eugène Laurent and Manilal doctor. They thought, in their simplistic analysis based uniquely on ethnicity as the Colonial Office papers indicate, that the Creole leaders and other Creoles were going to be '*assimilated*' by the Indians:

"Laurent, a Creole leader of Indian origins, was an example of that assimilation which alarmed the officials. But they soon found a new enemy. Creole leaders were not the only threat to Indian loyalty. There was Manilal Doctor, a lawyer from Gujarat who was favoured by Mahatma Gandhi and had helped Indian workers to complain against ill-treatment. The procureur-general thought he was trying to 'stir the Indian element'." [11]

The movement for retrocession to France gathered momentum among the opponents to the Parti de l'Ordre of the sugar barons, thus raising again British fears of a rebellion, but this time unlike the 1832 rebellion of the slave-owners and coming from the other side of the political divide: the French-speaking, educated professionals and petite bourgeoisie suffering from unemployment and discrimination from the ruling classes.

As will be shown in this section, immediately after the retrocession movement died out, London was expressing fear that the Indo-Mauritians were being influenced by '*terrorists*' who got their inspiration from the pro-independence movement in India. In both cases, those fears were imaginary as the retrocessionists submitted themselves to the electoral process, while the Indian nationalists had been seeking financial help, as some researchers have established, from Indo-Mauritians who could afford to support them.

"Official attitudes were losing touch with reality. What the Congress party wanted from Indians in Mauritius was financial help for its campaigns in India." [12]

---

10 Robertson, C.J., ***The Sugar Industry of Mauritius***, Economic Geography, Vol. 6, No. 4 (Oct., 1930), pp. 338-351, Clark University. <http://www.jstor.org/stable/140527>. Accessed 26 February 2012.
11 Ballhatchet, in ***The Historical Journal***, op cit, page 999.
12 Ibid., page 1004.

Anti-Oligarchs

Joseph Chamberlain (left), Secretary of State for the Colonies from 1893 to 1903, wrote: "The Indians are I think in a majority of the population & it is most desirable that their interests shd. be represented. I will face the storm. When it has settled down we shall be stronger in Mauritius than we have ever been & the French oligarchy will be kept in order by the other races." Similarly, Edouard Nairac (above) won in Port-Louis at the general elections against the Party of the Oligarchs. Below, a picture of the Royal College Curepipe at the beginning of the 20th century, when most of the locale elite studied there.

affairs of their new island home. It surprised and pleased Lutchumun that people from so many communities should be speaking from the same platform." [1]

In those years, two other major leaders of the 20th century mass movements were in their twenties: Maurice Curé, who became a laureate of the Royal College in 1907 and left the country to study medicine, and Cashinath Kistoe who, in 1908, led a protest movement of labourers in the South. Kistoe was prosecuted for sedition and thrown in prison, where he was visited by a pious man, Pandit Bhagath. The latter helped him obtain his release and go to India in 1912 where he made advanced studies and qualified as a religious leader. [2]

The growing political awareness of the new generation of Mauritians was a direct result of the action of the Action Libérale. The Bissoondoyal family, who were to play a major role in Mauritian politics, settled in Port-Louis in 1913, two years after the riots. It is no wonder that in their political message, consider

---

1 Bissoondoyal, Uttama, ***Promises to Keep***, Editions de l'Océan Indien 1990.
2 Peerthum, Satteeanund, ***Pandit Cashinath Kistoe***, op cit.

This was only part of the truth as later, in the 1940, Emmanuel Anquetil appointed his trusted friend Basdeo Bissoondoyal as the Mauritius Labour Party representative with the independist Indian Congress Party.[13] It was a purely political alliance. In the 1920s, already fear of Indian influence continued to haunt the British after the retrocession movement collapsed.

This retrocessionist initiative, following the electoral impasse that maintained the less fortunate classes of Coloured and Creoles and the 'petits blancs' in a sort of blocked society without hope of progress, where most of them could not vote, was yet another way to challenge the colonial authorities and the sugar barons. Many believed that integrating the French fold would bring them a better social status and jobs and the ensuing well-being that they were being deprived of. A serious study of the causes of that curious episode of Mauritian history is needed, but what can be established already is the constant influence of ideas of freedom from overseas, especially Europe and India, has always played a role in the island's history.

One cannot dissociate the events in Europe where socialism was on the rise, especially in France with such great leaders as Jean Jaurès, assassinated in 1914, and who had probably influenced Dr. Maurice Curé, who had studied in Britain, then had participated in the Balkan War as a doctor, and other intellectuals of his days. The same can be said of influences brought to Mauritian shores by Gandhi and Manilal Doctor and of the considerable influence of Indian nationalism on great Mauritian leaders like Cashinath Kistoe the later Curé and Anquetil and Basdeo and Sookdeo Bissoondoyal.

Communalist historians have argued otherwise and it is known that the British and the sugar magnates did play the game of divide-and-rule that explains the surge of communalism in 20th century Mauritius, based, on the one hand, on the Retrocession Movement presented as anti-Indian, and on the other hand, on the role that *'Mother India'* played positively in influencing Dr. Eugène Laurent, Manilal Doctor, Kistoe and the Bissoondoyals. The latter have always expressed their admiration for Laurent as one of the great liberators of Mauritius. Racism and considerations of social status, caste, etc. did exist among the ethnic communities, but the political history of the island has been mainly a matter of class-based struggles.

The Retrocession Movement

The Franco-Mauritian sugar barons opposed retrocession to France and so did the affluent leaders of Indo-Mauritian businesses and they monopolised the right to vote except in Port-Louis where there was a large number of self-employed people and middle- and low-ranking government employees who could satisfy the property franchise. At the Colonial Office, there was a lot of head-scratching, observes researcher Ballhatchet on the basis of an examination of the frantic correspondence between the governor in Mauritius and the officials in London in those days on the topic of retrocession and then on imaginary Indian *'terrorists'*. It is extremely unfortunate that such people were defining the destinies of the colonies.

For those officials, the partisans of retrocession were being disloyal. They had the same reaction when Manilal Doctor, Gandhi's envoy, mobilised the Indian small planters and labourers and disturbances broke out before and after the 1911 general elections and the influence of India started to be felt in the island. In 1922, following the demise of the retrocession movement, the Colonial Office was considering action against the Indo-Mauritians being inspired by Indian nationalism and C.O. (Colonial Office) files contain references to those persons as *'sedition-mongers.'* [14]

Cashinath Kistoe had organised strikes in the south of the island and had been sentenced to prison and then upon liberation went to India from whence he came back a priest and an even more resolute militant. Later, the independence movement in India started to inspire more Indo-Mauritian leaders who were not close to the oligarchy and were active rather at the grassroots level of the community. More serious disturbances would come in the 1930s from the masses of Indo-Creoles militating under the banner of Curé's Labour Party and one of the names that come up in the Colonial Office papers was going to be that of the young Pandit Sahadeo:

"Then Bede Clifford, the governor, told the secretary of state that Pandit Sahadeo, Curé's 'principal assistant', was in India 'going through a course of instruction with Nehru and the terrorists'. Bede Clifford thought he was 'a rank seditionist' who wanted 'to induce Mauritius Indians to follow the

---
13 On November 16, 1938, Mauritius Labour Party wrote a letter to Basdeo Bissoondoyal in India, asking him to inform the Indian National Congress about the situation in Mauritius and the MLP. The young missionary wrote a memorandum which he communicated to the Congress and also sent a letter to Mahatma Gandhi, according to U. Bissoondoyal. His memorandum was given publicity in some Indian newspapers, namely T*he Amrita Bazar Patrik*a and *The Statesman*.
14 Ballhatchet, Kenneth, op cit.

anti-British policy prevalent in India'. He was 'cunning', whereas Curé was 'mentally unbalanced'." [15]

In both cases, the perceived threat from France and subsequently one from India led to quite harsh measures. A warship, HMS Comus, was sent to cruise off Mauritius to intimidate the retrocession partisans and they were also not allowed to campaign freely. Governor Sir Hesketh Bell had been allowed to interdict public meetings for retrocession according to a despatch to him from Viscount Milner, Secretary of State at the Colonial Office. [16] Governor Bell was accused even in London of having interfered with the freedom of the press: two newspaper editors (those of **Le Mauricien** and **Le Progrès Colonial**) who were supporting retrocession had to assert their loyalty to the British Crown As for the Indians and their allies in the following years, they were arrested, imprisoned and sued in court and some strikers lost their lives.

Retrocession and the rise of ethnic prejudice

The retrocession-to-France movement, just as the influence of India on the Indo-Mauritian leaders from Kistoe to the Bissoondoyal brothers, has been used to stir communalism in the country. This section will show how. However, it must be also admitted that there has been in the course of such political movements, excessive language used on various sides. Such excesses were literally made available to the communalist strategists like when a supporter of retrocession argued that in Réunion Island the Indians had been assimilated and that it should be the same in Mauritius to avoid an Indo-Mauritian majority that would rule the country. This came from a district cashier, one Abel Loumeau in his *'La rétrocession et les aliens,'* a publication smacking of anti-Indian racism, published in 1919 in Port-Louis under the pseudonym of Elba L. He was for good reason sacked by the British administration. [17]

"The retrocessionists were defeated in the elections. This at least was the official view, though they were never allowed to campaign for retrocession." [18]

Nevertheless, the policies *'keep-them-apart'* of the oligarchy to divide the work force, and, its equivalent, the *'divide-and-rule'* [19] of the British colonial administration were being tested and put into practice, and the ultimate result is today's ethnic politics, pushed to the extreme, unashamedly, by the Mauritian political establishment to this date, in independent Mauritius. And yet, scholarly studies have established that Mauritius has remained an *'integrated'* society to such an extent that the greatest geniuses in the science of statistics have never been able to solve the problem of ethnic classification and demographics with so many intercultural and interethnic marriages, the blurring of the divide between the Indian castes following immigration to Mauritius, etc. This has led to such conclusions as this one:

"The very problems of the census commissioners derived from the fact that throughout the nineteenth and twentieth centuries the variously defined communities lived as an integrated society, notably in Port Louis, the capital, making segregation and separation impossible." [20]

The retrocession movement was supported by **Le Mauricien** newspaper where Raoul Rivet, a young journalist, had been recruited by the then owner, E. Henry. Several Coloured intellectuals belonging to the middle and lower middle classes supported the movement But the Retrocessionist platform was not of a nature to rouse the sympathy of either the non-voting working classes of Creoles and Indians, or the wealthy Indo-Mauritian voters, who generally sided with the essentially White plantocracy, with whom they had common business interests.

The true nature of the retrocession movement

Retrocession to France, it must be said, was also, despite the underlying class-based antagonism between the rich and the poorer sections of Coloured and Creoles, motivated by a mixture of nostalgic ideas about French colonisation that had left in the island a major cultural heritage. Anand Mulloo writes, **"With the long World War I over, the bottled up feelings of sympathy for France – La douce France (sweet France) – exploded."** [21]

U. Bissoondoyal sees the more political aspect of the movement:

15 Ballhatchet, op cit.
16 Ibid. **Milner, telegram to Bell, 12 Oct. 1920**, quoted by Ballhatchet, op cit.
17 Ibid.
18 Ibid.
19 The maxims divide et impera and divide ut regnes were utilised by Caesar and Napoleon and meant divide and rule or divide and conquer. The British applied them in their colonies, mainly India. There are theories that say either they created the principle or that it existed already and they used what they saw.
20 Christopher, J.A., **Ethnicity, community and the census in Mauritius**, 1830-1990. In: The Geographical Journal, Vol. 158, No. 1 (Mar., 1992), pp. 57-64. Published by: Blackwell Publishing on behalf of The Royal Geographical Society (with the Institute of British Geographers) Stable URL:< http://www.jstor.org/stable/3060017 >.Accessed: 09/03/2012 22:32.
21 Mulloo, Anand, Our Struggle, 20th Century Mauritius, Vision Books 1982.

"During the 1921 elections, the main issue was the retrocession of Mauritius to France. Some liberal politicians of Mauritius campaigned in favour of the annexation of Mauritius to France in the hope that this would give Mauritius a larger measure of autonomy in internal affairs."[22]

In Madden and Darwin's ***'Select documents'***,[23] it is observed that Colonial Office documents mentions the case of an Indian who was a retrocessionist: *"**The son of the deputy mayor of St. Louis (Port-Louis), a wealthy Indo-Mauritian, had been treated in an offensive way in Cape Town: his father had become an enthusiastic 'retrocessionist'.**"*

What ethnic bias prevents some writers from saying is that the defeat of the retrocession movement was not the work of the Indo-Mauritian electorate which was only composed of a very tiny number of voters that were rich enough to qualify as electors and most of them sided with the conservatives. In fact, in Port-Louis, for instance, the anti-retrocessionists Edouard Nairac and Jérôme Tranquille defeated not just the two retrocessionist candidates, but also those of the oligarchy. Of course, there were Indo-Mauritian voters on both sides, as per one example cited above. Class politics prevailed in Port-Louis over other considerations. Nairac (later Sir Edouard Nairac) was a liberal like René Mérandon du Plessis, and came from a modest family like many Indo-Mauritians and, later, he rose to be the Chief Justice of Mauritius.

'**The Dependent Empire**' reveals the Franco-Mauritian Oligarchs' hostility to retrocession.[24] Sir Henri Leclézio, knighted by the Queen, also wrote to acting governor Sir John Middleton in 1919:

"There were some 5,000 'gentry of colour', attached to England and opposed to retrocession – equal in intellect with the whites. There are some 15,000 coloureds of middle class and 'pretty well educated' with some French blood: clerks, professors, traders, doctors, attorneys &c. – where in particular retrocessionists could be found, but not many. The promoters had indeed neither influence nor prestige to lead this section (…) [Leclézio and elected members of the Council of Government asked for the advocacy of retrocession to be treated as disloyalty, believing that the leaders knew it was a 'chimera'…" [25]

The Oligarchy controlled a majority of the electoral votes from 1886 to 1948 and so, the defeat of the Retrocessionists was primarily their doing and that of the liberal candidates like Edouard Nairac and Jerôme tranquille and not particularly of the Indo-Mauritian labourers, who simply did not have the right to vote. The abusive, if not simplistic assertions by historians and politicians that the Indo-Mauritian community defeated the retrocession movement are not accurate. Leclézio, the leader of the multiethnic conservative electorate, descending from an old French family, led the battle against the retrocessionists - and that's the plain historical truth. It was class-based politics, or politics, simply put, based on class interests as the liberals, on the left side of politics, also fought against retrocession to France.

This being said, revolutionary trade unionism and "social" or leftist Catholicism were challenging the conservative French establishment as from 1905. The rise of the leftists in France had resulted, following an intense anticlerical campaign, in the ousting of the Catholic Church from the State apparatus and the separation of Church and State had been proclaimed in 1905. [26] A left-leaning man like Curé would have probably envisaged a French type of socialism for Mauritius at the time he stood as a candidate for the Retrocession Movement, especially as, in Mauritius, he opposed the practices of the Catholic establishment in the field of education because in his eyes (as in those of Raoul Rivet) they were discriminatory and favoured a small minority of privileged persons.

The author of this book has seen in the historical documents held by a former Labour Party leader, now defunct, copies of letters Curé had been constantly, not to say obsessively, sending to the governor in the 1920s in the defence of Indo-Mauritian labourers who were ill-treated and the actual written responses of the Colonial Secretary on behalf of the British governor. There is absolutely no reason to believe that Curé or Raoul Rivet, the man who introduced Dr. Seewoosagur Ramgoolam in the political arena as a man of great promise, could have ever viewed retrocession with the sectarian blinkers worn by a small number of supporters of that movement.

Curé's pro-workers behaviour explains why, once back from his studies, during which he witnessed the rise of socialism in France and served as a doctor in the Balkan wars, he took up the cause of the Indo-Mauritian and Creole

22 Indians Overseas. The Mauritian Experience, op cit..
23 Madden, A. Frederick & Darwin, John, ***The Dependent Empire, 1900-1948, Colonies, Protectorates, and Mandates Select Documents on the Constitutional History of the British Empire and Commonwealth*** - December 1994.
24 Ibid. "***SIR HENRI LECLÉZIO TO ACTING-GOVERNOR JOHN MIDDLETON, 21 April 1919 [Apart from a very few, the white population descending from the old French families was opposed to a return to France.] They have personal feelings of strong affection and admiration for the country of their origin, but they are loyally attached to England by bonds of gratitude for the blessings which they enjoy under the British rute: liberty of conac1ence 1 freedom of speech, social peace...*"
25 ***Ibid***.
26 Le grand livre de l'histoire du monde, op cit.

labourers and artisans. He experienced the rise of the Labour Party while in the UK and became a Fabian socialist. [27] After his defeat at the 1921 general elections, he followed with keen interest the rise of trade unionism in Britain where, eventually, the Labourites, backed by the Liberals, conquered power in 1924 under the leadership of James Ramsay Macdonald. The latter came back to power in 1929 and from 1931 to 1935, Macdonald headed a coalition government. Curé was, at the same time, in Mauritius, setting up a formidable trade union movement, the first one to gather widespread support in the island's history, and he launched the Mauritius Labour Party in 1936. Once more, events and ideas outside Mauritius were going to rock the country.

Born in 1886 from a middle class Coloured family, Curé studied brilliantly at the Royal College, some of his exceptional performances attracting media attention. He became a laureate of the English Scholarship in 1907 and went on to study medicine in Great Britain. There also, he was a brilliant student and a gold medallist. A career in medical research opened before him. But he then went to serve as a medical practitioner in the war in the Balkans before finally going back to Britain, then returning to Mauritius for family matters. [28]

When Curé was candidate with Edouard Laurent in Port-Louis, in 1921, for the Retrocession Movement, the 'great' Laurent, Dr. Eugène Laurent, had already left the country on August 14, 1919, to migrate to Britain, where he died in London on February 13, 1926, at the age of 67. His deputy in Action Libérale, Edouard Nairac, and Jerôme Tranquille, another Liberal, stood, as already mentioned, as candidates for the Legistive Council against the Oligarchs and the Retrocessionists. All the Retrocessionist candidates lost, while Curé, some time afterwards, left the movement, which, meanwhile, gradually slipped into oblivion and disappeared altogether.

The Oligarchs won in all the rural districts, supported by the rich Indian voters, while two Liberals, the heirs of Dr. Eugène Laurent, Edouard Nairac and Jerome Tranquille were elected in Port-Louis. Edouard Nairac, observes Yvan Martial, **"turned his back on his Coloured voters and espoused the anti-retrocession cause."** [29] R. K. Boodhun, who had also lost, was nominated by the governor to the Legislative Council where he joined Hassen Sakir as another official representative of the Indo-Mauritian community.

Boodhun thus became the deserving leader of part of the elite of the Indo-Mauritian community. At the base of that section of the population, among the lower middle and working classes, Kistoe paved the way for Curé and the Bissoondoyal brothers to create and lead a significantly far more radical political movement, based on trade unionism, and inspired by the British Labour Party as well as by the Congress Party of India, which was struggling for independence.

First Indo-Mauritians in the Legislative Council

Within the Legislative Council, two other prominennt members of the Indo-Mauritian community made history at the general elections of 1926, Rajcoomar Gujadhur, the owner of two sugar estates, and Dhunputh Lallah, attorney-at-law who were elected in Flacq and Grand Port respectively. They were the first members of the Indo-Mauritian community to be elected to the legislature in Mauritian history. The contest had been tough in Grand Port where there was a three-cornered fight, but Lallah came out first, winning a total of 424 votes against L. Maurel's 306 votes and G. Gebert's 230 votes, the total number of electors being 1,031, of whom 335 Hindus, 128 Muslims, 564 General Population and four Chinese. In a pamphlet about Dhunputh Lallah published in 1992, Premdath Bhujun writes:

"The daily cry of the electoral campaign of Mr. Dhunputh Lallah was 'khoon par khoon - khoone khoon'. The political slogan was repeated not only by Hindus and Muslims but also by a few members of the General Population." [30]

This is not surprising as Dr. Eugène Laurent was of Indian origin and, as seen before, was suspected by the Colonial Office in London, on the basis of his ethnic mix, of creating an Indo-Creole alliance to overthrow the established political order in the island in favour of the majority.

Following the successive defeats of the anti-Oligarchy parties (the Liberals led by Dr. Beaugeard, the Democrats led by Dr. Eugène Laurent and the Retrocessionists led by Armand Esnouf), there was a vacuum which was quickly filled by a "unionist" party, the Union Mauricienne of "the other Laurent": Dr. Edgar Laurent, who had been elected in Port-Louis together with a former Retrocessionist, Arthur Rohan, at the 1926 general elections.

---

27 Peerthum, Satteeanund, unpublished research work on the life of Dr. Maurice Curé.
28 Ibid.
29 Ile Maurice: Edouard Nairac - De la caisse de savon à la Cour suprême, in L'Express, May 17, 2010.
30 Bhujun, Premduth, Dunputh Lallah (1885-1947), Mauritius 1992.

Actually, it was with Raoul Rivet as his deputy that Dr. Edgar Laurent (not to be confused with Dr. Eugène Laurent, the Liberal, or Edouard Laurent, the Retrocessionist) structured the U.M. as a real political party, which obtained its successes mainly in the Port-Louis legislative and municipal elections. However, in spite of such prominent figures as were its leaders as well as the young Jules Koenig, Razack Mohamed and Dr. Seewoosagur Ramgoolam who was introduced by Rivet into active politics, the Union Mauricienne was incapable of seriously challenging the domination of the Oligarchs over Mauritian politics.

Just like its liberal-leaning predecessors (Beaugeard's movement and Action Libérale) the Union Mauricienne was not very successful at the national level, apart from electing for two successive terms Dr. Edgar Laurent and Raoul Rivet, in 1931 and 1936, to the Legislative Council. It provided, nevertheless, the breeding ground for a new generation of moderate politicians like Dr. Seewoosagur Ramgoolam and Jules Koenig, who both stood as municipal candidates under the banner of the UM and fought elections against the Labour Party in the 1940s.

However, the U.M. preached elitism as its main political objective on the eve of the very era when the masses would enter abruptly the political arena. Even Dr. Seewoosagur Ramgoolam later accused the UM of anti-Indo-Mauritian "***machinations***" in an article entitled "***We Stand for our Rights***" and a series of others under the heading "***In the World of Mr. Rivet***," published in 1940 and 1941. Ramgoolam left the party which, even before the general elections of 1948, disbanded and disappeared completely from the political scene, when the right to vote was granted for the first time to the working classes, in the 1947 Constitution.

Until that time, at the general elections of 1931 and 1936, Indo-Mauritian candidates were not elected any more, producing a feeling of intense frustration among the intellectuals and leading business people of the community. The number of electors surprisingly decreased again by 800 from 1926 to 1931, with the Indo-Mauritian electorate diminishing by as much as 500. From 1931 to 1936 the decrease was about 1,000. Professor Hansraj Mathur, of the University of Mauritius, writing in ***L'Express***, attributed the decrease to two causes, first the economic crisis of the 1930's which impoverished a number of electors who thus lost the property qualifications required by the 1886 electoral law still in force, second to the deliberate striking off of electors' names from the electoral roll under pressure from the Oligarchs.

Chapter 37
Class, community and elections in the 1920's

In an article that smacked of sectarianism, Roger Pezzani had, in 1914, written that *"Indo-Creoles are not the meek lambs that the armchair politician takes pleasure in picturing himself."* He described them as *"a servile horde yet unreclaimed from heathendom and barbarism."* He was one of those who believed that only the intellectual elite should have the right to vote. However, as will be seen later, Pezzani was not a racist in the true sense of the word, but wanted the Indo-Mauritians to produce their own elite that would join the other elites in the various other ethnic communities so as to govern the country. Elitism was thrust forward in the various ethnic groups as a new political ideology - and elitism can be viewed as a sectarian approach favouring elites, in this case, the educated elite in legislative representation and regarding the rest of the people as being servile and barbaric.

It was the same Pezzani who, during a special session of the Legislative Council, on March 29, 1927, presented a motion as follows: *"The Council of Government is of opinion that this Colony is now ripe for representative government."* [1]

It was a fact that the country badly needed an electoral reform to reflect the major change in the composition of the population brought about by the massive Indian immigration of the previous decades. In 1922, there had been an attempt by Emile Sauzier to bring about a reform of the Constitution to give more power to the representatives of local interests. A committee subsequently recommended a Council comprising six elected members and three officials, and a House of Representatives of 17 members of the General Population and four Indo-Mauritians. But no major reform was actually carried out. [2]

The only solution would have been a far-reaching reform of the Beaugeard Franchise of 1886. The Democrat Edgar Antelme's 1887 formal legislative proposal for what he called *"universal suffrage"* (excluding indentured workers who had not permanently settled in the country) would have had more far reaching effects than some timid proposals of reform made in the 1920's.

Whatever the shortcomings of the Antelme Franchise, it would have probably given liberal/democratic parties decisive victories over the Oligarchs. In contrast, Pezzani's representative government formula was based on the 1886 franchise and would not have produced a really representative Legislative Council.

As the core of the democratic problem was the nature of the franchise. Historians are often perplexed by the lack of propositions within the Legislative Council for a franchise revolution, particularly during the years when the British Labour Party under Ramsay Macdonald from 1924 to 1931 was in power (from 1931 to 1935, though, Macdonald headed a coalition government with the Conservatives).

It was only when the Labour Party was re-elected to power in Britain for the period 1945-1951, under Clement Richard Attlee as Prime Minister, that the franchise was enlarged in Mauritius where the Mauritius Labour Party led by Guy Rozemont (who succeeded Emmanuel Anquetil in 1946) managed to obtain an enlarged franchise that brought onto the electoral registers most of the small planters and a major section of the working classes of Creoles and Indo-Mauritians.

But that does not mean that the members of the Legislative Council did not debate about constitutional reforms and the question of franchise. Actually, there were two proposals made in 1925 and 1927, respectively, for constitutional reforms. And a lowering of the 1886 franchise requirements was suggested by Dr. Edgar Laurent during the 1927 debates in Council. It is interesting to study what went on during those debates, which throw light on the class aspects of Mauritian society in those days.

The first of the two proposals for electoral reform was made by Edouard Nairac. The latter had worked together with Dr. Eugène Laurent and Manilal Doctor in the Action Libérale from 1911 up to the departure of Laurent from the country in 1919. Nairac was re-elected in Port-Louis, this time with Jerome Tranquille, at the 1926 general elections. One year before the 1926 general elections, Nairac, a veteran of Action Libérale, proposed to the Council

---
1 Legislative Council, Debate, 29 March 1927.
2 Legislative Council, Debate, 1922.

a motion the first clause of which read:

"This Council is of opinion that it is necessary to amend the Constitution of the Legislative Council of Mauritius so as to ensure a more extensive representation of the community and give it a larger share in the management of the affairs of this Colony." [3]

So far, so good. But Nairac's colleague Tranquille, after supporting only that first part of the motion, refused to caution the rest of it. And the rest of that motion restricted the first part to just the following changes in the electoral law: that the vote be given to *"the owner of shares in landed property or factories in the rural districts, of face value of Rs 3,000"*; and that the Council should be composed of six unofficial members with freedom to vote representing all sections of the Mauritian community, plus 12 official members and 12 elected members instead of 10 (he proposed a third member for Port-Louis and a second one for Plaines Wilhems, while the other seven districts would continue to be represented by one elected member each). The motion went on to propose also that the decision of the majority of members should be the final decision of the Council save in exceptional circumstances decided by the governor, and that the governor should still have the final word in financial matters.

Prior to that motion in Council, there had been in Mauritius a debate about *"communal representation."* During the debates on his motion, Edouard Nairac referred to the that debate by saying that it was anyone's duty *"not to follow the extremist views of those who wanted communal representation for all those who want to call themselves Indians or non-Christians."*

He then went on to say that the majority of votes in seven out of the nine districts of the country (each district was considered as one electoral constituency) were controlled by *"the landed interests,"* while in the two others, Plaines Wilhems and Port-Louis, the majority of votes reflected *"the salaried and commercial interests."* As for the *"landed interests,"* Edouard Nairac explained:

"That landed interest, so far as the ownership of the soil goes, is shared by two sections of the community, the one which hitherto has sent almost invariably representatives to the Council and the other which is the growing Indian element."

He stated also that the Constitution, for 40 years, *"has given to all owners of landed property equal electoral rights."* But he recognised that in spite of that and except *"for a few recent tendencies,"* the Indo-Mauritians had not resorted to *"ultranationalism"* But the problem was that in the seven above-mentioned rural districts, electoral representation belonged only to the *"landed interests,"* whereas, *"the salaried or commercial interests are reduced practically to nothing as compared with the agrarian element, that element made up of the owners of the soil, of sugar factories and their descendants."*

The debates on the motion give us today an interesting insight into the class conflicts that were occupying the minds of the opinion leaders of those days. Actually, Edouard Nairac's motion was proposed to strike a balance within the existing system between what he termed agrarian and landed interests, on the one side, and salaried and commercial interests on the other side (especially small and medium traders of Port-Louis).

Moreover, it is also interesting, whatever the shortcomings of some of his proposals, to note that Nairac stated in Council that the people who owned company shares were not recognised by the electoral law as owners who were qualified to vote, contrary to the situation of the owners of land who, even in the case of small fragmented portions of land, were registered as voters. Revealing what was going on in his mind, he said that those owners often belonged to *"the illiterate classes"* who, he added, *"were acquiring votes daily."* He wanted to place the Rs 3,000-shareholders on an equal footing with the Rs 3,000-movable property owners, as the latter already had the right to vote since 1886, under the Beaugeard Franchise.

But Nairac would also have increased plural voting, that is, an elector voting in more than one district, wherever he/she had shares of the required value. Referring to that two years later, that is, in 1927, Dr. Edgar Laurent would criticise Nairac (who had come back to the Council this time as a nominated member), saying that plural voting, which already existed, should not be encouraged.

---

[3] Mauritius Legislative Council, Debate 28 April 1925.

When put to vote, the following voted for the whole motion: Henri Leclézio, the leader of the oligarchy faction, Samuel Fouquereaux, R.K. Boodhun, L.H.A. Noel, L.A.M. d'Unienville, A. Duclos, M. Martin, P. Raffray, L. Rouillard, C. Antelme, Edouard Nairac. But the 1926 elections were near and no action followed the motion.

After the 1926 elections, Dr. Edgar Laurent and Arthur Rohan were the rnembers elected for Port-Louis, replacing, as such, Nairac and Tranquille. Pezzani, who had been elected in Plaines Wilhems, tabled the motion which read:

"The Council of Government is of the opinion that this Colony is now ripe for Representative Government" [4]

It must be stressed here that representative government means a government composed of a majority of elected members within the colonial system, whereas responsible government means a government not only composed of a majority of elected members, but able to legislate on a number of vital local affairs and to carry out the application of its legislative decisions, but still within the colonial system though independence would by then be upcoming.

Quite surprisingly, during the 1927 debates on his motion, the same elitist Pezzani who had written about the *"servile horde"* of Indo-Creoles in 1914, in **Mauritius Illustrated**, addressed the Indo-Mauritian community as one which, in his view, would one day give to Mauritius politicians of the calibre of Sir William Newton and Sir Virgil Naz. He also asserted that it was time for Mauritians to unite and said also that Mauritians of all ethnic groups could represent the interests of the Indo-Mauritian population, and not necessarily just the Indo-Mauritians. The man had mellowed with time and age.

In the Council in which he was speaking on March 29, 1927, there were the two elected members of the Indo-Mauritian community, Rajcoomar Gujadhur and Dhunputh l.allah. G.M.D. Atchia had also joined the ranks of the Indo-Mauritian representatives as a nominated member after the 1926 elections, in replacement of Dr. Hassen Sakir.

Pezzani asked for a Council composed of 23 members, of which five would be officials, six nominated and 12 elected. [5] That would have given, for the first time, a majority to the elected component of the Legislative Council. But there were four other interventions worth reading today to understand what went on in the minds of the members of the legislature in the 1920's: those of Dunputh Lallah, freshly elected in 1926 in the district of Grand Port, Dr. Edgar Laurent, the future founder of the Union Mauricienne, Arthur Rohan, and G.M.D. Atchia, nominated to represent the interests of the Indo-Mauritian community after Hassen Sakir retired.

Dhunputh Lallah clearly stated that he would vote against the motion. He spoke of *"the population to which I have the honour to belong"* as forming the majority of the population of the country. He found *"danger"* in the motion which, he said, *"does not (...) meet with the wishes of the majority of the people or of the inhabitants of this island."* He went on: *"I submit that it would be absolutely rash at this stage of our political development, being given the heterogeneous composition of our population, to grant representative government to this island."*

Dunputh Lallah recalled that Pezzani had suggested, during the debates, a Council of 23 members, composed of five officials, six nominees and 12 elected representatives, which meant, he said, that *"whatever may be the decision of the official and nominated members and whether the latter would be willing to vote with the government or not, the elected members would always be in majority (...) Representative Government in such circumstances would be nothing but Government by a minority of the people, because, anyhow, it is only a minority that would be elected and it would be very easy for them to come here and pass any resolution or measures detrimental or disadvantageous to any section of the population. "*

Referring to the 1925 motion of Edouard Nairac, he said that it would have meant the *"jeopardising of the interests of the Indian population by giving the right of vote to shareholders in the different districts in which they possess property."* He spoke of the objection of the proprietors living in Curepipe, Quatre Barnes, Beau Bassin and Rose Hill to the establishment of elected town boards. *"If we have such systematic opposition to obtain freedom for small townships, how then can I, a son of India, who sees around me 250,000 Indians, vote a measure which I am sure in the future will prove detrimental to that population?"* he asked.

Dr. Edgar Laurent made a lengthy speech. He said there were three types of reform: one proposed in 1925 by Edouard Nairac, another one termed *"communal representation"* and the third one the Pezzani motion. He said that the *"communal representation"* formula would mean *"going backwards"* and it would *"divide"* the country. The objective of equal political rights was better, he said, and a "union mauricienne" was a goal that was quite attain-

---
[4] Mauritius Legislative Council, Debate 22 March 1927.
[5] Ibid., 29 March 1927.

able, though not in the immediate future. However, he found that a reform of the electoral law should bring about a change in the franchise. Apart from Port-Louis, he said, all the electoral districts were dominated by the "*landed interests.*" But what about the interests, he asked, "*of the little proprietors, the artisans, the workers, the small tenants?*" Laurent then expressed the opinion that the franchise should be lowered, particularly as regards the requirement of movable property of a minimum value of Rs 3,000 which should be fixed instead at Rs 2,000. He was in favour of granting the right to vote to people "*having a certain degree of education,*" but he immediately stressed that he was against any attempt to prevent people expressing themselves in their own languages from enjoying the right to vote. He then asked that the number of elected members for Port-Louis be increased from two to three and that of the elected representatives of Plaines Wilhems be increased from one to two, giving a total of 12 elected representatives for the nine electoral districts in the Legislative Council.

Dr. Edgar Laurent attacks anti-Indian slogans

He was also against the 1925 proposal of Edouard Nairac in favour of the right to vote on the basis of shareholding interests in companies. Then Edgar Laurent gives the answer to a problem which has puzzled many modern historians: the diminishing numbers of voters, election after election, under the 1886 electoral law. He criticised magistrates and other authorities who harassed people who claimed their right to vote under the movable property franchise of Rs 3,000. Magistrates interpreted that right at their own discretion, he said, and took upon themselves to strike off the names of voters from the electoral registers. He spoke of the risk that the country "*would be left entirely in the hands of the rich.*"

A part of Dr. Edgar Laurent's speech focused on the question of the so-called "*Indian peril*" [6] raised in some quarters. It is quite revealing and has to be quoted here for the reader to gain more insight into that particular aspect of the political debate in those days:

"*There is another objection which has not been raised in the Council, but about which much has been said in the press. I mean the 'peril indien, non-IndoMauricien', or also, the 'Indian spectre.' I must remark that already in 1883-84, those who were hostile to any Reform, like Sir Celicourt Antelme, had mentioned that Indo-Mauritian spectre. Sir Célicourt Antelme was saying that if the Reform was accepted as was asked by Naz, Newton, Guibert, Raoul and others in 1883, the Council would quickly be submerged by the Indo-Mauritian element.*

"*Nothing of that sort has happened; forty years have had to elapse for two Indo-Mauritians to be elected, and I do not believe that a majority of seats will, in the immediate future, be obtained by Indo-Mauritians. An even if that was to be the case, from the moment that we agree on the principle that the Council should not be representative of the various sections of the population, but should rather be representative of the various interests, whoever be our representatives at this Council table, the members of the seven districts where the agricultural interests are predominant will always be the representatives of the landed interests. The representatives of Port Louis will represent, with other interests, those of the artisans and the workers (...)*

"*I must say that among those who cannot refrain from raising all the time the question of the Indian spectre, there are some who, as in 1884-85, do not at all believe in such peril but rather form part of that handful of Mauritians, of those handful of 'reactionaries,' who do not want any change at all, and who are partisans of the status quo. (...) the large majority of the inhabitants of this country want our Constitution to be seriously overhauled (...)We know that since the Reform and up to now, only the landed interest had been represented in the Council, with one or two exceptions.*"

Edgar Laurent referred to the stand taken by Dunputh Lallah:

"*My honourable friend of Grand Port does not want the Constitution to be changed because, he says, that change would constitute a disadvantage for his two hundred and fifty thousand countrymen, the Indo-Mauritians. I confess that I do not understand by what sudden reasoning my friend has come about to think that if we had representative government, the right of access to this Chamber would be refused to the Indo-Mauritians. Having the advantage of their number, of an immense share of the riches of the country, enjoying the same rights and considered as equals, I do not see how Indo-Mauritians would suffer a disadvantage.*

"*We do not have the right to determine the real motive which explains the stand taken by our friend the Member for Grand Port; we do not want to believe even for one moment that it is because he does not think that the Indo-Mauritians will not be able to play an important part in the affairs of the country and that they do not want any change. On the contrary, their newspapers claim for them*

---

[6] Chamber of agriculture proceedings, 8 Apr. 1908, C0882/9/1 IO, op cit, cited in Ballhatchet: the original expression 'the Asiatic peril' was coined by oligarch leader Sir Henri Leclézio. It would be taken up by communalist political forces until the early 1960s. Here Laurent goes further back to Sir Célicourt Antelme when was raised an issue of the so-called 'Indian spectre.'

everyday a larger share in the management of our affairs (...) how can it be that a representative government which would offer them a direct and sure control over our destinies, may frighten them?"

He contested also the right for any member to claim representation for a particular ethnic group. The members for Port-Louis, according to him, represented all ethnic groups. Port-Louis, he also stressed, had by far the largest number of voters and the legislative representation of the district cut across ethnic barriers, he said, adding that the Port-Louis members were not representatives of the Coloured population.

A. Rohan, second member for Port-Louis, expressed his intention to vote for the motion, remarking that it did not go as far as asking for a change in the voting qualifications. "*The question of franchise has altogether been left aside,*" he said.

He added that there was a need for an evolution as the 1886 constitution was not meant to create a stagnant situation. It was an encouragement, he said, for further changes. However Rohan argued that the country was not ripe enough for "*responsible government,*" not yet, though at a later stage that would come. In the meantime, there should be "*representative government,*" according to him, especially for dealing with local affairs, with the governor keeping his so-called "*Reserve Power.*"

Rohan then went on to make a sort of sociological analysis of the composition of the Council. The member for Savanne, L. Rouillard, was a "*big man*" who represented landed interests, banks and insurance companies. The member for Flacq, R. Gujadhur, was an owner of two sugar factories and was voted also by small landowners of his district. All the other districts were represented, according to him, by big bosses of the financial, trading and industrial interests in the Council, except for the Plaines Wilhems district whose member, R. Pezzani, represented clerks, traders, the middle classes, a few small planters and "*a certain number of Indo-Mauritians,*" and the Port-Louis representation was supported by "*clerks, petty traders, big traders, house-owners, merchants,*" that is, "*all interests.*" Rohan claimed that he, personally, came from the "*lower rung of the ladder, being more in contact with the poorer and working classes than any other member of this Council.*"

Rohan, who had trained in an attorney's study to become an attorney in 1911, and who, after his marriage in 1922 to Olga Manuel, had gone to Britain where he was called to the bar in 1925 at the age of 42, said he was "*formerly a workman*" who had found his way into the legal profession. He was, however, a partisan of elitism applied to all communities, whether "*Christians, Hindoos or Mussulmans,*" he said, contemptuously speaking of the "*big mass of comparatively ignorant, backward people outside,*" in contrast to the elites of those communities. But it was the same Rohan who had seconded Dr. Eugène Laurent and helped Willy Moutou set up a trade union movement after a workers' strike in Plaine Lauzun in 1921 (see next chapter). Still, one must bear in mind that a category of specialised workers belonged to a rather well educated small bourgeoisie.

The elitist ideology was eventually incorporated in the programme of the Union Mauricienne founded by Dr. Edgar Laurent and Raoul Rivet and to which Rohan and other contemporary leaders like Dr. S. Ramgoolam and Jules Koenig among others, adhered to struggle as much against the Oligarchy as against the Labour Party of Maurice Curé.

G.M. D. Atchia, who had been nominated to represent the interests of the IndoMauritians, said he agreed with D. Lallah and E. Laurent that there should not be a shareholding qualification as proposed by Nairac in 1925 as that was aimed at "*counter-balancing the Indo-Mauritian vote.*"

The motion was rejected by 10 votes to five. Voted against: E. Nairac, G. Robinson, M. Brodie, L. Rouillard, R. Gujadhur, D. Lallah, M. Martin, S. Fouquereaux, P. Raffray, A. Noel. Voted for: Dr. Ferriere, G.M.D. Atchia, R. Pezzani, A. Rohan, E. Laurent.

Dr. Maurice Curé: "No great man in this world will (...) make me bend.""

During that time, what was Dr. Maurice Curé doing after having left the retrocession movement? After the defeat of the movement, Curé took up the problems of the Indian immigrants in 1926. As stated previously. The author of this book has consulted hitherto unpublished manuscripts of Curé dating from the 1920's to the 1940's thanks to files passed on to him by a leading member of the Labour Party in the 1970s, who passed away several years ago.

For instance, in an exchange of letters with the Colonial Secretary, Curé took up the case of an immigrant who had been wounded on the Bel Air St. Félix Estate and who had been sacked from his job. He wrote to the governor and to the Protector of Immigrants about the case. In a reply dated December 4, the Colonial Secretary stated, "*I am directed by the Governor to acknowledge the receipt of your letter of the 30th November last and to inform you, in reply, that your letter to the Protector of Immigrants has been referred by the latter to the Inspector General of Police for enquiry and that a further communication will be addressed to you in due course."*

Another letter from the Colonial Secretary followed announcing to Curé, "*I am directed by the Governor to inform you that, after enquiry, Government is not prepared to intervene in the matter reported in your letter of the 30th November last.*" But Curé, in a letter dated December 24, 1926, on the eve of Christmas, insisted,

"I wish I could know the reasons why that man was not examined medically as I suggested and why his aggressor was not prosecuted. It is not possible to admit a single instant that his wounds were the result of an accident or that they were self-inflicted. I intend to bring the case before the Department of Emigration of the Government of India as the latter will decide whether immigrants in this colony are to be treated as other human beings."

That incident tells everything about the kind of man Curé was. It happened a decade before he founded the Mauritius Labour Party. And in January 1926, when he was a candidate at the general elections in the Savanne district and where he once more lost, he drafted a political manifesto addressed to the voters. That one-page document, which were among the papers consulted and is available at the Mauritius Archives, is quite revealing about his political philosophy, already.

He said first of all that he had been forced to retire from the electoral race in Plaines Wilhems. The member for Savanne in the Legislative Council who was standing for re-election had followed, he wrote, "*an essentially conservative policy.*" He assured the electors that "*no great man in this world will ever be able to make me bend.*" After that, the manifesto, which he signed, goes on to explain that he is "*preoccupied by the necessity of bringing about a reform of our Constitution so that it may be more democratic, with a view to give satisfaction to all sections of the population.*"

Curé predicted correctly that the country was entering a period of unprecedented crisis and that the cost of living would rise so much that "*to protect from the effects of the high cost of living the middle class and the large mass composed of the working classes, the State must be brought to abolish the tax on rice as has happened in England where there are no duties on basic food items.*"

The manifesto proposed also protective social laws "*which exist in all civilised countries,*" for example, the law on accidents on work sites and that concerning workers' pension "*presently being studied by government.*" He also gave the assurance that he would defend the monopoly of the English Scholarships detained by the Royal College (the Catholic Church and the Oligarchy wanted to extend the scholarships to the private colleges created for the rich children following the opening of the Royal College to the Coloured population): "*Nobody will attack this monopoly,*" he wrote in defence of the Royal College.

Nevertheless, Curé, like most democratic and liberal candidates from 1886 to 1936, would be defeated due to the 1885 franchise which prohibited the under-privileged classes from voting.

history from its very beginning. Sookdeo Bissoondoyal, who had been illuminated by Evenor Hitié's work on Mauritian history, believed in the oneness of the country's historical evolution, from its very beginning to modern times. In his political speeches, he told the Indo-Mauritian masses that they should consider their struggle for emancipation as a continuation of those led by the slaves, the Coloured population, and, in particular, by Jacmin, Tabardin, Rémy Ollier, and Jean Lebrun, whom they considered as great heroes of the historical evolution of the island.

They even rewrote history in books and pamphlets to counter-balance historical accounts they felt distorted by the Oligarchs and others, and in their writings, the sufferings of those great Coloured and Creole leaders at the hands of the Oligarchs were described. De Plevitz also was a model and they have compared him to Gandhi. U. Bissoondoyal has found echoes of Gandhian philosophy before Gandhi in the words of de Plevitz.

Basdeo and Sookdeo successfully helped Curé, through their Jan Andolan, to assemble vast crowds of Indo-Mauritian labourers under the banner of the Labour Party.

Dr. Seewoosagur Ramgoolam, Jules Koenig and Razack Mohamed, who were to become prominent leaders of major political parties themselves, stood as candidates for municipal elections under the unionist banner, against the Labourites as much as they stood also against the candidates of the Oligarchy. Ramgoolam was appointed, in 1940, as successor to S. Seerbookun, who had been the British governor's nominee chosen to represent the Indo-Mauritians in the Legislative Council.

Ramgoolam was nominated in a period of intense social tension when the colonial administration was being assailed from the streets and the sugar cane fields by strikes, demonstrations and other protest movements organised by the Labour leaders. He drew criticism from the Unionists as well as from the Labour Party leaders, including the Bissoondoyal brothers who severely contested his assertions that he was the rightful leader of the Indo-Mauritian community.

With considerable political skill, and the support of the intellectual bourgeoisie that had opposed a number of radical ideas professed by Curé and the Bissoondoyal brothers, he sought, as an independant candidate at the 1948 general elections, the support of the Labour Party where the more flexible Rozemont had succeeded Anquetil. In the two years after the 1948 general elections, he became a full-fledged member of the MLP. His full membership of the party dates from the early 1950's, fifteen years after the party had been founded by Curé.

After Rozemont's death in 1956, and that of Renganaden Seeneevassen, the next in the line of succession, the rise of Ramgoolam to the Labour leadership became a reality. The Bissoondoyal brothers broke away to form their own party, the Independent Forward Bloc, which put an end to Labour's quasi-monopoly of the rural votes and nearly toppled the Labourites from their leading position on the political chess-board, a possibility that would be barely averted by Ramgoolam through his considerable skill in behind-the-scene manoeuvring to forge or undo political alliances in his favour.

Actually, there had been three Bissoondoyal brothers: Soogrim, Basdeo and Sookdeo. After having moved from the South of the island to Port-Louis, they lived and studied in the best melting pot of races, cultures and religions in the island. They developed a lifelong admiration, found in their writings and reported also by U. Bissoondoyal, for the Coloured and Creole teachers who were among the best the country offered then. "**The major influence on the three brothers was that of Villiers René who was continu**The call for a comprehensive and really democratic reform of the franchise was finally going to come from the streets, in the 1930's, from the revolt of the "**lambs**." Dr. Curé would be the first to head a mass political movement in the history of Mauritius to claim the right to vote on behalf of the working classes in February 1936, when a resolution to that effect was voted by a large crowd in the Champ de Mars, gathered for the foundation of the Mauritius Labour Party.

Anyway, contrary to what has been generally believed, the evolution of Mauritian politics from the 1930's to date cannot be understood without an understanding of what went on in the minds of the prominent political personalities of the second half of the 19th century and of the less-studied two first decades of the 20th century.

What followed after that, as contained in the next chapters, is a much easier story to tell – and better known to most Mauritians, albeit being most of the time distorted by the political elite of the nation for the purpose of ethnic politics. The fact is that the foundation of the Labour Party in 1936 marked the beginning of the modern era and it provided the momentum that led to the independence of the country in 1968.

The events that followed the foundation of that party will be easier for anybody to understand after a careful study, in the preceding chapters, of the way classes and ethnic groups related to each other between the elections of 1886 and February 1936. During that period of 50 years, an oligarchy held firmly the reins of political power and deprived of the right to vote a large mass of people that can be described as a multiethnic petite bourgeoisie-and-working classes. From 1936, the balance of forces would definitely change as Curé's Labour Party and its trade unions ignited a social upheaval that can be best described as a major political and social revolution.

The Aapravasi Ghat, World Heritage Site

Engravings on the walls of the Apravasi Ghat built in 1849 as the point of landing for indentured labourers. The site was renovated in 1986 by the government led by Prime Minister Sir Anerood Jugnauth. The Aapravasi Ghat website (aapravasighat.org/) recalls: "In 1987, the historical importance of the Immigration Depot was recognized by the government and it was declared a National Monument." In 2001, a committee of historians chaired by Deputy Prime Minister Paul Bérenger decided that the date 2 November be proclaimed a public holiday in memory of the arrival of the first indentured labourers who came to Mauritius on that date in 1834 on board the Atlas. In 2001, the Jugnauth government set up the Aapravasi Ghat Trust Fund which "led to the implementation of a project to document, excavate, conserve and restore the Aapravasi Ghat site." In 2006 the building was declared a World Heritage Site by UNESCO, in the wake of PM Navin Ramgoolam's efforts to complete the project.

Basdeo Bissoondoyal, a national figure

Pandit Basdeo Bissoondoyal, pictured here, was, along with Dr. Maurice Curé, one of the leading figures of the social and political struggles to improve the lot of the masses of workers and small planters. In addition, he preached the values of Hinduism to his co-religionists and educated them in politics, together with his brother Sookdeo. Both worked with the Labour Party and Emmanuel Anquetil, a close friend of his, appointed him as the representative of the party, during his studies in India, with the Congress Party of Jawaharlall Nehru, which was fighting for Indian independence. Two major political leaders of Mauritius emerged from the Bissoondoyal fold: Sookdeo Bissoondoyal, leader of the Independent Forward Bloc, and Sir Anerood Jugnauth, who was Prime Minister for 16 years.

Chapter 38
The revolt of the "lambs"

In the end, the "*lambs*" revolted. The "*servile horde*" or the "*big mass of comparatively ignorant, backward people outside*" - who frightened as much the Oligarchs as the elitist Unionists - rallied around Dr. Maurice Curé, Cashinath Kishtoe, Guy Rozemont and the Bissoondoyal brothers, who successfully masterminded the first great mass political movements of Mauritian history.

Kistoe as well as, later, the Labour Party leaders, used political journalism to promote their ideas and mobilise the large classes of small planters and workers. The Conservatives as well as the Unionists (Union Mauricienne) were strongly entrenched in the journalistic world, defending forcefully their interests. Since Adrien d'Epinay had obtained the freedom of the press in 1831, political journalism had become a major player in the political development of the island. All the major political forces founded newspapers and periodicals to convey their respective messages.

Like Adrien d'Epinay, Rémy Ollier or Manilal Doctor, Cashinath Kistoe founded a newspaper, the Arya Vir, in 1929. In that paper, Kistoe published articles in English and Hindi and supported Dr. Maurice Curé's political struggles which led to the formation of the Mauritius Labour Party in 1936. Kistoe and Curé were particularly interested in the fate of the workers and the underprivileged small planters and small employees.

Concerning the organisation of workers, there had been attempts in the 1920's by Edgar Laurent and Arthur Rohan to establish trade unions following a strike in Plaine Lauzun, in Port-Louis. From the time of Beaugeard, the workers of Port-Louis had supported democratic and liberal politicians. The petite bourgeoisie and the workers in Port-Louis had voted successively for Dr. Onésipho Beaugeard, Dr. Eugène Laurent and Dr. Edgar Laurent. The latter, who always stressed that he came from the working class, tried to obtain from the authorities the necessary legal measure to allow the formation of trade unions. They had helped Willy Moutou organise, in 1921, a public meeting to claim that right in the name of the workers. Moutou had actually failed in trying to get the Legislative Council, dominated by the Oligarchs, to vote a motion to introduce industrial legislation similar to the one existing in Britain. They then petitioned the government, which, on August 31, 1926, introduced a bill "*to provide for the regulation and registration of trade unions,*" then back-pedalled and the bill never came up for the second reading. It was referred to a Law Committee where it was forgotten altogether.

As Kistoe, followed by the Bissoondoyal brothers, set out to mobilise the underprivileged classes and joined forces with Maurice Curé, a group of intellectuals of the Indo-Mauritian community, gathered around R.K. Boodhun, who had studied law in Britain. They decided to start a socio-political action so as to take the lead of their community and press upon the colonial administration to recognise them as its official representatives. Eventually, those two movements representing respectively a new intellectual Indo-Mauritian bourgeoisie and a new generation of radical intellectuals within the same community were to clash in the press and in the political arena.

It was a sort of replica of the divisions within the other communities, whether White, Coloured or Creole. As already seen in previous chapters, those who believed that class conflicts superseded ethnic rivalries, clashed with those on whose agenda communal representation by the intellectual elites was the priority. Those elitists of various ethnic groups would be strongly supported by the British governors during the 1930s and 1940s as the latter seemed to believe that ethnic representation would attenuate class conflicts that played in favour of the Labour Party. To the non-radical Creoles and Indo-Mauritians of the first half of the 20th century, such communal representation was the sine qua non condition, within the colonial legislative system, for promoting the welfare of the respective ethnic groups of the country. Mass political demonstrations and trade unionist activism were not their cup of tea.

The Union Mauricienne, for some time, carried the hopes of that group of Indo-Mauritians, Creoles and a number of White salaried employees who could not reconcile themselves with the idea of joining the Labour Party of Dr. Maurice Curé, Guy Rozemont and Pandit Sahadeo, and the Jan Andolan Movement of the Bissoondoyal brothers.

Those mass movements advocated an ideology comprising socialism and a brand of nationalism which was strongly influenced by the Indian independence struggle, especially when Basdeo Bissoondoyal was asked by the Labour Party president, Emmanuel Anquetil, in 1938, to represent the party at the Indian National Congress while he was studying in India.

In his book "***Promises to keep***," U. Bissoondoyal explains the philosophy propagated by Professor Basdeo Bissoondoyal:

"He decided that he must preach Indianism rather than Hinduism. Naturally, in his view of Indianism, the place of the Hindu Dharma was central." [1]

The Bissoondoyal brothers were among the finest intellectuals of their generation who, in addition to their advanced knowledge of their ancestral culture and religion, studied thoroughly Western literary, philosophical, historical and political works. Most of all, they had an intimate knowledge of Mauritian history from its very beginning. Sookdeo Bissoondoyal, who had been illuminated by Evenor Hitié's work on Mauritian history, believed in the oneness of the country's historical evolution, from its very beginning to modern times. In his political speeches, he told the Indo-Mauritian masses that they should consider their struggle for emancipation as a continuation of those led by the slaves, the Coloured population, and, in particular, by Jacmin, Tabardin, Rémy Ollier, and Jean Lebrun, whom they considered as great heroes of the historical evolution of the island.

They even rewrote history in books and pamphlets to counter-balance historical accounts they felt distorted by the Oligarchs and others, and in their writings, the sufferings of those great Coloured and Creole leaders at the hands of the Oligarchs were described. De Plevitz also was a model and they have compared him to Gandhi. U. Bissoondoyal has found echoes of Gandhian philosophy before Gandhi in the words of de Plevitz.

Basdeo and Sookdeo successfully helped Curé, through their Jan Andolan, to assemble vast crowds of Indo-Mauritian labourers under the banner of the Labour Party.

Dr. Seewoosagur Ramgoolam, Jules Koenig and Razack Mohamed, who were to become prominent leaders of major political parties themselves, stood as candidates for municipal elections under the unionist banner, against the Labourites as much as they stood also against the candidates of the Oligarchy. Ramgoolam was appointed, in 1940, as successor to S. Seerbookun, who had been the British governor's nominee chosen to represent the Indo-Mauritians in the Legislative Council.

Ramgoolam was nominated in a period of intense social tension when the colonial administration was being assailed from the streets and the sugar cane fields by strikes, demonstrations and other protest movements organised by the Labour leaders. He drew criticism from the Unionists as well as from the Labour Party leaders, including the Bissoondoyal brothers who severely contested his assertions that he was the rightful leader of the Indo-Mauritian community.

With considerable political skill, and the support of the intellectual bourgeoisie that had opposed a number of radical ideas professed by Curé and the Bissoondoyal brothers, he sought, as an independant candidate at the 1948 general elections, the support of the Labour Party where the more flexible Rozemont had succeeded Anquetil. In the two years after the 1948 general elections, he became a full-fledged member of the MLP. His full membership of the party dates from the early 1950's, fifteen years after the party had been founded by Curé.

After Rozemont's death in 1956, and that of Renganaden Seeneevassen, the next in the line of succession, the rise of Ramgoolam to the Labour leadership became a reality. The Bissoondoyal brothers broke away to form their own party, the Independent Forward Bloc, which put an end to Labour's quasi-monopoly of the rural votes and nearly toppled the Labourites from their leading position on the political chess-board, a possibility that would be barely averted by Ramgoolam through his considerable skill in behind-the-scene manoeuvring to forge or undo political alliances in his favour.

Actually, there had been three Bissoondoyal brothers: Soogrim, Basdeo and Sookdeo. After having moved from the South of the island to Port-Louis, they lived and studied in the best melting pot of races, cultures and religions in the island. They developed a lifelong admiration, found in their writings and reported also by U. Bissoondoyal, for the Coloured and Creole teachers who were among the best the country offered then. "***The major influence on the three brothers was that of Villiers René who was continuing the work of Jean Lebrun a century later,***" writes U. Bissoon-

---
[1] Op cit.

United they stood

Dr. Maurice Curé (centre), flanked by his closest collaborators (Pandit Sahadeo is on the left) faced the might of the sugar estate owners and of one of the most repressive governors of the history of Mauritius: Sir Bede Clifford, who tried to break the back of the Labour movement and its trade unions.

doyal. [2]

In Port-Louis, the Arya Samaj was also well implanted and the three brothers felt the influence of Swami Dayanand, which led Basdeo to feel that his vocation was to become a missionary.

Under the guidance of Villiers René, Soogrim and Basdeo topped the list at the teachers' examinations. Soogrim, however, died prematurely, after the three of them had become teachers. Basdeo went to India where he brilliantly passed his Master's degree exams and qualified also as a missionary. Sookdeo, after passing the extremely difficult examinations of those days to qualify as a teacher, worked in the government service where he constantly rebelled against every single case he perceived as resulting from injustice and prejudice.

One of his first really political protest actions, described by U. Bissoondoyal as his "*first Satyagraha*," was a walk-out he and a few friends successfully orchestrated in 1943, at the Port-Louis theatre during a conference by the Director of Education, Ward, who was in favour of the teaching of Indian languages by cultural organisations rather than by the government schools. He left the civil service in 1945 and became a reputed private teacher, which gave him independence and thus enabled him to enter the political arena.

Basdeo studied in Lahore Calcutta. His contact with India was illuminating. He lived in the exciting 1930's in a country where the independence movement had gathered considerable force. He saw the great Indian leaders of those days, including Jawaharlal Nehru There was also an extraordinary cultural renaissance in India. **"He had seen the great Indian leaders and experienced Indian politics. Gandhiji had come to Lahore in 1934 (...) Gurudev Tagore had come in 1935,"** writes U. Bissoondoyal.

Basdeo Bissoondoyal was also in contact with his motherland. The Mauritius Labour Party in 1938 was suffering such severe repression following the strikes it had organised, that it was on the point of collapsing. On November 16, 1938, the party wrote a letter to Basdeo Bissoondoyal to ask him to inform the Indian National Congress about the situation in Mauritius and the MLP. The young missionary wrote a memorandum which he communicated to the Congress and also sent a letter to Mahatma Gandhi, according to U. Bissoondoyal. His memorandum was given publicity in some Indian newspapers, namely *The Amrita Bazar Patrika* and *The Statesman*.

Different political backgrounds for two future Prime Ministers

It is also important in any study of modern Mauritian history to know the background of Ramgoolam, who became the island's first Prime Minister, as well as that of the political movement of' the Bissoondoyal brothers where the second Prime Minister and future President of the Republic of Mauritius, who was one of their students, Anerood Jugnauth, started his political career.

Writing about the preparation of Basdeo and Sookdeo Bissoondoyal for their political career, U. Bissoondoyal states:

"It lay not in living the life of the poor which they knew already, but in looking at things from the vantage point of history. The volume of Hitié had conjured up before their eyes the past history of the island with its glorious heroes. Their acquaintance with the life of Gandhi and with the freedom struggle in India provided the other reference. As Sookdeo said in the Legislative Council in 1957, 'I have read the history of the Indian National Congress. I have read Mahatma Gandhi and I know how politics should be done with the English people. There is no power in this country, there IS no power in the Colonial Office that can curtail the rights of the People'. The history of Mauritius provided the vision of one people."

He advised his colleagues on March 30, 1965, in the Legislative Assembly, to read Mauritian history:

"All the fanaticism, all the blindness, all the stupidity that now prevails would evaporate' (...) Three figures dominated the scene: Maurice Curé, Emmanuel Anquetil and Basdeo Bissoondoyal. The three of them found themselves in jail, placed under house arrest or deported." [3]

A significant section of the Indo-Mauritian intellectual bourgeoisie of the 1930's and 1940's refrained from taking part in the confrontational tactics of the trade unions rallied around Curé's Labour Party and the Bissoondoyal brothers, Basdeo and Sookdeo. Their moderation won them the admiration of their middle-class Creole, Coloured and White counterparts in the island's class structure. Raoul Rivet praised the young Ramgoolam as somebody

---
[2] Bissoondoyal, U,op cit. Tributes to teachers like Villiers René are also found in: Bissoondoyal, Basdeo (Pandit), *Life in Greater India – An Autobiography*, Bharatiya Vidya Bhavan, India 1984; Bissoondoyal, Sookdeo, *A Concise History of Mauritius*, Bharatiya Vidya Bhavan, India 1968. Sookdeo Bissoondoyal writes: *"Villiers René, a man of character, was the headmaster. Much of the credit for moulding the character of the three brothers goes to him. They could never fully repay that obligation. He loved self-respecting students."*
[3] Mauritius Legislative Council, Debate 30 March 1965.

Historical documents: Labour Party alerts the UK and India

The news of the 1937 killings during the labour unrest in Mauritius were spread to the rest of the world by the Labour Party by Dr. Maurice Curé and Emmanuel Anquetil through their contacts with the Labour Party in Britain and the Congress Party of India. Above, scanned original copies of their telegram covers with Anquetil's original signature. (see further the content of the messages).

who "*indulges in politics rather than in agitation,*" and "*a highly valued professional.*" [4] Rivet introduced the young doctor as a municipal candidate under the unionist banner in 1943 and 1946.

The newspaper **Le Radical** of Loïs Lagesse, Leon Lautret and other members of the upper middle class of the General Population, which was extremely critical of Dr. Curé and of the agitation that was gaining ground among the Indo-Mauritian small planters and working classes, heaped praise upon K. Hazareesingh and Anauth Beejadhur in an article entitled "***Les plaisirs de l'esprit***" ("***Intellectual pleasures***"). [5] K. Hazareesingh, who enjoyed the confidence of the British governor, writing biographical notes on King George V, admiringly described the latter as "*our beloved sovereign*" in the same newspaper, [6] which contrasted radically with the strong anti-colonialist language of the Bissoondoyal brothers with regard to the head of the British colonial empire.

1930s to 1960s: The pace of History 'accelerates'

The film of events from the 1930s to the 1960s, when there was a sort of acceleration of Mauritian history through the foundation of the Labour Party, is worth exploring in the rest of this chapter as a prelude to the march of the country to Independence. Dr. S. Ramgoolam, born on September 18, 1900, at Bois d'Oiseaux, was the son of Indian immigrant Moheeth Ramgoolam, from the village of Hurgawo, in the State of Bihar, India. Moheet Ramgoolam was a '*sirdar*' (supervisor of workers) on the Queen Victoria Sugar Estate, in the east of Mauritius. His mother was Basmati Ramchurn, a widow who lived in a large house in Belle Rive, where the family had been staying as from 1898. Seewoosagur Ramgoolam, also called Kewal, wanted to become the governor of Mauritius according to his childhood friends of Belle Rive. [7]

He studied at the Roman Catholic Aided School of the locality and then went on to stay in Curepipe with relatives, the Bhaguth family, who had remarkably succeeded in business. There, he studied at the Royal College, before leaving the country in 1921, while Mauritius was enjoying a formidable economic boom due to high sugar prices. He stayed in Britain for nearly a decade and a half, exactly 14 years, qualifying as a medical practitioner, while taking a keen interest in politics and literature and cultivating his lifelong taste for classic and sober British suits, as much as he admired the Westminster system of parliamentary government. At one point, sugar prices went down, family revenues plunged and he was in need of financial help. G.M.D. Atchia, a member of the Legislative Council who had travelled to London and met him, organised financial help that enabled him to complete his studies.

One of his admiring biographers, Anand Mulloo, writes that he looked like a "*prosperous gentleman*" while in London. Another one, Marcel Cabon, found in him "*the manners of a perfect British gentleman.*" A third one, M. Varma, described him in his books as a real "***Britisher***." [8]

He came back in 1935, like the young Gandhi in 1901, with a belief that evolution was better than revolution and that the British democratic system could be applied in the colonies to meet the demands of the people. Mauritius having already a parliamentary tradition, Dr. S. Ramgoolam managed to integrate it five years later as a nominee of the British governor to the Legislative Council to replace S. Seerbookun as an official representative of the Indo-Mauritian section of the population.

His nomination was criticised by the Labour Party press organ, **Le Peuple Mauricien**, editor Guy Rozemont, in an article published on November 18, 1940, in which he was blamed for not having chosen a political career in opposition to the government as "*he was destined to do,*" and for having opted "*when faced with the prospect of a difficult political life, in favour of an easy and less useful career.*" Clearly, the party would have liked to have Ramgoolam within its ranks, but was highly critical of him for having opted to join the politicians of the middle bourgeosie who actually stood for election under the banner of Raoul Rivet's Union Mauricienne against the Labour Party at the Port-Louis municipal elections.

But the young Dr. S. Ramgoolam had already, in 1935, the same year when he came back to Mauritius, chosen his path: he had participated in the celebration of the centenary of the great wave of Indian immigration to Mauritius in company of the moderate Indo-Mauritian intellectuals, including K. Hazareesingh, all gathered around R.K. Boodhun, who had founded, in April 1936, the Indian Cultural Association which published the **Indian Cultural Review**.

The Bissoondoyal brothers later criticised certain aspects of that event because they would have wished a more radical

---
4 Le Mauricien, 8 December 1943.
5 Le Radical, 16 January 1936.
6 Ibid., 24 January 1936.
7 Selvon, S. Ramgoolam, Editions de l'Océan Indian (1st ed.) 1986 ; MDS Editions (2nd ed.) 2006.
8 Ibid. The citations were from: Mulloo, A., Dr. S. Ramgoolam, his life, his work, his ideas, 1980; Cabon, Marcel, Biographie de Ramgoolam, Les Editions Mauriciennes, Port-Louis 1983; Varma, Mohindra Nath, The Struggle of Dr. Ramgoolam, Quatre Bornes, 1975.

stand from the Indo-Mauritian intelligentsia. U. Bissoondoyal writes:

"The centenary celebrations of Indian immigration were like the last convulsion of a culturally dying race. There was not a single speech in Hindustani." [9]

Dr. E.F. Twining, the director of Labour, Information and Censorship (he was also a member of the British Intelligence Service for East Africa, according to his biographer H.E. Bates in "*A Gust of Plumes*", [10] and governor Sir Bede Clifford, had found in Dr. S. Ramgoolam, who had spent 14 years (at that time, more than a third of his life) in London, a perfect choice, due to his moderation. His nomination was effective in November 1940.

Meanwhile, across the country, the effects of an economic crisis which begun at the end of the 1920's and raged throughout the 1930's, had created a considerable degree of poverty. Unemployment had set in and wages had decreased. Thousands of poor people depended on the meagre allowances granted under the Poor Law Ordinance. Deaths, in the early 1930's, outnumbered births; disease was rampant among the working classes and, combined with undernourishment, significantly increased mor- tality. In 1944, the average expectation of life at birth was only around 32 years for males and about 34 for females.[11]

The country's situation during the economic crisis was so serious that a delegation to request financial assistance was sent to London composed of J. Leclézio, Dr. Edgar Laurent, P. Raffray, R. Gujadhur and G.M.D. Atchia, the latter being chosen to rep- resent the Muslim community. A loan was guaranteed by the British government to bring relief following the 1931 cyclone which had considerably damaged the island's agriculture. G.M.D. Atehia obtained that all Indian civil servants be given leave for a number of religious festivities.

It was during that period, in 1932, that Ramgoolam suffered such difficulties that his landlady, one Mrs. Jacob, helped him and G.M.D. Atchia also collected a sum to come to his help.[12]

But living conditions were made so infernal by poverty and disease among the working classes that the latter were not at all attentive to the political message of the moderate politicians of the country like Rivet or Ramgoolam or Koenig. The majority of them turned rather to those of the Labour Party formed in 1936 at the Champ de Mars by Dr. Maurice Curé, and of the Jan Andolan of Basdeo and Sookdeo Bissoondoyal. It was the revolt of the "*Iambs*", starting in the 1930's

Dr. Maurice Curé in action

Well-known historian Satyendra Peerthum writes, "*Curé was "the father of Modern Mauritius"* (or the period in Mauritian history between 1936 and 1968) as well as the founder and first president of the Mauritian Labour Party."[13]

This is no exaggeration in this statement made in one of the best scholarly tributes to the founder of the Labour Party: Curé was the first politician to introduce successfully socialism as an effective tool to mobilize the working masses of Mauritius and lead them to force constitutional and labour law reforms. It was this popular, multiethnic movement that ultimately brought about the independence of the country.

He sacrificed everything, even his career and personal life to enable the country to achieve that end and, as a consequence, was persecuted by the British and boycotted as a doctor by the ruling classes and the rich in general. He was sued and incarcerated, his reputation was damaged by a hostile radio campaign and he was financially ruined to the extent that he was forced to withdraw from politics. When the Labour Party kept him at arm's length in the 1950s and 1960s, he was given a ticket to be a candidate of the Independent Forward Bloc (IFB) by his old friend and admirer Sookdeo Bissoondoyal, the IFB being in those days a formidable electoral force that had seriously curtailed Labour's supremacy in the rural areas.

Dr. Maurice Curé had been elected for the first time to the Legislative Council in a by-election in Plaines Wilhems in 1934, in replacement of R. Pezzani, who migrated to Britain (he died after in a car accident in 1940). Moderates like Edgar Laurent and Rajcoomar Gujadhur, himself owner of two sugar estates, had also addressed the problem of rampant poverty at the Legislative Council.

However, Curé wanted more meaningful welfare policies. He advocated a welfare state for the working classes and the poor in general. He requested a form of financial aid to the workers whose welfare, he said, was guaranteed by the Treaty

---

9 Indians Overseas…, op cit.
10 Bates, Darrell, *A Gust of Plumes: A Biography of Lord Twining of Godalming and Tanganyika*, London, Hodder and Stoughton 1972.
11 The Titmuss Report, op cit.
12 See Selvon, S, Ramgoolam (1st and 2nd eds.), op cit.
13 Peerthum, Satyendra, *Tribute to a maker of Mauritian history. Remembering the struggle of Dr.Maurice Curé (1886-1977)*, in Week-End, 3 October 2004

The contents of the 1937 Labour Party telegrams

Above: the original text of the cable sent to "the Indian Congress Party Legislative Assembly Delhi." Below: the original cable sent "Doctor Lewis"in London" asking him to report the 1937 killings to the newspaper The Herald Chronicle. The original documents are now with the author of this book.

of Versailles.

He urged the government to establish a department of Labour to replace the post of '*Protector of Immigrants and Poor Law Commissioner*' as there were no longer immigrants. He believed a Department of Labour was the ideal organisation to provide help to the working classes. Curé also militated for a minimum wage to be determined by an advisory body. Edgar Laurent and even the sugar magnate Gujadhur concurred that daily wages were insufficient. The latter was militating at the same time for measures that would bring about an increase in the price of Mauritian sugar. [14]

The wages were then 40 to 50 cents daily for the inter-crop season and 40 to 60 cents daily during the crop season. Gujadhur had proposed that the wages be raised to about 60-75 cents daily. But when the labourers were sub-contracted by contractors or sirdars (supervisors), the latter deducted such profits that the money earned by a worker were even lower than if he/she had been directly employed on the estate, amounting to Rs 5 to Rs 8 a month, plus food rations of about Rs 3 to Rs 8 monthly, during intercrop, and Rs 8 to Rs 10 monthly plus the same food rations during the crop season. Actually, the wages were reduced in 1931 according to the International Labour Office: *"According to the latest Government report on Mauritius, wages were reduced in 1931 owing to the difficulties created in all local industries by the low selling price of sugar."*[15]

The small planters, for their part, in addition to being dissatisfied with the weighing of their canes at the sugar mills, feeling cheated of large amounts of their sugar, were forced to accept arbitrary deductions on their money. The millers, moreover, formed a cartel in various regions to compel the planters to sell their canes to specific mills, prohibiting them from having any bargaining power that would have allowed them to sell at the best prices.

The small planters, like the workers, suffered enormously at the time of the Great Depression that started during the second half of the 1920's and persisted in the 1930's. Their number was constantly being reduced (as in the case of the Coloured planters of the 19th century during times of economic crisis, with falling sugar prices). They cultivated just over 45 per cent of the total sugar plantations in Mauritius in the 1910's, but in the 1930's, that figure was reduced to around 38.6 per cent.

Curé wanted important reforms, like, for example, wages amounting to Rs 3 daily for the field workers during the crop season and Rs 1.60 during the inter-crop season. He wanted an inquiry into the situation of the small planters, the elimination of middlemen who eroded their revenues, and protection against abuses by the sugar millers.

At first, he asked for a second member to represent the Plaines Wilhems district in the Legislative Council. After the general elections of 1936 where he did not get elected, but was nominated, he started mobilising the workers and small planters around petitions addressed to the governor. In one petition containing 1,650 signatures, he asked for an Indo-Mauritian nominee in the Legislative Council to represent the labourers and for another one to represent the artisans. In the second, containing 1,200 signatures of people belonging to the working classes, a revision of the Constitution was asked for a Legislative Council more representative of the population, especially the working classes.

As his movement gained momentum, he presented five more petitions and continued to press government to nominate members to represent the workers in the Legislative Council. Finally, on February 23, 1936, at the Champ de Mars, he organised the biggest public meeting to be held in those days where about 8,000 enthusiastic people, mainly from the urban and rural working classes, labourers and artisans, approved the foundation of the Mauritius Labour Party with Curé as its first president (today the title of leader is more usual).

Resolutions were passed asking for: *two nominated members on the Legislative council for the labouring classes; the right to vote for the workers; the right to organise trade unions; the establishment of social protection for the underprivileged classes as recommended by the International Labour Bureau, including the necessity for old age pension; a dispatch to be sent to the Secretary of State for the Colonies to inform him of the formation of the MLP with the object of discussing about minimum wages and problems concerning labour; the enforcement of the Minimum Wages Ordinance through a Department of Labour to be created in replacement of the Immigration Department and of the Office of the Protector of Immigrants as there were no more immigrants in Mauritius.*

Those demands were revolutionary for those times. They reflected the philosophy of the British Labour Party during that period.

Curé was a methodical leader who followed up all resolutions with letters and petitions to the authorities in Mauritius and in London. Thousands of workers and small planters signed those petitions. He toured the country to inform the people of the activities of the MLP and was helped by a team of intellectuals and workers including Dr. Edgar Millien,

---
14 Mauritius Legislative Council, Debate, period from 1934 to 1936.
15 Industrial and Labour Information, International Labour Office, vol 35, 1933.

Osman Hassenjee, Pandit Sahadeo Rama, Swaminathan, Gaston Pierre and Godefroy Moutia, both editors, Dr. Piarroux and, as from 1937, Emmanuel Anquetil, and from 1938-39, Basdeo Bissoondoyal. He attacked the 1885 Constitution still in force as a document ensuring the domination of the Oligarchy over the country's affairs to the detriment of the rights of the workers and the small planters.

Satyendra Peerthum explains:

"The campaign of the Labour Party under the guidance of Curé, Anquetil, and Sahadeo was indeed the first school of mass political education. The working masses, by attending the political rallies of the Labour Party and listening to the passionate speeches of its leaders, were fast becoming a powerful, organized, and enlightened social force. During the late 1930s, this social process was taking place even though the workers neither had the right to vote for a representative on the Council of Government." [16]

Curé and his team were energetically critical of the moderates who flocked around some Creole and Indo-Mauritian intellectuals who preferred a type of political action which privileged constant consultation with the British governor. He denounced the excessive hours of work imposed on workers and the lack of social protection against old age and sickness, as well as the absence of labour inspectors to check whether the employers respected the law. He claimed a substantial increase in wages for the working classes, especially the labourers who, it was admitted by one and all, could no longer meet both ends.

In those days, sending petitions was a major method for trying to obtain redress from the authorities and the British government used to react to them by sending an answer or comment. Curé intensified his campaign by sending more of them to the British government, the British Labour Party and the governor. He did not cease to criticise the 1885 Constitution which excluded the vast majority of the members of the working classes from the electoral registers.

He asked, for instance, for unemployment benefits; financial help for the small planters; control of the weighbridges of the millers where fraud was obvious as regards the weighing of their canes; control, also, of a system of middlemen who managed to reduce the income of the small planters; the abolition of the allocations paid to the members of the Legislative Council since 7,000 people out of a total population of 400,000 voted at the elections, etc.

In a letter on June 10, 1936, the Secretary of State for the Colonies in reply to the letter informing him of the foundation of the MLP, made it known that there was no objection from the British government. However, as for the other resolutions, they had to be submitted to the legislature. But soon, the impatience of the workers and the small planters was such that conflict became inevitable, as wages, sugar prices, and small planters' receipts took the plunge in the 1930's.

The 1937 unrest across Mauritius

Small planters in the Flacq district were particularly infuriated in 1937 when, to add to their woes, notices were posted by the Sans Souci and Bel Etang estates announcing a 15 per cent reduction of the price of Uba varieties of cane which grew exceedingly well on their mostly marginal lands, optimising their production, albeit the fact that those varieties had a high fibre and lower sucrose content than other varieties preferred by the estates. Actually, the sugar barons had only themselves to blame regarding the reasons why the small planters had to do their own biotechnological search that led them to use those varieties. In fact, those big estate owners were officially blamed for that following the unrest that ensued, as will be seen later on in this chapter.

A quite interesting academic paper has been produced explaining the whole issue in 1995, entitled **Small-Scale Sugar Cane Farmers and Biotechnology in Mauritius: The "Uba" Riots of 1937**. Essentially, the paper demonstrates that the local Chamber of Agriculture in Mauritius had monopolised biotechnology and was indifferent to the small planters' needs although the latter's canes were crushed by the large sugar estates:

"The Chamber was, in many ways, the shadow government of Mauritius, and it usually succeeded in badgering the colonial state into doing its bidding, except on several occasions when its plans encountered opposition from the Colonial Office in London… When large-scale, capitalist agricultural companies attempted to monopolize biotechnology in colonial Mauritius, they met with popular resistance." [17]

This study dwells on the refusal by the Chamber of Agriculture and the estates to share biotechnological research facilities set up from the 1890s with the small planters. It points out that after the riots and the inquiries that were made by the colonial government, the big estate owners were compelled to work with the government's Department of Agriculture and the small planters in the dissemination of well researched cane varieties. Previously, the small planters had done their

---
16 Peerthum, Satyendra, op cit.
17 Storey, William Kelleher, *Small-Scale Sugar Cane Farmers and Biotechnology in Mauritius: The "Uba" Riots of 1937*, in: Agricultural History, Vol. 69, No. 2, [Agribusiness and International Agriculture](Spring, 1995), pp. 163-176. Published by: Agricultural History Society. Stable URL: http://www.jstor.org/stable/3744263 .Accessed: 11/03/2012

own search for varieties:

"These canes resulted from natural hybrid crosses between noble canes or Saccharum officinarum and a variety of S. spontaneum which Hindu immigrants imported during the nineteenth century to plant near temples and use in religious ceremonies. The estates called the new hybrids Uba because they resembled S. sinense in their vegetative vigor, high fiber, and low sucrose. One of these varieties was called Uba Marot, named after the owner of an estate in the Black River district who found it growing in his fields. The manager of the "Rich Fund" estate in the Flacq district also found similar seedlings of a cross between S. officinarum and S. spontaneum growing in his fields. The estate named these canes Uba de Rich Fund, and after planting them on up to twenty hectares during 1926 and 1927, it also found them to have great vigor but too little sugar for the factory to make a profit. Nonetheless, up until 1937 the estate continued to cultivate several hectares of Uba de Rich Fund because it grew well on marginal lands."

The contracts between the sugar estates and the small planters allowed the former to reject any cane variety brought for crushing. It was found out by the Hooper Commission of Inquiry that the refusal of Uba canes, including the Uba de Rich Fund that had considerably spread and covered 1,600 acres of plantations of the small planters, was the original trigger of the violent incidents that ensued on the Gujadhur's property. The estates had decided to refuse all Uba canes brought for crushing, whereas in Natal, South Africa, owners had adapted their crushing equipment to those varieties to adjust to the high fibre content. [18]

In July 1937, the small planters were shocked when, bringing their canes to a weigh bridge at Rich Fund, they saw a sign that notified them that they would be paid 15% less for their Uba canes in comparison with what was paid for the other varieties. They were desperate actually because they barely broke even with the Uba canes, their best choice with regard to their lands. They had important sums of money to pay to creditors and this in turn was to lead them into an unending debt cycle of borrowing at even higher interest rates.

In fact, biotechnology was not the only cause of discontent, as explained already in the present chapter, as the '*Uba riots*' starting from the Gujadhur sugar estate, was the result of a culmination of factors from unscrupulous exploitation to discriminatory attitudes from the sugar estates in their relations with the small planters, who, in their majority, suffered poverty. The latter joined the Labour Party campaign of agitation for better conditions led by Curé who had systematically militated for them and the working classes in general. The estates had done nothing, while the economic crisis worsened due to declining prices.

"Between 1913 and 1937, the small planters were faced with some of the same problems as the estates, but the state did little to help them. The price of sugar declined steadily, except during the unusual years of 1914 to 1921, and the chronic lack of finance capital squeezed all producers. By 1936, when the price of sugar hit rock bottom, the small planters merited more government attention than ever." [19]

When the planters protested after the refusal of their canes at Rich Fund weighbridge and elsewhere, the Union Flacq Sugar Estate owners' family, "***the most Indo-Mauritian family of the island***" [20] refused to negotiate with the planters, who spontaneously started a movement of resistance by setting fire to estate sugar cane fields, tipping over vehicles and demonstrating in front of the factory. The owners called the police for protection, but the police refused to intervene, making vague remarks about how staff could '***mobilize themselves***'. When, on August 13, several hundred planters marched on the factory, the owners and staff had weapons (pistols and rifles) ready to be used. The staff stood outside holding their weapons. The only policeman who had arrived there tried in vain to mediate as angry words were exchanged between the planters and the estate people. The crowd started then to throw rocks and stones and wield sticks and stormed the factory. Fearing for their lives, according to their version of facts, the staff started firing into the crowd, killing four protesters and wounding six of them. The protesters fled, set cane fields on fire and retired to their villages. [21]

For their part, the labourers on various estates also became restless due to declining wages, during the same year, 1937, and thousands of them had joined Curé's trade union movement which was demanding an increase in wages. A first strike occurred at Chebel sugar estate on July 17. Then discontent spread to various other estates. On August 9, there was a procession of small planters and labourers from Brisée Verdière to Port-Louis. Labour Party activists took part in the demonstration and handed over a petition of labourers and small planters to the police.

After the Union Flacq Estate killings, crowds assembled at other estates on the East to march on the factories. Panic spread among the sugar barons while the police asked for help from the military, but the latter soon withdrew to their barracks. There were demonstrations at Solitude also, in the North, as well as in the Plaines Wilhems, especially at High-

---
18 Ibid.
19 Ibid.
20 Ibid.
21 Hooper, Charles Arthur, et al, ***Colony of Mauritius, Report of the Commission of Enquiry into Unrest on Sugar Estates in Mauritius, 1937***, Port Louis: R. W. Brooks, Government Printer 1938.

lands, Trianon, and Réunion, where Pandit Sahadeo, a member of the MLP was arrested. Crowds gathered also in the West, at Medine, Albion and Bambous, to demonstrate. Creole and Indo-Mauritian workers took part together in those demonstrations in various places. The South was also affected by several strikes and at L'Escalier one man killed by the police who fired to disperse a crowd blocking the road.

The employers panicked during the strikes and demonstrations by hostile, stone-throwing and stick-carrying crowds on various estates. The Chamber of Agriculture tried to convince the authorities to relieve the employers of any responsibility on their part, should the situation further deteriorate. The police refused. Newspapers supporting the sugar barons attacked the workers and their leaders, especially those who belonged to the Labour Party.

The Mauritius Labour Party immediately internationalised the tragic events. Two telegrams were dispatched by Anquetil who went to the Postal & Telegraph Department office. [22] One was addressed to the "Leader Congress Party Legislative Assembly Delhi," on behalf of Dr. Curé, President of the Mauritius Labour Party. It read,

"Unarmed Indian Labourers shot by staff Sugar Estate whilst attempting negotiation for better wages than fifty-five cents daily. Six killed several wounded. Claim Royal Commission to establish responsibility."

The other one was signed by Anquetil himself and addressed to one of the Labour Party's contacts among the supporters of British Labour Party, in London, and read as follows: "Doctor Lewis please report Herald Chronicle Times unarmed labourers shot by staff sugar estate whilst attempting negotiation for better wages than equivalent nine pence daily. Six killed several wounded. Royal Commission necessary establish responsibility. Anquetil."

Both telegrams are dated August 23, 1937. The documents still exist. The way they were written indicates haste and a desire to get as quickly as possible help from overseas friends and movements, especially the British Labour Party and the Congress Party of India, both having close links with Curé, Anquetil and Basdeo Bissoondoyal (the Bissoondoyal brothers were still tightly associated with the Mauritius Labour Party and they would only break away after Dr. S. Ramgoolam and his group of moderate pro-British intellectuals entered the party with Rozemont's support).

Finally, the government appointed a Commission of enquiry to study the cause of the unrest on the sugar estates. It was the Hooper Commission, composed of the following members: C.A. Hooper, Procureur and Advocate General, chairman of the Commission, Dr. E. Laurent and P. Raffray, members of the Legislative Council, L. Collet, Protector of Immigrants and member of the Legislative Council, and Monk, general manager of the Anglo-Ceylon Company. The Labour Party severely criticised the composition of the commission as the workers were not represented.

Several witnesses deponed. Dr. Maurice Curé, president of the MLP was the first one and he reiterated the demands of his political movement formulated already in public meetings and petitions sent to the authorities. He asked for the extension of the right to vote to the working classes, and the establishment of proper structures, including a Department of Labour, to provide welfare for the underprivileged classes.

Emmanuel Anquetil, who was considered as a "**bolshevist**," that is, an ardent communist in the Soviet style, because of his activities in the British leftist political circles and trade unions, manoeuvred skilfully as one or two of the commissioners tried to corner him on that aspect of his political activism. He was reputed to be ***persona non grata*** in British India because of his views and risked severe penalties had he been tied directly to the unrest on the sugar estates and presented himself as an avowed communist.

But Anquetil, who was already past 50 when he arrived in Mauritius, mellowed into a rather moderate socialist by the time of his death in 1946, and so did Rozemont, afterwards, in the 1950's, more or less reconciled with the British gradualist approach as regards the evolution of the colonies. Gradualism was also the philosophy of Dr. S. Ramgoolam and of all the other moderate Indo-Mauritian and Creole intellectuals.

Curé and the Bissoondoyal brothers refused totally to bow before the British political agenda with which they practically refused the slightest compromise when it came to questions like universal suffrage and the pace of political change. They wanted major concessions that would produce a completely new structure of power derived, at general elections, from mass movements like the Labour Party, the Jan Andolan and the trade unions. They also wanted major wage increases, at least two-thirds of the sucrose content of the canes of the small planters to be paid to the latter and the establishment of a Welfare State, since the Poor Law was only a derisory remedy to the serious problems of social and economic underdevelopment like malnutrition, disease, and dire poverty.

The Hooper Commission could not link Curé directly to the demonstrations and the violence which ensued, though everybody knew that he had campaigned in such an efficient way that the working classes and the small planters had

---
22 See scanned copies of the telegrams in this chapter.

mobilised to protest openly against their living and working conditions. Governor Bede Clifford stated in his correspondence with the Colonial Office, on November 9, 1937, quoted by U. Bissoondoyal:

"Nevertheless, I do not think anyone would be justified in asserting that the recent disturbances were entirely economic and devoid of political significance. For some months past, Dr. Curé, Comrade Anquetil and Pandit Sahadeo have been holding meetings in public and in camera. The authorities have reliable information regarding what has taken place in both classes of meetings. It would appear that the utterances of Curé are mainly concerned with local politics, those of Anquetil with international Bolshevism, while Sahadeo who is frankly seditious appeals to the religious fanaticisms and racial animosities of the Indians with the obvious aim of arousing Anglophobia and of provoking a disturbance of the peace." [23]

The term "*comrade*" in the case of Anquetil is a reference to the latter's adhesion, in the UK, when he militated as a trade unionist, to the radical British left.

The moderate faction of the Indo-Mauritian intellectuals. inclluding Dr. Ramgoolam, who were Anglophiles was approached by the governor to conduct a policy of appeasement after the Hooper Commission Report so as to avoid what was happening in India, where nationalism had reached new heights around the theme of independence.

Hooper's report contained accusations against Curé concerning his political campaign. The commissioners, however, recommended some reforms to meet a number of demands made by the Labour Party, but not to the full extent as had been requested by Curé and his political aides and supporters. The creation of a Department of Labour, legislation more protective of workers' rights and the setting up of industrial associations were recommended. The arming of estate personnel was criticised.

As regards the tragic incidents during the strikes, the conclusion was that pointing rifles towards the demonstrators at Union Flacq was a provocative act, but that the people inside the estate premises had feared for their lives due to *"the hostile action of the crowd in the estate yard."* At L'Escalier, concluded the report, the police had no choice and the incident could not be avoided. [24]

An important conclusion of the report was that the law concerning strikes was obsolete "*and not in keeping with modern conditions by which a man was free to sell his labour for the highest price he could get.*" In fact, the Penal Code stipulated that "*any coalition among workmen, servants, labourers, or others either in town or in country to cease from working at the same time at their work or to prevent others from proceeding to or remaining at their work, before or after certain hours, or generally to suspend or prevent any work to raise the price thereof shall be punished by imprisonment not exceeding three months.*" The same penalty was provided for *"the principals or ringleaders."*

The millers were blamed for having made announcements at the last hour concerning the 15 per cent cut on two varieties of sugar cane cultivated by the small planters and the Commission recommended the establishment of a board of experts to solve questions relating to the share due to the small planters from the milling of their canes. Information should circulate among all parties concerned about their respective problems, whereas the government should control the accuracy of the weigh-bridges periodically to ensure that the canes of the small planters were properly weighed before the milling operations.

Concerning the workers, the Commission recommended a 10 per cent increase of wages of casual and estate labourers. The estates would have, henceforth, the obligation to pay directly the casual workers instead of going through middlemen. Trade unions would be allowed to bargain with the employers about the conditions of employment. A Department of Labour to attend to problems relating to old age pension, sickness insurance and the welfare of widows and orphans, as well as an institution to encourage conciliation in trade disputes were to be appointed in order to create better industrial relations. A committee to fix wages was also recommended.

23 *Secret despatch Sir Bede Clifford to the Secretary of State for the Colonies, 9 November* 1937, cited in: Peerthum, Satyendra, in *Remembering a Historical Figure. The struggle of Pandit Sahadeo*, in *L'Express*, 21 October 2003. Peerthum publishes in this article the extract of an obituary written in February 1967 by Dr. Maurice Curé in L'Express, after the passing away of Sir Ramparsad Neerunjun, a renowned figure of Mauritius history and one of his best friends: « **Pandit Sahadeo avait été arrêté aux Vacoas, détenu aux Casernes centrales et il allait passer en jugement. J'avais retenu les services de Me Koenig et Me Neerunjun pour le défendre. Le jour fixé, je me rendis au tribunal. La situation dans tout le pays était tendue à l'extrême. Des gens n'avaient qu'une idée, mettre le feu dans tous les champs de cannes; ma femme et moi, nous avions eu toutes les peines du monde pour les détourner de pareils excès.**"
« J'étais debout dans la cour du tribunal quand je vis passer Pandit Sahadeo encadré de plusieurs policiers, les menottes aux mains. On ne pouvait prendre plus de précautions s'il s'agissait d'un malfaiteur dangereux.
J'étais sous l'empire de l'indignation quand je vis Neerunjun s'approcher de moi. Il me fit part du désir du procureur général Hooper de me voir avant l'enquête sur les troubles où il devait présider. Je déclarai à Neerunjun que je n'accéderai au désir de Hooper qu'à une condition : que Pandit Sahadeo fut remis en liberté immédiatement. Neerunjun retourna voir le procureur général. Quels furent leurs propos ? On peut le deviner. L'ordre fut donné par Hooper de libérer Pandit Sahadeo qui allait être jugé par le magistrat Brouard. J'accompagnais alors Neerunjun au bureau de Hooper, avec qui j'eus une longue conversation. Neerunjun avait épargné au pays beaucoup d'heures critiques et peut-être sanglantes. »
24 *Hooper Commission Report*, op cit.

After the Hooper Commission

Following the Commission of Inquiry, the Department of Labour was set up in 1938 to assist workers in ensuring the respect of their rights. The department could access a number of relevant employers' records, report offences against the labour laws and provide advice during trade disputes. The Department of Labour recommended wages to be fixed at 66 cents daily during inter-crop and Rs 1.25 daily during the crop season, whereas estate labourers were to be paid Rs 20 monthly, plus housing, medical services, fodder, fuel for domestic purposes, normal wages on holidays decreed by the estates, plots of land for cultivation, an annual gratuity and sheds for their animals.

An Industrial Associations Ordinance and a Labour Ordinance were voted in 1938 and the Minimum Wages Board of 1934 was reactivated and given more power to fix minimum wages where an independent study established that they were too low and could produce industrial conflicts. The Industrial Associations Ordinance made it illegal for an employer to *"make it a condition of employment of any employee that the employee shall not be or become a member of an industrial association."* The employment of children was prohibited, work on Sundays was limited to three hours before 9 a.m. and paid according agreed rates, maternity allowances were to be paid to female workers and some other protective provisions were included.

But several of the provisions of the new pieces of legislation voted by the Legislative Council were not respected in the following years, especially after the Second World War started in 1939. The cost of living shot upwards, but the employers refused to comply even with government demands that wages be readjusted accordingly. Housing conditions did not improve on several big estates, with several 'camps sucriers' inherited from slavery remaining intact until near the end of the 20th century, while the food allocated to workers was insufficient and of bad quality.

The moderate Indo-Mauritian leaders had believed that the changes brought about by the governor after the 1937 riots were sufficient to appease the working classes. When the Colonial Office sent a new governor, Sir Bede Clifford, to replace Sir Wilfrid Jackson in 1937, they had approached the latter as representatives of the Indo-Mauritian community at large and participated in his vigorous policy of appeasement.

Bede Clifford has been described in most admiring terms by K. Hazareesing in various history books published long after the independence of Mauritius in 1968, especially in his History of Indians in Mauritius, where he refers approvingly to a garden party at Le Réduit where were invited *"hundreds of Indians of all classes in the community."*

Bede Clifford severely criticised in Westminster

In contrast, Bede Clifford's conduct was severely criticised in the British Parliament, especially by the Labour MPs. One of them, Creech-Jones, addressed *"six strong letters"* according to Hugh Tinker, to Secretary of State for the Colonies Malcolm MacDonald and his assistant, Lord Dufferin, on the labour unrest in Mauritius. [25]

Curé did everything to obtain the return of Anquetil from exile in Rodrigues, and he wrote to Rajmohunsing Jomadar, who had been sent by the Labour Party to study law in Britain, to approach the British Labour leaders and Members of Parliament. He also wanted to have an English barrister to come to Mauritius, but Jomadar wrote that it would entail heavy expenses. [26]

In a handwritten letter dated October 8, 1938, to Dr. Curé from his address at 112, Gower St., London W.C. 1, Jomadar stated,

"... as regards Anquetil I have put the matter before the Trade Union Congress and the Labour Party. They have written to the Colonial Secretary (...) I have high hopes that Mr. Creech-Jones to whom I have given all the necessary details and information will not fail to see the Colonial Secretary (...) I am sorry to hear about the way in which Hassenjee, Abel, Pandit Sahadeo and yourself have been treated."

Eventually, Creech-Jones wrote a letter dated November 7, 1938, to Lord Dufferin in the Colonial Office about *"the matter of the Mauritius strike and associated events."* In that letter, the British M.P. stated also, *"I have thought over (...) the points you put to us and would like to be assured that (...) it is the intention of the Government to give immediate attention to political reforms"* which would allow *"some political representation either direct or indirect in the legislature, of the masses of workers at present excluded from all form of political expression."*

Creech-Jones also criticised in his letter the enormous powers which Governor Bede Clifford had assumed to crush the strikes and asked for assurances that *"in future there will be no deliberate breaking of strikes initiated by a union and restric-*

---

25 *Separate and unequal: India and the Indians in the British Commonwealth*, 1920-1950, University of British Columbia Press, 1976.
26 The author of this book consulted the original letters in a private collection.

tions placed on peaceful picketing provided the working classes suffering from grievances place, when their negotiations have failed, their dispute to the approved conciliation machinery." He added that *"strikes, when conciliation fails, are not regarded as illegal."*

In contrast to what was happening at Westminster, Dr. K. Hazareesingh, who helped Bede Clifford during those events, wrote retrospectively in his History of Indians in Mauritius (op cit.):

"The authorities were faced with a serious dilemma; the dockers had openly flouted the Industrial Ordinance by not referring their dispute to arbitration and the Government felt that if the law were to remain on the statute book, immediate action must be taken."

Creech-Jones protested against the deportation of Anquetil, the arrest of workers and the confinement imposed to Dr. Curé. He added, in the same letter to Lord Dufferin, that he was prepared to *"urge on the people concerned the observance of legal and constitutional forms, but that always assumes that fair and reasonable liberty is enjoyed by people to act in combination both politically and industrially for the improvement of their lot and to find direct expression in political and industrial forms in order that their grievances can be known and pressure for redress secured."* He went on:

"I can only add that even after your explanation I am profoundly disturbed at the disabilities and conditions of these people, at the way in which the strike was broken and the harsh sentences imposed upon the people prosecuted."

In the House of Commons, Creech-Jones and another Labour MP, Sorensen, were very active at Question Time and during their speeches on the subject of the Mauritius riots and the harsh treatment received by the Labour Party leaders and members. Creech-Jones raised the fundamental questions related to freedom in the colonies and the deportation of local leaders 'merely because they strike':

"If we believe in freedom we should demand now that some of the oppressive ordinances which have recently characterised the Statute Books of many of the Colonial territories should be removed. We should release Grant from prison in Barbados, where he is now suffering a ten-years' sentence for labour agitation; we should stop deporting and prosecuting people merely because they strike, as was recently done in Mauritius; we should practise civil liberty, even with men like Pratt and Johnson in Sierra Leone; we should remove the colour bar in Southern Rhodesia and other parts of Africa; we should reverse the segregation policies that mar our work in the Continent of Africa. In all these ways let us declare for democracy and freedom. Let us carry out these changes, and be true to those noble sentiments so often expressed in the early records of our Colonial Empire. These are the immediate tasks of statesmanship, whether war is on or not." [27]

The records of the House of Commons show that the question was further dealt at question time on July 29, 1938, by M. P. Sorensen regarding the Commission of Inquiry of 1937 and the question of wages. The government answered that the increase of wages was being attended to under proposed arrangements. A written answer was afterwards given to a question by Creech-Jones regarding the Commission of Inquiry of 1937. But MacDonald in reply to the M. P.'s desire to know *"whether further consideration has been given to political reform?"* stated:

"No change has been made in the constitution, but the Governor has nominated representatives of small planters to the Council of Government during the current session."

Creech-Jones in the House of Commons, spoke about the labour situation in the colonies in the following terms, arguing that racism was part of the British government's colonial policies:

" (...) every effort on the part of the workers to create an organisation has been frustrated by the authorities. Meetings have been broken up or prevented by the police. In Trinidad and Mauritius the workers have been obliged to adopt subterfuge in order to get some form of organisation (...) There is the recent case which came before the Privy Council. In fact, one may say that so wide an extension has now been given to the legal meaning of sedition that almost any searching criticism of a Colonial Government by a black man or even of the conditions of employment in a Colony has become a punishable offence. How can there be effective trade unionism when many of the Colonies still have remnants of Master and Servant Ordinances on the Statute Book?

"Labour conditions have created problems in many colonies, often resulting in disturbances and bloodshed. Such unsatisfactory labour conditions usually have, as one common feature, the absence of effective machinery for collective bargaining. I am glad that the right hon. Gentleman is going to set up machinery for conciliation, in the form of labour bureaus which will function as an institution whose help is much needed throughout the West Indies. Mauritius and Trinidad have suffered greatly from the absence of such machinery lately. Commissions which have been set up in both those islands have on every occasion recommended that facilities should be provided for collective bargaining." [28]

The 1937 disturbances seen by a UK news correspondent in Mauritius

The events of 1937 as seen by *'Our own correspondent'*, in *The Scotsman*, one of UK's most widely read newspapers, is interesting and revealing, especially the part regarding the visit of the Marquess of Duffferin and Alba in 1938 during which the appointment of an Indo-Mauritian to represent the Indo-Mauritians in the Legislative was discussed in camera.

---

[27] Debate On The Address, HC Deb 30 November 1939 vol 355 cc291-411
[28] Colonial Office, HC Deb 14 June 1938 vol 337 cc79-189.

In a telegram dated September 7, 1937, after the riots at Union Flacq Sugar Estate, the correspondent reported,

"The Governor Sir Bede Clifford, has proclaimed a state of emergency throughout Mauritius, after giving the striking dockers an opportunity of returning to work. It is expected that drastic action will be taken against them. Police and military have been mobilised (...) 19 strikers on one of the sugar estates were brought to Court. They were remanded for three days.

"Several more factories in the central area have ceased work because the docks cannot accommodate any more sugar, now that loading of vessels has ceased. It is estimated, however, that half of the factories will be able to carry on for a few more days.

"The island dependency of Rodrigues, 400 miles from Mauritius, is in serious need of food, and it has been arranged that a steamer shall leave for there to-morrow. It is confidently expected that she will be loaded in spite of the strikers."

On September 9, under the title *"**Drastic Measures by Governor. 300 dockers arrested**,"* the correspondent in Mauritius wrote,

" Drastic measures have been taken by the Governor of Mauritius, Sir Bede Clifford, to end the disorders throughout the island caused by the dockers' strike. The 300 dockers who have been arrested, and the many others who have fled, have been replaced by hundreds of volunteers from the sugar estates.

"They arrived in the capital during the night under police protection, and have been loading ships with sugar all day. So much sugar had accumulated waiting for shipment that the docks could not accommodate any more.

"(...) One of the chief agitators, Georges Anquetil, has been deported to the island of Rodrigues, 400 miles from Mauritius, with his son."

In the same issue, the fate of the "socialist leaders" is announced:

"Dr Maurice Curé, Pandit Sahadeo, and other Socialist leaders have not been allowed to leave certain areas of Mauritius.

"The police, who have been concentrated in Port Louis, have been relieved by special constables mobilised from the local volunteer regiment. All liquor shops and many other shops have been closed as an additional precaution.

"(...) Dr. Curé has cabled to London requesting the dispatch of a Royal Commission to inquire into conditions in the island. He has also asked for a British Lawyer to defend the agitator, Anquetil.

"A commission of inquiry has already been at work. In its report, published in April, it recommended wage increases, sickness insurance, old-age pensions, and conciliation orders."

The newspaper report in *The Scotsman* of 10 February 1938, stated, under the pen of 'our own correspondent':

"The Marquess of Dufferin and Ava, Parliamentary Under Secretary for the Colonies, has written a letter to Bede Clifford thanking him "for giving him so many opportunities during his recent stay of meeting members of all sections of the population. Lord Dufferin remarked on the spirit of loyalty to the Throne, so proudly displayed by the people (...) Lord Dufferin added that he was convinced that a far closer co-operation between employer and employee was essential for the peace and prosperity of the island. He referred to the necessity of ensuring representation in the Legislature of the views and interests of all sections of the community and said that the Governor had proposals to that effect. Work on these lines must be done quickly, he concluded. Sacrifices would have to be made and patience exercised by all."

In the opinion of Pandit Basdeo Bissoondoyal, who at the time, thought that he should have been nominated (he told this to the author of his book in the 1970s at his home in Port-Louis), Ramgoolam was not representative of the larger masses of Indo-Mauritian small planters and workers toiling in the sugar cane fields and never defended their interests during the 1930s and 1940s, when he was a candidate for the Union Mauricienne with Edgar Laurent, Raoul Rivet, Jules Koenig and others. Pandit Bissoondoyal resented the role of the governor, who was close to Ramgoolam and his group, and wrote that Bede Clifford *"started a communal 'hare'."* [29]

Two years later, in 1940, there would be furious protests from the left of the political arena when a politician who vehemently opposed the Labour Party and the Bissoondoyal brothers, was announced as the governor's appointee: Dr. Seewoosagur Ramgoolam, recommended by Dr. E.F. Twining, the director of Labour, Information and Censorship, member of the British Intelligence services, a fact revealed by Twining's biographer Sir Darrell Bates. [30]

Curé and Bissoondoyal blast Dr. Ramgoolam's relations with Governor Clifford

Twining did not recommend Professor Basdeo Bissoondoyal or any other Indo-Mauritian working at the grassroots level and probably found in Dr. Ramgoolam the moderation they needed on the part of somebody they were appointing. This was criticised, at the time, by the press organ of the Labour Party, *Le Peuple Mauricien*, editor Guy Rozemont. For his part, Ramgoolam was campaigning in his newspaper *Advance*, and he was targeted by severe criticism as well from Basdeo Bissoondoyal and his followers and they were openly critical of the nomination.

Dr S. Ramgoolam (then a fierce adversary of the Labour Party and vying for a post of nominee from the governor in the

---
29 Bissoondoyal, Basdeo, Life in Greater India, Bharatiya Vidya Bhavan, India 1984.
30 Bates, A Gust of Plumes, op cit.

Council), K. Hazareesingh, J.N. Roy and H. Ramnarain became, for the governor, *"precious assets at this critical juncture,"* writes U. Bissoondoyal who recalls that those moderates had for mouthpiece, as from 1940, the newspaper *Advance* owned and controlled by Dr. S. Ramgoolam (the Labour Party had its own newspaper, *Le Peuple Mauricien* and *Advance* became the party's mouthpiece much later in the 1950s when Ramgoolam took control of the MLP).

Actually, the conflict between the moderate Indo-Mauritian leaders, on the one hand, and the leaders of the Labour Party on the other hand, had become quite virulent towards the end of 1938, particularly when Dr. Ramgoolam and a group of his moderate friends went to see the very controversial and virulently anti-MLP governor, Sir Bede Clifford, at Le Réduit, to express their solidarity with him in the face of severe criticism of his policies and of those of the Procureur General Hooper.

On December 6, 1938, Dr. Ramgoolam, the future British-appointed nominee, wrote, in reply to the outcry caused by his visit to the governor that "we did not want the Government to believe that the greater majority of the Indian community shared in any way the unwarranted attack against the Procureur General and the Governor."

On December 9, he wrote,

"I spontaneously accepted to form part of the delegation (...) because of my strong conviction that a high official was being unjustly attacked, and it was high time that we denounced the war-mongers who were arrogating to themselves the right to speak in the name of the great majority of the Indian people."

That was a clear reference to the radical leaders who had been accused by Bede Clifford of creating unrest among the workers. Dr. Ramgoolam explained further that the delegation of which he formed part went to see the governor in the name of the Indo-Mauritian community. Dr. Maurice Curé's response was quite severe in the face of those criticisms.

Replying on December 14, in a letter to *Le Mauricien*, Curé said that *"even I were a 'self-appointed leader,' what about the delegation led by Dr. Ramgoolam which met the governor and which was supposed to represent the Mauritians of Indian origin of this country?"* He asked, *"Was that delegation authorised to speak in the name of the Indo-Mauritians?"*

On December 19, Dr. S. Ramgoolam, severely attacked Curé who had reminded him that he had advocated *"an alliance with the French community."* Ramgoolam explained that he had done it because he thought that Indo-Mauritians should cooperate with all sections of the population *"provided that each one respected the ideals of his neighbour and did not trespass upon the legitimate rights of one another."* He added, further,

"Dr. Curé seems to think that the 'intellectuals' of my community are a class apart from the Indian proletariat, and that their interests are opposed to those of the working section of the community. Nothing is further removed from the truth. Let me remind Dr. Curé that these 'Intellectuals' take root in the ranks of the working class, and that they are fully conscious of the desperate conditions of their fellow-countrymen."

Yet, Ramgoolam and his friends never dared depone in favour of the workers, small planters and labourers to defend them before the Hooper Commission. On December 16, 1938, Sookdeo Bissoondoyal, siding with the Labour leaders, Curé and Anquetil, in particular, because they had deponed for the proletariat before the Hooper Commission, attacked the moderate Indo-Mauritian leaders for not having done the same to defend the workers. Sookdeo Bissoondoyal wrote, in a letter signed with his usual pen name "Indo-Mauricien," published in Le Mauricien,

"Before the Commission of Inquiry, no Indian representative came to depone in the name of his co-religionists. There was then the danger for the one who dared do it to lose the good favours of certain big planters or to be judged as communalists by the government."

Curé received a letter, which was among the documents he preserved until his death, and which was signed S.B., dated November 6, 1939, belonging to a private collection, condemning *"the director of the Arya Vir who has brought before a tribunal a claim for the impression of a pamphlet."* That was an extremely strong-worded letter from S.B. who wrote that such a decision should not have been taken by somebody *"who boasts being at the head of a social institution which has as its motto the upliftment of the Hindu masses."* S.B. finds that the director of the paper is in the camp of those intellectuals *"of our community"* who have chosen to oppose Curé and to cause him *"all sorts of torments,"* and who have chosen to befriend *"the governor and the rich."* The letter was accompanied by a sum of money, praying Dr. Curé to accept it though it was quite insignificant, writes S.B., *"so that it may be some sort of compensation for the outrage which the prominent people of our community are heaping upon you just when you are in need support and encouragement around you."*

The two fundamental problems of it all were thus clearly expressed:
- Where does class politics stop and where communal political representation starts?
- Where did cooperation with the colonial power and even the Oligarchy stop and where did the fight for political

emancipation start?

The moderates and the radicals, in those days, had quite divergent answers to those questions. Less than two years after the virulent press polemic opposing Dr. Curé and Dr. Ramgoolam, Seerbookun resigned from the Legislative Council to work in the administration and the nomination of Dr. S. Ramgoolam in his place gave a boost to the moderate Indo-Mauritian intellectuals who went on to contest the municipal elections in Port-Louis in 1943 and 1946 on the same platform as the moderates of the White, Coloured and Creole middle classes which, U. Bissoondoyal rightly recalls, *"included Furcy Adèle, Gabriel Martial, Félix Laventure, René Humbert, A.R. Mohamed, Radhamohan Gujadhur, Maurice Poupard, Raymond Hein, Maxime de Sornay and Jules Koenig."* That was the Union Mauricienne platform which Ramgoolam preferred to joining the MLP.

But neither the new pieces of legislation meant for the welfare of the working classes, nor the gorgeous garden-parties at Le Réduit organised by Bede Clifford in honour of his friends and supporters of *"all classes in the community"* and *"members of other ethnic groups,"* really defused the explosive industrial situation.

In the Colonial Information Bulletin of the British trade unions, on page 8, the 1937 strike was commented just after the report of the commissioners was submitted, in those terms:

"It is believed in Mauritius that the Report does not really contain anything more than a semblance of concessions to the workers, although it is expected that the press will claim that the workers are obtaining fair treatment. The Report has attacked the Labour Party leader, Mr. Maurice Curé, to whom in reality the credit of having enabled the workers to realise their strength, belongs."

The governor lifted finally the deportation order against Anquetil who came back from Rodrigues with his son who had accompanied him there. Curé had protested his own confinement in a letter dated September 8, 1938, in which he stated that he had to attend his patients outside Curepipe and the order concerning him was curtailing *"my liberty to attend my professional duties."* Further, we read, his letter, now in a private collection:

"Your Excellency expressed his desire that the Executive Committee of the Labour Party should examine the New Bill on Labour and make any suggestion that they think fit, seeing that there is no direct representation of Labour in the Legislative Council. In the face of Your Excellency's order, there is now no possibility for the spokesmen of the working classes to participate in the framing of the contemplated legislation on labour. The responsibility of such legislation will rest entirely upon the Legislative Council where the interested parties have no voice."

In the face of the sharp criticism which his behaviour had brought upon him from a number of M.P.'s in the British Parliament, especially concerning his authoritarian way of dealing with the workers and the leaders of the Mauritius Labour Party, the governor had been forced to restrain himself from more excesses, to liberate both Anquetil and Curé, and to think about the question of political representation in the Legislative Council. He was to propose, later, a form of communal representation.

Bede Clifford: a highly controversial British Governor

Sir Bede Clifford, the man who, according to Professor Basdeo Bissoondoyal, started the *'communal hare'* (i.e. introducing and stirring politica. communalism) in Mauritius, revealed himself as a very controversial figure in his days as British governor, especially in the Caribbean where he was later posted and found himself involved in big financial scandals. Two of them still plague his gubernatorial legacy in the island-nations, and form part of their history.

Onf of those affairs is described by H. M. Kirk-Greene in a voluminous book on the European governors in Africa:

"Not that a private income necessarily insured a peaceful administration. In the Bahamas, His Excellency the Honourable Bede Clifford followed up his legislators' agreement to turn the island into a tax-free haven and tourist attraction by himself purchasing a hotel, a beach, and a golf course, which he then proceeded to sell to his own Bahaman government." [31]

A highly dubious project he set up and carried out in Trinidad is still commented today in this country and is widely known as the "***Caura Dam Scandal***" during which charges of bribery were heard. Clifford put an end to the existence of a historical indigenous village, expelling all the inhabitants, and this painful memory still lives on among the survivors and their descendants. The village had been renamed La Veronica which explains the two names used in the following account of the scandal during which this old village was razed to the ground by Bede Clifford:

"In 1943, the government, under Governor Sir Bede Clifford, acquired all the lands in and around the village of Caura or La Veronica. The purpose of this was to build a dam to supply the entire north of Trinidad with water, according to the authorities... This meant that the

---
[31] African Proconsuls. European Governors in Africa. L.H. Gann & Peter Duignan, eds. New York/London/Stanford. The Free Press/Collier Macmillan Publishers & Hoover Institution. 548 pages.

village had to be destroyed and its thousand-or-so inhabitants had to go. On November 4, 1945, the church, the presbytery and the school were all dynamited. By 1946 all the people and all the buildings had been cleared from the Caura site and workmen began laying down the foundations of the dam.

"... There were charges of graft and bribery and corruption involving even the governor, Sir Bede Clifford, a good number of expatriate staff such as the Director of Public Works and all sort of "experts" and "advisers" running through all ranks. Expensive machinery imported for the dam lay rusting in the sun and rain.

"It was the biggest financial scandal this country has ever known, up to this date. In April 1947, new governor, Sir John Shaw within a year the project was declared abandoned." [32]

This brief digression was needed to show that the man who was persecuting the leaders of the Labour Party and praised by those who attacked that party was not an official who has left only the nice memories we can find in the traditional historiography of Mauritius.

The British want a communal system of representation

Coming back to the British governor's plan to introduce communal representation, Jomadar informed Curé, in a letter dated December 1938, from London, in which he wrote,

"I spoke to Mr Cr. Jones about Constitutional reforms and inquired what kind of reform the Government is contemplating. He told me that the Colonial Secretary is rather inclined to the Communal Basis system. I am strongly in opposition to this and I dare say that you would agree with me that we have never thought of such a thing before. What we want is an extension of the franchise and we shall do our best to achieve our aims." [33]

In the next chapter, we will see that Bede Clifford did propose a form of communal representation and that Jomadar was right in his letter.

The fact was that the measures taken in 1937-38 to appease the working classes (who had been mistakenly taken as *"meek lambs,"* to use Pezzani's expression), did not work, was proved not only by the dockers' strike, but by widespread discontent among the labourers of the sugar estates, particularly in 1943. The official nominee for the Indo-Mauritians in the Legislative Council could do nothing to change that, as averred by the facts, in spite of the hopes placed in him by Bede Clifford, who had deliberately avoided to appoint anybody close to the Labour Party. In several cases, the minimum wage of Rs 20 was not being paid.

Even if the prospect of more unrest as in 1937 brought a number of employers to increase the wages, others refused or employed delaying tactics as on the Belle Vue Harel sugar estate in 1943, where the workers went on strike on September 23. Two days later, the estate owners gave them notice to vacate the estate camp, a decision which considerably worsened an already tense situation.

Some of the moderate Indo-Mauritian personalities of those years were, as U. Bissoondoyal puts it, like H. Ramnarain, were caught between two roles:

"Ramnarain was caught in his conflicting roles – he worked as a propagandist within the Department of Information and therefore could not really oppose his Head, the Acting Director of Labour who was the Chairman of a Conciliation Board (...) The explosion took place, the police fired on an unarmed and suspicious crowd which had become restive when it saw in the baithka a government officer. Three died and thirty-two were wounded. Among them Anjalay, a woman with child. Ramnarain, who had compromised years of service in a moment of weakness, retired to a temple in Goolands to fast for eight days."

The other victims were: Kistnasamy Mooneesamy, Moonsamy Moonien and Marday Panapen. The funeral rites were presided over by Professor Basdeo Bissoondoyal in front of a large crowd. R.K. Boodhun, the guru of the moderate section of the Indo-Mauritian community, was not able to convince Anauth Beejadhur to publish in *Advance* a poem for the occasion, according to U. Bissoondoyal, [34] precisely because of the embarrassment caused by the failure of the governor's policy of appeasement which some intellectuals had supported. But Boodhun went to *L'Oeuvre*, the newspaper of Dr. Millien, a noted figure of the Labour Party, where he was not censured. He wrote:

"Yesterday, I bore witness to a most lugubrious event in the annals of the Labour movement in Mauritius. It was a human procession of about 1,500 men, women and children which conducted the bodies of three agricultural workers of Belle Vue, Rivière du Rempart – a young man, 29 years old, a middle aged woman, and a boy, 14 years old to a cremation ground in the locality. Those three soldiers of Labour had been killed by shooting, it is alleged, in the course of an affray which occurred on Monday last (...) I will not travel over slippery ground and say more than this (...) Whatever be the motive of the shooting (or killing by other methods) (...) the Indian community or the working

---

32 As related on a Trinidad and Tobago website: <TrinbagoPan.com> under the title of Caura, on the history of a historical Arawak village that has now disappeared.
33 Jomadar's letter is in a private collection consulted by the author.
34 Op cit.

portion of it, at any rate has heard with a sense of horror and grief of the overwhelming threefold misfortune which has befallen it and will mourn it for a considerable time." [35]

In 1995, a statue of Anjalay was unveiled on the site of the shooting and commemorative speeches relating that tragic event were made by leaders of independent Mauritius. On 26 January 1991, Prime Minister Sir Anerood Jugnauth, a former disciple of the Bissoondoyal brothers and elected member of their party, the IFB, inaugurated the Anjalay Stadium near the spot where the shootings had occurred. R. K. Boodhun's prediction had come true: Anjalay has not been forgotten even if a '*considerable time*' has gone by.

The British authorities watched with much anxiety the religious sermons delivered in every corner of the island by Professor Basdeo Bissoondoyal. He was preaching and teaching, but at the same time mobilising the under-privileged classes of the Indo-Mauritian community. He was severely criticised not only by the British governors and the Oligarchy, but by the moderate Indo-Mauritian politicians who tried to wrest from him and from the Labour Party the political leadership of the Indo-Mauritian community. It was an intense power struggle between two sections within the intellectual elite of that community.

Vast crowds flocked to the sermons and other events organised by the Bissoondoyal brothers. They had their own policing methods, organised in the Indian way by means of a group of young responsible men grouped into an organisation called the **Swayan Sewak Samithi.** It reminded the British of Subhas Chandras Bose's Indian National Army, writes U. Bissoondoyal. But that movement was an efficient and peaceful force which successfully contained the great crowds assembled in various parts of the island to listen to Professor Bissoondoyal. One of those popular assemblies was the Maha Yaj of 1943.

What was even more disquieting to the British authorities was the strong bond of friendship and cooperation which existed between Basdeo Bissoondoyal and Emmanuel Anquetil. The religious man often called on the president of the Labour Party at Rose Hill. [36]

The authorities started to warn him not to organise any public event without obtaining the approval of the government, even for a type of religious gatherings. He protested that he was not the only religious person organising gatherings for prayer and sermons and that there was no reason, under the law, for the authorities to discriminate against him. He insisted that nothing would stop him from delivering his sermons, and such firmness of purpose only increased his already considerable popularity throughout the country.

Governor D. Mackenzie-Kennedy, who had succeeded Bede Clifford, was persuaded that the missionary was acting on racial lines. Anquetil and Dr. Millien challenged that point of view publicly. But Basdeo Bissoondoyal was prosecuted and brought to Court.

In October 1944, he was arrested following a sermon he had programmed in Vacoas and a public procession that had been spontaneously organised by the Hindus of the region. In Court, he refused to say yes or no to the magistrate's question as to whether he would plead guilty or not. He repeatedly answered: *"Find it yourself"*. He was condemned for contempt of court and sent back to prison. Then when the case came up for trial, he asked that the governor be summoned as witness. He was condemned to 12 months hard labour. Sent to prison on 3 November 1944, he was released on 18 July 1945.

The matter was so serious that it drew attention from overseas. A parliamentary question was put on the matter on 12 November 1946 to Pandit Jawaharlall Nehru in New Delhi, by Pandit K.D. Paliwal. During his prison term, Pandit Bissoondoyal went on a hunger strike while workers on several estates started a go-slow, a fact which was mentioned in a speech of the governor in Council. Dr. Millien and Jules Koenig believed that Professor Bissoondoyal had been victim of persecution. Millien wrote a virulent reply to the governor in his newspaper *L'Oeuvre*, another paper that, with Le Peuple Mauricien, was close to the Labour Party.

U. Bissoondoyal writes:

"In December 1944 another Hindu missionary was prosecuted holding a procession. Jules Koenig, appearing for him, said that Basdeo Bissoondoyal had been persecuted and not prosecuted". [37]

---
35 Op cit.
36 Op cit
37 Op cit. This chapter has drawn, regarding the Bissoondoyal brothers and their political action in context, information sourced from various publications edited or authored by U. Bissoondoyal, principally **Indians Overseas, The Mauritian Experience**, op cit.; **Gandhi and Mauritius, and Other Essays,** op cit; and **Indian Laboour Immigration,** op cit, Bissoondoyal, U. and Servansing, S.B.C. (eds.): papers presented at the International Seminar on Indian labour immigration at the Mahama Gandhi Institute, Mauritius, 1984.

It was then that Sookdeo Bissoondoyal finally decided to leave his teaching job in government and to enter the political arena as a full-fledged politician. The brothers acquired a small printing press from Dr. Rivalland in Curepipe and installed it in St. Denis Street, Port-Louis, where they started publishing tracts and pamphlets, as well as a montly periodical called *Sainik*, which was later followed by the *Zamana*, which became a quite popular publication.

What Basdeo Bissoondoyal was practising in those days, could, in some ways, be compared to the theology of liberation which motivated Catholic priests of the working classes of various parts of the world several decades later, especially in the 1960s.

Anyway, the "lambs" had revolted. Some of them had fallen. Others were to rise again and again and face oppression and repression. They did so each time withrenewed vigour to claim better conditions and more democratic freedoms.

Raoul Rivet, politician and journalist

One of the most important figures of journalism and politics in the 20th century was Raoul Rivet (left). He introduced Dr. Seewoosagur Ramgoolam to the electorate as a man with a great future and they stood together, with other candidates, at the Port-Louis municipal elections in the Union Mauricienne. TThey stood as candidates against both those of the plantocracy and the Labour Party and also joined their newspapers, Rivet's Le Mauricien and Ramgoolam's Advance, during and for a long time after World War II in one common newspaper together with Le Cernéen.

The Old Port-Louis Theatre

Top left: The Port-Louis Theatre in the 1950s in the days of Raoul Rivet. Below, the theatre in the early 1900s when the statue of Sir John Pope Hennessy was still in the middle of the square as shown in this old post card.

Chapter 39
The end of the status quo

The 1885 Constitution had maintained a complete *status quo* regarding the political evolution of the country for more than sixty years before the British government realised – or was made to realise – that it was time to loosen the local oligarchy's grip on the State apparatus and to give democracy a chance.

The strike of 1943 at Belle Vue Harel, just four years after the 1937 disturbances, had demonstrated the incapacity, if not the unwillingness of the ultra-conservative governor Mackenzie-Kennedy to bring the Oligarchy to respect even the frail protective net offered to the working classes by the 1938 Labour Ordinance and other measures taken in the wake of the 1937 strikes. A commission which inquired into the 1943 unrest had given conclusions that could be interpreted as a total failure of the institutions supposed to enforce the respect of the law. [1]

Obviously, neither occasional amendments of the Labour laws, nor the appointment of the governor's Mauritian nominees in the Legislative Council, had been adequate for good governance. The fact was that nearly 10 Indian workers had been killed in just 4 years. The shootings and the causes of the 1943 labour unrest were raised in the British Parliament again by Creech-Jones leading the offensive. Answering to one of his questions, Colonel Stanley, the Secretary of State for the Colonies, stated,

"Steps are being taken to amend the legislation with regard to the formation of industrial associations, and in the meantime no application to form such an association has been refused, and certain new associations have been added to the Schedule in the existing legislation." [2]

Another major factor motivating the desire for change was that the cost of living, according to members of the House of Commons and even the Secretary of State Stanley, had risen by between 100% and 200%. These figures came up during exchanges between Stanley and MPs Adams, Silverman, and Dr. Morgan. The Second World War was raging and world trade was disrupted. The MPs insisted that the government should apply price control in addition to rationing to protect the Mauritian population, but Stanley said prices could not be controlled and that wages should be made to adjust to inflation. Dr. Morgan suggested that the Colonial Office should *"limit the powers of the governors."*[3]

Governors did not often apply legislation voted in the UK to address unrest among workers in the colonies. A workers' movement in the West Indies had demanded immediate independence and the introduction of universal adult suffrage. One concrete example of the attitude of the governors is regarding the Colonial Development and Welfare Act that was voted in 1939 following unrest in the preceding years in Mauritius, Jamaica, spreading to the West Indies generally. The Act, which was not even exactly all that what was needed but was nevertheless a positive step, became law in July 1940 and provided for reform in welfare and development throughout the entire British Empire. It granted £5m to be spent yearly on colonial development and welfare for ten years and £500,000 annually for colonial research indefinitely.

During a parliamentary session in Britain, pressed by Creech-Jones, Colonial Secretary Oliver Stanley indicated that the colonial governments had been instructed that their legislation should contain provisions corresponding to various sections of UK legislation, including the United Kingdom Trade Union Act, the Trade Disputes Act, 1906. Creech-Jones wanted *"definite guarantee and assurance from the Colonial Government that such legislation will be enacted"* and all colonies be *"brought into line"* with this requirement. Stanley revealed that Mauritius was one of the *"territories which have trades union legislation which does not comply fully with the requirements of the Act."* [4] The Mauritius Legislative Council also failed to address this issue, while the local Labour Party and the Bissoondoyal brothers were treated as *"agitators"* and even *"terrorists"* for defending the interests of the masses and their rights to freedom of association, demonstration and strike were denied.

There were strong factors that finally caused the 1943 unrest: a lack of freedom to constitute trade unions, a rising

---

1 *Report of the Commission of Enquiry into the Disturbance which occurred in the North of Mauritius in 1943*, London 1944.
2 *Answers To Questions. Mauritius (Shooting Inquiry)* HC Deb 27 October 1943 vol 393 cc185-6
3 *Cost of Living*, HC Deb 03 March 1943 vol 387 cc544-5.
4 *Colonial Development And Welfare* HC Deb 05 May 1943 vol 389 cc174-6

cost of living that crushed the poorer classes of the population, a governor who sided always with the oligarchy. There was also the question of the total absence of political representation for the working classes under the 1886 Constitution still prevailing and under which the nominees of the governor were appointed. Overall, the system was barring access to the legislature to representatives of the workers.

The strikes and the well-attended public gatherings organised by the Mauritius Labour Party and the Bissoondoyal brothers everywhere in the country were clearly motivated by a desire of the working classes to choose their own representatives in the Legislative Council. There were also the legitimate nationalistic feelings growing within a large section of the local intelligentsia who aspired to take part in the management of the country, and rightly so.

The Hooper Commission had found that there had been political motivations behind Curé's actions. And so what? There was one of the most brilliant sons of the Mauritian nation who was, as the leader of a party supported by the majority of the population, legitimately interested in leading his country to political emancipation. He was being told by the British governors that he had no right to do so! How long could those governors, apart from having their policemen shoot and kill people as in 1937 and 1943 at BelleVue Harel, continue to assign to residence, arrest, imprison, deport, prosecute and persecute immensely popular leaders like Curé, Anquetil and Basdeo Bissoondoyal?

India was rapidly moving towards independence, which she obtained in 1947. The Second World War had been painful for the Mauritians. The 1943 shootings had deeply affected the morale of the working classes. Ruthless repression by Governor Mackenzie-Kennedy, a veteran of the British anti-independence efforts in India, was the order of the day.

Large numbers of Mauritians had volunteered or had been drafted to serve in the British armed forces on the various fronts of the war and many died, while at home, food was scarce and life was quite hard because of the consequences of the disruption of the world's economy and trade. The governor had even proposed to introduce compulsory labour on the sugar estates! Governors continued to be subservient to what the Colonial Office still called, in various papers, the oligarchy of Mauritius.

Governors were very powerful. The following exchange between MP Adams and Colonel Stanley in the House of Commons is typical of the government's reluctance to intimate to a governor to grant even a basic freedom to workers:

" Mr. Creech Jones asked the Secretary of State for the Colonies whether consideration is being given to a new Constitution for Mauritius; and whether, meantime, a more representative Executive Council can be set up, to include representatives of the unfranchised peoples and classes, including working people?

"Colonel Stanley : I am informing myself as fully as possible about the political situation in Mauritius (…).

"Mr. Creech Jones: In view of the long delay in bringing in constitutional reform in Mauritius and the strong local feeling, and the social and economic difficulties, will the right hon. and gallant Gentleman consider, as an interim arrangement during the war, a wider representation, particularly of workers, on the Executive Council of the Colony?

"Colonel Stanley : As I said in my answer, I am looking into the matter; but the hon. Gentleman must realise that Mauritius is still very close to the front line." [5]

It is obvious that Mauritius was in no way close to the front lines. But the war was a good pretext to avoid constitutional reforms and, again, the following exchange shows the government dragging its feet while the governors were appointing non-elected nominees as a panacea to all problems of the country:

"Mr. Creech Jones asked the Secretary of State for the Colonies whether he can make a statement on the recent consideration of the constitution of Mauritius?

"Colonel Stanley : No, Sir, but I have asked Sir Cosmo Parkinson, who is visiting Mauritius for personal discussions with the Governor on my behalf, to take the opportunity to discuss with him this among other matters. In the meantime, the Executive Council has been enlarged by the appointment of Mr. Osman, an Indian resident of the Colony, who, as a member of the Council of Government has already shown his interest in public affairs.

"Mr. Creech Jones: May I ask the right hon. and gallant Gentleman to bear in mind that the Under-Secretary of State for the Colonies gave a firm promise as far back as 1938 that there would be constitutional reform? Will he see that this matter is pushed on?

"Colonel Stanley : Of course, there has been a war since that time." [6]

So, after the 1937 disturbances there had been talk of constitutional reform to address the political situation in Mauritius. Then, four years after, just months before new disturbances and more killings, again pressed by MPs to

[5] *House of Commons: Mauritius (Constitution)* HC Deb 14 April 1943 vol 388 cc1206-7
[6] *Mauritius (Constitution)* HC Deb 21 July 1943 vol 391 cc888-9.

bring about constitutional reforms, the Colonial Office found nothing better than to use the war as a pretext: Mauritius was, too close... to the frontline!

The governors ruled like tyrants. Under Donald Mackenzie-Kennedy, Clifford's successor, a well-known activist among the Bissoondoyalists, Sukdeo Bishnu Dayal, was arrested and imprisoned for three weeks for having demonstrated publicly against racism in South Africa with a procession of bullock carts and images of Gandhi during a visit of South African tourists to Mauritius.[7] Nothing of this sort would have happened if the likes of Curé, Bissoondoyal and Rozemont had already achieved a legislative majority that could take decisions. Instead, the legislature continued to be dominated by the unelected nominees of the governor, and a handful of elected members dominated by the oligarchy's representatives who had been sent to legislate by voters constituting less than 2% of a population of over 424,000.

The governor's communalistic agenda

First, a definition of communalism is necessary. In the Merriam-Webster online dictionary, it is defined as *"1. Social organization on a communal basis; 2. Loyalty to a sociopolitical grouping based on religious or ethnic affiliation."* In Mauritius, the extreme pejorative meaning the word has taken equals it to prejudice and racism based on communal considerations.

Bede Clifford had toyed with the idea of communal representation in 1939, according to historian Satteeanund Peerthum, who believes, like the Bissoondoyal brothers, that the governor's proposals to that effect (like a similar system referred to in Council in the 1920's) would have resulted in institutionalising communalism. The formula would have created a Legislative Council where 21 seats, reserved for specific communities, attributed among the Franco-Mauritians, the Coloured-and-Creoles, and the Indo-Mauritians: 7-7-7 formula, as it was known. In his book **Proconsul**, Bede Clifford writes that his proposals did not satisfy the Franco-Mauritians and the Coloured, while the Colonial Office considered those proposals communally divisive.

In the same book, Clifford also bluntly states that he could not allow the Whites to be ousted from power by the Indians, arguing that the former constituted the indigenous Mauritians and the latter were newcomers whose strength was only based on their number and unskilled work.[8] This indicates that the governor was indulging fully in ethnic politics. Historian Kenneth Ballhatchet explains,

"Bede Clifford was unsettled: his notions of Indian politics were shadowy, and the spectre of Creole and Indian leaders working together was disturbing. He warned against rash constitutional change, and the old stereotypes of excitable and irresponsible Mauritians were refurbished in official discussions both at the colonial office and in Mauritius. For the foreseeable future, the officials agreed, Mauritius would need the steadying influence of the British."[9]

No wonder, therefore, about the delaying tactics employed by the British government in Parliament in Britain to ward off the spectre of majority representation in the Mauritius Legislative Council.

Supporting the 7-7-7 formula, Dr. Edgar Laurent, of the Union Mauricienne, declared, during the debates in the Consultative Committee which led eventually to the 1947 Constitution:

"We were given the definite assurance by the then Governor, Sir Bede Clifford, that the proposed new Constitution would offer liberal representation to each of the principal communities without permitting anyone of them to secure at the elections an absolute majority over the other two as might happen if a reasonable liberal expansion of the franchise were to take place without any safeguarding conditions."

Pandit Basdeo Bissoondoyal has a largely differing view of Clifford's action in Mauritius in a book[10] chapter entitled *"How communalism came to the island"*:

"It was a Governor who was not satisfied with the governorship of a little island who aspired to be one day governor of an Indian province no less important than Bengal, and later Viceroy of India, that set the people of Mauritius a-thinking by publishing an article on the three principal communities of the island. He deliberately went in for a feat that, he believed, could earn him the gratitude of his fatherland. He started a 'communal hare.'"

He does not mince his words regarding the actions of the governor and of a British official named Ward, Director of Education, who he said wanted the *"**banishment of Oriental languages**"*[11] and accuses both Clifford and Ward of profanation of a Hindu temple. He adds:

---
7 Incident mentioned in Ballhatchet, op cit. Source cited: ***Donald Mackenzie-Kennedy to A. CreechJones, 7 and 22 Mar. 1947***, C0537/2230/33, 40.
8 Clifford, Bede, *Proconsul: being incidents in the life of the Honourable Sir Bede Clifford*, Evans 1964.
9 Ballhatchet, op cit.
10 Bissoondoyal, Basdeo, *Life in Greater India. An Autobiography*, Bharatiya Vidya Bhavan, 1984. Page 145.
11 Ibid. Page 49.

"Governors and Directors do not lose a single opportunity that can enable them to sow the seeds of communalism." [12]

Bede Clifford was not able to carry out his plan of enlarging representative government the way he had proposed in 1939. He spent much time dealing with the considerable unrest created by the Labour Party activists who, throughout the country, were organising strikes for better wages and living conditions for the workers, and demanding the extension of the franchise to the majority of the population, that is the working classes.

His only consolation was that, in spite of being highly criticised by the Labour Party and the Jan Andolan movement of the Bissoondoyal brothers for his repression of the struggle by small planters and workers generally, he enjoyed the support of the one particular section of the Indo-Mauritian community. Hazareesingh in his *History of Indians in Mauritius* (op cit) explains:

"Ramgoolam backed most of the policies proposed by Sir Bede Clifford, as they generally aimed at wider participation of the Indian community in the affairs of the country (...) Sir Bede Clifford appointed Ramgoolam a member of the first Minimum Wage Board. He was also made a Director on the Board of the Mauritius Institute ..." [13] *That was in addition to naming him to the Mauritius Legislative Council as representative of the Indo-Mauritians."*

But the turning point for Dr. Ramgoolam was his stand during the debate on constitutional reforms initiated from 1945 to 1947 by the governor.

The war had ended. The Labour Party rose to power in Britain in 1945. Decolonisation and independence were the order of the day everywhere in the Third World. In 1946, Clement Attlee, the British Prime Minister declared that India was completing the process of self-determination. Then the British Parliament voted the Indian Independence Act which came into force on August 15, 1947, after decades of struggle by the Indians for their political emancipation. But the country split into two, with the formation of a new country by the Muslims, Pakistan.

The British already contemplated to give ministerial responsibility to a large number of their colonies, prior to self-government, which, in turn, would lead them to independence. In fact, by the end of the 1950s and in the 1960s, Britain had decided to give independence to its colonies in the so-called Third World and providing self-governing powers to the others like Canada and Australia. Decolonisation became a formal British policy under the pressure of the Foreign Office, itself acting under pressure from the United Nations. As official British policy, decolonisation was implemented while everything was put into place to prevent radicals, or elites perceived as radical, to accede to the political control of the former colonies. [14]

That explains the attitude of the Mauritian governors from the 1940s and 1950s, when pro- and anti-decolonisation elements expressed their views in Whitehall, to the mid 1950s and in the 1960s, when the pro-decolonisation officials (using divide-and-rule policies and other methods) became the decision-makers, albeit as a result of intense international pressure.

In Mauritius, the members of the Legislative Council who discussed the Constitution from 1945 to 1947 did not ask for self-government. The Labour Party and the Bissoondoyal brothers were being kept outside the unrepresentative Mauritius Legislative Council by an undemocratic franchise. The discussions, actually, revolved increasingly around racial and communal representation in relation to the franchise, a situation that later developed into full-fledged ethnic politics.

Jules Koenig: a man of the masses who went astray

Jules Koenig, who had until then sided with the Labour Party leaders and the Bissoondoyal brothers on several issues and had been accused of being a "bolshevist" by the oligarchs, joined the representatives of the latter and a few moderates to oppose the extension of the franchise to the working classes. That came as a surprise to many political observers as Koenig had been systematically opposed to the oligarchs. He had supported, at the age of 16, the Retrocession Movement in the 1920's because the French colonies appeared to him better integrated into the French republican system.

After his studies from 1920 to 1924 in England and France, he came back and later, like Ramgoolam, joined the Union Mauricienne founded by Dr. Edgar Laurent, Roger Pezzani and Raoul Rivet. It was an elitist and centrist party opposed to the oligarchs, but quite moderate and unwilling to ask for universal suffrage. But for a brilliant

---
12 Ibid. Page 148.
13 Op cit.
14 Heinlein, Frank, *British Government Policy and Decolonisation, 1945-1963: Scrutinising the Official Mind.* London and Portland: Frank Cass, 2002. See also: *Decolonisation,* A. P. Thornton, in: *International Journal* , Vol. 19, No. 1 (Winter, 1963/1964), pp. 7-29. Published by: Canadian International Council. Article Stable URL: http://www.jstor.org.virtual.anu.edu.au/stable/40198689

Franco-Mauritian lawyer to oppose the oligarchs, that was already a big political event in those days and Koenig was considered almost as a traitor by the sugar barons. [15]

He, nevertheless, stood as a candidate in January 1931, in the district of Rivière du Rempart, against one of the most prominent leaders of the Oligarchs and of the Franco-Mauritian community: Maurice Martin, President of the Chamber of Agriculture, influent member of the Mauritius Sugar Syndicate, director of the Mauritius Commercial Bank and of several sugar companies, President of the Mauritius Turf Club, the Mauritius Jockey Club, the Club de Curepipe, member of the Legislative Council for Rivière du Rempart for about two decades, owner of the right-wing newspaper *Le Radical*. He became the target of virulent attacks from that paper and *Le Cernéen*, another mouthpiece of the oligarchy.

Koenig had defended Dr. Maurice Curé in 1934 when the latter was sued by the magistrate Hanning after Curé had protested against the magistrate's decision to eliminate a number of persons from the electoral list. Curé had severely attacked Hanning and Koenig managed to reduce the damages claimed, while Curé was elected at the by-election of 1934. In August 1937, Koenig and R. Neerunjun successfully defended Pandit Sahadeo who had been arrested and prosecuted for having breached public peace on the Reunion Sugar Estate.

Curé was blamed for having loaned to Rajmohunsingh Jomadar, for his studies, money from a worker's welfare organisation, the Société de Bienfaisance des Travailleurs de l'Ile Maurice. Curé had founded that association to help workers in case of sickness or other urgencies, a sort of social insurance. Governor Bede Clifford ordered the dissolution of the association on January 13, 1939, as the loan had not been refunded. Koenig appealed to the Supreme Court against that decision and wanted to assign Bede Cliford as witness. But the Supreme Court turned down his demand. The welfare organisation disappeared, but the Labour Party became even stronger.

A brilliant orator, Koenig appealed to the centrists-elitists. His father was an employee of the Civil Service, as the Director of the Forest Department, and was attacked vigorously by Martin. During his 1931 electoral campaign, the sugar barons prohibited Jules Koenig from entering the estate premises to meet those employees who had the right to vote. Finally, Koenig lost, obtaining 181 votes and Martin 242.

Only three centrists were elected: Laurent and Rivet in Port-Louis and Pezzani in Plaines Wilhems. Five days after the election, Koenig was physically assaulted by Martin's son at the back of Saint Paul Catholic Church, Phoenix. The young oligarch hit him in the face and in the stomach. That incident was considered extremely serious and *Le Mauricien* of Rivet, which supported the centrist party, severely condemned the attack. [16]

Koenig quarrelled with the Union Mauricienne when, in December 1935, Goolam Mamode Dawjee Atchia was not elected mayor of Port-Louis for 1936. Initially, the post of mayor had been unanimously promised to Atchia, a prominent Indo-Mauritian leader in those days, by the members of Union Mauricienne. But the decision was suddenly reversed in favour of Rivet, and Koenig was furious, refusing to listen to allegations of betrayal against the party alleged against Atchia. Koenig left the Union Mauricienne and resigned from the municipal council, followed by Atchia, Savrimouton, Bour and Noormohamed, and Edgar Laurent was elected as mayor with Gabriel Martial as deputy-mayor.

It was only ten years later, in 1946, that Koenig joined once more the ranks of those who had been at the Union Mauricienne (which had fizzled out), but who had constituted the Group of Twelve, which comcomprised also Dr. S. Ramgoolam, who was taking part in the debates over constitutional reforms. This group defeated two candidates of the Mauritius Labour Party at the 1946 Port-Louis municipal elections. It comprised also: René Humbert, Abdul Razack Mohamed, Radhamohun Gujadhur, Raymond Hein, Maxime de Sornay. Today, no one remembers that Ramgoolam was an opponent of the Labour Party for several years. He was to seek support from the MLP when franchise was enlarged and Labour was, as a result, pretty sure of winning a majority after the 1947 Constitution was introduced, especially as the party was widely supported by the Indo-Mauritian community, which was not the case for the Union Mauricienne in which Ramgoolam had fought his first electoral battles.

What was happening in reality? The perspective of constitutional reforms had caused a general scramble among the

---

15 This part of the book on Koenig's life is sourced principally from J.A. Koenig, *Une vie pour la justice: biographie de Jules Koenig*, Mauritius Printing 1979. Koenig had strong support from the Indo-Mauritian electorate, especially small planters and workers, so much so that he was elected at the 1948 general elections when the Mauritius Labour Party swept the polls on a franchise enlarged to the majority of the population of Creoles and Indo-Mauritians. His opposition to universal suffrage, inspired from his days at the elitist Union Mauricienne, was the target of considerable criticism, but he was not the only politician of the 1960s that had been in the UM.
16 *Le Mauricien*, 26 January 1931.

Mauritian political class for communal leadership. The journalistic world had followed suit. **Le Cernéen** was openly defending the Franco-Mauritians. **Advance** had been founded, as Hazareesingh writes, by Dr. S. Ramgoolam, as a project *"which had the financial support and backing of all sections of the Indian community,"* and, as a matter of fact, the editor of the paper, Anauth Beejadhur, had written in his first editorial that it would *"claim with proper moderation, but without weakness, the rights of the Indo-Mauritian community."* The centrist-elitist **Le Mauricien** of Raoul Rivet became the rallying point of the Coloured and Creole intelligentsia, the Union Mauricienne doing its utmost, as during the 1946 municipal election, to attract the elite of the Indo-Mauritian and other communities.

Eventually, in this atmosphere, the predominantly Coloured and Creole centrist-elitist political current failed, like Beaugeard, to campaign for universal suffrage, which would have been the best weapon against the oligarchy at general elections. It panicked at the idea that the Indo-Mauritian majority would 'swamp' the ethnic minorities. Eventually Koenig would claim to be the champion of those minorities. The centrist politicians watched with mixed feelings, even with suspicion, as the Indo-Mauritian intellectuals led by Dr. S. Ramgoolam gradually integrated the Mauritius Labour Party and moved rapidly upwards within its structure during successive leadership crises following the death of Anquetil, then of Rozemont. The Indo-Mauritian elite siding with Dr. S. Ramgoolam and K. Hazareesingh, accepted the party's manifesto in favour of a radical transformation of the suffrage in favour of the workers, where the Indo-Mauritians formed an overwhelming majority.

A substantial part of the Creole and Coloured intelligentsia, among them Dr. Millien, who controlled the newspaper *L'Oeuvre*, Guy Forget, a young promising intellectual, Raymond Rault, and Mrs. R. Rochecouste, decided to militate under the banner of the Labour Party. Millien strongly attacked Jules Koenig, former lawyer of several Labour leaders and agents, for having, according to him, chosen to support the oligarchy. In Koenig's reply, the main arguments were the necessity to improve the economy with better prices for the Mauritian sugar production and his belief, from his days at Union Mauricienne that the masses had first to receive a proper degree of education before being allowed to vote.

The Mauritius Labour Party, which had asked for the right to vote for the working classes since its foundation in 1936, was going through serious problems. Curé was financially ruined by his political activities, his enormous sense of generosity which led him to devote considerable time to free medical care for thousands of poor labourers and artisans, and the boycott of his medical cabinet by the rich who were, in those days, the only people who could afford a private doctor. As a result, he had relinquished the leadership of the party to Emmanuel Anquetil. The latter died during the constitutional debates, in 1946.

Ramgoolam's courts the Mauritius Labour Party as franchise is enlarged

Dr. S. Ramgoolam had taken quite a moderate position, at first, during the Legislative Assembly debates in 1944. He commented on the governor's project to discuss constitutional reforms by saying:

"Starting with the revision of the Constitution, I shall stress upon the fact that we Indians – and when I say 'Indians' I do not mean to speak on racial grounds, but to emphasise that our people belong to the working classes of this Island – will be most affected by any changes that it might please His Majesty the King to bring about. I would urge Your Excellency to go into the revision of the Constitution as quickly as possible. I hope that by the time the life of this House comes to an end, you will have made up your mind on this matter, and that it will not be long before you will declare to the people of this Island the conclusions you will have reached; that your decision will have been arrived at in consultation with the various elements in the Colony, and no doubt you will have taken care of their interests and fully considered their share in the affairs of the Colony." [17]

He commented also the events of 1943, that is, the preceding year, by saying that *"these incidents were due to little things, and if those little things are not taken care of now how can we be sure there will be no recurrence?"* He blamed the Labour Department for not having been able to prevent *"such occurrences"* and stated that *"there is no reason to believe that the feeling of restlessness is dissipated and replaced by a feeling of harmony and peace."* In all fairness, it must be said that in the same speech, Dr. Ramgoolam did blame the authorities for having jailed a missionary, whose name he did not mention but it was presumably Pandit Basdeo Bissoondoyal, one of his implacable adversaries within the Labour Party circles.

He made a comment also about wages following the government's decision to the effect that in 1944 they should remain the same as in the preceding year:

"Despite my high regards for those who are concerned with the immediate Government of this Island, I must say that

---
[17] Legislative Assembly, 19 July 1944.

wages should have been increased this year because the cost of living has gone up. It is only reasonable."

He deplored that *"a Hindu missionary has been imprisoned for not paying his fine,"* pleaded for the freedom of every subject *"of the British Empire"* to *"exercise (...) his religion"* and added that *"I know that Government has no intention of jeopardising this right."* He welcomed the decision of the government to provide meals at school for children (as a result of a long battle by Curé and Laboour) and expressed the wish that the workers would be better represented on the Labour Advisory Board.

Dr. Ramgoolam was, at the same time that he went to the Port-Louis municipal elections on the list of the Union Mauricienne's centrist-elitist candidates, moving closer to the successors of Curé within the Labour Party, first Anquetil, and, as from 1946, Guy Rozemont. The latter was even more anxious about the rising communal tone of the political debate in the country than his predecessors had been.

During the continuing debate over constitutional reform before the Consultative Committee in 1947, Dr. S. Ramgoolam pleaded in favour of the *"direct representation"* of the Labour Party in the Committee and said that *"with the sudden death of Mr. Anquetil we do not know exactly what would be the view of the Labour Party on such a vital matter"* as constitutional reform. But he was still quite moderate in his views, adding that the proposed constitutional reform *"should make an advance towards the composition of a Legislative Council which should be truly representative, though perhaps without the power to change its own Constitution."* [18]

He proposed, in fact, the British approach to constitutional evolution, that is, a long process of change that would not hurt British interests. He stated,

"The only thing we decided was that the country is not prepared for yet is self-government, and that we should proceed by stages so that in due course we should be prepared to work towards self-government. For this purpose some progress should be made now towards representative government. This representative Council would not in any way endanger or in any way be against the interests of His Majesty's Government, because the Governor will still be there as the Governor of a Crown Colony, with all reserved powers and right of veto.

"If half of the members are elected, then to make good the plan, the other half would have to be reduced in number. We can, for instance, instead of having twelve nominated unofficial members and nineteen elected members, increase by one the elected members. Even reducing the number of official nominated members is a good step forward. We cannot, however, remove the Colonial Secretary. This is the only way to move towards self-government, and the Governor as the representative of His Majesty's Government will in time collect information to say whether the country is ready for further advance or not. Otherwise His Majesty's Government will have reason to claim in the future that the country is still not fit for self-government. We should make that advance. It is in the interest of the country to do so. It is also in the interest of the Imperial Government."

Dr. S. Ramgoolam was displaying considerable skill, actually, in trying to win over the support of the Mauritius Labour Party, with which he had clashed in the past, and, at the same time, to give assurances to the British that a gradual evolution was quite possible from the 1885 Constitution to a really representative Legislative Council which, at some future time, would give way to self-government.

His courtship of the Labour Party, which he had opposed until the election in Port-Louis in 1946, started from 1947, at the time when the British were already moving towards an enlargement of the suffrage to more voters. His speeches in the Legislative Council as the governor's nominee changed in tone towards the Labour Party, with which he had so much clashed until then. He stated in 1947, in the Consultative *Committee that was working on constitutional reform:*

"May I know whether it is the intention that a representative of the Labour Party should sit on this Committee? It is my firm conviction that the Labour Party in Mauritius should be given direct representation on this Committee, and in view of such an important matte as the revision of the Constitution, it is incumbent upon us, with your permission, to see to it that a representative of that party sits on our Committee. With the sudden death of Mr. Anquetil we do not know exactly what would be the view of the Labour Party on such a vital matter." [19]

The Labour Party, laminated by the loss of towering figures like Curé and Anquetil, was trying, under Jos Guy Rozemont, to keep up its faltering organisation in the face of mounting communal feelings generated by conflicting forces within the traditional political establishment. In reality, the Franco-Mauritian sugar and business barons, the predominantly Coloured and Creole centrist intellectuals of the former Union Mauricienne, and that part of the Indo-Mauritian intelligentsia which had gathered around Dr. Ramgoolam were discussing at Government House about the fate of the majority and of the minority communities in the future constitutional changes.

But Ramgoolam was, in a sense, the most astute politician of them all in that he skillfully and gradually, with considerable patience and using to his advantage internal party conflicts, won the support of the Labour Party.

---
18 Consultative Committee, 22 January 1947.
19 Consultative Committee, 22 July 1947.

After all, Labour, with its trade unions, was the major political force in the island. He correctly calculated that the Labour Party would be the biggest winner when the suffrage would be extended to the working classes where there was a huge majority of Indo-Mauritians and Creoles, plus the multiethnic petites bourgeoisies of the various other communities, waiting to reverse a historical evolution that had been most of the time painful for them.

Moreover, the British administration with which Ramgoolam – never did he make a secret of it – had close ties, was confident that the latter would eventually, by working an arrangement with the Labour Party, bring about a moderation of the political programme of its leadership – and that was what exactly happened, as some years later, the radical hard core of that programme made up of a series of nationalisations was scrapped in favour of a much milder brand of socialism coupled with free enterprise, the resulting ideology being, by the 1970s, termed the ***"mixed economy."***

Coming back to the constitutional debate, Dr. S. Ramgoolam, who had managed to obtain Anquetil's, and after him, Rozemont's support, started, in 1947, to speak a more radical language. The oligarchs had, for a long time, wanted female suffrage, which would have substantially increased the number of their electors and strengthened their control of the electoral process under the 1885 constitution. Dr. S. Ramgoolam, intervening on January 15, 1947, before the Consultative Committee, declared:

"We are not against female suffrage if it is extended to all the women in the country without distinction of creed or class. If the workers of this country are able to send their wives or sisters to toil in the fields, I am sure they will not object to their going to the polling booths to record their votes. What we object to in the present proposal for female suffrage is that it only serves the purpose of a class of people who have always insisted on keeping things as they are (...) But if female suffrage is awarded in a democratic manner, I do not think that there is anybody outside or in this Committee who will be against it." [20]

On the question of the literacy test for electors, at one moment it was considered that a Primary School Leaving Certificate should be requested. The centrist-elitist politicians, led by Raoul Rivet, and the oligarchs did not believe that the right to vote should be indiscriminately given as wanted by the MLP and the Bissoondoyal brothers, to all people who could, in any language, read and write a simple sentence. Dr. S. Ramgoolam intervened during the Legislative Council debates to support the MLP's and the Bissoondoyalists' points of view in favour of the simple literacy test in any language understood by the voter. [21]

He said, during that debate, that English as a compulsory language for the voter, had been accepted by the Franchise Committee of Trinidad but that **"this criterion has been done away with by the Colonial Office since February of last year, because after examination it was found that it would not stand the test of the people who are impartial and who today feel that the Colonies must advance. And by advancement it is meant that every class of the population should advance."**

He opposed wage qualification the more so that wages varied seasonally and annually, and depended on the will of the employer.

"I do not think that a wage qualification will be of any advantage to the workers, because it is set so high that with very rare exceptions, they will be left with hardly any political rights at all. I must point out to the Committee that even a big industrialist like Mr. Gujadhur, when submitting his memorandum to the Committee, suggested that the wage qualification should be brought down to four hundred and eighty rupees, knowing well from experience that the working man cannot earn enough to meet the wage qualification imposed here (...) Today we must do away with property altogether, and deal with a man as a man, as an essential and good citizen who is able to play his part in the life of the island just as everybody else."

Developing his ideas, he said there should be compromise on the question of suffrage.

"Franchise and education go together to a certain extent, but (...) illiteracy is no bar to voting ability or to the secrecy of the ballot. Adult franchise is quickest and best way of setting up an attack on illiteracy as everywhere the demand of the common people for education is strong. It is true that lack of political knowledge and experience will handicap the voters in the beginning, but this will lead to a revolution, as the likelihood is that they will vote for the same kind of people as were previously in power (...) The right to vote should be given to the man or woman who is able to fill in the electoral form in any language in use in the island (...) the final solution will be in adult suffrage. We cannot stick to the past like friends who oppose us today. They will say that this kind of qualification might give representation to a large number of people at the risk of leaving out useful people from the Council of Government. Historically that cannot be true because in every country where a change of Constitution has taken place, people have always taken a conservative stand."

Commenting on the communal question, he remarked that Indo-Mauritians and voters of other communities, had

---
20 **Consultative Committee**, 15 January 1947.
21 **Consultative Committee**, January 29, 1947.

not been voting on communal lines:

"The history of this Colony will also show that despite the fact that certain classes of people, even certain communities, are in the majority in certain districts, they have not made use of it to return members on communal lines in an election. The present Council of Government is an example of it. The District of Flacq only lately returned Mr. Gujadhur; they have always returned a man of another class, although the Coloured people are in the majority. Grand Port is another instance."

Then he skilfully cajoled the conservatives, telling them that they should not fear as they were resourceful and could hope to have a number of elected representatives and any imbalance would be corrected by the governor by his power to nominate members in the Council:

"The governor will judiciously make his selection and see that the community which is not otherwise represented will be represented. He can make good any defect in the electoral maturity of a people." [22]

Dr. Ramgoolam finally proposed a Legislative Council on the following lines:

"We must be given a representative form of government with perhaps half of the number elected on the franchise decided by the Secretary of State, with the provision that it should not be given the power to change the Constitution. The Governor as Her Majesty's representative would be given the necessary reserve powers in cases of emergency, for fit and proper cases. A system of that nature will make responsible government possible in a reasonable period, and will be an advance on what we already have." [23]

The British 'worried' by inter-communal cooperation and friendliness in Mauritius

After various schemes proposed by the governor and the Colonial Office to restrict the franchise in favour of the conservatives, there was an outburst against those manoeuvres from the "*progressive*" elements led by the Labour Party of Guy Rozemont who was supported by prominent intellectuals like Dr. S. Ramgoolam, Basdeo and Sookdeo Bissoondoyal and Dr. E. Millien. What amazed the British was the dominance of class over communal interests among people of all the communities who were on the lower rungs of the social hierarchy, especially the solidarity between Indo-Mauritians (Hindus, Muslims) and Creoles. Ballhatchet notes from colonial office correspondence papers:

"The officials worried about the friendly relations established by the Creole Dr Millien with Indian politicians. In 1948 the governor told Creech Jones how Millien was arguing that Indians were no threat to Creoles. The governor concluded with satisfaction: 'there is no evidence that his efforts are proving successful'. [24]

But when Millien ran into difficulties with the government in the following year the officials were disconcerted to find that Ramgoolam supported him. Millien published criticisms of prison administration made by an inquiry commission. He was found guilty of sedition and breach of the Official Secrets Act, sentenced to 15 days' imprisonment, fined and refused permission to publish his newspaper for a month. Aged 66, he was carried shoulder-high from the court, and on appeal his prison sentence was commuted to a small fine. Ramgoolam was now a member of the executive council. He stood bail as one of Millien's sureties, and in the legislature he spoke up for him. This prompted the acting governor to summon Ramgoolam to Government House, where he was rebuked for supporting Millien.'" [25]

New constitution approved for enlarged franchise

The British finally conceded a large franchise and a substantial reform of the electoral system. The new Constitution approved by the Secretary of State in 1947 provided for a Legislative Council composed of the governor, 19 elected members, 12 nominated members and three officials appointed as ex-officio members (the Colonial Secretary, the Procureur and Advocate General and the Financial Secretary). The country was divided into five electoral districts:

- Plaines Wilhems and Black River (6 seats)
- Port-Louis (4 seats)
- Pamplemousses and Rivière du Rempart (3 seats)
- Moka and Flacq (3 seats)
- Grand Port and Savanne (3 seats)

---
22 Ibid.
23 **Consultative Committee**, 24 January 1947.
24 Ballhatchet, op cit., from **Mackenzie-Kennedy to Creech Jones,** 1 Oct. 1948, Co167/945/ j7715/ L
25 Ballhatchet, op cit. Documents cited attesting the factual content of this extract are the Colonial Office papers: **Mackenzie-Kennedy to Creech Jones**, 1 Oct. 1948, CO167/945/57715/I.; **J. D. Harford to Creech Jones**, 10 Mar. 1949, CO167/945/57715/I. 127 **Harford, note of a talk with Dr Ramgoolam at le Reduit**, 24 Mar. 1949, CO167/ 938/57249/9.

The franchise was redefined as follows:
- An elector had to be 21 years old or more and have resided in the country for two years preceding an election.
- Each elector had to be able to satisfy a simple literacy test in any language used in the country.
- Ex-servicemen with 13 months service in the army could vote.

That was quite an enormous change as compared with the 1885 Constitution, though plural voting was included, favouring especially the rich who could vote in more than one constituency.

The Labourites and particularly the Bissoondoyalists toured the country to ensure that a maximum of workers, especially labourers and artisans, would qualify to vote. The Bissoondoyalists gave lessons, teaching in record time thousands of illiterate workers how to write and read their names and simple sentences so that they could satisfy a simple literacy test. They succeeded admirably and finally, the number of electors jumped from less than 12,000 to 71,569 at the 1948 general elections.

The Mauritius Labour Party fielded its own candidates and recommended a number of independent candidates like Dr. S. Ramgoolam who were not members of the party. Ramgoolam was an independent candidate supported by the Labour Party in Pamplemousses-Rivière du Rempart, where two of his friends were also candidates, Anauth Beejadhur and Harilall Vaghjee, who were fighting the two actual Labour Party candidates. The Labour Party fielded only two candidates in Pamplemousses, Partab Algoo and Donald Francis, who were both beaten by Ramgoolam's two independent friends, Beejadhur and Vaghjee. This upset the Labour Party and the Bissoondoyal brothers especially as in the Grand Port/Savanne constituency, only Sookdeo Bissoondoyal was elected whereas his fellow candidates of the Labour Party, Philippe Rozemont, brother of Guy Rozemont, and Willy L'Etang, were defeated by two non-Labour candidates.

To keep its head above water, the party had to rely on the votes, in the Legislative Council, of members who had not been elected under its banner or if they had been, were not members of the party – or not yet, as in the case of Dr. Ramgoolam and his group.

The elected members at the 1948 general elections were:
- Port-Louis: Guy Rozemont (leader of the Labour Party), Dr. E. Millien, R. Seeneevassen, S.B. Emile.
- Pamplemousses-Rivière du Rempart: Dr. Seewoosagur Ramgoolam, H.R.Vaghjee, A. Beejadhur.
- Moka-Flacq: S. Balgobin, R. Balgobin, B. Gujadhur.
- Grand Port-Savanne: S. Bissoondoyal, J.N. Roy, J. Beedaysee.
- Plaines Wilhems-Black River: J. Koenig, R. Rault, D. Luckeenarain, G. Forget, R. Rivet and the first woman in history to be elected to the Mauritius legislature, former school headmistress Mrs. Marie-Louise Emilienne Rochecouste, born Orian.

The Labour Party could count on a majority composed by its own elected members and those it had supported, plus some independents and nominees like A.H. Osman and Dr. Maurice Curé. Some other members could support the party on a number of issues such as social assistance and education.

No Muslim elected, only 1 nominated on 12 appointees

Communal feelings ran high, eventually, after the 1948 general elections, stirred up by some people among the local political elite. This was due to the question of what was presented, by the conservative politicians, as the uncertain sociopolitical fate of the minority communities in relation to an electoral result that was depicted, by Labour's adversaries, as the political emancipation of essentially the majority ethnic community. The question had been raised by the elitists-centrists and the Oligarchs. Nevertheless, the fact that the enlarged electorate did not send any Muslim to the Legislative council created, as the conservatives wanted it to be, an atmosphere of discontent in the Muslim community, especially as the reality of this fact could not be rebutted and was embarrassing for Labour.

The governor made the situation even worse. He proceeded, after the election, as required by the new Constitution, to nominate 12 members in addition to the 19 elected members and the three ex-officio members (himself, the Colonial Secretary and the Financial Secretary). The twelve nominees included Dr. Maurice Curé and Dr. Edgar Laurent. The other ten were: R. Maigrot, Mme. D. de Chazal, J. Ah Chuen, , E. de Chazal, A. Gellé, A.G. Robinson, A.H. Osman, and A.L. Nairac. The governor nominated only one Muslim and, knowing the way the British used divide-and-rule tactics in the colonies, this was probably deliberate on his part. The end result was, any way, as divisive and harmful to Labour's image and future as London would have certainly wished. The conservatives started, from then on, an intense anti-Labour campaign on communal grounds that was to considerably weaken the party from the 1960s, while the Bissoondoyal brothers and their supporters were being elbowed out of Labour's circle of friends and collaborators by Ramgoolam's group.

Everything was made, from then on, by Labour's conservative adversaries, to make things appear as if Labour was anti-Muslim and anti-General Population. There were in all 34 members in the Legislative Council, of whom 17 elected ones were either members of the Labour Party or had been backed by that party or the Bissoondoyal brothers or were liberals, plus Dr. Maurice Curé. Labourites and Liberals could muster a majority in the new legislature, in spite of a number of nominees from the ranks of the oligarchs.

In any case, Labour Party leader Guy Rozemont had led his party to its first victory at legislative elections and, as a consequence, the history of the country completely changed course, with the evolution to self-government then independence becoming, henceforth, an inescapable political issue.

ᴴᴱᴺᴱᴿᴬᴸ NOTICE No. 501.

CENSORSHIP NOTICE

It is notified for information that *all* overseas postal or telegraphic ommunications are liable to censorship. The public is earnestly equested to co-operate with the Censor, in order to expedite the smooth vorking of the censorship, the sole object of which, it must be realised, s the preservation of the safety of the Colony and the Empire.

Bede Clifford, the Governor who repressed the struggle for freedom

Sir Bede Clifford (picture above) was the British governor who ruthlessly repressed the struggle for freedom and, according to the Bissoondoyal movement, started the 'communal hare' in modern Mauritius. He is revered, though, by the former Labour Party's and Jan Andolan's adversaries. Picture below: An official notice announcing the instauration of censorship in Mauritius in war time, in 1939. From 1943, he became mired in huge financial scandals in the Bahamas and Trinidad and was accused of taking bribes.

Chapter 40
The march to Independence (1)
The rise of ethnic politics: N.M.U. attacks Ramgoolam and Koenig

The ethnic question became the dominant theme of the defeated oligarchs after the 1948 general elections. Their mouthpiece, *Le Cernéen*, launched a full-scale attack on the Labour Party and its allies, in particular Dr. Ramgoolam, who had switched sides and sought the support of the Labour Party where he was not far from seizing the leadership as the party was mired in crisis following general elections. It had suffered some backlashes as described in the previous chapter.

Jules Koenig, Ramgoolam's former fellow candidate backed by the Union Mauricienne, was violently attacked also from 1949 to February 1950 by the new editor-in-chief of that paper, an avowed extreme-right advocate going by the name of Noël Marrier d'Unienville (better known by his initials N.M.U.). The latter blasted Koenig for having refrained from attacking, as a *"communist"* and *"totalitarian"* force, the Labour parliamentary group of the Council. Koenig was also the subject of N.M.U.'s mockery for having proposed a formula called *"social Christianism,"* which suggested limits to both socialist and capitalist programmes, but was still too anti-capitalistic to the taste of any fanatical extreme-rightist. [1]

Historically, N.M.U. can be regarded, like Bede Clifford, as one the most efficient promoters of communalism in Mauritian politics. Born in Baie du Tombeau in 1888, he had spent some time in France. He came back in 1949 from France, where he had been a partisan of the extreme-right forces under the banner of Action Française, and adhered to an extremely virulent racist ideology. He wrote articles which were openly motivated by racism against Dr. Ramgoolam and the Indo-Mauritian community in general and then started to lead a campaign requesting the formation *"of a Christian political party, a Muslim political party and a Chinese political party, associated through a common interest, which is to prevent the Hindu hegemony,"* so that those parties *"could fight on the same platform in the next general elections."* The title of the article was: *"The Indian menace."* [2]

Campaigning in his newspaper during the municipal elections against the Labour Party and its allies, N.M.U. wrote, in the same year:

"If the Ramgoolam-Rozemont list is elected in Port-Louis, you must consider that it will be the first communist victory in this country. If you allow this, you will contribute to assassinate your country."

Ramgoolam was attacked as *"ramgooloo-labourite, ramgooloo-nationalist,"* etc. On July 22, 1950, he called Ramgoolam *"the future Prime Minister"* and the following year, when Dr. Ramgoolam was appointed Liaison Officer for Education, he wrote that with such an appointment, the governor *"has insulted the 150,000 Christians and the Muslims of Mauritius by naming that notoriously subversive person at the Department of Education, so that he may influence the souls of our children."*

He heaped insults also upon the Creole and Coloured politicians, whether independent or members of the Labour Party, who defended Dr. Ramgoolam against his fanatical and racist attacks. On May 12, 1951, he wrote that *"when we see members of the Christian community like Rozemont, Rault, Forget allying themselves with Dr. Ramgoolam (...) we cannot help from thinking that they are unconsciously selling their brothers to the extremist Hindu hegemony that is being cultivated here."*

He was such an efficient propagandist that his articles troubled the minds of a number of politicians and opinion leaders of various political denominations. His insistence on the so-called *"Hindu hegemony"* as an inevitable result of the introduction of universal suffrage gained ground among moderate politicians like Jules Koenig. And that question of *"Hindu hegemony"* dominated the political debates in Mauritius for a very long time, reaching an intolerable climax towards the end of the 1960s, long after NMU's death in 1959.

The NMU 'factor' in Mauritian politics

---

[1] Editorial views published in *Le Cernéen* daily from the election results in 1948 to February 1949.'
[2] *Le Cernéen*, 'La menace hindoue', 28 April 1950.

One interesting question which deserves attention from history students is whether ethnic politics, which already preoccupied the minds of Mauritian politicians and public opinion during the debates leading to the 1885 Constitution and in the 1920's, would have been as virulent as it came to be in the 1960's without N.M.U.?

There is no doubt that the man was a skilful propagandist of the ideology of racism and some commentators have seen in him a Mauritian Goebbels.

It is also true, though, that even excluding N.M.U.'s influence, ethnic considerations have constantly influenced politics. This has been the case in Mauritius and in the rest of the world. In Eastern Europe, communist regimes used force to hold power during a few decades, efficiently repressing ethnic rivalries in the Balkans until the 1980s, when communism was defeated and those rivalries erupted violently again, causing war, genocide and destruction. And we have not spoken of the Americas, Africa and Asia where numerous examples of the influence of ethnic considerations on politics were provided on an almost daily basis in the world news reports during much of the 20th century.

As Mauritius was developing its parliamentary system and enlarging its franchise, ethnic, religious and tribal conflicts rocked various parts of the colonial world. Whereas conflict has existed in all human societies, in Africa, the violence of colonialism and of post-independence neocolonialism, is still very potent today. It results from the centuries of scramble by colonial powers to grab and control the continent's riches. Neocolonial policies have caused the nature of the traditional African conflicts to change radically. From a system of conflict management by the elders and even women, conflict regulation by codes of honour and other traditional conflict resolution systems, Africa, under the colonial and post-independence neocolonial regimes set up and maintained by the former colonial masters and other world powers coming from East and West, plunged into bloody and devastating conflicts as in the Congo, Biafra, Rwanda and other parts of the continent. This is well explained in a research paper on the origin of those conflicts, and which is summed up as follows by the author.

"The problems of violent conflicts in Africa today can be traced back to situations deeply rooted in exploitation and colonial domination of Africa. As far back as the days of the Atlantic slave trade to the period of colonial subjugation, Africa witnessed one form of violent conflicts or the other virtually unprecedented in the life of a typical African. Further on was the scrabble for African territories which eventually created artificially bounded nation-states. Similar was the divide and rule method, which alienated Africans from Africans. This method characterized the policies of the various colonial administrations. This paper admits that conflicts, not on a large scale, existed in pre-colonial Africa. It also examines the traditional methods of resolving these conflicts in pre-colonial Africa particularly among the Yorubas. However; the paper traces the incessant ethnic/tribal conflicts or the civil wars on a large scale that have pummelled various African societies since independence to the invasion of the continent by European colonialism. It examines the implication of the partitioning and creation of artificial boundaries in Africa and how it leads to a breakdown of communication among artificially bound natives. The paper submits that the various violent conflicts in Africa are a direct consequence of colonial domination." [3]

The traditional African rules of war imposed, according to the researcher, a number of practices like the choice of weapons, no war to be fought during harvests and other specified periods, protection of women and children with conflicts settled far away from the villages, etc, while there are no records of wars being fought on the massive scale like those that were fought in Europe during the corresponding period of world history. It was the divide-and-rule policy of the colonisers in Africa that was one of the main causes of the African conflicts that raged during much of the 20th century and spilling over into the 21st century.

Based on the arch-conservative governor Bede Clifford's actions, the divide-and-rule policy in Mauritus can be regarded as having been as successful as in Africa because, in the long run, blood was shed in the 1960s and in 1999 during what can be assessed as '***tribal***' conflicts.

Ethnic political representation, in one way or another, whether in the United States or India, which are large multi-ethnic societies, has to be attended to. And that was why even Dr. S. Ramgoolam, for instance, adopted a very limited form of proportional ethnic representation in the Mauritian Constitution at the time of Independence in the form of the Best Loser System. Nonetheless, there is a limit to the role of ethnicity in representation as the ethnic element should not go beyond people's reasonable sense of their original identities and indulge, by speech and acts, into sectarianism and the refusal of diversity and mutual tolerance. The problem is the use of the individual's sense of identity in the political debate not with a view to enrich it and promote tolerance, but to feed intolerance and

---

[3] Afisi, Oseni Taiwo, ***Tracing contemporary Africa's conflict situation to colonialism: A breakdown of communication among natives,*** Philosophical Papers and Reviews Vol. 1 (4), pp. 059-066, October, 2009, Academic Journals, Department of Philosophy, Faculty of Arts, Lagos State University, Ojo, Lagos, Nigeria. Web:< http://www.academicjournals.org/PPR>. Accessed 7 July 2012.

mutual fear and reap the electoral and other perceived benefits of the resulting hate-mongering. [4]

However, in the second half of the 19th century and in the early 20th century, there had not been an equivalent of N.M.U. in the ranks of the Mauritian **White oligarchs'** political leaders, who, in fact, used to cooperate with the wealthy Indo-Mauritians. No one as extremist as N.M.U. emerged among them to occupy a prominent position in the Legislative Council or in the media, however deep were the racial or class-based prejudices they entertained against the working classes.

One question that needs academic investigation is whether N.M.U. was or was not an agent '*planted*' in Mauritius by a colonial power like England or France or both to help the local conservatives and the British governor counter the rise of the Labour Party. Pezzani spoke of the "*servile hordes*" of workers and labourers, but he had, in the 1920's and 1930's, mellowed into a centrist-elitist who proclaimed that the country should be governed by members of its intellectual elite whatever their racial origins (in French, the slogan he invented was: "*L'élite d'où qu'elle vienne*".

The influence of N.M.U. over Mauritian politics was clearly enormous, judging by, among other things, the fact that his initials are still currently used today, even by academics, to convey the horrors which communalism and racism can produce within the Mauritian political system.

Even those political leaders who believed, like him, that the country was not ripe for universal suffrage, held him in contempt and attacked him for his virulently racist articles. Conservatives and moderates were often embarrassed by his extremist views, especially as a number of them, including Franco-Mauritian sugar and business barons like Fernand Leclézio came to look upon Dr. Ramgoolam as a great politician, the same Leclézio saying in 1963 (quoted by one of Ramgoolam's biographers, M.Varma) that *"no government has done better in Mauritius than the Ramgoolam government."*

Actually, Dr. Ramgoolam was such a moderate politician that there was no reason for N.M.U. to attack him as he did, with a degree of virulence rarely surpassed in Mauritian political history. Dr. Ramgoolam was very close to the British and had intimate contacts with British leaders in London throughout his political career, starting in 1935. N.M.U. knew that.

This proximity of Ramgoolam and Hazareesingh with such figures as Bede Clifford and the British Censor officer and secret agent Twining [5] even led Bissoondoyalists and historian U. Bissoondoyal in his book ***Promises To Keep***, [6] to speculate whether those attacks against Dr. Ramgoolam, which in reality made him even more popular, could have been deliberately carried out to help the moderate faction led by him to take over control of the Labour Party. Actually, under him, the Labour Party eventually discarded its hardest nationalisation projects before the 1960's to the acclaim of both London and Fernand Leclézio.

It is a fact that N.M.U. had exceptional skills as a propagandist bent on dividing the new electoral majority of Mauritians, using its multiethnic character to further his communalist agenda. One of the main weaknesses of the constitution of 1947 was that, while ethnic politics intensified, it had no check, in the first electoral round, that could have prevented any minority group from finding itself without a representative in the Legislative Council, albeit the fact that the nomination system, as a second round of the electoral process, was supposed to provide for that. The governor, as seen above, chose to appoint only one Muslim to the new legislature, exacerbating the communal tension. Historians have pointed out that Razack Mohamed was, for that reason, closely associated with Jules Koenig and his Ralliement Mauricien, later Parti Mauricien, then PMSD before the 1960s. [7]

The Labour Party and its allies, after their 1948 electoral victory, presented a list of candidates at the Port-Louis municipal elections of 1950 where Dr. Ramgoolam was a member of the party, which was then under the leadership of Rozemont, successor of Emmanuel Anquetil. The Labour Party presented 10 candidates among whom were G. Rozemont, and supported some independent candidates, while a Group of Thirteen, among whom there were Jules Koenig and A.Razack Mohamed stood against them.

The Labour Party and its allies won nine of the 16 municipal seats, though they failed to remain united and take over the mayorship. In 1951, backed by the Labour Party at a by-election in Moka-Flacq, independent candidate

---
4 Author's analysis.
5 Bates, Darrell, *A Gust of Plumes, A Biography of Lord Twining of Godalming and Tanganyika*, op. cit..
6 Op cit at page 89
7 Emrith, Moomtaz, *Sir Abdool Razack Mohamed:His life and times. A political biography*. ELP 2006.

Veerasamy Ringadoo was elected and entered the Legislative Council. Those electoral victories led *Le Cernéen* to redouble its efforts to create an atmosphere of panic and fear of what it alleged to be the threat of Hindu hegemony. That campaign gained some ground in even usually moderate circles of former Union Mauricienne members and supporters as well as among the Muslim community, and affected the popularity of the Labour Party especially in Port-Louis. Razack Mohamed and Jules Koenig led the rallying cry for a coalition of minority communities against Labour.

In 1953, Labour was defeated at the municipal elections in Port-Louis, and even Dr. Ramgoolam lost his seat of councillor, failing to be elected, under the intense campaigning of the Koenig's Ralliement Mauricien, which had been joined by many former members and supporters of the Union Mauricienne. *Le Cernéen* intensified its campaign against the Labour candidates and Dr. Ramgoolam in particular, stating that *"here as in Guyana (...) the revolutionary movement is led by subversive Hindus."* In 1956, after Rozemont had died at the age of 41, leaving Guy Forget as the president of the party, the Labour candidates won a decisive victory at the Port-Louis municipal elections. But in the other towns, the Labour Party lost to the Parti Mauricien, created in 1955: in Curepipe and Beau Bassin/Rose Hill, the Parti Mauricien won all the seats and in Quatre Barnes, it obtained a majority of 5 seats on a total of 7.

In Port-Louis, Dr. Millien became mayor and Dr. Ramgoolam his deputy in 1957. In the following year, Dr. Ramgoolam became mayor, after which he retired in December 1958 to focus on politics at the national level.

By that date, however, the Mauritius Labour Party was suffering from serious losses caused by major divisions among its own ranks. Ethnic politics took its toll, while the permanent opposition between radicals and moderates within the party led to splits.

Ethnic politics, even excluding N.M.U's viciously racist campaign, had received much attention during constitutional debates leading to the 1886 general elections as well as after that. Expecting an almost total absence of the ethnic element during discussions in the political life of a multiethnic society would have seemed unrealistic to leaders like Beaugeard, Rajcoomar Gujadhur, Dunputh Lallah, Dr. Edgar Laurent, Raoul Rivet, Pezzani, A. Razack Mohamed, and others. But the level of sectarianism that ensued in the wake of the 1948 general elections in spite of the Labour Party's truly national composition, was unprecedented and, as a result, the country was on the brink of disaster in the 1960s as the PMSD used ethnic politics vigorously and brought the entire political establishment into the same game.

Jules Koenig's mistake: opposing universal suffrage

Jules Koenig was going to be the target of a campaign for his elitist views on the right to vote, which, as seen already, was the leitmotiv of the Union Mauricienne where he was not alone in sharing such a views. But after Ramgoolam moved away from the UM and obtained, on the eve of the 1948 general election, Labour's support, Koenig reaffirmed his elitist philosophy on voting, especially as he remained refractory to universal suffrage. In all fairness, it must be recalled that he could not be described as a racist. It was obvious that he had ceded to fear that the Labour Party and some radical views expressed by a number of Hindu leaders entering that party, that led him to express such a reactionary position on the extension of the franchise. In his biography (op cit), matters are set in their proper perspective, including his divergence with Gaëtan Duval's excesses that included mass demonstrations with slogans that offended the Hindu community in the early 1960s (albeit, prior to starting a campaign of appeasement with a new slogan, "Hindu, my brother" in the late 1960s). [8]

He had not only been a member of Edgar Laurent's, Pezzani's and Rivet's Union Mauricienne, but had defended Indo-Mauritian and Creole workers as well as small planters during the great strikes of the 1930's and 1940's. He had stood in court, sometimes with Rampersad Neerunjun, to defend their leaders, Dr. Curé, Basdeo Bissoondoyal and Dr. Millien. [9] In September 1938, he defended 19 Indo-Mauritian labourers who had taken part in the strike on Trianon estate and had been condemned to forced labour: he appealed to the Supreme Court and won the case on November 14. Regarding his defence of Professor Basdeo Bissoondoyal, he had been imprisoned under a law restricting the freedom of the Hindu religious preachers. [10] Koenig was for the small man of any ethnic group and a devout Christian. He was the only Franco-Mauritian to be elected, with substantial support from Indo-Mauritian

---
8 Une vie pour la justice, op cit.
9 Ibid.
10 Bissoondoyal, U, op cit.

small planters' and workers' in his home district of Plaines Wilhems, during the political tsunami of 1948, where the oligarchy was ousted by the enlarged electorate of multiethnic petit bourgeois and working classes, from the elected component of the Legislative Council.

Koenig and his political successor Gaëtan Duval worked eventually in successive coalitions with Dr. S. Ramgoolam, his former friend within the Union Mauricienne and the Group of Twelve in the 1940's during municipal elections in Port-Louis. Elitism in the 1950s regarding the right to vote considerably damaged his image as Labour leaders campaigned to link him to his arch-enemy N.M.U. His biography has helped to rehabilitate his image and it is remarkable that Dr. S. Ramgoolam kept his esteem for him until his death after the lost the 1967 general elections when it was rumoured that the Prime minister had actually considered means to have his old friend appointed to the legislature.

Razack Mohamed's deal with the Labour Party

A. Razack Mohamed, feeling that his community did not have a fair deal with Koenig's political team, later struck a deal with the Labour Party where Dr. S. Ramgoolam made specific concessions to satisfy his demands for better representation for the Muslim community, a historical event which once more showed the importance of ethnic considerations in the political sphere.

In his book *History of the Muslims in Mauritius* Moomtaz Emrith writes about the "***shock***" which was felt, by the Muslim community following the elections of 1948 where "***all the Muslim candidates – five in all – bit the dust.***" He adds,

"Their debacle, which was expected, was felt with serious concern by the Muslim community (...) Muslim representation in the Legislature suffered another serious set-back when only one Muslim was appointed as a Nominee by the Governor (...) a series of meetings were held across the island to apprise the Muslims of the seriousness of the situation, culminating with a mass rally of Muslims at the Champ de Mars on September 26, 1948, to demand justice for the community (...)Muslim ineffective representation in the Legislative Council would continue for another decade." [11]

It would be unfair to attribute to Koenig's or Edgar Laurent's or Rivet's preoccupations with ethnic politics the same racist motivations that were behind N.M.U.'s writings. Actually, the moderate politicians from the former Union Mauricienne were trying to build what they hoped to be a serious political platform on the necessity perceived by them to avoid a radical socialist change and to obtain guarantees concerning the so-called rights of the minorities. The political debate in those days in Mauritius was influenced by, among other things, the rise of communism as well as the ethnic tensions and confrontations in Africa and Asia, in particular in Kenya. In trying to steer a middle course, however, the centrist politicians wrongly opposed universal suffrage on the basis that guarantees for the respect of minority rights were, in their eyes, insufficient.

Even some of the oligarchs of the old days, like Fernand Leclézio, were not always by their side, choosing to support, for reasons like economic priorities and social stability, the moderate Labour leaders, a fact that motivated the major splits in Labour in the 1950s and 1960s, during which the Bissoondoyal brothers and some Creole trade-unionists left the Labour Party – and which, in the late 1960's, led to the creation of an even more radical leftist party, the Mouvement Militant Mauricien (MMM) which former Bissoondoyalists like Anerood Jugnauth joined enthusiastically.

Another defection was that of André Masson, formerly at *Advance*, Ramgoolam's newspaper, then editor-in-chief of *Le Mauricien*, who in 1967 opposed Independence, and then wrote twice, in the 1970's, that such opposition on his part had been one of the greatest mistakes of his life. Anyway, the political forces that had opposed the Labour Party in the 1950's and 1960's under Koenig's and then G. Duval's leadership joined several governments of Dr. S. Ramgoolam to work together, and N.M.U., who had died in 1959, was not there to comment!

Ramgoolam and the sugar barons

An article of Hervé de Sornay, who was editor-in-chief of *Le Cernéen* as from 1934 and had followed Ramgoolam's political career very closely, speaks a lot about the absence of racism in its worst forms in the relations which most conservatives, dubbed oligarchs, entertained with Dr. S. Ramgoolam. That article about the author's souvenir of Dr. S. Ramgoolam, was published by the Indian Cultural Association with the unflinching official support of a pow-

---
[11] Moomtaz, E. Op cit.

erful group belonging to the sugar barons, the Weal Group of companies led by Sir Emile Series. [12] For instance, it gives details about the years, during the Second World War, when Ramgoolam, de Sornay and Rivet joined forces to combine into one daily issue, their three newspapers: Advance, founded to defend the interests of the Indo-Mauritians in the 1940s (the MLP after World War II), Le Cernéen, the voice of the conservatives, and Le Mauricien, which supported Rivet's centrist political formation then the Ralliement Mauricien of Jules Koenig, Razack Mohamed and others.

De Sornay, writing retrospectively in 1981, states that he was against any attempt to impose radical socialism, or communism on the country. He sincerely admitted, in his article, that he was a conservative, "inspired by the right-wing" and that he held leftists in suspicion. However, Ramgoolam, who was not yet a member of the Labour Party in the 1940's, entertained excellent relations with his colleagues of Le Cernéen and Le Mauricien. They all decided to move to the office of Advance, which had a better press, at Dumas Street, and to produce one newspaper containing the daily editions of all three publications. This partnership survived for several years, which tells a lot about Mauritian politics:

"That common paper prolonged its life until after the 1948 legislative elections. It survived, therefore, the riots of September 1943 at Belle Vue Harel, the dockers'strikes in the harbour, the polemics about ethnicity regarding the (Mauritius) regiment of Whites and the one for non-Whites, the debate on the necessity of a new Constitution and then on the 1947 Constitution, and the legislative elections of 1948." [13]

In the Indian Cultural Review, de Sornay recalled that Rivet used to predict that Ramgoolam had a bright future. The former editor of Le Cernén and successor to N.M.U. (with whom his views sharply constrasted) admitted that he gradually learned, as the years went by, that,

"... many of my preconceived ideas were unjustified, that they were sometimes false, that reason and sincerity were not the exclusive property of one side only, and that it is not necessarily one's own opinion which one reveres which can and should be the only basis of human felicity." [14]

He had privileged and friendly relations with Dr. S. Ramgoolam in the 1950's and 1960's, had the opportunity to interview him and obtain assurances that there would be no radical socialist revolution in Mauritius, and he even met him in London where the future Prime Minister dedicated a lot of time to support him personally as his brother had suddenly died in the British capital. That article of almost 10 pages in the Indian Cultural Review by the former chief-editor of Le Cernéen is full of praise for Dr. Ramgoolam and his political action and the only comment which such things would derive from a Mauritian historian who is well acquainted with his country's political traditions might well be:

"This is Mauritius, where mountains do meet each other!"

Notwithstanding the prejudices bluntly expressed by some Mauritian leaders of various communities, there was, in the 1950's, a need to address seriously the communal question. Dr. S. Ramgoolam did address it after an initial period during which he and his group of moderate friends took gradually control of the Labour Party, still in a radical phase and advocating a project of nationalisation of sugar estates. He needed to address the strong suspicion raised among the sugar barons, mostly its majority of Franco-Mauritian owners, which disturbed the colonial authorities as well. Sugar barons and British governors were wary of Labour Party's intentions towards the Franco-Mauritian sugar magnates as an ethnic group and their properties should Labour obtain full political control of the country as was already expected at some time in the future. Ramgoolam ensured that those nationalisations disappeared altogether from the manifesto of the Labour Party by the end of the 1950s, when he consolidated his hold on the Labour leadership, so much so that Sir Hilary Blood wrote in The Times British Colonies Review:

"Other interesting cross-currents are to be the official disowning by the Labour Party of any plans for nationalising sugar estates, thus tacitly accepting the efficiency of the politically conservative minded companies who own the industry." [15]

It was during that same period that Hervé de Sornay, chief editor of Le Cernéen, as already mentioned, interviewed Dr. S. Ramgoolam at Government House in Port-Louis, while he was Chief Minister. He recalled asking Ramgoolam if he would formally give him the assurance that as long as he would hold the destiny of Mauritius in his hands "no communist regime would ever be set up in the country." De Sornay writes:

---
12 Indian Cultural Review, special issue, 1976.
13 In: L'Express, February 14, 1981, L'hommage de Hervé de Sornay à Anauth Beejadhur, article recalling in detail a moving tribute written in 1987 by Hervé de Sornay, former chief editor of Le Cernén, in an obituary following the death of his former colleague of the common newspaper, Anauth Beejadhur, former chief editor of Ramgoolam's Advance.
14 Indian Cultural Review, op cit.
15 Blood, Hilary (Sir), Times British Colonies Review, 1960.

"That assurance, he gave it to me without hesitation." [16]

Rozemont, the man who paved the way for Ramgoolam

The man who made possible the accession of Ramgoolam to the highest levels of the Labour Party establishment was undeniably Guy Rozemont. His success in the political arena became legendary even during his lifetime. Guy Rozemont was revered by the working classes as a champion of their struggle for political emancipation and better working and living conditions. From the Labour victory at the general elections of 1948 to his death on March 22, 1956, Guy Rozemont only confirmed his reputation as one of the greatest Mauritian politicians of the 20th century.

Born on November 15, 1915 in Port-Louis, Joseph ("Jos") Guy Rozemont was the son of a clerk. He studied at St. Enfant Jesus School in Rose Hill and then at the Royal and St. Joseph colleges. He abandoned his studies because of the death of his father and, at the age of 16, did several jobs and for some time worked also in the Chagos Archipelago. He enthusiastically joined the ranks of the Labour Party and militated in its trade unions. In January 1940, Anquetil asked him to work as editor of the official press organ of the Labour Party Le Peuple Mauricien.

Dr. Maurice Curé abandoned active politics for financial reasons and Anquetil became president of the party in 1941. He offered the charismatic Rozemont, a master orator who thrilled the crowds of workers across the country during public meetings, the post of secretary-general. In 1946, after Anquetil's death, Rozemont took over the leadership and brilliantly led the party to three successive electoral victories at the general elections of 1948 and 1953 and the Port-Louis municipal elections of 1950.

When Anquetil died, the priest in charge of the St. Jean Church, Father Nealon, C.Sp., had blamed Rozemont officially, in three hand-written letters dated 3.12.46, 3.1.47 and 5.1.47 [17] for having made a speech at the cemetery contrary to instructions which had been given to him by the same priest. But there was such a large crowd of mourners of all communities, especially workers, that Rozemont, in his answer dated January 7, 1947, to the priest, wrote, that

"...only circumstances compelled me to violate the directions of the ecclesiastical authorities. On receiving your letter dated 31 st ultimo, I was placed with the following situation: Not to speak and give reasons publicly, in reading to those who attended the funeral the letter I received from you, which, in my humble opinion would have caused uneasiness and discontent (...)"

On 20 July 1949, according to a report in the newspaper Le Mauricien Rozemont and a labour activist Choytun held a public meeting at Plaine Verte, Port-Louis, to denounce an attempt by a number of persons claiming to be the communal

1908,[18] on a total Mauritian population of 368,791. [19]

Prior to that, there had been 4,061 electors, as already mentioned, in 1885, on the eve of the first general election in the history of the island, out of a population that had already reached 359,874 in 1881. Six years later, at the elections of 1891 the number increased only slightly to 4,717 registered voters, of whom 4,029 voted, the total population being then 370,588, according to Governor Sir Charles Cameron Lees. [20]

In 1911, at the time of the general elections, the Indo-Mauritians plus those still classified as Indians had reached a total of 257,697 (the Indians: 35,396; the Indo-Mauritians.: 222,301). The Creoles and Coloured '*petites bourgeoisies*' and working classes were also seriously underrepresented as their number was about 100,000 if the figures provided by Sir Henri Leclézio are considered: *"In 1919 Sir Henri Leclezio thought the general population included 6,000 white French, 5,000 upper-class Creoles (he called them 'gentry of colour'), and 15,000 middle-class Creoles."* [21]

Those 100,000 were not represented and this was also the case for over a quarter of a million Indo-Mauritians and Indian residents most of whom were settling down in the country.

At the Colonial Office, a radical liberal politician, J. Chamberlain, the Secretary of State for the Colonies, was

---
16 Indian Cultural Review, op cit.
17 Letters from a private collection consulted by the author in 1978.
18 *"The number of registered electors on 31st December, 1908, was 6186..."*: In: *The Dominions office and Colonial office list ...: comprising historical and statistical information respecting the overseas dominions and colonial dependencies of Great Britain*, Waterlow & Sons, London 1910; see also Madden and Darwin, op cit.
19 Mauritius Central Statistics Office, vol. 36. **Population and Vital Statistics, Table2 - Population growth in intercensal periods - Island of Mauritius**, 1851–2000.
20 *Lees to Knutsford, no. 76, 18 Feb. 1891.* CO 167/661, cited in Ballhatchet, op cit.
21 In Ballhatchet,T*he Structure of British Official Attitudes: Colonial Mauritius, 1883-1968* in *The Historical Journal,* Vol. 38, No. 4 (Dec., 1995), pp. 989-1011, Cambridge University Press, <http://www.jstor.org/stable/2640097> Accessed: 09/03/2012. The author cites *Leclézio to J. Middleton*, 21 Apr. 1919, CO167/826/34921. Leclézio's analysis of the ethnic groups is similar to the one he did at that time in *Mauritius Illustrated*, op cit.

thinking of ways to reduce the influence of what was formally referred to as the Mauritius oligarchy of French descent over the affairs of the country by suggesting more Creole and Indian participation and appointments as K. Ballhatchet observes. [22]

Chamberlain (who was the father of future British P.M. Neville Chamberlain) minuted the following on a despatch from Mauritius Governor Sir Charles Bruce as follows (written in 'minuting' style):

"The Indians are I think in a majority of the population & it is most desirable that their interests shd. be represented. I will face the storm. When it has settled down we shall be stronger in Mauritius than we have ever been & the French oligarchy will be kept in order by the other races." [23]

The '*other races*' alluded to the lower bourgeoisies of Coloured and Creoles, not to the Coloured elite that was allied to the Oligarchy. [24]

Lutchumun Bissoondoyal, the father of Basdeo, born in 1906, and Sookdeo, born in 1908, had witnessed the events. Uttam Bissoondoyal, in his book **"Promises to Keep"** has written about the reminiscences of his grandfather, which gives the true atmosphere of hope and of a budding political awareness among the Indians as they attended the meetings of the Action Libérale:

"The dim awareness of politics was already there in the Indians and Lutchumun Bissoondoyal was no exception. He had seen Manilal Doctor ill-treated in Rivière des Anguilles when he was addressing a public meeting there (...) In 1908, he had followed a procession headed by the roulotte of the Action Libérale proclaiming assertively 'La vérité en marche.' The procession had left Port Louis at noon on 1ˢᵗ June and went through Nouvelle France and Grand Bois to Souillac where the meeting was held on Sunday. It was the first time he had really listened to a public meeting. He did not very much understand the main orators.

"René Mérandon and Willie Dawson were making a case for a Royal Commission.

"He was, however, more impressed by Boodhun Lallah who spoke in Hindustani (...) Edouard Nairac who was to preserve his reputation of a liberal politician and professional throughout his career appealed to the Indo-Mauritians to get themselves interested in the affairs of their new island home. It surprised and pleased Lutchumun that people from so many communities should be speaking from the same platform." [25]

In those years, two other major leaders of the 20th century mass movements were in their twenties: Maurice Curé, who became a laureate of the Royal College in 1907 and left the country to study medicine, and Cashinath Kistoe who, in 1908, led a protest movement of labourers in the South. Kistoe was prosecuted for sedition and thrown in prison, where he was visited by a pious man, Pandit Bhagath. The latter helped him obtain his release and go to India in 1912 where he made advanced studies and qualified as a religious leader. [26]

The growing political awareness of the new generation of Mauritians was a direct result of the action of the Action Libérale. The Bissoondoyal family, who were to play a major role in Mauritian politics, settled in Port-Louis in 1913, two years after the riots. It is no wonder that in their political message, considerable importance was given to the contribution of the party of Eugène Laurent and Manilal Doctor as well as the former Democratic Party of Beaugeard to the cause of democracy in Mauritius. They lived through those difficult but exciting years and Sookdeo Bissoondoyal recalled the Port-Louis of 1913 thus:

"There was no electricity, no sewerage, no tarred roads. At night, the streets were lighted up with lanterns. Oil or candles were used. A man used a ladder to climb and light the lanterns one by one." [27]

An important economic factor was to come into play. As already mentioned, the sugar industry has been periodically going through problems of a declining labour force and dips in the prices of sugar. Those two factors were among the principal causes of an increase of '***morcellements***' by which large sugar estates sold or rented parts of their lands to obtain revenue and to address the labour shortage. C. J. Robertson writing in 1930, observes:

"Amongst economic causes the chief is the progress of 'morcellement,' the breaking-up of the estates into small holdings, which results in a scarcity of hired labour on the remaining estates. The rapid extension of this process began after 1910, under the stimulus of low prices, many of the estates selling land to former labourers on easy terms, usually on condition that the land remains under cane. In this way the proportion of cane land held by Indians increased from 30.3 per cent in 1909 to 43.1 per cent in 1917, and then more slowly to 46.2 per cent in 1922." [28]

By becoming self-employed planters, the Indo-Mauritians, albeit the fact that a majority of them were not rich, were becoming an economic community with similar interests and, therefore, a force to be increasingly reckoned with. Action Libérale had obtained the support of the majority of them, but they still did not enjoy the right to vote

---

22 Ballhatchet, Kenneth, ibid.
23 **J. Chamberlain, minute,** 18 Jan. [1900], COI67/724/I065 as quoted by Ballhachet, K, ibid.
24 Ballhatchet, K. ibid.
25 Bissoondoyal, Uttama, **Promises to Keep**, Editions de l'Océan Indien 1990.
26 Peerthum, Satteeanund, **Pandit Cashinath Kistoe**, op cit.
27 Ibid.
28 Robertson, C.J., *The Sugar Industry of Mauritius*, Economic Geography, Vol. 6, No. 4 (Oct., 1930), pp. 338-351, Clark University. <http://www.jstor.org/stable/140527>. Accessed 26 February 2012.

Figures of the 1940s and 1950s

Clockwise, from top right: Emmanuel Anquetil, Renganaden Seeneevassen, Guy Rozemont and Dr. Seewoosagur Ramgoolam were involved in various historical events of the 1940s and 1950s, in different contexts.
Photos: Courtesy of the Mauritius Government Information Services (GIS)

and would not do so until Curé's Labour Party would rock the colonial establishment and the big barons of the sugar industry and obtain the necessary constitutional reform in 1947.

Similarly, there were the lower bourgeoisies of Creole skilled workers and clerks, teachers, civil service employees and manual workers, small meat and other agricultural producers, etc. They also supported the Liberal Party of Laurent and Manilal Doctor and, later, Curé's Labour Party.

Then the First World War (1914-1918) broke out. The Mascarene Islands were barely affected by the major military operations, though in the case of the Seychelles, which had been detached from Mauritius in 1903 and depended on a significant amount of trade with Germany, the situation was different: the Seychellois suffered from a major economic and financial crisis and Mauritius granted to their administration a sum of Rs 100,000 voted by the Council of Government at the request of the British Colonial Office in London. A large number of Mauritians went to serve in the war among the British and French forces in Europe against the Germans and in Mesopotamia against the Turks. Many of them were killed in action or wounded.

On purely economic grounds, the First World War was a golden opportunity for the sugar industry, as Mauritian sugar fetched high prices in England. The trading classes, in particular the Indo-Mauritians who had trading houses in Port-Louis, increased the country's commercial links with the East, especially as regards the import of food items, mainly cereals of all sorts. Important fortunes were thus built in the island from sugar and trade, and the country prospered until the mid-1920s when the price of sugar fell abruptly. The boom reinforced the social stratification that was occurring within the Indo-Mauritian community, with the gap increasing between the top and the bottom of the social hierarchy on the basis of class interests.

At the 1916 elections during the war and the economic boom, the Oligarchs, under the banner of their Parti de l'Ordre, won once more a large majority among a total electorate of about 6,000 voters, except in Port-Louis where the liberal leaders, Dr. Eugène Laurent and Edouard Nairac were re-elected. But in the following years, the ranks of the Action Libérale were deprived of several of its members and supporters who decided to support a rather unexpected and surprising political movement in favour of the retrocession of Mauritius to France.

London worried by retrocession to France and Indian 'terrorists'

The British in London and Mauritius had been seriously worried by Action Libérale's leaders Dr. Eugène Laurent and Manilal doctor. They thought, in their simplistic analysis based uniquely on ethnicity as the Colonial Office papers indicate, that the Creole leaders and other Creoles were going to be '*assimilated*' by the Indians:

"*Laurent, a Creole leader of Indian origins, was an example of that assimilation which alarmed the officials. But they soon found a new enemy. Creole leaders were not the only threat to Indian loyalty. There was Manilal Doctor, a lawyer from Gujarat who was favoured by Mahatma Gandhi and had helped Indian workers to complain against ill-treatment. The procureur-general thought he was trying to 'stir the Indian element'.*" [29]

The movement for retrocession to France gathered momentum among the opponents to the Parti de l'Ordre of the sugar barons, thus raising again British fears of a rebellion, but this time unlike the 1832 rebellion of the slave-owners and coming from the other side of the political divide: the French-speaking, educated professionals and petite bourgeoisie suffering from unemployment and discrimination from the ruling classes.

As will be shown in this section, immediately after the retrocession movement died out, London was expressing fear that the Indo-Mauritians were being influenced by '*terrorists*' who got their inspiration from the pro-independence movement in India. In both cases, those fears were imaginary as the retrocessionists submitted themselves to the electoral process, while the Indian nationalists had been seeking financial help, as some researchers have established, from Indo-Mauritians who could afford to support them.

"*Official attitudes were losing touch with reality. What the Congress party wanted from Indians in Mauritius was financial help for its campaigns in India.*" [30]

This was only part of the truth as later, in the 1940, Emmanuel Anquetil appointed his trusted friend Basdeo Bissoondoyal as the Mauritius Labour Party representative with the independist Indian Congress Party.[31] It was a purely political alliance. In the 1920s, already fear of Indian influence continued to haunt the British after the

---
29 Ballhatchet, in *The Historical Journal*, op cit, page 999.
30 Ibid., page 1004.
31 On November 16, 1938, Mauritius Labour Party wrote a letter to Basdeo Bissoondoyal in India, asking him to inform the Indian National Congress about the situation in Mauritius and the MLP. The young missionary wrote a memorandum which he communicated to the Congress and also sent a letter to Mahatma Gandhi, according to U. Bissoondoyal. His memorandum was given publicity in some Indian newspapers, namely T*he Amrita Bazar Patrik*a and *The Statesman*.

retrocession movement collapsed.

This retrocessionist initiative, following the electoral impasse that maintained the less fortunate classes of Coloured and Creoles and the 'petits blancs' in a sort of blocked society without hope of progress, where most of them could not vote, was yet another way to challenge the colonial authorities and the sugar barons. Many believed that integrating the French fold would bring them a better social status and jobs and the ensuing well-being that they were being deprived of. A serious study of the causes of that curious episode of Mauritian history is needed, but what can be established already is the constant influence of ideas of freedom from overseas, especially Europe and India, has always played a role in the island's history.

One cannot dissociate the events in Europe where socialism was on the rise, especially in France with such great leaders as Jean Jaurès, assassinated in 1914, and who had probably influenced Dr. Maurice Curé, who had studied in Britain, then had participated in the Balkan War as a doctor, and other intellectuals of his days. The same can be said of influences brought to Mauritian shores by Gandhi and Manilal Doctor and of the considerable influence of Indian nationalism on great Mauritian leaders like Cashinath Kistoe the later Curé and Anquetil and Basdeo and Sookdeo Bissoondoyal.

Communalist historians have argued otherwise and it is known that the British and the sugar magnates did play the game of divide-and-rule that explains the surge of communalism in 20th century Mauritius, based, on the one hand, on the Retrocession Movement presented as anti-Indian, and on the other hand, on the role that **'Mother India'** played positively in influencing Dr. Eugène Laurent, Manilal Doctor, Kistoe and the Bissoondoyals. The latter have always expressed their admiration for Laurent as one of the great liberators of Mauritius. Racism and considerations of social status, caste, etc. did exist among the ethnic communities, but the political history of the island has been mainly a matter of class-based struggles.

The Retrocession Movement

The Franco-Mauritian sugar barons opposed retrocession to France and so did the affluent leaders of Indo-Mauritian businesses and they monopolised the right to vote except in Port-Louis where there was a large number of self-employed people and middle- and low-ranking government employees who could satisfy the property franchise. At the Colonial Office, there was a lot of head-scratching, observes researcher Ballhatchet on the basis of an examination of the frantic correspondence between the governor in Mauritius and the officials in London in those days on the topic of retrocession and then on imaginary Indian '***terrorists***'. It is extremely unfortunate that such people were defining the destinies of the colonies.

For those officials, the partisans of retrocession were being disloyal. They had the same reaction when Manilal Doctor, Gandhi's envoy, mobilised the Indian small planters and labourers and disturbances broke out before and after the 1911 general elections and the influence of India started to be felt in the island. In 1922, following the demise of the retrocession movement, the Colonial Office was considering action against the Indo-Mauritians being inspired by Indian nationalism and C.O. (Colonial Office) files contain references to those persons as '***sedition-mongers***'.[32]

Cashinath Kistoe had organised strikes in the south of the island and had been sentenced to prison and then upon liberation went to India from whence he came back a priest and an even more resolute militant. Later, the independence movement in India started to inspire more Indo-Mauritian leaders who were not close to the oligarchy and were active rather at the grassroots level of the community. More serious disturbances would come in the 1930s from the masses of Indo-Creoles militating under the banner of Curé's Labour Party and one of the names that come up in the Colonial Office papers was going to be that of the young Pandit Sahadeo:

"Then Bede Clifford, the governor, told the secretary of state that Pandit Sahadeo, Cure's 'principal assistant', was in India 'going through a course of instruction with Nehru and the terrorists'. Bede Clifford thought he was 'a rank seditionist' who wanted 'to induce Mauritius Indians to follow the anti-British policy prevalent in India'. He was 'cunning', whereas Curé was 'mentally unbalanced'." [33]

In both cases, the perceived threat from France and subsequently one from India led to quite harsh measures. A warship, HMS Comus, was sent to cruise off Mauritius to intimidate the retrocession partisans and they were also not allowed to campaign freely. Governor Sir Hesketh Bell had been allowed to interdict public meetings for retro-

---

32 Ballhatchet, Kenneth, op cit.
33 Ballhatchet, op cit.

cession according to a despatch to him from Viscount Milner, Secretary of State at the Colonial Office. [34] Governor Bell was accused even in London of having interfered with the freedom of the press: two newspaper editors (those of *Le Mauricien* and *Le Progrès Colonial*) who were supporting retrocession had to assert their loyalty to the British Crown As for the Indians and their allies in the following years, they were arrested, imprisoned and sued in court and some strikers lost their lives.

Retrocession and the rise of ethnic prejudice

The retrocession-to-France movement, just as the influence of India on the Indo-Mauritian leaders from Kistoe to the Bissoondoyal brothers, has been used to stir communalism in the country. This section will show how. However, it must be also admitted that there has been in the course of such political movements, excessive language used on various sides. Such excesses were literally made available to the communalist strategists like when a supporter of retrocession argued that in Réunion Island the Indians had been assimilated and that it should be the same in Mauritius to avoid an Indo-Mauritian majority that would rule the country. This came from a district cashier, one Abel Loumeau in his '*La rétrocession et les aliens,*' a publication smacking of anti-Indian racism, published in 1919 in Port-Louis under the pseudonym of Elba L. He was for good reason sacked by the British administration. [35]

"The retrocessionists were defeated in the elections. This at least was the official view, though they were never allowed to campaign for retrocession." [36]

Nevertheless, the policies '*keep-them-apart*' of the oligarchy to divide the work force, and, its equivalent, the '*divide-and-rule*' [37] of the British colonial administration were being tested and put into practice, and the ultimate result is today's ethnic politics, pushed to the extreme, unashamedly, by the Mauritian political establishment to this date, in independent Mauritius. And yet, scholarly studies have established that Mauritius has remained an '*integrated*' society to such an extent that the greatest geniuses in the science of statistics have never been able to solve the problem of ethnic classification and demographics with so many intercultural and interethnic marriages, the blurring of the divide between the Indian castes following immigration to Mauritius, etc. This has led to such conclusions as this one:

"The very problems of the census commissioners derived from the fact that throughout the nineteenth and twentieth centuries the variously defined communities lived as an integrated society, notably in Port Louis, the capital, making segregation and separation impossible." [38]

The retrocession movement was supported by *Le Mauricien* newspaper where Raoul Rivet, a young journalist, had been recruited by the then owner, E. Henry. Several Coloured intellectuals belonging to the middle and lower middle classes supported the movement But the Retrocessionist platform was not of a nature to rouse the sympathy of either the non-voting working classes of Creoles and Indians, or the wealthy Indo-Mauritian voters, who generally sided with the essentially White plantocracy, with whom they had common business interests.

The true nature of the retrocession movement

Retrocession to France, it must be said, was also, despite the underlying class-based antagonism between the rich and the poorer sections of Coloured and Creoles, motivated by a mixture of nostalgic ideas about French colonisation that had left in the island a major cultural heritage. Anand Mulloo writes, *"With the long World War I over, the bottled up feelings of sympathy for France – La douce France (sweet France) – exploded."* [39]

U. Bissoondoyal sees the more political aspect of the movement:

"During the 1921 elections, the main issue was the retrocession of Mauritius to France. Some liberal politicians of Mauritius campaigned in favour of the annexation of Mauritius to France in the hope that this would give Mauritius a larger measure of autonomy in internal affairs." [40]

In Madden and Darwin's '*Select documents*', [41] it is observed that Colonial Office documents mentions the case of an

---

34 Ibid. **Milner, telegram to Bell, 12 Oct. 1920**, quoted by Ballhatchet, op cit.
35 Ibid.
36 Ibid.
37 The maxims divide et impera and divide ut regnes were utilised by Caesar and Napoleon and meant divide and rule or divide and conquer. The British applied them in their colonies, mainly India. There are theories that say either they created the principle or that it existed already and they used what they saw.
38 Christopher, J.A., ***Ethnicity, community and the census in Mauritius***, 1830-1990. In: The Geographical Journal, Vol. 158, No. 1 (Mar., 1992), pp. 57-64. Published by: Blackwell Publishing on behalf of The Royal Geographical Society (with the Institute of British Geographers) Stable URL:< http://www.jstor.org/stable/3060017 >.Accessed: 09/03/2012 22:32.
39 Mulloo, Anand, Our Struggle, 20th Century Mauritius, Vision Books 1982.
40 Indians Overseas. The Mauritian Experience, op cit..
41 Madden, A. Frederick & Darwin, John, ***The Dependent Empire, 1900-1948, Colonies, Protectorates, and Mandates Select Documents on the***

Indian who was a retrocessionist: *"The son of the deputy mayor of St. Louis (Port-Louis), a wealthy Indo-Mauritian, had been treated in an offensive way in Cape Town: his father had become an enthusiastic 'retrocessionist'."*

What ethnic bias prevents some writers from saying is that the defeat of the retrocession movement was not the work of the Indo-Mauritian electorate which was only composed of a very tiny number of voters that were rich enough to qualify as electors and most of them sided with the conservatives. In fact, in Port-Louis, for instance, the anti-retrocessionists Edouard Nairac and Jérôme Tranquille defeated not just the two retrocessionist candidates, but also those of the oligarchy. Of course, there were Indo-Mauritian voters on both sides, as per one example cited above. Class politics prevailed in Port-Louis over other considerations. Nairac (later Sir Edouard Nairac) was a liberal like René Mérandon du Plessis, and came from a modest family like many Indo-Mauritians and, later, he rose to be the Chief Justice of Mauritius.

'The Dependent Empire' reveals the Franco-Mauritian Oligarchs' hostility to retrocession.[42] Sir Henri Leclézio, knighted by the Queen, also wrote to acting governor Sir John Middleton in 1919:

"There were some 5,000 'gentry of colour', attached to England and opposed to retrocession – equal in intellect with the whites. There are some 15,000 coloureds of middle class and 'pretty well educated' with some French blood: clerks, professors, traders, doctors, attorneys &c. – where in particular retrocessionists could be found, but not many. The promoters had indeed neither influence nor prestige to lead this section (…) [Leclézio and elected members of the Council of Government asked for the advocacy of retrocession to be treated as disloyalty, believing that the leaders knew it was a 'chimera'…" [43]

The Oligarchy controlled a majority of the electoral votes from 1886 to 1948 and so, the defeat of the Retrocessionists was primarily their doing and that of the liberal candidates like Edouard Nairac and Jerôme tranquille and not particularly of the Indo-Mauritian labourers, who simply did not have the right to vote. The abusive, if not simplistic assertions by historians and politicians that the Indo-Mauritian community defeated the retrocession movement are not accurate. Leclézio, the leader of the multiethnic conservative electorate, descending from an old French family, led the battle against the retrocessionists - and that's the plain historical truth. It was class-based politics, or politics, simply put, based on class interests as the liberals, on the left side of politics, also fought against retrocession to France.

This being said, revolutionary trade unionism and "social" or leftist Catholicism were challenging the conservative French establishment as from 1905. The rise of the leftists in France had resulted, following an intense anticlerical campaign, in the ousting of the Catholic Church from the State apparatus and the separation of Church and State had been proclaimed in 1905. [44] A left-leaning man like Curé would have probably envisaged a French type of socialism for Mauritius at the time he stood as a candidate for the Retrocession Movement, especially as, in Mauritius, he opposed the practices of the Catholic establishment in the field of education because in his eyes (as in those of Raoul Rivet) they were discriminatory and favoured a small minority of privileged persons.

The author of this book has seen in the historical documents held by a former Labour Party leader, now defunct, copies of letters Curé had been constantly, not to say obsessively, sending to the governor in the 1920s in the defence of Indo-Mauritian labourers who were ill-treated and the actual written responses of the Colonial Secretary on behalf of the British governor. There is absolutely no reason to believe that Curé or Raoul Rivet, the man who introduced Dr. Seewoosagur Ramgoolam in the political arena as a man of great promise, could have ever viewed retrocession with the sectarian blinkers worn by a small number of supporters of that movement.

Curé's pro-workers behaviour explains why, once back from his studies, during which he witnessed the rise of socialism in France and served as a doctor in the Balkan wars, he took up the cause of the Indo-Mauritian and Creole labourers and artisans. He experienced the rise of the Labour Party while in the UK and became a Fabian socialist. [45] After his defeat at the 1921 general elections, he followed with keen interest the rise of trade unionism in Britain where, eventually, the Labourites, backed by the Liberals, conquered power in 1924 under the leadership of James

---

Constitutional History of the British Empire and Commonwealth - December 1994.
42 *Ibid.* "SIR HENRI LECLÉZIO TO ACTING-GOVERNOR JOHN MIDDLETON, 21 April 1919 [Apart from a very few, the white population descending from the old French families was opposed to a return to France.] They have personal feelings of strong affection and admiration for the country of their origin, but they are loyally attached to England by bonds of gratitude for the blessings which they enjoy under the British rute: liberty of conaclence 1 freedom of speech, social peace..."
43 *Ibid.*
44 Le grand livre de l'histoire du monde, op cit.
45 Peerthum, Satteeanund, unpublished research work on the life of Dr. Maurice Curé.

Ramsay Macdonald. The latter came back to power in 1929 and from 1931 to 1935, Macdonald headed a coalition government. Curé was, at the same time, in Mauritius, setting up a formidable trade union movement, the first one to gather widespread support in the island's history, and he launched the Mauritius Labour Party in 1936. Once more, events and ideas outside Mauritius were going to rock the country.

Born in 1886 from a middle class Coloured family, Curé studied brilliantly at the Royal College, some of his exceptional performances attracting media attention. He became a laureate of the English Scholarship in 1907 and went on to study medicine in Great Britain. There also, he was a brilliant student and a gold medallist. A career in medical research opened before him. But he then went to serve as a medical practitioner in the war in the Balkans before finally going back to Britain, then returning to Mauritius for family matters. [46]

When Curé was candidate with Edouard Laurent in Port-Louis, in 1921, for the Retrocession Movement, the 'great' Laurent, Dr. Eugène Laurent, had already left the country on August 14, 1919, to migrate to Britain, where he died in London on February 13, 1926, at the age of 67. His deputy in Action Libérale, Edouard Nairac, and Jerôme Tranquille, another Liberal, stood, as already mentioned, as candidates for the Legistive Council against the Oligarchs and the Retrocessionists. All the Retrocessionist candidates lost, while Curé, some time afterwards, left the movement, which, meanwhile, gradually slipped into oblivion and disappeared altogether.

The Oligarchs won in all the rural districts, supported by the rich Indian voters, while two Liberals, the heirs of Dr. Eugène Laurent, Edouard Nairac and Jerome Tranquille were elected in Port-Louis. Edouard Nairac, observes Yvan Martial, "*turned his back on his Coloured voters and espoused the anti-retrocession cause.*" [47] R. K. Boodhun, who had also lost, was nominated by the governor to the Legislative Council where he joined Hassen Sakir as another official representative of the Indo-Mauritian community.

Boodhun thus became the deserving leader of part of the elite of the Indo-Mauritian community. At the base of that section of the population, among the lower middle and working classes, Kistoe paved the way for Curé and the Bissoondoyal brothers to create and lead a significantly far more radical political movement, based on trade unionism, and inspired by the British Labour Party as well as by the Congress Party of India, which was struggling for independence.

First Indo-Mauritians in the Legislative Council

Within the Legislative Council, two other prominennt members of the Indo-Mauritian community made history at the general elections of 1926, Rajcoomar Gujadhur, the owner of two sugar estates, and Dhunputh Lallah, attorney-at-law who were elected in Flacq and Grand Port respectively. They were the first members of the Indo-Mauritian community to be elected to the legislature in Mauritian history. The contest had been tough in Grand Port where there was a three-cornered fight, but Lallah came out first, winning a total of 424 votes against L. Maurel's 306 votes and G. Gebert's 230 votes, the total number of electors being 1,031, of whom 335 Hindus, 128 Muslims, 564 General Population and four Chinese. In a pamphlet about Dhunputh Lallah published in 1992, Premdath Bhujun writes:

"The daily cry of the electoral campaign of Mr. Dhunputh Lallah was 'khoon par khoon - khoone khoon'. The political slogan was repeated not only by Hindus and Muslims but also by a few members of the General Population." [48]

This is not surprising as Dr. Eugène Laurent was of Indian origin and, as seen before, was suspected by the Colonial Office in London, on the basis of his ethnic mix, of creating an Indo-Creole alliance to overthrow the established political order in the island in favour of the majority.

Following the successive defeats of the anti-Oligarchy parties (the Liberals led by Dr. Beaugeard, the Democrats led by Dr. Eugène Laurent and the Retrocessionists led by Armand Esnouf), there was a vacuum which was quickly filled by a "unionist" party, the Union Mauricienne of "the other Laurent": Dr. Edgar Laurent, who had been elected in Port-Louis together with a former Retrocessionist, Arthur Rohan, at the 1926 general elections.

Actually, it was with Raoul Rivet as his deputy that Dr. Edgar Laurent (not to be confused with Dr. Eugène Laurent, the Liberal, or Edouard Laurent, the Retrocessionist) structured the U.M. as a real political party, which obtained its successes mainly in the Port-Louis legislative and municipal elections. However, in spite of such prominent figures as were its leaders as well as the young Jules Koenig, Razack Mohamed and Dr. Seewoosagur Ramgoolam

---
46 Ibid.
47 Ile Maurice: Edouard Nairac - De la caisse de savon à la Cour suprême, in L'Express, May 17, 2010.
48 Bhujun, Premduth, Dunputh Lallah (1885-1947), Mauritius 1992.

Makers of history

Top left, Sir Abdool Razack Mohamed, who started the struggle for guarantees in the electoral system for seats for the Muslim minority following the 1948 general elections where no one from that community was elected.

Above: Sir Harilall Vaghjee who had a distinguished career in the Mauritius legislature before and after independence. He was elected for the first time as an independent candidate in the PamplemoussesRivière du Rempart electoral district.

Left, Mrs. Emilienne Rochecouste who was the first woman to be elected to the legislature in Mauritius. She was an independent candidate in 1948 and was supported by Guy Rozemont's Mauritius Labour Party.

Photos: Courtesy of the Government Information Services (GIS).

who was introduced by Rivet into active politics, the Union Mauricienne was incapable of seriously challenging the domination of the Oligarchs over Mauritian politics.

Just like its liberal-leaning predecessors (Beaugeard's movement and Action Libérale) the Union Mauricienne was not very successful at the national level, apart from electing for two successive terms Dr. Edgar Laurent and Raoul Rivet, in 1931 and 1936, to the Legislative Council. It provided, nevertheless, the breeding ground for a new generation of moderate politicians like Dr. Seewoosagur Ramgoolam and Jules Koenig, who both stood as municipal candidates under the banner of the UM and fought elections against the Labour Party in the 1940s.

However, the U.M. preached elitism as its main political objective on the eve of the very era when the masses would enter abruptly the political arena. Even Dr. Seewoosagur Ramgoolam later accused the UM of anti-Indo-Mauritian "*machinations*" in an article entitled "***We Stand for our Rights***" and a series of others under the heading "***In the World of Mr. Rivet***," published in 1940 and 1941. Ramgoolam left the party which, even before the general elections of 1948, disbanded and disappeared completely from the political scene, when the right to vote was granted for the first time to the working classes, in the 1947 Constitution.

Until that time, at the general elections of 1931 and 1936, Indo-Mauritian candidates were not elected any more, producing a feeling of intense frustration among the intellectuals and leading business people of the community. The number of electors surprisingly decreased again by 800 from 1926 to 1931, with the Indo-Mauritian electorate diminishing by as much as 500. From 1931 to 1936 the decrease was about 1,000. Professor Hansraj Mathur, of the University of Mauritius, writing in ***L'Express***, attributed the decrease to two causes, first the economic crisis of the 1930's which impoverished a number of electors who thus lost the property qualifications required by the 1886 electoral law still in force, second to the deliberate striking off of electors' names from the electoral roll under pressure from the Oligarchs.

In contrast, Bede Clifford's conduct was severely criticised in the British Parliament, especially by the Labour MPs. One of them, Creech-Jones, addressed "*six strong letters*" according to Hugh Tinker, to Secretary of State for the Colonies Malcolm MacDonald and his assistant, Lord Dufferin, on the labour unrest in Mauritius. [49]

Curé did everything to obtain the return of Anquetil from exile in Rodrigues, and he wrote to Rajmohunsing Jomadar, who had been sent by the Labour Party to study law in Britain, to approach the British Labour leaders and Members of Parliament. He also wanted to have an English barrister to come to Mauritius, but Jomadar wrote that it would entail heavy expenses. [50]

In a handwritten letter dated October 8, 1938, to Dr. Curé from his address at 112, Gower St., London W.C. 1, Jomadar stated,

"*... as regards Anquetil I have put the matter before the Trade Union Congress and the Labour Party. They have written to the Colonial Secretary (...) I have high hopes that Mr. Creech-Jones to whom I have given all the necessary details and information will not fail to see the Colonial Secretary (...) I am sorry to hear about the way in which Hassenjee, Abel, Pandit Sahadeo and yourself have been treated.*"

Eventually, Creech-Jones wrote a letter dated November 7, 1938, to Lord Dufferin in the Colonial Office about "*the matter of the Mauritius strike and associated events.*" In that letter, the British M.P. stated also, "*I have thought over (...) the points you put to us and would like to be assured that (...) it is the intention of the Government to give immediate attention to political reforms*" which would allow "*some political representation either direct or indirect in the legislature, of the masses of workers at present excluded from all form of political expression.*"

Creech-Jones also criticised in his letter the enormous powers which Governor Bede Clifford had assumed to crush the strikes and asked for assurances that "*in future there will be no deliberate breaking of strikes initiated by a union and restrictions placed on peaceful picketing provided the working classes suffering from grievances place, when their negotiations have failed, their dispute to the approved conciliation machinery.*" He added that "*strikes, when conciliation fails, are not regarded as illegal.*"

In contrast to what was happening at Westminster, Dr. K. Hazareesingh, who helped Bede Clifford during those events, wrote retrospectively in his History of Indians in Mauritius (op cit.):

"*The authorities were faced with a serious dilemma; the dockers had openly flouted the Industrial Ordinance by not referring their dispute to arbitration and the Government felt that if the law were to remain on the statute book, immediate action must be taken.*"

Creech-Jones protested against the deportation of Anquetil, the arrest of workers and the confinement imposed to Dr.

---
49 ***Separate and unequal: India and the Indians in the British Commonwealth***, 1920-1950, University of British Columbia Press, 1976.
50 The author of this book consulted the original letters in a private collection.

Curé. He added, in the same letter to Lord Dufferin, that he was prepared to *"urge on the people concerned the observance of legal and constitutional forms, but that always assumes that fair and reasonable liberty is enjoyed by people to act in combination both politically and industrially for the improvement of their lot and to find direct expression in political and industrial forms in order that their grievances can be known and pressure for redress secured."* He went on:

"I can only add that even after your explanation I am profoundly disturbed at the disabilities and conditions of these people, at the way in which the strike was broken and the harsh sentences imposed upon the people prosecuted."

In the House of Commons, Creech-Jones and another Labour MP, Sorensen, were very active at Question Time and during their speeches on the subject of the Mauritius riots and the harsh treatment received by the Labour Party leaders and members. Creech-Jones raised the fundamental questions related to freedom in the colonies and the deportation of local leaders 'merely because they strike':

"If we believe in freedom we should demand now that some of the oppressive ordinances which have recently characterised the Statute Books of many of the Colonial territories should be removed. We should release Grant from prison in Barbados, where he is now suffering a ten-years' sentence for labour agitation; we should stop deporting and prosecuting people merely because they strike, as was recently done in Mauritius; we should practise civil liberty, even with men like Pratt and Johnson in Sierra Leone; we should remove the colour bar in Southern Rhodesia and other parts of Africa; we should reverse the segregation policies that mar our work in the Continent of Africa. In all these ways let us declare for democracy and freedom. Let us carry out these changes, and be true to those noble sentiments so often expressed in the early records of our Colonial Empire. These are the immediate tasks of statesmanship, whether war is on or not." [51]

The records of the House of Commons show that the question was further dealt at question time on July 29, 1938, by M. P. Sorensen regarding the Commission of Inquiry of 1937 and the question of wages. The government answered that the increase of wages was being attended to under proposed arrangements. A written answer was afterwards given to a question by Creech-Jones regarding the Commission of Inquiry of 1937. But MacDonald in reply to the M. P.'s desire to know *"whether further consideration has been given to political reform?"* stated:

"No change has been made in the constitution, but the Governor has nominated representatives of small planters to the Council of Government during the current session."

Creech-Jones in the House of Commons, spoke about the labour situation in the colonies in the following terms, arguing that racism was part of the British government's colonial policies:

" (...) every effort on the part of the workers to create an organisation has been frustrated by the authorities. Meetings have been broken up or prevented by the police. In Trinidad and Mauritius the workers have been obliged to adopt subterfuge in order to get some form of organisation (...) There is the recent case which came before the Privy Council. In fact, one may say that so wide an extension has now been given to the legal meaning of sedition that almost any searching criticism of a Colonial Government by a black man or even of the conditions of employment in a Colony has become a punishable offence. How can there be effective trade unionism when many of the Colonies still have remnants of Master and Servant Ordinances on the Statute Book?

"Labour conditions have created problems in many colonies, often resulting in disturbances and bloodshed. Such unsatisfactory labour conditions usually have, as one common feature, the absence of effective machinery for collective bargaining. I am glad that the right hon. Gentleman is going to set up machinery for conciliation, in the form of labour bureaus which will function as an institution whose help is much needed throughout the West Indies. Mauritius and Trinidad have suffered greatly from the absence of such machinery lately. Commissions which have been set up in both those islands have on every occasion recommended that facilities should be provided for collective bargaining." [52]

The 1937 disturbances seen by a UK news correspondent in Mauritius

The events of 1937 as seen by *'Our own correspondent'*, in *The Scotsman*, one of UK's most widely read newspapers, is interesting and revealing, especially the part regarding the visit of the Marquess of Duffferin and Alba in 1938 during which the appointment of an Indo-Mauritian to represent the Indo-Mauritians in the Legislative was discussed in camera.

In a telegram dated September 7, 1937, after the riots at Union Flacq Sugar Estate, the correspondent reported,

"The Governor Sir Bede Clifford, has proclaimed a state of emergency throughout Mauritius, after giving the striking dockers an opportunity of returning to work. It is expected that drastic action will be taken against them. Police and military have been mobilised (...) 19 strikers on one of the sugar estates were brought to Court. They were remanded for three days.

"Several more factories in the central area have ceased work because the docks cannot accommodate any more sugar, now that loading of vessels has ceased. It is estimated, however, that half of the factories will be able to carry on for a few more days.

"The island dependency of Rodrigues, 400 miles from Mauritius, is in serious need of food, and it has been arranged that a steamer shall leave for there to-morrow. It is confidently expected that she will be loaded in spite of the strikers."

On September 9, under the title *"Drastic Measures by Governor. 300 dockers arrested,"* the correspondent in Mauritius

---

[51] Debate On The Address, HC Deb 30 November 1939 vol 355 cc291-411
[52] Colonial Office, HC Deb 14 June 1938 vol 337 cc79-189.

wrote,

"Drastic measures have been taken by the Governor of Mauritius, Sir Bede Clifford, to end the disorders throughout the island caused by the dockers' strike. The 300 dockers who have been arrested, and the many others who have fled, have been replaced by hundreds of volunteers from the sugar estates.

"They arrived in the capital during the night under police protection, and have been loading ships with sugar all day. So much sugar had accumulated waiting for shipment that the docks could not accommodate any more.

"(...) One of the chief agitators, Georges Anquetil, has been deported to the island of Rodrigues, 400 miles from Mauritius, with his son."

In the same issue, the fate of the "socialist leaders" is announced:

"Dr Maurice Curé, Pandit Sahadeo, and other Socialist leaders have not been allowed to leave certain areas of Mauritius.

"The police, who have been concentrated in Port Louis, have been relieved by special constables mobilised from the local volunteer regiment. All liquor shops and many other shops have been closed as an additional precaution.

"(...) Dr. Curé has cabled to London requesting the dispatch of a Royal Commission to inquire into conditions in the island. He has also asked for a British Lawyer to defend the agitator, Anquetil.

"A commission of inquiry has already been at work. In its report, published in April, it recommended wage increases, sickness insurance, old-age pensions, and conciliation orders."

The newspaper report in *The Scotsman* of 10 February 1938, stated, under the pen of 'our own correspondent':

"The Marquess of Dufferin and Ava, Parliamentary Under Secretary for the Colonies, has written a letter to Bede Clifford thanking him "for giving him so many opportunities during his recent stay of meeting members of all sections of the population. Lord Dufferin remarked on the spirit of loyalty to the Throne, so proudly displayed by the people (...) Lord Dufferin added that he was convinced that a far closer co-operation between employer and employee was essential for the peace and prosperity of the island. He referred to the necessity of ensuring representation in the Legislature of the views and interests of all sections of the community and said that the Governor had proposals to that effect. Work on these lines must be done quickly, he concluded. Sacrifices would have to be made and patience exercised by all."

In the opinion of Pandit Basdeo Bissoondoyal, who at the time, thought that he should have been nominated (he told this to the author of his book in the 1970s at his home in Port-Louis), Ramgoolam was not representative of the larger masses of Indo-Mauritian small planters and workers toiling in the sugar cane fields and never defended their interests during the 1930s and 1940s, when he was a candidate for the Union Mauricienne with Edgar Laurent, Raoul Rivet, Jules Koenig and others. Pandit Bissoondoyal resented the role of the governor, who was close to Ramgoolam and his group, and wrote that Bede Clifford "*started a communal 'hare'.*"[53]

Two years later, in 1940, there would be furious protests from the left of the political arena when a politician who vehemently opposed the Labour Party and the Bissoondoyal brothers, was announced as the governor's appointee: Dr. Seewoosagur Ramgoolam, recommended by Dr. E.F. Twining, the director of Labour, Information and Censorship, member of the British Intelligence services, a fact revealed by Twining's biographer Sir Darrell Bates.[54]

Twining did not recommend Professor Basdeo Bissoondoyal or any other Indo-Mauritian working at the grassroots level and probably found in Dr. Ramgoolam the moderation they needed on the part of somebody they were appointing. This was criticised, at the time, by the press organ of the Labour Party, *Le Peuple Mauricien*, editor Guy Rozemont. For his part, Ramgoolam was campaigning in his newspaper *Advance*, and he was targeted by severe criticism as well from Basdeo Bissoondoyal and his followers and they were openly critical of the nomination.

Curé and Bissoondoyal blast Dr. Ramgoolam's relations with Governor Clifford

Dr S. Ramgoolam (then a fierce adversary of the Labour Party and vying for a post of nominee from the governor in the Council), K. Hazareesingh, J.N. Roy and H. Ramnarain became, for the governor, *"precious assets at this critical juncture,"* writes U. Bissoondoyal who recalls that those moderates had for mouthpiece, as from 1940, the newspaper *Advance* owned and controlled by Dr. S. Ramgoolam (the Labour Party had its own newspaper, *Le Peuple Mauricien* and *Advance* became the party's mouthpiece much later in the 1950s when Ramgoolam took control of the MLP).

Actually, the conflict between the moderate Indo-Mauritian leaders, on the one hand, and the leaders of the Labour Party on the other hand, had become quite virulent towards the end of 1938, particularly when Dr. Ramgoolam and a group of his moderate friends went to see the very controversial and virulently anti-MLP governor, Sir Bede Clifford, at Le Réduit, to express their solidarity with him in the face of severe criticism of his policies and of those of the Procureur General Hooper.

---
53 Bissoondoyal, Basdeo, Life in Greater India, Bharatiya Vidya Bhavan, India 1984.
54 Bates, A Gust of Plumes, op cit.

On December 6, 1938, Dr. Ramgoolam, the future British-appointed nominee, wrote, in reply to the outcry caused by his visit to the governor that "we did not want the Government to believe that the greater majority of the Indian community shared in any way the unwarranted attack against the Procureur General and the Governor."

On December 9, he wrote,

"I spontaneously accepted to form part of the delegation (...) because of my strong conviction that a high official was being unjustly attacked, and it was high time that we denounced the war-mongers who were arrogating to themselves the right to speak in the name of the great majority of the Indian people."

That was a clear reference to the radical leaders who had been accused by Bede Clifford of creating unrest among the workers. Dr. Ramgoolam explained further that the delegation of which he formed part went to see the governor in the name of the Indo-Mauritian community. Dr. Maurice Curé's response was quite severe in the face of those criticisms.

Replying on December 14, in a letter to **Le Mauricien**, Curé said that *"even I were a 'self-appointed leader,' what about the delegation led by Dr. Ramgoolam which met the governor and which was supposed to represent the Mauritians of Indian origin of this country?"* He asked, *"Was that delegation authorised to speak in the name of the Indo-Mauritians?"*

On December 19, Dr. S. Ramgoolam, severely attacked Curé who had reminded him that he had advocated *"an alliance with the French community."* Ramgoolam explained that he had done it because he thought that Indo-Mauritians should cooperate with all sections of the population *"provided that each one respected the ideals of his neighbour and did not trespass upon the legitimate rights of one another."* He added, further,

"Dr. Curé seems to think that the 'intellectuals' of my community are a class apart from the Indian proletariat, and that their interests are opposed to those of the working section of the community. Nothing is further removed from the truth. Let me remind Dr. Curé that these 'Intellectuals' take root in the ranks of the working class, and that they are fully conscious of the desperate conditions of their fellow-countrymen."

Yet, Ramgoolam and his friends never dared depone in favour of the workers, small planters and labourers to defend them before the Hooper Commission. On December 16, 1938, Sookdeo Bissoondoyal, siding with the Labour leaders, Curé and Anquetil, in particular, because they had deponed for the proletariat before the Hooper Commission, attacked the moderate Indo-Mauritian leaders for not having done the same to defend the workers. Sookdeo Bissoondoyal wrote, in a letter signed with his usual pen name "Indo-Mauricien," published in Le Mauricien,

"Before the Commission of Inquiry, no Indian representative came to depone in the name of his co-religionists. There was then the danger for the one who dared do it to lose the good favours of certain big planters or to be judged as communalists by the government."

Curé received a letter, which was among the documents he preserved until his death, and which was signed S.B., dated November 6, 1939, belonging to a private collection, condemning *"the director of the Arya Vir who has brought before a tribunal a claim for the impression of a pamphlet."* That was an extremely strong-worded letter from S.B. who wrote that such a decision should not have been taken by somebody *"who boasts being at the head of a social institution which has as its motto the upliftment of the Hindu masses."* S.B. finds that the director of the paper is in the camp of those intellectuals *"of our community"* who have chosen to oppose Curé and to cause him *"all sorts of torments,"* and who have chosen to befriend *"the governor and the rich."* The letter was accompanied by a sum of money, praying Dr. Curé to accept it though it was quite insignificant, writes S.B., *"so that it may be some sort of compensation for the outrage which the prominent people of our community are heaping upon you just when you are in need support and encouragement around you."*

The two fundamental problems of it all were thus clearly expressed:
- Where does class politics stop and where communal political representation starts?
- Where did cooperation with the colonial power and even the Oligarchy stop and where did the fight for political emancipation start?

The moderates and the radicals, in those days, had quite divergent answers to those questions. Less than two years after the virulent press polemic opposing Dr. Curé and Dr. Ramgoolam, Seerbookun resigned from the Legislative Council to work in the administration and the nomination of Dr. S. Ramgoolam in his place gave a boost to the moderate Indo-Mauritian intellectuals who went on to contest the municipal elections in Port-Louis in 1943 and 1946 on the same platform as the moderates of the White, Coloured and Creole middle classes which, U. Bissoondoyal rightly recalls, *"included Furcy Adèle, Gabriel Martial, Félix Laventure, René Humbert, A.R. Mohamed, Radhamohan Gujadhur, Maurice Poupard, Raymond Hein, Maxime de Sornay and Jules Koenig."* That was the Union Mauricienne platform which Ramgoolam preferred to joining the MLP.

But neither the new pieces of legislation meant for the welfare of the working classes, nor the gorgeous garden-parties at Le Réduit organised by Bede Clifford in honour of his friends and supporters of *"all classes in the community"* and *"members of other ethnic groups,"* really defused the explosive industrial situation.

In the Colonial Information Bulletin of the British trade unions, on page 8, the 1937 strike was commented just after the report of the commissioners was submitted, in those terms:

"It is believed in Mauritius that the Report does not really contain anything more than a semblance of concessions to the workers, although it is expected that the press will claim that the workers are obtaining fair treatment. The Report has attacked the Labour Party leader, Mr. Maurice Curé, to whom in reality the credit of having enabled the workers to realise their strength, belongs."

The governor lifted finally the deportation order against Anquetil who came back from Rodrigues with his son who had accompanied him there. Curé had protested his own confinement in a letter dated September 8, 1938, in which he stated that he had to attend his patients outside Curepipe and the order concerning him was curtailing *"my liberty to attend my professional duties."* Further, we read, his letter, now in a private collection:

"Your Excellency expressed his desire that the Executive Committee of the Labour Party should examine the New Bill on Labour and make any suggestion that they think fit, seeing that there is no direct representation of Labour in the Legislative Council. In the face of Your Excellency's order, there is now no possibility for the spokesmen of the working classes to participate in the framing of the contemplated legislation on labour. The responsibility of such legislation will rest entirely upon the Legislative Council where the interested parties have no voice."

In the face of the sharp criticism which his behaviour had brought upon him from a number of M.P.'s in the British Parliament, especially concerning his authoritarian way of dealing with the workers and the leaders of the Mauritius Labour Party, the governor had been forced to restrain himself from more excesses, to liberate both Anquetil and Curé, and to think about the question of political representation in the Legislative Council. He was to propose, later, a form of communal representation.

Bede Clifford: a highly controversial British Governor

Sir Bede Clifford, the man who, according to Professor Basdeo Bissoondoyal, started the *'communal hare'* (i.e. introducing and stirring politica. communalism) in Mauritius, revealed himself as a very controversial figure in his days as British governor, especially in the Caribbean where he was later posted and found himself involved in big financial scandals. Two of them still plague his gubernatorial legacy in the island-nations, and form part of their history.

Onf of those affairs is described by H. M. Kirk-Greene in a voluminous book on the European governors in Africa:

"Not that a private income necessarily insured a peaceful administration. In the Bahamas, His Excellency the Honourable Bede Clifford followed up his legislators' agreement to turn the island into a tax-free haven and tourist attraction by himself purchasing a hotel, a beach, and a golf course, which he then proceeded to sell to his own Bahaman government." [55]

A highly dubious project he set up and carried out in Trinidad is still commented today in this country and is widely known as the ***"Caura Dam Scandal"*** during which charges of bribery were heard. Clifford put an end to the existence of a historical indigenous village, expelling all the inhabitants, and this painful memory still lives on among the survivors and their descendants. The village had been renamed La Veronica which explains the two names used in the following account of the scandal during which this old village was razed to the ground by Bede Clifford:

"In 1943, the government, under Governor Sir Bede Clifford, acquired all the lands in and around the village of Caura or La Veronica. The purpose of this was to build a dam to supply the entire north of Trinidad with water, according to the authorities... This meant that the village had to be destroyed and its thousand-or-so inhabitants had to go. On November 4, 1945, the church, the presbytery and the school were all dynamited. By 1946 all the people and all the buildings had been cleared from the Caura site and workmen began laying down the foundations of the dam.

"... There were charges of graft and bribery and corruption involving even the governor, Sir Bede Clifford, a good number of expatriate staff such as the Director of Public Works and all sort of "experts" and "advisers" running through all ranks. Expensive machinery imported for the dam lay rusting in the sun and rain.

"It was the biggest financial scandal this country has ever known, up to this date. In April 1947, new governor, Sir John Shaw within a year the project was declared abandoned." [56]

---
55 African Proconsuls. European Governors in Africa. L.H. Gann & Peter Duignan, eds. New York/London/Stanford. The Free Press/Collier Macmillan Publishers & Hoover Institution. 548 pages.
56 As related on a Trinidad and Tobago website: <TrinbagoPan.com> under the title of Caura, on the history of a historical Arawak village

This brief digression was needed to show that the man who was persecuting the leaders of the Labour Party and praised by those who attacked that party was not an official who has left only the nice memories we can find in the traditional historiography of Mauritius.

The British want a communal system of representation

Coming back to the British governor's plan to introduce communal representation, .Jomadar informed Curé, in a letter dated December 1938, from London, in which he wrote,

"I spoke to Mr Cr. Jones about Constitutional reforms and inquired what kind of reform the Government is contemplating. He told me that the Colonial Secretary is rather inclined to the Communal Basis system. I am strongly in opposition to this and I dare say that you would agree with me that we have never thought of such a thing before. What we want is an extension of the franchise and we shall do our best to achieve our aims." [57]

In the next chapter, we will see that Bede Clifford did propose a form of communal representation and that Jomadar was right in his letter.

The fact was that the measures taken in 1937-38 to appease the working classes (who had been mistakenly taken as *"meek lambs,"* to use Pezzani's expression), did not work,was proved not only by the dockers' strike, but by widespread discontent among the labourers of the sugar estates, particularly in 1943. The official nominee for the Indo-Mauritians in the Legislative Council could do nothing to change that, as averred by the facts, in spite of the hopes placed in him by Bede Clifford, who had deliberately avoided to appoint anybody close to the Labour Party. In several cases, the minimum wage of Rs 20 was not being paid.

which existed between Basdeo Bissoondoyal and Emmanuel Anquetil. The religious man often called on the president of the Labour Party at Rose Hill. [58]

The authorities started to warn him not to organise any public event without obtaining the approval of the government, even for a type of religious gatherings. He protested that he was not the only religious person organising gatherings for prayer and sermons and that there was no reason, under the law, for the authorities to discriminate against him. He insisted that nothing would stop him from delivering his sermons, and such firmness of purpose only increased his already considerable popularity throughout the country.

Governor D. Mackenzie-Kennedy, who had succeeded Bede Clifford, was persuaded that the missionary was acting on racial lines. Anquetil and Dr. Millien challenged that point of view publicly. But Basdeo Bissoondoyal was prosecuted and brought to Court.

In October 1944, he was arrested following a sermon he had programmed in Vacoas and a public procession that had been spontaneously organised by the Hindus of the region. In Court, he refused to say yes or no to the magistrate's question as to whether he would plead guilty or not. He repeatedly answered: *"Find it yourself"*. He was condemned for contempt of court and sent back to prison. Then when the case came up for trial, he asked that the governor be summoned as witness. He was condemned to 12 months hard labour. Sent to prison on 3 November 1944, he was released on 18 July 1945.

The matter was so serious that it drew attention from overseas. A parliamentary question was put on the matter on 12 November 1946 to Pandit Jawaharlall Nehru in New Delhi, by Pandit K.D. Paliwal. During his prison term, Pandit Bissoondoyal went on a hunger strike while workers on several estates started a go-slow, a fact which was mentioned in a speech of the governor in Council. Dr. Millien and Jules Koenig believed that Professor Bissoondoyal had been victim of persecution. Millien wrote a virulent reply to the governor in his newspaper *L'Oeuvre*, another paper that, with Le Peuple Mauricien, was close to the Labour Party.

U. Bissoondoyal writes:

"In December 1944 another Hindu missionary was prosecuted holding a procession. Jules Koenig, appearing for him, said that Basdeo Bissoondoyal had been persecuted and not prosecuted". [59]

It was then that Sookdeo Bissoondoyal finally decided to leave his teaching job in government and to enter the political

---

that has now disappeared.
57 Jomadar's letter is in a private collection consulted by the author.
58 Op cit
59 Op cit. This chapter has drawn, regarding the Bissoondoyal brothers and their political action in context, information sourced from various publications edited or authored by U. Bissoondoyal, principally **Indians Overseas, The Mauritian Experience**, op cit.; **Gandhi and Mauritius, and Other Essays,** op cit; and **Indian Labour Immigration,** op cit, Bissoondoyal, U. and Servansing, S.B.C. (eds.): papers presented at the International Seminar on Indian labour immigration at the Mahama Gandhi Institute, Mauritius, 1984.

arena as a full-fledged politician. The brothers acquired a small printing press from Dr. Rivalland in Curepipe and installed it in St. Denis Street, Port-Louis, where they started publishing tracts and pamphlets, as well as a montly periodical called *Sainik*, which was later followed by the *Zamana*, which became a quite popular publication.

What Basdeo Bissoondoyal was practising in those days, could, in some ways, be compared to the theology of liberation which motivated Catholic priests of the working classes of various parts of the world several decades later, especially in the 1960s.

Anyway, the "lambs" had revolted. Some of them had fallen. Others were to rise again and again and face oppression and repression. They did so each time withrenewed vigour to claim better conditions and more democratic freedoms.

Chapter 41

Independence of Mauritius still to be completed

In 2015 Mauritius won a case at international level against UK

Mauritius won against the UK a judgment from the International Tribunal of the Law of the Sea (ITLOS) on a complaint lodged on April 1, 2010, against the UK's unilateral decision to create a marine park around the Chagos Archipelago without consulting the Mauritian authorities. The judgment was published on March 18, 2015. ITLOS stated in an official press release[1] on that day that, *"The Tribunal went on to find unanimously that, as a result of undertakings given by the United Kingdom in 1965 and repeated thereafter, Mauritius holds legally binding rights to fish in the waters surrounding the Chagos Archipelago, to the eventual return of the Chagos Archipelago to Mauritius when no longer needed for defence purposes, and to the preservation of the benefit of any minerals or oil discovered in or near the Chagos Archipelago pending its eventual return. The Tribunal held that in declaring the MPA, the United Kingdom failed to give due regard to these rights and declared that the United Kingdom had breached its obligations under the Convention."* As of date Mauritius has expressed the intention, based on its victory before ITLOS where two judges held a dissenting judgment stating that Mauritius should be awarded sovereignty on the Chagos, to ask the UN's International Court of Justice for an opinion on the continued occupation by the UK of the Mauritian territory of the Chagos. UK and Washington consequently tried to persuade Mauritius not to go to the ICJ by using threats of retaliation,[2] then obtaining from Mauritius acceptance of a negotiated solution in 2017 to the illegal occupation, which violates various UN resolutions on decolonization and several international conventions *(see further details in this book)*. The following is an excerpt from the reply by Mauritius in its '*Mauritius Memorial*' (MM in the footnotes) to a "Counter Memorial" (UKCM) by the UK during the court case before ITLOS.

"In a 2009 judgment rendered by the UK's highest court (the House of Lords, as it then was), Lord Hoffmann offered the following description of the Chagos Archipelago: "The islands were a dependency of Mauritius when it was ceded to the United Kingdom by France in 1814 and until 1965 were administered as part of that colony."[3] *The UK now disagrees with the views expressed by its own highest court. Mauritius agrees with Lord Hoffmann's view that the Chagos Archipelago was administered as part of Mauritius until its unlawful detachment. The fact that the Chagos Archipelago has always been an integral part of Mauritius is also evident from (a) the constitutional, legislative and administrative arrangements; (b) the economic, cultural and social links between the Chagos Archipelago and Mauritius; (c) the practice of the UK; and (d) the fact that it is recognised as such by the international community. (...)*

Chagos, Tromelin: Mauritian territory from British Conquest

Below is an extract, cited verbatim, from '*The Colonial List 1903*', one of many publications, official, quasi-official or privately published, that listed the Chagos Archipelago and Tromelin Island as integral parts of Mauritius, based on the official and legally sound and internationally accepted records of the Colonial Office in London. European colonialism, British, American and French colonialism across the world illegally denied, from the 1950s onwards, the sovereignty of independent Mauritius over parts of its territory that they decided to seize in violation of decolonization legislation passed by the United Nations, while those powers accuse and even declare war against other countries for similar violations. The extract from this well-known annual publication widely circulated across the world speaks for itself on the unfinished decolonisation of Mauritius. In 2016, Mauritius was still struggling for independence from France and the UK, which deported its citizens, the Chagossians, to a life of poverty and suffering in exile since 1965.

Excerpt of the document lodget at ITLOS by Mauritius:

The St. Brandon, or Cargados Islands (Albatross, Tromelin, and Coco), lie between 16° 20' and 16° 50' S. lat., and 59° 26' and 59° 41' E. long. Most of them are mere sandbanks, and their only produce is a little salt fish.

"*Constitutional, legislative and administrative arrangements confirm that the Chagos Archipelago has always been an integral part of the territory of Mauritius. Throughout the period of French rule, from 1715 to 1810, the Chagos Archipel-*

---

[1] PCA PRESS RELEASE, CHAGOS MARINE PROTECTED AREA ARBITRATION (MAURITIUS V. UNITED KINGDOM) The Arbitral Tribunal Renders its Award. THE HAGUE, 19 March 2015
[2] Press release 24 June 2016 "Joint Press Statement from the British High Commission and the Embassy of the United States of America" The communique stated, "Referral of this matter to the International Court of Justice would cause lasting damage to Mauritius' bilateral relations with both the UK and the USA."
[3] Lord Hoffmann in R (Bancoult) v Secretary of State for Foreign and Commonwealth Affairs (No.2) [2008] UKHL 61, [2009] 1 AC 453 ("Bancoult (No.2)"), at 475-476, para. 4 (emphasis added).

ago was administered as part of Mauritius. This continued without interruption throughout the period of British rule, from 1810 until 8 November 1965. As noted in the Memorial, the 1814 Treaty of Paris, which formally ceded Mauritius to the UK, recognised the Chagos Archipelago a part of the territory of Mauritius.[4] In its Counter-Memorial, the UK concedes that the Chagos Archipelago was "included for some purposes within the definition of the 'Colony of Mauritius'"[5] Succesive constitutions of the dependent territory of Mauritius defined Mauritius as including its dependencies.[6] Under British colonial rule the Governor of Mauritius was granted legislative authority over the Chagos Archipelago. In 1815 the first British Governor of Mauritius, Sir Robert Farquhar, issued a proclamation by which UK Acts of Parliament abolishing the slave trade "extend to every, even the most remote and minute portion, of the Possession, Dominion and Dependencies of Her Majesty's Government"[7] Two Ordinances of 1852 and 1853, referred to by the UK in its Counter-Memorial, granted the Governor of Mauritius the power to extend the laws and regulations of Mauritius to the Seychelles and other Dependencies (including the Chagos Archipelago).[8] The limited evidence relied on by the UK to argue the Chagos Archipelago was not part of Mauritius does not support its position."

"Rodrigues, the most important dependency of Mauritius after the Seychelles, is situated in latitude S. 19° 41' and longitude 63° 23', and is 344 nautical miles from Mauritius. The island is 18 miles long by 7 miles broad, and is surrounded by coral reef extending in some places 5 or 6 miles from the shore. It is under the administration of a magistrate, who takes his instructions from the Governor of Mauritius. Laws for the island are made in the form of regulations framed by the Governor of Mauritius in executive council. The population (census 1901) is 3,162 (author's note: of the Mauritian document).

"The Agalega Islands (2) are midway between Mauritius and Seychelles. The population is about 350, and they are engaged in a prosperous oil factory. Amongst other detached islands may be named Assumption, Astove, St. Pierre, Providence, Cerf, Farquhar, and the Aldabra, but none of these have any permanent population.

"The Chagos Islands, the Trois Frères or Eagle Islands, and the Cosmoledo Islands, which are known generally as the Oil Islands, lie between 6° 40' and 9° 40' S. lat. and 72° 22' and 47° 48' E. long. The chief are North, South, Polyte, Wizard, and Menai.

"The island, which is volcanic, mountainous, and in some parts well wooded, is beautiful and picturesque in the extreme. The highest land is 1,760 feet above the level of the sea, and may be seen in clear weather at a distance of 10 or 12 leagues. The temperature differs little from that of Mauritius, although the breezes are stronger and hurricanes more frequent and severe. Theclimate is healthy. The principal industries are fishing and the rearing of cattle and goats, for which latter the pasturage is excellent. The soil is good; sugar-cane, cotton, coffee, rice, maize, beans, and vanilla grow luxuriantly.

"The numerous dependencies of Mauritius comprise about a hundred islands scattered over the IndianOcean, and contain a total population of 24,117 inhabitants (census 1901). They may be roughly divided into four groups, the Seychelles (see separate description under that heading), the Amirantes Group, the Oil Islands and St. Brandon Group, and detached islands, such as Eagle Island, Peros Banhos, and the Solomon Islands. The Amirantes Group lie between 4° 24' and 6° 13' S. lat., and 53° 27' and 53° 7' E. long. They are coral islands, producing cocoanut oil and a little maize, and some of them are used as fishing stations. The chief are Poivre, Darros, African,mEagle, lies des Roches, Boudeuse, Alphonse, Coetivy, and Platte.

"During the time of slavery fortunes were made in this island by agricultural pursuits; but of late years cultivation has been neglected, owing to want of regular communication and insufficent labour. There is an abundance of fresh water springs in the island, and wild guinea fowls and partridges are plentiful. There are also deer and wild pigs. Fruit abounds, such as mangoes, bananas, guavas, pineapples, avocas, custard apples, wild raspberries, and tamarinds, while the island is famous for oranges, citrons, and limes. The palmiste and vacoa trees are to be found all over the island.

"The principal exports at present are beans, maize, salt-fish, cattle, goats, pigs, poultry, and fruit. Diego Garcia (population, 526), the most important of the Oil Islands group, consists of four islands, at four days' steaming from Mauritius, the chief one

---

4 4 MM, paras. 2.15-2.16: see Article VIII of the 1814 Treaty of Paris (UKCM, Annex 1): "His Britannic Majesty, stipulating for Himself and His Allies, engages to restore to His Most Christian Majesty, within the terms which shall be hereafter fixed, the colonies, fisheries, factories, and establishments of every kind which were possessed by France on the 1st of January, 1792, in the Seas and on the Continents of America, Africa, and Asia, with the exception however of the Islands of Tobago and St. Lucie, and of the Isle of France and its Dependencies, especially Rodrigues and Les Séchelles, which several Colonies and Possessions His Most Christian Majesty cedes in full right and Sovereignty to His Britannic Majesty, and also the portion of St. Domingo ceded to France by the Treaty of Basle, and which His Most Christian Majesty restores in full right and Sovereignty to His Catholic Majesty" (emphasis added). During the period of French rule, Mauritius was known as Ile de France and is referred to as such in the Treaty. For convenience, the name Mauritius is used throughout this chapter.

5 UKCM, para. 2.32

6 Section 52 of the Letters Patent (16 September 1885) altered the constitution of the Council of Government and defined the Colony of Mauritius as "the Island of Mauritius and its Dependencies" (Annex 4). Section 2(1) of the Mauritius (Constitution) Order in Council, 1958 defined the colony of Mauritius as "the Island of Mauritius (including the small islands adjacent thereto) and the Dependencies of Mauritius" (Annex 16). There is a similar definition provided for in section 1(1) of Mauritius (Legislative Council) Order in Council, 1947 (Annex 8). Section 90(1) of the Mauritius (Constitution) Order, 1964 defines Mauritius as "the island of Mauritius and the Dependencies of Mauritius" (Annex 28)

7 Edis, R, "Peak of Limuria – The Story of Diego Garcia" (Reprinted Edition, 1998) (Extract), (hereinafter "Edis"), p. 35: Annex 104. Slavery was abolished in Mauritius and its dependencies in 1835.

8 Mauritius and Dependencies, Ordinance No. 14, 23 March 1853, (UKCM, Annex 3) and Mauritius and Dependencies, Ordinance No. 20, 2 June 1852 (UKCM, Annex 2). The 1853 Ordinance is virtually identical in its terms to the 1852 Ordinance, except that the earlier ordinance empowered "the Governor" rather than "the Governor in his Executive Council".

being about 30 m[il]es in length, extending in an irregular horse-shoe shape, and embracing between its extremities three minor islets. It is a cor[al] atoll, fifteen miles by six-and-a-half, nowhere over ten feet high, but forming a spacious bay, roomy enough for large vessels t[o en]ter, being fifteen miles in length from end to end, and from two to five miles in breadth. Situated as Diego Garcia is, at 7° [latit]ude S. And between 72° and 73° longitude E., on the straight line between the entrance to the Red Sea and Cape Leeuwin, [it af]fords great convenience for coaling purposes to steamers, and coal depots have been established on the island by commer[cial] companies.

"In 18[?] was placed under the jurisdiction of a magistrate, with a small force of police from Mauritius, which was, however, with[draw]n in 1888."

Chagos, a priority in the Mauritius Parliament from 2015

[Th]e issue of the Chagos is a priority in the Mauritius Parliament since 2015. The Hansard shows many issues were raised particularly the need for Mauritius to complete its decolonization. This started with the Presidential [s]peech at the opening of the new Parliament. Then in her speeches proposing, then summing up the debates on [t]he new Lepep Alliance government's programme on February 10, 2015, and 10 March 2015, Member for Grand River North West/Port-Louis West Danielle Selvon highlighted the issue. Soon after, Prime Minister Sir Anerood Jugnauth appointed an all-party committee and appealed to national unity on the question of the Chagos in the name of national interest. Leader of Oppposition Paul Bérenger intervened several times at Private Notice Question time on the issue. On March 18, Mauritius learned that it had won its case, lodged by the previous government of Dr. Navin Ramgoolam against the UK before ITLOS. On July 5, 2016, Danielle Selvon[9] again raised the issue at ajournment, blamed the UK and the US for violating several international conventions and asked the Mauritian government to press more vigorously for the return of the Chagos and offer a plan for the relocation of the Chagossians in the archipelago. Labour parliamentary leader Shakeel Mohamed, following this, pleaded to the media in favour of such a plan. The PM took Chagossian leader Olivier Bancooult for the first time to the UN General Assembly in September 2016, where Sir Anerood Jugnauth raised vigorously Mauritius"s claim of sovereignty.

The rape of the Chagos: Double responsibility of Mauritian leaders and the Anglo-American alliance

Events at the Constitutional Conference at Lancaster House were mainly centred on two main issues: (1) independence; and (2) the detachment by Great Britain of the Chagos Archipelaqo, an integral part of the historical and national territory of Mauritius. The responsibilities for this illegal action and the human tragedy rest on:

1. London and Washington, who violated international law and, in addition, as revealed by the Wiki Leaks in 2009-2010 and publicised by the international media, have systematically used lies and deceit (a) to deport the inhabitants of the island to a life of poverty, misery and heartbreaking exile from their native land and (b) then, in the 21st century, to try to put an end to the claim of the islanders to return to their homes.
2. The Mauritian political leadership, albeit acting illegally (i.e. in contempt of international law), gave the green light to London to detach the Chagos from Mauritius, something no true freedom fighter would accept regarding the integrity of the national territory – a book published 2011 by a former minister and chairman of a Select Inquiry on the excision of the Chagos.[10] The book allegesthat the British used 'bribery' to obtain Chagos.

However, what was well known across the world and of which Mauritian leaders of 1965 have denied knowledge, is that the purpose of the cession of the Chagos was to build an American base for defence purposes. It was not just for communications facilities as Ramgoolam, for instance, argued before the 1983 Select Committee inquiring over the Chagos affair. The following exchange in the House of Commons (just as happened in the Lok Sabah in India and elsewhere in the world) is quite clear in answer of Anthony Greenwood, Secretary of State for the Colonies:

"Mr. Biggs-Davison: Can the Minister say how the Government's discussions are going on with a view to establishing an Anglo-American base?

---

9 D. Selvon attributed to the UK and the US multiple violations of international law. Hansard, 5 July 2016 http://mauritiusassembly.govmu.org/English/hansard/Documents/2016/hansard1516.pdf
10 L'Estrac, J.C. de, *L'an prochain à Diego Garcia*, ELP 2011.

"An Hon. Member: Very well.
"Mr. Biggs-Davison: In that event, may I be assured that there will be no effect on the sovereignty of the territory?
"Mr. Greenwood: The question of the defence use to which the island is to be put is a matter which should be referred to my right hon. Friend the Secretary of State for Defence. There is certainly no question of any derogation from Britain's sovereignty of these territories." [11]

In world politics, it was well known, from the end of the 1960s, that the Americans were about to send a formidable fleet into the Indian Ocean and that was also several times invoked in Indian media and houses of Parliament. The Americans were preparing to replace the declining British power in the Indian Ocean. As far back as 1957, this decline and the necessity for Washington to deploy a formidable military force in the Indian Ocean was strongly recommended by American analysts specialised in geopolitics, among whom George Fielding Eliot, writing in the U.S. Marine Corps Gazette, on the basis of a detailed analysis of the military situation and of the communist penetration in south-east Asia:

"The military and political problem which faces the United States in the Indian Ocean area and in its Middle Eastern bastion is how to provide a reliable substitute for the British-Indian power system which will be visibly reassuring to Asian-African fears of Communist penetration, while arousing no counter-fears of American imperialism entering by the back door as British imperialism departs by the front.
"The first requirement necessitates: 1) short-term capabilities sufficient to bring effective aid to any threatened state of the area against limited or localized Communist or Communist-inspired threats and 2) long-term capabilities which could defeat a major Communist penetration should one be attempted.
"The second requirement rules out the presence of American troops in the territory of any Asian or African state on anything like a permanent basis. Our Indian Ocean strategy cannot be founded, as was the British, by American presence on its shores, but rather by American access when and as required, associated with the development of friendly local forces." [12]

The American intentions in the Indian Ocean were the talk of the town in all the world's capitals. How could an entire government not know the geopolitical issues being discussed across the world and major indications coming out that an American alternative was being prepared to occupy military strategic positions in the Indian Ocean? Most analysts today contend that the Chagos were simply given away, and one factor that contributed to this was that the Premier, freshly knighted on 12 June 1965 on the occasion of the queen's birthday, described by Colonial Office in documents recently declassified as "the old man in a hurry" [13] and eager to become, in the wake of the constitutional conference, the first Prime Minister of Mauritius, ceded the precious part of the national heritage in a remarkably short time, but he was not the only one responsible as all the other Mauritian political leaders and delegation members, did nothing to oppose the cession, Duval only wanting economic and trade advantages that were never accepted by the Americans. [14]

The Chagos affair, based on declassified official documents

Narainduth Sookhoo's research based on declassified official documents in London gives a valuable insight into the events during the negotiations on the independence of Mauritius and the fate of the Chagos and it is important to integrate his findings to this chapter for a complete view of what really happened. Based on such formerly *'Top Secret'* British documents, here is what this researcher has discovered and wrote in *Le Mauricien*: [15]

"And it was during highly confidential discussions away from Lancaster House in the grand offices of Whitehall and in Downing Street with a last-minute personal intervention by the British Prime Minister, Harold Wilson that these issues were settled on British terms. Let us see how events unfolded...
"At a meeting held at 9.00 a. m. on Monday 20th September 1965 in the Colonial Office (C.O) and chaired by the Secretary of States for the Colonies, Anthony Greenwood and attended by five top British officials (Sir H. Poynton, Permanent Secretary, C.O ; Sir J. Rennie, Governor of Mauritius, and Messers Trafford-Smith, A.J. Fairclough and J. Stacpole all from the CO) and five political delegates (SSR, Messrs J. Koenig, A.R. Mohamed, S. Bissoondoyal and J.M. Paturau) Greenwood expressed his desire to keep the discussion of the proposal to establish defence facilities in the Mauritian dependencies (Chagos) separate from the Constitutional Conference. He mentioned his own double role as a spokesman of Her Majesty's Government's interest in this matter and as custodian within the British Government of the interests of Mauritius. SSR said that the Mauritian Government was not interested in the excision of the islands and would stand out for a 99-year-lease. He envisaged a rent of about £7m. a year for the first twenty years and estimated £2m. for the remainder. SSR regarded the British offer of a lump sum of £1m as derisory and said he would rather make the transfer gratis than accept it. The alternative was, SSR said, for Britian to concede independence to Mauritius and allow Mauritius Government to negotiate thereafter with the British and United States Governments over Diego Garcia. Bissoondoyal and Mohamed expressed their support for the views expounded by the Premier, SSR. Koenig spoke of Mauritius record of loyalty to Britain in

---

[11] *Future*, HC Deb 18 November 1965 vol 720 cc1308-9
[12] Eliot, George Fielding, *American Seapower and the Indian Ocean, Marine Corps Gazette* (pre-1994)41, 12 (Dec 1957): 8-18.
[13] Sookhoo, N., *Diplomacy: SSR's style*, article sourced, from British Colonial Papers. In *Week-End*, 16 January 2011..
[14] *The 1983 Select Committee on the Chagos*, op cit.
[15] Sookhoo, Narainduth, *Mauritius Independence. Marginalism and political control* (), in: *Le Mauricien*, 26 February 2012.

two World Wars and his own natural inclination to advocate that the facilities required for Commonwealth defence should be made available free of charge. Against this the grave economic needs of Mauitius made him anxious to find some middle way between a generous gesture of this kind and what SSR had proposed. Paturau pleaded for an increase in the sugar quota imported by USA from Mauritius.

"Intimidated SSR facing Wilson

"From a note in file written the same day, Monday 20 September 1965 and signed by J.O. Wright of PMO, we learn that Harold Wilson, the Prime Minister, held a meeting at 10 Downing Street at 5.00 pm on 20 September. Were present the Colonial Secretary, the Defence Secretary and officials (not named). The note reads "The Colonial Secretary reported on the latest stage of the Constitutional conference on Mauritius. He said that the Mauritians had opened their mouths very wide over compensation for the detachement of Diego Garcia. It was agreed that the Prime Minister would have a private word with Sir S. Ramgoolam on the following day. SSR was convened at 10 Downing Street on Thursday 23 September 1965 at 10.00 a. m.

"J.O. Wright wrote a strong steering brief dated 22 September 1965 for Harold Wilson for his meeting with SSR. It reads "Prime Minister, Sir Seewoosagar Ramgoolam is coming to see you at 10.00 tomorrow morning. The object is to frighten him with: hope that he might get independence. Fright lest he might not unless he is sensible about the detachement of the Chagos Archipelago. I attach a brief prepared by the Colonial Office, with which the Ministry of Defence and the Foreign Office are on the whole content... I also attach a minute from the Colonial Secretary, which has not been circulated to his colleagues, but a copy of which I have sent to Sir Burke Trend. In it the Colonial Secretary rehearses arguments with which you are familiar but which have not been generally accepted by Ministers".

"The CO brief attached to Wright's note is a 3-page comprehensive unsigned document giving a biographical note on SSR and his political position, details about Diego Garcia defence facilities, its cost and Mauritius reaction to it, report on MCC and finally notes to Wilson on how to handle the interview with SSR. Extracts reads as follows : "Call him 'Sir Seewoosagar' or 'Premier' his official titles. He likes to be called 'Prime Minister'... Getting old. Realises he must get independance soon or it will be too late for his personal career. Rather status-conscious. Responds to flattery".

Report on the MCC reads "The gap between the parties led by Sir S. Ramgoolam wanting independence and Parti Mauricien and its supporters who seek continuing association with Britain will not be closed by negotiation. HMG will have to impose a solution. The remaining conference sessions will be devoted to bringing the position of all parties on details of the constitution as close together as possible and, in particular to securing the agreement of all the parties to the maximum possible safeguard for minorities. The Secretary of State's mind is moving towards a decision in favour of independence, followed by a General Election under the new Constitution before Independence Day, as the right solution, rather than a referendum to choose between independence and free association, as the Parti Mauricien has demanded".

"British policy of continued dismemberment

"On handling the interview CO recommends Wilson : "The Premier should not leave the interview with certainty as to HMG's decision as regards independence, as during the remaining sessions of the conference it may be necessary to press him (SSR) to the limit to accept maximum safeguards for minorities".

"Record of the meeting of Wilson and SSR at 10.00 am on Thursday 23 September 1965 in Downing Street is a revealing and important document. Only three persons were present : the British Prime Minister, Harold Wilson, the Mauritian Premier, SSR and J.O. Wright of PMO.

"As expected Wilson was very tough towards SSR. He told SSR, clearly and forcefully that he (SSR) "and his colleagues could return to Mauritius either with independence or without it. On the Defence point, Diego Garcia could either be detached by Order in Council or with agreement of the Premier and his colleagues. The best solutions of all might be Independence and detachement by agreement". An intimidated SSR said he was "convinced that the question of Diego Garcia was a matter of detail ; there was no difficulty in principle".

The official documents reveal a sad tale of division on the issue of independence, an intimidated and weak SSR in the face of British pressures, blackmail, deceit and duplicity on the part of the British to dismember the Mauritius national territory, the flat refusal by the Anglo-Americans to even accept a lease. We are far from the claims of courageous struggle for independence as, obviously, Mauritians struggled against each other on the issue of independence and never against the colonial master.

The uphill battle to get back the Chagos

Today, after the British had their way quite easily as seen above, Mauritius is engaged in a very difficult, uphill battle, to get back its right of sovereignty over the archipelago and to obtain from the British government the right for its inhabitants, condemned for decades to a life of dire poverty, to settle back at least in those islands that are not used for military purposes. Both London and Washington continue to ignore resolutions voted by the United Nations that condemn the illegal dismemberment of the national Mauritian territory prior to giving the country independence.

On the question of the excision of the Chagos Archipelago (it is to be noted that some islands belonging to the Seychelles were excised also from the Seychellois territorial patrimony for the same military, not communications, reasons), the principle of excision accompanied by some conditions was not questioned by any Mauritian party present, save that the PMSD was for a higher financial compensation while the pro-independence parties later stated that they were made to understand that only *"communications facilities"* would be set up and nothing else - and this is absolutely not the truth as seen above, based on documentary research.

The Labour Party leader and Prime Minister of Mauritius, Sir Seewoosagur Ramgoolam, came up, nearly two decades later, with the explanation that the U.K. blackmailed the pro-independence delegation by accepting to give independence in exchange of the archipelago. [16]

The excision of the Chagos Archipelago violated two U.N. resolutions on the question of decolonisation:

1. Resolution 1514 of 1960, interdicting the breaking up of national territories prior to their independence, [17] *and*

2. 'Resolution 2066 (XX) Question of Mauritius' of 1965, urging the U.K. "to take no action which would dismember the Territory of Mauritius and to violate its territorial integrity". [18]

Britain and the United States later led bloody wars in Afghanistan and in Iraq on the basis of violations of United Nations resolutions, but they have to this day refused to accept repeated appeals made by Mauritius at the United Nations, as an independent state, to put an end to their occupation of the Mauritian territory of the Chagos Archipelago as per the resolutions 1514 of 1960 and 2066 (XX) of 1965. Or, at least, acknowledge Mauritian sovereignty.

Moreover, the excision of the Chagos in 1965 was accompanied by the brutal depopulation of the islands. Hundreds of families who had lived on the islands for several generations were exiled manu militari to the Seychelles and Mauritius where they lived in extreme poverty, a shocking situation which, for decades, has caused and is still causing a formidable public outcry in Mauritius and internationally.

In March 2005, a documentary on Canadian public television compared this depopulation of the Chagos with the expulsion of thousands of Acadian families from their homes and their country in North America during eight years, from 1755 to 1783. [19] These families were dispersed everywhere. About 10,000 families were forced to put foot on board and sail down to Louisiana, while many headed to France. Still others ran away to Quebec, or hid with the Mi'kmaq Indians in Nova Scotia where they still are; half of those who fled died on the high seas. British historian Mark Curtis who coined the term '*unpeople*' in a book he wrote in 2004, [20] in reference to peoples who have been violently chased out of their homeland, has included the Acadian people in this category and publicly compared them to the Chagossians who suffered the same fate.

Hunger strikes, legal actions, public demonstrations, international information campaigns, a film released on the B.B.C. and numerous other documentaries, protests by the African Union and the NonAligned Conference and at the U.N., and other such actions have highlighted the proven illegality of the excision in international law and the violation of human rights by the expulsion by force of the inhabitants of the Mauritian archipelago – but to no avail, the Anglo-American stand has been systematically opposed to Mauritius' and the displaced islanders' claim on the archipelago.

The Chagos, integral part of Mauritius

Legal and historical documents from French to British rule in Mauritius show that the Chagos Archipelago was part and parcel of the Mauritian historical, cultural and territorial patrimony. Mauritius was always defined as a main island with its dependencies and in 1826, following a formal request made through a resolution voted by the House of Commons in Britain on March 21 of that year, a compilation of the list of islands forming part of Mauritius was submitted by Governor Sir Lowry Cole to Lord Bathurst. [21] The Chagos Archipelago was included in the list, as in all previous ones established at the signature of international treaties

---

16 Mauritius Legislative Assembly, *Report of the Select Committee on the Excision of the Chagos Archipelago (No. 2 of 1983),* Government Printer, Port-Louis, June 1983. Will be referred to as: *Report of the 1983 Select Committee: Chagos.*
17 Declaration on the Granting of Independence to Colonial Countries and Peoples, voted by the United Nations General Assembly on 14 December 1960.
18 1398th Plenary Meeting, 16 December 1965.
19 Canadian Broadcasting Corporation, *Expulsion: The story of Acadia,* 2004.
20 Curtis, Mark, *Unpeople: Britain's secret human rights abuses*, Vintage 2004. Much of the book is based on declassified documents. His comment was reported on the peace activists site ufppc.com on 8 November 2005.
21 *Dependencies of the Mauritius. Return of the Government of Mauritius laid before Parliament agreeable to an address to His Majesty's by the House of Commons and printed by order of the House*, 27th February1827. In: T*he Asiatic Journal and Monthly Register of British India and its Dependencies*, Vol. XXIII, January to June 1827, Farbury, Allen & Co, Booksellers to the East-India Company, London 1827.

involving Mauritius and its dependencies.

The Chagos were always referred to by Britain as a dependency in Mauritius as in 1944, in the House of Lords when the population of the two main islands was mentioned by Lord Faringdon as totalling about 700:

"There is in addition the island of Agalega, 580 miles to the north, and the Chagos Archipelago, nearly 1,200 miles to the north-east, both with a population of about 450. Then there is Peros Banhos island, 32 miles north of Diego Garcia, the principal island in the Archipelago, with a population of about 330, and the Solomon and six other small islands with a population of about 250." [22]

The first survey of Diego Garcia in view of setting a nuclear base occurred at the end of the 1960s with the participation of a Mauritian scientist, Dr. Alfred Orian. In the 1970s, outside the scope of a series of articles on his scientific research by the author of this book, Dr. Orian told the latter that at the time he was sent to the Chagos, he was totally unaware that the mission he carried out in the island had any link with a military project. With hindsight, he said, he could conclude that there was a relation. The survey had in fact been ordered in the period during which Washington and London were seeking, in the wake of decolonisation, safe outposts for their military, to face the perceived threat from the then communist bloc of nations led by the former Soviet Union. [23]

The global perspective: the Chagos and the deadly Polaris missiles

In fact, the British were going through a phase of decolonisation of which they had taken the initiative for reasons already mentioned in this book, which comprised economic and financial factors in addition to diplomatic pressure from rising decolonisation requests from the United Nations and rising militancy among pro-independence forces in the colonies. The Cold War opposed the West to the huge, expanding Communist bloc led by Moscow. Perceiving that as a major threat, the Western powers reorganised their military deployment. As Britain retreated from its colonies, it gave them independence in a neo-colonial setup where London pushed into the seats of power so-called moderate leaders to the detriment of other political forces less willing to accept the new imperialism. [24]

At the same time, regarding the Indian Ocean, which had the sea lanes crucial to the commercial interests of the big European powers for oil, raw materials, etc., Britain created an airforce base in the Maldives, and then accepted to negotiate with the United States various defence arrangements. As far back as 1958, the House of Commons and the House of Lords in the U.K. started debating about the acquisition of the new Polaris missiles developed by the United States, indicating diplomatic and military contacts between London and Washington on that topic.

In January 1958, the Lords were debating about the North Atlantic Treaty Organisation (NATO) conference held a few weeks back in Paris in December 1957 between the Western powers. Lords Teyham and Merrivale spoke about the powerful Polaris missiles that could cover huge distances to strike an enemy either from submarines or land bases and the debate covered also the question of density of population in the UK because there was apprehension that ground bases would create fear among the population. Lord Merridale stated,

"I should like to see consideration given by the Government to the fitting of certain of our surface vessels or submarines of the future with launching platforms."

From that time, Polaris missile acquisition from the United States became a major topic in the UK and would eventually become an important part of the upcoming deal between the two countries over the Chagos Archipelago. In one debate, the long range of the Polaris missile was mentioned by an MP referring to information that made it understood that **"a Polaris submarine could hurl a half-megaton warhead 1,200 miles into the heart of metropolitan Russia."** [25]

---

22 ***Mauritius***, HL Deb 19 April 1944 vol 131 cc453-78
23 Orian, Alfred, ***Report on a Visit to Diego Garcia, Revue agricole et sucrière***, 1959.
24 Routledge, op cit.
25 ***The North Atlantic Treaty Organisation***, HL Deb 25 January 1961 vol 227 cc1195-298, Lord Boothby.

Independance in exchange of democracy, minorities' rights

PHOTO: Harold Macmillan addressing both Houses of the South African Parliament at Cape Town, 3 February 1960 [1]

The UK wanted to give independence to its colonies. UK PM Macmillan told the parliamentarians of the 'winds of change: *"In the twentieth century and especially since the end of the war, the processes which gave birth to the nation states of Europe have been repeated all over the world. We have seen the awakening of national consciousness in peoples who have for centuries lived in dependence upon some other power. Fifteen years ago this movement spread through Asia. Many countries there of different races and civilisations pressed their claim to an independent national life. Today the same thing is happening in Africa and the most striking of all the impressions I have formed since I left London a month ago is of the strength of this African national consciousness. In different places it takes different forms but it is happening everywhere. The wind of change is blowing through this continent and, whether we like it or not, this growth of national consciousness is a political fact. We must all accept it as a fact, and our national policies must take account of it."*

An official British document[2] stated in February 1960, *"1. The goal is freedom and independence. 2. We recognise as legitimate the aspirations of the peoples of the African territories to manage their own affairs. 3. But before transferring power, we would wish to be satisfied that certain basic principles of just and democratic rule will be respected: –There must be no discrimination on grounds of race, colour or creed. Merit alone is the criterion of the place of the individual in society. –The rights of minorities, whether racial, political or religious, must be safeguarded."*

Most problems arose later with racial, and tribal conflicts occured in the colonies and the threat of communist influence and insurrection became serious threats to Western interests.

Minister for the Colonies Iain Macleod said on the 'winds of change' speech,

"I think the difficulty with Harold Macmillan in relation to Africa was that he had all the right instincts, as his 'Winds [sic] of Change' speech showed quite clearly. He was more than prepared for a rapid move to independence—as his appointment of myself showed."[3]

---

1 Macmillan, Harold, *Pointing the way, 1959-1961,* Macmillan, 1972 - Biography & Autobiography - 504 pages
2 DO 35/8039, no 14 [27 Apr 1960] 'British colonial policy in Africa': draft CRO declaration.1 Minutes by G B Shannon, Sir A Clutterbuck, Lord Home and Sir H Lintott
3 R Shepherd, Iain Macleod (London, 1994) p 199.

Two meetings were held in March and April 1961 between US President John Fitzgerald Kennedy and British Prime Minister Harold Macmillan and defence was at the centre of their discussions and of an agreement. The following exchange in the House of Commons of an MP with Conservative government minister Selwyn Lloyd, came as a result of what was widely interpreted as the submission of Britain to the will of the USA from then onwards:

"Mr. Selwyn Lloyd: As the House knows, my right hon. Friend the Prime Minister met President Kennedy at Key West and subsequently at Washington in March and April. The agreed joint communiqué issued after these talks, and my right hon. Friend's answers to Questions in the House, made it clear that these discussions covered a wide range of matters of mutual interest. In addition to these personal talks, there are, of course, consultations at all times in the normal way between Her Majesty's Government, the American Government and other allied Governments.

"Mr. Rankin: Since we do not hear very much about what happened at Vienna as a result of the previous conversations at Key West, could the right hon. and learned Gentleman – without violating anything that happened between the President and the Prime Minister later – tell us a little about any agreements that were reached at Key West, or are we to conclude that the identity of interest between ourselves and America on foreign affairs is now so complete that our foreign policy can be adequately expressed by President Kennedy?" [26]

Chagos deal "outside the process of decolonisation"; population "to be entirely removed"

Selwyn Lloyd did not reveal the content of the agreement reached at those two important summits during which Britain gave away to the United States the leading role in her own defence. This was a secret agreement to which the British Parliament could not have open access. Scholars like Professor André Marc Oraison have highlighted it as being the start of a relationship between in London and Washington that led, some years later, to the detachment of the Chagos following various surveys and measures agreed on between the two powers with the express purpose of

"...setting up an important military base (...) to defend the interests of the West under the double condition that the English colony retained for that purpose be placed outside the process of decolonisation and that its population be entirely removed for reasons of security. In exchange, they (the Americans) offered a discount of 14 million US dollars on the Polaris missiles that the British were then envisaging to purchase for their nuclear submarines." [27]

Oraison cites the revelation of the deal in 1975 by the New York Times [28] This revelation made headlines across the world and gave a clue to academics about the real origin of the Chagos tragedy: a shameful financial gain for Britain against the forced deportation of an entire population to a life of dire poverty and severe moral and psychological distress.

"As an incentive to British participation, the United States agreed to lower the cost of a group of Polaris submarines that it was selling to Britain by $14 million." [29]

London: Mauritian and Seychellois leaders agreed to cession of islands

The Seychelles group of islands evolved independently of Mauritius as from 1903 and constituted a new national entity. The Seychelles obtained independence in 1976 and the British agreed to a request of the Seychellois political parties to return those islands (Aldabra and Desroches) which, together with the Chagos, had been detached for military purposes to constitute the British Indian Ocean Territory (B.1.0.T). Secretary of State for Foreign and Commonwealth Affairs Luard, explained, in the House of Commons in 1977 that in the case of Mauritius as well as the Seychelles the local executive bodies gave their assent to ceding their islands to Britain:

"The Seychelles Executive Council confirmed their agreement in October 1965 to the detachment of the islands of Aldabra, Desroches and Farquhar in return for Britain's agreement to construct an airfield on Mahé Island, Seychelles, to compensate the landowners and to resettle the inhabitants. The islands reverted to Seychelles on that country's independence in 1976 (...)

"The Mauritius Council of Ministers agreed to the detachment of the Chagos Islands after discussions which concerned the negotiation of a defence agreement between Britain and Mauritius – since terminated by agreement – and the grant of £3 million additional to the cost of compensating the landowners and a grant to resettle the islands' inhabitants. Understanding was also reached on rights to mineral, oil and fish resources and there was agreement that, in certain circumstances and as far as was practicable, navigational, meteorological and emergency landing facilities on the islands were to remain available to the Mauritian Government. In the event of the islands no longer being required for defence purposes it was agreed that they should revert to Mauritian jurisdiction." [30]

At the London constitutional talks in 1965, the subject of excision of the archipelago was nothing new to the Mauritian political parties which were represented. The Council of Ministers of Mauritius had, on July 14, 1964, taken

---
26 *Prime Minister And President Kennedy (Consultations)*, HC Deb 08 June 1961 vol 641 cc1390-1
27 Oraison, André Marc, ***Diego Garcia:enjeux de la présence américaine dans l'océan Indien***, in : *Afrique contemporaine*, 2003, pages 115-132.
28 New York Times, 17 October 1975, p.3
29 In: *Air University Review,* March-April 1978, *The United States on Diego Garcia, a question of limits.*
30 ***British Indian Ocean Territory***, HC Deb 23 June 1977 vol 933 cc549-50W.

note of Governor Sir John Shaw Rennie's statement to the effect that a survey of some islands including the Chagos Archipelago was going to be made in view of improving defence facilities. This was raised in 2010 by the Mauritius High Commission protesting the establishment of a marine park in the Chagos Archipelago, in a written evidence recorded (as of March 2012) and published as '*uncorrected evidence*' on the website of the British House of commons:

"1964: August – A joint US/UK military survey of the islands took place. The UK/US first choice was the island of Aldabra, north of Madagascar.

"Unfortunately, Aldabra was the breeding ground for rare giant tortoises, whose mating habits would have probably been upset by the military activity and whose cause would have been championed noisily by publicity-aware ecologists.

"The alternative was the Chagos Islands, part of Mauritius, then a British territory campaigning for independence and inhabited by Chagossians." [31]

On April 5, 1965, in the House of Commons, the question had been raised in a Parliamentary question and answered as follows:

"Mr. James Johnson asked the Secretary of State for the Colonies what approaches have been made to the Mauritian Government regarding certain facilities for an Anglo-United States base in the Indian Ocean.

"Mrs. Eirene White The Premier of Mauritius was consulted in July last about the joint survey of possible sites for certain limited facilities that was then about to begin. In November the Council of Ministers, who had been kept informed, were told that the results of the survey were still being examined and that the Premier would be consulted again before any announcement was made in London or in Washington."

Reactions in the Mauritius Legislative Assembly

In November 1964, in the Mauritian Legislative Assembly, a member, B. Ramlallah, asked for a prompt explanation by government on the question of the survey going on in Diego Garcia. The Chief Secretary, Tom Vickers, C.M.G. confirmed in a written reply on December 14 of the same year, the presence of a joint British-American team doing survey works *"on certain islands, including the Chagos Archipelago, Agalega, but not including Mauritius,"* and he added that prior notification of that survey had been given to the Mauritius Council of Ministers. [32]

On June 15, 1965, Dr. Maurice Curé, the founder of the Labour Party, who had no party affiliation and had been nominated, asked the government if the U.S. had military interests in the Mauritian dependencies and pressed the government to convey to the British government *"the inadvisability of entering into any agreement with the United States of America before a change in our Constitution as envisaged by the London Conference of September next"* and to make sure of *"the presence of oil fields in our dependencies before alienating them."* The Chief Secretary, Tom Vickers referred him to the reply he had already given B. Ramlallah. [33]

All the members of the Legislative Assembly were therefore aware of the question and the strategic, economic and military issues, and so were public and international opinion as proved by the vigorous protests which occurred in the Mauritian press, in the British press by Mauritian immigrants, in the Indian Parliament and at the United Nations.

At the Constitutional Conference held in London in September 1965, the question of the excision of the Chagos was not raised in the open conference, but the decision of the British government to excise the island from Mauritian territory was first communicated to Dr. S. Ramgoolam, as Premier of Mauritius, who shared the news with other party leaders and the independent member Maurice Paturau present at the conference. [34]

They were informed of the British-American joint project to establish defense facilities on the Chagos and, subsequently, the deputy-leader of the Labour Party, Guy Forget, the leader of the PMSD, Jules Koenig, and the leader of the CAM, A. Razack Mohamed, and Maurice Paturau formed a delegation that called at the American Embassy in London where they met the official in charge of economic affairs. They tried to obtain, in return for the excision of the Chagos, guaranteed access and prices for Mauritian sugar on the American market. Deponing before a Select Committee of the Mauritian Parliament set up to inquire on the subject, Paturau recalled that the Americans turned down the request and stressed that matters relating to the Chagos were to be discussed only between the U.K. and the U.S., excluding Mauritius. [35]

---

31 OT 423: **Written Evidence from HE Mr Abhimanu Kundasamy, High Commissioner of Mauritius,** Mauritius High Commission London, 2010, published on the British Parliament's website: www.parliament.uk.
32 Mauritius Legislative Council, 10 November 1964.
33 Ibid. 10 June 1965. This was also reported by the Mauritian media, including **Le Mauricien**, so the population was adequately informed.
34 **Report of the 1983 Select Committee: Chagos**, op cit..
35 Ibid.

Mauritian documents on the Chagos excision

On September 23, 1965 a British delegation led by the Secretary of State for the Colonies, Anthony Greenwood, and a Mauritian delegation comprising the Premier, Dr. S. Ramgoolam, the Minister for Social Security, A. Razack Mohamed, the Minister of Industry, Commerce and External Communications, Maurice Paturau, and the minister for Local Government, Sookdeo Bissoondoyal, discussed in detail the excision of the Chagos Archipelago by Britain.

An official document of the Mauritian Council of Ministers made public in 1983 contains paragraphs 22 and 23 of the minutes of that meeting at Lancaster House, and which read thus:

"22. Summing up the discussion, the Secretary of State asked whether he could inform his colleagues that Dr. Ramgoolam, Mr. Bissoondoyal and Mr. Mohamed were prepared to agree to the detachment of the Chagos Archipelago on the understanding that he would recommend to his colleagues the following:

i. negotiations for a defence agreement between Britain and Mauritius;

ii. in the event of independence an understanding between the two governments that they would consult together in the event of a difficult internal security situation arising in Mauritius;

iii. compensation totalling up to £3m, should be paid to the Mauritius Government over and above direct compensation to landowners and the cost of resettling others affected in the Chagos Islands;

iv. the British Government would use their good offices with the United States Government in support of Mauritius' request for concessions over sugar imports and the supply of wheat and other commodities;

v. that the British Government would do their best to persuade the American Government to use labour and materials from Mauritius for construction work in the islands;

vi. the British Government would use their good offices with the U.S.

"*Government to ensure that the following facilities in the Chagos Archipelago would remain available to the Mauritius Government as far as practicable:*

a. Navigational and Meteorological facilities;

b. Fishing Rights;

c. Use of Air Strip for emergency landing and for refuelling civil planes without disembarkation of passengers;

vii. that if the need for the facilities on the islands disappeared the islands should be returned to Mauritius;

viii. that the benefit of any minerals or oil discovered in or near the Chagos Archipelago should revert to the Mauritius Government.

"*23. Sir S. Ramgoolam said that this was acceptable to him and Messrs Bissoondoyal and Mohamed in principle, but he expressed the wish to discuss it with his other ministerial colleagues.*"[1]

The Colonial Office in London sent to the governor in Mauritius the "*secret*" Colonial Office Dispatch No. 423, dated October 6, 1965, another document made public in June 1983.[2] It referred to the minutes quoted above of which a copy was enclosed with the precision that

"*...this record has already been agreed in London with Sir S. Ramgoolam and by him with Mr. Mohamed, as being an accurate record of what was decided.*"

The Colonial Office asked the governor for his

"*...early confirmation that the Mauritius Government is willing to agree that Britain should now take the necessary legal steps to detach the Chagos Archipelago from Mauritius on the conditions enumerated in (i)-(viii) in paragraph 22 of the enclosed accord.*"

The Chief Secretary T.D. Vickers presented a Memorandum to the Mauritian Council of Ministers on November 4, 1965, confirming the London discussions and listing, once more, the eight conditions contained in the above-mentioned paragraph 22 of those discussions. The unfolding of events has been welldocumented by the 1983 Select Committee as follows:[3]

On November 5, 1965, the Council of Ministers of Mauritius composed of the members of the all-party government comprising Labour, Parti Mauricien, CAM, IFB and independent ministers met and discussed the excision of the Chagos and the eight conditions proposed. The two official documents show that there was serious dissent and that the PMSD was resigning from the government.

The first document is the Telegram No. 247, dated November 5, 1965, sent by the office of the Governor of Mauritius to the Secretary of State for the colonies. The telegram referred to the record of the discussions at Lancaster House as quoted above, with the eight conditions it contained. It read as follows:

"*Your Secret Dispatch No. 423 of 6th October. United Kingdom/U.S. Defence Interests.*

"*Council of Ministers today confirmed agreement to the detachment of Chagos Archipelago on conditions enumerated, on the understanding that*

(1) statement in paragraph 6 of your dispatch "H. M.G. have taken careful note of points (vii) and (viii)" means H.M.G. have in fact agreed to them.

(2) As regards (vii) undertaking to Legislative Assembly excludes (a) sale or transfer by H.M.G. to third party or

(b) any payment or financial obligation by Mauritius as condition of return.

(3) In (vii) "on or near" means within areas within which Mauritius would be able to derive benefit but for change of sovereignty. I would be grateful if you would confirm this understanding is agreed.

"*2. PMSD Ministers dissented and (are now) considering their position in the government. They understand that no disclosure of the matter may be made at this stage and they also understand that if they feel obliged to withdraw from the Government they must let me have (resignations) in writing and consult with me about timing of the publication (which they accepted should not be before Friday 12th November).*

"*3. (Within this) Ministers said they were not opposed in principle to the establishment of facilities and detachment of Chagos but considered compensation inadequate, especially the absence of additional (sugar) quota and negotiations should have been pursued and pressed more strongly. They were also dissatisfied with mere assurances about (v) and (vi). They also raised points (1), (2) and (3) in paragraph 1 above.*"[4]

The second document is an extract from the Minutes of Proceedings of the Meeting of the Council of Ministers held on November 5, 1965 and reveals that the PMSD was envisaging to resign from the government:

---
1 Ibid.
2 Ibid.
3 Ibid.
4 Ibid.

"UK/US Defense Interests in the Indian Ocean.

"No. 553 Council considered the Governor's Memorandum CM (65) 183 on UK/US Defence Interests in the Indian Ocean.

"Council decided that the Secretary of State should be informed of their agreement that the British Government should take the necessary legal steps to detach the Chagos Archipelago on the conditions enumerated on the understanding that the British Government has agreed to points (vii) and (viii) that as regards point (vii) there would be no question of sale or transfer to a third party nor of any payment or financial obligation on the part of Mauritius as a condition of return and that "on or near" in point (vii) meant within the area within which Mauritius would be able to derive benefit but for the change of sovereignty.

"The Attorney General, the Minister of Sate (Development) and the Minister of Housing said that, while they were agreeable to detachment of the Chagos Archipelago, they must reconsider their position as members of the Government in the light of the Council's decision because they considered the amount of compensation inadequate, in particular the absence of any additional sugar quota, and the assurance given by the Secretary of State in regard to points (v) and (vi) unsatisfactory." [5]

As for the Mauritian ministers, Dr. S. Ramgoolam and H. Walter, who took part in the negotiations, they have argued later in the media that they were forced by Britain to accept the cession of the Chagos in exchange for independence. This is the same argument used by Sir Seewoosagur Ramgoolam, deponing before the 1982-83 Select Committee of the Mauritian Parliament on December 6, 1982. Sir Seewoosagur Ramgoolam, who had lost the 1982 general elections, said,

"A request was made to me. I had to see which was better - to cede out a portion of our territory of which very few people knew, and independence. I thought that independence was much more primordial and more important than the excision of the island which is very far from here, and which we had never visited, which we could never visit (...) If I had to choose between independence and the ceding of Diego Garcia, I would have done again the same thing." [6]

In fact, not ceding the Chagos would have meant complete independence, whereas the choice was, at the end of the day, an incomplete independence whereas a real struggle should have been put up, calling the people of Mauritius to take to the streets, to claim the liberation of the entire national territory, just as the Labour Party did to oppose (successfully) the Banwell Report. Anyway this answer given by Ramgoolam also confirms that there was an element of constraint and blackmail used by a strong and superior military colonial power with a view to tamper with Mauritian "territorial integrity" in contravention with the United Nations Resolutions guaranteeing all colonies against such abuse.

According to Professor A. Oraison, this use of superior force is sufficient to invalidate in law the cession of the archipelago. [7] At one moment, Dr. Ramgoolam had refused to give in to British pressure according the *Le Mauricien* newspaper in an article dated July 27, 1965, and had proposed, instead, that the British pay a rent.

"Sir Seewoosagur has objected to the demand that the Chagos Archipelagos be detached from Mauritius. The Premier and leader of the Labour party wants rather a leasing agreement which, in his opinion, would provide additional revenues," wrote the newspaper while also congratulating the Mauritian Premier for his objection, and noting that the British would try to impose its will on Mauritius. It is also worthy to note that *Le Mauricien* congratulated Dr. Ramgoolam on this issue, though it was supporting the Parti Mauricien's demand for integration with Britain instead of independence.

Another article dated August 9 in the same newspaper confirmed once again that there was opposition to the cession of the Chagos and that the talks on independence were linked to that question. Nevertheless, what has come out finally is that none of the delegates at the Constitutional conference opposed the British proposal and they even, in the end, accepted the cession of the Chagos. This was why the British government announced officially to the House of Commons, on 10 November 1965, that the government of Mauritius had agreed to the cession. This historical fact cannot be disputed today, though Mauritius was not then independent and even if it was, any cession of territory would have been illegal in interna-

---

5 Ibid.
6 Ibid.
7 Oraison, André Marc, ***Les avatars du B.I.O.T (British Indian Ocean Territory): le processus de l'implantation militaire américaine à Diego Garcia***, 1979.

tional law.[8]

In the 1990's, Britain has recognised a number of the rights preserved by Mauritius under the 1965 arrangements, including the return of the archipelago to Mauritius whenever it would not serve any military purpose. Nevertheless, in 2010, the British have created a marine park in the area which has attracted a major controversy and official protest from Mauritius.[9] The marine park was clearly intended to prevent the return of the islanders and to further ensure the strict control of the military facilities by the Anglo-Americans. The following excerpt gives an idea of the huge importance that the base has become in the global military infrastructure of Washington and London:

"Diego Garcia, a coral atoll in the British Indian Ocean Territory (BIOT, last-born of British colonies, established by order-in-council in 1965), happens to be the site of one of the most valuable (and most secretive) U.S. military bases overseas, strategically situated at the center of the Indian Ocean, close to the Middle East and to its vital oil supply routes. Following a series of UK-U.S. bilateral agreements since 1966, the island was developed from an "austere communications facility" into a naval support facility, a satellite tracking station, and a bomber forward operating location, under a $2.5 billion construction program. The Diego Garcia airfield – with the world's longest slipform-paved runway built on crushed coral (12,000 feet, also designated as an emergency landing site for the U.S. space shuttle) – played a central role in all offensive combat missions against Iraq and Afghanistan from 1991 to 2006, and was used as a staging area for twenty B-52 bombers prominently deployed as "calculated-ambiguous" tactical nuclear deterrent against any chemical or biological weapons use by Iraq against U.S. forces. The Diego Garcia internal lagoon – a gigantic natural harbor, 48 square miles wide and dredged to a depth of 40 feet as turning basin for aircraft carriers and nuclear submarines – is currently being upgraded under a $200 million, 5-year construction program to accommodate the U.S. Navy's new SSGN (nuclear-powered, guided-missile) attack submarines and a 23,000-ton submarine tender. The Diego Garcia base has also been confirmed by the U.S. Central Intelligence Agency as destination/transit point for several "extraordinary rendition flights" delivering suspected terrorists. (While the BIOT is subject to British colonial legislation, neither the UK Human Rights Act, nor Britain's ratifications of the Geneva Conventions or the UN Convention against Torture are applicable to the territory)." [10]

The establishment of a marine park: 'deceit' used

On the basis of secret official British documents made public by the Wikileaks in 2009, Prime Minister Navin Ramgoolam told the international press that the British had used deceit to establish a huge marine park that would prevent the Chagos islanders from returning to their homeland.

"Navinchandra Ramgoolam spoke out after the Labour government's decision to establish a marine reserve around Diego Garcia and surrounding islands was exposed earlier this month as the latest ruse to prevent the islanders from ever returning to their homeland." [11]

The entire world came to know of secret documents in which British officials clearly state that the purpose of the marine park was more precisely motivated by a claim lodged before the European Court of Human Rights (ECHR) by the Chagossians to be given the right to return to their homeland. Wikileaks revealed the following extracts from diplomatic cables, in which the British official has been identified as Colin Roberts (HMG: Her Majesty's Government):

C O N F I D E N T I A L LONDON 001156

Classified By: Political Counselor Richard Mills for reasons 1.4 b and d

¶1. (C/NF) Summary. HMG would like to establish a "marine park" or "reserve" providing comprehensive environmental protection to the reefs and waters of the British Indian Ocean Territory (BIOT), a senior Foreign and Commonwealth Office (FCO) official informed Polcouns on May 12. The official insisted that the establishment of a marine park -- the world's largest -- would in no way impinge on USG use of the BIOT, including Diego Garcia, for military purposes. He agreed that the UK and U.S. should carefully negotiate the details of the marine reserve to assure that U.S. interests were safeguarded and the strategic value of BIOT was upheld. He said that the BIOT's former inhabitants would find it difficult, if not impossible, to pursue their claim for resettlement on the islands if the entire Chagos Archipelago were a marine reserve...»

<u>*Protecting the BIOT's Waters*</u>

¶2. (C/NF) Senior HMG officials support the establishment of a "marine park" or "reserve" in the British Indian Ocean Territory (BIOT), which includes Diego Garcia, Colin Roberts, the Foreign and Commonwealth Office's (FCO) Director, Overseas Territories, told the Political Counselor May 12. Noting that the uninhabited islands of the Chagos Archipelago are already protected under British law from development or other environmental harm but that current British law does not provide protected status for either reefs or waters, Roberts affirmed that the bruited proposal would only concern the "exclusive zone" around the islands..."

¶3. (C/NF) Roberts iterated strong UK "political support" for a marine park; "Ministers like the idea," he said. He stressed that HMG's "timeline" for establishing the park was before the next general elections, which under British law must occur no later than May 2010. He suggested that the exact terms of the proposals could be defined and presented at the U.S.-UK annual political-military consultations held in late summer/early fall 2009

---

8 See: Oraison, André, *Le contentieux territorial anglo-mauricien sur l'archipel des Chagos revisité*, 83 **REVUE DE DROIT INTERNATIONAL ET DE SCIENCES DIPLOMATIQUES ET POLITIQUES 109** (2005).
9 OT 423: **Written Evidence from HE Mr Abhimanu Kundasamy, High Commissioner of Mauritius**, op cit.
10 Sand, Peter H., **African Nuclear-Weapon-Free Zone in Force: What Next for Diego Garcia?**, American Society of International Law, 28 August 2009. The article discusses the implications for the Diego Garcia base on the entry into force of the "Treaty of Pelindaba" for an African Nuclear-Weapon-Free Zone (ANWFZ).
11 The Guardian, Tuesday 21 December

(exact date TBD)..."

<u>*Three Sine Qua Nons*</u>: U.S. Assents

¶4. (C/NF) ... Roberts asserted that the proposal would have absolutely no impact on the right of U.S. or British military vessels to use the BIOT for passage, anchorage, prepositioning, or other uses. Polcouns rejoined that designating the BIOT as a marinepark could, years down the road, create public questioning about the suitability of the BIOT for military purposes. Roberts responded that the terms of reference for the establishment of a marine park would clearly state that the BIOT, including Diego Garcia, was reserved for military uses.

¶5. (C/NF) Ashley Smith, the Ministry of Defense's (MOD) International Policy and Planning Assistant Head, Asia Pacific... "shares the same concerns as the U.S. regarding security" and would ensure that security concerns were fully and properly addressed in any proposal for a marine park. Roberts agreed, stating that "the primary purpose of the BIOT is security" but that HMG could also address environmental concerns in its administration of the BIOT. Smith added that the establishment of a marine reserve had the potential to be a "win-win situation in terms of establishing situational awareness" of the BIOT. He stressed that HMG sought "no constraints on military operations" as a result of the establishment of a marine park.

...Mauritian Assent...

¶6. (C/NF) Roberts outlined two other prerequisites for establishment of a marine park. HMG would seek assent from the Government of Mauritius, which disputes sovereignty over the Chagos archipelago, in order to avoid the GOM "raising complaints with the UN." He asserted that the GOM had expressed little interest in protecting the archipelago's sensitive environment and was primarily interested in the archipelago's economic potential as a fishery. Roberts noted that in January 2009 HMG held the first-ever "formal talks" with Mauritius regarding the BIOT. The talks included the Mauritian Prime Minister. Roberts said that he "cast a fly in the talks over how we could improve stewardship of the territory," but the Mauritian participants "were not focused on environmental issues and expressed interest only in fishery control." He said that one Mauritian participant in the talks complained that the Indian Ocean is "the only ocean in the world where the fish die of old age." In HMG's view, the marine park concept aims to "go beyond economic value and consider bio-diversity and intangible values."

...Chagossian Assent

¶7. (C/NF) Roberts acknowledged that "we need to find a way to get through the various Chagossian lobbies." He admitted that HMG is "under pressure" from the Chagossians and their advocates to permit resettlement of the "outer islands" of the BIOT. He noted, without providing details, that "there are proposals (for a marine park) that could provide the Chagossians warden jobs" within the BIOT. However, Roberts stated that, according to the HGM,s current thinking on a reserve, there would be "no human footprints" or "Man Fridays" on the BIOT's uninhabited islands. He asserted that establishing a marine park would, in effect, put paid to resettlement claims of the archipelago's former residents. Responding to Polcouns' observation that the advocates of Chagossian resettlement continue to vigorously press their case, Roberts opined that the UK's "environmental lobby is far more powerful than the Chagossians' advocates." (Note: One group of Chagossian litigants is appealing to the European Court of Human Rights (ECHR) the decision of Britain's highest court to deny "resettlement rights" to the islands' former inhabitants...

"Je Ne Regrette Rien"

¶8. (C/NF) Roberts observed that BIOT has "served its role very well," advancing shared U.S.-UK strategic security objectives for the past several decades. The BIOT "has had a great role in assuring the security of the UK and U.S. -- much more than anyone foresaw" in the 1960s, Roberts emphasized. "We do not regret the removal of the population," since removal was necessary for the BIOT to fulfill its strategic purpose, he said. Removal of the population is the reason that the BIOT's uninhabited islands and the surrounding waters are in "pristine" condition. Roberts added that Diego Garcia's excellent condition reflects the responsible stewardship of the U.S. and UK forces using it.

Administering a Reserve

¶9. (C/NF) Roberts acknowledged that numerous technical questions needed to be resolved regarding the establishment and administration of a marine park, although he described the governmental "act" of declaring a marine park as a relatively straightforward and rapid process. He noted that the establishment of a marine reserve would require permitting scientists to visit BIOT, but that creating a park would help restrict access for non-scientific purposes. For example, he continued, the rules governing the park could strictly limit access to BIOT by yachts, which Roberts referred to as "sea gypsies."

BIOT: More Than Just Diego Garcia

¶11. (C/NF) Yeadon stressed that the exchange of notes governed more than just the atoll of Diego Garcia but expressly provided that all of the BIOT was "set aside for defense purposes..." She urged Embassy officers in discussions with advocates for the Chagossians, including with members of the "All Party Parliamentary Group on Chagos Islands (APPG)," to affirm that the USG requires the entire BIOT for defense purposes. Making this point would be the best rejoinder to the Chagossians' assertion that partial settlement of the outer islands of the Chagos Archipelago would have no impact on the use of Diego Garcia. She described that assertion as essentially irrelevant if the entire BIOT needed to be uninhabited for defense purposes.

¶12. (C/NF) Yeadon dismissed the APPG as a "persistent" but relatively non-influential group within parliament or with the wider public. She said the FCO had received only a handful of public inquiries regarding the status of the BIOT. Yeadondescribed one of the Chagossians' most outspoken advocates, former HMG High Commissioner to Mauritius David Snoxell, as "entirely lacking in influence" within the FCO. She also asserted that the Conservatives, if in power after the next general election, would not support a Chagossian right of return. She averred that many members of the Liberal Democrats (Britain's third largest party after Labour and the Conservatives) supported a "right of return."

¶13. (C/NF) Yeadon told Poloff May 12, and in several prior meetings, that the FCO will vigorously contest the Chagossians' "right of return" lawsuit before the European Court of Human Rights (ECHR). HMG will argue that the ECHR lacks jurisdiction over the BIOT in the present case. Roberts stressed May 12 (as has Yeadon on previous occasions) that the outer islands are "essentially uninhabitable" and could only be rendered livable by *modern, Western standards with a massive infusion of cash.*

Comment

¶14. (C/NF) Regardless of the outcome of the ECHR case, however, the Chagossians and their advocates, including the "All Party Parliamentary Group on Chagos Islands (APPG)," will continue to press their case in the court of public opinion. Their strategy is to publicize what they characterize as the plight of the so-called Chagossian diaspora, thereby galvanizing public opinion and, in their best case scenario, causing the government to change course and allow a "right of return." They would point to the government's recent retreat on the issue of Gurkha veterans' right to settle in the UK as a model. Despite FCO assurances that the marine park concept -- still in an early, conceptual phase -- would not impinge on BIOT's value as a strategic resource, we are concerned that, long-term, both the British public and policy makers would come to see the existence of a marine reserve as inherently inconsistent with the military use of Diego Garcia -- and the entire BIOT. In any event, the U.S. and UK would need to carefully negotiate the parameters of such a marine park -- a point on which Roberts unequivocally agreed. In Embassy London's view, these negotiations should occur among U.S. and UK experts separate from the 2009 annual Political-Military consultations, given the specific and technical legal and environmental issues that would be subject to discussion.

¶15. (C/NF) Comment Continued. We do not doubt the current government's resolve to prevent the resettlement of the islands' former inhabitants, although as FCO Parliamentary Under-Secretary Gillian Merron noted in an April parliamentary debate, "FCO will continue to organize and fund visits to the territory by the Chagossians." We are not as sanguine as the FCO's Yeadon, however, that the Conservatives would oppose a right of return. Indeed, MP Keith Simpson, the Conservatives' Shadow Minister, Foreign Affairs, stated in the same April parliamentary debate in which Merron spoke that HMG "should take into account what I suspect is the all-party view that the rights of the Chagossian people should be recognized, and that there should at the very least be a timetable for the return of those people at least to the outer islands, if not the inner islands." Establishing a marine reserve might, indeed, as the FCO's Roberts stated, be the most effective long-term way to prevent any of the Chagos Islands' former inhabitants or their descendants from resettling in the BIOT. End Comment.

Angry reactions in Mauritius

In Mauritius, the reaction has been one of anger, especially among the leading political leaders and the media. The Guardian reported that despite British assurances that the Chagos will be retroceded to Mauritius **'when it is no longer needed for defence purposes,'** according to a statement in April 2010 by then Foreign Secretary David Miliband, Mauritius is suspicious of the real British intentions. Quoting the Mauritian Prime Minister, the newspaper reported:

"I feel strongly about a policy of deceit," Ramgoolam said, adding that he had already suspected Britain had a 'hidden agenda.'

Asked if he believed Miliband had acted in good faith, he said: "Certainly not. Nick Clegg said before the general election that Britain had a 'moral responsibility to allow these people to at last return home.' William Hague, now foreign secretary, said that if elected he would 'work to ensure a fair settlement of this long-standing dispute."

Chagos and Tromelin: neo-colonial tactics defying international law

The Western powers have violated international law to seize colonial lands prior to decolonisation so as to build neo-colonial outposts. The worst case is that the the Chagos, involving, in addition to an illegal detachment of the territory prior to independence, the expulsion of the entire population of the islands. The case of Tromelin is no less a violation of the territorial integrity, even if the island was not populated. The violation was so flagrant that France proposed co-management of the island and Mauritius accepted.

From 2006 to 2012, more developments in the Chagos affair (see also Chapter 41):

- The world discovers that the excision of Chagos was based on deceit

- The illegal excision of the Chagos from the national territory of Mauritius and the marine park created four decades afterwards by the British authorities were all based on deceitful tactics that have been uncovered in several official documents revealed in Court matters from 2000, and by the Wikileaks in 2009. The recent developments in the matter can be summed as follows:

November 2000: The UK High Court ruled that the expulsion of the Chagossians was an illegal act. One of the aspects of the case was that several documents that had been declassified after 30 years indicated the extent of the bad faith of those who organised the crime of deportation. While the British government had to amend the law of deportation to accept the resettlement of the former inhabitants, it still persisted to defy international law by arguing defence arrangements it had made with Washington that would block the actualreturn of the islanders. Pleasure yachts continue to stop in the archipelago and 2,000 foreign personnel are employed on the base, but London and Washington continue to argue against the return of the islanders.

June 2002: The Foreign and Commonwealth Office completed a feasibility study on the resettlement of the islanders on their islands that concluded against such resettlement on the ground that such a return would cost too much, the islanders would not be able to earn a living and would be threatened by various natural hazards like flooding and various effects of global warming. The UK Chagos Support Group has demolished this kind of reasoning:

"(...) Harvard resettlement expert Jonathan Jenness said the study's conclusions were "erroneous in every assertion" He also criticised the study for its lack of data, lack of objectivity, and a complete failure to consult the Chagossians themselves. It has been pointed out that a settled population lived there happily for generations, and that the Americans live there now without worrying unduly about natural disasters." [12]

10 June 2004: A secret Order in Council (a means casually used by the UK to reverse embarrassing decisions by the judiciary and turn illegality into legality) was issued that banned any person from setting foot in the Chagos. There was another setback:

"This blow was followed a few days later by the refusal of permission to appeal a High Court ruling from October 2003 which denied the Chagossians compensation." [13]

11 May 2006: The Order in Council of 2004 was overturned by the High Court, which restituted to the Chagossians their right of return acquired by the 2000 judgment. The UK Chagos Support Group recalls,

The islanders' solicitor Richard Gifford said: *'The British Government has been defeated in its attempt to abolish the right of abode of the islanders after first deporting them in secret 30 years ago…This is the fourth time in five years that Her Majesty's judges have deplored the treatment inflicted upon this fragile community."* [14]

2007: UK government defeated again in Court: The Chagossians fought against an appeal by the UK government against the latest decision of the High Court and once more they won.[15]

2008: Nevertheless, the government appealed in the House of Lords and the decision, against the islanders, was announced in 2008: this time the government had won by a 3-2 majority. The UK group comments:

"In short, it means that the highest court in the land has decided the 'Orders in Council' used secretly to renew the islanders' eviction in 2004 (after they had won the right to return four years earlier) were indeed legal, despite the High Court and Court of Appeal having said they were not. But the islanders haven't given up, and are taking their case to the European Court of Human Rights." [16]

2010: Mauritius accuses Britain of '*dishonesty*': At one point, Prime Minister Paul Bérenger threatened that Mauritius would leave the Commonwealth due to the violation of the country's sovereignty, and his successor, Dr. Navin Ramgoolam and the latter's minister for Foreign Affairs, Arvin Boolell, spoke of the '*dishonesty*' of the British. The *Guardian* reported on Bérenger's threat,

"The Mauritian deputy high commissioner, Haymandoyal Dilium, said there were a number of options under consideration, but leaving the Commonwealth was the only way Mauritius could take Britain to court.

"Mr Berenger said at the weekend: 'The Commonwealth is not the property of London. It is a democraticclub, and we will miss the annual summit which gives rise to important exchanges, but [on] other things like technical and educational assistance we can live without it.'" [17]

In 2010, Ramgoolam expressed the view that the British had been '*dishonest*'. He was also quoted in *The Guardian* in December of that year when he confirmed his strong reaction that the British had adopted a '*policy of deceit*'. [18] Deceit is synonymous with dishonesty according to the Thesaurus (English, United Kingdom). In fact, Mauritian Foreign Affairs Minister Arvin Boolell echoed Ramgoolam when he told *L'Express* that the British had been '*dishonest*' and '*hypocritical*'. [19]

- In the same month, Mauritius launched a legal action contesting Britain's creation of a Marine Protection Area around the Mauritian territoro of the Chagos Islands, in the wake of the Wikileaks revelation of documents indicating that the British was setting up the park to prevent any return of the Chagossians back to their islands.

How the French seized Tromelin from Mauritius

In the 1950s and 1960s, another part of Mauritian territory, historically recognised, like the Chagos, byinternational treaties, as a dependency of Mauritius, was occupied by France following a decision of the World Meteorological Organisation (WMO) to ask that country to take charge of a meteorological centre there, with the agreement of the British authorities which were administering Mauritius. The French landed for the first time since the British con-

---

12 *History, Recent developments*, <chagossupport.org.uk> Accessed 28 March 2012.
13 Ibid.
14 Ibid.
15 "*Exiled islanders win 40-year battle to return home as judges accuse UK of abuse of power,* by Julian Borger, diplomatic editor, *The Guardian,* Thursday 24 May 2007 https://www.theguardian.com/world/2007/may/24/politics.topstories3 Accessed 2.3.20
16 *History, Recent developments,* op cit.
17 The Guardian, *Mauritius may sue for Diego Garcia*, Ewen MacAskill, Diplomatic Editor, 7 July 2004.
18 *The US Embassy cables: Chagos Islands – Mauritius launches legal action against UK,* Guardian, 22 December 2010, cited in: Jon Lunn, *The Chagos Islanders*, House of Commons Library, International Affairs and Defence Section, SN/IA/4463, 10 June 2011.
19 In: *L'Express, Arvin Boolell: 'Nous condamnons avec force la malhonnêteté des Britanniques',* 3 December 2010.

quest in 1810 on Tromelin, a dependency of Mauritius where Mauritius sent ships to fetch guano - bird dejections - to fertilize its sugar cane fields. Guano increased cane yields and sugar production for several decades in Mauritius. The French seized Tromelin illegally, setting foot for the first time since they lost the island in 1810, in April 1954 from the ship Marius-Moutet to set up the meteorological station and never leaving the island. That the island was British is even understood by the French captain of the ship who is featured in a report in a well-known French magazine, '*Tout Savoir*',[20] and he even draws a map in the magazine report which, in addition, describes Tromelin as a '*foreign land*", meaning it was not a French island. The British colonial master of Mauritius had granted the WMO permission to set up a regional weather station. The author of this book was asked to submit a copy of this publication to the Prime Minister's office to be included, he was told, in a file that Prime Minister Sir Anerood Jugnauth was taking along with him as he headed a delegation to meet French President François Mitterand in Paris with whom he discussed the Tromelin conotroversy.

Back in 1976, following intense pressure by the main opposition party, the MMM, and public opinion like in the case of the Chagos, the Mauritian government of Sir Seewoosagur Ramgoolam, in a correspondence with the French embassy, claimed the island back from the French authorities for the first time since it was taken over in the 1950s. He went on to make a statement that was reported internationally.

"Mauritian Premier Sir Seewoosagur Ramboolam reaffirmed a claim to the French-owned Indian Ocean island of Tromelin in a speech to parliament yesterday." [21]

Subsequently, Mauritius did a research of ship log books and other proofs of continued use of Tromelin by Mauritius in the 19th and early 20th century, which established formal proof that Mauritius had exercised its sovereignty over the island, albeit in a relationship of a colony and its dependency under British law.

Tromelin was officially one of the dependencies of Mauritius included officially by the British government as Isle de Sable, another name by which it has been known for a long time. [22] Moreover, hydrographic charts of the British government portray Tromelin/Isle de Sable as part of the dependencies of Mauritius.

It is also worth recalling here the most important event in the history of this tiny island, an exiguous stretch of sand barely emerging above the surface of the ocean:

Tromelin, scene of one of the worst tragedies of this part of the Indian Ocean

The history of the island is quite short, but it was the theatre of one of the worst tragedies of the Indian Ocean islands' history. Tromelin was first reportedly discovered by a French navigator, Jean Marie Briand de la Feuillée, in 1722 and that was when it started to be known by the name of Isle de Sable. During the night of 31st July to 1st August 1761, the French ship Utile, leaving France with a crew of 142 and carrying 160 men, women and children as slaves from Madagascar to Mauritius, ran into the reefs of the island.

About 122 crew members, in majority European, and about 60 slaves survived whereas most of the slaves who were in the hold of the ship where they had been confined, perished. Two separate camps were set up, one for the Europeans and the other for the slaves, who were maintained in the servile state and barely had enough water on an island where the precious liquid was almost nowhere available except haphazardly, when some rain water had accumulated – a rare occurrence. Captain Lafargue lost his mind and was replaced by First Lieutenant Castellan.

The survivors, including the slaves, built a rudimentary ship which, leaving most of the slaves behind, managed to leave the island for Madagascar, then Bourbon and Isle de France. Castellan had, before departure, promised crew members and all the 60 slaves who had been left behind that he would come back to save them. He did plead with the authorities, but the Isle de France Governor Desforges-Boucher never acceded to his request to send him with a ship to rescue those people, who were, after, that completely ignored by the colonial administrators after Castellan went back to France. There was a lot of indignation for some time among French intellectuals after they learned what had happened.

France's conduct in this sad historical episode was utterly shameful and criminal. Later, attempts to reach the island to find out if there were survivors were not successful due to difficult landing conditions and it was only on 29 No-

---

20 *"En exclusivité mondiale. Notre envoyé accompagne des naufragés volontaires sur l'île des cyclones"*, in: **TOUT SAVOIR-Toute la vie du Monde par le texte et par l'Image** N°15 AOÛT 1954.
21 "Mauritius Reaffirms Claim to French Isle, The Washington Post, 27 October 1977, p. A12.
22 Dependencies of the Mauritius. Return of the Government of Mauritius laid before Parliament agreeable to an address to His Majesty's by the House of Commons and printed by order of the House, 27th February 1827, op cit. Page 641.

vember 1776, 15 years after the shipwreck, that the Chevalier de Tromelin on the ship La Dauphine landed on the island, finding only 7 women and one child, all from the slave population, who had survived. They were in attire made of bird feathers and had kept a fire alive during all those years on the island. All the survivors were freed, baptised into the Catholic faith, and the child survivor was christened Moïse. The most moving reconstruction of those tragic events has been carried out byIrene Frain, while other works have been based on recent research. [23]

The Franco-Mauritian controversy

The French claim the island on the basis of its discovery by La Feuillée and the fact that in the French language version of the Treaty of Paris that finalised the cession of Mauritius, Tromelin is not specifically mentioned but the words "Isle de France et ses dépendances nommément Rodrigues et les Séchelles." In the English version, the words are as follows: "especially Rodrigues and the Seychelles." But this play on words was not followed by the facts, where Britain exercised jurisdiction over the Tromelin from the time of the capitulation of Mauritius and only granting France the right to set up station there at the invitation of the World Meteorological Organisation, which the French did, as was reported even in the French media in the 1950s where it was clearly stated by special envoys to the island covering the event that the French were operating on foreign territory.

Nevertheless, arbitration by the Indian Ocean Commission (in French: Commission de l'Océan Indien, COI) has led to a decision in principle, on 3 December 1999, implemented on 7 June 2010, ensuring the comanagement of the island by France and Mauritius. Professor Oraison has suggested that there should be a further arrangement that would detach the Iles Eparses of the region (Glorieuses, Juan de Nova, Europa and Bassas da India) from the French Overseas Territories, an entity that includes French Antarctica, and group them with Tromelin under the supervision of UNESCO's World Heritage Committee. [24]

Tromelin has an Exclusive Economic Zone (EEZ) of 280,000 square kilometres. The island's weather station has been operated by France from 1954. In the meantime, whereas France had been claiming that Mauritius never used the island even in the face of evidence produced from the 1970s by researchers and the Mauritian government. The evidence made it clear that Mauritian ships carried guano as one of the main fertilisers that were used for agricultural activities in Mauritius during decades. The guano was collected on a massive scale in Tromelin and was instrumental in boosting sugar production in Mauritius. [25]

This appears to have been evidenced by the French 3rd archeological mission on the shipwreck of 1761 on Tromelin in 2010. A building dating after the final departure of the last eight victims of the shipwreck in 1776 has been discovered and tentatively attributed, pending further research, to Mauritians who were exploiting guano under licences delivered by the government in Mauritius. [26] The confirmation would demolish further an important pillar of the French claim based on the assertion that Mauritius never exercised its sovereignty over the island.

On the balance of facts, there is no doubt about the sovereignty of Mauritius over the island. Mauritius has been victim, once more, of the neocolonialism that scholars have amply described as the alternative sought and developed by the Western powers as the wave of decolonization and liberation movements swept the planet. [27] It appears that once more, the ecological pretext has been used to ward off the rights of sovereignty of Mauritius over yet another of the islands traditionally forming part of its national patrimony.

Tromelin: the Franco-Mauritian compromise:

In June 2010, the Tromelin issue was partially addressed when Mauritius, France agreed to jointly manage Tromelin, a Mauritian island occupied by the French after they were sent there by the World Meteorological Organisation to set up a meteorological station in 1954. Despite the fact that from the start the French formally acquiesced that they were going to a British Island (ceded by France together with Mauritius in 1810), in later years, they finally decided to occupy formally the island where Mauritius ships used previously to collect guano, deposits of bird droppings that had

---

23 "Irène Frain, Frain,Irène, Les Naufragés de l'île Tromelin, Paris, Michel Lafon, 2009; also: Guérout Max and Romon, Thomas, Esclaves oubliés de l'île Tromelin, Paris, CNRS Éditions, octobre 2010.
24 Oraison, André, "Plaidoyer pour l'inscription des îles Tromelin, Glorieuses, Juan de Nova, Europa et Bassas da India au Patrimoine mondial naturel de l'UNESCO. Prochaine étape logique et décisive : l'inscription des îles Éparses au «Patrimoine mondial naturel» de l'UNESCO, in: temoignages.re 10 March 2011.
25 Walter, A. op cit.
26 TAAF : la 3e mission archéologique du naufrage de « L'Utile » sur Tromelin en 1761, Lemonde.fr, 05 janvier 2011
27 Routledge, op cit.

accumulated over the centuries and constituted an excellent fertilizer that contributed to the rapid development of the Mauritius sugar industry from the 19th century.

Chapter 42

The march to independence resumes amidst controversy
MLP, CAM, IFB ask for reserved seats, PMSD for PR

During the 1965 Constitutional Conference at Lancaster House, in London, the pro-independence parties were opposing a demand by the Parti Mauricien Social Démocrate in favour of a referendum on the question of independence. A referendum, according Dr. S. Ramgoolam, would have considerably decreased the chances of the Labour Party and its allies to win independence. At the general elections, two years later, the Parti Mauricien lost, albeit winning 44 % of the national vote. Ramgoolam's statement to the 1983 Select Committee inquiring into the cession of the Chagos that his choice was only, according to him, between independence and a referendum (allusion to a threat brandished by the British) [1] was an attempt to show that a referendum could have been a risky gamble. It was, as the result was rather close percentage-wise, albeit the fact that the PMSD was under-represented in Parliament with 27 seats for 44% of the popular vote, against 43 seats for the Independence party with 54.66% of votes - a problem that will plague the opposition thereafter and remain unsolved as of 2017, when this book was published despite repeated demands by the MMM for correction by a dose of proportional representation with party lists submitted to the Electoral Commissioner for that purpose.

Yet, the result of the 1967 general election showed also that Ramgoolam was right in assessing that there was a large section of the population that could vote against independence in a referendum. With about 44% of the votes, or nearly half of Mauritius supporting the PMSD, it was clear that the anti-independence vote was multiethnic and not just composed of the votes of Creoles and Coloured as some politicians continue to suggest in their efforts to cultivate ethnic politics even in the 21st century. These minorities make up well less than 30% of the population and Labour had obviously support among them, though not as massive as from the 1930s to the 1950s, as Millien observed regarding '*ethnic*' voting trends.[2]

The argument about the British blackmail on the referendum issue was still out of context with regard to the fact that the entire Mauritian delegation at the talks accepted to link the Chagos question to matters of military security, as documentary evidence as shown (see the previous chapter). The security question had obviously nothing to do with the issue of national sovereignty on the Chagos archipelago as it had to do only with the post-independence arrangements with the UK on military cooperation, albeit without any link whatsover to be accepted by Mauritius with the question of sovereignty over the Chagos. The attitude of the entire all-party Mauritius delegation has been heavily blamed later for that accepting the link made by the UK between independence and sovereignty on the Chagos.

A big lie

Then there was the argument of the Mauritian leaders that they did not know there would be a military base but knew there would be only a communications station. Evidence clearly shows that the whole world, including the political leaders of Mauritius, knew that there would be an American military base in the Chagos and this was widely debated globally. They all lied in that respect.

Ramgoolam had, in fact, a choice other than caving in to the British exigencies: he could choose the path of the freedom fighters of India, Africa and other colonies, that is, just as he had his party take to the streets to protest against the Banwell report, a lesser issue, organise national resistance. He did not. British official documents indicate London assessed him as an *"old man in a hurry,"* as Sookhoo points out (see previous chapter).

He could have asked for complete independence, with all Mauritian dependencies included, and not the partial independence that was obtained, excluding one of the most precious parts of the Mauritian national heritage. One way to start putting up resistance would have been to walk out of the constitutional conference. He did not.

He was not, though, the only one responsible for such a serious absence of will to struggle for complete indepen

---
1 1983 Select Committee on Chagos, op cit; see also: Oraison, A., Les avatars du B.I.O.T., op cit.
2 See The triumph of ethnic politics in Chapter 40 where Millien provides some statistical estimates of 'ethnic' voting patterns.

dence. Not a single one of the leaders who were at the table have any sacrosanct immunity to criticism of the way they acted in the name of the people of Mauritius, unless some people believe that history has to be censored or not even taught to the youth of the nation. The other leaders of the independence parties and the anti-independence leaders had, like Ramgoolam, the same duty of protection of the national territorial integrity. They could have all joined their efforts to preserve national interests in alerting the international community, which, they well knew, commanded a majority in the General Assembly of the United Nations. The objective would have been to muster support against the multiple violations of international law by the UK and the US by the detachment of the islands and the massive depopulation that was contemplated.

It is clear that nothing of the sort happened, nor was any protest even contemplated by the Mauritian political parties. They paid this omission very dearly after independence, because neocolonialism and the Chagos letdown were among the main reasons that in the 1970s, young Mauritians of all ethnic groups rallied around a new political party, the MMM, which, in the early stages of its history, went to great lengths to denounce the 'neo-colonial' setup in which Mauritius gained its independence. It is a historical fact that the MMM initiated the first political campaigns to claim the lost islands of Chagtos and Tromelin in the 1970s, especially through its newspaper *Le Militant* and its various electoral manifestos and other published documents and newspaper articles. The Labour Party finally joined the move and, as of the 21st century, the Labour government, then, from 2014, the MSM government and the MMM opposition were presenting to the rest of the world a united front on matters of national sovereignty. Today, in 2017, the nation is unanimously claiming back the Chagos Archipelago.

Back in the 1980s, as the MMM-PSM alliance won the 1982 general election, it initiated the Parliamentary Select Committee inquiry that shed a new light on the whole affair. Subsequently, through successive prime ministers, to raise the issues of illegality of the cession and of the mass deportation of Chagossians. Mauritius, under Sir Anerood Jugnauth's prime ministership, has also reinforced, together with the MMM, its Constitution as written by the British and approved by the first Mauritian government at independence. SAJ and Paul Bérenger initiated a much needed and justified amendment that has ensured the inclusion, into the Constitution of Mauritius, of both the Chagos Archipelago and Tromelin in Chapter XI, Section 111, as follows:

"'Mauritius' includes –

(a) the Islands of Mauritius, Rodrigues, Agalega, Tromelin, Cargados Carajos and the Chagos Archipelago, including Diego Garcia and any other island comprised in the State of Mauritius;

(b) the territorial sea and the air space above the territorial sea and the islands specified in paragraph (a);

(c) the continental shelf; and

(d) such places or areas as may be designated by regulations made by the Prime Minister, rights over which are or may become exercisable by Mauritius."

Former Supervising Officer at the Ministry for Foreign Affairs, Mauritius, commented that *"it was only in 1982 that the Constitution was amended to incorporate the Chagos Archipelago, including Diego Garcia in the State of Mauritius."* [1]

Back home, to ethnic politics

The independence issue was thickly clouded, during the constitutional talks, by the cession of the Chagos, which was widely reported in the local media. What happened was that once back in Mauritius, the entire political establishment just went back to their day-to-day business of ethnic politics. There developed across the country a charged atmosphere that would eventually cause the blood bath that happened three years later in January 1968, in addition the deaths caused by sporadic communal strife from 1965.

The communal tension was quite disquieting for several members of the British Parliament, as the British government still ruled the country and what happened at Westminster was crucial to the future of Mauritius. Generally speaking, the mood there was to give independence to Mauritius within the Commonwealth together with a defence agreement linking the two countries. Mauritius enjoyed considerable popularity among the members of the Commons and the Lords, especially from the British Labour Party members of Parliament who, at times, blasted Duval.

MP Russell Johnston, on 27 May 1965, stated, during debates on disturbances occurring in Mauritius,

"May I draw my right hon. Friend's attention to the fact that there is no such party as the Social Democrat Party in Mauritius, that Mr.

[1] *Chagos Strategy,* by Krish Ponnusamy, in L'Expess, 12 June 2010.

Duval, the self-styled leader, only masquerades as leader." [1]

On 1st June of the same year, MP James Johnson, also a strong supporter of Mauritius and of the Mauritius Labour Party, in a lengthy intervention, attacked Duval and attributed to his actions the bloody incidents that occurred in the island necessitating the sending of British troops to restore order. [2] Reacting to this virulent frontal attack on Duval, Conservative Party MP Nigel Fisher stated, even though he did not see that Mauritius could be integrated to the UK as requested by the PMSD,

"(…) the hon. Gentleman's strictures upon Mr. Duval were very strong and somewat unfair. This gentleman, who is the Minister of Housing in Mauritius, represents very genuine fears there…" [3]

The incidents that were being discussed were quite serious and the situation was quite explosive in Mauritius. The speeches of Koenig and Duval inciting the minority communities, including Indo-Mauritian minorities like the Muslims and Hindu minorities like the Tamils, to seek sectarian representation, added to caste dissensions that led to the migration of a number of Hindus to the PMSD. The Labour Party was being elbowed into a situation where its problems in promoting the cause for independence were compounded with retaliation by some of its increasingly radical partisans who, often in defiance of Ramgoolam's well known conciliatory approach to the minorities, were bent on responding to PMSD's inacceptable provocations by engaging in open conflict, verbal and physical.

The PMSD under Duval's actions was engaged in a dangerous game of populist politics that Jules Koenig's biographer denounces, confirming rumours that there were, in fact, serious divergences between Duval and Jules Koenig on the methods of protest. [4] Duval's populist tactics of moving huge, angry crowds into the streets on the basis of ethnic politics could only be organised, obviously, with strong financial support. Those private sector financiers seemed to hold sway over the entire community of sugar sector leaders, albeit the fact that a few of these, like Emile Series, Amédée Maingard, Maurice Paturau and Guy Sauzier had friendly links with Ramgoolam who, later, knighted most of them. In the House of Commons, speaking about Duval's activities in relation to the racial clashes in Mauritius, Labour MPsJames Johnson commented,

"Over the past months allegations have been made, with some evidence, about his demagogic activities, on a platform leading to violence. Under the banner of the Parti Mauricien, by means of speeches splitting and dividing the people, he has done much damage." [5]

In spite of the disturbances in Mauritius, the talks on the future Constitution of Mauritius and the electoral system in September 1965 in London between the British government and the multi-party Mauritian delegation resulted in a report published on 21 October 1965. [6] The official summary was presented to the House of Commons a week later. One of the important features of it is that separate electoral rolls for the different communities had been rejected:

Summary of the constitutional proposals after the London talks (sub-titles by author):Human rights, Judicature, Ombudsman

"The outline constitutional scheme includes provisions for the preservation of Human Rights; for securing the continued impartiality of the judicial system and the Commissions concerned with the Public Service, the Legal and Judicial Service and the Police; and for dealing with prosecutions and the exercise of the prerogative of mercy. For the first time in such a constitution provision is made for an Ombudsman.

Electoral system: 'no communal rolls', a Commission appointed

"A Commission will be appointed to make recommendations on:
1. (i) the electoral system, and the method of allocating seats in the Legislature, most appropriate for Mauritius; and
2. (iii) the boundaries of electoral constituencies.

'The Commission will be guided by the following principles:—
1. (a) The system should be based primarily on multi-member constituencies.
2. (b) Voters should be registered on a common roll; there should be no communal electoral rolls.
3. (c) The system should give the main sections of the population an opportunity of securing fair representation of their interests if necessary by the reservation of seats.
4. (d) No encouragement should be afforded to the multiplication of small parties.
5. (e) There should be no provision for the nomination of members to seats in the Legislature.

---
1 Hansard, *Incidents*, HC 27 May 1965.
2 *Commonwealth And Colonial Affairs*, HC Deb 01 June 1965 vol 713 cc1549-652
3 Ibid.
4 *Jules Koenig:Une vie pour la justice*, op cit.
5 *Common Commonwealth And Colonial Affairs*, HC Deb 01 June 1965 vol 713 cc1549-652.
6 *UK Parliament, Cmmd. Paper 2797*, 21 October 1965.

1. *(f) Provision should be made for the representation of Rodrigues.*

'When the electoral Commission has reported, a date will be fixed for a general election under the new system, after which a new Government will be formed. In consultation with this Government, Her Majesty's Government will be prepared to fix a date and take the necessary steps to declare Mauritius independent, after a period of six months full internal self-government, if a resolution asking for this is passed by a simple majority of the new Assembly. Her Majesty's Government would expect that these processes could be completed before the end of 1966.

All parties agree on Anglo-Mauritian defence agreement

'In the course of the Conference, it became clear that all parties wanted Mauritius to continue her collaboration with Britain in matters of defence; and Her Majesty's Government agreed that they would be willing in principle to negotiate with the Mauritius Government, before independence, the terms of a defence agreement which would be signed and come into effect immediately after independence.

"Her Majesty's Government envisage that such an agreement might provide that, in the event of an external threat to either country, the two governments would consult together to decide what action was necessary for mutual defence. There would also be joint consultation on any request from the Mauritius Government in the event of a threat to the internal security of Mauritius. Such an agreement would contain provisions under which on the one hand the British Government would undertake to assist in the provision of training for, and the secondment of trained personnel to, the Mauritius Police and Security forces; and on the other hand, the Mauritius Government would agree to the continued enjoyment by Britain of existing rights and facilities in H.M.S. "Mauritius" and at Plaisance Airfield."

The Parti Mauricien had been asking for separate electoral registers for the various minorities as a guarantee they would be adequately represented in Parliament. As U. Bissoondoyal recalls, the CAM was also in favour of those separate lists, but Sookdeo Bissoondoyal, the leader of the IFB provided support to his long time adversary Ramgoolam by using the magnificent example of an IFB Muslim candidate elected in a constituency with a large Hindu majority. This was recalled in ***L'Express*** in a tribute to the IFB leader:

"At the Constitutional Conference held in London in 1965 the example of the election of the IFB candidate Abdool Wahab Foondun in a predominantly Hindu constituency was used to prevent the imposition of separate communal electoral rolls in Mauritius. At the conclusion of the Conference Dr K.Hazareesingh went to congratulate Dr Ramgoolam. But Dr Ramgoolam, showing his magnanimity at that moment in history, asked him to congratulate Sookdeo instead, adding: "He deserves a statue in gold for his contribution". [1]

At one stage, it could have been feared that Labour, under pressure, would accept separate lists for Muslims and Sino-Mauritians to save its alliance with the CAM, but the leader of that party, Sir Abdool Razack Mohamed stayed in the coalition with Labour, having obtained an important concession in terms of the recommendation in favour for reservation of seats (see summary of 1965 Constitutional Conference report above). That principle of reservation of seats was introduced very early in the Indian Constitution as pointed out below:

"Phase one was that of constitution-making after the achievement of independence in 1947. In India, caste-based reservations were introduced under the 9th Schedule (articles 330 and 331)5 of the Indian Constitution in the first instance for 50 years, but under the 62nd Amendment Act of 1989 were extended for another 40 years, demonstrating the political sensitivity of the removal of reservations once they have been established." [2]

A footnote to the article cited above states,

"Article 331 stipulated a reservation of seats for the Anglo-Indian community for two years if the president thought it to be under-represented in Parliament." [3]

It was not difficult for the British to have the principle of the reservation of seats introduced in the report based on the solution found in India in an even more complex multiethnic context than in Mauritius. Greenwood, the Secretary of State for the Colonies, officially announced the composition of the electoral commission as per the report of the Constitutional Conference on 1st December 1965 in a statement to the House of Commons:

"I am glad to report that Sir Harold Banwell has accepted my invitation to be Chairman and Professor Colin Leys and Mr. T. G. Randall, C.B.E., have agreed to be members of the Mauritius Electoral Commission. The Commission will leave for Mauritius on 2nd January." [4]

The Banwell Report: the demands of the political parties

The report sums up the demands of the respective parties as follows (author's own sub-titles):

Mauritius Labour Party for 'reservation of seats' in some constituencies

"The M.L.P. advocated the formation of twenty constituencies by grouping the present 40-single-member constituencies in pairs, each constituency to return four members by simple majority voting and all electors being obliged to cast all the four votes to which they were entitled,

---

[1] *SookdeoBissoondoyal (1908-1977). The long battle for dignity and justice*, in L'Express, 26 September 2008.
[2] Rai, Shirin M., *Reserved seats in India:A Regional Perspective*, at: idea.int/publications.
[3] Ibid.
[4] *Electoral Commission (Membership)*, HC Deb 01 December 1965 vol 721 c215W 215W.

failing which their ballot paper would be void. Rodrigues would form an additional constituency returning two members. As a temporary measure to allay the anxieties of the two communities (Muslim and Chinese) who, by reason of their dispersion over the island had in their view little or no hope of returning members by the use of their own votes in the ordinary process of election, they advocated the reservation of seats in a number of constituencies for which only candidates drawn from those communities would be eligible to compete, coupled with a prohibition against members of those communities from standing as candidates in any constituencies.

P.M.S.D.: Proportional representation plus compulsory multiethnic lists of candidates

"*The P.M.S.D. recommended that the number of members of the Legislative Assembly should be forty for Mauritius and two for Rodrigues, and emphasised the burden on the economy of any material increase above this figure. They favoured the party-list system of proportional representation with two constituencies, one for Mauritius and one for Rodrigues, members being declared elected from each party's list in proportion of votes cast, but expressed themselves as willing to consider other systems, provided that proportionality was preserved and that the number of seats was not so high as to create an unreasonable financial burden. They were opposed to the reservation of seats to any community, because they held that under the system which they advocated parties would be obliged to include in their lists candidates from all communities if they were to have any hope of attracting votes from them all.*

I.F.B.: 'Temporary' reservation of seats for Muslims and Chinese

"*The I.F.B. proposed thirteen five-member constituencies with election by simple majority, (but without the obligation on the elector to cast all five votes), and a separate constituency for Rodrigues returning one member. They favoured, as a temporary measure, the reservation of seats for the Muslim and Chinese communities. They were also concerned that staff concerned with the registration of electors and the conduct of elections should be drawn from more than one community in order to ensure impartiality, and that any changes proposed in the rules governing registration, the revision of electoral rolls, and the sitting of polling stations should be the subject of consultation with the leaders of political parties before final decisions were taken.*"

C.A.M.: Reservation of seats plus a minimum of 13 Muslims in a Parliament of 80 MPs

"*The proposals submitted to us by the M.C.A. were essentially similar to the M.L.P. but they laid stress on the reservation of seats and urged that the specific mention of reservation in our terms of reference was a clear pointer to the way in which the absence of Muslim representation, through the termination of the procedure of nomination, should be met. They asked that a minimum of 13 seats in a house of 80 representatives should be reserved for Muslim candidates.*"[1]

The core of the demands by the Mauritian political parties focused on ethnic representation. Essentially, the PMSD demanded proportional representation and mandatory multiethnic lists of candidates while Labour, CAM and IFB requested the 'reservation of seats' system. All four parties were addressing, in this way, the question of representation of the minority communities.

The Banwell Report: main recommendations

Excerpts of the Banwell recommendations: [2]

First-past-the-post: We recommend that the method of allocating seats should remain as at present; in three-member constituencies, therefore, the three candidates who receive the largest numbers of votes should be declared elected. We also recommend however, that each voter should be required to cast all 3 of his votes, one for each seat to be filled.

The following part of the report, though, was going to be the most controversial:

The variable corrective

"*We recommend that if any party receives more than 25 per cent of the total votes cast at a general election, but secures less than 25 per cent of the seats in the Assembly; and if, after the operation of the "constant corrective", it still does not have 25 per cent of the seats, then sufficient further seats should be allocated to that party to bring its share of the total number of seats in the Assembly up to the nearest whole number exceeding 25 per cent; the total number of seats being, of course, the total which will result from the requisite addition of seats under this form of corrective. Each of these additional seats would be allocated in turn to the 'best loser' (i.e. the candidate who received the largest number of votes) among the party's remaining defeated candidates, regardless of community. This corrective might be described as a "variable corrective". In other words any party which gains more than 25 per cent of the total votes cast in an election should be assured that no change in the entrenched provisions of the Constitution can be made without its assent. If the "variable correction" comes into operation it will cause an increase in the total size of the Assembly for the life of that Assembly. In practice we do not think that it is likely that this provision would often operate, or involve more than a few seats.*"

The constant corrective:

The commission then addressed the "*question of inducements to minority parties to seek intercommunal support, the representation of the smaller communities, and safeguards against severe under-representation*" with another corrective mechanism:

---

[1] Mauritius Legislative Assembly, *Report of the Banwell Commission on the Electoral System with Despatch from the Secretary of State, Session Paper* No. 5 of 1966.
[2] Ibid.

"In order to deal with the first two of these questions, we recommend that there should be a "constant corrective" consisting of further seats in the Assembly... the "constant corrective" does not, and in our view should not, promise complete proportionality. Any party which seeks to establish itself as a majority party cannot rely on the corrective to enable it to achieve this aim."

Labour/CAM/IFB' demands for reserved seats for communities rejected

"We are sure that the reservation of seats for any specific community is bad in itself and should if possible be avoided; the electoral system should encourage Muslims and Chinese voters to get what representation they can by the normal process of politics, however much this may require supplementing by other means... a prohibition on Muslims or Chinese from standing in constituencies in which seats were not reserved would be repugnant to the political traditions of Mauritius, and might also exclude good potential candidates of all parties who preferred to stand in such constituencies."

The Banwell Report: protests from 3 out of the 4 political parties

The report was accepted *'in full'* by the Secretary of State for the Colonies Fred Lee in a despatch dated 28 may 1966 accompanying the document addressed to Mauritius Governor Sir John Shaw Rennie. In the House of Commons, he stated, after the protests against the report within the coalition government of all parties, especially regarding proportional representation:

"The hon. Members will have seen from the dispatch printed in the White Paper (Colonial No. 362) that I reached the conclusion that the Commission's recommendations were fair and satisfactory in the circumstances of Mauritius and that I accepted them in full. Publication of the Report in Mauritius on 31st May resulted in immediate protests from the three parties forming the Government. The Premier has now sent me a memorandum giving the reasons of these parties for opposing the Commission's recommendations and asking me to call a fresh Conference to discuss the points at issue and I am giving this careful consideration." [1]

The reaction to the report was, in fact, motivated by the Labour Party's belief that formula of proportional representation proposed as the *'variable corrective'* formula would weaken its already receding electorate as per the trend in results noted after the 1959 general elections and the increasing perception that Labour was essentially a Hindu party, which was entertained among the population by the presence of a strong PMSD and a rising CAM, both enshrined as representatives of the minority communities. This explains Labour's support for the system of reservation of seats to reassure CAM. Labour then organised massive political rallies to oppose the proportional system and advocated another constitutional conference.

John Stonehouse in Mauritius: Proportional representation scrapped

On 23 June 1966, Secretary of State for the Colonies Frederick (Fred) Lee announced in the House of Commons that he had decided to send to Mauritius his assistant, Under Secretary of State John Stoneouse. The latter, he explained, **"should visit Mauritius to examine on the spot the various points raised and views expressed in the Mauritius Legislative Assembly and report to me on their implications."** [2]

On 30 June, Labour MP James Johnson spoke ironically of the PMSD:

"Is it not a fact that the Mauritius Parliament have formed a coalition Government since the election, of the Labour Party, the Muslim Party and the Independence bloc, who are deeply shocked by the findings of the Commission; further, that the only party in opposition, the Parti Mauricien, which is usually termed the "capitalist bourgeoisie", is delighted? Would my right hon. Friend consider convening a conference in London to look at the whole matter?" [3]

John Stonehouse carried out his mission with remarkable celerity. He was able to report to Lee, from Mauritius, within a short time and the latter approved promptly "*variations*" proposed by his assistant. Lee reported to the House of Commons as follows, in reply to further questioning about the post-Banwell Report situation and again he reaffirmed that he had approved the Banwell Report and that the changes focussed on the '*correctives*.' Those changes instituted the Best Loser System. Excerpts of Lee's statement:

"(...) After full discussion with the Mauritius Premier, Sir Seewoosagur Ramgoolam, his Ministerial colleagues and with leaders and members of the Opposition in Mauritius, full agreement was reached on certain variations of the recommendations of the Banwell Report which would make it generally acceptable. I immediately informed Mr. Stonehouse that I was willing to accept these variations and he announced this before leaving Mauritius on Monday last, 4th July.

"(...) In brief, whilst the scheme proposed by the Commission for constituency elections is to be retained in full, changes have been made in the "correctives" recommended by the Commission. In place of these, eight Specially Elected Members will be returned from amongst unsuccessful candidates who have made the best showing in the election. The first four of these seats will go, irrespective of party, to the

---

1 Ibid.
2 ***Banwell Report.*** HC Deb 23 June 1966 vol 730 c120W 120W.
3 ***Banwell Report,*** HC Deb 30 June 1966 vol 730 cc2162-3

'best losers' of whichever communities in the island are underrepresented in the Legislative Assembly after the constituency elections. The remaining four seats will be allocated on the basis of both party and community.

"Only two other important changes are to be made in the Banwell recommendations. Party alliances, as well as parties, will be permitted to qualify for the 'best loser' seats (the Commission had proposed that only individual parties should be permitted to qualify for their recommended corrective seats); and the Commission's recommendation that a party should secure certain minimum results in the constituency elections in order to qualify for certain of the proposed corrective seats will be dropped and no corresponding provision will be made in relation to the "best loser" seats.

"The general effect of the electoral system now accepted by all parties in Mauritius will be that, as a result of the allocation of theeight "best loser" seats, all communities will be better able to obtain a fair share of the seats in the Legislative Assembly in accordance with their strength in the population."

Labour rightly claimed victory as, in fact, PR was scrapped from the report, save the non-controversial (in those days) BLS which was reinforced by adding three additional members to the proposed five in the Banwell Report. The report was adopted. The future Constitution of Mauritius having been determined, the entire nation focused on the upcoming general elections where the PMSD hoped to stop the march of the country towards independence and persisted in its attempt to convince both the Mauritian population and the British authorities in London that Mauritius should be integrated to Britain. This proposal attracted not just the minorities, but a good number of Hindus, probably because many of them contemplated immigration to the UK and were settling there attracted, in those years, by the training and job offers, more particularly in the field of nursing.

As a matter of fact, official figures tabled by Secretary of State Greenwood in the House of Commons in December 1965, revealed that on an estimated Mauritian population of 751,000, there were 5,240 Mauritians migrating overseas, and out of this figure, 3,550 left for the UK and only 502 left for Australia as of December 1965. [1] The number of migrants to Australia as well as to the UK would increase in the ensuing years. The population in 1965 had doubled in just 60 years (1905-1965) and the very serious problem of overpopulation and unemployment as pointed out in the Titmuss Report (op cit) explained in great part the widespread poverty that prevailed in those days in an island that was still quite under-developed. Emigration was viewed even by government, both as an escape from the difficult socio-economic context and a solution to overpopulation.

Hindu candidates who stood against independence

Meanwhile, the Parti Mauricien had undergone an important metamorphosis. From a party dedicated to fighting for the rights of minorities, it transformed itself into a *"national party"* appealing to the Hindus to join its ranks with the slogan *"Hindu, my brother."* A number of Hindus, who accepted the liberal economic model of the PMSD, and who came especially but not necessarily from the minority subgroups of that community, joined the PMSD as future candidates or followers. The party then seemed to be in a position, particularly because of the rapidly rising popularity of Gaëtan Duval, the deputy-leader, to challenge seriously the Labour Party for the first time at general elections.

Moreover, as from 1964, the party had also changed its name into Parti Mauricien Social-Democrate (PMSD) to showcase political in lieu of racial ideology as its main driving force. On November 14, 1966, Koenig finally resigned to hand over the leadership to Gaëtan Duval, who was only 36 years old, and whose popularity was then at its highest point in his career. According to Koenig's biography, the transitiondid not happen smoothly. [2]

Duval forged links with the Hindu community with consumed skill and obtained an impressive number of Hindus as PMSD candidates against independence in 1967: Narainduth Sookoo, B. Dusowuth, M. Jeeraz, A. Bhujun, S. Chetty, K. Bablee, S. Nandoo, H. Ramchurn, J. Poonith, S. Ramkissoon, S. Ramen, J. Jhurry, H. Gungah, R. Dookhun, M. Jootun, C. Lobin, J. Seegobin, D. Lalji. Most of them stood in rural constituencies and obtained honourable scores, from around one third of the votes to nearly one half in some cases. 40 years after the 1967 general elections where he stood as candidate against independence, Jodun Poonith said, in a newspaper interview, that he did not regret it because it was an *'ideological'* battle between PMSD and Labour and not one based on ethnicity. [3]It was obvious he had, like thousands of other members of his community, apprehensions as to the future of the country due to the appalling economic conditions of those days. Anyway, emigration from the 19th century to the

---

1 *Mauritian migrants who left the colony permanently during the last 10 years (from year 1955 to year 1965) Population*, HC Deb 09 December 1965 vol 722 cc144-5W.
2 *Une vie pour la justice*, op cit.
3 *Les élections de 1967. Plus une bataille idéologique qu'une lutte des ethnies,* in *Week-End* 5 August 2007.

1960s and 1970s, to Australia and other countries had been mainly prompted by economic distress, albeit the fact that the PMSD used also the ethnic argument of '*Hindu hegemony*' to stimulate the immigration of members of the Coloured community and a number of Creoles to Australia. It was unfortunate was that Australia was implementing an immigration policy officially called "*Keep Australia White*" and refusing prospective immigrants of Indian descent. That racist policy, which was obviously not the doing of the PMSD, was only scrapped in the 1970s after the Australian Labour Party rose to power.

Another Hindu candidate against independence, Narainduth Sookhoo, was one of those members of his community who were disillusioned with what he saw as sectarianism literally invading the Labour Party establishment. He wrote on November 3, 1966:

"After the death of Anquetil, Rozemont, Seeneevassen, the Labour Party became the breeding ground of communalism, casteism, opportunism and all sorts of social and political ills." [1]

That was a quite severe comment. The truth is that all the main parties in Mauritius have caved in to the pressure of sectarian lobbying. As one form of sectarianism invariably and logically breeds another and extends to ethnic sub-groups like castes, ethnic politics sinks its roots deeper in the political arena. Invariably, this leads to cronyism and nepotism, worse, power ultimately becomes a family affair. K. Hazareesingh, who was the intellectual mentor of the Ramgoolam group since the 1930s, has stressed the rise of ethnic consciousness in politics, described as '*solidarité communautaire*' in his ***Histoire des Indiens à l'île Maurice***, [2] but it is not only the community of Indian origin that this applies to. The other ethnic groups and sub-groups living in an atmosphere of vigorous ethnic politics the Mauritian way, are not immune.

Supreme Court quashes Legislature's legality; royal intervention prevents crisis

The country seemed to be heading straight to the polls when, arguing an extremely difficult economic situation caused by a drop in sugar prices, the government tried to choose a later date than expected. The PMSD counterattacked to force early elections by contesting the legality of the Legislative Council in the Supreme Court. A petition was presented by Clement Roussety claiming that Rodrigues had been left out of the constitutional developments including universal suffrage, as the island had no right to choose its representatives to the Council.

The Supreme Court accepted the petition on May 30, 1967, a decision which meant that the Council had not been legally constituted at the general elections of 1959 and 1963. But an Order in Council issued by the Queen in extremis validated the constitution of the Legislative Council at the two previous general elections, so that the judgement in favour of Roussety had no effect. The information was announced to the House of Commons by the Secretary of State for the Colonies, Fred Lee:

"An Order in Council entitled the Mauritius (Former Legislative Council) Order, 1966, has been made today providing that the fact that the forty electoral districts established for the purposes of the 1958 Constitution of Mauritius were situated wholly in the island of Mauritius shall not be held to have affected the validity of the elections and the Legislative Councils under that Constitution or anything done by those Councils or their Members.

"It was never the intention that the island of Rodrigues and the other dependencies of Mauritius should be included in the electoral districts established under the 1958 Constitution, nor have they in fact been included in the electoral districts established under the present Constitution granted in 1964. This Order prevents the 1958 Constitution from being 371W construed in a contrary sense. The new Constitution for Mauritius made today provides for elections to be held for Rodrigues as well as in the island of Mauritius." [3]

The PMSD announced the imminent resignation of its members from the Legislative Council at a meeting at the Champ de Mars on April 24, 1967. The next day, the party's legislators walked behind Koenig as the party's sympathisers applauded in the streets of Port-Louis, taking their letters of resignation to Government House, which was heavily guarded because of the prevailing political tension. Such demonstrations considerably helped the PMSD reduce the lead which the Labour Party had taken on the Ralliernent Mauricien and then the Parti Mauricien at previous general elections.

Tension rises, date of general elections fixed

With huge crowds flocking, week after week, at rallies organised by the PMSD and the pro-independence parties, the political tension became unbearable until the general elections were fixed for August 7. In the House of Com

---
[1] *Le Mauricien*, 3 November 1966.
[2] Op cit.
[3] *Legislative Assembly (Elections)*, HC Deb 21 December 1966 vol 738 cc370-1W 370W.

mons, it was announced, as the PMSD had requested, that foreign observers would monitor the elections. The Secretary for Commonwealth Affairs, Mrs. Hart, stated:

"The General Election will be held on 7th August. Mr. Maurice Abela of Malta has agreed to be Chairman of the independent team of observers and Mr. A. N. Kashyap of India and Mr. Charles Ross of Canada have agreed to serve as members. All were members of the previous team who observed the registration of electors.

"I also hope to appoint a fourth Commonwealth member to the team. His name will be announced later.

"In addition, the Government has decided that in view of the crucial nature of the coming Election and the responsibilities of Parliament for the territory, it will be valuable to add to the team two Members of this House. This decision has been conveyed to the Governor, and my hon. Friend the Member for Wandsworth, Central (Dr. David Kerr) and the hon. Member for Antrim, North (Mr. Henry Clark) have agreed to serve as members of the team." [1]

The PMSD was supported, in its opposition to independence, by a number of newspapers of which *l.e Cernéen* and *Le Mauricien* were the main ones, while *Advance* and *L'Express* were the biggest papers supporting independence.

A new radical Hindu party was formed, the ***All-Mauritius Hindu Congress***. Its members comprised Anerood Jugnauth, who had defeated the political veteran Anauth Beejadhur to the surprise of the whole country, at the 1963 general elections in the electoral district of Rivière du Rempart.

On June 7, 1966, during a sitting of the Legislative Council, an incident had occurred during which the PMSD leader had alleged that his supporters had voted for Bissoondoyal, Jugnauth and Padaruth, IFB candidates in 1963. Bissoondoyal and Jugnauth denied strongly on June 10, Anerood Jugnauth stating that despite the fact that he was a member of the Hindu Congress, Duval had asked him to join the PMSD, which he refused for "***ideological***" reasons, and that the same Duval had even told him he should not have opposed A. Beejadhur in Rivière du Rempart as the latter was a "***nice man.***" Jugnauth explained, on June 10, 1966, that his adhesion to the Hindu Congress was motivated by the fact that he perceived the PMSD as a conservative party which was encouraging communalism against the Hindu community. Otherwise, he said, *"the Congress would never have come into being."* [2]

Victory of the pro-independence coalition Labour/CAM/IFB

The electoral campaign was tense. The pro-independence parties, grouped under the banner of the Independence Party, won 54.13 per cent of the votes and 39 seats out of a total of 62 seats in direct elections. The PMSD obtained 43.99 per cent of the votes and 23 seats, prior to the nomination of the Best Losers.

The defeat of Jules Koenig at La Caverne/Phoenix and that of Razack Mohamed in Port-Louis Maritime/Port-Louis East, two adversaries who had once been under the same political banner at the Union Mauricienne and the Ralliement Mauricien, stunned political observers. But Mohamed returned to Parliament with a Best Loser Seat. Koenig died nine months later, deeply regretted by friends and adversaries.

Foreign observers: elections were not so ethnic in character

It was obvious that both sides of the electoral divide were multiethnic. In fact, the foreign observers, despite the tension that prevailed and the communal riots that had occurred in the 1960s, both sides received a largely multiethnic support and this impressed the foreign electoral observers. One of them, British MP Henry Clark, speaking to the House of Commons during discussions on the Mauritius Independence Bill, stated that,

1 *Mauritius (General Election)*, HC Deb 18 July 1967, vol. 750 c217W 217W.
2 *Le Mauricien*, June 1966.

Cover photo (left) of a widely circulated and respected French monthly periodical, dated 15 August1954, referred to in this chapter, containing a 'world exclusive' exclusive report of a trip to Tromelin of a French government team to Tromelin. The report contains an article of the journalist which features government-sourced information that the team sent officially by Paris was aware of going to work on a 'foreign territory', that is not belonging to France - in this case, Britain. The cover is a painted colour image of the landing of the French government team landing in Tromelin Island from the French ship 'Marius-Moutet' in 1954. This is among substantial evidence (official documents) that have forced France to propose a compromise that Mauritius shares management of the island. Mauritius accepted to sign a proposed arrangement of co-management of the island with France. In 2017, France had abstained to put the signed agreement into practice, while Mauritius has continued to claim that French occupation is illegal in international law.

"(…) whatever may be said about the percentages of voters, it cannot be disputed that the election was well and truly won by the present Government. The really refreshing fact about it was that, for the first time in the history of Mauritius, people began to some extent to vote away from race and religious affiliations."

From this viewpoint, the PMSD Hindu candidate Jodun Poonith [3] was right in that the dividing line was more related to ideology rather than being a purely ethnic confrontation. This is not to say that the ethnic element was not entirely absent, but it was not a purely and entirely racial vote. The question remains, though, as to whether the racial riots of January 1968, six months after the elections and three months prior to independence, was caused by the electoral campaign having occurred in a tense atmosphere due to campaigning on ethnic lines.

Why do a large number of voters refuse to respond, even to this day, to such campaigns and what is the percentage who do so, the fact being that the divide continues to be 50:50 as in 1967 and the political establishment still practises ethnic politics, even to a larger extent? Research is needed on this resistance to the ethnic vote.

The January 1968 racial riots

It has been officially stated by the Secretary of State for Commonwealth Affairs, Thomson, in the House of Commons that, gang warfare rather than politics, burst into full scale inter-ethnic riots between Creoles and Muslims in January 1968, just three months ahead of independence which was due to be celebrated on 12 March 1968. Nevertheless, later on, he did not exclude political causes.

Thomson, replying to parliamentary questions on January 23, refuted allegations that the origin of the disturbances was political (allegedly PMSD's reneging on an engagement to appoint a Muslim mayor in Port Louis). He stated,

"I would content myself with quoting to the House the explanation that the Governor gave to the people of Mauritius in his broadcast on Sunday evening. He said: I do not want to go too deeply into the causes of this violence at this stage. He said that there was nothing at all to suggest that this was politically inspired and motivated and added: It appears to have its roots in gang rivalry." [4]

The economic situation, which was extremely difficult in those days with widespread unemployment (as revealed in official reports and highlighted in the House Commons during debates on Mauritius) must have contributed also to a social atmosphere that made it easy for violence to flare up. British MP Wall actually hinted at that during question time in the House of Commons:

"Is it not a fact that the root cause of the trouble in Mauritius is growing unemployment? Would the Secretary of State consider bringing forward the financial talks that he is to have with the Mauritius Government?" [5]

Secretary of State George Thomson summed up succinctly the events:

"I very much regret to inform the House that there has been rioting leading to loss of life in Mauritius. A state of emergency has been declared and British reinforcements despatched. On 21st January the Governor informed me that there had been a series of brawls between communal gangs in Eastern Port Louis and these had escalated in violence and extent. After consultation with the Prime Minister of Mauritius the Governor decided to declare a state of emergency in the eastern part of Port Louis.

"By yesterday, 22nd January, the violence had spread still further and the total number of dead had reached 14. The Governor therefore extended the state of emergency to cover the whole island. In these circumstances, both the Governor and the Prime Minister agreed that it was necessary to request military reinforcements. A small contingent of the King's Shropshire Light Infantry was sent to Mauritius and the first elements have already arrived in Mauritius. Two frigates are also on their way.

"Within the last half hour I have been in telephonic communication with the Governor. I regret to say that the death roll has now reached 17. The Governor however, tells me that the island is now quieter though there is still danger of outbreaks. Some shops remain shut in Port Louis, and there is a refugee problem with which the Government are coping.

"Political leaders of the Mauritius Government and of the Opposition in Mauritius have both deplored this outbreak of violence. The whole House will share my hope that the Mauritius security forces will soon succeed in restoring order." [6]

On January 30, Thomson reported more casualties to the House and attributed the violence to the economic situation, but this time, he did not exclude *'political factors'*:

---
3 Op cit.
4 HC Deb 23 January 1968 vol 757 cc216-21 216
5 Ibid.
6 *Mauritius (State Of Emergency),* HC Deb 23 January 1968 vol 757 cc216-21 216

"The disturbances in Mauritius had, in the first instance, an economic rather than political origin, although I do not exclude the fact that there were political factors involved. The situation is now calm, and I would not like at this stage to speculate on the future there.

"Following are the details: I regret to say that the death roll has now risen to 24; 43 people have been seriously injured. Up to yesterday morning, 344 people had been arrested. Those against whom no substantive evidence was established have been released and the remainder are being brought to trail as soon as possible. First judgments were given yesterday. Sentences of up to five years' penal servitude were imposed on two persons convicted for possession of offensive weapons; 19 other persons are now before the court. I should like to pay tribute to the officers and men of H.M. Ships "Euryalus" and "Cambrian" and of the King's Shropshire Light infantry for the help they have given to the local security forces in dealing with the disorders. H.M.S. "Euryalus" has now left Mauritius." [7]

Social and religious leaders appealed for peace. The country's leading journalists, irrespective of political or other divergences, contributed substantially to reduce the tension. The riots were fortunately limited to Port-Louis and some parts of the north, but they caused a large number of victims. It is a popular belief to this day that the number of casualties, including persons unaccounted for, was higher than the official figures, but this has never been proved.

Independence Day: intense emotion at the Champ de Mars

One week prior to Independence Day, the situation had not been stabilised enough for the British and Mauritian authorities to give the green light for Princess Alexandra to represent the queen during the festivities. The announcement was made by Secretary of State George Thomson to the British Parliament about the agreement between the two countries that such a visit could not take place:

"Owing to the continuation of violence in Mauritius, we felt anxiety about whether it would be desirable to carry on with the visit. Accordingly, my noble Friend the Minister of State, Lord Shepherd, flew out to Mauritius last Sunday to investigate the situation on the ground and to report. The decision which I have just announced has been made on the basis of his advice and after the fullest consultation by him with the Government of Mauritius.

"Both we and the Mauritius Government had hoped that the state of emergency could have been terminated before Her Royal Highness' visit, but this has not proved possible and, in these circumstances, we have decided that we would be prudent not to add at this time to the responsibilities of the security forces in the islands.

"The Government of Mauritius have issued a statement referring to the regret with which they have learnt of this decision and the great disappointment which will be caused to the people of Mauritius. We share this regret and disappointment that this decision should have been necessary." [8]

The British Minister of Housing and Local Government Anthony Greenwood was selected to represent the queen and there was never a security problem during his stay. As for Alexandra, as will be seen, she did have a security issue that caused her to enter the political history of Mauritius in a rather spectacular manner.

The country proceeded peacefully to become an independent State at noon, on March 12, 1968, when the Union Jack was lowered and replaced by the new Mauritian national flag. The crowd at the Champ de Mars numbered 150,000, the largest ever to assemble in one place in the history of the country as of that time.[9] The crowd remained impressively silent as this part of the ceremony was carried out. Sir Seewoosagur Ramgoolam and Governor Sir John Shaw Rennie appeared both gripped by emotion during the lowering of the Union Jack carried out by Lieutenant D.E. Wenn, for the British, and the raising of the national flag by Inspector Palmyre of the Special Mobile Force (SMF), for the Mauritian side.

After the ***"God Save the Queen"*** the crowd heard for the first time the sound of the Mauritian national anthem, ***"Motherland."*** The words were by Mauritian poet Jean-Georges Prosper and the music by Police Band musician Philippe Gentil. Warships in the harbour fired 31 salvos. The crowd broke into a long applause.

At the same time, in London, at Westminster Abbéy, a prayer service was being held with Princess Alexandra and her husband Angus Ogilvy in attendance. In Mauritius also, religious services had been held by all religions across the country, culminating into major ones in Port-Louis at the Catholic church's St. Louis Cathedral, the Anglican Church's St. James Cathedral, the Jummah Mosque and Hindu temples.

In Rodrigues, there were incidents due to the hostility of a crowd of anti-independence supporters of the PMSD. Rodrigues had voted for the first time in 1967. This kind of climate had been created by a campaign of the PMSD against independence that resulted in a massive vote for integration with Britain.

---

[7] ***Mauritius***, HC Deb 30 January 1968 vol 757 cc1082-4 1082.
[8] ***Mauritius*** HC Deb 08 March 1968 vol 760 cc838-41 838
[9] The author of this book, who was a young journalist with the pro-independence ***L'Express*** newspaper, watched with emotion, like the big silent crowd, as the British flag was brought down and replaced for the first time ever by the Mauritian quadricolor.

After the defeat of the PMSD, in January 1968, Guy Ollivry travelled London and the *Times* reported that he was advocating that Rodrigues be detached from Mauritius. His visit and meeting with British officials were mentioned in the House of Commons with one MP stating that Ollivry was acting on behalf of the leader of the Opposition, Sir Gaëtan Duval. It was clear that the British rejected entirely the idea of any secession by Rodrigues, although they did watch the situation with some concern following what had happened in Anguila, [10] a small territory that, after several massive votes against federation with other islands, brought the British to accept, in 1971, its secession from Nevis and St. Kitts. It became a British dependency, while St. Kitts and Nevis went on to become an independent nation in 1983.

The temptation to ask for independence remained quite strong for several years in Rodrigues until it was granted constitutional autonomy with its own Rodrigues Regional Assembly.

---

10 *Mauritius Independence Bill,* HC Deb 19 January 1968 vol 756 cc2133-56 2133.

Chapter 43

Priorities: nation building and the economy
St. Guillaume: Duval was for independence, 'deep within himself'

The PMSD quickly reconciled itself with the reality of political independence. There was no other option and its financiers, mainly the private corporations that controlled the large sugar estates and their related companies in other sectors of business, together with the leading Western capitals (namely London, Washington and Paris) wanted political stability. Private sector leaders and Western politicians and diplomats engineered a coalition project that would bring the PMSD into the government.

PMSD member seconds Independence motion

The PMSD had organised a boycott of the Independence Day ceremony at the Champ de Mars. Otherwise, the crowd would have been much larger. However, **Le Mauricien** newspaper, which had campaigned against independence, decided to not to participate in the boycott and reported on the events. Two members of the PMSD took part in the festivities, Yvon St. Guillaume and Tangavel Narainen, in defiance of Duval's decision. St. Guillaume even seconded Ramgoolam's motion subsequently asking the Queen to approve the independence of Mauritiius – a formality that acquired considerable importance as it was a PMSD Member of Parliament who had taken a stand that was totally contrary to the party's years of campaigning against independence.

Four decades later, St. Guillaume confided in a press interview that he believed that Duval was, *"deep within himself, for independence"* and had privately told him that *"he wanted to turn the page but that he was being subjected to too much pressure."* [1]

One may speculate, then, if St. Guillaume (who was a religious official in 2008, and was probably telling the truth), on whether there had been some forces, financiers, backers of some kind, secret service operatives of some foreign powers, who were in a position to dictate to the PMSD its policies and decisions. It appeared to the author of this book during a visit to London in 1972 to meet British officials, that Duval had strong ties inside the British state apparatus and that he could rely on them for support – as he has confirmed in his book of reminiscences **Une certain idée de l'île Maurice** [2] regarding a secret meeting in New York *"at the Wardolf Astoria"* where the *"Western powers"* managed to convince him to join Ramgoolam in a coalition to fight the communist threat. That has been the only time that Duval openly revealed such discreet contacts that could invite him to New York to tell him to join the government. The fact that subsequently Ramgoolam readily dropped the IFB to take the PMSD into his government was also quite unexpected in 1969, but did reinforce the idea of neocolonialism at work – neocolonialism meaning *"the control of less-developed countries by developed countries through indirect means. The term neocolonialism was first used after World War II to refer to the continuing dependence of former colonies on foreign countries, but its meaning soon broadened to apply, more generally, to places where the power of developed countries was used to produce a colonial-like exploitation—for instance, in Latin America, where direct foreign rule had ended in the early 19th century. The term is now an unambiguously negative one that is widely used to refer to a form of global power in which transnational corporations and global and multilateral institutions combine to perpetuate colonial forms of exploitation of developing countries."*[3]

This was actually the analysis of the MMM, a new leftist political party founded in 1969 with, at its beginnings, Marxism as its main inspiration.

Anyway, to the great surprise of the country, after independence, it was not long before it was known that Duval and Dr. Ramgoolam had started to discuss the possibility of forming once more a coalition government. Top sugar industry leaders, principally Claude Noel, as well as foreign dignitaries, mainly the French Minister and representative of Réunion Island at the French National Assembly, Michel Debré, as well as American and British diplomats,

1 Yvon St. Guillaume, l'homme qui défia son parti au nom de son pays, Week-End 16 March 2008.
2 Op cit.
3 Halperin, Sandra, **Neocolonialism**, in: *Encyclopædia Britannica*, inc. March 23, 201 https://www.britannica.com/topic/neocolonialism, accessed 2 February 2017.

were the the intermediaries. In his reminiscences on his political career that he wrote in 1976, Sir Gaëtan Duval explained that the Western powers made known to him that their main concerns were to stop the advance of communism in the region. [1]

They were encouraged also by a young student, Paul Bérenger, who wrote articles in *L'Express*, to ask for a coalition government. [2] His view was that Duval represented the interests of the Western countries and that would help Mauritius on the economic front, while a Labour/PMSD coalition would also help soothe the wounds left by ethnic politics during the long struggle between the two parties. Nevertheless, Bérenger would, in the following years, make a spectacular entry in the Mauritian political arena by fighting the Ramgoolam-Duval tandem and what he called the '*neocolonial*' nature of their government, proposing a formula of "*direct democracy*" inspired from Marxism and the Student Revolt of 1968 in Paris.

Western geostrategy and the Labour/PMSD coalition

What could be described as '*obscure*' forces behind the coalition were, in the end, not so obscure, after all. While Duval revealed, seven years later, the Western '*connection*' in his book of reminiscences. [3] Michel Debré, the French Foreign Affairs Minister until 1969, and from 1969, Defence Minister, had not hesitated, in that same year, to publicly betray the link between Western diplomacy and the proposed coalition. He did it in front of a large crowd in Curepipe, by joining the hands of Sir Sewoosagur Ramgoolam and Duval in his own, a clear and unambiguous signal of an impending coalition. France was, for sure, not alone in this enterprise.

As earlier stated, the Americans were contemplating, already in the 1950s, as decolonisation swept across the planet and, at the same time, communism was advancing rapidly, the dispatch of important military and naval forces to stay permanently in the Indian Ocean. This is clear in the following excerpt from a 1957 research paper in an American Marine Corps publication:

"(...) with the translation of India, Pakistan, Ceylon, Burma and Malaya into independent states, the specifically British military responsibilities in the Indian Ocean have greatly diminished. Today they may be defined as the protection of commerce, notably that of the oil-trade of the Persian Gulf; the extinguishing of the last embers of Communist revolt in Malaya; and the security of sea-communications with Australia and the Far East. In all of these, the United States also has an interest of varying degree. All of them are connected with the continued security of the Indian Ocean and of the nations around its shores. The basic requirement of that security may be stated in a single phrase - exclusion from the Indian Ocean area of Communist power and influence.

"This is also a vital consideration to the global strategy of the struggle against the Communist coalition - a strategy in which Britain bears an important part, but of which the power of the United States is the mainstay. Thus today, for the first time in history, the United States has a definite long-term strategic interest in the Indian Ocean; and because of the diminished power and authority of Britain in that area (as elsewhere) the United States is required to support that interest with its own power, or at least to be visibly prepared to do so." [4]

This was the setting of the Cold War that raged from the 1950s, throughout the 1960s and beyond and it has been replaced by the so-called Western '*war on terrorism*" that has seen full scale warfare launched by America against the pro-Taliban regime in Afthanistan and that of Saddam Hussain in Iraq. [5] Those conflicts were the kind of situations, anticipated in the 1957 paper cited above, that would invite a response from the U.S. Additionally, as of 2017, tensions have risen between the US and NATO on one side, and Russia on the opposite side, once more.

France-Nato: secret arrangements that include Mauritius

In the 1960s, France left the Northern Alliance Treaty Organization (NATO), which to this day ensures the military defence of the Western nations and their alliesunder American leadership (France has now rejoined) but Paris made secret defence arrangements that, among other things, include Mauritius. NATO has been fighting communism everywhere on the planet in both cold and hot conflicts. Several secret arrangements were made by the French and American political and military top brass to maintain joint military and intelligence operations, including covert operations. To this day, those agreements, one of which is known as the Ailleret-Lemnitzer agreements (also called, inversely, the Lemnitzer-Ailleret agreements) have remained secret. What is known to scholars has been summed up in various papers and books. The following excerpt from a book by researcher Anand Menon gives some idea of the importance of those secret arrangements:

"Between 22 November 1966 and February 1967, a series of meetings occurred between French Chief of Staff General Charles Ailleret, and the

---
[1] Duval, Gaëtan, *Une certaine idée de l'ile Maurice,* Le Trèle 1976. Pages 155-156.
[2] *L'Express*, 5 and 10 August 1967
[3] Op cit.
[4] Elliot, George Fielding, *American Seapower and the Indian Ocean,* Marine Corps Gazette 1957, op cit, Chapter 41.
[5] Sand, Peter H., op cit.

Supreme Allied Commander, Europe (SACEUR), General Lyman L. Lemnitzer, culminating in the signing of agreements on military co-operation between France and NATO. The exact details of their discussions have remained confidential. It seems clear, however, that the Ailleret-Lemnitzer agreements, signed on 22 August, were both detailed and far-reaching. (…)

"On 2 December 1970, the Fourquet-Goodpaster agreements were signed. These improved coordination between NATO and French air defence systems and included provision for French membership in the NATO Ace High network, eight of whose stations were placed on French soil. In July 1974, the Valentine-Feber accords were signed between the commander of the French First Army and the commander of the Allied Forces Central Europe. (…)

"It is striking how low a profile was accorded the instances of cooperation between France and its Allies. As the Ailleret-Lemnitzer agreements went almost unnoticed, so too were subsequent agreements between France and its allies shrouded in secrecy. Cooperative initiatives towards NATO were undertaken almost surreptitiously." [1]

In actively advocating a coalition government in Mauritius, Michel Debré, Foreign Affairs Minister of France until 1969 when he was appointed Minister of Defence, was obviously abiding by the above mentioned agreements. He enjoyed the additional advantage of being a close friend of Duval and, after the coalition, of Ramgoolam also, who chose the capitalist course of economic development that was deeply and naturally embedded in Duval's mindset. Debré was an elected member for nearby Réunion Island in the French National Assembly. Debré was, the word is not too strong, ferociously fighting the very popular Communist Party of Reunion, the PCR, then in its early historical phase when it was close to Moscow and wanted Réunion to be independent. An independent Mauritius under communist influence represented a risk France would not take in the midst of the Cold War. This was the true context of the joining of hands of Ramgoolam and Duval, which Debré performed in person in front of a large crowd in Curepipe in 1969, inviting them to work together.

From that moment, the Labour/IFB coalition could be considered already dead. Ramgoolam embarked on a policy that he personally took control of, even to the detriment of Duval: a policy of very close rapprochement with France. Under the secret agreements, France was the '*gendarme*' of the South West Indian Ocean islands and region, with the blessing of NATO and Washington. The word '*gendarme*' has in fact been widely used in the media and academia since that time, and the French role has been well explained by French researcher Guillaume Burdeau. [2] As for Britain, on January 12, 1968, the government of Harold Wilson had announced that the British were retreating from East of Suez. That expected move resulted in placing more strategic responsibilities in the care of the Americans and of the French. The British retreat from Southeast Asia and the Persian Gulf were spectacular developments in view of Britain's huge role in those parts of the world for centuries. The moves have been amply documented and analysed by analysts like Saki Dockrill and Sato Shohei. [3]

The post-independence coalition was effectively the chef d'oeuvre of Western neocolonialism in the sense given to this word by academia in Routledge's voluminous work on decolonisation. [4] Ramgoolam and Duval could invoke realpolitik considerations in the interest of Mauritius, with regard to the enormous economic benefits their government reaped from entering literally into association with the European Union and being able to secure markets not just for Mauritian sugar, but the future exports of the industrial free zones they successfully created in the 1970. This strategy finally, in the 1980s, enabled the country to emerge from widespread poverty – albeit the criticism aptly levelled at the coalition to this day about its repressive measures during the 1970s.

Many people thought, like Bérenger, that a coalition comprising the PMSD, which saw itself as the representative of the minorities and of Western interests, and the Labour-led government, which often claimed to speak in the name of '**Hindu unity**' and was also well considered in Westminster, would promote a sense of national unity among the population, thus helping nation-building. Sir Seewoosagur Ramgoolam would argue with insistence, at the local level, that he wanted Gaëtan Duval in his government in the name of national unity. Duval would do the same, but

1 Menon, Anand, *France,NATO, and the limits of Independence, 1981-97: the politics of ambivalence*, MacMillan, Great Britain 2000.
2 Burdeau, Guillaume, *Les relations entre la France et les Seychelles d'après la presse française (1977-2004)*, Université Paris Ouest - Nanterre - La Défense - Master 2 Histoire 2010 : « *La France est la garante de la sécurité des voies maritimes de l'océan Indien. En dominant le trafic maritime, la France entretient des relations commerciales avec l'ensemble des pays riverains. En tant que principale puissance militaire étrangère présente dans l'océan Indien, la France est mise en cause par les pays qui cherchent à créer une « zone de paix » dans la région. Pourtant, on a accepté de maintenir la présence militaire française « au nom de la paix ». En effet, elle joue un rôle de stabilisatrice et son retrait aurait été profitable à l'hégémonie d'autres puissances, surtout celle de l'URSS. De plus, la France est une puissance navale moyenne et non hégémonique, elle rassure les pays alliés face à ses agresseurs et évite aux pays riverains d'être confrontés sans cesse à l'URSS : elle attire plus facilement la sympathie des États. Cela permet à la France de jouer son rôle de gendarme de l'océan Indien et d'affirmer son statut de puissance riveraine. Position que l'URSS a vainement tenté de supplanter.*»
3 Dockrill, Saki, ***Britain's Retreat from East of Suez***, London, Palgrave Macmillan 2002. Also: Sato, Shohei, ***Britain's Decision to Withdraw from the Persian Gulf, 1964–68: A Pattern and a Puzzle***, Journal of Imperial and Commonwealth History Vol. 37, No. 1, Routledge, March 2009, pp. 99–117
4 Rothermund Dietmar, ***The Routledge Companion to Decolonization***, op cit.

would find it much more difficult to persuade his electorate and even his party.

Bérenger's arguments, published just three days after the elections, were: firstly, a multiethnic country must necessarily be governed by coalitions and Mauritius was then living in a very tense atmosphere, and, secondly, the economic interests of the country would be better served by a coalition in which Duval would have the duty, he wrote, of keeping *"close contacts with Great Britain and the European Common Market, in particular with France."* Mauritius should associate itself with the Common Market, he argued. [5] Bérenger was not in a position, though, to have any real influence in the political arena – not yet.

'Terrifying' population explosion, large scale unemployment and poverty

It must be borne in mind also that, in those days, Mauritius was still a poor, underdeveloped country. The 1960s had started with two violent cyclones, *Alix* and *Carol*, which, within three months, had brought the country down on its knees. Three exhaustive reports ordered by the government reveal the extent to which life was miserable for the majority of Mauritians at the end of the 1950s: the Luce Report,[6] the Meade Report [7] and the Titmuss Report. [8] Studying Mauritian unemployment in March 1958, Professor R.W. Luce observed that out of the people who could be economically active, 15.1% were unemployed. Luce commented that *"the figures indicate unemployment on a very severe scale judged by any standard."*

What worried Professor James Meade, for his part, was the '*terrifying*' population explosion that was in the making: the natural rate of increase of the population had evolved from about half per cent per year in the years following World War II, to reach 3% a year in 1958. The population had multiplied by about six times. At such a rate, the population of such a poor country like Mauritius would increase from 600,000 in 1958 to 3 million at the end of the 20th century. That was the reason why Meade, who won the Nobel Prize for economics in 1977, predicted a Malthusian future for Mauritius. How could a nation with an economic growth rate that was around 1% annually, at even at times negative, meaning no growth at all, feed 3 million persons?

The gross national product (GNP), at constant prices, between 1953 and 1958, was less than Rs 590 million a year and the per capita GNP had gone down from Rs 1, 058 to Rs 956 rupees a year. Looking at the extent of the poverty that affected the majority of the population, and, like Meade, based on the demographic explosion that was in the making, Titmuss spoke of *'the emerging crisis.'* Meade had found the labour force was growing by 1% only in 1958. Due to the lack of natural resources, Meade recommended industrialisation. He proposed a major diversification of the economy, which from then on, became the leitmotiv of all Mauritian governments from the 1960s to date. From the early 1960s, the government had adopted a policy of encouraging manufacturing activities for import-substitution industries (ISIs) by granting export development certificates and protected them from external competition by means of tariff barriers.

This created less than 2,000 jobs, while the demographic bomb continued to tick and unemployment continued to rise. Gradually, business and government in Mauritius were made aware that small territories like Taiwan and Hong Kong were being quite successful in adopting what became known as an export oriented industries (EOIs) strategy consisting in providing low costs of production through fiscal and other incentives for production oriented activities that targeted the large affluent markets, meaning those of the Western countries, Europe and the United States. [9]

"By the time of independence unemployment was unofficially estimated at over 20 per cent and the GDP was only Rs 840 million or a mere Rs 1,086 per capita, even less than in 1963 when it was Rs 1,283 per capita. The country had a mono-crop economy, relying mostly on the annual sugar cane harvests and sugar production. The population had reached nearly 800,000 and there were dire predictions as to the future when the one-million mark would be reached." [10]

There was a convergence between the needs of Mauritius to escape from under-development and the diplomatic and strategic manoeuvres of the Western nations to work with governments of the region while finding a means to ward off the threat of a rapidly advancing communist bloc.

Malnutrition, disease, cyclones and housing crises

---
5 *L'Express*, 10 August 1967, op cit.
6 Luce, R.W., **The Luce report: A time for decision, Sessional Patper No. 7 of 1958,** Mauritius Legislative Council.
7 Meade, J.E. & Others, **The Economic Structure of Mauritiius, Sessional Paper No. 7 of 1961**, Mauritius Legislative Council.
8 Titmus, Richard M., and Abel-Smith, Brian, **Social Policies and Population Grrowth in Mauritius**, op cit.
9 Yeung LamKo, Louis, **The Economic Development of Mauritius Since Independence**, School of Economics University of New South Wales, Sydney NSW 2052, Australia 1998.
10 Ibid.

In the decade leading to independence, the 1960s, living conditions were very difficult for the majority of the population. Many villages had not yet been electrified. In most villages, and even within some town boundaries, people, mostly women and young boys and girls, had to obtain water from public fountains and carry it in large, heavy recipients often precariously placed on their heads.

Based on a population estimated at 600,000 in 1959 from the official figures of population in the inter-censal period 1952-1962, nearly 6% of Mauritians, or 35,203, were receiving outdoor relief from the Public Assistance. [11] Malnutrition was widespread:

"A high proportion of manual labourers suffer from anaemia and a high proportion do not get an adequate diet... Government medical officers have told us frankly that the primary cause is usually economic and not medical. Applicants (for poor law relief) have failed to find work which brings in enough money to provide an adequate diet for themselves and their families." [12]

The rapid increase of population coupled with the spread of poverty caused a fifteen-fold increase of poor law relief expenditure from 1945 when the figure stood at under half a million rupees (Rs 465,496), to nearly Rs 7 million in 1958 (Rs 6,984,786). Life was hard on the sugar estates. Titmuss observed that there was '*reluctance*' among workers to work on the sugar estates, many of them because of malnutrition that affects seriously their health, but others, especially the young ones, because of the attitude of the employers who offered no security of employment nor training and promotion, all reserved to a handful of employees. [13]

Titmuss concluded:

"(..) the growth of population and other factors have led to a reduction of living standards among certain sections of the people, to growing unemployment, and to a heavy drain on the budget from a creaking system of not discriminate aid." [14]

Cyclones Alix & Carol, 1960: in 2 months 12% of the population become refugees[15]

What was worse at the beginning of the 1960s was the passage of several violent cyclones at the very moment when the colonial authorities in London had despatched to the island the various experts who were proposing population control, poor law reforms and economic diversification to combat poverty and unemployment. In just the year 1960, the British Parliament was already working on a programme of aid following a first cyclone, **Alix** (16-20 jan 1960) when the second, **Carol** (25-29 Feb 1960) even more violent, struck. There were many casualties and nearly 12% of the total population became refugees. The Secretary of State for the Colonies, reported to the House of Lords the extent of the damage from despatches sent by the Governor of Mauritius:

"My Lords, cyclone "Carol" which struck Mauritius on the 27th and 28th February was the most severe ever recorded in the island's history. There were over 1,700 casualties; 42 people were killed and 95 seriously injured. Over 100,000 buildings and huts were destroyed or seriously damaged. Nearly 70,000 of the island's total population of 600,000 are now in refugee centres. The House will recall that cyclone "Carol" was preceded in January by cyclone "Alix", which killed eight people, injured over a hundred and destroyed over 20,000 buildings and huts.

"It is estimated that as much as 60 per cent. of the year's sugar crop may prove to have been lost, though the size of the final crop will naturally depend on the weather during the remainder of the season. About 30 per cent of this season's tea crop has been lost, but I am advised that no serious damage has been suffered by mature tea bushes. The Government's tea factory is likely to be out of action for some months, but the remaining factory capacity of the island will be able to handle this season's reduced tea crop.

"It is not yet possible to give any estimate of the total value of the losses suffered, though it runs into many millions of pounds. My right honourable friend the Secretary of State for the Colonies has made arrangements for a team of his advisers to visit Mauritius to look into the cyclone damage and measures for reconstruction, this in consultation with an economic survey mission which is now visiting the Island to consider a long-term development programme." [16]

11 Author's estimate based on: Outdoor Relief Cases, Titmus Report, op cit, page 11 and: Table 1.3 - Population growth in intercensal periods - Republic of Mauritius, 1851 – 2000, Ministry of Finance and Economic Development, Digest of Demographic Statistics 2010.
12 Titmuss Report, op cit, page 11.
13 Ibid.
14 Ibid.
15 *List of Historical Cyclones,* Mauritius Meteorological Services - several severe cyclones struck Mauritius between 1960 and 1962, URL http://metservice.intnet.mu/publications/list-of-historical-cyclones.php

Year	Date-Month	Name	Classification	Nearest Distance from M'tius	Highest Gusts km/h	Lowest Pressure hPa
1960	16 - 20 Jan	Alix	Intense Cyclone	30 km off Port Louis	200	970
1960	25 - 29 Feb	Carol	Intense Cyclone	Over Mauritius	256	943
1961	22 - 26 Dec	Beryl	Intense Cyclone	30 km West	171	992
1962	27 - 28 Feb	Jenny	Intense Cyclone	30 km North	235	995

16 *Cyclone Damage In Mauritius*, HL Deb 17 March 1960 vol 221 cc1267-8.

Titmuss observed,

"The effect of the cyclones has been to magnify the social and economic problems of Mauritius. On the morning after cyclone Carol on 29th February, about 80,000 people – one-eighth of the population – had taken shelter in schools, village halls, churches, social welfare centres and other buildings. In addition, a larger number of people took refuge with friends and relations. Well over half of the houses on the island were damaged… The major casualties of the cyclones were the wood and straw huts. A plan was quickly improvised to build temporary 'terraces' of family units in wood and corrugated iron. Within three weeks of the second cyclone some of these units were ready for occupation. At the same time longer-term plans were worked out for cyclone-proof housing." [17]

People lived in those rudimentary shelters for years. Government put into practice extensive housing schemes throughout the 1960s, creating the '*Cités*' which were new agglomerations of cyclone proof houses for the working classes, who had suffered the most from the cyclones. That was also the time when the majority of Mauritians practically stopped building houses made of wood and iron sheets, and resorted to concrete houses that started to radically transform the towns and villages. Aesthetic considerations were pushed aside as people frantically set up houses that were mainly made to be cyclone proof in those days when poverty was still rampant and housing loan schemes still in their infancy. The private financial sector was not really interested in taking part in special loan schemes for the poor, so the government took upon itself the main responsibility to offer new housing units to the working classes.

Economic situation at the time of independence

Prior to independence, the Malthusian prediction of Professor Meade loomed large over the island. With a predicted population of 3 million by the end of the century, efforts had been stepped up to control demographic growth and this had been the priority throughout the 1960s. The Mauritius Family Planning Association played a major role in the process and those, who for religious reasons, preferred other means of birth control, went to the very active Action Familiale, a catholic organisation that promote birth control methods acceptable to their faith. Referring to Meade's prediction, Bheenick and Schapiro observe:

"A population explosion of that magnitude would have large-scale economic and social effects. For example, the working age population (aged 15 years and over) was projected to increase by some 50 % during 1957-72; a situation that would present Mauritius, then exclusively dependent on sugar to provide employment and output growth, with a bleak prospect. Population control could provide some hope, but while family planning can decrease the size of families in the future given sufficient motivation to restrict fertility, it offers no help for those already born who would soon be seeking employment." [18]

Between 1965 and 1970, the number of unemployed (only those who registered) soared from 7,795 to 19,794. The government had introduced from the 1960s a system of relief work as a measure to attenuate the levels of unemployment and poverty, the relief workers working four days a week doing various jobs as labourers/manual workers. Relief workers' numbers increased as unemployment went up and by 1970, they numbered 16,094. Registered unemployed and relief workers, who received very low wages, totalled 35,848 by 1970 or 8% of the population of working age. [19]

"The late 1960s were characterized by relatively slow economic growth: the GDP grew at an annual average of less than 4.5 % during 1965-69, and fell in two of these years. In addition, unemployment grew substantially as the labor force was increasing at almost twice the rate of population increase, a direct consequence of the high fertility rates of the 1940s and 1950s. Although the country's dependence on sugar to balance its external payments position was less than earlier, it was still considerable: this sector accounted for 16 % of GDP in 1970 compared to 34 % in 1959. In short, forecasts of the future continued to be depressing." [20]

While the opposition parties in the 1960s argued that relief work was also conveniently used by the government to give jobs to its supporters – governments in Mauritius, most major political parties included, are known to practice, since independence, this kind of politically biased recruitments especially during the period leading to general elections. Nevertheless, excluding such alleged unfair practices by which deserving unemployed persons were left out, the relief work system did alleviate poverty to a certain extent among the recipient families of the meagre wages (paid partly in kind). Unemployment was one of the main causes of rampant poverty and it has been said that the unemployment rate far exceed the official figures that show only the registered unemployed and most unemployed women who wanted to work were not registered. This would mean that the real figure was more or less

---
17 *Titmuss Report*, op cit. pages 14-15.
18 Bheenick, Rundheersing; Schapiro, Morton Owen, Mauritius: *A Case Study of the Export Processing Zone, Economic Development* Institute of the World Bank, Successful Development in Africa. Case Studies of Projects, Programs, and Policies, World Bank 1989.
19 Ibid, quoting figures from the Central Statistics Office, Mauritius.
20 Ibid.

20% as some analysts have pointed out. [21] Such a situation was inevitably explosive and, as observed in the British Parliament during the 1968 racial riots, economic problems must have been among the triggering factors.

Industrialisation goes hand in hand with a political coalition

In 1969, following what Duval has called the intervention of the Western powers in his reminiscences published seven years later, [22] pressures from the private sector also intensified. Among the private sector pundits involved, there was Amédée Maingard, a former British secret agent during World War II who played a major role in the French resistance after being dropped by the Special Operations Executive and had received several distinctions as a war hero. Maingard was a pioneer of the Mauritius tourism industry, having started the first large scale tourism hospitality activities with the New Mauritius Hotels and participated in the creation of Air Mauritius, the national airline, of which he was one of the founders and the first chairman and executive director. [23]

He and various Franco-Mauritian personalities from the sugar industry sector who were closely associated with Sir Seewoosagur Ramgoolam and the latter's friend Dr. K. Hazareesingh, were the intermediaries between SSR and Duval that helped forge a Labour/PMSD coalition. It was obvious that the British, especially through Maingard, as well as the Americans and the French were not so far behind, acting in the name of shared Western geostrategical interests.

There was a pre-coalition arrangement made in March 1969 at the level of the lists of candidates for the municipal elections. In a statement in April 1969 to the mayors of the towns, Dr. Ramgoolam promised that the voting age would be lowered to 18 years. On April 19, at the annual congress of the Labour Party, he announced that there would be a *"honourable coalition."* [24]

Before the coalition was sealed, the PMSD had seemed to be playing cat and mouse with Ramgoolam. There was in reality divided opinions, particularly with regard to the proposed postponement of general elections until 1976 by a constitutional amendment. Within the PMSD, the opposition was quite strong against this and would eventually lead to a split that, in the following years and decades, would cause a rapid decline of the party in terms of voter support.

At that time, Duval was arguing that the PMSD's mission by entering a coalition government was to help build national unity, following the deep divisions on ethnic lines that, according to him, had torn the country apart at the 1967 general election. He also wanted the PMSD to be given a chance to participate in the social and economic development of the nation.

Before joining the government, Duval tested his electorate at a huge rally at the Place du Quai, Port-Louis, on June 2, 1969. The media reported him as having said *"No to the coalition"* under enthusiastic applause by the large crowd. [25] The next day, though, he tried to correct himself by stating to the media, *"Yes, it can happen."* The media also reported that Duval added that for the coalition to happen, *"the Prime Minister has only to drop his decision not to have the general elections organised before 1977, and we would then not hesitate to say 'Yes' to the coalition."* [26]

Duval's handling of his communication with his electorate proved, with hindsight, to have been a total disaster as that electorate was going to leave him quite soon, recalling that he had said a categorical *"No"* at the Place du Quai, as reported by the media, and that he had then reneged on this promise.

The coalition had formidable opponents from the start. The principal opponents in the PMSD to the postponement of the general election due in 1972 comprised prominent members of the party's top leadership like Maurice Lesage, Raymond Rivet and Cyril Leckning and later on Guy Ollivry. The IFB, for its part, denounced the major role it believed the sugar barons, who backed the PMSD, would play in the new government.

The most formidable opposition to the coalition, though, came from the streets, where discontent was high due to rampant poverty, frozen wages and unemployment, especially among the younger generations and the work-

---

21 Yeung LamKo, op cit.
22 *Une certaine idée de l'île Maurice*, op cit.
23 The Air Mauritius website pays tribute to him in the web page on the Amédée Maingard Lounge at the Sir Seewoosagur Ramgoolam International Airport in these words: *"Mauritius owes its blooming tourist industry to the vision of some of its famous children; they were armed with the energy and determination to cultivate interaction amongst peoples of various horizons. Amédée Maingard, one of the founders and first Chairman and Managing Director of Air Mauritius, was one of those few."*
24 *Le Mauricien* and other newspapers, 20 April 1969.
25 Le Mauricien and other newspapers, 3 June 1969.
26 Ibid. 4 June 1969.

ers. The PMSD had left a vacuum in the opposition, especially street opposition, after it entered government, but neither the IFB nor the PMSD dissidents who formed a new party, the Union Démocratique Mauricienne (UDM) were able to capitalize on that situation.

Commenting on those days of intense diplomatic and political activities, Duval wrote in 1976,

"I travelled to Paris, London and New York. The Western nations feared that unless a coalition was formed, communism would be established in Mauritius encouraged by the desperately high level of poverty of the population. They promised, in exchange, their unconditional financial support." [27]

Coming back from his long overseas tour, together with Ramgoolam, on 18 October 1969, both men paused on the plane's gangway for a historic photo each with a hand raised in triumph and holding each other with the other hand. It was obvious that both of them had been pressured into yet another coalition.

Ramgoolam abruptly rid his government of the IFB, though party leader Sookdeo Bissoondoyal, on the same day that Ramgoolam announced IFB's exclusion from the coalition government, stated in a note handed over to *L'Express* newspaper[28] that he and his IFB colleagues had left the government over serious disagreements. It appears that both parties desired to get rid of each other, the IFB having sacrificed its considerable popularity to join Labour on the independence platform. Members of the party defected in and outside Parliament to Labour together with a large part of its electorate, a heavy price indeed. The extent of the defections were such that the IFB never won, from the next elections in 1976, a parliamentary seat again and disappeared from the political scene, in spite of the leaders' decisive contribution to the Labour Party from its creation by Curé and to the country's march to independence.

Ramgoolam, as a shrewd politician, arguing that the coalition needed more time that the Parliament's current mandate, asked and obtained that Duval accept the postponement of the general elections due in 1972 as one of the conditions for the formation of the coalition government. Duval later publicly regretted having made that concession in his book *"Une certaine idee de l'Ile Maurice,"* written after his party was expelled from the Ramgoolam government (with the exception of a number of parliamentarians who crossed over to Labour). [29]

In November 1969, the new Labour-CAM-PMSD coalition modified the Constitution to give the 1967-elected Parliament a supplementary mandate of five years, which meant that the 1972 elections were postponed to 1976, that is for 7 years, thus extending Parliament's mandate to a total of nine years (1967-1976). The PMSD obtained key ministries: Foreign Affairs, Tourism, Industry, Trade, and Economic Planning.

The coalition actually led to the sharp decline of the party, starting from a major split led by some of its most popular leaders on the issue of the postponement of the elections and, later on, the state of emergency that the coalition used to repress leftists and which also curtailed basic democratic rights and allowed the instauration of press censorship. All of the PMSD's attempts, throughout the following decades, to recover its status as the largest party of the country, which it acquired at the 1967 general election, were to fail.

The 'economic miracle' of the 1970s

The pro-business policies of Duval and Ramgoolam were to result in quite positive results on the economic front: as they implemented their ambitious economic agenda, the national economy soared. The country had record annual economic growth rates, with an average of 8.2 per cent between 1971 and 1977, while, in the meantime, in 1974, the PMSD had been expelled from the coalition government. Nevertheless, the PMSD's contribution had been decisive and enduring, lasting well beyond its departure from government.

The Ramgoolam-Duval coalition (with CAM's Razack Mohamed) accomplished what can be also described as a '*miracle*' that translated into a formidable boost to industrialization and the tourism industry as well. Duval's PMSD, which had key ministries (Foreign Affairs, Tourism, and Trade) played a prominent role in attracting to the country a large amount of foreign investment in the industry and tourism sectors.

The tourism policies were successfully defined and applied in that period, virtually reserving the island to affluent tourists and rejecting the backpacker style. This paid off in a spectacular manner, making of tourism one of the key economic pillars of the nation. In addition, a major boom in the sugar industry caused by a sharp rise in the price of sugar also helped the Ramgoolam regime in the mid-1970s to show positive economic results until an extremely

27 Une certaine idée de lile Maurice, op cit.
28 To the author of this book, then a young sub-editor at office of *L'Express*
29 Op cit.

1936-1968: The long road to Independence

Two photos taken 32 years apart mark the two of the most most important historical events of a turbulent 20th century. Above, Dr. Maurice Curé is pictured on February 23 at the Champ de Mars at a massive popular meeting of labourers, small planters, workers and thousands of employees of all sectors, during the formation of the Mauritius Labour Party.

Sir Seewoosagur Ramgoolam the fourth leader of the MLP after, successively, Maurice Curé, Emmanuel Anquetil and Guy Rozemont, the latter of the mover of the motion for 'greater self-expression' in 1953, is seen (photo, left) with British Governor Sir John Shaw Rennie, also at the Champ de Mars on March 12, 1968, a few moments after the Mauritian flag replaced the Union Jact as Mauritius obtained independence.

violent cyclone (*Gervaise*) in 1975, destroyed most of the sugar harvest. This was followed, until the beginning of the 1980s, under Labour governments, by an economic and social situation that deteriorated due to skyrocketing inflation and double-digit unemployment rates.

14, 000 Mauritians migrate to other countries, including Australia, from 1966-1972

The fear of independence and economic recession entertained by the PMSD among the population had led large numbers of Mauritians to migrate overseas prior to and in the years following independence. A substantial number of Franco-Mauritians and Coloured persons (due to the *Keep Australia White policy*) migrated to Australia. The Australian government has kept track of this important wave of migrants:

"By the early 1960s, there were about 1,580 Mauritians living in Australia. As Mauritius progressed towards universal suffrage, self-government and finally independence, some Mauritians found themselves in a less privileged position and were more inclined to emigrate. About 14 000 Mauritians left their homeland between 1966 and 1972, some migrating to Australia.

"Given the size of Mauritius, the number of Mauritians in Australia is surprisingly substantial. Numbers have increased steadily over the past 30 years. The 1971 Census recorded 7630 Mauritius-born living in Australia; and by the 2001 Census their number had increased to 16 910 making up 0.4 per cent of the overseas-born population." [30]

Australia that barred from entry immigrants who could not prove they were 75% European. That policy is recalled by the Australian government on its website as follows, regarding Mauritians who migrated in the early 1960s:

"Most of those who migrated were Franco-Mauritians, as the Immigration Restriction Act 1901 introduced policies excluding non-Europeans from entry to Australia, required that prospective settlers be 'at least 75 per cent European.'" [31]

At the end of the 1960s, there were not just Franco-Mauritians, as a large number of migrants were Coloured Mauritians, that is, Creoles who satisfied the 75% requirement with the birth certificates of their grandparents. It is a falsification of the truth to repeat *ad nauseam*, like some communalist-minded politicians still do, that '*Creoles*' abandoned Mauritius for Australia out of ethnic prejudice. In reality, the majority of Coloured and Creoles could not even contemplate migration to Australia, firstly because they had no means to do so, secondly most of them did not want to go there and thirdly they did not qualify racially and, even if they did, they could not care less. Many Creoles were candidates or voted for the Labour/CAM/IFB coalition. In addition, as already stated, the Truth and Justice Commission has rehabilitated the Coloured population denying the right for people to call them '*traitors*.' Relatives of future Prime Minister Sir Aneerood Jugnauth also migrated to Australia and, eventually, thousands of non-Creoles migrated there and to Europe and other destinations, from even before the 1960s and continue to do so.

A large majority of Mauritians who left for Australia in the 1960s, settled in Victoria, mainly in Melbourne. In the 21st century, the Australian authorities stated on Mauritian immigrants, which continued after the end of the *Keep Australia White Policy* when families of all other ethnic groups migrated there:

"The trend changed in the post-war period, with Mauritian immigration peaking during the late 1960s, coinciding with the country's declaration of independence in 1968. By 1971, Victoria was home to the largest population of Mauritius-born immigrants in Australia, with 3,791 people. Their population continued to grow until the early 1990s.

"In 2006, Victoria still had the largest Mauritius-born community in Australia with 9,050 members. This mainly French-speaking, catholic population is based in Hampton Park, Noble Park, Endeavour Hills, Narre Warren and Dandenong. Of those employed 36% are engaged in clerical, sales and service roles while a further 25% work in professional roles. Although many Mauritians participate in the activities of the broader French community, they also have their own distinct identity, born out of a mix of African, Malagasy, Indian, Chinese and French cultures." [32]

The Mauritian diaspora in Australia have kept close links with Mauritius, though the younger immigrants are mainly English speaking with French increasingly becoming a second language.

In the 1970's, thousands of Hindus and members of other communities also migrated because of the prevailing difficult economic conditions in Mauritius. Thousands of Mauritians of all ethnic groups, including large numbers of people of Asian descent, went to work as nurses in Great Britain or to take up other jobs as workers in France, many of them (they belonged to all communities) being scared by the socioeconomic state of the nation before and just after independence, without being branded as traitors. Dr. Ramgoolam himself discussed the possibility of

---
30 *Community Information Summary, Mauritius,* Australian Government, Department of Immigration and Citizenship, all data sourced from the Australian Bureau of Statistics Census of Population and Housing. Website: immi.gov.au Accessed 23 March 2012.
31 Ibid.
32 *Museum Victoria, Origins, Immigrant Communities in Victoria, History of Immigration from Mauritius,* museumvictoria.com.au Accessed 23 March 2012.

facilitating Mauritian immigration in France with the French government. His government set up a ministry of immigration that actively encouraged Mauritians to migrate to other countries because of the severe unemployment problem in the island. Gaëtan Duval, who also held the portfolio of the Ministry of Immigration, helped thousands of Mauritians, irrespective of their ethnic origins, to migrate to Europe, particularly France where he had contacts at the highest levels.

There have been attempts by Mauritian governments in the 21st to adopt an approach that differs from that of the communalist lobbies from the 1960s onwards that have heaped sharp criticism, even abuse on the Mauritians who left during the march of the country to independence just before and after the 1967 general elections. In 2006, Foreign Minister Madun Dulloo indicated the interest Mauritius was taking in its diaspora worldwide. He said that the government was considering ways to tap the skills of those people, and stated:

"Over the years, the Mauritian population was constituted of the European, African, Indian, Chinese and other Asian diasporas. During the second half of the last century a reverse process started. Mauritian born citizens started migrating to reach out to other parts of the world. With the result that we have forged our own Mauritian diaspora spanning the globe and stretching across oceans and continents. The population of the Mauritian diaspora, I am told, is estimated to be about 120,000 i.e. about 10% of the actual Mauritian population." [33]

Rehabilitation came at last in November 2011, initiated by the Truth and Justice Commission:

"No person should have to fight inch by inch for equal rights, equal education, and equal political representation. The waves of emigration of the 1960s and 1970s were, partly at least, caused by the leaders of the Creoles insisting on their 'malaise' and instilling fear into a community. Once the Gens de couleur had left to ensure "a better life for their children", Mauritian cultural life suffered a serious blow. Yet, others grew stronger to take the place of our artists, singers, writers, teachers and intellectuals who had emigrated. Today, Gens de Couleur are expecting that in a spirit of reconciliation, Mauritians in Mauritius ensure that those Mauritians who have emigrated, and continue to do so for family and professional reasons, are not branded as 'traitors' – a sad term used during a Diaspora convention a few years ago.

"Numbers, especially numbers of votes, should matter less, if we are to evolve as a nation; smaller communities, such as the 'General Population', and the Gens de Couleur within it, and Sino-Mauritians, may not have the numbers. However, the Mauritian people must recognise the fact that all communities have made a vital contribution to our history, irrespective of their origins.

"History is philosophy teaching by examples," declared LordBolingbroke. Educating the young through the teaching of a balanced History of Mauritius is the way forward. Only then, can cultural memory take on its true significance for young Mauritians – seeing the present through the past and envisioning the future through the present. Otherwise, old clichés will persist." [34]

---

33 Dulloo, Madun, **Keynote Address, Migration Dialogue for Southern Africa Workshop,** Le Maritim Hotel, 11 October 2006.
34 **Truth andJustice Commission,** op cit. Page 253.

Some leaders at the time of independence
Top, from left: Sir Satcam Boolell, Sookdeo Bissoondoyal, Sir Gaëtan Duval.
Middle, from left: Sir Guy Forget, Sir Veerasamy Ringadoo, Sir Raman Osman.
Third row, from left: Sir Kher Jagatsingh, Sir Jean Moilin Ah Chuen, Raymond Rault.
Left: Hurryparsad Ramnarain.
Photos: Courtesy of the Government Information Services (GIS).

Chapter 44
A new political force emerges

The partnership between the private sector and the coalition government within the western postcolonial strategies was bound to upset the members of a new leftist movement created by Jooneed Jeerooburkhan, Dev Virah Sawmy and Paul Bérenger, who founded the Mouvement Militant Mauricien in 1969 and vowed, during the first years of its existence, to establish a regime of direct democracy inspired from Marxism as well as from the 1968 Student Revolution in Europe. Their aim, they stated, was to eradicate capitalism and Western imperialism and neocolonialism, and to diversify the country's international relations by developing new relationships with the Communist bloc, the Scandinavian countries and other regions of the world where Paul Bérenger claimed there were interesting markets for Mauritian exports.

In an article published in *Le Mauricien* back in 1968, Paul Bérenger had advocated *"peaceful revolution,"* but *"permanent political agitation"* by the workers, the unemployed and the youth. He expressed the wish that Mauritius adhered to the revolutionary trends in the Third World in the struggle against *"Western imperialism."* He advocated the formation of *"revolutionary trade union movements"* so as to induce the workers to leave the *"traditional parties and leaders"* and professed the necessity of a cultural revolution in favour of the emergence of a *"culture populaire et tiers-mondlste."* At the top, the revolutionary organisation would be rather *"fluid."* [1]

That was to be the first stage of the revolution, wrote Paul Bérenger, Then, there would be the second stage during which there would be, this time, a well-structured revolutionary executive organisation at the top. That second stage would be one of *"permanent popular agitation, accelerated to its highest pitch."* Then there would be two further stages consolidating the revolution whereby power would be shared by a *"triple alliance"* consisting of the New Left (the revolutionary party), the youth and the workers grouped in *"revolutionary trade unions."* That article was signed by Paul Bérenger in the name of the Club des Etudiants Militants (CEM).

In 1968, Paul Bérenger, who rapidly became the strong man of the *"new left"*, first under the banner of the CEM then under that of the MMM, sent a collection of articles of the CEM to the press entitled *"What the CEM wants,"* where the *'failure of orthodox Marxists'* was criticised. The emerging political group showed interest for the Marxist experiences in Cuba, China and Tanzania, quoting prominent writers and thinkers like Gunnar Myrdal and René Dumont. Parliamentarism, according to those articles, was bankrupt and had to be replaced by the Marxist formula of direct democracy. [2]

After completing his studies in philosophy and journalism in Europe, Bérenger had come back to Mauritius in 1969, taken part in the foundation of the MMM with his group of friends and emerged with Virahsawmy and Jeerooburkhan as the leading trio of the party. Their main concern, judging from their several statements in the media and during their public appearances, was the *'neocolonial setup'* of independent Mauritius, the role of the big capitalist groups, foreign and local and the ethnic politics practised by the *'traditional'* political parties, which they designated as PMSD, CAM and also Labour, the latter being accused of having *'betrayed'* its original ideals of the 1930s and 1940s that prevailed under Maurice Curé, Pandit Sahadeo and others. This led them to clash violently with the police on 12 September 1969, led by their main animators, among whom Bérenger, at the St. Jean roundabout while they protested an official visit of Princess Alexandra, accompanied by her husband Angus Ogilvy, of the transnational conglomerate Lonrho that had invested considerably in the Mauritius sugar industry.

The multiethnic crowd of young people shouted anti-imperialist slogans and stones were thrown at the car of the royal couple from a nearby sugar cane field by persons that, according to the participants, were unknown to them, and had not been noticed by them. The police arrested twelve of the demonstrators, among whom Bérenger, Sushil Kushiram and Heeralall Bhugaloo, who had been wounded during the confrontation. From that day onwards, the future MMM and the coalition government engaged in a battle that was going to cost the life of one of the MMM militants who was assassinated in 1971, and the death, in allegedly mysterious circumstances according to the

---
[1] Bérenger, Paul, *L'ABC de notre révolution,* Le Mauricien, 11 september 1968, Paul Bérenger.
[2] Le Mauricien, from 16 September 1968.

MMM, of another one in a car accident. There were innumerable street protests and violent clashes between militants and bouncers of the MMM and those of mainly the PMSD of whom three went to prison in relation to the 1971 murder of MMM militant Azor Adelaide.

It was actually when the Labour/PMSD coalition government was being discussed, in September 1969, and after the St. Jean demonstration against Alexandra, that the CEM had mutated into a '***revolutionary***' party, the MMM. This party immediately started to apply the first stage of its plan by campaigning against the '***traditional***' parties, unions and political leaders. The MMM sums up its early history as follows:

"*1968: Mauritius obtains its independence, but there is no popular euphoria as such. The sequels of the racial conflict are still very much in the minds of a deeply divided population. During a holiday in Mauritius from his studies, Paul Bérenger made acquaintance with Dev Virahsawmy, Jooneed Jeerooburkhan, Tirat Ramkisoon, Krishen Matis, Ah-Ken Wong, Kreeti Goburdhun, Vella Vengaroo, all of them members of the Club des Etudiants. They had discussions, following which it was decided to transform the Club des Etudiants into the Club des Etudiants Militants. This club was organising discussions and holding ideological sessions at the Tennyson College and the City of London College in Quatre Bornes. Less than a year later, the Club des Etudiants Militants mutated into the Mougement Militant Mauricien.*" [3]

The party militated on several issues that included the diplomatic relations that existed then between Mauritius and Israel in spite of the occupation of Palestinian lands by that state, as well as the relations of the coalition government with the apartheid regime in South Africa.

The country kept close, though non-diplomatic ties with South Africa mainly because it depended heavily for its tea exports to that country and, as well to sustain its budding tourism industry. Mauritius also maintained the links with Pretoria to satisfy its need for cheap imports in key sectors of the economy, which, according to the government's version of facts, would have otherwise collapsed and brought economic disaster should Mauritius have applied economic sanctions. Later, while condemning strongly apartheid, Mauritius would plead for recognition as being in a similar position as the *"front-line"* African states also dependent on South Africa for economic reasons. The argument was that South Africa was the closest industrialised economy and, as such, a major market for exports and imports. The MMM would, for several years, advocate alternative sources for trade and business that would help to reduce the country's dependency on the apartheid regime. A boycott of the South African oranges ***Outspan*** was even decreed by the militants.

Moreover, large communities of Mauritians, Whites, Coloured and Indo-Mauritians, had lived for generations in South Africa and had (they still have) close ties with their relatives in Mauritius. Some opponents of apartheid in South Africa could not understand the economic dependency of Mauritius on the South African economy and the impossibility of finding an alternative strategy.

In those days, the country was economically extremely fragile and poverty was rampant. Traditionalpolitical leaders and even some trade union bosses seemed to have rallied around Western values while being allegedly complacent towards the private sector leaders, and the impression was cultivated by the MMM in the public opinion that they had left the masses to their fate. That was the major reason why the brand of *"marxisme libertaire"* proposed by Paul Bérenger and his group appealed strongly to the youth and the workers. Hundreds of people flocked to the political forums organised by the emerging Marxist leaders and those meetings sometimes degenerated into incidents with the police. Some were interdicted, the result being still more popularity for the new political leadership and the party.

Within a few years, even politicians known for their moderation joined the MMM. One was Aneerood Jugnauth, who had abandoned politics, but returned in 1971 to join the MMM, attracted by *"direct democracy,"* which he advocated at several press conferences in the 1970s. Nevertheless, a number of moderate political leaders who were left of centre, like Sookdeo Bissoondoyal and Guy Ollivry were against any attempt to establish a Marxist regime in Mauritius and vigorously expressed their views to that effect. Nevertheless, they also strongly condemned what they considered the coalition government's over-reaction which consisted in the systematic and brutal repression of the leftist movement, including the suspension of basic constitutional freedoms.

As the 1970s went by, Bérenger developed contacts within the government even while his party was suffering from repression and envisaged with insistence an alliance with Labour provided the PMSD was kicked out of government. He was entering mainstream politics[4] while his party was changing the political landscape and changing the

---
3 ***Histoire du MMM de 1969 à 2006,*** at mmmparty.org Accessed 23 March 2012.
4 Whatever can be said about the postponement of the general election of 1972 and the subsequent harsh repression of the growing Marxist movement in Mauritius, one of their leaders, Paul Bérenger himself, once confided to the author of his book at the editorial office of the party newspaper, ***Le Militant***, that it was a good thing the MMM did not accede to power in 1976 with an electoral manifesto that would have

way people perceived their own history, in many ways positively and in other ways not without serious mistakes like, according to many critics, Bérenger's often controversial approach to ethnic politics into which he was dragged as decades flew by.

Nevertheless, he has had with him nearly half of the electorate who voted him as Prime Minister at general elections in 1983, 2000 and 2010, which certainly means that his support cut across the ethnic divide, despite the fact that the situation has persisted where more of the minorities vote MMM (as they voted PMSD in 1967) and, among the other multiethnic half of Mauritus voting Navin Ramgoolam (or Aneerood Jugnauth in the 1980s), there is a majority of Hindus together with other communities. This is only what can be speculated, the vote being secret and ethnic considerations being impossible to translate in figures.

For their part, Sir Seewoosagur Ramgoolam and Duval claimed that their achievements as leaders of the coalition were considerable: they later highlighted that they engineered the successful diversification of the economic base of the country, which enabled the *"economic miracle,"* an era of unprecedented economic prosperity starting in the mid-1980s when unemployment vanished and foreign workers had to be called in under Aneerood Jugnauth's successive prime ministerships until 2003.

---

resulted in a wave of nationalisations and a *"direct democracy"* experiment that would have *"**us being booted from power sooner than we would have expected.**"*

Chapter 45
Agitated times - and political assassination

The coalition government quickly became unpopular in spite of the positive economic transformation that it had kickstarted. New opposition leader Sookdeo Bissoondoyal, and UDM leader Maurice Lesage systematically blasted the Labour-CAM-PMSD regime for postponing the 1972 general election. Outside parliament, the MMM was on a spectacular uptrend course, attracting large crowds, mostly young, but also disgruntled supporters of PMSD, Labour, CAM and PMSD.

The party was also becoming extremely active on the trade union front, setting up new unions that rapidly obtained the majority support of the workforce in several key sectors of the national economy, especially the port, the transport industry and the Central Electricity Board (CEB). Those unions were brought together under the banner of a new organisation, the General Workers Federation. Bérenger manoeuvred successfully to take over the control of both the party and its unions. He displayed political skills that comprised a mixture of charisma that attracted voters, and ruthlessness applied within party ranks and little known outside - both characteristics being typical of the leaders of the large parties in Mauritius.

In 1969 and 1970, the "*Militants*" popularized their manifesto entitled *"Pour une Ile Maurice possible."* In that document and in other public statements made to the media, the party advocated the nationalization of key-sectors of the economy, namely the sugar industry, the banks, the port, as well as the transport and insurance industries. It was clear the party was then campaigning to curtail the economic might of the sugar barons, who, the MMM repeatedly over the years, *"control the key sectors of the national economy."* Little did people suspect, then, that as time flew by, Marxist regimes would collapse all over the planet (with some exceptions) and the MMM would not just conclude an alliance with the PMSD, but also adopt neo-liberal policies set down by the International Monetary Fund (IMF) and the World Bank in Washington DC.

In 1969, it was a completely different world and the MMM's slogan *"Yes to class struggle yes, no to ethnic conflict"*[1] was the ideology that was being successfully propagated from coast to coast in Mauritius. The MMM organized systematically special courses *"to educate the masses"* focused on class-based politics meant to replace ethnic politics. About one year later, it had a golden opportunity to show its strength in a parliamentary by-election.

MMM's first electoral victory: Triolet-Pamplemousses

Lall Jugnauth, member of the National Assembly for Triolet/Pamplemousses, had died and the whole country focused on the upcoming by-election to replace him. Incidents of an increasingly violent nature opposed agents of the coalition government parties and those of the MMM. The workers across the country became more and more restless as the MMM-related unions stepped up efforts to force wage and salary increases. Bérenger had become, by then, so popular among all ethnic groups, particularly the working classes, that Sookdeo Bissoondoyal proposed, at one point, that his mother, Mrs. Bérenger, one of the party's most dedicated activists, should be a candidate at the by-election in defiance of communalism in a constituency with a large Hindu majority,

"... as a sign of solidarity with Paul Bérenger and the other leaders of the MMM who were imprisoned at that time. This did not happen for one reason or another, but he campaigned for the MMM candidate, Dev Virahsawmy, who won a landslide victory." [2]

Bissoondoyal campaigned for the MMM, whose candidate, finally, was Dev Virahsawmy who, nevertheless, did not fit the ethnic profile required in those days and even in the 21st century, of candidates in that constituency which was the prime minister's stronghold. Virahsawmy crushed his Labour opponent Boodram Nundlall, obtaining 71.5 % of the votes. This caused panic within the ranks of government and later Duval was to reveal that the coalition regime was on the verge of collapsing.[3] Duval, Satcam Boolell and Razack Mohamed, were to be among a small group of ministers who were instrumental in preventing this.

Duval also resigned for a short period from the Cabinet to constitute, albeit with very little success, a *"Black Power"*

---
[1] In French, "***Lutte des classes et non lutte des races***".
[2] In: ***L'Express***, 26 September 2008, ***Sookdeo Bissoondoyal (1908-1977)***, op cit.
[3] *Une certaine idée de l'île Maurice*, op cit.

movement to try and woo back into the ranks of the PMSD thousands of Creole workers who had flocked to the MMM and its trade unions. The movement quickly fizzled out, but serious incidents followed between his bodyguards and agents, and those of the MMM-GWF. Those incidents were increasingly violent and at times occurred on an almost daily basis. Tension reached a high pitch, especially in Duval's stronghold of Curepipe.

Virahsawmy was sworn in as member of the National Assembly in November 1970, in a safari suit, in defiance of conventional dress code requiring suit and tie. He managed to have this casual attire accepted in Parliament, arguing also that Guy Sauzier had done it before him. Within the coalition government, the first days of panic were followed by the adoption of a harder stance towards the MMM.

Legislation was passed in the following months and years to, among other measures, abolish altogether parliamentary by-elections and allowing vacant seats to be filled by candidates who had lost the previous general election. Another measure taken was the Public Order Act (POA) that practically interdicted public meetings that were not wanted by the government. Even one Labour member of the National Assembly, B. Gokulsingh, voted against that law. The IFB and the UDM opposed it vehemently in the National Assembly while in the media there was severe criticism that a *'police state'* was in the making. [4] The law was voted by the Labour-CAM-PMSD coalition regime by a majority of 43-13.

The government argued that the country would become unmanageable without such a law. Investment would not be forthcoming, especially from overseas, Ramgoolam and Duval warned, if social instability persisted. They pointed to the repeated strikes organized by the leaders of the MMM and GWF that paralysed the national economy and cost the nation hundreds of millions of rupees in lost economic activities.

The social situation actually worsened as PMSD and MMM agents engaged in violent skirmishes in the towns. In December 1971, the worst happened: there were assassination attempts by PMSD agents against the MMM leaders Bérenger and Virahsawmy in Curepipe, in front of the municipal building and the restaurant **Welcome**, at Rue Chasteauneuf, respectively. Shots were fired during both incidents barely missing the two MMM/GWF leaders, but killing on the spot, in Chasteauneuf Street, Virahsawrny's companion Azor Adelaide, a dock worker and MMM/GWF activist. Bérenger and bodyguards Said Mungroo and Désiré Carre had barely escaped moments before, when they had been attacked, by fleeing to the yard of Dr. Soreefan's residence, where they heard the shots of the second assassination attempt during which Adelaide died.

The attackers were identified by witnesses as Shummoogum, Paul Sarah, who was accused of firing the shot that killed Adelaide, and Ignace Balloo, but doubts still subsist about Balloo's culpability. They were later arrested, convicted and condemned to long terms in prison. Prior to that, while the three men had been awaiting trial, Duval had started a campaign against the death penalty, which they risked. Actually, Duval was both proving his loyalty to his agents and expressing his lifelong, philosophical opposition to the death penalty. The nation was in a state of shock after Adelaide's death. The country had no tradition of political assassinations. The MMM and other opponents to the coalition regime started a campaign accusing the PMSD of having a tradition of violence. The PMSD's image deteriorated further, with the MMM writing graffitis on walls across the country during several years, especially at election time, accusing the party of being one of "*assassins*". Duval's position within government gradually weakened while his **"Black Power"** movement evaporated, leaving no significant trace in the nation's political evolution.

As for the MMM, it continued to rise in popularity, benefiting from the PMSD's decline and the increasing discontent of workers and of the middle classes as well, in the face of economic austerity. Low wages and salaries and inflation that often reached into double digits fuelled the discontent.

The wage freeze blasted by the MMM/GWF

Actually, the MMM and the GWF managed to break the wage freeze that had been in place in the transport industry by obtaining, on November 9, 1971, a Supreme Court decision by Judge Droopnath Ramphul who ordered a 12% wage increase for transport workers. This led to wage increases in other sectors, which helped the MMM and GWF increase their influence and support from the salaried employees, especially among middle and lower middle classes.

Nevertheless, the party and its unions hardened their stance after that, especially in the last two months of 1971. Sensing that the unpopularity of the government was on the increase, a trend developed within the MMM and the

---
4 *Le Mauricien*, 11 December 1970.

GWF that clamoured for the two to associate further and bring down the government through agitation. A group of dissenting militants wanted to continue the *"education of the masses"* through the propagation of Marxism before any attempt was made at overthrowing the government.

The MMM and the GWF finally triggered, on December 16, 1971, a general strike nationwide, with the clear objective of bringing down the government. Bérenger publicly claimed that the government was about to fall. The situation was made worse by a series of attacks against electric transformers across the country and the burning of sugar cane fields. The government promptly accused the MMM of *"acts of sabotage"* in addition to having paralysed the national economy with strikes that completely immobilized crucial sugar and other exports as well as much needed imports. Production in several sectors was disrupted by the strikes that affected transport and electricity. [5]

At the Supreme Court, Judge Ramphul, who had been asked to arbitrate once again the industrial dispute, said he would not work in a climate marked by strikes. In the ministerial cabinet, a majority emerged to strike back at the MMM and GWF with force. The private sector was vigorously urging government to take action to stop the strikes, while its mouthpiece *Le Cernéen* was campaigning against the ideology of Marxism and its Mauritian torchbearers.

The coalition government strikes back

The government did not take long to react – and it was a very strong reaction indeed. The para-military force of the police (the Special Mobile Force - SMF) was brought to help the normal force and the Riot Unit to put an end to the strikes. Workers were bused through picket lines into the port in military transport vehicles. Hundreds of strikers were sacked across the island. Duval, who was the Lord Mayor in Port-Louis, sacked dozens of strikers at the municipality. On December 22, Parliament voted by a majority of 48 against 10 and five abstentions, a government bill setting up a nationwide state of emergency. On December 28, even though the GWF's general assembly had called off the strikes after the proclamation of the state of emergency and legislation introduced to curtail severely the rights of trade unions and workers, all unions of the MMM-GWF were interdicted while Bérenger, Dev Virah Sawmy, HervéMasson and several other militants of the two organizations were arrested and imprisoned.

Calm was restored across the country. The police, the Riot Unit and the SMF patrolled hot spots. But the MMM and the GWF actually prospered by going completely underground, organizing clandestine meetings at night and multiplying its militant cells in towns and villages all over the island. Repression gave the militants an aura of glory in the eyes of their supporters and even attracted to them the bourgeois that had been so often criticised by the most radical elements of the party. However, the secret service, then the State Security Service (SSS) infiltrated several cells and the government was rather well informed of several decisions the party took during clandestine meetings. Bérenger and Masson spent the year 1972 in prison, attracting further support in the middle classes.

Among those bourgeois the MMM attracted to its ranks there was a lawyer called Anerood Jugnauth, who had entered history by defeating in 1963, as an IFB candidate, an iconic leader of the Labour Party, Anauth Beejadhur, at Rivière du Rempart. He had been shortly a Cabinet minister and resigned, he said, after disagreeing with other ministers on some issues that he was deeply concerned with, namely favouritism practised, he said, by government. In 1971, Jugnauth resurfaced from his *"retreat"* – he had worked as a Crown Counsel, then as a magistrate before setting up his own private practice. He entered the party's book of legends by visiting the political prisoners and meeting Bérenger during the latter's one-year stay in prison. Those contacts transformed him into a militant of the MMM.

Meanwhile, the press suffered a strict regime of government censorship. All chief editors had to submit a proof of their newspaper before printing to allow the police censors to cut out things like the mere mention of the names of MMM and GWF leaders and even the slightest criticism of the government. At one point, censorship was made more severe by forcing newspapers to fill in the blanks left by the police '*scissors*' so as to hide from the eyes of the public the work of the censors. After three years, censorship was gradually relaxed.

One newspaper was interdicted from the time the state of emergency was voted. It was **Le Militant**, which at that time was edited by Hervé Masson, a popular MMM figure and former Labour Party supporter and pro-independence militant, who had come back from Paris, where he was a reputed artist, to Mauritius to take up a job offered to him by Ramgoolam. He later defected to the MMM because of his strong hard line Marxist convictions. The MMM was authorized in 1975 to again publish a newspaper.

---

5 *Le Mauricien* issues from 17 September has extensive day-today news coverage of those events.

Prison had a considerable impact on the MMM. Courting the middle classes became a leitmotiv for Bérenger and this was one of the reasons given by Dev Virahsawmy, his brother Raj, Peter Craig and other radical militants of the party to break away and form the MMMSP (Mouvement Militant Socialiste Progressiste) after Dev Virahsawy was freed from political prison. All of those radical Marxists veered sharply to the political right a few years later in alliances with the PMSD.

From the point of view of the national economy, though the government damaged the democratic fabric of the nation and its own popularity by the state of emergency, the POA, press censorship, political imprisonment and repression. It could express satisfaction that industrialisation had successfully been kickstarted in the EPZ, exports were growing and tourism was flourishing. The trio of leaders, Ramgoolam, Duval, Mohamed and some top ministers like Satcam Boolell, Harold Walter and Kher Jagatsingh have always defended their actions in those days as having been inspired above all by the national interest. They have shored up their arguments with the economic achievements of the coalition government.

Chapter 46
Successful economic diversification

The Meade report initiated the concept of economic diversification as far back as 1961. It led to the setting up of the ISIs (import substitution industries) from 1963 and, seven years later, Mauritius moved a step further by setting up the EOIs (export oriented industries). A study by Rhundeersing Bheenick and Morton Morton Schapiro published by the Economic Development Institute of the World Bank recalls that this '*famous*' report had recommended the diversification of the economy through industrialisation as one of the key measures in the face of the population explosion, and acknowledges that the Mauritian govenments performed well in applying this solution. [1]

Set up by legislation in 1970, the export processing zone (EPZ) started creating hundreds, then thousands of jobs each year. The new coalition government's policies regarding the EPZ and the tourism industry, gave the country a new start with high rates of economic growth never achieved previously. The average growth rate of the gross domestic product reached 10 per cent yearly from 1971 to 1975 while the balance of payments recorded considerable surpluses.

The main engines of economic growth in the first half of the 1970s were, in addition to the sugar industry (boosted by booming prices and record harvests) the EPZ and the tourism industry. In the second half of the decade, though, there was a slowdown in the EPZ and the national economy was in crisis due to a number of factors.

"Perhaps the most basic measure of the EPZ's success is the number of enterprises established. After being officially launched by the EPZ Act of December 1970, nine units were set up within one year of the scheme's initiation... beginning in 1971, the sector expanded rapidly because of the buoyant economic conditions accompanying the record sugar crop. With the economy liquid and capital funds plentiful, investors took advantage of the incentives available under the EPZ proposition, the result being an impressive number of new units added each year until 1977.

"The second phase, 1977-82, was marked by a deceleration in EPZ expansion. The momentum created in the earlier phase was lost. In general the number of units operating continued to increase but at a much slower pace. During this time, nearly one-third of the existing firms shut down, with the highest number of closures in any one year being 15 in 1978. The EPZ had borne the brunt of the recession in the industrialized countries and of their increasingly protectionist policies. Plus, on the domestic front, the expansionary fiscal policy the government pursued in the wake of the boom conditions of the mid-1970s raised wages faster than productivity, leading to higher unit labor costs and pricing some EPZ products out of world markets." [2]

Diplomacy: a key element of the economic revival

At the time the Labour/PMSD coalition was formed, Mauritius was struggling on all fronts trying to safeguard its sugar export markets, most of the production being sold to the U.K. Ramgoolam, Duval and the Mauritian diplomats in Europe worked hard to obtain the necessary support, especially from France. Their objective was to obtain that the European Common Market (now the European Union) accept Mauritian sugar exports on a preferential basis after the U.K.'s entry into the European community and the phasing out of the Commonwealth Sugar Agreement (CSA), which had benefited Mauritius for decades. In addition, Mauritius was vying for economic association with Europe to sell its EPZ products, dominated by textiles, at preferential tariffs. The European Union, originally the European Common Market, had, under the Treaty of Rome that created it in 1958, developed special economic links for the former French, Belgian and Italian colonies that had been consolidated by the Yaoundé conventions of 1963 and 1969.

The arduous diplomatic effort, led by Ramgoolam, Duval, Agriculture Minister Satcam Boolell, assisted by accredited officials like Guy Sauzier, Ambassador Raymond Chasles in Brussels, and High Commissioner Leckraj Teelock in London, was going to bear its fruits. Mauritian diplomacy obtained support from the African and Caribbean countries associated with the EU under Yaoundé in addition to strong diplomatic support already guaranteed by France. The counterpart was that France became deeply involved in Mauritius, promoting close cultural links while protecting her and NATO's geopolitical and strategic interests under the benevolent patronage of the coalition government.

Ramgoolam announced to Parliament in March 1970 that the negotiations regarding the continuation of sug-

1 Bheenick, Schapiro, op cit.
2 Ibid.

ar exports at preferential prices after Britain's entry in the EU (then the European Common Market) comprised meetings in London and other European capitals as well as discussions with other Commonwealth countries that resulted in widespread support for Mauritius as *'a special case'* due to the country's reliance *'for more than 96% on the export of sugar.'* He added, regarding the diplomatic efforts of Mauritius:

"It was wise for us to go and explain our position and we succeeded (...). We worked like a team and did everything in an atmosphere of goodwill and understanding (...) We have established friendly relations with many countries and these countries are prepared to sympathise with our efforts. Britain will do her best to see that the Sugar Agreement is maintained as far as a lot of Commonwealth countries and New Zealand are concerned." [3]

Two years later, on March 2, 1972, negotiations started in Brussels during which Mauritius asked for admission to the Yaoundé Convention. Five ministers, five government technocrats and two representatives of the private sector as well as several diplomats formed part of the Mauritian delegation. Mauritius was admitted to the Yaoundé convention in October.

Mauritius had benefited from 1953 from a guaranteed export quota under the Commonwealth Sugar Agreement (CSA) that allowed most of our sugar exports to be absorbed by the British and Canadian markets. That quota rose from 470,000 tons in 1953 to 570,000 tons in 1974, at the time the CSA expired. It was only during eight years that the prices obtained under that agreement fell under the world price of sugar. During the 1972 sugar harvest, the sugar industry suffered, paradoxically, from a labour shortage though there were 40,000 people registered as unemployed. The industry had a record harvest of 600,000 tons, which explained the need for a larger labour force.

Mauritius was finally admitted to the Lomé Convention that succeeded Yaoundé in 1975, with a guaranteed export quota of half a million tons of sugar annually, in addition to export preferences for its industrial production and financial support to economic development from European development funds, among a range of opportunities offered by the convention. Harvard University Kennedy School's Jeffrey Frankel observes:

"Even though the EEC price was well below the world price then, during most of the time, since, it has been far above, due to the political power of European farmers domestically. Thus the decision by Mauritius to place priority on quantity turns out to have been a brilliant strategy. Sugar exports to Europe produced large rents for many years thereafter,70 part of which the government was able to capture and use for social spending and part of which went to investment." [4]

The national economy, which had stagnated during the period 1968-1970, improved considerably in the first half of the 1970s as a result of economic diversification as well as the maintenance of sugar exports at preferential prices. From 1971 to 1977, a total of 64,000 jobs were created and the total number of employed people rose from 142,485 in 1971 to 194,762 in 1977. Most of those jobs were being created in the export processing zone and the tourism industry. [5]

In 1971, there were only nine factories in the EPZ, with a total of 644 employees and exporting about Rs. 4 million worth of manufactured goods, mainly garments. In 1977, the figures had risen to 89 factories employing 18,169 persons and exporting products for a total value of Rs. 433 million.

In the tourism industry, progress was remarkable also. The number of foreign visitors to the country, which was 15,533 in 1968, more than doubled in 1971. It continued to rise and in 1977 went over the 100,000 mark to reach 102,510. The yearly percentage increases recorded between 1969 and 1973 were unprecedented. In 1969, the number of visitors went up by 32.4 %; in the following year the increase was 31.6 %; in 1972 it was a 34.1 % increase; and in 1973 there was an all time record increase of 39.3 %.

Sugar production also progressed significantly. It reached 621,000 tons in 1971, 686,000 the following year, 718,000 tons in 1973 and 697,000 tons in 1974. Those record figures of production brought into the country huge receipts in foreign exchange, the more so that, at that time, the price of sugar was increasing on the world market, where Mauritius was selling its production that was in excess of its guaranteed quota on the European market.

Highs and lows of a tumultuous decade – the 1970s

The negotiated sugar price went from 57 pounds sterling per ton for 1972-1973 to 79 pounds in 1974. Mauritius, was also able to sell, in addition to its guaranteed EU quota, over 100,000 tons yearly at high prices on the world

---
[3] Hansard, *Debate* 17 March 1970.
[4] Frankel Jeffrey, ***Mauritius: An African Success Story***, Harvard Kennedy School, September 7, 2010, HKS Working Paper No. RWP10-036
[5] The figures and facts, here, have been extracted and summarised by the author from diverse Government of Mauritius statistical data for the years in focus, including Central Statistics Office and Ministry of Economic Planning reports. See also: Dinan, Pierre, ***Dix ans d'économie mauricienne***, Editions IPC, Port-Louis 1979.

market during those boom years, until 1974. However, in 1975, the harvest was destroyed to a great extent by cyclone Gervaise, one of the most violent in the nation's history. As a result, Mauritius could not even reach a production figure that could enable it to respect its commitment to the export quota of 500,000 tons to Europe under the Lomé Convention (which had replaced the Yaoundé Convention).

Nonetheless, with an average economic growth rate of 8.2 % yearly from 1971 to 1977, Mauritius remarkably progressed on the economic front. The foundations of economic diversification had been successfully laid.

If, in the final years of the 1970s decade, a major economic crisis was to hit the country, during the first half of the decade, workers had benefited from the economic prosperity of the nation through hefty bonuses paid by the sugar industry. Also, tens of thousands of unemployed people and their families had revenues from the new jobs created in the EPZ. At that time, the sugar industry was the nation's biggest employer, with 62,000 employees, while the EPZ employed 2,588 persons and the tourism industry 1,559.

All in all, 1972, 1973 and 1974 were years of appeasement for the nation. The end-of-year bonuses that were paid out, especially in the sugar industry, the sugar boom, and the jobs created by the economic upturn created an air of general prosperity. In 1974, a 35 % wage increase was granted to the dockers by Judge Vallet. A bonus equivalent to 12 months of their salary was granted to the administrative personnel of all sugar estates across the country, after the industry obtained record revenues of over one billion rupees. During the period 1974-1979, salaries increased by 30 %. The welfare state was reinforced with, among other things, the introduction of a national pension scheme, the abolition of school fees and constantly increased subsidies to basic food supplies, rice and flour.

One must bear in mind, though, that Mauritius was still a poor country and parts of the urban and the rural areas had important pockets of rampant poverty mainly due to a still high figure of 65,000 registered unemployed people. Nevertheless, the basis of the future Mauritian economic miracle of the 1980s was already in place with tourism and manufacturing continuing to grow. The Labour-led government that continued to lead the country after 1976 seemed to be suffering from so much internal instability and power games, especially within Labour itself, that it was increasingly divided. It was unable to respond as a team to a better organised and more dynamic, younger generation of opposition politicians that dominated the parliamentary debates, raising, for instance, major issues like the cession of the Chagos, the Tromelin Island affair, the economic decline of the second decade of the 1970s and the subsequent '*brutal*' devaluations of the Mauritian rupee that caused spectacular increases of the cost of living. It could not also respond to the younger elements who became restless and rebellious within Labour itself, pressing for internal reform and restructuration of the party.

One major problem in those years was the state of democracy after the paralyzing strikes of 1971, in the light of a new situation where the threat of political and social upheaval was already history. The government appeared still wary of the MMM and its trade unions, though everybody could notice that the party was increasingly moderating its ideology to attract the bourgeois classes. This was obvious with the recruiting, during the years leading to the 1976 general election, of Anerood Jugnauth, Rajesh Bhagwan, Vishnu Lutchmeenaraidoo, Ram Pyndiah, and other people.

What still worried Ramgoolam and Duval, even after the latter joined the ranks of the opposition and formed a "*Front commun*" of trade unions with Bérenger, was that those bourgeois cadres of the party supported direct democracy and nationalization policies that remained the hard core of the MMM's manifesto. How could such bourgeois cadres of the party propose, until the 1976 general elections, a Marxist agenda, even of a '*libertarian*' type, and entertain close links with Madagascar where the regime practised hard line communism under Didier Ratsiraka, leading that island into dire poverty; the Seychelles, which, under President Albert René who was no better, then, than his Malagasy counterpart; and other similar regimes in Algeria, Cuba and Lybia?

In 1974, the last of the boom years of the decade for the sugar industry and the national economy, few people would imagine that the following year would be one of the worst of the nation's history, with cyclone ***Gervaise*** hitting hard Mauritius in February 1975.

Meanwhile, the political struggles continued, but this time, the MMM, like the rest of the opposition parties, used the constitutional institutions to attack the regime. The MMM petitioned the Supreme Court asking the judges to scrap the constitutional amendment that had postponed the 1972 general elections. But the judges refused to listen to the arguments in favour of the restoration of democratic elections presented by the party's lawyers, Anerood

Jugnauth and Kader Bhayat. The Supreme Court judges in those days rejected all demands by various opposition parties, including the UDM and, later the PMSD, to restore the electoral system, abolish press censorship and allow public meetings.

There being no other constitutional way to obtain general elections, the MMM, after losing its case in the Supreme Court, did not opt for street action and strikes again to try and get rid of the government. It was clear that Jugnauth and Bhayat, among the many new middle class recruits of the party, were having a major influence within the ruling circles of the MMM.

For their part, the UDM and the IFB voted against another undemocratic piece of legislation introduced in Parliament. That was the law, already mentioned, abolishing legislative by-elections and motivated by the victory of the MMM in Triolet/Pamplemousses. It authorised the appointment as members of the National Assembly of candidates who had lost the 1967 general election and having obtained the highest percentage of votes among non-relected candidates. The parliamentary opposition parties, however, lost several seats when a number of their members defected to the other side of the House. The UDM lost several members in this way and, as a result, on October 13, 1973, the party leader, Maurice Lesage, ceded to the IFB leader Sookdeo Bissondoyal his position as leader of the opposition. Switching allegiance was increasingly a matter of enjoying the perks and priveleges of power than anything else and the future was going to see an increase of this kind of behaviour among all political parties. Rumours of corruption, favours being dished out in exchange for switching sides, big sums changing hands and blackmail used against parliamentarians trapped in some murky matters, even of a personal nature, spread, always unverified, always talked about, never proved and never the subject of serious inquiry so thick and opaque were (and still are) the curtains protecting the secrets of politburos of various hues and ideologies.

Towards the end of the 1970s, and during the 1980s, ideologies disappeared altogether among the mainstream political establishment, to which the MMM finally adhered. The party was sucked as all the others into traditional politicking, particularly meticulous ethnic screening of candidates, ethnic politics, and secretive financing of operations. Politics among this mainstream became more than ever a hunting ground for perks and privileges and all such matters pertaining to self-gratification through politics, and less and less to genuine consideration for the national interest. An inflation of a new kind appeared on the political stage in the ensuing decades: an increasing number of allegations and counter-allegations of corruption within the political establishment that have continued well into the 21st century. [6]

Another piece of legislation that was going to be blasted by the MMM for several decades and which its members actually failed to scrap when in power on various occasions, was the Industrial Relations Act (IRA) that severely restricted the freedom of workers and their unions. Later, Duval, who had participated while in government, in the preparation of that legislation, expressed his regrets in his memoirs. [7] In truth Duval never voted for the IRA. The reason was that just before it was brought to Parliament, his party was expelled by Ramgoolam from the coalition government. This happened in 1973, at a time when the national economy was improving, an indication that the government was on the defensive in the face of a popular opposition.

The social scene remains troubled

Mauritians, despite the booming years 1973-1974, did not feel happy in their own country, according to a poll organised by the Joint Economic Council (JEC) which revealed that 62 per cent of the population wanted to migrate to another country. A total of 42 per cent of people polled wanted an office job.

The suspects in the murder of Azor Adelaide were convicted and sentenced to heavy prison terms. On the political front, the government, having already abolished legislative by-elections, postponed the municipal elections which would only be held five years later, in 1977.

In December 1972, the MMM and GWF members, including Paul Bérenger and Hervé Masson, held as political prisoners since 1971, were released. The social atmosphere was then more relaxed than during the previous year and the nation was busy celebrating by the end of the year following the payment of substantial bonuses to all employees.

In February of that year, the Bank of Mauritius announced that the annual growth rate of the economy had reached

---

6 This paragraph is the author's analysis (based on observations made during 44 years of jounalistic career).
7 *Une certaine idée de l'île Maurice*, op cit.

10 % and that the balance of payments had recorded an excess of Rs. 88 million, while reserves in foreign exchange were at Rs. 295 million. World Bank President Robert Macnamara visited Mauritius and expressed admiration for the *"pragmatic realism"* of the government. Air Mauritius was growing spectacularly also and opened a direct link with the U.K., which boosted the tourism industry. On April 28, the Bank of Mauritius revealed that the balance of payments surplus had reached Rs. 125 million. On January 19, the headlines of the local media indicated that 9,000 jobs had been created in only one year.

On the international front, a major event was the holding, in Mauritius, in 1973, of the summit of the heads of state and of government of the Organisation Commune Africaine, Malgache et Mauricienne (OCAMM), a francophone international club patronized by France. The second "M" of the abbreviation stood for Mauritius and was actually added during the Mauritius summit. This adhesion of Mauritius to the international francophone community despite being a member of the Commonwealth, was an illustration of the resolutely francophile foreign policy of the Ramgoolam/Duval regime that, the latter pointed out, helped Mauritius to obtain economic association with the European Union. The summit was organised under the aegis of Paris which was trying to create a kind of French Commonwealth of nations in the wake of the decolonisation movement, just as Britain did with much more success and institutional stability and durability. Whatever the economic advantages that may have accrued from it to Mauritius, the OCAM meeting was an assembly of many dictators, some sanguinary presidents like, for example, Jean Bedel Bokassa who wore medals covering his breast and going down almost to his abdomen, like innumerable, ridiculous trinkets. [8]

Ramgoolam had spelt out clearly beforehand the diplomatic agenda of his government regarding the upcoming OCAM conference, and the adhesion of Mauritius to the OAU (not the African Union) in his New Year message in January 1973:

"... Mauritius took the historic and decisive step of signing the Port-Louis Convention to enter the the Eruropean Economic Community through Yaoundé, a step which was made possible by the cooperation of OCAM and OAU to which Mauritius belongs as a sovereign independent state. And in this context, it is significant that the next OCAM meeting will be held here ion April and May of this year, and it will be attended by ministers and heads of state and of government. I am sure the people of Mauritius will give these leaders a most cordial and warm welcome. They will be coming here as brothers and well-wishers of our people." [9]

Larry Bowman and some other researchers have placed this kind of diplomatic events that included the organisation of a meeting of Francophone states in Mauritius in 1975, in the context of the efforts made by Mauritius to adhere to the Yaoundé Convention and to gain entry for its products in the EU at preferential tariffs. [10] Those researchers believe that the strategy paid off as Ramgoolam and Duval said it would at the time. Bowman points out that Mauritius had an average economic growth rate of 10 % annually from 1971 to 1979, successfully implementing – a rare feat internationally – most of what was recommended in a social-economic plan, the "***1971-1975 Four-Year Plan.***" That plan set out the objectives that were largely achieved as indicated by the high growth rates of the economy.

Ramgoolam stressed the remarkable success of the planification that translated into the boom years of the early 1970s in his January 1973 New Year message that was delivered in a buoyant mood (the MMM political prisoners were going to be released after one year in prison):

"I can say with confidence that 1972 has been a year of considerable achievement for Mauritius both on the domestic and international fronts. All around us there are signs of intense activity both in the private and public sectors, and everybody is happy, although the Jeremiahs will always be with us. Industries are going up everywhere, more schools are being set up, moreand better houses are being built, and the whole of Mauritius is humming with creative activity. These, my countrymen, are the first fruits of our economic and social policies (...) We are entering the New Year with fine economic prospects. In fact, the great boom is already here (...) Most important of all, the price of sugar is good and our production is rising. We have made a substantial dent in unemployment and more men and women are finding work daily (...) the future is bright. A large number of jobs have been created in the course of the Development Programme and still more jobs and more opportunities will be created as economic growthgathers further pace and momentum..." [11]

Government instability sets in, coalition breaks up

---

8 The author of this book, then a journalist at *Le Mauricien*, recalls covering the conference and Duval appealing to the Mauritian media not to make disparaging references that would offend the presidents like Bokassa. This reflected perfectly the anxiety of the Mauritian leaders to do everything to please Paris, the patron of the Mobutu's and Bokassa's of that era.
9 ***New Year Message, 1973***, from Dr. K. Hazeereesingh's original manuscript of SSR's speeches from the beginning of his political career and from which the content of his book was selected (Hazareesingh, K., ***Selected Speeches of Sir Seewoosagur Ramgoolam***, Macmillan, London 1979.) The manuscript was given to the author of this book by the late Dr. K. Hazareesingh.
10 Bowman, Larry W., ***Mauritius: Democracy and Development in the Indian Ocean***, Westview Press, 1991.
11 Original manuscript, ***Speeches of Sir Seewoosagur Ramgoolam***, op cit.

Good economic results were not synonymous, though, with stable government. There had been considerable infighting within the coalition government between Duval and the Labour leadership. Pressure to oust him grew. Some Labour leaders wanted their party to take a left turn and strike a deal with the MMM and were negotiating secretly with Bérenger. Many had been upset by the so-called '*scandals*' that were alleged to have occurred during OCAM, related to summit expenses and the '*scandalous*' conduct of a number of African VIPs. Allegations reached such a pitch that Ramgoolam had to table in Parliament a document refuting various allegations of misconduct by delegates. The opposition, especially Sookdeo Bissoondoyal and other members, were highly critical of some aspects of the event, including '*excesses*' that were alleged to have been committed by Duval and the people around him. Ramgoolam was forced to come up with a speech trying to give the official version, especially as inside Labour, discontent with the conference was also brewing:

"OCAM has assured us support in our efforts to bring the E.E.C. to accept more of our sugar and at a remunerative price... OCAM and OAU conferences will help us to increase jobs for our people, increase tourism, increase investment and further strengthen our economy. The success of the OCAM is due a great deal to the endeavours (...) of the Minister of External Affairs, Honourable Gaëtan Duval to whom I pay tribute for his great efforts." [12]

Duval reacted strongly against his critics within the government but a few months after the unconditional praise he received from Ramgoolam, the latter sacked him, responding to severe disagreement within the Labour Party over several issues pertaining to Duval's '*excesses*' and other internal problems. Indirectly, the sacking gave credibility to the opposition parties, including the MMM, in their criticism of the way the PMSD was behaving in government. Three other PMSD ministers and three parliamentary secretaries of that party were also sacked along with their leader on September 17, 1973 and the left wing of the Labour Party could not contain their satisfaction and congratulated Ramgoolam warmly at subsequent official functions.

Several members of the PMSD continued, nevertheless, to support Ramgoolam and, after they were excluded from the PMSD, joined the Labour Party. They became popularly known as "*transfuges*" in the most pejorative meaning of that word, meaning literally "*turncoats*". Some of them, like Raymond Devienne, were closely associated with Ramgoolam in the freemason movement. Devienne had actually patronised Ramgoolam when the latter joined the movement in Paris.

The PMSD 'hoisted by its own petard'

As the popular Shakesperian expression goes, the PMSD, which had helped engineer the repressive laws of the early 1970s, was '*hoisted by its own petard.*' [13] It was the turn of that party to suffer bitterly the severity of the repressive laws it had initiated and helped to vote while in government. The party tried to set up trade unions and organize strikes. It was restricted by those same laws it had defended tooth and nail when in power. Worse, the PMSD lost control of the municipalities, including that of the City of Port-Louis, when the government sacked all municipal councils and replaced them by non-elected boards of nominees. At the same time, a commission of inquiry revealed serious improprieties and abuses committed by the PMSD municipal administrations.

Municipal elections, like legislative elections, having been abolished, at least for 8 years, government had appointed municipal commissions, chaired in Port-Louis by Hamid Mollan, in Beau Bassin/Rose Hill by Roland Armand, in Quatre Bornes by Harry Tirvengadum and in Curepipe by Gaëtan de Chazal.

The PMSD asked the Supreme Court to scrap the interdiction of public meetings and press censorship it had itself helped to establish. The judges refused and went even as far as upholding that Parliament is supreme and, as such, has the right to even abolish democratic rights. This stance was one of the main reasons why, after winning the 1982 general elections, the MMM and the PSM immediately amended the Constitution to make it virtually impossible to abolish or postpone general elections.

One of the key problems was that the judiciary in Mauritius is not totally sheltered from the influence of the government of the day, especially as it is the government who, to this day, decides the salaries and perks of the judges and the recruitment of retired judges enticed by hefty contracts. I

On the political front, from 1974 to 1976, the government realized that a general election was inevitable. The state of emergency was gradually relaxed and was not renewed, allowing the first free political meetings in four years

---
12 Legislative Council, **Debate** 18 May 1973.
13 *'For 'tis the sport to have the engineer*
Hoist with his own petard.' (**Hamlet**, Act 3, Scene 4).

from 1976, when the MMM and its unions assembled a record crowd at the Labour Day rallye it organised in Rose Hill. Huge crowds flooded into the town from every part of the country.

MMM shadow Prime Minister: Bérenger steps down, Jugnauth steps in

Within the MMM, in 1973, Bérenger had voluntarily stepped down as shadow prime minister of the party arguing to his central committee that *"Mauritian realities"* dictated his replacement by a Hindu of a particular caste.[14] Bérenger himself proposed Jugnauth as shadow PM and that was accepted by the central committee.

Nevertheless, it was not easy to have that decision approved by all the party's cells/branches across thecountry. Jugnauth's past career in the Hindu Congress weighed heavily against him in some branches, especially at Quinze Cantons, Vacoas, where approval was obtained only after considerable efforts by the executive members of the Vacoas branches of the MMM.[15]

Party discipline prevailed finally and Jugnauth's appointment was approved by a general assembly of MMM delegates, many of them reluctantly accepting Bérenger's decision to step down and bow to what they described as the old rules of traditional ethnic politics. Jugnauth was, nevertheless, a candidate that Labour realized could help sway its traditional electorate towards the MMM. Labour started portraying him, after he became president and shadow PM of the MMM in 1973, as a *"puppet"* of Bérenger, one that would be *"manipulated"* by the party to pave the way for the country to enter the international communist camp.[16]

Mauritius ended the year 1974 in an atmosphere of euphoria on the economic front. The country was developing a second development plan, the *"1975-1980 Five-Year Development Plan"* that the authorities hoped would be as successful as the one that had covered the preceding four years. The new plan targeted the creation of 76,000 more jobs by 1980.

Cyclone ***Gervaise***, in 1975, whose centre crossed the entire island, put an end to the euphoria. During the night of February 6-7 of 1975, gusts reaching 256 km/h and, at one point, a maximum of 275 km/h, killing ten persons, wounding 59 and depriving 10,000 persons of their homes, set the national economy several years back. In March, 70,000 families still had no electricity. The authorities had to distribute cheap construction materials to 8,000 families to help them reconstruct their homes. The sugar harvest, which had reached record heights in the previous years, was almost completely destroyed.

The nation was again on its knees. ***Gervaise***, then four years later, cyclone ***Claudette***, whose éye' or centre also crossed Mauritius, contributed significantly to the economic downturn that followed until the early 1980s.[17]

---

14 The author of this book, who was then a member of the shadow cabinet as information minister and each fortnight accompanied party colleague Jugnauth to central committee meetings (both resided in Vacoas) was witness of the historical change that then occurred.
15 The author's personal recollection of events as one of the former leading members of MMM in the 1970s. In 1978, the author resigned and left politics to go back to independent journalism.
16 Media reports of repeated criticisms by the parties in power throughout that period until 1983.
17 *"Dans les années 70, Gervaise détruit de nombreuses maisons et cause un long arrêt de l'alimentation électrique. Il fait 10 morts, tandis que des milliers de sans-abri errent dans les rues. En 1979, l'œil du cyclone Claudette traverse l'île de part en part et cause d'affreux dégâts. Des vents de 231 km/h sont enregistrés à Plaisance, un record. Six personnes trouvent la mort, 34 sont blessées, et 3 706 Mauriciens se retrouvent sans abri,"* recalled *L'Express* newspaper on 13 January 2015.

Chapter 47
From May 1975 student revolt to the 1976 general election

In addition to cyclones *Gervaise* and *Claudette*, other factors contributed to the economic downturn of the second half of the 1970s decade.

The world economic context was more difficult, especially due to the oil shock that saw prices of petroleum products rise to unprecedented heights. There occurred a major rise in prices of all imports. At about the same time, sugar prices declined on the world market.

Ramgoolam's government, which barely survived the December 1976 general election by a last-minute post-electoral coalition, with the PMSD,[1] was blasted by its critics for having overspent during the boom years. The World Bank and International Monetary Fund experts were of the opinion that salary increases had been excessive, averaging 30 % from 1971 to 1979.[2] The MMM, which had played a major role, together with the PMSD, in pushing up the salaries of the workforce, focussed its attacks on the government, especially Finance Minister Sir Veerasamy Ringadoo. Nevertheless, as seems to be usually the case in the Mauritius political arena, the MMM and the Labour Party were, during second half of the 1970s, exploring the possibility of an alliance and contacts occurred between top members of the two parties (see footnotes).

Ringadoo had to bear, after the 1976 general election, the brunt of the attack against government on the subject of the economy by the new, strong MMM parliamentary opposition. This was despite the fact that during his mandate as finance minister, the national economy had progressed spectacularly until cyclone Gervaise and the international oil shock hit the country.

Four major events, which were real political cyclones, occurred during the period 1975-1983, impacting deeply on the political history of Mauritius:

1. The Student Revolt of 1975, comparable to the May 1968 Student Revolt in Europe, especially France, essentially targeting the government's education policies.

2. The 1976 general election which Ramgoolam lost while the MMM carne out with the highest number of seats, 34 on a total of 70, forcing Labour 928 seats) into a last minute post-electoral coalition with Duval's PMSD (8 seats) to barely maintain itself in power.

3. A major split in the Labour Party led by an emerging young leader, Harrish Boodhoo, the ultimate result being the defeat of Labour at the 1982 general election.

4. A deep split within the ranks of the MMM after it won the 1982 general election, leading the new Prime Minister Aneerood Jugnauth to form a dissident party, the MSM, and maintain himself in power, while Bérenger went from being a powerful finance minister to take over the leadership of the parliamentary opposition (as a '*best loser,*' ironically after the rank and file of his party has claimed the abolition of the '*best loser system*' in the wake of the previous year's electoral victory of the MMM-PSM alliance).

Former Marxist party turned into a major national electoral force

---

1 After the 1976 elections, there were reports of coalition talks between the three main parties, MMM (34 seats), Labour (28 seats) and PMSD (8 seats). Malenn Oodia writes that the MMM proposed to Labour a coalition government with MMM in power and Ramgoolam president of a proposed Mauritian Republic, which Ramgoolam refused (*Quelle voie choisir ? Mouvement Militant Mauricien, 20 ans d'histoire*, Port-Louis 1989, p. 79. *L'Express* on 24 December 1976 and *Week-End* on 24 May 1977, reported a failed Labour-MMM coalition attempt. Indian researcher Ajay Kumar Dubey, in a PhD thesis where those sources are quoted, adds his own interviews of Labour and PMSD '*activists*' he says he met in July 1990, to write that Duval refused a coalition proposal from the MMM and adds that Boolell favoured a Labour-PMSD alliance. (*Shodhganga : a reservoir of Indian theses* - Jawarharlall Nehru University, published 1 January 2015 - URL http://hdl.handle.net/10603/100526) There have also been rumors that Jugnauth turned down a PMSD offer of an MMM-PMSD coalition government to oust Labour from power. There is a lack of official statements by the parties involved to confirm MMM-PMSD discussions while the late Sir Veerasamy Ringadoo, governor-general of Mauritius, told the author of this book at Le Réduit, off the record, in the 1980s, when he was governor-general, that Sir Harold Walter and himself had actually been delegated by Ramgoolam, prior to the 1976 general election, to engage in discussions with Bérenger, but that at the last minute, when talks were going to conclude, the PM instructed them to put an end to the negotiations. SSR, he added, gave no explanation. "*It was a sudden decision. There had been, to my knowledge, no other persons delegated by him to engage in coalition talks with the MMM at that time, contrary to what some people may have believed then.*"
2 See also Bheenick and Schapiro, op cit

In the second half of the 1970s, the MMM mutated into a successful electoral machine that dramatically changed the balance of forces in the political arena. Gone were the days when a faction of the party saw a violent upheaval as a means to seize power. Its president, Aneerood Jugnauth, described himself in the media as a monarchist, attended the royal wedding of Prince Charles and Lady Diana in London, in 1981, and after becoming PM in the 1980s accepted such perks as a membership on the Queen's Privy Council and a knighthood. He retained his title of "Sir" after the country became a republic and, in 2003, when he became President of the Republic of Mauritius.

Bérenger also mutated fast as from the 1976 general election where the MMM was the actual winner but was deprived of power by a new Labour/PMSD coalition. He donned his street militant's black jacket and casual safari wear for expensive business suits after being elected to Parliament.

His party had reduced the PMSD to 16.5 % of the national vote at the 1976 general election, beating Labour to the finish, while the IFB and the UDM were wiped out for good from the parliamentary scene. Bérenger spent the rest of the 1970s decade preparing himself and his party to obtain power only through election and to manage the country the way the IMF and the World Bank like it, that is, through liberalization of the national economy, the scrapping of the hard core of nationalizations in the party's 1976 election manifesto and working in conjunction with the private sector.

The party was to make history in the 1980s and 1990s with massive electoral victories, two 60-0 wins in 1982 with Boodhoo's PSM, and in 1995 with Navin Ramgoolam's Labour Party (Navin Ramgoolam is the son of Sir Seewoosagur Ramgoolam), and a 56-4 victory in 2000 with Jugnauth's MSM that led Bérenger to a short mandate as PM of less than two years, followed by the return of Labour to power at the July 3, 2005, and again at the May 5, 2010 general elections, where the MMM still had 44% popular support with Bérenger as candidate for Prime ministership. The MMM was also in control of all the nation's five municipalities from 1982 to 2001, winning up to 100% of the seats, then losing just a handful until 2001, after that losing massively (by securing a mere 4 seats) in 2005 to a Labour/MSM/PMSD alliance.

May 1975 student revolt took MMM, former CEM, by surprise

As the political chessboard was changing in the mid-1970s, in May 1975, a major student revolt flared up at the University of Mauritius and a large number of secondary schools across the country. Its leaders made it a point to state that they were not from the MMM and, actually, that party had been surprised by the uprising. This indicates at least one thing: the MMM, created from a student revolutionary group, the Club des Etudiants Militants in 1969, was, in 1975, fully engaged in the electoral process and preparing for the upcoming general elections expected at any time (they took place in 1976), and was less active among the students, most of whom were only secondary students

The MMM, though, had a youth movement that promptly expressed support for the students, especially after the government sent anti-riot forces to stop thousands of students who tried to enter Port-Louis by the Grand River North West bridge on May 20,1975. The clash was violent.[3] Agitators had apparently infiltrated the movement and the police was attacked with stones.[4]

Police charged and dispersed the student demonstrators using teargas on the GRNW bridge that led into Port-Louis. The students had been protesting, according to what their leaders told the media during those events, against the educational system. They felt it did not respond to their aspirations and that they had few hopes of finding jobs after their studies. One could not see, from the demonstrations they held, why they would attack the police.

The student revolt increased tension across the country, especially as cyclone **Gervaise** had severely crippled the national economy and popular discontent was brewing due to a return to hard times.[5] There was some relief, however, on the social front, when in August of the same year, the National Remuneration Board (NRB) granted a wage increase of 20 to 23 %, plus an additional bonus equivalent to three months' wages to the labourers and artisans of the sugar industry.

The MMM/PMSD common front

Other sectors of work also wanted wage hikes to face the rising cost of living following the cyclone. The MMM stepped up political pressure on the government by entering into a "common front" of trade unions with the PMSD, trying to

---

3 The author of this book was an eye-witness, being a news reporter working right in the middle of the action on the bridge.
4 It has been speculated in unverified affirmations that there had been '**agents provocateurs**' who started throwing stones while being hidden in the adjoining cane fields, during the 1969 anti-Princess Alexandra demonstration, and also in later disturbances in Mauritius where, for instance, in the 1999 riots, there appeared to be a number of seemingly '**agents provocateurs**' who poured fuel into the fire.
5 Each year, this student revolt is commemorated and the events are reviewed and analyzed in the media. For instance, in *L'Express* on 20 May 2014, https://www.lexpress.mu/article/246314/20-mai-1975-il-y-39-ans-etudiants-descendaient-dans-rue and *Le Mauricien* on the same date, http://www.lemauricien.com/article/20-mai-1975-la-colere-d-jeunesse-revendicatrice

force more wage increases. The PMSD was particularly active among the workers of the EPZ where wages were the lowest of all the major sectors of the economy. This front was hotly opposed within the MMM by a large faction led by a leftist militant, Jack Bizlall, already very critical of the party's "deviation" to the right, as he called it. Bérenger won the approval of the general assembly of MMM delegates, a mandatory process under the party's constitution, by an extremely thin margin when the "common front" was put to the vote at a meeting at New Devton College, in Beau Bassin.

A story was circulated by Labour and its allies, regarding the common front, and both Berenger and Duval confirmed, indicating how close the two leaders were, despite years of violent street clashes between their respective bouncers and partisans. Duval was invited to a reception during a new visit by Princess Alexandra, wearing a pair of socks borrowed from Bérenger prior to that function. Duval boasted of this to the royal visitor, who had been invited by the government with a view to make up for the 1969 anti-Alexandra protests. The incident bounced back to Mauritius from diplomatic circles. Critics of the common front promptly took it up and the story made headlines in the pro-government media. The two parties did not forge any electoral alliance as this would have probably caused a deep split within the MMM and its electorate, most likely in the rural districts.

Labour Party prepares for first general elections in 9 years

Ramgoolam extended the right to vote to the 18-year-old's through a bill voted by Parliament on December 16, 1975. This was expected to appease the nation's younger generations following the May 1975 student revolt.

The Labour Party was mobilizing itself for the upcoming general election expected any time in 1976. They would be the first to be held since 1967 – in nearly a decade. At the Labour Party's 40th anniversary general assembly on February 23, 1976, one of the former key leaders of the MMM, Heeralall Bhugaloo was in attendance, having defected to Labour's ranks.

In April 1976, the IFB leader, Sookdeo Bissoondoyal, proposed a common front of all opposition forces. But this was never going to happen, though as far as March 11, 1976, Bérenger told the media that there was an atmosphere of "*détente*" between the MMM and the PMSD.[6] One would have expected the IFB and other opposition parties to join forces with them without any major problem.

The fact is that, at the same time, Labour leaders were discussing a possible Labour/MMM alliance at the forthcoming general election. Ramgoolam had, as previously mentioned, given the green light to Ringadoo and Walter to negotiate with Bérenger.

The IFB was, some time later, pressed by the MMM to enter into an alliance as the election campaign was about to start. Bissoondoyal declined, expressing reservations about the party's manifesto which was still inspired by Marxism, prescribing specifically direct democracy as the next political system. That meant handing over government decisions to popular assemblies – if not to the streets – and the business world would be made subservient to assemblies of their workforce.

In the end, all the opposition parties, PMSD, MMM, UDM and IFB went separately into the 1976 general election while Labour, CAM and the elements that had crossed the floor from the PMSD went together.

Labour had, during that election year, scored some good marks with the successful organization in Mauritius of the summit of the heads of state and of government of the Organization of African Unity (OAU), now the African Union, of which Ramgoolam became the president. The event was somewhat marred by the presence of Ugandan dictator Idi Amine. While Amine was in Mauritius, an Israeli commando freed the passengers of an aircraft who had been taken hostage at the international airport at Entebbe, Uganda, while his government was seen to be friendly to the hostage-takers. Amine was already notorious within the international community for having expelled the Indian community of Uganda with his characteristic brutality.

During the OAU summit, Mauritius also broke diplomatic ties with Israel to conform to the policies of the OAU on the Palestinian question.

Ramgoolam's presidency of the OAU gave him the international glamour that did, to a certain extent, play in his favour

---

6 This '*détente*' is often referred to as the '*front chaussettes*' (literally meaning: *alliance based on a pair of socks*), an MMM-PMSD truce was sealed after Duval borrowed a pair of black socks from the MMM leader on his way to a cocktail at Le Réduit in honour of Princess Alexandra who was visiting Mauritius. A defiant Duval apparently boasted to the Princess that he was wearing socks offered by Bérenger, who demonstrated against her with other hostile militants, at the St. Jean Roundabout in 1969. The subject is now a national joke with such media references four decades later as in an article in *Week-End* on 20 July 2014, entitled "*On a Point of Order*", and a historical recall in *L'Express* of 31 December 2016, entitled, "*Analyse: une alliance PTr-MMM-PMSD est-elle possible ?*" Bérenger personally confirmed the 'socks' incident to the author of this book at the *Le Militant* daily newspaper office where the latter was chief editor in those days.

on the local political scene. Another major diplomatic success was when Ramgoolam, with the help of Satcam Boolell, a key negotiator during discussions, obtained the adhesion of Mauritius to the Lomé Convention in 1975, which, as already mentioned, allowed the national economy to prosper considerably through guaranteed quotas and prices for its sugar and EPZ exports and cooperation programs financed by the European Union.

Labour argued, during the campaign leading to the December 12, 1976 general election, that 65,000 new jobs had been created since independence and put forward its successes on the diplomatic front. The party promised that if it came back to power, it would grant free education to the student population of the country. Ramgoolam and his colleagues also pointed out the benefits of the large welfare state that they had set up.

The PMSD campaigned in favour of liberal economic policies. Both Ramgoolam and Duval alleged that the MMM had foreign allies like the Soviet Union and other communist countries that were ready to come over should that party win the election to help set up a communist regime.

The MMM proposed a new Mauritian society that would be entirely controlled by voters and workers through direct democracy. Nationalisation of key sectors of the economy was the hard core of its manifesto. A higher status for the Creole language to put it, according to critics, on an equal footing with English and French, was proposed. Jugnauth was presented as future PM. The party did its utmost to woo voters among the middle classes.

At the general election, the MMM came out first with 38.7% of the popular vote against 37.6% for the Labour/CAM alliance. The PMSD obtained 16.5% (this would shrink to under 10 % in future elections), a major drop in comparison with the 44% obtained at the previous general election in 1967. Duval lost his own reelection battle.

The MMM's seats were equally divided between the rural and urban areas. At the direct election for the first 60 seats in Parliament, the MMM won 30 of them, against Labour's 25 seats and the PMSD's seven seats, of which two in Rodrigues (Cyril Guimbeau, Nicol François), With the nomination of eight best losers, the MMM's share was 34 seats, while the Labour/CAM alliance obtained 28 and the PMSD a total of eight seats.

Ramgoolam asked and obtained the support of the PMSD to stay in power with a total of 36 seats against the MMM's 34. Later, during the debates on the motion of thanks for the Speech from the Throne delivered by the governor-general, the Queen's representative in Mauritius (the country was not yet a republic), Jugnauth, the new Leader of the Opposition, claimed that Duval had approached him just after the general election to offer him the prime minister's seat, but that he had refused.

1982 election results by main parties

Alliance/Party	Total votes	No voters	% votes	Elected seats	Best loser seats	Total seats	% seats
Alliance MMM/PSM	906,900	302,300	64.16	60	0	60	90.91
Parti Alliance Nationale (PAN)	364,410	121,470	25.78	0	2	2	3.03
Parti Mauricien Social Démocrate (PMSD)	110,129	36,710	7.79	0	2	2	3.03
Others	32,148	10,716	2.27	*2	0	2	3.03
Total	1,413,587	471,196	100.00	62	4	66	100.00

Note: These two seats in "Others" were won by the Organisation du Peuple Rodriguais (OPR - Organization of the People of Rodrigues. Kasenally 2009, 299).

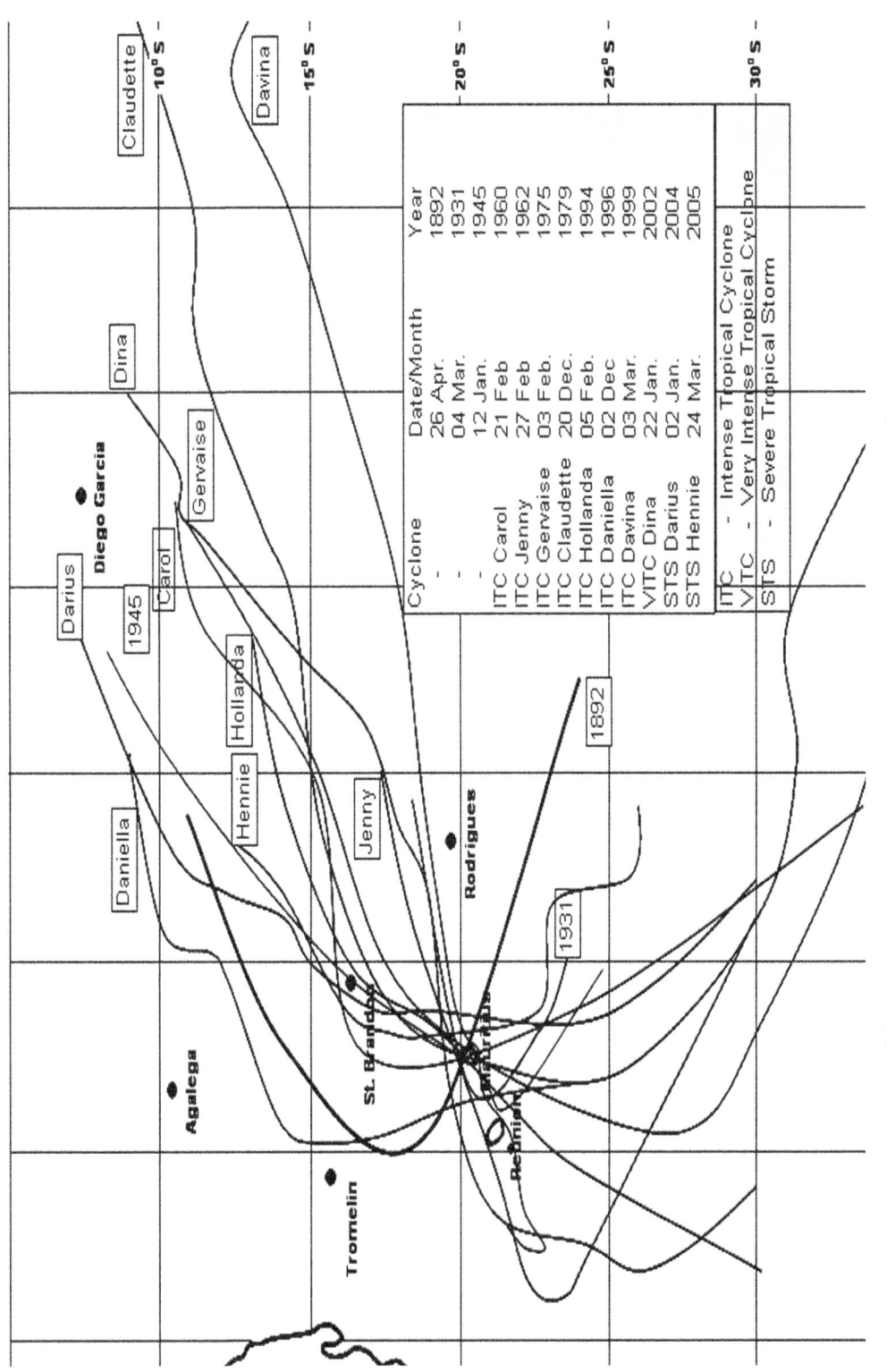

The Met's list of the worst cyclones to hit Mauritius from 1832

Cyclone	Date/Month	Year
—	26 Apr.	1892
—	04 Mar.	1931
—	12 Jan.	1945
ITC Carol	21 Feb	1960
ITC Jenny	27 Feb.	1962
ITC Gervaise	03 Feb.	1975
ITC Claudette	20 Dec.	1979
ITC Hollanda	05 Feb.	1994
ITC Daniella	02 Dec	1996
ITC Davina	03 Mar.	1999
VITC Dina	22 Jan.	2002
STS Darius	02 Jan.	2004
STS Hennie	24 Mar.	2005

ITC — Intense Tropical Cyclone
VITC — Very Intense Tropical Cyclone
STS — Severe Tropical Storm

The Mauritius Meteorological Services keeps track of the cyclones affecting the Mauritius region and has listed (above) the worst among them that hit the island. The effect of cyclones are devastating and those of the past even more so when the island was a monocrop economy.

Chapter 48
Years of crisis: 1977-1983 (1)

After the 1976 general election, the Ramgoolam regime weakened considerably. There was crisis in various areas of the nation's life as well as a *"scandal"* that led to the downfall of two Cabinet ministers and one of the most serious splits to hit the Labour Party. This situation was to make it quite difficult for Ramgoolam to have his budgets and other government bills voted by Parliament, especially during the last years of the government's mandate.

Dissent within the MMM

Within the MMM also, there was a serious wave of dissent in 1977. On May 27, Rajiv Servansing, Habib Mosaheb and Jack Bizlall left the party politburo protesting what they alleged to be the MMM's *"deviation"* in accepting the rules of ethnic politics and caving in to considerations that smacked of a *"communal"* approach in its various choices (mayors, shadow ministers and other appointments). They gave statements that made screaming headlines in the media, but later the movement, which had described itself as the *'left wing'* of the party, fizzled out as its members went back into the formal structure of the party.

Bizlall was, however, the exception. He believed, he said, he had a mission to bring back the party to the left, failing which he would leave Parliament and join the trade union movement where he would re-kindle the leftist militancy of the early 1970s. In 1980, Bizlall, who had entered Parliament under the BLS system, decided to leave his seat to the next BLS in line,[1] who promptly declined to cross over again from independent journalism to politics. The last MMM best-loser, Jacques de Commarrnond also declined when subsequently approached and Bizall then announced he had no choice but to remain in Parliament because the seat would revert to the right, a PMSD BLS, thus changing the result obtained at the polls.

Labour splits, the dissidents form a new party, the PSM

The dissent that was to split Labour would be much more serious than the internal problems of the MMM in 1977. Harrish Boodhoo had entered Parliament at the 1976 general election after a very successful career, together with his wife Sarita, on the social-cultural front within the Seva Shivir, a movement that covered the whole island and focused on keeping alive Hindu cultural and religious traditions. Young and extremely active on the ground, Boodhoo resented the role of Kher Jagatsingh, secretary general of Labour, to whom he attributed the disastrous electoral results Labour at the 1976 general election and the general decline of the party. He pointed out that Jagatsingh had lost his own re-election and did not deserve to keep his key position as general secretary.

The so-called "old guard" Labour leaders opposed fierce resistance to Boodhoo's campaign against Jagatsingh. Several young party members, agents and supporters rallied around Boodhoo and the clash between the two camps was becoming inevitable as the 1982 general election was looming ahead.

Between the general election of 1976 and that of 1982, some of the most prominent leaders of the nation passed away. Dr. Maurice Curé, founder of the Labour Party, and Sookdeo Bissoondoyal, the IFB leader died in 1977, while Sir Abdool Razack Mohamed, the CAM leader, who had been in the Union Mauricienne with Jules Koenig and Raoul Rivet, then in Koenig's Ralliement Mauricien before forming the CAM, died the following year. A huge chunk of national history was going away with them.

Alleged 'affairs' that shook the political arena

The government faced, during its mandate, allegations of impropriety related to a *"jewellery scandal"* dubbed the *"the Singhania affair"* that led the opposition to request a probe into the matter. Singhania was an Indian businessman who was stopped by customs officers at the international airport at Plaisance. Expensive jewellery was impounded and sold by auction in London in July 1978. In April 1980, however, a report from the Director of Audit indicated that 14 pieces of jewellery were missing when the sale took place. This gave rise to rumours and allegations of impropriety even from among rebellious elements in government ranks, but finally, the Director of Public

---
1 The author of this book was the next possible choice.

Prosecutions (DPP) found there was no ground for taking legal action.

Previously, another major affair had broken out in 1978, the so-called Sheik Hossen affair, from the name of a young man of Mauritian origin, Jean-Paul Sheik Hossen, who came from Belgium and worked for some time as a part-time policeman (paid five rupees a day when on duty, these policemen were popularly known as the '*five-rupee policemen*').[2] He also worked for some time for right-wing daily *Le Cernéen* where, according to Editor Jean-Pierre Lenoir[3] he brought articles blasting communism that, it was later found out, came from the offices of the police at the Line Barracks in Port-Louis. Those articles were part of an anti-MMM campaign. It was later discovered that Sheik Hossen was the son of a former member of the Mauritius Police top brass. This made him lose all support from *Le Cernéen.*

In 1978, the newspaper *Le Militant* published an article where the young man said he worked for the State Security Service (SSS), which was heavily engaged in the political arena trying to curb the rise of the MMM. The newspaper published nothing more than those allegations of infiltration and spying of the MMM. But the man was going to say even more.

Sheik Hossen was fully taken in charge by some members of the MMM leadership, with Amédée Darga taking the initiative of giving him shelter and ensuring his security. One day, talking to his new MMM friends he claimed having set fire to the old, wooden, colonial-style building of the daily *Le Mauricien*, which had been completely destroyed in January 1978 by a fire. MMM general secretary Paul Bérenger took the matter in his hands. Even *Le Militant*'s editorial team was not informed of those *"secret revelations"* until the news gradually infiltrated outside the little circle of friends of Sheik hossen within the MMM.

Bérenger ordered a search for a witness in the matter, the former security guard at *Le Mauricien* at the time of the fire. The man was found and, when confronted with Sheik Hossen, he did not confirm the latter's allegations that he played a part in setting fire to the newspaper building. Bérenger made the mistake, though, of believing what Sheik hossen had told him and made extremely serious allegations that the government had utilized the SSS and Sheik hossen to commit the crime of arson. Within the ranks of the MMM, Aneerood Jugnauth, even as Leader of the Opposition, abstained from going as far as Bérenger who had sworn that he had uncovered the truth. Even the party newspaper,[4] called in a top party leader, lawyer Kader Bhayat, to help weed out parts of Bérenger's speech so serious and unsupported had been the allegations against Ramgoolam.

Deeply shaken, the Ramgoolam government ordered a fire inquiry presided by Magistrate Namdarkhan. Sheik Hossen, Bérenger and Darga were unable to prove their allegations and the inquiry concluded that Sheik Hossen had fabricated his "revelations" and was a psychopath. Bérenger was forced to apologize publicly for his mistake.

MMM unaffected by setbacks

Although those alleged '*affairs*' did not topple the government for obvious reasons, the DPP having concluded in its favour in the Singhania case and Bérenger having had to apologise for his allegations based, albeit mistakenly, on incorrect information, the MMM seemed unscathed by the government's strong reactions targeting the party's credibility. The MMM, which had won control of three municipalities (Port-Louis, Beau Bassin/Rose Hill and Vacoas/Phoenix) at the April 1977 municipal elections, was not very much affected in its progression on the political scene even by a number of defections that saw four of its parliamentarians cross the floor after the 1976 general election: Suresh Moorba, Krishnalall Coonjan, Jean-Claude Augustave and Vijay Venkatasamy.

The government battered by criticism from the opposition parties and from dissenters from its own ranks, threatened by a deteriorating economic situation, increasingly found itself faced with mounting impopularity, even though it had respected its electoral promise to introduce free schooling. An interim structure was put into place in January 1977 and it was replaced afterwards by a better organised system, with a Private Secondary Schools Authority (PSSA) that centralised the payment of all teacher salaries and various allowances used to improve school infrastructure. The MMM, while not opposing free schooling, attacked the government alleging that it had been a desperate move to get votes before the election and stemmed from a decision that had not been adequately planned prior to implementation. To some extent, this proved to be true as it was not easy to overcome a number of prob-

2 "*La polis 5 roupies*".
3 In a statement to the author of this book and fellow chief editor at *Le Militant*, despite both being of very different political views. Ethics counted first for both editors.
4 Then led by the author of this book as chief editor.

lems that the teachers discovered regarding their conditions of work within the new system, and this gave way to public protest by a number of frustrated teachers through their union leaders.

Notwithstanding the birth pangs of the system, the removal of school fees constituted a significant relief for most families. In 2005, a new Labour government, this time led by Dr. Navin Ramgoolam, granted free transport for students (and to the elderly), another significant cut in overall schooling expenses.

On the regional front, the MMM developed close ties with two communist regimes that had taken power by staging violent coups in Madagascar and the Seychelles in the 1970s. President Didier Ratsiraka of Madagascar and President Albert René of the Seychelles and Paul Bérenger in Mauritius developed close relationships on the basis of a need for the islands of the Southwest Indian Ocean should develop cooperation. The MMM also entertained a close relationship with Libya, another country then in sharp political and ideological opposition to the Western nations. The advent of communism had destroyed the budding economy of Madagascar dramatically increasing poverty, while the Seychelles only survived that era of dictatorship and state violence mainly because of its tourism industry that kept that nation's economy afloat.

Labour weakened further by dissidence

The Mauritian government suspected the MMM of trying to organize a coup in the country and systematically attacked the party for its close relationship with the then Union of Socialist Soviet Republics (USSR), Cuba, Madagascar, Libya and the Seychelles. During election campaigns, one photo of Bérenger surrounded by the Seychellois military during one of his frequent visits to the Seychelles was widely circulated by government agents.

The problem for the regime, however, was that the economic situation of the country was fast deteriorating. In addition, there was one scandal where it was revealed that examination papers were being fraudulently smuggled and sold to candidates on a thriving black market prior to examinations. The media exposed the fraud and there was a national uproar as this put into question the future of the youth and the parents were furious. Such matters reduced considerably the impact, if any, of the government propaganda. Actually, at the same time that Labour was alleging that the MMM was communist, it was also stating that it was a party that was the vassal of capitalism, a contradiction that was quickly and effectively exploited by the MMM top brass.

In the end, Boodhoo's dissidence was an additional factor that helped the MMM to deal the fatal blow to the government at the upcoming elections. From 1978, Boodhoo took the leadership of a group of ministers and members of the National Assembly who supported his drive for a revamp of the Labour party's structure and the ousting of secretary general Kher Jagatsingh. Boodhoo openly proposed to take up the latter's responsibilities and reorganize the party with his group. By July 1978, this protest movement had amplified, but Jagatsingh was re-elected for the 17th time as secretary general with the support of the so-called *"old guard"* surrounding SSR.

Boodhoo and his group from then on intensified their campaign against the party leadership and even voted with the opposition in Parliament. In December 1978, SSR was defeated during a vote on a motion presented by MMM member Vijay Jandoosingh.

Meanwhile, across the country, a 15 % hike of the bus tickets was extremely unpopular. Worse, at the behest of the World Bank, electricity tariffs went up by 25 %. And there was more ahead.

In 1979, following allegations of corruption levelled by Boodhoo against two Cabinet ministers, Gyandeo Daby and Lutchmeeparsad Badry, a commission of inquiry presided by Judge Victor Glover found the two elected public officials guilty of various charges of impropriety. Both Daby and Badry had to resign under the threat of being revoked by the PM. For his part, Boodhoo promised more revelations against other ministers.

Under pressure from the IMF and the World Bank, which had been called in by Ringadoo to help redress an ailing economy, the government started adopting stringent budgetary measures, saying an era of austerity was inevitable before prosperity could return. The MMM as well as Boodhoo and his group vehemently opposed Ringadoo's budget, which was only voted after concessions of about Rs. 100 million that he had to make due to opposition pressure. The Mauritius Tax Payers Association had added its voice to the protest against the budget, attracting even more middle class support for the opposition.

After the budget vote, Ramgoolam rallied the party around him for the expulsion of Boodhoo and other dissidents, who then went on to form the Parti Socialiste Mauricien (PSM).

Economic downturn at the end of the 1970s

Industrial relations had become extremely tense all over the island as the national economy took the plunge in the last years of the 1970s. As Larry Bowman recalls, from 1974 to 1978, the country's imports had doubled while exports fell. The external debt was multiplied by nearly four, with government borrowing massively to pay for the import bill and sustain social welfare programs. Foreign exchange reserves collapsed from 183 million U.S. dollars to a mere 14 million U.S. dollars by August 1979. [5]

In 1981, the budget deficit reached Rs. 982 million. In the following year, the balance of payments deficit topped Rs. 1.12 billion. Inflation reached a record high of 42 % in 1980, while the number of registered unemployed reached 73,000. The current account deficit reached a record 14.4 % of the gross national product (GNP).

In November 1978, then in August 1979 strikes again paralysed crucial sectors of the economy including the port and the transport industries as well as the Central Electricity board. Bérenger took the leadership of the strike action in 1979 and participated in a hunger strike with other union leaders. He was the accredited negotiator of the General Workers Federation (GWF) in addition to being the MMM general secretary and a Member of Parliament. Government negotiated with him to end the strikes and the matter was resolved in an atmosphere that still smacked of intense bitterness long afterwards. The IMF and the World Bank, for their part, continued to exert pressure and obtained two devaluations of the rupee totalling 50 % within two years (30 % in October 1979 and 20 % in 1981). Those devaluations increased popular discontent against the Ramgoolam regime, especially due to the huge impact they had on the cost of living, sending prices spiralling upwards.

In January 1981, a World Bank report published in the Mauritian media and subsequent World Bank studies during that year revealed that 12 out of 100 Mauritians were living in absolute poverty conditions and that 5 % of Mauritian families controlled 31 % of the national revenue. On report stated that "*Income is... relatively concentrated at the top end, with the top decile receiving almost 40%.*" [6] Those figures were like fuel added to the fire, shoring up the claims of the MMM and the PSM that the government was governing in the interest of a privileged few. However, a more substantial report repeated more about the dramatic socio-economic situation was published by the World Bank in May 1982. This second report also predicted an economic recovery from 1982.[7]

The government accused the MMM of having again irreversibly harmed the nation's economy by the 1979 strikes, with sugar exports being delayed by up to five months. Ringadoo argued that the devaluations had been inevitable and were needed to boost exports and, in the long run, redress the economy and the nation's finances.

Labour's partner PMSD splits

Within the government, minister Eliezer François, who had been entrusted with the leadership of the PMSD parliamentary group, started agitating against the party leader, Gaëtan Duval, and eventually there was a split with François being driven out of the party and remaining in government while Duval and the PMSD formally entered into opposition to the regime – despite the fact that Ramgoolam had Duval elevated to knighthood in December

---

5 Bowman, Larry, op cit.
6 World Bank, *Mauritius -Urban Sector Memorandum*. Report No. 3127-MAS, March 1981. "*In Mauritius average income per capita in 1979 was Rs 5,900 (over US$1,100 at the pre-devaluation exchange rate)... In 1979, average household income was about Rs 2,770 per month, with a median of almost Rs 1,000 per month. Income is thus relatively concentrated at the top end, with the top decile receiving almost 40%. The absolute poverty household income level based on World Bank definitions... is Rs 500 per month (1979) which includes almost 12% of households; the relative poverty level is Rs 770 per month (1979), about 34% of households.*" Page 13.
7 World Bank, *Mauritius Economic Memorandum Recent Developments and Prospects,* Report No. 3857-MAS, Country Programs Department Eastern Africa Region May 26, 1982. This economic report is more substantial and detailed than the one mentioned in the media. It is found at http://documents.worldbank.org/curated/en/478921468281694658/pdf/multi-page.pdf Accessed on 24 February 2017.

1980.

The government majority was dwindling. In December 1979, it had survived a motion of blame in Parliament by 35 votes against 33. In 1980, it lost on a vote on a supplementary budget. From then on, government members had to explore the National Assembly building each time there was a vote to ensure that all members found loitering in the corridors or even in the toilets would be made to attend and vote with discipline.

The situation was becoming desperate for the Labour-led regime as the next general election became due. The MMM and the PSM were touring the country, campaigning on the sad state of the national economy and rising prices and capitalizing on several "affairs" that had rocked the government.

Chapter 49

Years of crisis: 1977-1983 (2)

One of the most important political events of the period leading to the 1982 general election was the alliance deal struck on January 23, 1981 between the MMM and the PSM of Harrish Boodhoo. The latter was appointed shadow Deputy Prime Minister in the opposition's shadow cabinet while Bérenger, going against Jugnauth's advice,[1] accepted to become the shadow Finance Minister and third in rank after Boodhoo. Jugnauth thought the MMM was going to win the general election anyway and the party should not grant major concessions to the PSM.

The members of the MMM gave a lukewarm approval to this arrangement where Bérenger appeared to have sacrificed himself in favour of Boodhoo whom many leftist and not-so-leftist militants suspected to be a Hindu fundamentalist. This perception would increase later, during the 1983 political crisis, but Bérenger was accused by MMM left-wingers of having entered fully into the game of ethnic politics, not just with Boodhoo's appointment, but on the basis of the choice of the MMM candidates for general elections since 1976. Bérenger confronted them with the argument that Boodhoo, who belonged like Jugnauth to the Vaish caste, a majority within the Hindu community, would give double assurance to the Hindu voters that an MMM-led government would not go against their interests.

As the 1970s drew to an end and the 1980s dawned, pressure was mounting against the government of SSR from several quarters. In addition to the opposition parties, including Boodhoo's newly formed PSM, the Mauritius Tax Payers Association (MTPA) and the Catholic Church had their say in the criticism of the government.

While the MTPA resented the high cost of living, the Catholic Church protested against what it perceived as the *"slow death"* of its schools due to measures taken when free schooling was introduced, deeming their financing inadequate. Such criticism increased the support of the middle and upper bourgeoisies for the MMM and also the PSM, as those schools were attended by all ethnic and religious groups, as in India, in spite of their stated mission of promoting Catholic moral values.

Another side from which the government was attacked was its policy regarding the former inhabitants of the Chagos Archipelago. Their land had been taken up to build a huge American naval air base which, years later, was used to launch military campaigns in Iraq and Afghanistan as University of Oxford's Sarmila Bose, quoting a book by David Vine, explains:[2]

"Now an impressively researched book that details its secret history goes even further and argues that Diego Garcia, and what happened in the Chagos Islands, lies at the heart of a global American empire that employs some 1,000 bases outside the United States. Their purpose: To ensure that no matter who governs in Asia, Africa or around the world, the US military would be in a position to "run the planet" from its chain of strategic island bases.

"For several decades, the shadowy presence of Diego Garcia and a whiff of its disreputable acquisition lurked in the misty fringes of Western security studies. David Vine's meticulously researched Island of Shame: the Secret History of the US Military Base on Diego Garcia (Princeton University Press, 2011) enables us to engage with the "strategic islands concept" and its consequences for the Chagossians and others. It provides a level of information about both the US and British policymakers and the human beings at the receiving end of their global power ambitions that had not been accessible before."

The focal point of the Labour campaign was the alleged relations of the MMM with communist countries, especially the U.S.S.R. and Cuba, and those of the region, Madagascar and the Seychelles, both led by hard-line dictators. The Labour strategists tried to make voters believe that an MMM-led government would lead the country into the communist camp. At the same time, though, they also accused the opposition of Those

---
[1] He confided this to a number of journalists, including the author of this book, who covered and editorialized on all the nation's political events from the 1970s to the 1990s.

[2] *Chagos, the heart of an American Empire?* by Sarmila Bose, Senior Research Fellow in the Politics of South Asia at the University of Oxford. 15 March 2012, http://www.aljazeera.com/indepth/opinion/2012/03/2012314114930627518.html, Accessed 14 July 2012.

Historic first 60-0 and aftermath

The victory of the MMM-PSM Alliance at the June 12, 1982 general elections (above table) was a first in the political history of the island and one that was unexpected by the framers of the Constitution. No opposition was elected. The Best Loser System enabled one to be formed with the appointment of four defeated candidates. Top: new government leaders: Kailash Ruhee, Sir Anerood Jugnauth, Paul Bérenger, Kader Bhayat and J.C. de l'Estrac.

"*Ilois*" or Chagossians, deported to Mauritius from their native land, lived in conditions of extreme poverty. They undertook in 1978 one of the longest hunger strikes in the country's history and Ramgoolam, under such intense pressure, had a compensation totalling Rs. 3 million paid out to them and promised to send a delegation to London for talks with the British authorities.

In April 1981, Cambridge University in the United Kingdom confirmed that examination questionnaires had been sold in Mauritius prior to the examinations being held in the island under the aegis of the university. The media revealed also that those question papers had been purchased for Rs. 500 to Rs. 1,000 each. A total of 71 of question-naires had to be changed during the examinations. This scandal was yet another one that gave the government an extremely negative image in the eyes of many voters.

Cracks in the opposition's ranks

For a short time in January 1982, rumours of secret talks between Boodhoo's PSM and Labour surfaced, but Boodhoo publicly denied. Those rumours had followed a cold snap within the MMM-PSM alliance in September of the previous year when Boodhoo had criticized the relations the MMM entertained with the Libyan government, accused by the Labour government of financing that party.

In those days, Jugnauth was privately assuring people around him that should he become PM, he would rein in Bérenger, who was perceived generally as having the upper hand over him within the party organization. To some journalists who questioned him on that subject, he confided, off the record, that he would react vigorously if Bérenger *"were to challenge my authority as PM after an election victory."* He did not want to be quoted then,[3] but it was not long before he would put to the test.

Bérenger seemed never to have received the message even from inside his party, as events following June 1982 were to prove. He was going to the general election with two colleagues who were both suspicious of his future behaviour and intentions once they would all be in power - Jugnauth and Boodhoo. This prefigured the crisis that actually followed their 1982 massive electoral victory, but the general public was unaware that the rot had already started developing within the fruit.

Labour hires an American electoral consultant

SSR was preparing his election campaign with the help of an American consultant, Eric Ekvall, who, to the journalists covering politics in those days, made all the mistakes that were necessary for the regime to sink deeper into unpopularity.

threatening the welfare state and defending the interests of the capitalists. Those contradictory messages did not serve the best interests of Labour and its allies, the CAM, and a small party of mostly Coloured bourgeois created by Philippe Blackburn, the Rassemblement pour la liberté (RPL), all grouped into a Parti de l'Alliance Nationale (PAN).

The Labour strategists were also unable to defend their economic austerity policies imposed by the IMF and the

---

[3] He said it to the author of this book who worked at *Le Mauricien* in 1978. It was an off-the-record statement at the time.

World Bank, starting with the devastating immediate effects of two devaluations of the rupee. While those devaluations were to help the country's exports and help usher the economic improvement of the mid-1980s, they were still negatively impacting the lives of the people across the country and, later, Bérenger, who pursued the World Bank and IMF policies, would suffer the same kind of attack as Minister of Finance.

Negative figures like the public debt reaching Rs. 7.2 billion had more impact on the public mind than the fact that the EPZ accounted already for over a quarter of the exports of the nation and tourism was flourishing. The theme "*Changement*" ("Change") chosen by the opposition became hard to oppose as the electoral campaign drew to its end and the government showing clear signs of what the French call the *'usure du pouvoir'* (power fatigue) due to a too long stay in power.

Two big blunders that also contributed to the rout of PAN at the June 1982 general election were: firstly, documents that the government officially claimed to be authentic documents proving the MMM-Libya link but which were discovered to have been fabricated; and secondly, the recruitment of over 20,000 workers by the government about which the opposition claimed there were insufficient funds to employ them even in the wake of an electoral victory and described as 'electoral bribery.'

The first 60-0 of political history: an MMM-PSM tsunami

The election result was a historic, first time electoral victory score of 60-0 at the direct election, pending the nomination of best losers, while in Rodrigues also, it was a 2-0 for a truly Rodriguan party, former Catholic priest Serge Clair's Organisation du Peuple Rodriguais (OPR), against the incumbent Mauritian members elected in 1976 under the PMSD banner. The winning alliance obtained 64.16 % of the popular vote while Ramgoolam's PAN obtained only 25.78 % and the PMSD a mere 7.79 %, the lowest in the party's history since the general election of 1967 and a figure that was to continue to go down in the next decades.

Since the Constitution of the country had been written, no one had imagined a scenario where a party or alliance would win all the seats at the direct election. Could best losers be appointed in such a situation as all of them would be from the opposition and there would definitely a change of the balance of forces in Parliament whereas the Constitution guaranteed that such a balance should not be disturbed by best loser appointments? Best losers could effectively reduce the government majority by up to eight seats. This was one of the questions that had to be resolved.

The matter was sent to the Supreme Court for advice and the judges decided that two best losers should be appointed for each of the PAN and the PMSD. This brought the number of members in Parliament to only 66, instead of the maximum of 70, because the maximum number of eight best losers could not be appointed following the Supreme Court ruling. Sir Gaëtan Duval thus went back to Parliament where he became the leader of the opposition constituted by his PMSD and Labour. The government brought into its ranks the two elected members of the OPR whose leader Serge Clair was appointed minister for Rodrigues. The government majority was reduced from 62-0 to 62-4 with the appointment of the best losers.[4]

Few people imagined, at that time, that this balance of forces would radically change within months and another general election would be held the following year, in August 1983.

The MMM-PSM alliance had been brought to power by the national electorate on a political manifesto promising change. But few of those changes were to be implemented as, within weeks, tensions were high within the Cabinet with Boodhoo disapproving the treatment meted out to the Leader of the Opposition, Sir Gaëtan Duval, banned after some time from official receptions at the behest of the MMM. Boodhoo was also against the high number of public servants sacked because of their alleged allegiance to the former regime. Among the most prominent figures sacked at the bidding of the MMM was Hervé Duval, brother of the PMSD leader, forced to go into premature retirement after long years of service to the state. It was only a matter of months before Hervé Duval would inflict a humiliating defeat on MMM candidate Gérard Ahnee at a municipal by-election in Beau Bassin/Rose Hill, a result that showed the disapproval by the voters of the treatment he received from the MMM. Hervé Duval would rise to political prominence by defeating the MMM at successive elections within an alliance with Labour and MSM

---

[4] Only 4 best losers have been appointed in subsequent elections with total or massive victories as Dr. Rama Sithanen, elecctoral expert, noted: *"In 1982, 1991 and 1995 only four Best Loser Seats were distributed as the winning party did not have any unreturned eligible candidate. During those years, there was a Parliament of only 66 members instead of 70 MPs as provided for in the Constitution. As a matter of fact, the Electoral Supervisory Commission did not know whether to appoint any Best Loser in 1982 as it could upset the balance of political forces...",* In: *A critical appraisal of the Best Loser System,* by Rama Sithanen, L'Express, 5 June 2008.

Within the Labour Party there was a serious dissent movement led by Sir Satcam Boolell, a long timecontender for succession to the leader, Sir Seewoosagur Ramgoolam. Unable to force the issue and get himself elected as leader, Boolell, who had formerly given discreet support to the Boodhoo group of dissenters without sticking out his neck and joining them, went on to create another party, the MPM or Mouvement Patriotique Mauricien, on 19 December 1982 at Patten College, Rose Hill.

Jugnauth and Boodhoo question Bérenger's economic policies

After the 1982 defeat, Labour did not wait long to be again in the corridors of power at Government House.[5] Another clear indication was given by Prime Minister Aneerood Jugnauth himself at a reception at the Chinese embassy where he said in a private comment[6] that weeks later went public, that he was impatiently waiting for Finance Minister Bérenger to return from mission in Washington at the IMF and World Bank headquarters to query him about his *"caving in to pressure"* from those organizations *"to the detriment of the population."* Jugnauth was furious that Bérenger, as finance minister, had refused a substantial general wage increase as promised, according to him, during the electoral campaign, and that he was accepting to reduce the welfare state, particularly the subsidies to rice and flour. This became a major issue.

Another bone of contention was a mission that Jugnauth led to Libya believing that the oil-rich Libyan government, which had close relations with Bérenger, would grant a massive financial package of one billion rupees to help redress the Mauritian economy and national finances. The mission did not yield anything substantial result while the communist bloc, from which Bérenger had said Mauritius would look to with a view to diversify its aid sources and trade links, also gave nothing that would compare to what Mauritius obtained from the Western nations.

With Bérenger being increasingly perceived as having the upper hand over the PM, Boodhoo manoeuvred to defend himself and the PSM from Bérenger as well as from hard-line militants who had never accepted him as deputy PM. He started also to counter aggressively the policies, decisions and role of the finance minister.

Jugnauth became increasingly restless also, especially as during a press conference, Bérenger cut him short to make a statement. Incensed by the fact that Jugnauth had told the media that the government would grant a general salary increase. For his part, Bérenger kept arguing that, as finance minister, he could assure one and all that the country's economic and financial state was *"worse"* than anticipated during the electoral campaign and a salary increase was out of question.

In fact, one of the most important defects in the MMM-PSM Alliance was that it was based on ethnic politics, that is, as Boodhoo bluntly expressed it in June 2012:

"... the MMM/PSM alliance itself was based on communalism. It is a Mauritian reality. We should not make a fuss of it... In 1982, the MMM presented Aneerood as Prime Minister, Harish as the VPM and fielded all 60 candidates with profiles so as to satisfy all races, religious beliefs and even castes... So, only fools will say that no communalism was present in politics." [7]

First major crisis in the MMM-PSM regime

The first crisis occurred in October 1982, less than 100 days into the new regime's mandate. It was immediately clear that on both sides of the line of fracture, communalism was the essential explanation of what was happening. There were repeated attacks from the PSM mouthpiece, Le Socialiste, and various members of the party, including Boodhoo, accusing him of working for the interests of his 'cousins,' the Franco-Mauritian sugar barons or 'grands Blancs.' This was replied to by the MMM in the same vein: communalism was Boodhoo's motivation because Bérenger is a White man. The economic issues becamesecondary to the new surge of ethnic politics. This was occurring ironically after an electoral tsunami that had been hailed by Jugnauth, Bérenger and their supporters as a harbinger of national unity and the death blow to ethnic politics. As seen above, Boodhoo's version to this day is that the alliance of the MMM with the PSM started as a kind of ethnic venture: it was 'based on communalism.' The crisis has leny credence to this view of things that prevailed among skeptics and critics, even at the time that

---

5 Even in the plane that was taking him to London in November 1982, Sir Seewoosagur Ramgoolam confided to the author of this book, who was on his way to an OAU summit in Tripoli, Libya, that a breakup of the MSM-PSM alliance government was in the making. Together with another journalist, Mitradev Peerthum of *Le Militant*, and the author, journalist at *Le Mauricien*, met SSR at his residence in London on their way back from the OAU summit where the former PM discussed the political situation in Mauritius.

6 Comment made to the author of this book, journalist at *Le Mauricien.*

7 http://defimedia279.rssing.com/chan-4398911/latest.php, Boodhoo's interview. Accessed 25 February 2017.

alliance was born and its shadow cabinet and list of candidates announced. It was predicted that it had all the ingredients to be highly volatile. Those critics and skeptics were both inside and outside the alliance, especially the left wing of the MMM and a group led by Ram Seegobin that went on to set up their own party, Lalit, and the opponents of that alliance mainly in the Labour Party and the PMSD.

In the end, Bérenger and a majority of MMM members of the National Assembly voted to oust Boodhoo and his party from government, trying to undo a political alliance that they had painstakingly negotiated and then defended for over a year. The crisis was so serious that, at that meeting held at Government House on October 21, 1982, to expel the PSM, Ramdath Jaddoo, member of the party's top brass, was believed by the media, the opposition parties (Labour, PMSD) and, later, Jugnauth himself, to have been told by Bérenbger to await the outcome of the meeting as a possible candidate for prime minister in case Jugnauth would have to step down. Jaddoo has never confirmed that, and Bérenger was going to oppose a strong denial after the event. Anyway, the situation at the time of that meeting, held on October 21 at Government House, was extremely tense.

Jugnauth emerged from the meeting visibly shaken and talked to the media in the main lounge of Government House, to announce the decision he had been entrusted with by his party: to sack the PSM and Boodhoo from the government. He gave the impression that he had accepted the decision. However, between that statement to the media and his residence at La Caverne, Vacoas, Jugnauth stopped at Le Réduit to meet the governor-general, Sir Dayendranath Burrenchobay, apparently, for many observers, to advise the latter to revoke the PSM ministers.

This was a crucial meeting from which Jugnauth emerged and decided not to revoke Boodhoo and the PSM from his Cabinet. It turned out that Jugnauth had been advised that, as Prime minister he was expected, under the Constitution, to ensure that it was the Cabinet and not his party and its politburo that should have the upper hand in decision-taking by the government. He appeared that same evening on the state-controlled television station making a statement that fell short of his party's expectation following its demand that the PSM be revoked.

On top of his attempt to force Jugnauth to revoke the PSM from the government based on what he perceived as that party's unjustified attacks against him, Bérenger had made yet another mistake in entering into a serious conflict with yet another member of the MMM's top brass, Trade Minister Kader Bhayat. On October 21, Bérenger had told *Le Mauricien* that the crisis opposed him and Jugnauth and that Bhayat was "*insignificant*" in that context, a reference to a controversy he entered into with the latter over his ministry's policies. The word '*insignificant*' with regard to a man who had been one of the main pillars of his party during over a decade of MMM history, was seized upon by Bérenger's opponents inside and outside government as being highly contemptuous and offensive.

Jugnauth, for his part, told the media that the crisis revolved essentially around the presence of the PSM in his government. The next day, the PSM told the media that the country had to go to another general election as the electorate had voted to power an alliance of two parties and not just the MMM. The MMM politburo then met without Jugnauth, absent for *"health reasons"* and decided that **"the party and the PM will work in consultation with each other to designate the new ministers."** Later, it became known that Jugnauth had been seriously ill during the crisis. Nevertheless, on Friday, October 22, Boodhoo, who had meanwhile met Jugnauth twice, and his party were still in the government. Jugnauth had clearly stood his ground with Boodhoo's support and by October 25, that first crisis appeared to have been resolved when Bérenger took back his seat in the Cabinet after having briefly left the government.

The MMM-PSM government explodes

The MMM has always been hostile to any criticism of its behaviour during the 1982-83 crisis. But even people who believed strongly in its core values have blasted the party for its strategy and actions in those days and months that seriously damaged national unity and the hopes of a vast national electorate. The conclusion of an article published thirty years later, in 2012, states that the MMM has, due to its errors and mistakes, **"has spent more time dominating the political arena than the time it has spent steering the country's affairs."** [8]

In truth, the wounds from that period never healed. Bhayat was still deeply hurt after his conflict with Bérenger. Jugnauth and Boodhoo still resented Bérenger's fiscal and economic policies whereby he had agreed to hike the prices of rice and flour, introduce for the first time a sales tax, which amounted to five per cent, and reduce the

---

[8] *APRÈS LES "60-0" DE 1982: Le MMM et le Pouvoir,* Article paru dans *Le Mauricien* | 11 juin, 2012, Par Shabana Raman-Caunhye, Parvèz Dookhy, Yannick Cornet et Med Doba.

export tax on sugar to the tune of 57 million rupees, regarded as a concession to the sugar barons. Those measures may have been inevitable, but successive governments were to apply the same medicine of austerity in exchange of improved economic growth with more dexterity, starting from Vishnu Lutchmeenaraidoo, Bérengers successor as minister of Finance. One explanation could be that Bérenger, when he is in power, has very poor media relations and not-so-experienced advisers on information matters.

Both inside government circles close to Jugnauth and Boodhoo, and among the opposition parties, the Rs 57-million concession was viewed as a "*gift*" by Bérenger to the White plantocracy. Then, Bérenger approved the sale, to a South African group, of two hotels, Touessrok and La Pirogue. The attack against the finance minister took a new turn: he was accused both from within and from outside government of being the stooge of white capitalism, of playing to the tune of his White "*cousins*" in Mauritius and in the country of apartheid, South Africa, while agreeing to a policy of austerity that made life more difficult for the masses of workers who had suffered from slavery and the indenture labour system for centuries. Those attacks, often excessive and irrational, went viral as he took charge of his own public image.

Responding, Bérenger tried to explain his policies, but he also counterattacked, together with his supporters in and outside Government House, by, not only defending his economic policies, but by also portraying himself as being victim of ethnic prejudice. This made his supporters even more aggressive in their attitude towards Jugnauth and Boodhoo. Both sides of the divide were, at the end of the day, fully engaged in a serious argument with a strong ethnic content that only made things worse.

On yet another front, Bérenger was losing ground: his relations with the trade unions and the left of his party. Within the trade union movement, there was resentment against his economic policies. Leftist militants led by Jack Bizlall and Ram Seegobin severely criticized those policies as a "*betrayal*" of the working classes that had brought the MMM to power and an indication that he had caved in to pressure from the world's main temples of western capitalism, the World Bank and the IMF..

What was really happening was considered by the unions and the political left as a clash between two ideologies. Neo-liberalism was the first one, coming from Washington, through the World Bank and the IMF. It commanded countries that relied on those two bodies to get funds for development, to slash social expenditure ruthlessly, and this even caused violent upheavals across the world as the cost of living soared far beyond the reach of the masses. The other ideology was the British/European moderate form of socialism that supported the existence of a welfare state of the kind that had been developed in Mauritius from the 1940s through the action of successive Labour leaders: Maurice Curé, Guy Rozemont, Emmanuel Anquetil and Sir Seewoosagur Ramgoolam.

Bérenger came to symbolize, in the eyes of Jugnauth's and Boodhoo's supporters and those of the Labour Party and the PMSD, as a leader who had betrayed his former socialist ideology to become a champion of neoliberalism and of his rich White '*cousins*' in Mauritius. That was how he was depicted by his adversaries, as the crisis deepened, albeit the fact that Mauritius has never stopped, even to this day, liberalising its economy to the tune of the World Bank and the IMF. The crisis was basically a struggle for power, which is a constant wherever there is political power. Bérenger and his opponents were all jostling for a greater share of power and the next victim, just a few years later, of this permanent infighting inside political establishments and governments, would be Harish Boodhoo in 1987, Bérenger in 1993 and again in 1997, both revoked by prime ministers wary of their political maneuvers perceived as sapping their authority and weakening them in a deliberate manner. Bérenger even entered into alliances with MSM, Labour and even the PMSD... in the ensuing decades.

An explosive mix: ideology, ethnic politics, social and economic issues

Bérenger's standpoint in the face of his opponents' criticism in 1983, was that he was applying rigour to the management of the economy and finances of the country. In 1982, it was true, as he pointed out on various occasions, that the new government was faced with a budget deficit representing 13% of the gross domestic product (GDP) and the former Labour-led government had left a public debt of Rs 6.3 billion, while the trade balance and the balance of payments were recording high deficits and the reserves in foreign exchange represented only two to three weeks of imports. [9]

---

9 *Bilan économique de Sir Aneerood Jugnauth*, in *L'Express* 30 September 2003, a review of Jugnauth's governments' performance from 1982 to 2003 with quotes from various sources, including economist Georges Chung Tick Kan who stressed that unemployment was eliminated "*for the first time ever*" under SAJ's prime ministership in the 1980s.

On the social front, official unemployment was 21% or a total of about 70,000 unemployed, according to the Central Statistics Office and the IMF. [10] Poverty was rampant and there could eventually be a risk of social explosion. During the election campaign, in a desperate bid to push down the figure, the former Labour government had recruited thousands of workers in what a Supreme Court judge, Rajsoomer Lallah, would later conclude to have been an illegal exercise.

There was a necessity, Bérenger argued, in Parliament [11] and outside, to adopt measures of austerity to redress the financial situation. Those measures comprised the creation of a uniform sales tax of 5% for the first time in line with modern fiscal trends across the world, linking the rupee to a new basket of currencies, withholding abrupt wage increases, giving fiscal respite to the sugar industry to maintain its productivity, etc. His decisions, according to him, made economic sense in a brave new world where to get assistance from international financial institutions like the IMF and the World Bank, nations had to apply rigorous financial management and reduce expenditure such as, in the case of Mauritius, the subsidies on rice and flour.

With hindsight, Bérenger, albeit the fact that he could have resisted socially sensitive changes as those regarding the price of rice and flour, was essentially right in his macroeconomic approach in the context of a liberalising world, if we are to believe the economic experts, for example Bheenick (future Labour government finance minister) and Schapiro, commenting on the way the government addressed, in the1980s, after Ringadoo in 1979, the problems faced by industry, including tourism, as their receipts sharply declined, alluding positively to Bérenger's decision concerning the rupee:

"Therefore, in February 1983, the government delinked the Mauritian rupee from the Special Drawing Rights and linked it instead to a basket of currencies that are more representative of the country's trade patterns. The change in the basket and the implementation of a flexible exchange rate policy gradually restored the real effective exchange rate to its September 1981 level, thereby improving the competitiveness of Mauritian exports internationally.

"Simultaneously, the government liberalized lending and deposit rates, initially with respect to nonpriority sectors (which excluded agriculture, tourism, and industry). Finally, it lifted all ceilings on interest rates and bank credit to introduce greater competition in the credit market..."

Bheenick and Schapiro observe further that the difficult economic situation started to improve from the beginning of 1983 (Bérenger was the Minister of Finance) and part of the credit goes to his much maligned predecessor, Sir Veerasamy Ringadoo: *"(...) beginning in 1983, the situation was reversed under the impact of the stabilization and structural adjustment programs that the authorities initiated in 1979 with the help of the IMF and the World Bank. Economic forecasts for the world economy became more optimistic and the demand for EPZ products, particularly knitwear and garments, grew. The government reinforced these positive developments by putting in place appropriate institutional and policy reforms. The combined effect of these events was a sudden surge in new applications for Export Enterprise Certificates, along with an expansion of existing units. By March 1987, the number of enterprises operating in the EPZ increased to 437, nearly a five-fold rise over 1977."* [12]

Far from politicking on the basis of actual economic and financial facts, Jugnauth and Boodhoo, just as prior to 1982, the Jugnauth-Boodhoo-Bérenger trio had done, were light-years beyond facts and figures of economic management. They were engaged in traditional Mauritian politics – so was Bérenger, Duval and the Labour party. With hindsight, they also praised Bérenger in later years and decades for his record, each time they were reconciled with the MMM and its leader and the latter in return heaped praise on his former foes. In 2012, when that book was published, the game was still ongoing, with deliberate political amnesia continuing to be rampant. Back in 1982-1983, during the government crisis, ideology, ethnic politics and social and economic issues constituted a highly explosive mix.

In December 1982, the MMM did not go to the municipal elections with its partner in government, the PSM. The party won a crushing victory over Labour and PMSD with 115 seats out of a total of 126 for the four towns plus the City of Port-Louis. Labour won six seats in Vacoas-Phoenix and the PMSD five in Ward 3 of Beau Bassin/Rose Hill. The MMM took the control of all five municipalities.

Bérenger may have overestimated the significance of this easy victory – or not. His behaviour in the following months betrayed an overconfidence that led him to even challenge Jugnauth to organize another general election if the PM wanted to work with Boodhoo's PSM.

---

10 In: *Mauritius: Unemployment and the Role of Institutions*, Issues 2003-2011, by Calvin A. McDonald, James Y. Yao. Page 3: *"The unemployment rate plunged from 21 percent to less than 4 percent between the early 1980s and the early 1990s."* See also the table based on CSO and IMF figures, page 10, showing the downward trend of unemployment from 1982-83.
11 *Budget Speech* by Paul Bérenger, 20th August 1982, Government Printing Port-Louis.
12 Bheenick, Schapiro, op cit.

The second crisis that shook the government arose from tension built up as both sides again criticized each other publicly. Reading through their media statements during the first few months of 1983 *(Le Mauricien, Le Militant, L'Express)* one gathers that instead of abating, the mutual hostility deepened week after week and the pace of events suddenly accelerated after the celebration of the 15th anniversary of independence on March 12, 1983.

The demise of the MSM-PSM government

Bérenger was continually complaining about the state of law and order in the country, while this area fell under the responsibility of Jugnauth as the minister in charge of the police. Jugnauth retorted at a meeting he expressly invited the media to at Triolet, to hear his criticism of the Customs Department, which, he said, was not run as it should, as a result of which large volumes of drugs were entering the country. It was Bérenger who was the minister responsible for that department.

Prior to the independence anniversary celebrations, a group led by Rama Poonoosamy, the minister of Culture, had produced a creole version of the national anthem "*Motherland*" that was broadcast by the MBC, whose director-general, Gaëtan Essoo, was a member of the group and an MMM appointee. Originally intended to be played at the Independence Day celebration, that new version of the national anthem was dumped in favour of the original one, in English. Boodhoo resented Essoo's close links with the MMM and campaigned against him on the ground that the MBC director-general was an agent of that party who was helping to elevate Creole to the status of official language, to the detriment of French, English and the oriental languages.

Pierre Benoit, at *Le Mauricien*, condemned what he perceived as a utilization of Creole that was detrimental to French, the main language of the Mauritian media and of an increasing number of families of all ethnic backgrounds.Boodhoo asked Jugnauth to sack Essoo and this was done on March 22, 1983. It was clear that Jugnauth wanted, by this decision, to challenge Bérenger on the subject of his prerogatives as PM under the Constitution. It was also obvious that Jugnauth was prepared for the worse and Bérenger had underestimated the PM's desire to set the record straight regarding his authority as head of the government, one that would not accept to be dictated by the central committee of the MMM, where Bérenger reigned supreme, with a comfortable majority.

On March 23, Bérenger, arguing he had not been consulted prior to Essoo being sacked and stating that the PSM had gone too far, resigned from the Cabinet together with 10 other ministers. Of those ministers, two were later to go back to the Jugnauth/Boodhoo fold, Kailash Ruhee and Jocelyn Seenyen of the PSM, while the others were: Jean-Claude de l'Estrac, Swaley Kasenally, Cassam Uteem, Rama Poonoosamy, Prem Koonjoo, Shirin Aumeeruddy-Cziffra, Krishna Baligadoo and Jayen Cuttaree. Two MMM ministers stayed in government, Kader Bhayat and Dr. Diwakar Bundhun, while Ramduth Jaddoo, absent from the country, would resign upon returning from mission, after which he would join a new political party set up by Jugnauth and Boodhoo, the Mouvement Socialiste Militant (MSM).

After the resignation of 11 of his ministers, Jugnauth's position in the MMM was challenged by the group supporting Bérenger. The situation worsened to the point that the PM was heckled by a vociferous crowd of pro-Bérenger militants as he stepped out of his car to attend, at the Quatre Bornes municipality, on March 24, 1983, a joint meeting of the MMM's parliamentary group and central committee. Jugnauth obviously feared for his security and was accompanied by his police bodyguards.[13] He said afterwards, he received an ultimatum from the pro-Bérenger group: either he organized a general election or he had to leave the MMM and form his own party. He also said he would never again attend MMM meetings.

That was the end of the MMM-PSM government. The MMM suffered a major split and Jugnauth had hardened his stand and was now unwilling to have Bérenger back in his Cabinet. One MMM meeting subsequently organized at Eden College Rose Hill at the initiative of party members was intended to end the rift between Jugnauth and Bérenger, It failed despite people shuttling between the meeting and Jugnauth's residence at La Caverne in desperate attempts to reconcile the two men.

Fresh elections in August 1983: Jugnauth wins

Bérenger then focused on ousting Jugnauth from power by way of a general election, which he was confident to win. This again betrayed his over-confidence which even blinded him to the fact that Jugnauth and Boodhoo were

---
13 The author of this book covered the event and was witness to insults being hurled at Jugnauth, accused to be a "*traitor*" to his party.

already at work building a new political coalition with Labour and the PMSD. They were also working on the setting up of a new party, the Mouvement Socialiste Militant (MSM).

In the meantime, the governor-general, Sir Dayendranath Burrenchobay, refused a request by Bérenger to call a general election. Burrenchobay followed Jugnauth's advice by appointing a new Cabinet under Jugnauth as PM. Jugnauth was biding his time to go to elections on his own terms. Jugnauth, supported by Boodhoo, founded the MSM at a popular rally in Vacoas. Boodhoo had dissolved his PSM and invited its followers into the new party led by Jugnauth with himself taking over organizational matters. Jugnauth then called a snap general election to be held on August 21, 1983.

Labour and PMSD as well as Sylvio Michel's Organisation Fraternelle/Les Verts joined the new government coalition. Bhayat was presented at the shadow deputy PM and Sir Seewoosagur Ramgoolam, who was denied a comeback as leader of that alliance, was presented as the country's future president after the proposed setting up of a republic. For its part, the MMM went into the electoral campaign with the pledge to set up a republic, the shadow president of which was presented to the electorate as Harichand Bhagirutty, a respected former magistrate. Bérenger, then Leader of the Opposition, was bidding for Prime Minister for the first time.

A very tense electoral campaign

The split of the 1982 government had deeply divided the country on ethnic lines.

During the electoral campaign, tension was extremely high, especially in certain areas of the south. An alleged plot to assassinate Boodhoo was "*revealed*" as the campaign was drawing to its close and nothing was ever heard of it after the election. In many respects, the 1983 electoral campaign was like that of 1967.

The government alliance obtained 51.9 % of the national vote and the opposition 45.6 %, a result almost similar to the 1967 general election, with the rural areas voting mainly for the government and a majority in the towns voting for the opposition, this time the MMM instead of the PMSD and with Bérenger losing his reelection bid at Quatre Bornes and returning to Parliament under the BLS. The MMM retained its position as the country's biggest party.

Chapter 50

Economic "miracle" – and more political upheavals: 1984-1989

The MMM came out of the 1983 general election severely shaken. Bérenger and his party had lost power and were down to about half the number of parliamentary seats they had obtained at the June 1982 general election. Worse, national unity was compromised and ethnic politics had returned and was being practised to a larger extent than ever before on both sides of the political divide, with Jugnauth settling scores with the Muslim community by reason of its support to the MMM and using Duval and Michel to rally Creoles, while Bérenger was going to persist in his belief (and in practice) that ethnic sub-groups within the Hindu community could be one by one wooed over to the MMM, including the Vaish majority, with a Prime Minister from that caste (even if Jugnauth and Ramgoolam would deny it, but that was Bérenger's thiking in1991, 1995, and the upcoming 2012 elections).

Jugnauth would always refer to the return to ethnic politics as being the result of Bérenger's role in the breakup of the MMM-PSM government, while Beronqer consistently threw back the blame on Jugnauth's and Boodhoo's shoulders. In subsequent government alliances, it became clear that Bérenger's desire to have the upper hand in the Cabinets in which he served led to him to be repeatedly sacked (1992, 1997) until he finally obtained the top job by compromising with Jugnauth at the 2000 general election. This was followed by a mandate with two PMs, Anerood Jugnauth until 2003, then himself until the 2005 general election, which he lost as PM and Pravind Jugnauth as PM in waiting.

American researcher Larry Bowman has aptly summed up the MMM's short incursion into power during nine months in 19821983 as having been essentially marked by political crises lasting over several months that led the party to lose the support of the Hindus.[1]

Positive views on the 1982-83 MMM-PSM government

In addition to the economic and fiscal reforms introduced by Bérenger seen by economic analysts like Bheenick and Schapiro, who consider that they contributed, like those of Ringadoo from the end of the 1970s and of Lutchmeenaraidoo after Bérenger, to the economic progress of the next decade,[2] some researchers believe that the 1982-1983 regime had some positive aspects, after all.

The positive results were on the democratic front, where the 1982 regime amended the Constitution to prevent any repeat the events of the 1970s when a general election was postponed for almost a decade (1967-1976), and legislative by-elections and local government elections abolished.

Bowman[3] also points out that the Constitution functioned remarkably well during this period of political crises, with ministers resigning voluntarily (a rare occurrence in developing countries) and a snap general election to give legitimacy to a new parliamentary majority.

Another positive factor was the coming of a younger generation of politicians in the MMM and the PSM. Labour and the PMSD had to look for new blood as a result of this major generation shift as they recruited candidates for the other elections of the 20th century and beyond.

Instability of the new government but economy grows

One saying goes that where there is power, there is struggle for power. This was true in the case of the new regime that won the 1983 general election and Jugnauth would be forced, even before the end of his mandate, to call another snap general election in 1987. His government was again threatened with losingits parliamentary majority following several internal upheavals. He never made it to the last year of his legal mandate, actually, and this was the case after the 1991 general election when he was forced to call a general election in December 1995 following more crises in government.

---

1   Bowman, op cit.
2   Bheenick and Schapiro, op cit.
3   Op cit.

However, this did not destabilize the country and the MSM/Labour/PMSD alliance engineered the so-called economic "miracle" that took Mauritius out of the list of poor countries by the end of the 1980s decade. Some observers see that as a continuation of the diversification efforts undertaken from as far as the 1960s after Professor James Meade recommended diversification and the first industrial establishment of Mauritius was established with the ISIs (import substitution industries), followed in the 1970s by the EOIs (export oriented industries). There seems to be a continuum irrespective of party lines, which tends to invalidate theories of great politician-saviours and luck as a factor as some in academia have discussed should be excluded in favour of various concrete elements as pointed out by Jeffrey A. Frankel, analysing the Mauritius success story:

"Some fundamental geographic and historical determinants of trade and rule of law help explain why average income is lower in Africa than elsewhere, and trade and rule of law help explain performance in Africa just as they do worldwide. Despite those two econometric findings, the fundamental determinants are not much help in explaining relative performance within Africa. The fundamental determinants that work worldwide but not within Africa are remoteness, tropics, size and fragmentation. (Access to the sea is the one fundamental geographic determinant of trade and income that is always important.) A case in point is the high level of ethnic diversity in Mauritius, which in many places would make for dysfunctional politics. Here, however, it brings cosmopolitan benefits. The institutions manage to balance the ethnic groups; none is excluded from the system. It is intriguing that the three African countries with the highest governance rankings (Mauritius, Seychelles and Cape Verde) are all islands that had no indigenous population. It helps that everyone came from somewhere else." [4]

In the case of Jugnauth, though, strong leadership qualities added to the positive factors in the above extract from academia, were decisive in the making of the 'economic miracle.' One should not also underestimate his minister of finance, Vishnu Lutchmeenaraidoo's remarkable skills in forging budgetary decisions and formulating social, financial and economic policies that were attractively package and won public approval, unlike Ringadoo's and Bérenger's somewhat abrupt styles.

Project of republic dropped

Jugnauth forged new, sometimes unexpected alliances that maintained him at the helm of the country from 1982 to 1995, without any interruption, and, in 2000 to come back to power and be PM for a further three years before retiring to Le Réduit as president of the republic.

After the 1983 general election, the new MSM-Ied regime replaced OPR leader Serge Clair as minister of Rodrigues by his colleague France Félicité and this was to cause a rift in that party at the next general election, but Clair would again triumph and Félicite would find himself out of the OPR by the time of the 1987 general election.

Then government's commitment to appoint Sir Seewoosagur Ramgoolam as the first president of a proposed republic could not materialize without the support of the MMM opposition. Discussions with Bérenger centred on the latter's request that the president be granted additional powers to those held by the governor-general. The government accused him of trying to actually prevent SSR, "the father of the nation's independence," from acceding to the highest office in the proposed republic. The stalemate wasnot resolved and Jugnauth dropped the republican project altogether.

The new regime focused much on the external relations of the country. The MMM had, in 1982-1983, stepped up efforts to have Mauritian sovereignty re-established over its archipelago and interdicted the sending of workers and provisions from Mauritius to the huge air and naval base the Americans had set up after having the population removed manu military from their native islands. The MMM-led government had also interdicted ships carrying nuclear material in the Port-Louis harbour, which meant such U.S. military ships were unwanted.

A complete reversal of the policy regarding sending workers and provisions to the Chagos Archipelago was decided by the government that emerged from the 1983 general election. Jugnauth and Duval had the embargo lifted, but the Mauritian claim over the archipelago was maintained.

Jugnauth then turned his attention to the relations between the MMM and Libya.

After the MMM-PSM government split, Tripoli had concentrated its relations with Mauritius on the Port-Louis municipality, entirely controlled by the MMM. When LordMayor Bashir Khodabux visited Tripoli officially, he was offered a grant of Rs. 1 million to the municipality. When summoned to provide explanations to the government

[4] Mauritius: African Success Story, op cit.

over this matter, the Libyans refused any discussion. The government reacted vigorously by expelling all the Libyan diplomats from the country, the ambassador being led manu militari to the airport.

Another major diplomatic incident occurred when PM Jugnauth secretly visited Taiwan, which was a departure from the official position of Mauritius recognizing only one China. Ministers Duval and Kadress Pillay also visited Taiwan and Jugnauth said his visit helped Mauritius to have a good deal for rice imports. The government made considerable efforts to bring into Mauritius investors from Taiwan, even offering them Mauritian passports. The operation was, overall, successful, bringing into the export processing zone several Taiwanese investors, in addition to those that were lured from Hong Kong, India, Singapore and Europe.

China and the MMM, which invoked "morality", protested following the Taiwan visit, but Jugnauth made a statement that was going to be used for a long time against him: "Morality does not fill one's tummy." ("Moralite napa rempli ventre.") Jugnauth and Duval managed to reassure Beijing that Mauritius had not put into question its one-China policy and pointed out that the relations with Taiwan remained trade-based, with no formal diplomatic ties. The Chinese accepted this explanation, though remaining quite nervous about the links between Port-Louis and Taipeh.

The making of the 'Mauritius miracle'

The MSM-led coalition government (comprising also Labour and PMSD) took advantage also of the panic that was prevalent in Hong Kong, as this territory's restitution to China was a certainty and investors there were looking for alternatives overseas. Mauritius was the place where many of them invested at the bidding of the MSM-Labour-PMSD government's business missions that travelled to various Asian countries, including Singapore, where a number of investors were also lured to Mauritius.

A key player in the government was Vishnu Lutchmeenaraidoo, ideologically a liberal in spite of his long years in the MMM where he was quite close to Bérenger. Playing much with the packaging of his fiscal and economic policies and giving a popular twist to the actual content, Lutchmeenaraidoo brilliantly succeeded at the helm of the nation's economy and finances. He was helped by the constant devaluation of the rupee in relation to a basket of foreign currencies, a system set up by Bérenger with the help of World Bank and IMF experts, which increased dramatically the receipts in rupees from Mauritian exports. His budget presentations were well prepared and were instrumental in the making of the economic miracle, which started to give fruits from around 1985-1986 and saw unemployment vanish almost completely and prosperity reach the working classes, especially those in the construction industry.

The government was successful in attracting investors after restoring business confidence some time after the 1983 general election. Tourism grew rapidly with the number of foreign visitors, which had declined from 121,620 in 1981 to 118,360 in 1982, probably due to two general elections within nine months, climbing back to 123,820 in 1984.

In the EPZ, export receipts increased to Rs. 2.25 billion in 1984, as compared to Rs. 1.3 billion in 1983, while the number of factories increased from 146 to 195 during the same period. By 1988, the number of factories reached nearly 600 and the export receipts of the EPZ amounted to Rs. 8.18 billion. The number of jobs increased each year by 30 % in the EPZ, from 1983 to 1987.

The economy of the country was being literally restructured. EPZ exports, in terms of value, accounted for 39.1 % of the value of total exports in 1984 and in 1988 the figure had risen to 58.8 %.

In the sugar industry, reform was undertaken with the preparation of an action plan that focused on increasing the yield of the lands of the small and medium planters, the rationalization of factory operations through the closing of some of them, the improvement of others, the setting up of new units to produce electricity from bagasse, the fibrous sugar cane residue, and efforts to diversify the industry's production base and promote research to improve cane yields.

The government reduced the export tax on sugar to a uniform rate of 18.75 % for producers of more than 3,000 tons of sugar, while the tax affecting the smaller planters was simply scrapped, as were those on molasses exports and the sugar milling tax. The small planters also obtained from the reform a higher proportion of the sugar extracted from their canes: it was increased from 74 to 76 %. Several fiscal concessions were granted to the industry to facilitate mechanization, reduce import taxes on agricultural equipment and spare parts.

This manner of proceeding in such a socially sensitive area as the sugar industry was significantly different from Bérenger's Rs. 40 million-concession perceived by critics as a "gift" to the sugar barons. Jugnauth and Lutchmeenaraidoo were better a packaging series of measures into more attractive positions.

Another factor that added to the general prosperity of the country was several cyclone-free years of large harvests of sugar cane resulting in high sugar production figures. Production reached 707,000 tons in 1986, 691,000 tons in 1987, and 634,000 tons in 1988.

The rate of economic growth, as measured by the Gross National Product (GNP) was a mere 0.4 % in 1983. It increased to 4.7 % in 1984 and in the years leading to 1988, the figure was successively: 6.8 % (1985); 8.9 % (1986); 8.4 % (1987); and 5.8 % (1988). The budget deficit, which had reached almost 14 % of the GNP in 1979-1980, was brought down to only 3.7 % in 1985-1986. Inflation, which had reached highs of 33 to 42 % during the economic crisis at the end of the 1970s, was a mere 1.8 % in 1986.

Lutchmeenaraidoo presented seven successive "no-tax" budgets that boosted investment. The fiscal regime was made more attractive. The maximum income tax rate was brought down from 70 % to 30 %. The fiscal regime was revamped, rationalized and simplified. A Unified Revenue Board was set up and the government created the Stock Exchange of Mauritius (SEM).

<u>Political instability returns</u>

Nevertheless the economic upturn did not shelter Jugnauth's government from internal upheavals. Boodhoo, the former deputy PM now the government's Chief Whip in the National Assembly, wrote a document in two parts addressed to Jugnauth. In it, he requested more freedom of action to reorganize the MSM and an increased role in government for Deputy PM Sir Gaëtan Duval. The government's internal wrangling had started with the sacking, in February 1984, not so long after the 1983 general election, of Sir Satcam Boolell, leader of the Labour Party. Boolell was not followed into the opposition by his parliamentary group. At the same time, the government launched a strong campaign to curb the influence of the newspapers, particularly those with high circulations that, according to Jugnauth and his colleagues in government, were supporting the MMM, in particular Bérenger. On March 31, a bill was proposed to make a large cash deposit of Rs. 500,000 mandatory for newspapers to be allowed to continue to operate. The bill was opposed by the media whose members organized a sit-down in front of Government House in Port-Louis. 44 protesting journalists were arrested, detained for four hours and prosecuted. They were later proclaimed "Mauritians of the Year" by the daily L'Express.

The cash deposit was a huge sum for most newspapers in those days. The deposit was scrapped in favour of a written commitment for a value of half that sum, purportedly to guarantee the payment of fines and damages arising from legal action against the newspapers.

In April 1984, Minister Sylvio Michel resigned from Jugnauth's Cabinet and, together with his colleague Gaëtan Gangaram, joined the ranks of the parliamentary opposition.

As for ministers Michael Glover and Dr. Beergoonath Ghurburrun who had not followed Boolell into the opposition, they formed a new party, the Rassemblement des Travaillistes Mauriciens (RTM) but were incapable of rallying popular support. They eventually dissolved the RTM to join the MSM.

The year 1984 was all the more difficult for Jugnauth as the MMM went before a commission of inquiry presided by Judge Goburdhun to accuse several ministers of corruption. The judge rejected the allegations, but the MMM nevertheless continued to campaign on the theme of corruption. The MMM insisted that corruption was rampant within government ranks. The accusation was proved right when four members of the Jugnauth government in the National Assembly were caught red-handed trafficking in drugs internationally – but their arrest and the convictions were obtained overseas, while in Mauritius the drug mafia had, since the 1983 general election, infiltrated the government circles and protected government candidates during election campaigns. Jugnauth would eventually react vigorously to that as will be seen below.

Death of SSR

In 1985, the MMM defeated the government alliance massively at the municipal elections. In December of that year, Sir Seewoosagur Ramgoolam died at Le Réduit, where he had replaced Sir Dayendranath Burrenchobay as governor-general. His appointment had followed government's failure to get sufficient votes from the opposition to change the constitution and make the country a republic. His health had seriously deteriorated over the years and he actually barely managed to give his last interview to the author of this book, [5] aided by Dr. K. Hazareesingh, his faithful companion till the very end.

The entire nation mourned him. The masses were grateful to him as he had, over several decades at the helm of government even from the pre-independence era, provided a welfare state that catered for the poor and the needy through various social aid allowances and programs, relief work, free schooling, universal and free health care, a national pension scheme, and more. Ramgoolam has joined the Pantheon of the nation's greatest leaders and a Samadhi at the Sir Seewoosagur Ramgoolam Botanical Garden at Pamplemousses has been erected in remembrance of his major role in the historical evolution of the nation.

The Amsterdam scandal rocks the government

Before the month of December was over, another shock occurred that shook deeply the country. Fourparliamentarians of the Jugnauth government were arrested at Schipol Airport, Amsterdam, in the Netherlands, with in their possession a suitcase containing over 20 kilos of heroin. They were Sattyanand Pelladoah, member for Grand Baie/Poudre d'Or; Ismael Nawoor, member for Port-Louis Maritime/Port-Louis East; Serge Thomas, member for Mahébourg/Plaine Magnien; and Kim Currun, member for Flacq/Bon Accueil.

The connection between the local mafia and Government House was revealed not only by those arrests overseas, but by the fact also that when they were released from prison, absolutely no action was taken against them in Mauritius. They were welcomed back home at the airport in the VIP lounge, stayed in government and were only punished by being left out of the list of candidates of the government at the following general election campaign.

The four government members represented only the tip of the iceberg. The drug mafia had also participated in the financing of the MSM, as was revealed at a commission inquiry on drug trafficking presided by Judge Maurice Rault. Other members of the National Assembly were accused by the commission of shady roles, including Suren Poonith and Lutchmeeparsad Ramsewak. Some of their colleagues whose names were persistently mentioned came out scot free.

After the Amsterdam arrests on December 31, 1986, a huge headline in Le Mauricien said: "The opposition: 'The government must resign.'" This was following a press conference held by the MMM opposition. Boolell also clamoured for the resignation of the Jugnauth government after the Amsterdam affair.

Inside the regime, Boodhoo moved for the kill, vigorously trying to oust Jugnauth.

Outside, SSR's son Navin Ramgoolam, started working together with a group within Labour led by Anil Baichoo, to forge an alliance with the MMM. Eventually, Baichoo was to form a dissident Labour group called the Moument Travailliste Démocratique (MTD) and enter into an alliance with the MMM, but Ramgoolam did not make the move expected by Baichoo at the 1987 general election and remained in London, lying in wait for a better opportunity to enter the political arena.

Jugnauth alleged in January 1986 that Boodhoo wanted to overthrow him by a coup during conversations with media leaders, including the author of this book. The two men had made contradictory statements to the Rault commission on the drug trade, mutually accusing of each other, in one instance, of having pocketed money offered by the mafia leaders of the country. In the end, Jugnauth sacked Boodhoo from his position as Government Chief Whip and banned him from the party. Meanwhile, Boolell had started negotiating his return to the Cabinet and this happened actually in August 1986, as Jugnauth was struggling to regain control of the MSM.

Boolell, as well as Anil Kumar Gayan, Kader Bhayat, Kishore Deerpalsingh and Kailash Purryag had given the impression at one time that they would join Boodhoo. In the case of the four "Ks" as they were dubbed (Kader, Kishore, Kailash, Kumar), they had blasted, during a discreet dinner they organized at La Pirogue to talk to the author of this book, then chief editor at Le Mauricien, for allegedly excluding candidates for jobs and promotions in the public service on a sectarian basis. Leaders of the Muslim community continue even today to recall those days when they felt their people were punished after 1983 for having supported the MMM.

The four "Ks" actually visited Boodhoo at his home in Belle Terre before submitting their resignation from Cabinet as the crisis deepened within the MSM. In fact, the ethnic politics game has started from the 1982-83 conflict opposing on one side, the MMM, and on the other side, the MSM/Labour/PMSD coalition. When the govern-

---

[5] Reproduced in: Selvon, Sydney, Ramgoolam, Sydney Selvon, 2nd edition Editions de l'Océan Indien 2006.

ment coalition won and believed that the Muslims had voted collectively as a community for the MMM, there was resentment towards them inside government and there followedretaliation due mainly to the fact that recruitments and appointments to hundreds, if not thousands of jobs in the Civil Service, were in the hands of the ministers, who had to get the vetting approval of the Prime Minister.

As the split in the MSM widened, Jugnauth felt that a general election was inevitable. He did everything to distance himself from the drug barons who had been his party's agents at the 1983 general election and he heaped the entire responsibility for this situation to Boodhoo. The latter hit back, putting the ultimate responsibility on Jugnauth himself, but he eventually resigned from government feeling having been unjustly associated by Jugnauth and the Rault commission with the drug scandal.

Another MSM member, Ramsahok, resigned also in the wake of the publication of the Rault report and, it must be said, a general election was near, anyway.

Jugnauth introduced the Dangerous Drugs Act in Parliament upon the recommendation of former Maurice Rault. The death penalty was provided for drug traffickers in that legislation and one mafia leader nicknamed "Alexandre" was hanged after being convicted for a murder that had remained unsolved for a long time though it had been committed in broad daylight, in front of dozens of witnesses, in the crowded Port-Louis market. Another of the mafia leaders managed to escape to Réunion Island where we was granted asylum because European Union laws interdict the expulsion of people to countries where they would risk the death penalty. Jugnauth managed to decapitate the mafia and to restore law and order to normal levels. Free from Boodhoo's influence, his authority became unchallenged inside the MMM.

The 1987 snap elections

As Jugnauth saw his majority shrinking, he announced snap general elections, hoping to take the MMM by surprise. The elections were announced in July for August of the same year. He entered promptly the campaign by pointing to the truly excellent economic and financial results the nation had achieved under his leadership, blasted Boodhoo on the question of drugs while highlighting his anti-drug trafficking legislation and other measures and attacked the MMM again on its 1982-1983 record that led to general elections within nine months of its taking power.

The MMM fired back, alleging the government had given a free rein to the drug traffickers, illustrated by the Amsterdam affair. On the economic front, the debate was taken to television, opposing Lutchmeenaraidoo to Bérenger. It mainly enhanced the profile of the finance minister who put forward the positive financial and economic results that had been forthcoming during his mandate, especially the thousands of jobs being created, while Bérenger, though a seasoned debater, did not appear to have overwhelmed his adversary.

Prior to the 1983 general election, Bérenger had ridiculed Duval for having predicted that construction workers would have so much work contracts that the typical bricklayer would ask his wife, before accepting a job: "Dear Suzanne, please check my diary first." This prediction literally materialized and there was already, by 1987, a scarcity of workers for a rapidly expanding economy. Jugnauth, Duval, Lutchmeenaraidoo and Boolell joined forces, while on the other side, the MMM presented Dr. Prem Nababsingh as shadow PM and Bérenger as the president of a proposed republic. The MMM seemed, at some times, well positioned for a victory with its ally, Baichoo's MTD.

A controversial point was whether the president designate, Paul Bérenger, would chair the Cabinet, and thus give Bérenger real executive power to override Nababsingh as PM, a radical change in the constitutional traditions of the country where power is essentially vested in the PM and not the president. A few days prior to Election Day, Bérenger was presented as a president who would chair the Cabinet meetings. This appears to have hurt Nababsingh's image as future PM and to have only served to highlightBérenger's perceived ambition to have the upper hand even without making it to the PM's chair.

The August 1987 general election saw again a victory of the MSM/Labour/PMSD alliance, which obtained 49 % of the popular vote and 39 seats at the direct election. The MMM/MTD Union won 47.3 % of the vote, but 21 seats only. After the appointment of eight best losers, the government had a total of 44 seats, the MMM 24 and the OPR two, Serge Clair and his party colleague Mrs. Zita Jean-Louis, the first Rodriguan woman to represent her island in the National Assembly.

For the MMM, defeat was the more bitter due to Bérenger's failure to be elected in his constituency of Belle Rose/

Quatre Bornes. This time he was too far behind to get a best loser seat and he remained outside Parliament while Nababsingh succeeded him as Leader of the Opposition.

The government continued with the same economic and social policies that had kickstarted the national economy from around 1984. Another major event in 1987, in addition to the general election, was the first major airline disaster in the history of the country since the 1950s when a Quantas plane had taken fire prior to takeoff at Plaisance, but there had been no victims. This time, it was a South African Airways (SAA) airliner that plunged into the ocean north of Mauritius where it was due to land on November 29, 1987. All 159 people on board were killed.

In 1988, the education system again revealed its flaws with a huge rate of failures at the Certificate of Primary Education (CPE): 44 %. Ruthlessly competitive and archaic in comparison with the education system of modern countries like Australia or Canada, the system imposed on young Mauritians aged from five to 12 years old a heavy regime of private tuition, huge heavy loads of books to carry everyday to school on their frail shoulders and over 16 hours of regular and private tuition several days during the week, plus weekend studies to try to make it to the top at the CPE exams. The clamour for the abolition of the rat race imposed by CPE system intensified. It was not before the 21 st century dawned that the problem was seriously addressed.

In June 1988, Jugnauth and businessman Deo Dookun were elevated to knighthood by the Queen. In the Catholic Church, Bishop Jean Marqeot was appointed Cardinal by Pope John Paul II during a ceremony in Rome.

More dissent in government

On the political front, the Jugnauth government was again shaken by dissent. Duval revealed that he and the PM were opposed on some matters. This included the Sinotex affair, from the name of a garments factory in the EPZ where Jugnauth had taken a tough stand against the workers protesting their work conditions, and the trade unionists involved. The PMSD favoured a more flexible stand and both the MMM and the PMSD blamed Jugnauth for having had trade unionist Algoo arrested and chained to a hospital bed where he was being administered treatment due to a medical condition and was suffering.

Duval and his party left the government in August 1988. Jugnauth sacked his sister, Ghislaine Henry, who was the Mauritian ambassador in Madagascar. This made the relations between Jugnauth and Duval worse.

In December 1988, a man called Sembhoo pressed a revolver against Jugnauth's head during an Arya Samaj ceremony at Trèfles in Rose Hill. Disarmed and arrested, the old man hired Duval to defend himself. It was revealed during court proceedings that he had no intention to kill the PM and had only wanted to draw the attention of the PM to some problems. Duval managed to have him acquitted. Months later, Jugnauth missed having his throat slashed when a young man, disguised as a pilgrim, attacked him during a ceremony at Ganga Talao (the sacred lake of Grand Bassin). The man was immobilized and arrested, tried and convicted. Another problem for the regime of Sir Anerood Jugnauth was the arrest of Nigel Soobiah, son of a close political ally, Soo Soobiah, the Mauritian High Commissioner in London. Nigel was a member of the mafia in the U.S. where he was arrested. Soo Soobiah said he had nothing to do with the activities of his son. The British authorities disagreed and accused him of alleged money laundering. While Soo Soobiah engaged in a long legal battle in the U.K., he resigned and said the media had campaigned against him. Finally, he was acquitted by the British justice system. Nevertheless, the affair had considerably embarrassed the Mauritian government at the time.

The government was once more the target of corruption allegations when Hanish Boodhoo said that Mauritian passports were the subject of a flourishing racket. In October 1986, the government had taken the decision to grant Mauritian passports to foreign investors who brought investment worth over 50,000 U.S. dollars into the EPZ. In December 1987, that figure was doubled and before the end of 1988, the practice was replaced by the grant of residence permits of unlimited duration.

However, about 200 passports had already been granted to people in Taiwan and Hong Kong. Press notices advertising the sale of Mauritian passports were brought to the attention of Boodhoo. He alleged that the government was involved in the traffic of passports. Jugnauth reacted swiftly and had both Boodhoo and Vedi Ballah, the editor of Le Socialiste, a daily that was then the mouthpiece of Boodhoo, arrested. The two men were later freed under the pressure of public opinion.

At the 1988 municipal elections, the MMM/MTD Union won all the 126 seats in all five towns. Jugnauth, who had feared a massive defeat of his government, had not fielded any candidate, but his partner in government, the

PMSD, took part but was unable to elect a single candidate,

The MSM was soon under pressure on a matter of corruption again. This time, it was alleged that Jalc Holdings, a company that controlled machines used for betting at the horse races at the Champ de Mars, financed the MSM and that the directors had received Mauritian passports from the government. In the international media, the company was linked with the apartheid regime in South Africa.

The opposition was also not spared by the scandals that from time to time emerged on the political front. Sol Kerzner, a rich businessman from South Africa, headed Sun International, the company that had taken control, with the support of the then MMM government back in 1982, of two jewels of the local tourism industry: the La Pirogue and Touessrok hotels. Allegations of corruption were never proved. This time, it was revealed that Kerzner had, on his passport request to the Mauritian authorities, the signature of MMM member of the National Assembly Ivan Collendavelloo, who represented the Vacoas/Phoenix constituency.

There were allegations of special relations between the MMM and the apartheid regime in South Africa. Notwithstanding the fact that after the crash of the SAA plane in the ocean north of Mauritius, Jugnauth had received South African Minister Pik Botha at his home in La Caverne, the MMM parliamentarian was subjected to such pressure from the government ranks that he resigned and presented himself for reelection. Jugnauth presented a new candidate, Cyril Curé. Collendavelloo was defeated and this was a serious blow to the MMM, where some leaders started wishing for a reconciliation with Jugnauth in view of the next general election.

The arrest of Sir Gaëtan Duval

Actually, Jugnauth, faced with a PMSD that was again quite active in the opposition after leaving his government, revived, when the opportunity presented itself, the Azor Adelaide murder by PMSD agents two decades back. One of the persons convicted during the trial of the murderers, Shummoogum, was taken by MSM members to the PM's residence at La Caverne where he alleged that Duval gave orders tokill Bérenger and this resulted in Azor Adelaide's death. Jugnauth sent him promptly to the police station in front of his residence where he recorded a statement formally incriminating Duval. The latter, who was in Madagascar, was arrested upon his return on the orders of the then Commissioner of Police Cyril Morvan, a man who was very close to the PM and Minister Michael Glover. Public opinion was clearly shocked and Duval's partisans could not repress their anger.

Duval spent some days in prison before being freed on bail. As Duval was tried by Magistrate Rashid Hossen during a preliminary inquiry at the Flacq Tribunal, crowds gathered near the court premises and expressed their protest and anger by stoning buildings. Le Mauricien published editorials under the signature of its then chief editor (the author of this book), who entertained with Duval close contacts due to the extremely explosive the situation in the country, and expressed repeatedly the view that the case should be prescribed as per European Union legislation. Duval provided the chief editor with criminal cases that had been prescribed in Europe because they dated too far into the past and proceeding with them would have been a violation of human rights.

He was finally released as the Director of Public Prosecutions did not find reasons to proceed with the case. The DPP does not usually give reasons for such decisions, but Duval confided to the author of this book, then chief editor of Le Mauricien, that he believed that the provisions of European law published in detail by Le Mauricien had prevailed in relation to that decision. In truth, Duval risked the death penalty, which was still in vigour in those days.

The MSM-MMM alliance takes the nation by surprise

After the Azor Adelaide affair during which many in the MMM had started pushing forward the idea of a reconciliation with Jugnauth, the latter managed to have a reluctant Bérenger at the table. Secret negotiations between the MSM and the MMM were arduous. The MSMwas hard pressed to find a new partner to stay in power and Boolell's Labour Party was already restless. Bérenger was already thinking of a possible alliance with Labour and the PMSD to give Jugnauth a taste of the medicine he had himself tasted in 1983 when Labour and PMSD were called in to support Jugnauth and defeat the MMM.

There were two trends inside the MMM. Nababsingh, de L'Estrac, Cassam Uteem and many other prominent members of the party favoured an alliance with the MSM. Bérenger was opposed initially. He allowed himself to be brought into this new arrangement after negotiations leading to a program that included some core elements of the

MMM manifesto and the appointment of Bérenger as shadow president of a proposed republic, though Bérenger would be again candidate at the general election.

The announcement of this new coalition in July 1990 took the nation by surprise.

Initially, both the MMM and the MSM had separately approached Dr. Navin Ramgoolarn in London. To one of the intermediaries sent to discuss a proposal for him to join the Jugnauth government, he said: "Lions don't feed on grass." (He actually used the Creole language: "Lions napa manze l'herbe." At the same time, the pressure on him to come and join the Labour Party grew. When the new MMM/MSM alliance was formed and decided to amend the Constitution to turn the country into a republic which he believed was a Jugnauth ploy to perpetuate his rule on the country, he decided to stick out his neck and act. His supporters gathered at the Sir Seewoosagur Ramgoolam airport upon his return.

Navin Ramgoolam promptly joined the Labour ranks under the leadership of Satcam Boolell and efforts were made to have him take over the position of leader.

His first major political action was to attack the government on the proposed republic project which Jugnauth and Bérenger had agreed to carry out without getting it approved by voters at a general election. The MMM/MSM alliance argued that the voters had already approved the project of a republic atsuccessive general elections from the 1980s. Ramgoolam said the matter needed a fresh vote. Ramgoolam canvassed the opposition ranks (the MMM had already crossed the floor, Boolell had left the Cabinet and joined the opposition and Nababsing had been appointed Deputy PM). Even a number of MSM members opposed the project.

Navin Ramgoolam obtained the support of the finance minister, Lutchmeenaraidoo, the social security minister, Dinesh Ramjuttun, and the Speaker, the MSM's Ajay Daby. Lutchmeenaraidoo had already entered into open conflict with the government over the conclusion of the alliance with the MMM. He felt he was being let down by Jugnauth and that he would not be included as the No.3 of the new regime after the election. Bérenger had made known to Jugnauth his hostility to the finance minister but, later, Jugnauth would deny that he let down Lutchmeenaraidoo and that the latter had a place in the new regime. But Lutchmeenaraidoo had already taken the decision that he would resign and support Navin Ramgoolam and he believed that the MSM/MMM alliance would be eventually defeated by Labour, PMSD and a group of MSM dissidents in a counter-alliance.

Duval was not so hostile to the republican project and at one point he tried to build a bridge with the government to obtain a non-partisan consensus vote on the matter. In 1991, Duval, a seasoned leader, no longer harboured the ambition of being prime minister. He had only five years to live and it was not impossible that he ambitioned the job at Le Réduit after retiring from politics. But his arbitration was not wanted and Jugnauth went ahead by putting the republic project to a parliamentary vote, hoping to get the three quarters majority required to change the Constitution, or a total of 53 votes.

The government failed by just one vote, with Lutchmeenaraidoo, Ajay Daby, Ramjuttun and a last minute recruit, Raj Virahsawmy voting against the bill. Jugnauth relieved all of them both from their positions in Parliament and from the MSM and the four men joined the opposition.

The Labour Party was at one point divided over whether to have Navin Ramgoolam take over the leadership from Satcam Boolell. Emissaries between the two men worked hard and, finally, Boolell ceded his seat to SSR's son while pointing out that he had revitalized the party during his mandate.

The general elections were delayed by the first Gulf War in 1991. Boodhoo had joined the opposition and was to be a Labour candidate. The new MSM/MMM government launched an intense campaign against its adversaries. At the general election of September 1991, the MSM/MMM Alliance won a massive victory, with 55.4 % of the popular vote, whereas the opposition alliance obtained 39.3 %. The government had a total of 57 seats and the opposition a mere three seats. The OPR once more won the two seats of Rodrigues. The Labour/PMSD opposition obtained four best loser seats.

Ramgoolam believed there had been "massive electoral fraud" but the various petitions submitted to the Supreme Court to validate this accusation were systematically rejected even if ballots found "lost" outside the polling stations were produced in a number of cases. He pledged to introduce transparent ballot boxes, which he did when it was his turn to be PM from 1995.

The new government had the required majority to turn the country into a republic.

Bérenger preferred to stay in the Cabinet as the No. 3 after Jugnauth and DPM Nababsingh. On March 12, 1992, when the republic was officially proclaimed, Sir Veerasamy Ringadoo, who had succeeded Sir Seewoosagur Ramgoolam at Le Réduit as governor-general in 1986, became the nation's first president of the republic. On June 30, 1992, Cassam Uteem succeeded him, with Sir Robin Ghurburrun as vice-president.

Nevertheless, behind the show of unity that the government displayed, with Bérenger even hitting hard at Le Mauricien when the daily revealed cracks within the alliance, a major crisis was in the making. In 1982-1983 the man in the middle between Jugnauth and Bérenger was Boodhoo. This time it was going to be Nababsingh.

Preserving memories of the past

Important works of restoration of buildings and structures from the past have been carried out in Mauritius in recent decades. Top: the newly restored Government House; above: a sugar industry windmill that was being restored near Goodlands (July 2012). Photos: Sheridan Selvon

Chapter 51[1]

From the 20th to the 21 st century – 1991 to 2005 (1)

Free trade: a major challenge to an economy based on protectionism

A brief overview of the evolution of the Mauritian economy is important here to understand the period from 1991 to 2005 during which Mauritius entered the era of globalization of the world economy, which meant the triumph of free trade lobbies across the world.[2] In the 1990s, Mauritius started focusing on regional trade blocs like the South African Development Community (SADC) and the Common Market for Eastern and Southern Africa (COMESA). Both the European Union and the United States pushed for the implementation of a free trade agenda which was entrusted to the World Trade Organisation (WTO). The idea of regional associations was to promote regional free trade and the emergence of regional trade blocs with huge regional markets open for global competition. Australia was a fierce proponent of free trade and was an adversary of Mauritius a international trade talks dominated by the free trade promoters.

Free trade thinkers believe that the abolition of trade barriers would bring down prices and boost national economies across the planet with more competitive practices. Nevertheless, the implementation of free trade agendas has been, and is still encountering major difficulties. In the North American Free Trade Association (NAFTA) making of the U.S., Canada and Mexico a huge common market without barriers, several trade conflicts have erupted. The U.S. has taken Canada to court on several occasions on the subject of Canadian grain and lumber exports. There have also been quasi-trade wars between the E.U. and the U.S. Accusations of violation of free trade have been mutually hurled in both directions from the two sides of the U.S.-Canada border and of the Atlantic. Once something has been sold as a commodity, even water, nothing can stop its sale in the future. This has aroused hostility in Canada where the purchase of Canadian water is believed to be threatened by such provisions that could hurt its ecosystem and cause other damage to the country's interests. This has been but one of the many issues that have resulted from the NAFTA treaty.

Nevertheless, small countries like Mauritius are in a difficult position to resist the dismantling of the trade preferences that enabled them to survive and feed their populations during the 20th century. Mauritian governments were hard pressed to push ahead a free trade agenda starting with the setting up of a regional common market in southern and eastern Africa. Mauritius even initiated, in 1995, a move to have a larger regional market grouping countries of the Indian Ocean basin within an organization called the Indian Ocean Rim Association for Regional Co-operation (IOR-ARC), but this initiative was marred from the beginning by opposing views especially in Mauritius and Australia and this regional initiative had not progressed in any significant manner by the beginning of the 21st century.

During the last decade of the 20th century, Mauritius had two successive governments, one led by Sir Aneerood Jugnauth from 1991 to 1995, the other by the third prime minister the nation has had since independence, Dr. Navin Ramgoolam, from 1995 to 2000. We are first looking here at the global evolution of the country over that period.

None of the two prime ministers of the last decade of the 20th century stayed in power for the full five-year term normally expected between two general elections. The country, it must be said, has known during that period an average economic growth rate of over five per cent. A peak of 8.9 % was recorded in 2000, but this figure was exceptional as in the previous year the rate had fallen to 2.3 % due to one of the worst droughts in the nation's history and comparison of growth rates between the two years 1999-2000 is non-applicable. The yearly growth rate of the

---

[1] This chapter and the following ones on modern Mauritius have been checked against multiple reports on current events by multiple Mauritian newspapers available at the Mauritius National Library in Port-Louis.
[2] *"Free trade is the opposite of trade protectionism or economic isolationism... Governments with free trade agreements (FTAs) do not necessarily abandon all control of taxation of imports and exports. In modern international trade, very few so-called FTAs actually fit the textbook definition of free trade..."* Read more: Free Trade Definition | Investopedia http://www.investopedia.com/terms/f/free-trade.asp#ixzz4ZmGvAT8E

Follow us: Investopedia on Facebook

economy, that is, the GOP (gross domestic product) growth rate, was, from 1991 to 1995, as follows: 4.4 % in 1991; 6.8 % in 1992; 4.9 % in 1993; 4.8 % in 1994; and 5.5 % in 1995.

After the Jugnauth-led government lost power, a new regime headed by Dr. Navin Ramgoolam took over and the nation's growth rates were as follows: 6.2 % in 1996; 5.6 % in 1997; 5.7 % in 1998; 2.3 % in 1999 (due to the drought); and 8.9 % in 2000 (due to the drought-related figure of the previous year, making the figure inapplicable also).

The economy, therefore, had grown constantly during the last decade of the 20th century.

In 2001, the economy grew by 5.8 %, but the rate fell to 2.1 % in 2002 one of the main causes being cyclone Dina which reduced sugar production.

So, the evolution of the yearly GOP growth rate has been as follows under the MSM/MMM regime that took power in September 2000: 5.8 % in 2001; 2.1 % in 2002; 3.9 % in 2003; 4.1 % in 2004. In mid-2005, the official prediction of growth for the year by the Central Stastistics Office of the Mauritian government was 3.8 %.

What has been disturbing, though, is the rise of poverty following a period when most people presumed it was receding to almost insignificance as the economic miracle unfolded in the 1990s. In a study carried out by the author of the present book in the weekly newspaper News On Sunday on July 25, 1999, under the title "Poverty: The Facts," that it was estimated, on the basis of official statistics from various government sources, including the Central Statistics Office, that the percentage of people living in poverty had dropped from 57.3 % in 1986-1987 to 17.8 % in 1989-1990. The article pointed out that this figure increased to 23.6 % during the period 1991-1997.

In 2005, Mauritius was on the eve of substantial reductions of the price of its sugar exports to the European Union as the latter bowed to pressure from the World Trade Organisation (WTO) and a group of countries led by Brazil and Australia to let go its policy of a relatively high guaranteed price to African, Caribbean and Pacific (ACP) countries. This special price had been obtained under the EU-ACP Sugar Protocol within the EU-ACP Cotonou Agreement, which had replaced the Lomé Convention.

Another threat under new WTO rules of free trade was the dismantling of the Multi-Fiber Agreement (MFA), which let loose the forces of free trade in the textile and garments sectors. That meant that world trade in those products became virtually free of customs duties as from January 2005. Mauritius and other countries that benefited from a special regime of low or no duty for their exports to the EU and the United States were placed, as regards access to those markets, on an equal footing with countries such as China and Bangla Desh which have much lower production costs due to extremely cheap labour.

From 1989 to 2005, Mauritian authorities focussed on setting up new "economic pillars" to capture foreign investment, reforming the sugar industry to reduce its production costs significantly, make the most of other products than sugar from sugar cane (alcohol, bagasse, special sugars, etc.), trying, on the diplomatic front, to limit the pace of reduction of the Sugar Protocol prices, and helping the EPZ to survive global competition as several factories closed and laid off thousands of workers.

Between those two dates (1989-2005), the following sectors were developed as new or future economic pillars: an international financial sector that comprised offshore banking; an information and communication technoloqies (ICT) sector with a cyber-city at Ebène, Rose Hill; and a regional/international fishing hub in Port-Louis harbour.

Politics: the issue of electoral fraud and other irregularities

After the 1991 general election, accusations of electoral fraud were many from the opposition. As we have seen, Labour's electoral petitions were thrown out. A motion in court to invalidate the electionresults on the basis of unsigned election posters that allegedly violated the electoral legislation was short-circuited when the massive MSM-MMM government majority voted a motion that was retroactive to 1967, nearly a quarter of a century back, legalizing all such posters purported to be illegal.

The Labour-led government that took power in 1995 introduced transparent ballot boxes. The opaque ones had become suspect in the eyes of a large section of the public after the 1991 general election and the opposition's allegations of massive rigging.

The death penalty

The matter of the death penalty was also a burning issue in the 1990s. There were three Indian drug traffickers waiting to be executed at the Beau Bassin prison. Prime Minister Jugnauth was a staunch supporter of the death penalty and had already sent to the gallows two convicted murderers during his previous mandates. He had introduced, as we have seen, the death penalty for drug traffickers in the Dangerous Drugs Act voted in the wake of the Rault Commission of Inquiry on drug trafficking after the Amsterdam affair in 1985-1986.

In February 1992, a judgement by the Privy Council in London invalidated section 30 of the Act, which made it impossible to hang the three Indians waiting in their death cells at Beau Bassin. Death penalty opponents were able to rejoice. The three Indians were then sentenced to 20 years in prison.

A singular surprise for everybody

In April 1992, a huge surprise awaited the population, and even the PM's wife, Lady Sarojni Jugnauth herself, for whom the surprise party was held. When her birthday came up for celebration during that month, Sir Anerood organized a birthday party during which he offered his wife a present consisting in the introduction on the market of a new banknote worth Rs. 20, an effigy of which was unveiled with MSM-MMM government leaders and bemused members of the foreign diplomatic corps applauding and chanting "Happy Birthday." That was truly something never seen before in any version of the truly Westminsterian system of government.

The affair reached such a pitch that Jugnauth blamed it on the former finance minister, Vishnu Lutchmeenaraidoo, who denied having made the decision the more so, he said, that after sacking him in 1990, Jugnauth had himself taken over the finance ministry and was the country's finance minister from 1990 to 1991. How this could have happened in a country that Jugnauth was ruling democratically baffled foreign observers as much as the local political analysts.

The party financing issue

Another controversial matter was a huge multi-storey building costing Rs. 80 million built by Jugnauth and managed by his family on prime real estate at Edith Cavell Street, in Port-Louis. He hosted the party headquarters and his newspaper The Sun in the building and rented the rest commercially. Jugnauth said he built the complex with party money collected from the business community and replied to critics that there were opposition leaders who, rather than show the money they collected in the same manner, hid it away from the public view for themselves to enjoy. At the inauguration of the building, MSM and MMM dignitaries of the alliance government lifted their glasses in a toast to the success of the new business-cum-SM-headquarters.

Both Labour and MMM, as well as the PMSD have accepted the Sun Trust as a reality that has not stopped them to enter into alliances with the MSM from that period to this day. Only when Labour or MMM are in opposition to the MSM do the former accusations against the Sun Trust come up again from either of them. The MSM, though, is the only party to have revealed the extent of private contributions, as of the 1990s, to the major political parties of Mauritius, and to have used the money to buildmodern headquarters. No relevant authority in Mauritius has ever question political parties as a result of such revelation, which means that none of the major political parties contest that system of financing, which remains legal under current legislation as long as it is not linked to any form of electoral bribery.

Nevertheless, the matter of party financing was submitted, after the September 2000 general election, to a constitutional commission chaired by a prominent South-African legal expert Albie Sachs, appointed by yet another MSM-MMM government. This commission's report on that subject had not been implemented at the end of the mandate of that government in 2005. The urgency of the matter has been clearly overlooked in spite of repeated appeals by local and foreign anti-corruption NGOs to Mauritius to tackle this matter, which is believed to be closely related to the perceived high level of corruption in the country.

No government has taken any strong action from that time to make party financing and election practices more transparent, despite the publicity obtained internationally by a case where a former minister was found guilty of abusing his ministerial position in the run up to the 2005 general elections by bribing voters to vote for him against promises of jobs and other favours. He lost the case in the Mauritius Supreme Court and before the highest court of appeal, the Privy Council and the matter was reported by several publications overseas including the Economist Intelligence Unit in 2008.

Other corruption matters

Ramgoolam had during his mandate as prime minister, between 1995 and 2000, set up an anti-corruption tribunal called the Economic Crime Office (ECO), which initiated proceedings against two of his own ministers following allegations of corruption regarding government contracts, and was also investigating two MMM ministers. It was dissolved by the MSM-MSM government elected in 2000 and its director Mrs. Indira Manrakhan left out of ICAC, another anti-corruption authority set up by the new Jugnauth government and which was headed by Navin Beekarry. ICAC started investigations of an MSM minister, who was even arrested and taken to court where he successfully pleaded against the charges laid against him.

From the 1980s to the general election of July 2005, in spite of several allegations of corruption against Mauritian ministers, none have been ever convicted and sentenced.

Yet, there was the Air Mauritius and the National Pension Fund scandal where funds under the supervision of government (which owns Air Mauritius) that totalled well over one billion rupees have been swindled and even paid to political leaders of all the major political parties from an illegal Air Mauritius secret fund. Top Air Mauritius and Rogers Group officials have been taken to court, but no government leader mentioned in the matter, even by the media, has been charged, nor will any one be charged after the case against former Air Mauritius Sir Harry Tirvengadum over this matter was dropped after his legal team convinced the Court that he was so seriously ill that he could not be tried.

ICAC is actually barred from inquiring about scandal allegations dating prior to the date on which it was created and this has left major corruption matters out of the scope of its investigations.

Another huge scandal involving over one billion rupees in government pension funds that have been swindled at the Mauritius Commercial Bank has resulted in court cases. The funds were those of the National Pensions Fund (NPF), a body that is under the responsibility of the social security minister.

Prior to 1995, a major scandal was revealed involving the responsibility of one of Jugnauth's ministers in relation to a huge contract to acquire turbines for the Central Electricity Board. An official report blaming the former minister of Energy was not followed by any legal action with regard to the minister, except that he had to resign. After its electoral victory in July 2005, the new government led by Dr. Navin Ramgoolam started reforming ICAC promising to make the anti-corruption body more than a toothless bulldog. Again, the anti-corruption body has been described by the opposition (MMM and MSM) as a body with a political agenda, especially in the 'Medpoint affair' in 2011 where arrested MSM ministers have maintained that a decision by the Labour-MSM-PMSD to buy a clinic belonging to the brother-in-law of Pravind Jugnauth, Dr. Malhotra for Rs 145 million was taken not by them but by the Labour Party itself. They were basing their defence in Court in 2012 with the relevant minutes of the Cabinet meeting documenting the decision. Pravind Jugnauth maintains that he left and took no part in the discussions and won a decision from the Supreme Court to produce the document for his defence.

The public perception is that the political establishment is in some ways shielded from punishment, and all studies indicate a strong perception in the public that corruption is widespread in the high spheres of political power. Transparency International, a body that employs a method to gauge public opinion on corruption, has in various reports highlighted the high level of public perception of corruption in Mauritius. The challenge for Mauritius is to truly work to reduce the actual level of corruption and to bring to justice political leaders who cross the line.

Mauritian citizenship

In the aftermath of the victory of the MSM-MMM alliance in 1991, Jugnauth was also under pressure for his policy of systematically refusing to grant Mauritian nationality to foreign wives of Mauritians and their children. The two parties in power actually voted a law granting discretionary powers to the PM to deport people of Mauritian descent, including children, often manu militari. An eight-month pregnant Sri Lankan woman, Sonia Medagama, was deported under this law and Paul Orian, son of illustrious Mauritian scientist Paul Orian, was refused Mauritian citizenship, the MSM-MMM government maintaining and defending a hardline policy that gave Jugnauth a free rein to take this kind of decisions. It was only after the MMM went back into the opposition and Jugnauth was in fear of losing his parliamentary majority at the end of 1994 that he bowed to a request from the PMSD's leaders, both Sir Gaëtan Duval and son Xavier, to change the Constitution, which he did, thus enabling a reversal of that citizenship policy.

Free radios at last

Another issue that was hot in the area of democracy was that of the liberalization of broadcast media, which had been remained a government monopoly since independence and been used (both radio and television) to promote the interest of the parties in power. The MSM-MMM government of the 1990s resisted public pressure to liberalise both radio and television and when liberalization came after 2000 under a new MSM-MMM government, television was left out, while MBC Radio and MBC Television remained the mouthpieces of the parties in power.

This was still the case in 2012 where government has actually increased to over a dozen channels its monopoly of the television airwaves. President Anerood Jugnauth, clashing with Prime Minister Navin Ramgoolam, has recently recalled that it was he who liberated the radio airwaves, allowing the setting up of free radios, and attacked the government for having maintained its monopoly on television.

The political scene from 1991 to 2005

During the period 1991-2005, various alliances were in power:
- 1991-1995: MSM-MMM, then MSM/RMM following yet another crisis in government and a new split in the MMM that produced the RMM, with the PMSD joining the regime in 1994. The PM during that period was Sir Anerood Jugnauth (MSM).- 1995-2000: Labour-MMM then, following a crisis in government during which the MMM went back into the opposition, Labour governed alone until it was joined by the PMXD in 1998. The PM during that period was Dr. Navin Ramgoolam (Labour).
- 2000-2005: MSM-MMM. The PM's seat was shared between Sir Anerood Jugnauth (2000-2003) and Paul Bérenger (2003-2005).
- 2005-2010: The July 3, 2005 general election brought back to power the Labour Party, with Dr. Navin Ramgoolam again as PM.

The MSM-MMM alliance government did not last long. A struggle for power within the MMM between Bérenger and Deputy PM Dr. Prem Nababsingh in some ways recalling to people's minds that between Bérenger and then DPM Boodhoo in 1982-1983, was again to cause a major crisis in the government.

Still, the two parties were united at first in trying to oust Dr. Navin Ramgoolam from his parliamentary seat after he stayed in London and away from Parliament allegedly for over three months, trying to finish his studies in law and to be called to the bar. The MSM and the MMM voted a motion in 1993 to have the matter submitted to the Supreme Court by MMM Attorney General and deputy-leader Alan Ganoo.

Court finds 'colourable' device to oust Ramgoolam

What was suspicious about the matter – and was to be later pointed out by the judges – was that the calling of the National Assembly meeting by Jugnauth occurred in unprecedented circumstances. The PM had Parliament summoned at 9 a.m., two hours earlier than is normally the case, at the beginning of January 1993, to discuss officially amendments to the Sugar Industry Efficiency Act. There was no emergency regarding this bill, but when the judges studied the dates that related to Ramgoolam's period of absence, it became clear to them that the summons to the members of Parliament was within a time frame calculated to push Ramgoolam out of Parliament.

While Bérenger had taken an active part in voting the motion to oust Ramgoolam in the context of what the judges later called "a colourable device," Bérenger was, surprisingly, going to put the blame for the whole scheme at the door of Jugnauth.

What had happened is that there was a constantly deepening divide within the MMM between two factions, one led by Bérenger and the other by DPM Nababsingh. Jugnauth's and Nababsingh's versions were that Bérenger had approached Jugnauth to have Nababsingh replaced by himself (Bérenger) as DPM and complained that Nababsingh was not delivering the goods as the Cabinet's second-ranking member. Later, Bérenger would tell another version that would win him the gratitude of Ramgoolam: he claimed he was opposed to the motion presented to the Supreme Court by Ganoo and he did not want Ramgoolam to lose his seat.

But the real opposition to Jugnauth's manoeuver came from the then chief editor of Le Mauricien (the author of this book) who, in several editorials, offered to his readers a flexible reading of section 35 (e) of the Constitution on cases of unduly long absences of members from Parliament (over three months in one session). Those editorials said the three months should not be necessarily consecutive calendar months, but three months of parliamentary time. The Supreme Court Judges Rajsoomer Lallah and Vinod Boolell retained this interpretation, refusing the government's version. The government lost the case, their argument that Ramgoolam's seat had been vacant from January 27 was thrown out.

The MMM splits and joins Labour

Bérenger and Nababsingh were at that time locked in a battle for control of the MMM at the pending central committee election. Cassam Uteem, Jean-Claude de l'Estrac, Dharam Fokeer, all top members of the MMM politburo, sided with Nababsingh. Jugnauth also supported Nababsingh in the struggle for power within the MMM. He sacked Bérenger following a dinner at the latter's home at River Walk in Floreal at which the MMM leader had invited Ramgoolam – one of initial meetings that later brought them into an alliance.

Jugnauth had probably in memory the evening when, without the knowledge of the MMM, he met secretly Sir Gaëtan Duval at the Quatre Bornes residence of an MSM agent in the presence of Azad Doornun, a staunch PMSD supporter. Jugnauth and Duval (who had retired from politics at that point in time) discussed that night the MSMMMM motion to oust Ramgoolam. Duval managed to convince the PM to ask his colleagues of the parties in power to accept that the motion be dropped. If they agreed, Jugnauth said, the motion will be dropped, otherwise it would proceed. The next day, the matter was leaked out to Boodhoo who made it public. Boodhoo made one little mistake: he spoke of a dinner, whereas there had been none, just around one hour of discussions.

Inside government, when he mentioned that the motion could be dropped, Jugnauth later said he was confronted with a formidable surge of hostility from both parties of the governing alliance, Bérenger and MSM leadership contender Minister Madun Dulloo included. Jugnauth found out that Bérenger and the other members of the top brass of his government were capable of putting him in minority in the Cabinet should he proceed with trying to drop the motion. He called Le Mauricien to have the news denied, but the newspaper refused. He sent the agent who had hosted the discussions with Duval to make a statement to the newspaper that "there had been no dinner." The meeting itself was never actually denied publicly.

So, the dinner at River Walk – dinner there was this time – so irritated Jugnauth that he sent to Bérenger his revocation letter from the Cabinet without even making a prior statement to the media. The MMM split over whether the party should follow Bérenger into the opposition. Nababsingh was unable to control the party even though he was supported by de L'Estrac, party president Fokeer and other members of the MMM's top brass. Those in opposition to Bérenger finally stayed in government and formed the Renouveau Militant Mauricien (RMM) under Nabansing's leadership, while Bérenger retained the leadership of the MMM and joined the opposition where, in order to get the support of Labour and Ramgoolam, allowed the latter to retain his position of Leader of the Opposition.

It must be pointed out that Bérenger had rightly sensed that the Jugnauth regime's image had considerably eroded over the years and that the MSM-MMM alliance was not a good bet. To be fair to the MMM leader, it must be recalled that soon after taking power in 1991, the MSM-MMM alliance went into another electoral campaign, albeit at the municipal level, but lost all three seats that were being contested in the town of Beau Bassin/Rose Hill to the PMSD then being led by Xavier Duval, Sir Gaëtan Duval's son. This defeat had apparently comforted Bérenger in his belief that Nababsingh, as the then leader the MMM, did not have the political clout that was necessary for the party to retain its electorate. Keeping the MMM's status then as the largest party of the country obviously counted much more in Bérenger's eyes than anything else, even more than remaining in power, at that time.

Bérenger and Ramgoolam soon started to negotiate a Labour-MMM alliance. The discussions were arduous and at one point in 1994, they even broke up but parted by shaking hands "like gentlemen" according to a statement made by Ramgoolam to the author of this book. Soon after, De L'Estrac and Bérenger were bidding for re-election following a row that opposed them in Parliament during which they challenged each other to be re-elected. This accelerated the Labour-MMM discussions and the two parties went together to legislative by-elections in the Stanley/Rose Hill constituency where Bérenger and Labour's Burty David won a decisive victory over Jugnauth's and Nababsingh's candidates, Jean-Claudede I'Estrac and Shirin Aumeeruddy-Cziffra and the candidates of the PMSD.

The PMSD joins Jugnauth

In 1994, as Labour and MMM were again discussing a common program and power sharing matters with regard to the next general election, the PMSD was negotiating with Jugnauth to enter government. Both Sir Gastan Duval and his son Xavier had discussions with Jugnauth and it was agreed that Xavier and Sir Maurice Rault would be appointed to the Cabinet, while Jugnauth would suspend the death penalty and, as stated earlier, change sections 22 and 23 of the Constitution to establish the right to Mauritian citizenship to any child born of a Mauritian mother married to a foreign citizen. The opposition voted with the government on that important bill, following which the deportation of such children of Mauritian women stopped.

Jugnauth has to call elections

The new MSM-RMM-PMSD alliance did not govern the country for long as Jugnauth again had to call a snap general election in December of the following year, his government falling in shambles because of the resignation of ministers belonging to the General Population after the PM was quoted as having made 'insulting' remarks about that section of the population, upon coming back from a visit to India. Those remarks followed a defeat of his government in Court on the issue of oriental languages and the resistance in some circles, more social than political, against the inclusion of those languages in the compilation of marks of the candidates at the Certificate of Primary Education (CPE) examinations. The final marks were crucial to obtain admission in the best secondary schools of the country and competition was extremely intense.

The events leading to his remarks at the airport started from when the Supreme Court delivered a judgment on the oriental languages issue. He visibly could not control his anger when the Court, represented by three judges, Vinod Boolell, Eddy Balancy and Lam Shang Leen decreed that counting the oriental languages to compile the CPE examination marks would be unconstitutional. In making the controversial remarks at the airport, he also pledged to appeal to the Privy Council against the judgment.

Jugnauth thought he had the support of the Hindu community and probably concluded that he would receive massive support from that section of the population at a general election fought over the status of the ancestral languages of the Hindus.

Xavier Duval and other Creole ministers, even MSM's Michael Glover and Karl Ottman resigned following those remarks.

The PMSD was being torn by a virulent quarrel between Sir Gaëtan Duval and his son Xavier. The latter had made a disparaging statement against his father that made screaming headlines in a weekly newspaper. Both wanted also to join the Labour-MMM alliance at the upcoming general election and both failed to come to an agreement with Ramgoolam and Bérenger. Xavier kept the PMSD out of the electoral campaign, presenting no candidate at all, while Sir Gaëtan formed a new party bearing his name, Parti Gaëtan Duval (PGD) which presented candidates across the country and allowed him to make a spectacular come-back to Parliament.

The MSM-RMM alliance was routed by the Labour/MMM alliance by another 60-0 score and did not even have the chance to get a best loser seat, Jugnauth himself being soundly defeated in his constituency of Piton/Rivière du Rempart. The Labour/MMM alliance won 65.1 % of the vote and all the 60 seats at the direct election, while the MSM obtained 19.9 %, or about one voter out of five, but was unable to secure a seat in Parliament. The BLS seats went to Gaëtan Duval, leader of the PGD, Cehl Meeah leader of the Hizbullah, an Islamic party, and two candidates from Rodrigues, Nicolas Von Mally, leader of the Mouvement Rodriguais (MR) and Jean Alex Nancy. Two candidates who were elected directly in Rodrigues were Benoit Jolicoeur, of the OPR and the leader of that party, Serge Clair.

Other major events during the period under study were the nomination as Cardinal, by Pope John Paul II, of the then Bishop of Port-Louis and head of the Mauritian Catholic Church, Jean Marqeot, in 1993, and during that same year, the summit of the bloc of francophone countries, which was attended in Mauritius by President François Mitterand of France.

Fishing, industrial and 'artisanal'
Top: Fishing port in Port-Louis. Above: a fisherman in Rodrigues.
Photos: Sheridan Selvon (top); detail from a photo taken for IBL's company Catovair.

Chapter 52

From the 20th to the 21 century – 1991-2005 (2)

From the early 1990s, the country experienced some positive events but also crisis situations in a number of crucial areas.

On the positive side, Mauritius was focusing, during the period starting in 2000-2001, on two economic sectors to make of them additional pillars of the national economy that would strengthen its base and diversify it further to make it more resilient to current changes caused by globalisation. Those sectors were information and communication technologies (ICT), with a project creating, from 2001, a Cybercity that generated thousands of jobs, and a fishing hub that was expected by government to grow in the following years.

On the negative side, during the last years of the 20th century, there were numerous issues, among which:

- The economic boom or '*miracle*' started in the 1980s and continued in the 1990s was, by the end of the century, seriously threatened as Mauritius started to adapt to the exigencies of the dominant global capitalist economy that required the abolition of trade preferences for Mauritian products on foreign markets;
- A deterioration of the social environment due to a decline in law and order that culminated in an explosive situation during which there had been widescale rioting in 1999;
- A deteriorating physical environment caused by the continuing destruction of the natural assets of the country;
- The incapacity of Mauritius to deal with the huge amount of waste and other environmental pressures produced by 1.2 million people plus over 800,000 tourists yearly on about 2,000 square kilometres of land and the surrounding lagoon, part of the damage being irreversible;
- The increasing concrete jungle in urban and rural areas, with many illegal practices – like hundreds of concrete constructions being built on riversides up to the water level that have completely wiped out unique wildlife species; constructions on natural brackish marshes on coastal lands that have been hastily filled and are now seriously flooded during heavy rains; blocked drainage systems that have dangerously increased flooding, particularly heavy and devastating flash floods, following heavy rains;
- The huge traffic jams that have become characteristic of the country's major roads, some of the worst of the planet with regard to the high frequency of fatal and other serious accidents;
- Looming economic and financial downturn/disaster, factory closures (EPZ, sugar industry) and thousands of job losses due to price cuts on export markets and decline of market shares induced by globalization;
- The unsolved cases of corruption despite the setting up of the Independent Commission Against Corruption (ICAC).
- A continuous rise in oil prices during 2004 and 2005 that showed no sign of abating and threatened the economy and the financial situation of the nation. There are questions that have to be answered regarding the medium and long term security for the nation's energy supplies when the planet's oil reserves start dwindling from around the 2030s/2050s.
- A housing crisis in the poorer rungs of the social hierarchy that, from the 1990s, saw people, including hundreds of immigrants from Rodrigues, increasingly living in overcrowded, unhealthy slums, some allowed, through corrupt governmental practices or sheer negligence and 'laisser faire'.

Some crucial issues: 1995-2005

Law and order

One of the concerns of Mauritians as well as of foreign embassies and consulates providing advice to their nationals visiting Mauritius was the rise of criminality in the island and aggressions against tourists during the end of the 1990s and the first years of the new century.

The sheer monstrosity of a number of crimes committed and the fact that many of crimes that dated back to several years were yet unsolved was considered extremely troubling by public opinion across the island. In 2005, the Cen-

tral Statistics Office (CSO), which is a government body, studied crime statistics, with admitted margins of error due to various factors (like unavailability of unreported criminal acts, withdrawal of complaints, etc..
Nonetheless, CSO did attempt to classify the Mauritian data *"according to the UN classification to allow some international comparison."* The CSO reports the following over the 10-year period 1993-2003:

"The rate for all offences for the Republic increased from 89 in 1993 to 159 in 2003.

"The crime rate, which was 4 per 1,000 inhabitants in 1993 increased, as the 20th century ended, by 50% to reach 6 per 1,000 in 2003. The misdemeanour rate decreased from 30 per 1,000 in 1993 to 28 per 1,000 in 2003. However, higher misdemeanour rates were registered during intervening years; rates as high as or higher than 30 were noted in 1993,1994 and 1997. The contravention rate increased by 123% from 56 in 1993 to 125 in 2003, with the highest rates being registered during the last three years in review. In 2003, the rate for all offences worked out 161 for the Island of Mauritius compared to 89 for Rodrigues. The crime rate was 6, that is, twice the Rodrigues figure of 3; tie misdemeanour rate was 28 compared to 23 and the contravention rate 127 compared to 63.

"During the period 1999 to 2003, homicides and related offences in the Republic increased by 21 % from 80 to 97 while sexual offences, which was 208 in 1999 increased by 43% to 298 in 2003. On the other hand, assaults and related offences stagnated around 12,700.

"Larceny increased by 4% from 13,955 in 1999 to 14,548 in 2003. Available data indicate that larceny on motor vehicles more than doubled during the period 2001 to 2003 increasing from 433 to 988 while larceny on cellular phone/pagers almost tripled from 334 to 928." [1]

Drug offences on the rise

During the 1990s and the first five years of the 21st century, recorded drug offences have spiralled upwards. Drug trafficking reached into the prisons of the country as revealed by the media in reports published over the years, including more reports during the first half of 2005. Drug consumption and crime have been shown to be closely inter-related in several cases brought to court. Statistics published in 2005 in the abovementioned report by the CSO are a source for concern as they show a sharp increase in recent years in the number of hard drug offences, accompanied, though, by a decrease in cannabis (gandia) related offences. CSO writes:

"The number of drug offences, which stood at 2,096 in 1999 in the Republic of Mauritius increased by62% to 3,387 in 2003. Offences related to heroin increased by nearly 300% from 550 in 1999 to reach 2,111 in 2003. During the same period, cases related to gandia (cannabis) declined by 19% from 1,439 to 1,159.

"The proportion of offences related to heroin increased from 26% in 1999 to 62% in 2003 while that related to gandia dropped from 69% to 34%."

The environment with regard to economic imperatives: a snapshot

The natural environment of the country has dramatically changed since the discovery of the island several centuries back by the Arabs around the 8th century of the modern era, then by the Europeans in the 16th century. The main cause of change has been the human being's activities on the island (including the Outer Islands), in particular economic activities. The growth of those activities has accelerated in the 20th century, especially in its three last decades, with rapid industrialization adding to the already considerable and irreversible damages caused by other sectors, especially agriculture. Less than one percent of the island's indigenous forests remained in the 1980s. That was why there was widespread protest in 2004-2005 against a highway project in the Ferney Valley that would have caused yet another major destruction of the island's original forest cover and its unique wildlife. The project was finally abandoned and the forest saved as a result of the protest.

From the statistical standpoint, the CSO, in its regular publications on the nation's environment, gave in 2005 the following snapshot of the environmental situation, starting with the expansion of the economic activities and human demographic pressures as evidenced by the rise in the GDP and the current population figure of over 1.2 million, with population density having reached 607 persons per square kilometre:

"From 1995 to 2004, Gross Domestic Product (GDP), which measures the total value of production, has increased in nominal terms by about 148%, from Rs 70,283 million to Rs 174,468 million. The share of agriculture in GDP fell from 10.3% in 1995 to 6.2% in 2004; that of manufacturing has decreased marginally from 22.9% to 21.0%, while that of financial and business services increased from 15.4% to 19.3%.

"During the same period, the population increased by 10.9% from 1,112,400 to 1,233,400 and the population density from 554 to 607 per km2.

"The proportion of land under agriculture in 1995 was 46.4% and that of forestry 30.6% whilst built-up areas constituted 19.5%.

"<u>Forests</u>: In 2004 the total forest area was 47,066 hectares, of which 22,066 hectares (47%) were state-owned and the remaining 25,000 hectares (53%) were privately-owned.

---

[1] Central Statistics Office, Mauritius, Statistics *Mauritius 1993-200*3.

"__Agriculture:__ *From 2003 to 2004, the effective area under sugarcane has shrunk by 3,332 hectares (-4.5%), to 70,785 hectares. During the same period area under tea plantation dropped to 674 hectares (-1%) from 681 hectares and area under tobacco fell to 356 hectares (-6%) from 379 hectares.*

"__Energy:__ *The total primary energy requirement of the country increased by 2.7% from 1,223 ktoe (thousand tons of oil equivalent) in 2003 to 1,256 ktoe in 2004. Around 78% of the total primary energy requirement was met by imported fuels (oil, LPG [gas] and coal) and the remaining 22%, obtained from local sources (bagasse and hydro): Final energy consumption increased by 2.8% from 815 ktoe in 2003 to 838 ktoe in 2004. The largest consumers were the transport and manufacturing sectors which accounted for 49% and 31 % of the total consumption respectively in 2004. It is interesting to note that the manufacturing sector only started consuming lesser energy than the transport sector as from 1998. Fuel oil is the most important input with its share rising from 35% in 2003 to 37% in 2004. On the other hand thecontribution of coal fell from 32% to 29%.*

"__Motor vehicles:__ *The number of registered motor vehicles has gone up from 276,371 in 2003 to 291,605 in 2004, a rise of 5.5%. This expansion has been accompanied by a corresponding growth in energy consumption and carbon dioxide emission in the transport sector. The number of vehicles per 1,000 population rose from 232 in 2003 to 243 in 2004. This translates to an increase of nearly 5%. In 2004, about 409 ktoe of energy were used for transport; diesel oil accounted for 166 ktoe or 41 %, aviation fuel 42 ktoe or 35% and gasoline 98 ktoe or 24%. From 2003 to 2004 the gasolene and diesel oil in the transport sector consumption rose by about 2% each.*

"__Greenhouse gas (GHG):__ *Carbon dioxide (CO_2) constituted 94% of total emissions and removals of greenhouse gases. The data indicate a marginal rise in net CO_2 emissions from 2,546 thousand tonnes in 2003 to 2,572 thousand tonnes in 2004.*

"*Net emissions take into account the removal of CO_2 by forests which act as 'sinks'. Carbon dioxide emission resulting from fuel combustion went up marginally from 2,781 thousand tonnes in 2003 to 2,794 thousand tonnes in 2004. The energy industries remain the principal source of CO_2 emission in the atmosphere. They contributed around 50% of the emissions, with 1,430 thousand tonnes in 2004 compared to 1,418 thousand tonnes in 2003 (+ 0.8%). They were followed by the transport sector which contributed 29% of the total emissions and the manufacturing industries with 13%. The number of notices to drivers of vehicles emitting black smoke rose from 3,666 in 2003 to 4,172 in 2004 (+ 14%).*

"__Water:__ *In 2004 the total water demand was estimated at 1,014 Mm3. The agricultural sector accounted for* most of the water *utilised with 490 Mm3 or 48%. Utilisation for the other purposes was as follows: hydropower 289 Mm3 or 29%, domestic, industrial and tourism 235 Mm^3 or 23%.*

"__Waste:__ *Solid waste has been tracked mainly as domestic, commercial and industrial. The total amount of solid waste landfilled rose to 381,204 tonnes in 2004 from 372,440 tonnes in 2003, representing an increase of 2.4%. In 2004 domestic waste constituted 96% of the total solid waste landfilled. The number of contraventions established in 2004 was 5,009, representing an increase of about 10 % over 2003. Most of the contraventions, (4,422 or 88%) were for illegal littering."* [2]

We have devoted a special chapter on the currently threatening dangers of an environmental nature that are hanging like a sword of Damocles on the future of Mauritius and its population, especially from the current dramatic changes in the global environmental conditions induced by climate change. In that same chapter, we deal with the local environmental changes as described for the period 2002 to 2010 in two reports of the Central Statistics Office.

The 2010 report indicates an improvement regarding Mauritius, mainly in terms of 'ecosystem vitality.'

Chapter 53
From the 20th to the 21 century, 1991-2005 (3)

Three regime changes occurred during the period 1995-2005 demonstrating the democratic nature of the Mauritian political system.

Labour and MMM shared power after they won the 1995 election. Dr. Navin Ramgoolam, the Labour leader became the new prime minister, the third in the nation's history after his father, Sir Seewoosagur Ramgoolam, who held power from independence in 1968 to 1982, and Sir Aneerood Jugnauth from 1982 to 1995. For the first time, Bérenger acceded to the NO. 2 rank in the Cabinet, being appointed Deputy PM.

However, it was not long before the government split, as has always been the case with coalitions until then, and the MMM was again back on the opposition benches in the National Assembly. The first budget of the new government, which Ramgoolam and Bérenger described as *"the dream team"*, was a disastrous exercise due to the MMM leader's opposition to additional taxation of the sugar industry. The government had to revise its first version of the budget prepared by Minister Ramdheersing Bheenick, who was severely and openly criticized by Bérenger, This incident and other clashes with the MMM in addition to an alleged *"huge hole"* in the finances of the country mentioned by Bheenick caused the latter to lose his position in the Cabinet. Berenger was severely criticised for his alleged support to the sugar barons, but the view from the MMM was that the sugar industry was still crucial to the economic well-being of the country and that overtaxing its profits could damage not just the industry, but the overall national economy.

Soon after that, Sir Gaëtan Duval, Leader of the Opposition, died at his home in Grand Gaube, plunging almost the entire country deep into grief. One of the largest crowds ever assembled in the nation's history lined the roads to watch or join the funeral procession to Curepipe. Commissioner of Police Raj Dayal stated that this was the *"biggest funeral procession in the country's history."* Duval was replaced by Nicolas Von-Mally, the first Rodriguan to accede to the position of leader of the parliamentary opposition.

Political assassinations

At that time, the Labour/MMM coalition was already in the throes of death, generating political instability at the highest level of government.

The situation was further complicated by the rise of Islamic fundamentalism, promoted by the Hizbullah, which had become a threat to the MMM in the then political stronghold of the latter, the Plaine Verte area. The MMM had won all municipal and legislative elections held there from 1986 onwards, with record majorities. The clashes between the MMM's and the Hizbullah's political agents deteriorated seriously, especially during the 1996 municipal election campaign. On October 26, 1996, the nation was deeply shocked to learn that three political agents of the government had been murdered by gunfire in Gorah Issac Street, Port-Louis, in the early hours of the morning, while they were campaigning.

Never before, in the history of the country, had there been such a bloody incident opposing political parties during an election campaign. The victims were: Babal Joomun, Yousouf Mourade and Zulfikar Bheeky.

Killing spree by a 'Death Squad'

Later, it was revealed also that there was a *"death squad"* whose members portrayed themselves as Islamic fundamentalists, who were executing people across the country. Some of the members had allegedly been trained in Pakistan and even Afghanistan and had gone as far as robbing banks and killing people to steal money from them, including a well-known horseracing bookie. Hizbullah leader Cehl Meeah has denied any involvement in the operations of the death squad, following allegations made against him mainly on the basis that the squad members were seen in several photos at his public meetings.

Meeah spent several months in prison after allegations of involvement in the Gorah Issac Street killings, but was allowed to go free after those allegations were dropped. His party moderated its stand after his release and Meeah was being increasingly perceived, in 2004-2005, as having entered the country's traditional mainstream political system.

The death squad was dismantled with then Chef Inspector Prem Raddoah and his men of the Curepipe CID playing a major role in tracking down its members. Several members of the squad including its chief, *"Bahim Coco"* committed suicide upon being surrounded by police, while others, including a former police officer, surrendered and accepted to be witnesses in court proceedings against those responsible for the creation and leadership of the group.

The failure of the Labour/MMM Alliance

The Labour/MMM alliance was a dismal failure. Even before the 1995 election, it had split a first time, after which the pieces were glued again together in view of the election campaign. Its weaknesses were inbuilt, with Bérenger disagreeing with several aspects of Ramgoolam's and other Labour ministers' policies indicating that the alliance had been dictated by circumstances more than by the sharing of common ideals and a common governmental programme of action.The tug-of-war continued until Ramgoolam sacked Bérenger from his cabinet in 1997.

Various reforms promised by the two parties during the 1995 election campaign were not carried out or if they were attempted, did not meet with much success. The reform of the education sector was planned by Education Minister Kadress Pillay, but was dropped by the Cabinet following strong opposition, especially from Deputy PM Kailash Purryag. The *"Action Plan",* which proposed a radical elimination of the CPE rat-race, was never implemented and education reform would only be carried out after a new MSM/MMM alliance came back to power in 2000, albeit with Labour disagreeing with various aspects of that reform that, according to Ramgoolam, once back in the opposition, was detrimental to the elite of the student population.

A radical revamping of the police force to eradicate corruption and unwarranted use of police violence against detainees and to resolve a long list of criminal cases gone cold did not happen under two different regimes, Labour/MMM and MSM/MMM. The in-depth reform had yet to be undertaken by 2012 and the police have complained about promotions and appointments being unduly delayed to the point that during the Independence Day celebrations in March 2012, the President of the Republic Sir Aneerood Jugnauth, albeit being aleady contemplating a return in the political arena, attacked his Prime Minister, Dr. Navin Ramgoolam, at celebrations held at the Hindu House, Port-Louis.

Local government is not autonomous as they are in greater democracies

Another expected area of reform after the 1995 general election was local government. A report on the matter was not followed by any action and in July 2005, back in power, Labour was committed to re-introducing village elections allegedly *"abolished"*[1] by the MSM/MMM regime of 2000-2005. Whatever touches that were brought over the years to the legislation on local government, the crucial problem to date is that no central government has been really willing to truly decentralize local government, more particularly inthe rural areas, in contrast to countries with a higher level of democracy than Mauritius like Australia, the U.K. or Canada, for example. Government House controls all local administrations to this day, in 2017.

In addition, local councillors are deeply mired in national politics whether in the town or district councils and real decentralization is impossible unless independent candidates are elected. The voters have an important share of the responsibility with regard to the country's inability to have truly independent local government councils as in more performing democracies.

More transparent voting, judiciary reform

The first Navin Ramgoolam government was successful, however, in other areas of reform like helping to make elections more transparent, kickstarting the long due reform of the judiciary with the help of a reputed British expert, Lord Mackay, who proposed over 200 recommendations and strengthening the financial system. During Ramgoolam's mandate from 1995 to 2000, measures were also envisaged to create a new economic pillar by developing the information and communication technologies (ICT) sector, but it was the next government that released

---

[1] The allegation was made on 7 December 2011 by MP A. Hossen as follows: « *En juillet 2002, le gouvernement MSM/MMM renvoie ces élections villageoises pour la première fois pour 2003, avec peut-être raison à cette époque vu l'avènement bientôt du New Local Government Bill… Mais arrivé en 2004, ces élections villageoises sont maintenant renvoyées pour les mêmes raisons pour l'année 2004. Donc, ça constitue le deuxième renvoi, M. le président. Tout à l'heure quelqu'un du côté de l'opposition avait mentionné l'abolition des by-elections municipales. Mais en 2004, on vient complètement abolir les élections villageoises, M. le président.* » http://mauritiusassembly.govmu.org/English/hansard/Documents/2011/hansardsecd3511.pdf Accessed 27 February 2017.

sugar land from the private sector in Ebène, near Rose Hill, where it started the building of a '*Cybercity*' that has from then, onwards, continued to grow and attract investment from overseas.

Economic Crime Office

Another major decision was the setting up of the Economic Crime Office under Mrs. Indira Manrakhan. Two ministers were accused of impropriety and ECO initiated legal procedures which led to their exit from the Cabinet. Former MMM ministers were also under investigation by ECO but in 2000, Labour lost the general election and the new MSM/MMM government disbanded ECO and set up ICAC, which was not given the power to investigate cases prior to its creation date.

On the plus side also, Navin Ramgoolam's regime had kickstarted the biggest infrastructure project in the history of the island, albeit one that had been initiated by the previous regime: the Midlands Dam. Like the Cybercity, this indicated the continuity of projects from one government to another, whoever was first to initiate the project. Lonrho company lands purchased for the Cybercity were not put into question by the following Ramgoolam governments who nevertheless claimed paternity of the project and even discussed a new coalition with Bérenger against who Labour had many innumerable accusations on the purchase of Lonrho. The Midlands Dam was destined to provide adequate irrigation water to the northern plains of Mauritius.

Ramgooolam's government also initiated major wastewater projects that were long overdue to relieve the island of increasing pollution of its underground water and the lagoon surrounding the island.

Racial riots in 1999[2]

The Ramgoolam regime of 1995-2000 suffered its worst setback in the area of law and order when riots broke out in February 1999 following the death in a police cell of a popular singer Joseph Reginald Topize, popularly known as Kaya. The latter, a Rastafarian was (as all members of the Rastafarian movement across the world) an advocate for the decriminalization of marijuana. He had created "*seggae*", a fusion of Mauritian sega music and the Caribbean reggae and had a good audience in the country.

He attended a meeting on February 18, 1999, in Rose Hill in favour of striking out the local marijuana species, gandia, from a list of prohibited drugs in the local legislation or, according to the organizer of the meeting, Rama Valayden, leader of the Mouvement Republicain (MR), in widely reported media statements, reducing penalties to a strict minimum while keeping the interdictions and heavy penalties on the harder drugs like heroin and crack.

Some people were reported by the media to have smoked gandia during the meeting. Acting on the media's and the MMM's insistent claims that the police had not applied the law, police officers tracked down suspects, including Kaya, who was arrested and, upon reportedly admitting having smoked gandia, was detained in a police cell. In any democratic country, this kind of offense is immediately bailable and today in the some of the more democratic countries, police actually do not prosecute consumers of small quantities of '*weed*'. Kaya was kept in detention for days and died in suspicious circumstances. The same newspapers that had blamed the police and the MMM, also attacked Valayden for having allegedly invited the crowd at his meeting to smoke gandia. MMM leader Berenger, obviously appealing to an electorate with very conservative views on the matter of even gandia, albeit the fact that most politicians of his generation (like Clinton) have at least '*tasted*' gandia, in Mauritius mainly in the form of "*bhang*", launched a campaign against Valayden and the MR for their support of the legalization of gandia. In February 2017, major political parties still shared the MMM's stand on gandia.

However, as the news of Kaya's death leaked out, his supporters and fans, drawn for the most part from the Creole community, took to the streets. In a matter of hours riots occurred in various places across the island. Rapidly, they turned into racial riots between Creoles and Hindus mainly in Quatre Bornes, Goodlands, Triolet and Rose Belle, while in the village of Bambous it was an ethnic mix of people comprising Hindus as well as Creoles that attacked the police station and were fired on by panicked police officers, with two young men in the crowd, a Hindu and a Creole, being left dead as the crowd dispersed. In various places, rioters consisting of a mix of ethnic groups attacked shops and supermarkets, which they looted.

Another tragic death was that of yet another singer, Berger Agathe, shot by the police at the Roche Bois roundabout in Port-Louis during a demonstration motivated by the suspicious circumstances in which Kaya died in police

2 Every year the event is recalled in the media. Le Mauricien published a recap ot the riots on 23 February 2012 here: http://www.lemauricien.com/article/%C3%A9meutes-1999-des-blessures-toujours-vives Accessed 27 February 2017.

custody.

In the north, several houses of Creole families were blown up and there were reports of police officers siding with the rioters in some cases.

The country was almost entirely paralysed by those riots. Had it not been for the intervention of President Cassam Uteem in the central part of the country, of Labour MLA Dr. Arvin Boolell in Rose Belle, and a number of prominent citizens in several hot spots, the riots would have degenerated into full scale civil war according to most observers. The police was unable to maintain order and the Special Mobile Force (SMF) proved to be helpless in the face of such chaos, as was later found by a commission of inquiry on those events.[3] The riots finally lost momentum largely due to the intervention of volunteers in the hot spots.

In 2003 an official report claimed that the singer had not died as a result of police brutality. Kaya's wife Veronique Topize and his lriends and fans have never accepted that official version. The police was unable to prove that Valayden had invited the crowd at his meeting to smoke gandia.

Navin Ramgoolam was blamed by the opposition and the media for not having quelled the riots earlier, but he replied that it was his address on television together with Veronique Topize and the instructions he gave to the police forces that played the decisive part in the restoration of peace. This has remained a controversial matter ever since between Ramgoolam and his political adversaries, while Kaya is now a revered artist in the same newspapers that had clamoured for police action against Valayden and the people who smoked gandia at his meeting. In Canada and the United States as well as in other democracies, the decriminalization of marijuana is not as virulently opposed at it was in Mauritius by the MMM and some newspapers at the time Valayden was leading the movement. Valayden had to drop this issue altogether from his party's political manifesto – and he was appointed justice minister in July 2005 in Navin Ramgoolam's new government.

The demise of a regime

Months before and after the 1999 riots, PM Navin Ramgoolam managed to win two legislative byelections. The first one was in 1998 when he fielded as candidate who was a newcomer to politics, former magistrate Satish Faugoo, in the Flacq/Bon Accueil constituency, against former PM Sir Aneorod Jugnauth, who was defeated. Faugoo won, defeating also a former contender to the SAJ's succession as MSM leader, Madun Dulloo, who had formed his own party, the MMSM and was in alliance with the MMM.

The second time it was when, in alliance with the PMXD, Labour helped Xavier Duval defeat the MMM candidate Francoise Labelle in Beau Bassin/Petite Rivière and then appointed him as industry and financial services minister.

Ramgoolam and Bérenger, though, maintained contact with each other keeping open the possibility, during most of the year 2000, of another Labour/MMM alliance.

The Sabapathee affair

January 2000 had started on a bad note for Ramgoolam. A man called Rajen Sabapathee, a former bodybuilding champion who had held the national Mr. Mauritius championship title and had ranked among the 10 top final candidates at Mr. Universe in London in the 1980s, had worked as bodyguard to an MSM minister. Subsequently he was engaged in drug trafficking and also committed acts of violent aggression that led him to the island's high security prison for the most dangerous criminals, La Bastille, in Phoenix. He managed, with other prisoners, to escape from there and to resist police for several days until he was surrounded and shot by police.

His funeral was attended by a huge crowd of supporters in Rose Hill as he had been a very popular figure and had remained so despite his criminal record.

A New MSM/MMM Alliance in 2000

On the political front, the MMM, which had formed a "federation" with the MMM in 1998, decided to leave this alliance in 2000 and to either go into a new coalition with Labour or fight alone the next general election. Bérenger negotiated an alliance with Labour until the very day he struck a deal for an alliance again with the MSM in view of

[3] After Ramgoolam left power, the report of the Commission of Inquiry, released by new Prime Minister Sir Aneorod Jugnauth revealed that it blamed former PM Ramgoolam for the riots. This made headlines in the international media, like the Panafrican News Agency (PANA) in an article entitled "Mauritius: Report Blames Former Premier Over 1999 Riots". http://allafrica.com/stories/200010230260.html The report is marked as available on the site of Lalit Party: "The February 1999 mass riots - The Matadeen Report and Human Rights" at http://www.lalitmauritius.org/en/publications.html

the general election in September 2000.

The Stauffer affair

Ramgoolam's regime had started to dip in public opinion following charges of corruption that led to the demise of two of his ministers, albeit the fact that the PM himself had taken the initiative to uproot corrupt members, if any, within his own Cabinet. The "Stauffer affair" was, however, a quite serious blow to the government.

A Swiss national, Eric Stauffer, was a close friend and business partner of Xavier Duval, together with a Frenchman, Jean-Pierre Fleury, who was well connected in Paris, was an expert in election campaigning and had considerable experience aiso in Africa. Stauffer resided for some time in Xavier Duval's cottage on the coast of Grand Gaube in the north of the island while they set up an investment management business in an office at St. James Court, St. Denis Street, in Port-Louis. The three men spent much time together planning and organizing Xavier Duval's campaign at the legislative election in Beau Bassin/Petite Rivière, which Xavier won, in part due to their contribution and actually, Fleury and Stauffer worked together with Labour campaigners and Ramgoolam's chief election strategist Christian Rivalland.

Stauffer was also owner, in Switzerland, of a company which was involved in attracting and managing funds, sometimes involving African political personalities. Later, he would deny some wrongdoings attributed to alleged shady dealings and would claim they had occurred in his absence. He would even land in prison where he spent some time in 2005 with a Swiss business partner before being released, after which he vowed to take to court his accusers and claimed he had been all the time working for the Swiss secret service. Later, after he left Mauritius, he became a prominent political party founder and leader in Switzerland where he was elected to the State Council of the Canton of Geneva.

After Xavier Duval's victory at the by-election, Stauffer had expected to be rewarded with an appointment as consul for Mauritius in Switzerland or special adviser to the new minister and leader of the PMXD. He was not appointed to any special position, but took the initiative of accompanying Xavier Duval during two ministerial missions in Europe and flying him to France at one point on a private aircraft he piloted, to enjoy, among other things, the famous '*bouillabaisse*'in Marseilles. Stauffer had also advised the minister that the government should support a project he devised in order to relocate to Mauritius an entire spinning factory from Switzerland as one of the means to face the looming crisis in the garments and textile sector in the EPZ as the world moved towards the abolition of export quotas.

This plan was never carried out because Ramgoolam, for unclear reasons, wanted to get rid of Stauffer. One day Duval advised Stauffer that Navin Ramgoolam was very upset with him. Duval then kept aloof from his Swiss partner, and ignored his repeated requests to be appointed adviser to him. Staufier learned that he could even be arrested and deported. He hastily left the country leaving behind a political bombshell: a media interview granted to a weekly where he made a number of allegations that Xavier Duval had illegally imported, through him, a firearm and he went on to add, at a later stage, still in media interviews, that Mauritian ambassador in Paris Marie-France Roussety, Finance Minister Vasant Bunwaree and Ramgoolam himself had been allegedly involved in discussions to invest government funds with the investment firm he used to work for in Switzerland in return for commissions to be paid to Labour leaders.

Navin Ramgoolam and Xavier Duval reacted strongly and the PM produced at a public meeting a "*report*" allegedly from Interpol to shore up their claims that Stauffer was a "*crook*." A local media report said Interpol had denied. Stauffer initiated legal proceedings against Ramgoolam in Switzerland and for some time rode on a wave of popularity among the supporters of the MMM, with Bérenger himself using his allegations to slam Ramgoolam and the Labour/PMXD regime in and outside Parliament. Jugnauth and the MSM joined the chorus and the pressure, generated especially by parliamentary questions put by Bérenger, reduced Ramgoolam and Duval to a defensive role. The government and the Commissioner of Police were quite embarrassed with the conditions in which the firearm had been imported by Stauffer, photos of Stauffer allegedly distributing banknotes during the byelection at Beau Bassin/Petite Rivière and his claims regarding allegedly shady discussions on the proposed investment.

Though no wrongdoing on the part of Ramgoolam and Bunwaree was eventually proved, the price they paid was heavy: the affair was one of the causes of the downfall of the Ramgoolam regime at the September 2000 general election. The whole affair continued to be the subject of parliamentary questions for several months. [4]

---

4 Mauritius NationalAssembly, Debate, 2002. The whole matter was detailed during several sessions of the National Assembly, particularly at

'Elections claires et nettes': Ramgoolam goes to snap elections

Believing, nonetheless, that he would win an electoral victory, Ramgoolam said he wanted "***des elections nettes et claires***" and envisaged at some point an alliance with the MMM. Actually, Bérenger was in favour of this alliance while MMM general secretary Ivan Collendavelloo was fiercely opposed to it and wanted the party to face the election alone. Intermediaries had a hard time convincing Collendavelloo and even more Bérenger to strike a deal with the MSM. Jugnauth refused even a 50-50 share of tickets at first, but then ceded and Bérenger, still in contact with Ramgoolam, came with the demand that the prime ministership should be shared between himself and Jugnauth. Finally, at the Medpoint Clinic in Phoenix, a deal was signed under which Jugnauth would be PM for three years and Bérenger for the remaining two years of the government mandate. Then Jugnauth would be appointed President of the Republic. He and Bérenger agreed on a common manifesto and a share of various government appointments.

Three smaller parties joined the alliance: Rama Valayden's Mouvement Républicain, Sylvio Michel's Organisation Fraternelle/Les Verts as well as the PMSD (of which Hervé Duval, Sir Gaëtan Duval's brother had taken control after a court battle with Xavier, and had then handed over leadership, for health reasons, to Maurice Allet). Those small parties have a tradition of moving to and fro between Labour, MSM and MMM to strike coalition deals.

This coalition won 54 out of the 60 available at the direct election. The Labour/PMXD alliance won two seats in Port-Louis, putting an end to an era where the MMM used to win all the 12 seats in the capital city, except one lost to Xavier Duval in 1987. One of the two seats that went to Labour in Port-Louis was won by Dr. Rashid Beebeejaun, who had refused to follow the MMM into the opposition benches when Bérenger had been sacked from Navin Ramgoolam's Cabinet in 1997.

Another surprise occurred in what had been considered as Jugnauth's stronghold, Piton/Rivière du Rempart: a newcomer to politics, Dr. Balkissoon Hokoom, managed to be elected in second position after Jugnauth. The election of two other Labour/PMXD candidates, Navin Ramgoolam and Arvind Boolell did not, obviously, surprise anyone, as they had, until then, been always elected in their constituencies, respectively in the north and in the south of the island.

Nevertheless, in September 2000, the MSM/MMM alliance did appear invincible to many with 52.07 % of the national vote, while the Labour/PMXD alliance won 36.48 % and a far lesser share of parliamentary seats, a problem that has seriously affected in the same way all the other major political parties of Mauritius, but corrected in Rodrigues in 2017 with a dose of proportional representation.[5] The new government immediately went into action in several areas. Nevertheless, the new opposition, though weak in number and overwhelmed by the huge government majority in Parliament, did not have to wait a long time for opportunities to find weaknesses in the hull of the MSM/MMM ship.

The rise and fall of the MSM/MMM: 2000-2005

Such weaknesses comprised: the emergence of a credible leadership through Beebeejaun within the Muslim community, the man also commanding respect outside of his community due to his brilliant medical career in the country; the role Bérenger took upon himself to play with regard to Mauritius Telecom, partly sold to French giant France Telecom, and the Illovo Deal where the sugar estate magnates benefited from a package to re-finance their businesses in exchange of which government obtained lands for housing projects and the Cybercity; education reform; the Catholic Church's view conflicting with that of government; and the poverty problem. Bérenger's and his supporters' and allies' response was that he was being targeted because he is a White person. They argued he was being denied the right to accede in 2003, as per the MSM/MMM Medpoint alliance, to the position of PM, until then occupied by a member of the Hindu community. They justified the above-mentioned measures as ones, particularly the Illovo deal, that would develop the country and produce jobs - which was effectively proven by such successes as the Cybercity, built thanks to the Illovo deal with over 20,000 jobs created in the ensuing years. Pravind Jugnauth, the minister of Agriculture, defended the Illovo deal in his media interventions.

A major constitutional crisis marked the MSM/MMM mandate when, after the September 11 terror attacks in New

---

PNQ time.

5 At the Rodrigues Regional Assembly elections in February 2017, a dose of proportional representation introduced by Prime Minister Sir Anerood Jugnauth has corrected this injustice without changing the overall First-Past-The-Post result.

York, Mauritius joined the U.S.-led coalition against terrorism as indicated by media statements by Foreign Minister Anil Gayan. Government went on to vote the Prevention Of Terrorism Act (POTA). The then President of the Republic, Cassam Uteem, who blasted the United States for, among other things, leading a coalition to war in Afghanistan, refused to sign the bill into Act. Uteem decided to resign rather than sign it. Vice President A. Chettiar also refused to sign and resigned, and this deepened the crisis. Supreme Court head Ariranga Pillay, who was then appointed as head of state pending the election of a new president, signed the law and the government majority in the National Assembly subsequently voted former Jugnauth's Cabinet member Karl Offman as president and Raouf Bundhun, former MMM member, as his deputy. Offman agreed to, and did, resign later to allow Jugnauth to move into the presidential role as per the Medpoint agreement.

The following is a summary of the actions taken by the MSM-MMM alliance in power from 2000-2005 (a number of them have attracted considerable controversy, at least from Labour):

Education: Steps towards the abolition of the CPE ranking system with an increase of the number of State Secondary Schools from 34 in 2000 to 70 in 2005[6]; setting up of the Zones d'Education Prioritaire (ZEP) for underperforming schools and low-achieving students; making education compulsory up to the age of 16; teaching of ICT from primary school.

Human resources: Creation of the Human Resource Development Council and the Mauritius Qualifications Authority (MQA).

Information and Communication Technologies: Liberalization of telecommunications; setting up of the first Cybercity at Ebene, near Rose Hill; passing of an ICT Act and setting up an ICT Authority plus legislation such as the Computer Misuse and Cybercrime Act and the Data Protection Act. First permits delivered for free independent radio stations, a major democratic advance.

Agriculture/Sugar Industry: Formulation of a Sugar Sector Strategic Plan aiming to ensure the long term viability of the industry through measures like the voluntary retirement of 8,200 workers, against over Rs 2 billion in compensation. This followed the Iliovo Deal, under which a Mauritian consortium purchased 80.25 % of the South African Iliovo Corporation's shares in the Mon Tresor/Mon Desert (MTMD) sugar estate for Rs. 1.6 billion in February 2001, soon after the new government took power. Genetically Modified Organisms Act: The law was voted to regulate biotechnology. EPZfManufaclruring: An Action Plan designed to restructure enterprises, promote vertical integration and encourage multi-skilling in the textile/garments sector.

Tourism: Green light to the construction of eight new hotels, with much focus on new tourist zones at Bel Ombre and St. Félix. Setting up of a Tourism Development Authority; an Integrated Resort Scheme aiming to attract high net-worth individuals to come and invest in Mauritius.

Fishing industry: attempting to put into practice the concept of Mauritius as a "seafood hub" so as to create a new economic pillar.

Financial/business sectors: Several new laws voted to create a new legal infrastructure: the Companies Act, the Securities Act, the Insurance Act and the Financial Services Development Act; setting up of a Financial Services Commission and a Financial Services Promotion Agency.

Poverty: Setting up of a Trust Fund for the Social Integration of Vulnerable Groups which provides aid to the poor.

Civil rights: Setting up of a Human Rights Commission in April 2001 with a Sex Discrimination Division created in 2003 to deal with cases of sexual harassment and sex discrimination; passing of a Sex Discrimination Act in December 2002.

Cultural centres: Setting up of Marathi, Tamil and Telegu Cultural Centres in addition to the Islamic Cultural Centre, the Nelson Mandela Centre for African Culture and the Mauritian Cultural Centre.

Historical holidays: Proclamation of February 1 and November 2 as public holidays to commemorate the Abolition of Slavery and the arrival of the Indian indentured labourers to Mauritius, respectively.Sports: A new Sports Act voted in December 2001; hosting of the 6th Indian Ocean Island Games in 2003; providing support to Mauritian world class athletes like Stephane Buckland and Eric Milazar.

Environment: Setting up of a ":Police de L'Environnement"; ending the extraction of coral sand from the coastal

---

[6] By 2017, SSS colleges have considerably improved and were competing successfully with the so-called 'star' secondary colleges reserved for the elite students.

lagoons.

Utilities: Setting up of a Utility Regulatory Authority Act in November 2004 and passing a new Electricity Act in March 2005.

Other major projects: Completing the Midlands Dam; carrying out several wastewater projects including those that have encompassed the mandates of different political regimes at Government House.

Constitutional reform project: Appointment of a Commission on Constitutional Reforms presided by internationally reputed Justice Albie Sachs. But the MSM-MMM government failed to achieve a concensus and to implement the report.

Rodriques/Agalega: Amendment of the Constitution to grant autonomy to the island of Rodrigues, with a Rodrigues Regional Assembly managing the affairs of the island; setting up the Agalega Island Council, through which the inhabitants can have a say in matters concerning their island.

First free radios: Setting up of an Independent Broadcasting Authority (IBA) which became operational on January 1, 2001, after which three private radios stations were created.

International conferences: Mauritius hosted the 2nd AGOA (Africa Growth and Opportunity Act) Forum in January 2003. AGOA ensures preferential treatment to exports to the United States market. Mauritius also hosted the SADC Summit in 2005 and this organization was chaired by Paul Bérenger, then Dr. Navin Ramgoolam who succeeded him in July 2005. The UN International Conference on the Small Islands Developing States was held in Mauritius in January 2005 in the presence of UN Secretary General and various heads of state and government.

On the subject of regional relations, it is to be noted that throughout the 1990s, the concept of regional partnership has been developing in the African and Indian ocean regions. The OAU was replaced by the African Union in July 2002. The New Economic Partnership for Africa's Development, commonly known as NEPAD, was launched to provide a new vision for sustainable development and the eradication of poverty on the African Continent.

After the cession to Paul Bérenger of the post of PM by Sir Aneerood Jugnauth three years into the government's mandate, it was just a matter of months before campaigning started for the upcoming general election. The resignation of Labour member Siddick Chady from the National Assembly triggered preparations for a byelection. It became obvious that the MSM-MMM coalition, which had suffered a crushing defeat already at a previous by-election in SAJ's constituency of Rivière du Rempart, did not wish to face another risky by-election closer to the general election. Bérenger could have dissolved Parliament after Chady's election and called a snap election, thus keeping control of the political agenda and a fair chance of winning. However, he waited a few months while DPM Pravind Jugnauth prepared a budget that they believed would lead them to electoral triumph. At one point, PMXD leader Xavier Duval was negotiating an alliance with both Labour and the MSM/MMM alliance, but in the end he went back to Labour and obtained the promise that a supplementary position of DPM would be created for him should a Labour-led coalition comprising the PMXD win the election. rations for a byelection.

Bérenger could have dissolved Parliament after Chady's election and called a snap election, thus keeping control of the political agenda and a fair chance of winning. However, he waited a few months while DPM Pravind Jugnauth prepared a budget that they believed would lead them to electoral triumph.

At one point, PMXD leader Xavier Duval was negotiating an alliance with both Labour and the MSM/MMM alliance, but in the end he went back to Labour and obtained the promise that a supplementary position of DPM would be created for him should a Labour-led coalition comprising the PMXD win the election.

At the 2005 general election, the opposition constituted the Alliance Sociale, a coalition led by the Labour Party with the PMXD, MR, MMSM and OF/Les Verts. Dr. Navin Ramgoolam, the proposed PM of this alliance, appointed Dr. Rashid Beebeejaun as shadow DPM and Xavier Duval and Rama Sithanen as two proposed additional VPMs.[7] He pledged to implement a series of popular measures during the first 100 days in power of the government mainly to alleviate poverty: the reintroduction of price controls that would ensure price cuts and free transport for all students were among the most immediate changes promised. Another one was a pledge to review the education reforms introduced by the MSM-MMM alliance so as to allow again the emergence of an elite among the student population.

---

7 Governments have taken liberties with the Constitution which does provide a constitutional post of Deputy Prime Minister in Article 59 (1) and not any position of Vice Prime Minister nor one invented in 2017, that of Mentor Minister. Technically, those two last positions are contrary to the Constitution.

A major criticism of the MSM/MMM by the Labour-led coalition was based on a number of government actions believed by the opposition and its supporters to have reinforced the "*traditional*" private sector, composed of the sugar barons who inherited their fortunes (now diversified to comprise trade, the EPZ and tourism) from the days of slavery and indentured labour. The opposition therefore pointed out with insistence that it would take action to "*democratize the economy.*"[8] This has been more talk than anything else, inspired from the 1930s and 1940s, as all governments, albeit some occasional confrontation with the sugar barons, have worked with them even reluctantly and in 2012, they were stronger than ever after consolidating their position in even more sectors in the preceding two decades, whoever was in government. Due to the blessing of all governments of all parties, they have a stronger presence in the banking sector, other financial services, real estate, retail and more with Prime Ministers of all governments inaugurating their largest projects without batting an eyelid despite fiery attacks on the '*oligarchy*'.

Even if government was willing, the prevailing dominance of neo-liberalism at the global level would stop them as nationalisations and wage hikes claimed by the trade union movements that would be of a nature to slow the pace of economic growth, are considered as an ideological mantra that constrains government action. On the contrary, government has been selling its assets and, in the 21st century, was suggesting the sale of government assets in the business world.

Weakening of MSM/MMM alliance as election looms

The MSM/MMM government led by Prime Minister Paul Bérenger went to the general election on July 3, 2005 after two splits within its ranks: Ministers Sylvio Michel, leader of OF/Les Verts, and Anil Baichoo resigned following disagreement with the PM and leader of the MMM. Michel made media statements revealing he was disappointed the government did not deliver on its commitment made in its 2000 election manifesto to work to obtain a compensation for the descendants of slaves.

Baichoo was dissatisfied with both the MSM and the MMM for being sidelined in the MSM by leader Pravind Jugnauth, who had succeeded to his father at the helm of the party in 2003, and in the government by Bérenger on major projects entertained by his ministry. He also said the government had reneged on its electoral commitments. Both Baichoo, followed by other MSM members, and Michel and his OF/Les Verts then joined the Alliance Sociale, the opposition coalition led by the Labour Party and comprising also the MMSM, the PMXD and the MR.

The MMM had also been affected by a top party member, Dev Hurnam, member for Pamplemousses/Triolet, a key constituency in the north, being caught in the web of a lengthy affair during which he was sent to prison for allegedly ordering an act of aggression against a Supreme Court judge, Bernard Sik Yuen. The allegation was made by a habitual criminal who had also made several revelations on unsolved criminal cases. But it was generally revealed that hit men were hired to kill or maim several people and a public notary was jailed after being charged of alleged criminal conduct in this context.

Another matter that created a major controversy during the MSM/MMM mandate was a threat by Prime Minister Bérenger to take Mauritius out of the Commonwealth. The reason was the refusal of the British government to accede to his demands that the U.K. takes measures in view of eventually recognizing the sovereignty of Mauritius over the Chagos Archipelago. He argued the illegality of the excision of the islands under international law and the British government's response was unusually harsh, giving the impression that London would never accept to hand back the islands to Mauritius, contrary to previous commitments. However, the Mauritian opposition did not agree with what it considered the "*hawkish*" and "*inappropriate*" manner in which the PM was handling the matter.[9] Nor did they agree also when Bérenger blasted the European Union when the MMM's then foreign affairs minister, Jayen Cuttaree, suffered defeat after losing his bid to be appointed director-general of the World Trade Organisation (WTO).

At the July 3, 2005 general election, the MSM/MMM government suffered heavy defeat, with the Alliance Sociale winning 38 seats in direct election and the outgoing government 22 out of a total of 60. MSM leader Pravind

---

[8] In 2017, the situation has not changed, even during 10 years of Labour in power, and concentration of capital has increased. However, the share of small and medium enterprises do have around 46% share of jobs, the highest one in comparison with government and the private sector.

[9] Once in power, the Labour Party followed the same policy as the MSM-MMM government, even going further in bringing the Chagos controversy before the International Tribunal of the Law of the SEA and even winning its case against the British illegal decision to create a marine park and to renege its position of recognizing Mauritius rights in the Chagos area. This has been related in detail further in this volume, in Chapter 41.

Modern Mauritius
Top: Inside view of the Mauritius Parliament (The National Assembly)
Above: The Ebene Cybercity as night falls.

Jugnauth, like several other ministers, lost his seat in Vieux Grand Port/Rose Belle. Bérenger was appointed Leader of the Opposition and Nando Bodha, former agriculture minister, became the parliamentary leader of the MSM. After the best losers were appointed, the 70 seats of the National Assembly were distributed as follows: Alliance Sociale 42; MSM/MMM/PMSD 24; OPR 2; Mouvement Rodriguais 2.

It is to be noted that for the first time in several decades, the third ranking party at the National Assembly with only 11 seats,[10] one less than its partner, the MSM. In August 2005, the MMM had only 10 seats after one of its elected members, Eric Guimbeau, resigned from the party to join its ally, the PMSD.

Soon after the election, a conflict opposed the new government and President Anerood Jugnauth. Prime Minister Navin Ramgoolam accused him of two violations of presidential ethics: a statement prior to the 2005 general election at an official function organized by the Sugar Investment Trust (SIT) at Belle Mare, Flacq, attacking the Labour Party and the participation of his wife, Lady Sarojni Jugnauth, in the MSM/MMM electoral campaign. Jugnauth was heckled by some members of the crowd at the swearing in ceremony of Dr. Ramgoolam's Cabinet in Port-Louis, an event organized for the first time in public.

Lady Jugnauth told the media she had been involved in the campaign because she was free to do so as a *"citizen"* and had seen *"shocking"* graffitis against her family to which she wanted to respond.

The PM refused also to meet the President every week and to provide him with a detailed account of government's proposed decisions. Only a brief was sent to Jugnauth. In addition, President Jugnauth had to read the traditional president's speech containing the programme of the new government where there were sharp condemnations of the previous MSM/MMM government, including a statement that *"the state machinery and electoral bribes"* were used in the 2005 electoral campaign (by the MSM/MMM alliance). Jugnauth retaliated soon afterwards by discarding the new PM's list of proposed nominations to the service commissions responsible for appointments to the public service, the disciplined forces and local government. Jugnauth appointed people from his own list, showing he was going to use all his presidential prerogatives whether the new government liked it or not.

In September, Dr. Navin Ramgoolam responded with his government coming forward with a bill to oust the president from the Appointments Committee that appoints the head and the other commissioners of the Independent Commission Against Corruption (ICAC), indicating that his regime would use its constitutional powers to curtail the powers of the president as much as is possible. Dr. Ramgoolam's parliamentary group was, at the beginning of September 2005, two members short of the required two-thirds majority to allow him to start proceedings to impeach the president. Even then, the procedure would be complex and the outcome would be uncertain.[11] Nothing finally happened.

Jugnauth's mandate was due to end in 2008 and, as of the beginning of September 2008, resisted all calls to resign and to let the new regime appoint a new president. In the meantime, Dr. Ramgoolam was activating a procedure by which his government would reform the Constitution with a view, among other things, to review the mode of election of the president (he is elected by simple majority in Parliament) and to reform also the electoral system to reflect *"more fairly"* party representation in Parliament. This reform would be then proposed to the voters at a referendum, the first one in the nation's history.

As soon as it took power in August 2005, the new regime had started implementing several measures promised during the first 100 days of its mandate. In September 2005, it was implementing, for example, its promise of free transport to all students, the restoration of universal pension to all retirees (the pension was scrapped by the previous regime for those earning over Rs. 20,000 monthly); the reconversion into Form 1 to Form VI secondary schools of exclusively Form VI secondary schools – created by the former regime – so as to cater for the needs of the elite among the student population; and the introduction of an emergency package of measures to boost investment and various sectors of the national economy in the face of declining economic growth.

Upon taking power, the new regime led by Dr. Ramgoolam pledged in the president's speech, to *"initiate a process of change at various levels of our society"* and *"to bring in a new economic model through the democratization of the Mauritian economy."* This *"new economic model"* is one, according to the speech, that *"reconciles economic efficiency*

---

[10] In 2010, the MMM regained at the general election, its second place held for decades prior to 2000, polling 42.02% of the national vote and obtained 22 seats in Parliament, against Alliance Sociale which polled 49.60% nationally and won 38 seats.
[11] See Article 30 of the Constitution of Mauritius where the procedure is set down for both the president and the vice-president.

and social justice."[12]

The state of the Economy in 2005 - *'Notable rise in GDP per capita'*

After the July 2005 general election where Labour won 42 seats, the MSM-MMM Alliance 24 and the PMSD who went alone, none, there was an assessment of the economy by the Mauritius Commercial Bank that was published. The part summing up the economy was as follows:[13]

"A further contraction in the EPZ amidst an increasingly unfavourable environment once again contributed to a below par economic growth of 4.1% last year with expansion excluding sugar estimated at 4.0%, representing a slight recovery from the corresponding rates of 3.9% registered in 2003. Economic performance was also marred by a weak growth in tourism and a downturn in the construction sector. On the other hand, activity was supported by appreciable expansion rates recorded in sugar, domestic oriented industry (DOI), transport, storage & communications and business & financial services amongst others.

"On a financial year basis, economic growth is estimated to have increased slightly from 4.0% in FY 2003/04 to 4.1% in FY 2004/05. Notwithstanding the subdued growth rate, a notable rise was observed in GDP per capita from Rs 128,283 in 2003 to Rs 141,422 last year, implying an increase of 12.8% in dollar terms to some USD 5,150 after accounting for a slight rupee appreciation against the dollar on an annual average basis in 2004. Consumption growth picked up to 6.8%, thereby prompting a fall in the Gross Domestic Savings to GDP ratio from 24.5% to 22.2%. Nonetheless, the economy continued to be characterised by a resource surplus situation on account of the persistent dampened investment climate, which does not augur well for significantly boosting the employment creation capacity of the country.

"Indeed, the ratio of Gross Domestic Fixed Capital Formation to GDP declined from an already low 22.7% in 2003 to 21.6% last year. Moreover, despite an appreciable growth in private sector investment in 2004, the latter is still deemed to be inadequate at around 15% of GDP.

"Against the backdrop of high oil prices and a general depreciation of the effective exchange rate of the rupee, the inflation rate has consistently risen during the past financial year to reach 5.6% in June 2005 despite important reductions in custom duties brought about since April last.

"Besides, soft conditions have persisted in the labour market on the back of lingering difficulties in the EPZ with the mid-year unemployment rate for 2004 standing at 8.5%, up from 7.7% in the previous year. As regards public finance, whilst latest estimates suggest that the budget deficit has declined from 5.4% of GDP in FY 2003/04 to marginallybelow 5.0% of GDP in FY 2004/05, the actual figure may be adjusted upwards on the basis of differing treatment regarding some items of expenditure.

A difficult external position and high oil prices

"In spite of a relatively favourable behaviour of the euro in FY 2004/05 on an annual average basis and a higher sugar production than one year earlier, the external position of the country deteriorated significantly in line with the dismal performance of the EPZ, coupled with a substantial rise in total imports fuelled by high oil prices on international markets and a depreciation of the effective exchange rate of the rupee on average. In effect, after four consecutive years of surpluses, the current account posted a higher than initially estimated deficit of 2.9% of GDP in the last financial year. Accordingly, the balance of payments registered a deficit of around Rs 3 billion in FY 2004/05."

Ethnic politics: more pronounced than in the 1960s

It must be acknowledged that in July 2005, the handover from outgoing Prime Minister Paul Bérenger to incoming PM Dr. Navin Ramgoolam was remarkable for the smoothness of the transition at this level of power. Never before had a change of government been marked by so much civility.

However, ethnic politics was being hotly debated after the election in several quarters. Some people are of opinion that it is worse today than in the 1960s due to the fact that on both sides of partisan politics, ethnic politics is the name of the game for the major political alliances. Small groups or parties like Resistans ek Alternativ, for example, have been fighting for years against ethnic politics.

Bérenger had been, from 1983, putting himself, albeit involuntarily and whether he agrees with this observation or not, into the shoes of former PMSD leader Sir Gaëtan Duval as a representative of the country's non-Hindu

---
12 In fact, Mauritius has retained essentially the same post-independence economic model of free enterprise with a large welfare state.
13 The full report was accessed on 1.3.2017 here: http://www.mcbgroup.com/en/media/AR_2005_A_Review_of_the_Mauritian_Economy_tcm12-1761.pdf

minorities, with the support of a minority among the Hindus, including Hindu minorities and other Hindus disillusioned with the Labour or MSM leaderships. Still, the MMM's Hindu electorate appeared to most observers and the general public to be a minority among the Hindus.[14]

Labour, for its part, had, since the mid-1960s, settled into the role of the political representative of the Hindu community, especially as it recognised the CAM as an official representative of the interests of the Muslims. From then on, Labour had the support of a minority among the the Coloured and Creoles. Nevertheless, with the CAM, it needed and obtained just an adequate number of Muslim votes to stay inpower until 1976, when it lost the election and only clung to power with the help of the PMSD.

Despite several electoral defeats, Bérenger still had substantial support in both the Muslim and Hindu communities for otherwise, how could he be voted as future prime minister by a little less than 50% of the population in 1983 and 2010 and voted as PM in 2000, albeit for the second part of one parliamentary mandate? Still, Labour's ethnic mix, just as the MMM's multiethnic electorate, do not seem convincingly '*national*' in character. There is, for any observer, exceedingly much more of the '*majority*' in the Labour electorate and as exceedingly much more of the '*minorities*' in the MMM electorate – even though the concept of a majority and of 'the' minorities is being increasingly blurred as decades go by.

The imbalance in his electorate is actually the reason why Navin Ramgoolam has been consistently trying to settle into the position that Bérenger enjoyed back in the 1970s when the MMM came out first at the 1976 general election and won equal numbers of rural and urban seats, its electorate cutting then across all ethnic groups as had been the case for Labour between the 1930s and the 1950s. The MMM became then an ideal situation of a truly national party never achieved after the 1982-1983 either by the MMM or Labour or the MSM.

The big question for Navin Ramgoolam in 2005 was whether Labour would succeed in losing its image of an essentially Hindu political party, at least in the eyes of a large section of the General Population, which explains his insistence in appointing to his Cabinet several members of that community (including Xavier Duval as an additional DPM) and several others as advisers to his office. In fact, as will be seen in Chapter 55 at the general election of 2010, he was far from achieving that objective with only 49.69% of the votes for a multipartite coalition of Labour, PMSD and MSM, against the MMM, the Union Nationale of Ashok Jugnauth, and the MMSD of MMM dissident Eric Guimbeau, 42,01%.

By the way, the exact percentage is difficult to calculate as, voting being by secret ballot, the calculation cannot take into account an unknown number of voters' practice of splitting their votes, or 'panachage' to use the French expression. Both of the main alliances present candidates reflecting proportionally the ethnic composition of the population. Individual candidates are placed in constituencies where their ethnic belonging is adequately represented in terms of numbers. Parties go to the extent of identifying communities, castes, 'carats' (an equivalence of caste in other communities) street by street, house by house, flat by flat, to organise private ethnic gatherings at night and to conduct the electoral campaign until election day. The exact mathematics of ethnic voting cannot be ascertained.

After the 2005 general election, there were discussions regarding the campaign led by Labour members against Bérenger on the ground that because he is a White man, he had no right to be the Prime Minister of the country – even if voters want it! Whether Ramgoolam was party to that remains unknown as all parties, whether Labour, MMM or the PMSD are known to talk ethnic politics in '*private*' nocturnal meetings with audiences selected on the basis of their respective communities and all leaders participate and/or are well aware of that. No effort has been made by the Electoral Commission or any member of the judicature to formally take up position against this practice of private ethnic meetings of often inflammatory nature that has been sapping national unity for decades. No one, except a handful of idealists and NGOs have attempted to find means to counteract ethnic politics of this type and magnitude.

Nevertheless, action needs to be taken regarding the electoral system according to many observers but as of March 2017, when that book was being written, no major reform intentions expressed by the major parties had materialised. Everything has been just talk for decades. Additionally, apart from ethnicity there is debate about other

---

14 Some researchers have noted that from the 1982-83 political crisis, the MMM became a party of ethnic minorities, e.g. See Jahangeer-Chojee, ***From Minority to Mainstream Politics:The Case of Mauritian Muslims***, J Soc Sci, 25(1-2-3): 121-133 (2010), Centre for Mauritian Studies, Mahatma Gandhi Institute, Moka, Mauritius. This view may not be shared by MMM sympathisers generally and is actually combated by the party whose support goes up to nearly half the population, an indication of support from all ethnic groups.

flaws of the system.

The EISA (Electoral Institute for Sustainable democracy in Africa) has highlighted on its website the following observations on the electoral process in Mauritius by Mauritian researchers and not just ethnicity:

"The FPTP frequently produces results which are grossly disproportionate"

"Post-independence electoral results (1976 onwards) have essentially favoured the larger or mainstream parties (MMM, LP and MSM). This can be explained by the presence of two factors: the existing electoral model and the systematic recourse to coalitions and alliances.

"The existing electoral model - the FPTP (first past the post) frequently produces results which are grossly disproportionate to the share of votes obtained by the different parties. This is clearly reflected in the outcome of the results and encourages a culture of 'winner takes all'. Observers have reflected on the unfairness of such a system which does not correlate percentage of votes obtained (by a party or an individual) with seats obtained in parliament. In fact, each major political party / coalition has fallen prey to such a system, yet it continues to be used.

"For their part, coalitions and alliances (most of the time pre-electoral ones) have become an inevitable feature of the Mauritian political landscape. The main aim behind these coalitions or alliances is to rally all the chances on the side of a particular coalition formation to win a given general election. The last eight post-independence general elections have seen a combination of the three main political parties as the dominant or equal partner. Smaller parties (usually splinter groups from the big three) have also been accommodated in these grand coalitions or alliances. Despite the popularity of coalitions and alliances, they have been a source of great instability and insecurity. In fact, many of the ruling coalitions (1982, 1983, 1987 and 2000) collapsed after a few years.

"Ethnicity is also a recurrent feature of the Mauritian political landscape and over the last decades it has significantly shaped the manner is which politics is understood and practised. In fact, it is visible in the choice, nomination and ultimate election of candidates who are chosen more for their ethnic value then anything else. Many observers believe that ethnicity has been exacerbated with the best loser system (see section on electoral system) and that there is an urgent need to de-ethnicise and de-racialise the current FPTP model." [15]

While Navin Ramgoolam and Bérenger reflected on the dilemma of ethnic politics and on how to polish the images of their parties as "*national*" political blocs, the country was moving into an era of economic uncertainty in 2005. The price of oil had jumped at one point to over 70 U.S. dollars a barrel of crude. There were fears in 2005 it would continue to surge and hit the $100-dollar mark. In addition to a dangerously rising oil import bill, the country was producing hundreds of thousands of tons of waste that it was dumping without any end in sight, and the last remnants, or less than one per cent of its original forests continued to be destroyed.

Alliance Sociale wins all 5 municipalities

At the municipal elections in 2005, the ruling labour-led coalition led by Dr. Navin Ramgoolam, Prime Minister, won total victory and gained control of ail five municipalities of the country, clinching 122 seats out of a total number of 126 councillor seats. In Port-Louis, Labour and allies won all 30 seats, another major historic event as this put an end to nearly three decades of control of the City of Port-Louis by the MMM. The same can also be said of the municipalities of Beau Bassin/Rose Hill and Vacoas/Phoenix, where the MMM had won ail elections since 1977. In 1982 the MMM gained control of both government and all five towns, becoming the first party in the country's history to do so. In 2005, this complete grip on power was achieved for the first time by Labour. The MMM's ally, the MSM, was also knocked down at the municipal election. It found itself in one of the worst post-electoral situations of the party's history.

The challenge for Dr. Ramgoolam was huge: putting back the national economy back on track and improving the municipal administrations needed, as of October 2005, considerable efforts, both by the govern-

---

15 Extracted from: Roukaya Kasenally 2009 *"Chapter 8: Mauritius"* IN Denis Kadima and Susan Booysen (eds) *Compendium of Elections in Southern Africa 1989-2009: 20 Years of Multiparty Democracy*, EISA, Johannesburg, 270-273.

ment and the whole nation, to succeed.

Chapter 54

The 21ˢᵗ century: serious threats from global warming and local factors as of 2015

Mauritius cannot and will not escape what is believed by many scientists as an impending global environmental disaster that could threaten in the medium to long term, during this century, the very existence of the human race. Environmental changes have been briefly mentioned over the period 1995-2004.

In Mauritius, from the first years of the century to date, there has been further evolution that is very important taking into account, particularly because environmental issues are going to be increasingly pressing. Momentous changes have been noticed across the planet, believed to be threatened seriously by global warming, a process many scientists believe to have already started.

<u>The global threat confirmed in 2012</u>

On the global front, the Reuters news agency had alarming news on 26 March 2012. Excerpts:

"The world is close to reaching tipping points that will make it irreversibly hotter, making this decade critical in efforts to contain global warming, scientists warned...

"Scientific estimates differ but the world's temperature looks set to rise by six degrees Celsius by 2100 if greenhouse gas emissions are allowed to rise uncontrollably.

"As emissions grow, scientists say the world is close to reaching thresholds beyond which the effects on the global climate will be irreversible, such as the melting of polar ice sheets and loss of rainforests.

"'This is the critical decade. If we don't get the curves turned around this decade we will cross those lines,' said Will Steffen, executive director of the Australian National University's climate change institute, speaking at a conference in London.

"Despite this sense of urgency, a new global climate treaty forcing the world's biggest polluters, such as the United States and China, to curb emissions will only be agreed on by 2015 - to enter into force in 2020." [1]

On March 25, Reuters had already reported on the latest scientific view based on a report in the journal Nature Climate Change:

"Extreme weather events over the past decade have increased and were 'very likely' caused by manmade global warming, a study in the journal Nature Climate Change said on Sunday.

"Scientists at Germany's Potsdam Institute for Climate Research used physics, statistical analysis and computer simulations to link extreme rainfall and heat waves to global warming. The link between warming and storms was less clear.

"'It is very likely that several of the unprecedented extremes of the past decade would not have occurred without anthropogenic global warming,' said the study.

"The past decade was probably the warmest globally for at least a millennium. Last year was the eleventh hottest on record, the World Meteorological Organization said on Friday.

"Extreme weather events were devastating in their impacts and affected nearly all regions of the globe.

"They included severe floods and record hot summers in Europe; a record number of tropical storms and hurricanes in the Atlantic in 2005; the hottest Russian summer since 1500 in 2010 and the worst flooding in Pakistan's history.

"Last year alone, the United States suffered 14 weather events which caused losses of over $1 billion each." "The high amount of extremes is not normal, the study said." [2]

Mauritius was confronted with some serious environmental issues during the period leading from the end

---
[1] *Global warming close to becoming irreversible-scientists,* Reuters 26 March 2012.
[2] *Link builds between weather extremes and warming,* Reuters 25 March 2012.

of the 20th century to the 21st century. First, there has been a serious drought in 1999, then, in the 21st century, the pattern of rainfall distribution appeared to change from 2010 and 2011 where the central plateau did not receive adequate rainwater to replenish the main reservoirs of the island located there, especially the Mare-aux-Vacoas, which nearly dried up. Severe cuts had to be applied to the supply of water and there were great fears that the island would be running out of potable water as well as water for other uses.

The authorities, apart from the supply cuts, applied several measures from investigating and trying to reduce leaks in the antiquated water distribution system where pipes had not been replaced for decades and large quantities of supplies were lost as was still the case when this book was published in 2012, the replacement necessitating a long period of works on the network. Drought and inadequate rainfall continue to constitute major environmental threats in the 21st century.

Maurice, Ile durable: Trying to avert disaster

Mauritius has seen its environment mercilessly depleted first by successive waves of visiting European sailors, then colonists who have wiped out, over the centuries, most of its magnificent ebony forests, followed by a population explosion and intensification of human activities that have put unbearable pressure from what remained of its original pristine forests and lagoons. From 2008 to 2011, the country has been working on a government project called *'Maurice, Ile durable. Towards a national policy for a sustainable Mauritius.'* The project has been presented in a Green Paper in April 2011. A 'facilitator', Professor François Odendaal was recruited to guide Mauritius on the way to developing appropriate policies to become a showcase in matters of environmental protection despite the serious and irreversible damage already suffered by the ecosystem.

Four years after the project was mooted at the Prime Minister's Office, it had yet to produce policy recommendations that would be adopted and applied. It is one of the rare projects in Mauritius that has been submitted to the public at large to participate. This is generally the practice required by eminent overseas personalities who come to Mauritius for major projects, as, otherwise, at the local level, public consultations is generally absent for such ambitious projects. There has been substantial public input through surveys and discussions. The Green Paper explains that the project is of an urgent nature in view of the currently deteriorating environmental state of the entire planet.

andfuture generations may not be able to meet their needs." [3]

The Mauritius environmental evolution up to 2015

In July 2016, Statistics Mauritius released *Environmental Statistics 2015*[4] which was the latest available document, as of March 2017, describing the state of the Environment in the Republic of Mauritius. The fiollowing was noted - Edited excerpts:

Land use, Forestry and Agriculture

In 2005, sugar cane plantations occupied 39% (72,000 hectares) of the total land area of the Island of Mauritius, forest, scrubs and grazing lands 25% (47,200 hectares), and built-up areas another 25% (46,500 hectares). During the period 1995 to 2005, the land occupied by sugarcane, tea plantations and forestry decreased while that of built-up areas, other agricultural activities, infrastructure and inland water resource systems went up.

Forest area is decreasing

Total forest area decreased by 34 hectares from 47,103 hectares in 2014 to 47,069 hectares in 2015. Some 22,069 hectares (47%) of the total forest area in 2015 was state-owned and the remaining 25,000 hectares (53%) was privately-owned. Out of the 22,069 hectares of state-owned forest area, 11,804 hectares (53.5%) were planted areas while the Black River Gorges National Park and the nature reserves accounted for 6,574 (29.8%) and 799 (3.6%) hectares respectively. "Pas Geometriques" covered about 625 hectares (2.8%), other nature parks, 906 hectares (4.1%) and other forest lands, 1,361 hectares (6.2%). The 25,000 hectares of privately-owned forest lands consisted of 18,447 (74%) hectares of plantation, forestlands, scrub and grazing lands, and 6,553 (26%) hectares of mountain,

---

[3] *Maurice Ile Durable, Towards a Policy for a Sustainable Mauritius*, Ministry of Environment and Sustainable Development, April 2011.
[4] Statistics Mauritius, *Environmental Statistics - 2015*, download site: http://statsmauritius.govmu.org/English/Publications/Pages/Environment_Statistics_Yr2015.aspx. Accessed 3 March 2017.

rivers and nature reserves.

Area harvested under sugar cane cultivation goes up

From 2014 to 2015, the area under sugar cane cultivation harvested increased by 3.3% from 50,694 hectares to 52,387 hectares. The area under tea plantation in 2015 was 574 hectares, representing a decrease of 14.6% over the figure of 672 hectares in 2014. The area under food crops harvested decreased by 3.8% from 8,459 hectares in 2014 to 8,137 hectares in 2015.

.Import of fertilisers goes down and that of pesticides rises

Intensive use of chemical based fertilisers and other agro-chemicals may contribute to the pollution of the environment through the leaching of nitrate to ground water. Between 2014 and 2015, import of fertilisers decreased by 38.3% (from 53,276 to 32,857 tonnes) and import of pesticides went up by 16.6 % (from 2,201 to 2,567 tonnes).

Energy and Greenhouse gas (GHG)

Though vital for economic development and households, the production and consumption of energy release greenhouse gases. Carbon dioxide is the main component of the greenhouse gases.

Total primary energy requirement increases

Total primary energy requirement (defined as the sum of imported and locally available fuels less re-exports and bunkering after adjusting for stock changes) was 1,534 thousand tonnes of oil equivalent (ktoe) in 2015, some 2.8% more than in 2014. Some 16% (251 ktoe) was met from locally renewable energy sources (hydro, wind, landfill gas, bagasse, fuelwood and photovoltaic) while 84% (1,283 ktoe) were from imported fossil fuels (petroleum products and coal).

Energy supply from local renewable sources increased by 18.4% from 212 ktoe in 2014 to 251 ktoe in 2015 and energy supply from imported fossil fuels went up by 0.3% from 1,279 to 1,283 ktoe.

Energy supply from petroleum products increased by 2.1% from 819 ktoe in 2014 to 836 ktoe in 2015. Supply of coal decreased by 2.8% from 460 ktoe in 2014 to 447 ktoe in 2015 (Table 6).

Net carbon dioxide emission increases

The national inventory of greenhouse gas (GHG) emissions by source category shows that:

• carbon dioxide remains the main contributor of greenhouse gas emissions and stood at 3,975.6 thousand tonnes, contributing 0.0096% to global emissions;

• removal of carbon dioxide (CO2) was around 295 thousand tonnes in 2015; and

• net carbon dioxide emissions, after accounting for the removal of CO2 by forests, went up by 0.1% from 3,675.6 thousand tonnes in 2014 to 3,681 thousand tonnes in 2015. In 2015, there was a rise in emission from the transport industries, manufacturing industries and other sectors, partly offset by a decrease in emission from the energy industries (electricity production).

Carbon dioxide (CO2) emission from the energy sector (fuel combustion activities)

In 2015, CO2 emission from the energy sector stood at 3,975.6 thousand tonnes, up by 0.2% from 3,968.8 thousand tonnes in 2014. Within the energy sector, the sub-sector that contributed most of the total CO2 emission was the energy industries (electricity generation) which accounted for 60.6% (2,407.5 thousand tonnes) of the total CO2 emissions. Next came the transport sector which made up 26.0% (1,032.1 thousand tonnes) of the total emissions, the manufacturing industries making up another 8.5% (337.8 thousand tonnes) and the other sectors accounting for the remaining 5.0% (198.2 thousand tonnes).

Energy industries (electricity generation)

- Carbon dioxide emission from the generation of electricity (energy industries) stood at 2,407.5 thousand tonnes in 2015 compared to 2,449.1 thousand tonnes in 2014, representing a drop of 1.7%. This is mainly attributed to decrease in the quantity of coal used to produce electricity.

- In 2015, around 39% of electricity was generated from coal, 38% from diesel and fuel oil and 23% from renewable sources. Electricity generated from coal decreased by 6.1% from 1,259 GWh in 2014 to 1,182 GWh in 2015; that from diesel and fuel oil together increased by 4.8% from 1,079 GWh in 2014 to 1,131GWh in 2015.

- Electricity generated from renewable sources increased from 596.2 GWh to 680.6 GWh, up by 14.2%. Photovoltaic

increased by 5.3% from 24.6 GWh to 25.9 GWh, bagasse by 11.7% from 456.2 GWh to 509.8 GWh and hydro by 34.3% from 90.8 GWh to 121.9 GWh. On the other hand, landfill gas went down by 4.2% from 21.3 GWh to 20.4 GWh and wind by 15.6% from 3.2 GWh to 2.7 GWh.

- In 2015, coal (50.2%) was the major fuel used to produce electricity followed by fuel oil (26.1%) and bagasse (23.5%);

• Between 2014 and 2015, fuel input increased by 3.0% from 820.3 ktoe to 845.0 ktoe;

• Input of fuel oil increased by 3.7% (from 212.5 ktoe in 2014 to 220.4 ktoe in 2015) while that of coal decreased by 3.8% (from 441.0 ktoe in 2014 to 424.3 ktoe in 2015); and

• Some 198.4 ktoe of bagasse was used to produce electricity in 2015 compared to 164.9 ktoe in 2014, up by 20.3%. It is to be noted that in 2014, sugar cane harvest was extended to the first week of February 2015.

Transport industries

In 2015, carbon dioxide emission from the transport sector stood at 1032.1 thousand tonnes compared to 996.5 in 2014, up by 3.6% due to higher fuel consumption (Table7). It is to be noted that the number of registered motor vehicles went up by 4.5% from 465,052 in 2014 to 486,144 in 2015 (Table 12). Consequently the energy consumed by land transport increased from 319.1 ktoe to 330.8 ktoe (+3.7%).

Manufacturing industries

The manufacturing sector registered an increase of 1.5% in CO2 emissions in 2014 (from 332.7 to 337.8 thousand tonnes) - (Table 7). The amount of fossil fuels consumed by the sector went up by 0.7% from 100.7 ktoe in 2014 to 101.4 ktoe in 2015 - (Table11).

Temperature

- The mean maximum temperature was above the long term mean (1981-2010) for all the months of 2015 except for January and February. On the other hand, the mean minimum temperature was above the long term mean for all the months of 2015. December was the warmest month, and July and August, the coolest month.

- The highest maximum temperature recorded was 35.4 °C, recorded on 28 February 2015 at Champs De Mars, Port Louis. The lowest minimum temperature was 9.7 °C which was recorded on 7 July 2015 at Mon Desir Alma.

Water

- Rainfall

During the year 2015, the mean amount of rainfall recorded around the Island of Mauritius was 2,377 millimetres (mm), representing an increase of 13.5% compared to 2,094 mm in 2014 and an increase of 18.7% compared to the long term mean (1981-2010) of 2,003 mm. The wettest month in 2015 was January with a mean of 455 mm, which represents a surplus of 73.0% relative to the long term mean (1981-2010) of 263 mm. September was the driest month with a mean of 46 mm of rainfall registering a deficit of 52.0% compared to the long term mean (1981-2010) of 96 mm (Table 14).

- Water Balance

In 2015, the Island of Mauritius received 4,433 million cubic metres (Mm3) of water from precipitation (rainfall), 13.5% higher when compared to 3,905 Mm3 in 2014. Only 10 % (443 Mm3) of the water went as ground water recharge, while evapotranspiration and surface runoff accounted for 30% (1,330 Mm3) and 60% (2,660 Mm3) respectively

- Water utilisation

Total water utilisation was estimated at 973 Mm3 in 2015. Around 85% (828 Mm3) of the total water utilisation was met from surface water and the remaining 15% (145 Mm3) from ground water.

The agricultural sector accounted for 35% (343 Mm3) of the water utilised, hydropower 37% (361 Mm3), and domestic, industrial and tourism sector 28% (269 Mm3).

Compared to 2014, water utilisation increased by 8.7%, from 895 to 973 Mm3 with changes as follows:

• domestic, industrial and tourism (+8.9%);

• hydropower (+31.3%); and

• agricultural (-8.0%).

Waste

The total amount of solid waste landfilled at Mare Chicose increased to 448,476 tonnes in 2015 from 417,478 tonnes in 2014, up by 7.4 %. Domestic waste constituted 96% of the total solid waste landfilled in 2015.

Complaints

Effective environmental management needs appropriate coordination and monitoring of environmental problems. The Ministry of Environment, Sustainable Development, and Disaster and Beach Management addresses complaints received from the general public according to a complaints handling protocol.

The number of complaints received goes down Complaints are received by the Pollution Prevention and Control Division of the Ministry of Environment, Sustainable Development, and Disaster and Beach Management. The number of complaints received decreased by 5.4% from 664 in 2014 to 628 in 2015. The complaints were mainly due to: air pollution (18%), noise (18%). waste water (12%), odour (12%) and solid waste (6%).

Environmental Impact Assessment Licences and Preliminary Report Approvals

In 2015, some 22 EIA licences were granted of which 4 were for industrial development, 3 for coastal hotels and related works and 2 each for land parcelling (morcellement), stone crushing plant and development in port area. During the same period, 13 PER approvals were issued of which 4 were for poultry rearing and 3 for industrial development.

Mauritius took in 2015 the radical measure of interdicting plastic bags which were consumed at the rate of 300 million annually and littered the country's terrestrial as well as inland waters, latgoons and seas already heavily polluted also by chemical fertilizers and pollutants brought mainly by runoffs during heavy rains and massive killing life forms, including corals. Mauritius takes an active part in the Conference of Parties, particularly COP 21 and COP 21 in Paris and Marrakech, respectively, presenting a long-term environmental effort up to 2030 and seeking international aid to finance it and new technoilogies to make the country *"cleaner, greener and safer.*

Chapter 55

2005-2012: Burning local and global issues and challenges

The highs and lows of the national economy

From a historical perspective, politics in Mauritius from 2000 to 2012 has been increasingly a confrontation of political alliances with more or less the same ideological mindset. The continuity of government policies is ensured at each regime change, with regard to the economic agenda of liberalization and globalization.

The Mauritian economy has been hit, from 2000, according to financial experts Patrick Imam and Rainer Köhler, by *"a series of external shocks."* In fact, they speak of a *"decade of shocks"* during the period 2000-2010.[1] The repeated *"shocks"* are echoed by the World Bank[2] and Minister of Finance Xavier-Duval.[3] As the millennium started, external factors like the end of protected markets for sugar and textiles, hit the country hard. Imam and Köhler observed:

"The phasing-out of the Multi-Fiber Agreement (MFA) for textiles in December 2004; drastic reductions in the European Union's sugar protocol prices (by 36 percent for 2006–09); and rising prices for imports of petroleum and other commodities caused a cumulative terms of trade shock of nearly 20 percent between 1999 and 2009."

In 2005, the Mauritius government responded to those shocks that had caused the buoyant growth rates of the economic miracle of the 1980s and 1990s to go down to 3%. The government applied reforms prescribed by the IMF and the World Bank to liberalise further the Mauritian economy for it to be in line with the global trends set down in Washington like abolishing further consumer price controls and tax reforms.

Rainer and Köhler observe with satisfaction:

"Trade was liberalized, various price controls were lifted, and business regulations were simplified, earning Mauritius the title "best place to do business in Africa" from the World Bank in 2008 and 2009. These structural measures were complemented by fiscal policy reforms. The government initiated far-reaching tax reform featuring a 15 percent flat tax and established a central revenue authority. It also adopted a fiscal consolidation strategy anchored in a new public debt law that stipulates that public debt is to be reduced to 50 percent of GDP by 2013, from a high of 80 percent in 2002. The appointment of a Monetary Policy Committee in 2007 was an important step in reinforcing monetary policy."

The two authors attribute to those reforms the recovery of economic growth to 5.5% and a rise in foreign investment that *"complemented far-reaching restructuring of the sugar and textile industries, with plantation land being converted to tourism facilities and rapid growth in the offshore financial sector."*

The sugar industry magnates in Mauritius were selling formerly sugar land to build luxury housing, a policy already started in the 1990s and which continued under both MSM-MMM and Labour-PMSD governments, each criticizing the other for doing essentially the same thing: a policy of helping the sugar industry to restructure itself and survive into the new century by entering the luxury real estate and set up large commercial malls. Leftist groups and trade unionists have criticized this policy, but the trend continued, the argument being that in the long term it would pay off.

Mauritian governments, though, whatever the parties that are in power, follow the reasoning at the IMF, theWorld Bank and also at the EU regarding the importance of ensuring the prosperity of the sugar industry. It was summed as follows, according to documentation on the Mauritius government website:

"For historical, economic and political reasons the sugar industry continues to play a very nimportant role in Mauritius, though its contribution in terms of GDP has been decreasing passing from 4.4% in 2000 to 3.7% in 2006 and 2.2% in 2009."[4]

The government of Mauritius launched a 10-year economic reform programmein June 2006. It was strongly supported by the EC (European Commission), the World Bank, the African Development Bank, the UNDP and the Agence Française de Développement (AFD), which were providing finance at the request of Port-Louis.

The financial crisis that everybody knew was behind the door happened in 2008. *"The global credit crisis in 2008/09 was only the latest shock; it hit tourism and textiles particularly hard,"* write Imam and Köhler. But they add that nobody knows when the crisis will end: *"It is difficult to predict when the current crisis will end."* For its part, the World Bank has observed:

---

[1] *Balance Sheet Vulnerabilitiesof Mauritius During a Decade of Shocks*, by Patrick Imam and Rainer Köhler, June 2006, IMF Working Paper WP/10/148.
[2] World Bank, *Mauritius Country Brief*, at worldbank.org Accessed 27 March 2012.
[3] Duval, Xavier-Luc, *Budget Speech 2012*, gov.mu.portal Accessed 27 March 2012.
[4] Multi-Annual Indicative Programme ForMauritius, Accompanying Measures for Sugar Protocol Countries 2011-13, at: gov.mu (Ministryof Finance and Economic Development).

"Global economic uncertainty is rising. The current external environment, with financial and debt concerns in the US and Europe, has triggered substantial fall of stock markets around the globe. The fiscal consolidation programs in the US and Europe to ease debt concerns will reduce already low growth prospects for 2011 and 2012. All this may affect FDI and the international financial sector, with concerns in the media that a double economic recession may take place in the US and Europe (65 percent of total export market for Mauritius), deteriorating global economic growth.

"In Mauritius, the economy is already showing signs of slowdown. National projections for GDP growth are less optimistic. While in late 2010, a gradual recovery of GDP growth was expected at 5 percent (4.5 percent by 2013), the economy is now projected to grow around 4 percent until .

"However, Mauritius has room of maneuver in the short run." [5]

Mauritian membership of SADC, COMESA and IOC

One of the solutions also prescribed is regionalisation, with countries surrendering more of their sovereignty, as in the case of the European Union, to a supra-government. This process has started mainly with the Southern African Development Community (SADC) which is being developed graduallyinto a common market and the Common Market for Eastern and Southern Africa (COMESA). At the end of the road, there will be the African Union that is expected to fully be engaged in the regionalisation process as the continent develops into an expected common market in the longer term. There seemed to be no hurry for the continental common market in 2015, albeit the ract the fact that is a project governed by a treaty.[6]

SADC launched a Free Trade Area at its 28th Summit in Johanesburg in August 2008, while COMESA has a Regional Integration Agreement (RIA) that also promotes the idea of a free trade area. COMESA defines as one of its objectives as, *"Promoting the COMESA FTA and a Common Investment Area and, more generally as follows: RIA seeks to optimize investment and trade opportunities in the region through developing and establishing synergies, networks, alliances, and co-operation with other Regional Economic Communities, co-operating partners and international institutions so as to achieve high investment levels that lead to rapid and sustainable economic growth and development."* [7]

IOC: Comorian opposition to French 'neo-colonial' action

There is a third regional organisation to which Mauritius is also a member, the Commission de l'Océan Indien or Indian Ocean Commission (IOC) which has received considerable French and European Union support over the years. Mauritius is a member nation of both organisations and participates in their regional integration activities.

Mauritius is also a member of another organisation engaged in the integration of the islands of the Southwest Indian Ocean, namely, four island states members of the ACP (African, Caribbean, Pacific group of countries associated to the EU), Comores, Madascar, Mauritius and Seyelles, and one *'ultra-peripheral region of the EU'*, Réunion, which is also a **French département**. Like Réunion, Mayotte, is also both a French départments and an ultra-peripheral region of the EU. However, Mayotte is not considered a member by the IOC because of objection by the Republic of the Comoros from which Mayotte seceded. The commission was founded in 1984 and has made substantial progress. Nevertheless, there seems to be renewed efforts on the European side to revitalise the organisation as can be observed in the incorporation of the IOC in the **Multi-Annual Indicative Programme ForMauritius**, *Accompanying Measures* for Sugar Protocol Countries referred to above. This programme has a section entitled *"Reorganization Of The Secretariat General Of The Indian Commission (IOC)"* stating:

"(...) the IOC is one of the first formal experiences of regional cooperation in this part of the vast region constituted by the Indian Ocean. In terms of development, however, these islands are not all on an equal footing and are in fact at various levels which are often, unfortunately, very far apart. Reunion, an ultra-peripheral region of the European Union, is part of the developed world; Comoros and Madagascar are members of the 23 group of Least Developed Countries; while Mauritius is classified as a Newly Industrialised Country (NIC) and the Seychelles a Middle Income Country (MIC).

"However, fast-increasing levels of globalisation, the emergence of new regional groups and changes in the situations of member countries have meant that regional cooperation has taken on a new dimension. All now believe that regional cooperation and integration, which require more effective solidarity, not only in economic terms but also in many other areas, are the key to greater cohesion and could close this gap. Work in this direction should be combined with enhanced integration of the countries of the region in the ultra-regional (COMESA, etc.) and global (EPAs,

---

5 World Bank, Country Brief, Mauritius, <worldbank.org>. Accessed 27 March 2012.
6 South African History Online website explains: *"According to the Abuja Treaty, regional economic integration is to be achieved in stages: Stage 1: creating new RECs and strengthening existing RECs (by 1999) Stage 2: stabilizing barriers to regional trade (by 2007) Stage 3: establishing a free-trade area (FTA) and a customs union for each REC (by 2017) Stage 4: coordinating tariff and non-tariff systems among RECs (by 2019) Stage 5: establishing an African Common Market and common policies among RECs (by 2023) Stage 6: establishing an African Central Bank, creating a continental monetary union and electing the first Pan-African Parliament (by 2028)* http://www.sahistory.org.za/article/african-union-and-regional-economic-integration *Accessed 2 March 2017.*
7 Regional Investment Agency, at <comesa.int>. Accessed 28 March 2012.

WTO) economy and, as a priority, with protection of insular individualities, the group's strong point.
"The IOC has yet to demonstrate its ability to assert its role as a driving force in this area." [8]

It is obvious that the attempt to revitalise the IOC is being carried out in the wake of globalisation with the European Union playing an active role in what were all former colonies of France, three of which, the Comores, Seychelles and Madagascar, having had serious political crises and a turbulent past including military coups and, in the case of the Comoros, partition of the national territory when one of the islands, Mayotte, voted to be annexed to France and was later integrated as a department of France. Madagascar was, in the 21st century, a still politically quite unstable country and so was the Comores after an attempted secession of another island, Anjouan, in 2006, which eventually failed.

France was still being accused of playing a neo-colonialist role in the region by projecting to turn the COI into an Indian Ocean Community (Communauté de l'Océan Indien) after completing the process of detachment of Mayotte. There is opposition in the Comoros to the French actions in Mayotte. The Comorian newspaper *Al-watwan* campaigned unsuccessfully in 2012 on the issue of Mayotte, asking the Comorian diaspora especially in France and the African Union to act against the procedure that was being used by France and the EU to complete the detachment of the island.[9]

Nevertheless, the same newspaper also announced in February 2012, *"the resumption of military between France and the Comoros".* [10]

U.S. military cooperation to 'democratise' Africa's governance

One major obstacle will be the instability of some African regimes, but Western powers have, in their drive to secure the planet's last important reserves of raw materials and precious metals and gems as well as strategic reserves of metals needed for the computer industry and nuclear power, adopted a policy of political and military interventions to '*democratise*' the continent – which means doing it the Western way.

A large number of African countries, including Mauritius, have adhered to military cooperation with the Western powers, especially the United States Africa Command (AFRICOM) which is based in Stuttgart in Germany. This organisation is extremely active over almost the entire continent.

France has continued its policy of defending Western strategic interests, as well as its own territorial interests in Africa and the Indian Ocean in the same manner as it has been doing it even before the 1960s. It has now joined NATO, which means greater economic cooperation and fighting piracy as well as waging the *'war on terror'* in the Indian Ocean. This created opportunities for the two to organise further military coordination in the region and to reinforce their geostrategic policies that include cooperation with the states and territories in Africa and the Southwest Indian Ocean.

Looking at those economic and strategic developments, it all looks like an ongoing process of reshaping the world just as the colonial powers did in the earlier centuries.

Highs and lows of the economy: the ministers of finance battle it out

Finance ministers of the governments that have succeeded each other at Government House have tried to prove that they were better than their predecessors. Between 2000 and 2012, there have been the following finance ministers: Paul Bérenger (2000-2003); Pravind Jugnauth (2003-2005); Rama Sithanen (2005-2010); Pravind Jugnauth (2010-2011); Xavier-Luc Duval (2011-2014). During those five tenures, the national economy has suffered, already mentioned, from 2000, three great shocks due to external factors: eenergy crisis, dismantling of the Multifibre Agreement and sugar price cut, while recovery from those events in a context of the global financial crisis was not a certainty.

It is interesting to have a look at the various assessments they made and criticism of their predecessors. Save for Xavier-Luc Duval, the other ministers of finance quoted below were presenting their last budget:

Bérenger (Budget Speech 2003-2004):[11]

"The last two budgets have been marked by unprecedented reforms and massive investment in key sectors… when we took office in September 2000, the Nation was without any sense of direction; the population was gripped by uncertainties about the future; national unity was under threat; and public finances were in shambles. We have

8 *Multi-Annual Indicative Programme For Mauritius,* op cit.
9 Al-watwan, 'Premier journal des Comores,' *La commission européenne se penchera sur le statut de Mayotte en juin, 9 February 2012* <al-watwan.net> Accessed 28 March 2012. See also: Extracts attributed to Al-watwan: *Commission de l'Océan Indien : Qui veut entériner la partition des Comores? "Les Etats de la COI devront faire le choix entre Mayotte ou les Comores,* <comoresonline.net> Accessed 28 March 2012.
10 Al-watwan, 9 February 2012, op cit, *Reprise de la cooperation militaire entre les Comores et la France.*
11 Downloadable here: mof.govmu.org/English/Documents/Budget%202003-2004/speechword.doc Accessed 3.3.2017

provided leadership, restored law and order, instilled new hopes, fostered social cohesion, established fiscal discipline, and brought the economy back on track. Above all, we have carved out a new vision to transform Mauritius into a diversified, hi-tech and high-income services economy."

Education

"… 33 additional State Secondary Schools have become operational through new construction, conversionor upgrading, while intake in Form I in public schools has more than doubled to reach 7,700. Never in living memory has so much been achieved in such a short time… We have also laid the basis for developing Mauritius into a technology and knowledge hub. The Ebène-Reduit-Telfair Corridor will soon host centres of higher learning and research co-existing side by side. Land has already been made available for this purpose under the Illovo Deal."

ICT and Free radios

"…We are now firmly engaged in creating a whole new sector of activity and transforming Mauritius into a cyber island. The Ebène CyberCity is taking concrete shape with the Cyber Tower scheduled for completion in December. World-renowned IT firms are already busy setting up operations in Mauritius.

"Liberalisation of telecommunication has become a reality. Together with the rapid fall in connectivity costs, it is opening up new vistas for ICT-enabled services, including e-business, e-education and e-government. Mauritius is on its way to feature proudly on the world ICT map.

"La libéralisation des ondes is another reality. We have thoroughly transformed the "paysage audio-visuel". Mauritians have now more venues to be informed and to express their views. Plans are in hand for digital broadcasting and private television as well as for optimising opportunities offered by the convergence of communication, IT and broadcasting technologies."

Voluntary Retirement scheme

"The Sugar Sector Strategic Plan, including the Voluntary Retirement Scheme (VRS), has been widely endorsed. Some 25 companies have implemented the VRS involving over 7,800 workers. They have obtained cash compensation of nearly Rs 2 billion. Each worker will also become the proud owner of seven perches of land. Some 780 arpents are thus changing hands. As in the case of the Illovo Deal, the VRS has been a major step forward towards the democratisation of land ownership..."

Financial services/Freeport

"We have strengthened the legislative and institutional framework for the financial services sector. The Companies Act, the Financial Services Development Act, the Trusts Act and the Anti-Money Laundering and Financial Intelligence Act have been passed. New institutions, namely the Financial Services Commission, the Financial Services Promotion Agency and the Financial Intelligence Unit, have been set up. We have laid the basis for sustained growth and sound development of the sector.

"We have restructured the Freeport sector and instilled new vigour in port activities. This is evidenced by rising investment in the Freeport and the phenomenal growth in transhipment traffic. Port Louis is now well poised to emerge as a distribution and transhipment hub for the region." [12]

Pravind Jugnauth (Budget Speech 2005-2006)[13]

"In the four years that we have been at the helm, we have dealt with the chaotic situation in law and order, brought it under control and made our country safer and more secure. We have delivered:

- the greatest number of jobs in any four-year period since the 1990s – 46,100 in all;
- the lowest inflation rate in 16 years;
- the highest level of foreign currency reserves in our history;
- the highest level of foreign direct investment in a long time: Rs 12.9 billion in all.
- We have turned around the rising trend in the budget deficit.
- We have introduced new budgeting principles through the Medium Term Expenditure Framework. We have implemented the most crucial reforms ever in the sugar sector, strengthened the tourism industry and set the financial services sector on solid foundations.
- We have defended our interests internationally. After intensive lobbying, especially by the Prime Minister, the third country fabrics derogation under AGOA was extended.
- We have, with the full cooperation of the private sector, implemented restructuring programmes to help the textile and clothing companies to maintain their competitiveness.
- We have created two new economic pillars to further diversify the economy: the ICT sector is now well entrenched in our economic landscape and the Seafood Hub is taking off.
- In education, where others have feared to tread, we have implemented the boldest, most effective reforms ever, introduced 16-year schooling, abolished ranking in the CPE, given oriental languages their rightful place and launched the Zones d'Education Prioritaires (ZEP).
- We have reached out to over 30,000 families through our social housing policy.
- We have started a strong economic democratisation process.
- We have put poverty and marginalisation firmly on a downward track.
- We have dealt with the inefficiencies at Customs and laid the basis for the establishment of the Mauritius Revenue Authority.

---

12 Mauritius National Assembly archives.
13 Downloadable here http://mof.govmu.org/English/Pages/Past%20Budgets%20Documents/2005-2006/Budget-.aspx Accessed 3.3.2017

- As promised, we took the decisions that were required to bring the Central Electricity Board, the State Trading Corporation and other parastatal bodies on more solid financial footing.
- And we have liberalised the airwaves."[14]

Rama Sithanen (Budget 2010)[15]

"(...) our country has survived the worst economic recession in many decades with minimum adverse impact. We are now seeing encouraging signs of a global recovery. We must seize the opportunities and shape our recovery so that the growth path can be more resilient... we must also consolidate the social progress that we have worked so hard to achieve and sustain the vision of Green Mauritius. These are the three pillars of future development and they are the main themes of this Budget...the four and a half years behind us were tough. Back in 2005, the population was facing the future with apprehension..."

"In 2006 we implemented the most fundamental, far reaching and bold reforms in the history of our nation. The development model relied too heavily on trade preferences in a globalizing world. It had become obsolete. We therefore replaced it with a paradigm centred on global competitiveness, supported by reforms aimed at greater openness of the country, a reengineered doing business environment, an accelerated diversification of the economy, a flexible labour market and a simple, more efficient and competitive tax system."

"In the very first year of our reforms, we saw encouraging signs of a major economic turnaround and noticeable social progress... FDI was surging. The textile industry regained its buoyancy after four years of despair when it slashed its output by some 35 percent and shed some 40,000 jobs. The sugarcane industry was reclaiming its role as a pillar of the economy. Employment creation was catching speed and the unemployment rate was coming down.

"By 2007 all the sectors of the economy were expanding, with tourism, banking, construction and real estate showing boom like performances...

"We have brought the SME sector to the forefront of economic development, by flattening the playing field and through direct support at every level of operations. The outcomes have been what we had hoped for. In the past four years, these enterprises have generated 24,000 new jobs, accounting for 60 percent of the total 40,000 jobs created.

"(...) we have made of regional integration a core objective of our strategy. Our role in realizing the Economic Partnership Agreement between the Eastern and Southern Africa group of countries and the European Community speaks of our commitment. We have also made of Mauritius a nucleus for activities that promote regional integration with countries of COMESA, SADC and IOC.

- The IMF has decided to locate AFRITAC, knowledge and training institution for countries of Sub-Saharan Africa, in Mauritius.
- Our country has recently been selected to host the COMESA Fund.
- The African Development Bank is finalising arrangements to post a resident country economist in Mauritius.
- UNIDO is setting up a regional office in our country.

"The dream of making of Mauritius a business gateway to Africa for countries like China and India is now a reality. The Jin Fei project, besides being the largest FDI our country has ever attracted, epitomizes the height that Mauritius has attained as a bridge between Asia and Africa. Global issues such as climate change and sustainable development are also an integral feature of our development model. Global problems need global solutions and we are doing our share through the Maurice Ile Durable vision of the Prime Minister. Another attribute of our development paradigm is the emphasis on empowering women."[16]

Pravind Jugnauth (Budget 2011)[17]

NOTE: This was first budget of the new government led by Dr. Navin Ramgoolam. He had dropped Sithanen who did not even obtain a ticket to present himself for re-election at the May 2010 general election. Sithanen's last budget recalled the performance of the government from 2005 to 2010, so Pravind Jugnauth, his critic and successor, presented his first budget for the new regime. Jugnauth presented essentially the philosophy of the Ramgoolam government and expected results during 2011. He resigned in that same year to join the opposition. Excerpts:

"The Great Recession and the euro-zone crisis have made us realize that upheavals on a global scale can open cracks in our own growth model and put our economy on a slippery slope. They have made us realize that our development policies must be anchored to new realities. And these realities are changing faster than ever before (...) now is the time to move from the legacy of a development strategy that is too euro-centric. As the world moves to a new multi-polarity of growth, as major countries in Europe recalibrate their policies, it is inevitable and indeed an imperative that we also rebalance our own economy."

"Our economy would expand by around 4.1 percent this year with positive growth in all sectors, going up slightly to 4.2 percent next year.

"On the expenditure side, as a ratio of GDP, Gross National Saving would be 15 percent and investment 25 percent this year. And total FDI inflows would be around Rs 11 billion by the end of this year.

"The trade and current accounts of the Balance of Payments, as a percentage of GDP, would show a deficit of around 20 percent and 8.6 percent, respectively this year. The overall Balance of Payments would show a surplus of around Rs 2 billion. The net international reserves of the country would be around Rs 99 billion, covering 8.8 months of imports.

"We expect to finish this year with an unemployment rate of 7.5 percent and an inflation rate of 2.7 percent."

---

14 Ibid.
15 Downloadable here: http://mof.govmu.org/English/Documents/Budget%202010/Budget%20Speech.pdf Accessed 3.3.2017.
16 Ibid.
17 Downloadable here: http://mof.govmu.org/English/Documents/Budget%202011/BudgetSpeech2011.pdf Accessed 3.3.2017.

Xavier-Luc Duval (Budget 2012) – First budget of the PMSD[18]

"In 2005, this Government inherited, in the words of the previous Prime Minister, an 'Économie en état d'urgence'. And since then, Mauritius has had to deal with one external shock after another. This included the worst food price inflation and biggest surge in oil prices in decades, the worst financial turmoil in a hundred years, the worst economic crisis Europe has seen in a very long time, and now the relapse of global economic recovery. It has been six years of assorted adversities."

"These adverse global events have left many countries counting their misfortunes. But Mauritius has withstood all the shocks.

"Since 2006, we have:
- created 9,400 jobs annually, compared to just 4,500 annually in the preceding 5 years;
- increased net international reserves to around 40 weeks of import cover;
- set out one of the simplest tax return systems in the world;
- made Mauritius one of the lowest income tax economies in the world;
- broadened the economic base with new sectors; and
- begun the democratisation of the economy."

"Three months ago I took office amidst fears that the world economy was once again in peril. These apprehensions have further intensified.

"The global economy is fragile and fraught with uncertainty. Global trade is losing momentum. And consumer confidence is waning.

"The wait for a robust upturn may be much longer than was anticipated." [19]

A major challenge: improving the quality of education

Despite continuity of government policies from one regime to another, there can be some modifications as in the case of the policies concerning education where the Obeegadoo reform was superseded by changes brought about by the Labour/PMSD alliance government that came to power in 2005 to preserve an elitist component in public institutions. There has been serious opposition to the previous government's reform from the Labour Party and when the latter came to power in 2005, new Minister of Education Dharam Gokhool refocused the reform more on creating and maintaining what he called an '*elite*' section of the student population that parents and teachers push, sometimes beyond measure and in defiance of modern concepts balancing education with sports and health as well as sound pedagogical principles. Partisan politics verging excessively on ethnic considerations prevailed during the electoral campaign, independently of purely pedagogical considerations.

In fact, whereas in countries like Australia, Britain, Canada or the United States students have, from an early age, to engage in sports activities at school, in Mauritius, schools are mostly deprived of decent sports grounds and there are even cases where the headmaster will advise students sternly to stay in class to study even at recess time. Most primary schools have had their playgrounds asphalted and sports facilities even indoors are totally nonexistent. Not practising sports togher with one's studies is considered the wrong attitude in the larger democratic countries.

The educational system needed reform in a truly efficient manner to provide adequate sports facilities to students so as to help them to balance the healthy practice of sports together with their studies. This is a sector that awaits revolution. The rat race seems to be still on and students continue to take private lessons at huge costs for their families in addition to going to school and this applies to both primary and secondary education, although a few secondary institutions do offer decent sports grounds and gymns. The problem is still with a wrong approach to education by educators and parents, encouraged by the system.

The quality of the Mauritian dietary habits is another problem for the students as well as of the rest of the population. Fatty, oily food and other dietary habits are blamed by doctors for growing number of overweight children and grownups. The most common diseases, because of those dietary habits, are diabetes and, for the population in their late 40s and up, often younger also, clogged arteries that cause cardiovascular disease.

What is somewhat curious is that over 30% failure at the Certificate of Primary Education (CPE) was still considered, at the end of 2011, a satisfactory result after an improvement of 0.02% was noted, the percentage of passes reaching 68.56 from the previous year's 68.54% figure. The Minister of Education held a national press conference to express his satisfaction. The rat race was still on as he announced that the result transcripts still mentioned the dreaded words '*no school*' for low ranking students. On the positive side, though, the minister had benefited from his predecessor's policy of building good secondary schools across the island and he announced that there were some 2,000 seats available for

---

18 Downloadable here: http://mof.govmu.org/English/Documents/Budget%202012/BudgetSpeech.pdf Accessed 3.3.2017.
19 Mauritius National Assembly, Budget 2012.

the *'no school'* category.

Thinking beyond the narrow-mindedness characteristic of party politics, this is an excellent illustration where two different approaches between two successive governments were finally reconciled: status quo for the *'elite'* and schools for all. What needs to be further considered with urgency is reconciling studies with health and regular sports at school with gyms and appropriate sports grounds. Fortunately, the private sector has been building schools and will continue to do it to provide a better balanced education in the medium and long term. Paid education has come back with greater force to stay, and, hopefully, it will force government to improve its own educational services.

Present day health problems waiting to be solved

Another area that needs to be seriously addressed is health. Whereas the diseases of the past have been controlled or eradicated through effective vaccination and other campaigns by the government, two diseases, real *'silent killers'*, diabetes and cardiovascular disease affect large sections of the population.

The National Service Framework for Diabetes (NFSD) observed in 2007:[20]

"Diabetes affects people of all socioeconomic and ethnic backgrounds. In Mauritius, over the past 20 years, a significant increase in the number of people with diabetes has been documented. Between 1986 and 1997, there was a 40% increase in persons with diabetes. At present around 15% of adults aged 20 years and over have the disease and many more are likely to suffer from it during their lifetime. In those aged above 30 years, nearly 20% have diabetes. Nearly half of the people with diabetes do not know that they have the disease.

"Diabetes is associated with huge human and economic costs, as it affects the physical, psychosocial and general well-being of those with the disease and their families, because of the associated complications such as heart disease, stroke, renal failure, amputation and blindness."

With regard to cardiovascular disease, at a Conference on the management of Cardiovascular diseases in Mauritius, where diabetes was again discussed, it was observed,

"According to the Non-Communicable Diseases Survey 2009, the prevalence of Type 2 diabetes in the population aged 20 to 74 years was 21.3% and almost 1 out of 2 Mauritians aged 25 to 74 years had either diabetes or pre-diabetes. The prevalence of current smoking was 21.7% while that of hypercholesterolemia was 33.5% in males and 29% in females. The Survey also showed that 16% of the population was obese and 35% overweight.

"Moreover, the cost of treating CVD and diabetes represents a huge financial burden to the Government. It is estimated that about 1 000 patients are under dialysis. Each year some 500 open heart surgeries, 2 500 angiographies and angioplasties and 400 lower limb amputations are carried out yearly due to diabetes. Furthermore some 175 eye surgeries are done every week." [21]

HIF/AIDS is another threat, although Mauritius has a low rate of prevalence nationally except in prisons where in 2012, it was revealed that the disease has been progressing at alarming rates. Dr. Saumtally of the AIDS Unit in Mauritius revealed to a conference attended by the Commissioner of Prisons Jean Bruneau stated that the rate of prevalence of the diseases in the prisons was 25%. [22] As for the country general, Dr. Saumtally has provided the following figures in a document of the Aids Unit:

"From 1987 to end of December 2009

•Detected cases of HIV/AIDS: with 4219 Mauritians (3429 males and 790 females).

•Sex ratio male to female is 4:1

•Deaths due to HIV/AIDS reported : 240among Mauritians (236 adults and 4 children).

•21 children (11 boys and 10 girls) of age 1 to 14 years: 4 died (1M & 3 F), 7 on ART *

•Roughly an average of 543 new infections yearly." [23]

---

[20] An interesting paper was written by Hemant Cassean of the University of Mauritius: *Towards more effective strategies for management of diabetes in Mauritius*, Open Journal of Preventive Medicine, Vol.2, No.2, 257-264 (2012) http://file.scirp.org/pdf/OJPM20120200019_76618953.pdf Accessed 3.3.2017

[21] Government Information Services, News and Events, *Conference on the Management of Cardiovascular and Reated Diseases*, 25 August 2010

[22] *Le Mauricien*, 5 March 2012.

[23] Saumtally, A, *HIV and AIDS Situation in Mauritius*, available on the government portal gov.mu Accessed 27 March 2012.

Figure 1 - Carbon dioxide emissions from energy sector (fuel combustion activities), Republic of Mauritius, 2006 - 2015

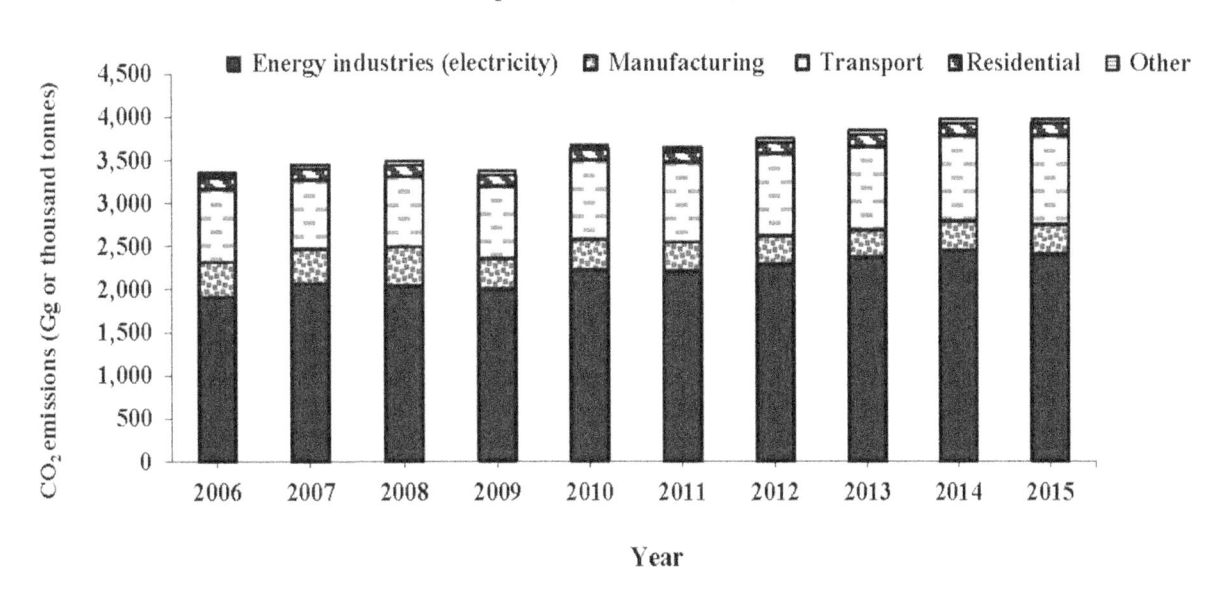

<?> Statistics Mauritius, *Environmental Statistics - 2015,* download site: http://statsmauritius.govmu.org/English/Publications/Pages/Environment_Statistics_Yr2015.aspx. Accessed 3 March 2017.

Figure 2 - Water utilisation, 2015

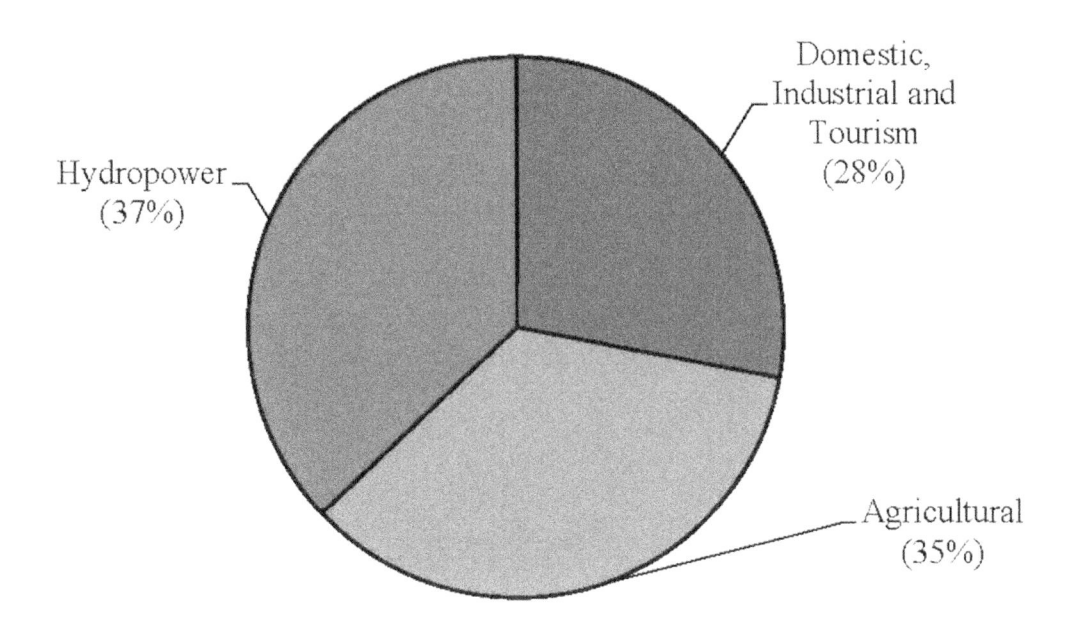

- Hydropower (37%)
- Domestic, Industrial and Tourism (28%)
- Agricultural (35%)

Figure 3 - Total solid waste landfilled at Mare Chicose, 2006 - 2015

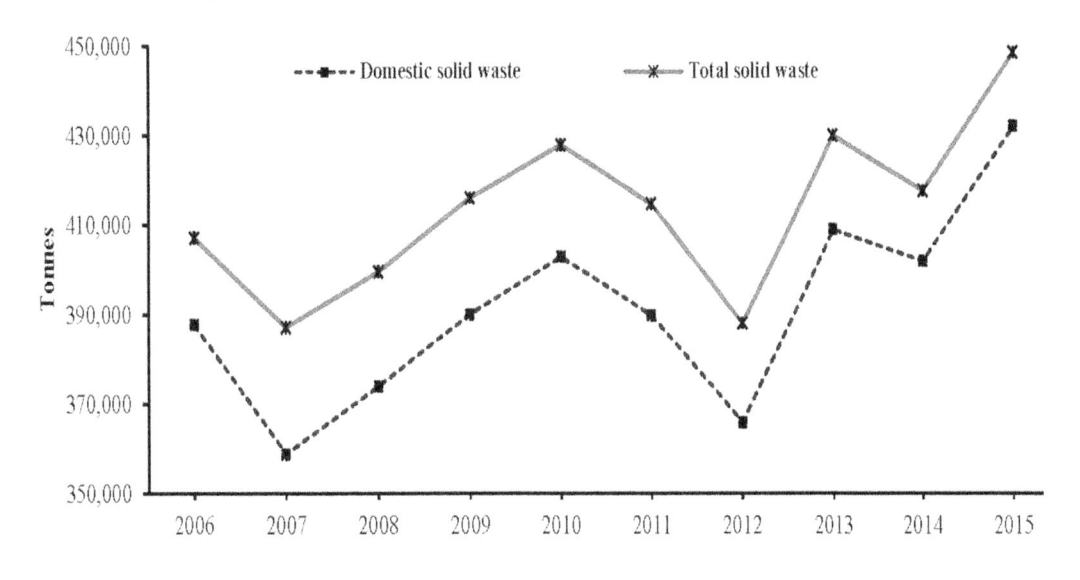

<?> Statistics Mauritius, *Environmental Statistics - 2015,* download site: http://statsmauritius.govmu.org/English/Publications/Pages/Environment_Statistics_Yr2015.aspx. Accessed 3 March 2017.

Chapter 56

Overview of some historical events 2005-2016
2005
TSUNAMI: THE AFTERMATH

The New Year was shrouded in an end-of-the-world atmosphere over that large part of the Indian Ocean countries that was affected by one of the planet's worst natural disasters in recorded history. It was a tsunami caused by a megathrust [1] undersea earthquake that had occurred a few days back, at 00:58:53 universal time on Sunday 26 December 2004, with the epicentre off the west coast of Sumatra, Indonesia. It caused major damage to Indonesia, India, Sri Lanka, Thailand, Malaysia, Myanmar, the Maldives, Somalia, Tanzania, Seychelles, Bangladesh, and Andaman. Deaths have been estimated between 235,000 and 285,000.

Mauritius and Rodrigues were affected, huge waves causing moderate damage on the coasts. Mauritius President Cassam Uteem was visiting the Maldives Islands which were severely affected with 82 persons killed and 42 missing. Prime Minister Paul Bérenger announced a USD 300,000 contribution by Mauritius in the context of the international effort to help the survivors. The tsunami showed to the world and to the Indian Ocean islands, including Mauritius, that every nation should be prepared in case of a recurrence of such a disastrous natural calamity. From that time a network was conceived and created for the better global surveillance, including warning systems. Mauritius participated fully.

'ECONOMIC TSUNAMI' THREATENS

Major factories like Sinotex and Sentex, as well as smaller ones were closing down during the first years of the 21st century. Regarding sugar, the EU announced in May that prices would be slashed by 23% to be increased to 37%. European Commissioner Peter Mandelson had previously stated,

"In January I was in the Caribbean where some small countries face an economic Tsunami, if the preferential quotas which have allowed them safe access to EU markets are suddenly swept away."[2] That was also the case regarding Mauritius, which had an export quota of half million tons in the EU.

In 2005-2006, the newly elected Alliance Sociale government initiated a package of reforms with the assistance and support of the World Bank and the International Monerary Fund and funds also from the European Union. This was meant to help the country to be more resilient to the prevailing global financial crisis, but the resurgence of the global crisis had created by 2012 a climate of incertainty for the future of Mauritius.

During its mandate, the MSM/MMM government had initiated some important reforms and projects. Those included the building of 33 new government secondary schools to end the CPE rat race. There was also the Cybercity project on land acquired from the Lonrho sugar company's plantations and the initial measures to provide for the reform of the sugar industry, threatened by the upcoming end of the preferential sugar prices on the European market and other decisions (see previous chapter). In 2005, the Cybertower of the EbèneCybercity near Rose Hill won the 'Intelligent building 2005' trophy awarded by the Intelligent Community Forum, New York, ranking ahead of countries like Singapore, Hong Kong and Ireland. [3]

CHALLENGE TO ELECTORAL ETHNIC IDENTIFICATION

Eleven political candidates of Resistans ek Alternativ, a small party on the far left of the political divide, tried in vain

---

[1] Natural Resources Canada of the Canadian government explains: *A megathrust earthquake is a very large earthquake that occurs in a subduction zone, a region where one of the earth's tectonic plates is thrust under another... two plates are continually moving towards one another, yet become "stuck" where they are in contact. Eventually the build-up of strain exceeds the friction between the two plates and a huge megathrust earthquake occurs.* < earthquakescanada.nrcan.gc.ca> Accessed 29 March 2012.

[2] February 4, 2005: Speech by Peter Mandelson, European Commissioner for Trade, on *"Trade at the Service of Development"*, at the London School of Economics (United Kingdom) 4 February 2005, copy provided on website: <http://europa.eu/rapid/press-release_SPEECH-05-77_en.htm> Accessed 3.3.2017

[3] Mentioned on the website of Business Parks of Mauritius Limited where the state-of-the-art building is described as follows: *"In operation since 2005, it offers state-of-the-art optic fiber datacom and telecom facilities in each floor and module."* <e-cybercity.mu> Accessed 29 March 2012,

to get registered as candidates because they refused to state to which community they belong on the election registration documents. They protested the rejection of their application in the Supreme Court where they won their case in a historic judgment delivered by Justice Eddy Balancy. Researchers have observed, recalling a precedent judgment by Justice Seetulsing in 2000:

"The criterion dealing with community is further reinforced in section 3 of the first schedule of the constitution, which deals with the official publication of the nominated candidate's community, and the subsequent bearing on the candidate if the validity of the claim is contested. In fact, the official requirement of nominated candidates having to disclose their com- munity has been the subject of numerous contestations by smaller political parties, such as Lalit and Resistanz Ek Alternativ, as it is believed in certain quarters to reinforce the notion of ethnic politics bent on segregation. Two cases filed by the above-mentioned political parties in the Mauritian Court in 2000 and 2005 (prior to the general elections) produced the 'Seetulsing Judgement' (2000) and the 'Balancy Judgement' (2005), which acknowledged the narrowness of the ethnic classification of Mauritian society. In 2006, Resistanz Ek Alternativ wrote to the United Nations Human Rights Commission to demand that the latter pronounces itself on the unconstitutionality of the first schedule of the Mauritian constitution." [4]

Resistans ek Alternativ then lost their challenge when the matter was taken to the Full Bench of the Supreme Court in 2005. The party and the Bloc 104, named after the number of candidates whose application to stand for election had been rejected, appealed to the Privy Council. In December 2011, the Privy Council ruled it had not the jurisdiction needed on the case, but left the door open to a further challenge:

"It remains open to the applicants to advance a constitutional challenge in the future. The Board expresses no concluded views as to the merits of any such challenge, especially since it will be based on evidence put before the Supreme Court or Court of Appeal and the Judicial Committee will then have the benefit of the views of the courts in Mauritius (...) The Board understands that the applicants wish to say that their existing constitutional rights have been infringed but does not think it right to reach any firm conclusions on the merits. It appreciates that, if the issues cannot be resolved politically, they may be raised before the Judicial Committee in the future."

WOMEN AND POLITICS

Soroptimist International expressed dissatisfaction with the fact that women are not well represented in the political arena and proposed that parties reserve at least 30% of their lists of candidates for women. Only 12 women were members of the new Parliament elected in 2005, among them, eight were from the opposition parties.

EDUCATION: TWO MORE KEY MEASURES

The year was also important because of two major decisions taken in succession by the MSM/MMM government that made education compulsory for children aged up to 16 years from January, and by its successor, the new Alliance Sociale government that provided free transport for students.

SIDS: SMALL ISLANDS UNITE

A modern conference centre, the Swami Vivekananda Convention Centre was opened by the government on Monday, January 10, and was first utilised by Mauritius to host a most important event: the summit of the Small Islands Developing States (SIDS), in the presence of Prime Minister Paul Bérenger, United Nations Secretary-General Kofi Annan, SIDS secretary-general Anwarul Chawdhurry and several heads of state and of government, 2,000 delegates and about 20 international organisations. Essentially, SIDS is the result of an initiative that aims to raise awareness globally regarding the excessive vulnerability of small island states in several spheres, regarding, among other things, economic matters in a globalising world as well as the effects of climate change and major natural disasters like the 2004 tsunami. The organisation is now well established in the international community.

On the sidelines of the conference, the Chagossian community exiled from their native islands had contacts with the British Secretary of State for the Foreign and Commonwealth Office, Bill Rammel, and the Commonwealth General-Secretary Don McKinnon. While London still maintained that it would not discuss the return of the Chagossians to their islands, they were organising a trip to the Chagos for the exiled community.

FERNEY VALLEY CONTROVERSY

A heated debate went on during 2005 over a government project to build a highway across the Ferney Valley, the site of one of the few last remnants of the island's unique original forests and of its flora and fauna, including some of the world's rarest and endangered species. Studies by the Mauritian Wildlife Foundation indicated in 2005 that Mauritius and its islands are left with no more than 2% of its original forest cover (1% according to some estimates).

---
[4] Roukaya Kasenally, 2009 "Chapter 8: Mauritius" IN Denis Kadima and Susan Booysen (eds) **Compendium of Elections in Southern Africa 1989-2009: 20 Years of Multiparty Democracy**, EISA, Johannesburg, 281-283.

In May, the organisation Nature Watch took the matter to the Supreme Court. After bulldozers had already been positioned to start work under the new Alliance Sociale government, the controversy took a new turn and opposition to the project was amplified locally and internationally. Finally, the Prime Minister, Dr. Navin Ramgoolam decided to stop the works altogether and to have a nature park created to protect the Ferney Valley forest.

SURVEY OF CITY'S CHRONIC TRAFFIC JAMS

A study by Luxconsult, entitled *'Origin-Destination Survey'* indicated in February 2005 that traffic congestion, already a serious problem with over 43,000 vehicles daily entering and exiting Port-Louis, would lead to a chaotic situation in a few years. It recommended measures to provide more fluidity of traffic in and around Port-Louis.

'PLURALISM WORKS'

India is a melting pot of races, cultures and religions and the appointment of Paul Bérenger was an occasion for Indian Prime Minister Manmohan Singh to make a remark on pluralism:

"India and Mauritius should lead the way in showing history and human kind that pluralism works, that pluralism is the order of the day and that in embracing pluralism, we embrace global security."

Manmohan Singh was paying an official visit to Mauritius with his wife Gursharan Kaur at the invitation of Mauritian PM Bérenger.

MAURITIUS MOURNS POPE JOHN-PAUL II

Pope John-Paul II died in April. His personal links and Vatican's diplomatic relations with Mauritius had been reinforced during a visit to Mauritius he made in 1989, when he had been warmly welcomed by the then Prime Minister Sir Anerood Jugnauth and the population. Those links had been established when Father Désiré Laval was beatified in 1979 and a delegation led by the then Prime Minister Sir Seewoosagur Ramgoolam had attended in Rome, while Mauritian Ambassador Radha Ramphul offered to Mgr Margéot a sculpted bust of the *'Saint of Mauritius.'* In 1988, when the Bishop of Port-Louis, Mgr Jean Margéot was elevated to the status of Cardinal, a Mauritian delegation led by the then PM Sir Anerood Jugnauth attended.

The pope's funeral was attended by Prime Minister Paul Bérenger.

NEW GOVERNMENT IN ACTION

The new Alliance Sociale government, after the July 3 election, started implementing a number of electoral pledges. It provided free transport to all senior citizens and entered into the commerce of milk by having the State Trading Corporation, the trade arm of the government, import milk of the brand Amul from India. Private companies engaged in the trade saw the competition from the government as a risk that there would no longer be a level playing field in this commercial sector. The government also amended the Prevention of Corruption Act (POCA) to give the prime minister the power to appoint the members of the Appointments Committee and to determine the conditions of service of the director-general. The parity in numbers in the parliamentary committee overseeing the Independent Commission Against Corruption (ICAC) was ended, with the government taking 5 seats against 3 to the opposition. Other measures included the approval by the National Assembly of a Law Review Commission.

DODO REMAINS DISCOVERED

In 2005 the first discovery of the 21st century of dodo remains was made by a Dutch-Mauritian team who found bones of about 20 dodos a in swampy area and two years later the most complete and well preserved dodo skeleton was discovered in a cave, and the British Broadcasting Corporation (BBC) speculated that DNA material may have been found intact and could create hope that the bird could be resurrected.[5]

2006

CHAGOSSIANS' EMOTIONAL VISIT TO THEIR ISLANDS

The moment of highest emotion in 2006 was probably the return of the exiled Chagossians for a visit to their islands in April 2006 on board the MV Trochetia. The visit was allowed by the Anglo-Americans following a judgment of the High Court in London quashing a queen's Order in Council obtained by Labour Prime Minister Tony Blair that

[5] BBC Knowledge, In search of the Dodo, < http://www.bbcworldwide.com/bbcworldwidewebsitessiteterms.aspx>

interdicted the resettlement of the islands in the Chagos. The islanders – about a hundred of them were on the ship – saw for the first time since 1971 their church now in ruins, the tombs of their dead and other remains of what used to form part of their daily lives.

Most of them shed tears on arriving on April 6 in the Chagos, recalling the days when, from 1965, they were let down by the Mauritian authorities and were in successive groups expelled from their islands and all their pets, including their dogs, killed. *"The Americans have arrived, you must go,"* had said Paul Moulinié, their boss who employed them to collect coconuts and extract coprah for the production of coconut oil. Lisette Talatte was told by their employer that the islands had been sold to be occupied by the American military.

The leader of the Group Réfugiés Chagos (GRC) Olivier Bancoult again reasserted to the media that the islanders will never abandon the struggle to get back to their islands, at least those not used for the purpose of military defence. He mentioned the appeal of the British government against the High Court judgment as well as a case his group has brought before the European Court of Human Rights (ECHR). The Mauritian and foreign media reported and commented the event as a major milestone in the struggle of the islanders. The following are three excerpts that went round the world both in the news media and in studies by academia:

Lord Justice Hooper and Mr Justice Cresswell: *"The suggestion that a minister can, through the means of an Order in Council, exile a whole population from a British overseas territory and claim that he is doing so for the peace, order and good government of the territory is, to us, repugnant. The defendant's approach to this case involves much clanking of the chains of the ghosts of the past."*[6]

Excerpt from the judgment: *"The power of the Queen in Council to legislate for the Territory is limited by the United Kingdom's obligation to respect the human rights of the Chagossian people, in particular their right to respect for private and family life and home, and the right to peaceful enjoyment of their possessions."*[7]

The Mauritian government:

"This historic victory over the UK Government banning their rights to return to their homeland, has instilled new hopes in the Chagossians and has also paved the way for an end to their long exile."[8]

2007

AND NOW AGALEGA?

On 26 November 2007 the **Times of India**, a respected newspaper in the Indian subcontinent, reported that the new Ramgoolam government had offered the Mauritian territory of Agalega to India '*ostensibly*' for tourism, but actually for "*strategic*" purposes. The article said,

"In a move that could give the country a strategic presence in the Indian Ocean, Mauritius has offered to hand over the Agalega Islands — which is closer to India than the African country — ostensibly for development as a tourist destination.

"The details of the offer, made during negotiations for a bilateral trade pact, are still being discussed. But its broad contours are something like this. Indian companies would develop hotels and resorts and also upgrade the existing airstrip in the island into an airport."[9]

Even though the news was denied by Mauritian officials as well as Prime Minister Ramgoolam in Parliament, Cable 89644, one of the *'India Cables'* of the United States revealed in the Indian press, indicated that Washington believed that there had been talks to have India develop the twin islands of Agalega for tourism and that India's intention was also to use them for strategic purposes. The cables were revealed in **The Hindu**, one of the most influential and respected Indian newspapers, on April 2, 2011 in two separate articles.[10]

What Ramgoolam revealed in Parliament was that India did a study at no cost for Mauritius on Agalega and Cable 89644 stated that two Mauritian government officials also denied, as Ramgoolam did in Parliament that the islands would be handed over to India:

"Ramgoolam's top two aides, his Chief of Staff Kailash Ruhee and the Secretary for Home Affairs Raj Mudhoo, have told the Embassy that this affair is much ado about nothing. They asserted that Mauritius was not going to cede Agalega to India and that the discussions were limited to economic and infrastructure development. Indian DCM, Sanjiv Ranjan, corroborated this account, adding that India initially did not agree

---
6 Snoxell, David, Cambridge Colloquium on the Royal Prerogative, 19 January 2008. *Political context (the Bancoult case) and Possible Solutions*.
7 Quoted in a comparative study of the Chagos and Pitcairn cases in: Farran, Sue, *Prerogative rights, human rights and island people: the Pitcairn and Chagos cases*, Public law, ISSN 0033-3565, Nº 3 (Autumn), 2007, págs. 414-424.
8 In: Cabinet Decisions taken on 12 May 2006, Government of Mauritius, http://pmo.govmu.org/English/Pages/Cabinet%20Decisions%202006/Cabinet-Decisions-taken-on-12-May-2006.aspx
9 *India eyes an island in the sun*, Times of India, 25 November 2006.
10 The articles of April 2, 2011 are: 1. *Mauritius denies plan to cede Agalega Islands to India, but issue shows Mauritian subordination*; 2. *U.S. saw Indian 'hidden agenda' in Mauritius* at <thehindu.com> **Accessed 29 March.**

to Ramgoolam's request but changed its position after he raised it with President Kalam. Nevertheless, Mauritian officials have displayed an unusual degree of nervousness and word parsing, which might indicate that there is more to these reports that the government has admitted."

There have been some hostile reactions to the rumours among the newspaper readership in newspapers that expressed fear of another affair like the 1965 cession of the Chagos. Nothing of the sort happened, though the Indian media again, in 2012, raised the possiblity of a cession by Mauritius, and once more the Mauritian Prime Minister denied the rumours.

CHIKUNGUNYA: A TERRIBLE EPIDEMIC STRIKES

The year 2006 has left bitter memories among the Mauritian population of a disease till then unknown that hit the island. The Mauritian authorities tried to minimise the impact as much as possible because of the importance of the tourism industry, according to some observers, including the political party Lalit.[11] It was going to be revealed in 2008 that a large number of people actually died from chikungunya. *(see 2009 below)*

PRICES: CONSUMERS CONCERNED

While the government did embark on a plan that successfully contained the effects of the financial crisis in the second half of the first decade of the 21st century, as acknowledged by the World Bank and the IMF, in 2006, after the new regime's budget, there was a series of price hikes that attracted criticism from the opposition and in the media. The government tried to step up efforts to get price reductions from the retailers, at times with mixed results due to a depreciating rupee at the time.

'IDENTITY-BASED POLITICS": "CHALLENGE FOR GOVERNANCE"

This expression from academia, signed Sheila Bunwaree, came up as follows in a report on Mauritius as yet another term in relation to ethnic politics:

"Reduced economic opportunities and a growing asymmetry in the distribution of entitlements have given rise to new forms of identity-based politics and pose important challenges for governance. Riots that occurred in February 1999 are largely attributed to the growing frustration and alienation of some segments of the Afro-Mauritian community."[12]

This is yet another of the many warnings to the nation of the dangers posed by the political elite pursuing the practice of ethnic-based politics, attacking adversaries on the basis of their ethnic identity.

THE CAMPEMENT TAX ISSUE

There was mounting protest against the National Residential Property Tax, frequently referred to as the Campement Tax, imposed by the new government. It affected bungalow owners in the coastal areas. It came into operation in October. An organisation was created, with the support of Eric Guimbeau, member of the National Assembly, to formally protest and even take the government to Court, arguing that the tax was disproportionate. In January 2007, the situation was summed up as follows in the media:

"The legal battle between the Association of Campement Owners and Users (Acou) and the government seems far from resolved. On the contrary, it appears even more serious with both sides keeping their stand. Minister of Housing and Lands, Asraf Dulull, has expressed his intention to go forward with the fees that campement owners have to pay to keep their bungalows while members of the Acou appear more than ever determined to fight their case.

"The latest legal weapon of the 700 Acou members is the difference between the rent they have to pay on their property and that paid by hotels and companies. Strangely enough, campement owners will have to pay 10,000 % more than hotels to rent a plot of land in the coastal areas.

"In fact, the parliamentary question by majority MP, Eric Guimbeau, made the Acou realise that the lease fee requested from industrialists and the one from individuals was far from being the same. 'How can they claim at the same time a lower amount from companies with higher revenues and higher amounts from individuals? This is not logical!'"[13]

It was also revealed in January that there were a total of 7,925 leases, out of which 1,288 were taxable under the NRPT.

LE MORNE: HERITAGE SITE

Governments in Mauritius had been working on the protection of a number of places as part of the national heri-

---

[11] *LALIT begins to be PROVEN RIGHT on Chikungunya Fever Epidemic*, 12 March 2008 <http://www.lalitmauritius.org/en/newsarticle/688/lalit-begins-to-be-proven-right-on-chikungunya-fever-epidemicbr/> **Accessed 5.3.2017.**
[12] The African peer review mechanism in Mauritius. Lessons from phase 1. June 2007, Sheila Bunwaree. (University of Mauritius). Downloadable here: http://www.sarpn.org/documents/d0002768/AfriMAP_APRM_Mauritius_Jun2007.pdf
[13] *L'Express* 23 January 2007.

tage, including both natural land and marine parks. The governments of the 21st century not only proclaimed two public holidays for, respectively, the commemoration of the abolition of slavery and that of indentured labour, but also asked UNESCO to inscribe on the World Heritage List, the Apravasi Ghat, a place where Indian immigrants coming mainly as indentured labourers landed in great numbers as from 1834. Mauritius then asked UNESCO to inscribe also Le Morne Mountain, which had, for centuries, been an important refuge for slaves struggling for freedom. In 2007, the Cabinet approved the Draft Management Plan for that project and the final step of the procedure. The Prime Minister flew to the top of the mountain to honour the memory of the 'esclaves marrons'.

POLITICS: SOME MAJOR CONTROVERSIES ERUPT

• Two separate events were quite unexpected during 2007. Finance Minister Rama
Sithanen threatened he would resign if Rundheershing Bheenick, one of his predecessors, were appointed as governor of the Bank of Mauritius. The tug-of-war opposing him and Prime Minster Navin Ramgoolam lasted for some time until he finally gave up. His relations with Ramgoolam seemed to have normalised, but in 2010, the latter did not give him a ticket for the general election.

• The other major event was when former minister Ashok Jugnauth's election in Moka-Quartier Militaire at the last general elections was invalidated by the Supreme Court. He had been accused of having contravened electoral legislation with regard to bribery and corruption of voters. He appealed to the Privy Council.

• Another matter, regarding the post of vice-president of Mauritius, retained attention. The Prime Minister, Dr. Navin Ramgoolam had expressed the desire to abolish this post, but had to admit that he could not do so because he did not have the necessary majority of three-quarters in the National Assembly for that purpose.

WASTE DISPOSAL NIGHMARE

The political establishment as well as the civil society were divided during the year on the question of how to dispose of waste. It was when a Rs5-billion project to incinerate all waste produced nationally was presented. One of main issues of the controversy centered on the emission of noxious gases from the plant, in particular dioxin. The debate also revolved about the costs to the government and so to the taxpayer.

MORE SUGAR FACTORIES CLOSE

One government decision which used to be controversial when it was the previous government that was in power, was to come up with the approval of the closure by the government that was now in power, of the closure of more sugar factories, with 7,500 workers losing their jobs and receiving, as in 2000-2002, land and money under a Voluntary Retirement Scheme and an Early Retirement Scheme. At the same time, the European Union was supporting the reform of the sugar industry and announced, in 2007, financial support at a higher rate than previously announced and that support was conditional upon centralisation of the industry to increase its declining efficiency trends. However, the agreement by government was reluctant during most of the year until an agreement was reached on 5 November 2007 and officially announced by government as follows:

«Following the successful conclusion of the win win deal between Government and the Mauritius Sugar Producers Association (MSPA) on 5 December 2007 regarding the sugar reforms, 25 growing companies, namely 18 members of MSPA, 4 members of Cane Growers Association, State Land Development Company (SLDC), Rose Belle Sugar Estate (RBSE) and State Investment Trust (SIT) applied for authorization to make an offer of VRS to their workers. Three milling companies around which there would be clusters, i.e. Belle Vue, Medine and Savannah, applied to offer ERS to their employees whereas factory closure procedures were initiated in respect of Riche-en-Eau, Mon Tresor and St Felix.»[14]

CONTROVERSY

• Student fees: A major area of controversy was the increase of student fees for taking School Certificate and Higher School Certificate exams and of admission fees to the University of Mauritius. After considerable tension between the student world and the authorities, the government managed to propose helping parents in the lower economic brackets.

• Tianli/Jinfei: Another controversy erupted and degenerated when planters evicted after Chinese investors proposed to build on agricultural land in Terre Rouge, north of Port-Louis, launched a protest movement, alleging that

---

[14] Ministry of Agro-Industry and Food Security, VRS 11 and Blueprint. http://agriculture.govmu.org/English/Pages/VRS-11-and-Blue-Print-.aspx Accessed 3.5.2017.

they were being inadequately compensated. It was the Tianli project that never materialised. Another company, Jinfei, later proposed to take up the project consisting of building a new town for Chinese businesses to operate from Mauritius and this had yet to materialise in 2012. In 2017, the new government elected in 2014 still had to make good an undertaking made by its former FinanceMinister Vishnu Lutchmeenaraidoo in 2015 to revive and revamp the project.

2008

CHIKUNGUNYA KILLS

In 2008, Mauritius looked back at the chikungunya epidemic that had created an atmosphere of panic in the island from the time it appeared (a small outbreak in 2005 followed by the 2006 epidemic). It must be said that the disease had not disappeared, though infections occurred on a much lesser scale. A study by a team including Mauritian and American researchers at Harvard University and the University of Alabama, revealed that, contrary to the belief spread by the Mauritian authorities among the population, in reality, chikungunya is a deadly disease that has killed a large number of persons, and this included Mauritius. Excerpts of a report they published:

"Human infections with chikungunya virus are associated with sudden onset of symptoms including headache, fever, rash, and muscle and joint pain. Before the outbreak in the Indian Ocean islands, deaths had not been associated with infections. However, Réunion Island reported >200 deaths during the 2006 chikungunya epidemic (January–April 2006), and India conservatively estimated 1,194 deaths since the virus reemerged in December 2005. (…)

"Mauritius Island had an initial outbreak of approximately 3,500 suspected cases of chikungunya fever from April through June 2005. With the onset of the drier season of winter, transmission of the virus subsided, but increased again during 2006. An outbreak began on Rodrigues Island in February 2006. The intensity of chikungunya fever outbreaks on Mauritius and Rodrigues Islands led us to explore the extent to which these outbreaks might have contributed to overall death rates…

"Chikungunya virus is transmitted to humans primarily by the bite of infected Aedes spp. mosquitoes. Aedes aegypti was effectively eliminated from the island of Mauritius during a malaria control campaign from 1949 through 1951. However, A. albopictus iswidely distributed on the island in rural and urban habitats; thus, A. albopictus may be the most likely vector for chikungunya virus. To determine whether a similar situation occurred in Mauritius, we compared expected number of deaths with observed number of deaths and estimated number of chikungunya cases from January through December 2006."[15]

The researchers noted *'excess deaths'* in relation to the normal death rate during the time the epidemic lasted. There were about 743 such deaths in Mauritius and the researchers also note that there were 200 deaths in Reunion Island.

WOMEN EMPOWERMENT

Mauritius has developed a National Gender Policy Framework to provide broad guidelines for the implementation of gender mainstreaming strategies. The Gender Unit within the Ministry of Women's Rights, Child Development and Family Welfare monitors the implementation of gender mainstreaming strategies for the empowerment of women and promotion of gender equality and equity. It conducts outreach activities at grassroots level through 15 Women Centres, the National Women's Council, the National Women Entrepreneur Council, the National Women Development Centre and some 1200 Women's Associations.

EQUAL OPPORTUNITIES ACT

The Equal Opportunities Bill was announced for introduction in Parliament in November 2008, incorporating all the different grounds of discrimination covered under sections 3 and 16 of the Constitution as well as age, pregnancy, mental and physical disability and sexual orientation in areas dealing with employment, education, the provision of accommodation, goods, services and other facilities, sports, the disposal of immovable property, admission to private clubs and premises open to members of the public. The Bill also provided for the establishment of an Equal Opportunities Commission and an Equal Opportunities Tribunal. It took a few years for the law to go through its proclamation stage and implementation.

FATHER GRÉGOIRE'S BIG CROWD

The traditional political parties were taken by surprise when Father Jocelyn Grégoire, president of the Fédération

---

15 Beesoon S, Funkhouser E, Kotea N, Spielman A, Robich RM. Chikungunya fever, Mauritius, *https://www.ncbi.nlm.nih.gov/pmc/articles/PMC2630048/* Accessed 6.3.2017. Emerg Infect Dis [serial on the Internet]. 2008 < wwwnc.cdc.gov/eid/article/14/2/07-1024.htm> **Accessed 30 March 2012.**

des Créoles Mauriciens (FCM) organized a Labour Day meeting that attracted a larger crowd than theirs. Advocating equal rights for the Creole community, Grégoire's popularity increased considerably during the years he spent within the group of leaders of the community. He emerged as the most influential one. Believed by his critics to be a fundamentalist, Grégoire, who has for a long time been a leading member of the *'charismatic'* groups of Catholics in Mauritius and the United States, displayed talents as an eloquent speaker at popular rallyes.

PRB REPORT GIVES WAGE HIKE: 36.8% AVERAGE

The long suspense that each time precedes the publication of the salaries report of the Public Research Report ended in 2008 with the document being released with a proposal of an average 36.5% wage hike. This was welcome news to public service employees, while a number of private sector companies did some adjustments to keep their wages attractive. Nevertheless, prices continued to rise and critics among the unions estimated that the salary gap between the top earners and those at the bottom of the hierarchy increased from 1:10.8 to 1:13.6.

HISTORIC FIRST MAURITIAN OLYMPIC MEDAL

At the 2008 Beijing Olympic Games Mauritius boxer Bruno Julie made history when he obtained thecountry's first Olympic medal. He was given a hero's welcome by a good crowd of friends and family and government officials. Mauritians sports, however, has not produced a large community of sports persons at this level mainly because sports is not part of the normal school activities in most of the country's schools, contrary countries like the U.S., Great Britain, Australia, New Zealand, Canada and other sports loving nations. Even the level of football, the national sport, has gone down dramatically. As already mentioned, Mauritius has one of the world's highest rates of diabetes and cardiovascular disease.

BHEENICK, LUTCHMEENARAIDOO: DIFFERENT VIEWS ON GOLD

Former Minister of Finance Vishnu Lutchmeenaraidoo, who had been involved in the *'economic miracle'* from 1983 to 1990, proposed that Mauritius converts in gradual stages a substantial chunk of its foreign exchange reserves into gold as the price of the metal had started rising abruptly in an atmosphere of financial uncertainty. Analysts worldwide indicated, on the basis of the global financial crisis, that it would continue rising for the coming years. This proposal was flatly rejected by former Finance Minister and later Governor of the Bank of Mauritius, Rundheersing Bheenick. In the following years, Lutchmeenaraidoo's proposal made sense and he alleged that Mauritius had missed the chance to make hefty profits that would have financed major projects including thousands of apartments according the government's project to build more public housing. He had calculated that in two years, the gain would have been about Rs 80 billion. Additionally, he suggested that government abolishes the tax on savings so that a sum of around Rs 10 billion would be brought back to Mauritius from deposits overseas.

HISTORIC FIRST: THE PRIVY COUNCIL SITS IN MAURITIUS

For the first time, the Privy Council decided to sit in Mauritius in its capacity as the ultimate court of appeal of the country. The first session was attended in September 2008 by Lord Hope of Graighead, Lord Mance, Lord Rodger of Earlsferry, Lord Caswell and Sir Paul Kennedy. This was not only a historic first, but also a decision that meant a substantial reduction of the costs of appeal for Mauritian citizens. The event was well received in the country.

First Mauritian to win the Nobel Prize

Mauritian and French writer Jean-Marie Gustave Le Clézio was awarded the Nobel Prize for literature. He was born in Mauritius from a French family who had migrated from Brittany in the 18th century. He proudly reaffirmed his Mauritian origins after receiving the prize. He had already won various prestigious literary prizes prior to the Nobel and had nearly half a century of career as a writer.

STIMULUS PACKAGE TO FACE CRISIS

A sum of 10.4 billion was made available during the year as *'stimulus package'* to private enterprise to be distributed over two years to help the country face the deepening global financial and economic crisis. Finance Minister Rama Sithanen stated that this was expected to positively affect the nation's economic growth by 1 to 1.5%. The measure was described by former Finance Minister and MMM spokesman Vishnu Lutchmeenaraidoo as *'too little, too late'* and the latter explained also that unemployment would continue to increase despite government's efforts.

2009

POLITICS : DEPARTURES

The year 2009 witnessed the dissolution of the Mouvement Républicain (MR) by its leader Rama Valayden. After some time, he started to focus on his professional activities as a lawyer and stayed away from active politics and the governmental alliance of which he had formed part under Navin Ramgoolam's leadership. On Sunday December 13, Labour Party Cabinet Minister James Burty David, member for the first constituency of Port-Louis, died suddenly during a function he was attending. He had been a loyal member of the party from his youth and was quite close to Prime Minister Ramgoolam. Previously, he had served under the latter's father, Sir Seewoosagur Ramgoolam.

In the MMM, deputy-leader and former MMM Cabinet Minister Jayen Cuttaree announced his retirement from politics. He had been elected seven times in succession in the constituency of Stanley/Rose Hill from 1982 to 2005. He wrote his memoirs in a book entitled *'Behind the Purple Curtain.'* Cuttaree had played key roles behind the scenes as his party engaged in discrete discussions leading to new alliances, especially with Labour.

TROMELIN: BOOLELL REAFFIRMS MAURITIUS SOVEREIGNTY

While Mauritius conceded to France a participation in the management of Tromelin Island in 2008, Mauritian Minister Arvin Boolell reaffirmed that the sovereignty of Mauritius on that territory had not been given away. The formal signature of the agreement was done in 2010, and in the meantime, Madagascar had reaffirmed its old claim on the island. Historically, though, the island belongs to Mauritius and had been recognised as such, as seen in the book, until the 1950s when France was allowed by Britain, then the colonial occupier of Mauritius and of its dependencies, to set up on the island a meteorological station for the World Meteorological Organisation (WMO). Mauritius traditionally used Tromelin as a source for guano, which played a major part in ensuring the prosperity of the Mauritian sugar industry.

2010

POLITICS: DEBATE OVER A LABOUR/MMM ALLIANCE

General elections were due that year and former President Cassam Uteem announced in the media (*Week-End*, January 3) that he was *'resolutely in favour of a Labour/ MMM alliance.'* Negotiations were held during a few months preceding the elections with *L'Express* director-general J.C. de l'Estrac involved by liaising between Ramgoolam and Bérenger and expressing his opinion editorially on the matter. The attempt failed after Ramgoolam decided to go to the polls in coalition with Pravind Jugnauth's MSM and the PMSD, which led him to be re-elected to power with a workable majority that soon proved to be more fragile than expected.

DIPLOMACY: GORDON BROWN RENEGES ON HIS PROMISE

The duplicity of British politicians in diplomacy, particularly in the case of the Chagos Archipelago, irritated the Navin Ramgoolam regime when his British counterpart Gordon Brown reneged on his word to the effect that London would not create a marine park that was projected around the archipelago. This promise was recalled again in January by the UK Chagos Support Association as *"a commitment which Gordon Brown had made to PM Ramgoolam at the Commonwealth Heads of Government Meeting in October 2009"* in an article on its website.[16]

MAURITIANS PERISH IN HAITI EARTHQUAKE

A major earthquake, one of history's worst, hits Haiti on January 12, causing the death of about 100,000 people. A Mauritian paramilitary police officer working with the United Nations in that island, Assistant Superintendant Bhojraj Luchmun was reported dead. He was given a funeral with full military honours on February 13 in Mauritius. Later it was reported that Cecilia Coreno, wife of Mauritian Patrick Hein, had also perished during the earthquake. Funds were raised in Mauritius to contribute to the recovery of Haiti after the earthquake.

16 January 2011 *Update*, < http://archive.chagossupport.org.uk/index.php/background/news-archive/january-2011-update/ Accessed 6.3.2010.

AFRICAN PEER MECHANISM REVIEW AND 'COALITION POLITICS'

The *African Peer Mechanism Review*, composed of the Nelson Mandela's wife Graça Machel (former President Samora Machel's spouse) and other personalities such as Professors Abebayo Adedeji and Babès and Domitille Mukantaganzwa, expressed, during the year, some concerns about Mauritius, namely: the way coalition politics is practised and the political elite turning itself into a kind of cartel that stifles the emergence of new leaders on the political scene and the use of coalition politics; the discriminatory treatment of of Rodrigues; and what they see as the risk for Mauritius to remain a few families-controlled democracy and economy and a country where corruption is rife:

«*The chemistry that exists between the country's political, ethnic and economic driving forces tends towards complicity and self-protection. Most importantly, however, this insularity has seen a trend develop whereby a few families control the island's economic and democratic resources... There is broad consensus at the national level that corruption still affects a number of key democratic institutions... as well as key institutions in the socio-economic sectors... Commonly the most likely occasion for corrupt practices, during the interface between the public and the private sectors, is in the awarding of public contracts However, POCA's scope for intervention is very limited in respect of corruption in the private sector...*"

"*The absence of a legal framework covering the financial activities of political parties as well as the corrupt behaviour of certain candidates are both elements that damage the very foundation of the Mauritian integrity system. Corruption in the realm of politicalfinance generally takes many forms, ranging from vote-buying and the use of illicit funds to the sale of appointments and the abuse of state resources. As the source of much of the money that funds political corruption, the corporate sector has a vital role to play in ending this abuse of power. In Mauritius, the private sector has taken*

the lead in promoting ethical standards and in calling on all those who wish to donate to political parties to record in their accounts the amounts given and the beneficiaries nominated. However, because political parties are not obliged to publish their accounts or to say how much they receive from the private sector, it is difficult to talk meaningfully about transparency in the financing of political

parties in Mauritius."[17].

vThe displacement, by the government, of the planters for the project earmarked and already financed with public funds for the Chinese Jinfei corporation to set up an industrial-residential complex at Terre Rouge, led to a long hunger strike by those planters. It lasted 30 days and ended after the government appointed a committee that comprised Alain Noel and Jayraj Ramkisson of the Food and Agricultural Research Council. The committee recommended Rs 500,000 in moral damages to be paid to each of the 28 planters and Rs 100,00 per year over 9 years. The governmment refused at first to publish the report and a new hunger strike lasting 19 days ended in the government publishing the report and making new proposals to the planters. In July 2012, it was claimed by the planters that they were given much inferior terms than initially promised to them, for instance a lease of 19 years in lieu of 65 years. Meanwhile, the government has invested heavily in infrastructure related to the Jinfei project described by Finance Minister Rama Sithanen as follows in his 2009 Budget Speech:

«*The dream of making of Mauritius a business gateway to Africa for countries like China and India is now a reality. The Jin Fei project, besides being the largest FDI our country has ever attracted, epito- mizes the height that Mauritius has attained as a bridge between Asia and Africa.*»[18]

As of 2017, the project has never materialised or been revived and revamped as promised by the new minister of Finance elected in 2014.

DEATH OF VICE-PRESIDENT CHETTIAR

Vice-President of the Republic Angidi Chettiar on September 15 at the age of 82. He was later replaced by Mrs. Monique Oshan-Bellepeau, the first woman to accede to this position.

2011-2012

The period 2011-2012 has been dominated, on the political front, by the resignation of President Anerood Jutnauth in March 2012, an event that had been preceded by clashes between his former party led by his son Pravind Jugnauth over the sale of the Medpoint Clinic belonging to the latter's sister and brother-in-law. In April, the MSM and the MMM formed an opposition to the Labour-PMSD government and it was named the Remake 2000, after the former MSM-MMM alliance that had won the 2000 general election.

17 *African Peer Mechanism Report, Republic of Mauritius*,. Country Report No, 13, July 2010.
18 *Budget Speech 18 November 2009 (Budget 2010),* **Government of Mauritius web portal,** <http://mof.govmu.org/English/Documents/Budget%202010/Budget%20Speech.pdf> **Accessed 3 March 2017.**

The water crisis: one of the worst of national history

First, there was a major drought, and a wave of panic swept the island as the nation's main reservoir, Mare-aux-Vacoas, nearly dried up. In 2009, the Mauritius Meteorological Services had produced a paper warning the country that the effects of the global climate change would result in an annual reduction of 8% of the annual rainfall, among other consequences. It was also observed that the usually heavy annual summer rainfall tended to come in December, late by at least two months.[19] In 2010-2012, those predictions more than materialised: there was almost no rainfall for months and the summer rains had not come.

The met report also stressed that climate change was causing disturbances that would make weather less predictable due to this kind of change in the usual weather patterns that had been observed over a long historical period.

The government had to take drastic measures to reduce consumption by severe daily cuts in the supply to consumers as the reservoirs continued to dry up. River water was pumped and treated in various parts of the island to add to improve supply and stringent regulations were passed interdicting the use of water for non-essential activities like car wash and watering of lawns. By mid-2012, the situation had eased substantially, but the authorities maintained a number of restrictive measures on supply and were ready to go back and proclaim emergency should the drought return. The news of the drought, like all other news about any event that could affect the national economy, was circulated worldwide by companies like Reuters and Bloomberg and other financial and economic media, warning the markets of the expected fall in the agricultural production of the island, especially sugar. One Bloomberg headline in January 2011 ran, «*Mauritius's 2011 sugar crop is unlikely to recover from drought.*»[20]

The authorities, though, managed well the water crisis with such additional intiatives like linking the Mare Longue reservoir to Mare-Aux-Vacoas several kilometres away.

THE MEDPOINT CLINIC 'AFFAIR'

President Aneerood Jugnauth and his son Finance Minister Pravind Jugnauth as well as Cabinet Minister Mrs. Maya Hanoomanjee, another member of their family have vigorously denied any wrongdoing in a decision taken by the Labour/MSM/PMSD government to purchase a clinic associated with their family. The two ministers were arrested by ICAC and released on bail for having allegedly participated in the deal despite conflicting interests as alleged. Both have explained that the decision was taken by the government even before they entered Parliament and government in May 2010 and that Pravind Jugnauth abstained from taking part in the Cabinet decision at its meeting during which it gave its final approval to the deal.

The clinic had been purchased for the purpose of turning it into a geriatric hospital and there were several allegations by MMM and Opposition Leader Paul Bérenger that the specifications in the government tender had been made to fit the clinic. Bérenger was to stop entirely attacking the MSM after he struck a deal with that party for an alliance with the MMM in view of the next general elections. He claimed to have been satisfied with the MSM leader's explanation that it was the government prior to the general election of 2005 that had decided to buy the clinic and not the new government which Pravind Jugnauth and Mrs. Hanoomanjee joined in May 2010. The Medpoint affair, however, became also a platform for the opposition and the President of the Republic Jugnauth, both believing that the Labour government was pulling the strings behind the scenes to attack the MSM. Bérenger has several times accused ICAC of acting on behalf of the government as a '*tool*' to attack its adversaries and Bérenger was himself interrogated by the police after he accused Ramgoolam of being responsible for a second evaluation of the clinic, prior to its sale, upwards to Rs 144 million.

As of July 2012, Pravind Jugnauth had obtained from the Court permission to use as evidence the highly confidential Cabinet minutes of proceedings regarding the Medpoint deal. He was waiting to prove in Court, on the basis of the Cabinet minutes his non-participation in the negotiations that led to government's decision to acquire Medpoint.

Looming threats for the economy from global crisis

---

[19] *Climate Change Imnpacts on Mauritius*, Mauritius Meteorological Services, Government of Mauritius, March 2009. http://31.222.186.27/fileadmin/multimedia_francais/centre_medias/dossiers_techniques/downloads/200903_Climate_Change_impacts_on_Mauritius.pdf Accessed 5.3.2017
[20] *Mauritius Beats Sugar Forecast, Warns on 2011 Harvest* <www.bloomberg.com> 10 January 2011.

While Mauritius had first seemed resilient to the shocks that the global financial and economic crisis generated across the planet, by the end of 2010 to mid-2012, different economic projections have been made as to the severity of the expected economic slowdown in Mauritius. Positive but lower economic growth rates were being anticipated and this was expected to put the Mauritian economy in an increasingly difficult situation according to those predictions, if the global context continued to worsen. One analysis by the Axys Group for 2012 was on the low side of those predictions, while mentioning them all:

"EXECUTIVE SUMMARY - BRACING FOR ANOTHER STORM

"While the Mauritian economy has been resilient thus far, the flip-flops in select Government policies have sent mixed signals to both the private sector and potential investors. Nonetheless, the economy grew at an estimated 4% in 2011 driven by a resurgent textile industry, and a strong performance by the financial sector. A year ago we had believed that the worst was behind; however, the issues surrounding the unsustainable levels of sovereign debt in Europe have now induced a localised mild recession. This will hurt demand and coupled with a weak EUR, we expect stagnation across a few sectors. Consequently, AXYS continues to adopt a conservative stance and projects a GDP growth rate of 3.4%. Our expectations are below that Statistics Mauritius' 4% and the IMF's 3.7% respective forecasts.

"2012 IN PERSPECTIVE

"While export manufacturing did recover in 2011, we expect a slow down for receipts from Europe-facing exports, although US-facing exports should show signs of improvement. The absence of major projects coupled with government-driven PSIP (Public Sector Investment Programme) delays will lead to a lethargic year for construction. On the Real-Estate front, we expect rentals to face downwards pressures in the coming years given the completion of several new malls, business parks, and residences. On the plus side, we believe the financial sector will become Mauritius' primary growth engine during 2012. Tourism will continue to struggle due to excess room capacity on the island; while the Sugar industry could see improved yields at adequate rates; although drought conditions and a weak EUR represent a threat.

"The current account deficit should remain under 9% of GDP increasing slightly due to lower export revenue; however with inflation set to drop under 5%, we would expect cuts in the Key Repo Rate during the upcoming months to alleviate the interest burden on leveraged enterprises. AXYS expects unemployment – whichremains a non-factor – to be contained at about 8%." [21]

2012: Overhauling the Constitution and political system

The most important event of 2012, as of 27 August 2012, was the announcement, on that date, by Prime Minister Navin Ramgoolam, following consultations with Leader of the Opposition Paul Bérenger and the representatives of the Electoral Commission and the Electoral Supervisory Commission of upcoming constitutional and electoral reforms.

Such reforms have been proposed and discussed over several years. There were various select committees of the National Assembly as well as constitutional experts who studied the political system of Mauritius and proposed reports on the electoral system, particularly proportional representation, the political funding of political parties and the judicial system.

There was also a select committee on fraud and corruption. The various reports submitted have been commented in detail over the years and public participation had been included, especially regarding proposed constitutional reforms. Those reports have been submitted to the National Assembly.

The select committee that studied proportional representation[22] was appointed in the wake of the Sachs commission on electoral reform.[23] The Sachs Commission was composed of Justice Albie Sachs, member of the South African Constitutional Court as Chairman, and B.B. Tandon, Election Commissioner of India and Robert Ahnee, a former Judge of the Supreme Court of Mauritius, as members. The Sachs Commission studied not just proportional representation, but looked at a series of measures intended to make elections more healthy, that is, devoid of the hate speech that characterises ethnic politics, particularly during election campaigns in Mauritius, and provide a basis to put an end to the absence of control on the funding of political parties, which appears to be among the main sources of corruption among the political establishment.

Initiated by the MMM within the MSM-MMM government elected to power in 2000, the report was referred to as a «*very good report*» on 22 June 2010[24] and other occasions by Navin Ramgoolam announcing his intention to

---

21 **The Mauritian Economy: 2012 Outlook,** Axys Group, Bhavik Desai, Vikash Tulsi**das, February** 2012 <http://www.axys-group.com/media/8762/mauritius_2012.02.21f.pdf> Accessed 6 March 2017.

22 *Report on Proportional Representation*, Mauritius National Assembly, 2002.

23 *Commission on Constitutional and Electoral Reform* 2001\2002, better known as the "Sachs" Commission. the funding of political parties, which appears to be among the main sources of corruption among the political establishment.

24 Navin Ramgoolam, stated, during Prime Minister's Question Time: *"When he* (Paul Bérenger) *was Prime Minister and was allied with the MSM, they did not manage to agree, although they had a very good report by Sachs and there were two committees. We also have some difficulties. But, I will certainly try to move this agenda forward."* Hansard, Mauritius Legislative Assembly, http://mauritiusassembly.govmu.org/English/hansard/Documents/2010/hansardsecd410.pdf Accessed 6.3.2017

propose major electoral and constitutional changes in the shortest possible delay.[25] The Sachs report was also the starting point for the appointment of a select committee of the National Assembly on the funding of political parties that submitted a report in 2004[26] and this topic could also form part of the changes announced by Ramgoolam.

Two more reports on constitutional and electoral reforms were produced, one in December 2011 by European constitutional experts Guy Carcassonne, Vernon Bogdanor and Pere Vilanova, at the request of Ramgoolam,[27] another one in January 2012 by former Finance Minister Rama Sithanen.[28] As seen also earlier in this book, there was the issue of the Best Loser System raised in the Supreme Court in Mauritius and before the Privy Council by Resistans ek Alternativ, where the focus was to eliminate the legal and constitutional obligation for candidates to declare their ethnic group when standing for elections.

The main thrust of the various reports has been, in fact, to attenuate, if not eliminate the ethnic and racial tensions that electoral campaigns raise, sometimes to an extremely high pitch, and which seems to havepolluted the entire nation. Another priority has been to make the practice of politics more transparent and ethical and root out corruption. There is another crucial question: revamp the entire political system to create a Second Republic. In 2012, newspapers widely reported that in this context, Ramgoolam and Bérenger had discussed a sharing of power between their respective parties, the first named being due to be appointed President of the Republic with increased powers and the MMM leader as the new Prime Minister, in the context of an new Labour/MMM coalition government. Ultimate confirmation of those reports was still pending as of 30 July, 2012 and would resurface later. What seemed to be still lacking was an initiative to teach the nation and its children their true national history, which, as the research leading to this book has demonstrated, unites more than it divides the population.

FORMER PRESIDENT JUGNAUTH ENTERS THE POLITICAL ARENA

The second half of 2012 was quite a busy time of the year on the political front. It was going to be the first test in a new political configuration for the Labour-PMSD alliance in power led by Navin Ramgoolam as well as for the main opposition parties, regrouped into a new MSM-MMM alliance led by the former President of the Republic who had resigned at the invitation of MMM leader Paul Bérenger *'to save the country',* as both of them put it.

The first major electoral test for the new alliance as well as for Ramgoolam' was to take place on December 9, 2012 at the municipal elections in the five towns of the island. Ramgoolam asked for a vote of confidence from the inhabitants of the municipal areas, representing around half of the population, in his government, at a public meeting in Curepipe, five days ahead of the elections. The MSM-MMM alliance,, led by the tandem Anerood Jugnauth-Paul Bérenger, denounced forcefully multiple affairs ("*scandals*") that made headlines in the media, as well as the '*mismanagement*' of the urban areas by the Ramgoolam regime.

A week prior to the municipal elections, 130 villages had elected 1,170 councillors, but while many groups and individuals showed some kind of affinity with the main national parties or alliances, several others were of unspecified or ambiguous political political affiliation at national level. Both the government and the Remake 2000 claimed they disposed of a majority in the rural areas following the results'

The government had counted on its national budget for 2013 presented in November 9, 2012, with the following economic indicators: Real GDP growth rates of 4% for 2013 against 3.4% for 2012; an unemployment rate of 8.0% for both years; an inflation rate of 6.0 for 2013 against 4.1% for 2012; a budget deficit of 2.2 and 2.5% of GDP for 2013 and 2012 respectively, while predicting a public sector debt that would decrease from 54.2% to 53.7%. Promises of a better economic situation from the government were strongly criticised by the Remake 2000 during the two successive electoral campaigns, the MSM-MMM alliance telling the population that the predicted growth of the economy was far from realistic and that the budget would not tackle positively the problems of unemployment and poverty.

The verdict of the urban electorate was as mixed as that of the rural voters. The municipal elections were won, overall, by the MMM-MSM alliance in three out of the five towns (Port Louis, Beau Bassin-Rose Hill and Quatre Bornes). Labour won in Vacoas-Phoenix. In Curepipe, fourteen of the fifteen seats were shared equally (7-7) between the Labour-PMSD and MMM-MSM alliances. However, the control of the municipality went to the gov-

---
25 Hansard, 27 July 2012; see also *Le Mauricien* and *L'Express* online, 28 July 2012.
26 Select Committee on the Funding of the Political Parties, Mauritius National Assembly 2
27 *Rapport à Monsieur le Premier Ministre sur la réforme électorale,* 11 December 2012.
28 *Initiative Citoyenne pour une réforme électorale réalisable à Maurice,* January 2012.

ernment alliance when the MMSD of Eric Guimbeau, which had one of its candidates elected, decided to support the Labour-PMSD alliance.

This finally gave three towns to the opposition and two to the government. From 2012, which marked a revival of the parliamentary and national opposition as it was joined by the MSM led by both Pravind Jugnauth, and its former leader Sir Anerood Jugnauth. They resigned from, respectively, the Ramgoolam Cabinet and the office of president of the Republic. They raised the issues of *'government by cliques'* and nepotism as main causes of a string of *'affairs'*, lack of transparency, corruption and *'scandals'* of all sorts and undemocratic practices.

The MSM-MMM alliance, called Remake 2000, prepared itself for the next general elections with Sir Anerood Jugnauth and Paul Bérenger sharing power equally in government if the opposition were to win at the poll.

Prior to the municipal elections, Navin Ramgoolam, in November, commenting on Budget 2012, had expressed confidence that he was supported by a majority of the electorate and had predicted an economic renaissance of the country in the next two years, with considerable development in, among other sectors, an ocean-based economy yet to come.

He held a press conference after the municipal elections to claim that the government had performed better than the MMM-MSM alliance and that overall, considering both the municipal and rural elections, the Labour-PMSD alliance was supported by a majority of the electorate. He then started a campaign based on his claim, expressed during a press statement he made on Saturday 19 September 2012, that the MMM's popularity in the electorate was declining *"because of its alliance with the MSM."*

Heads of State of Mauritius from Independence to 2017

12 March 1968 to 12 March 1992: Queen Elisabeth II, Queen of Mauritius and its Dependencies

Representing the Queen:

- Sir John Shaw Rennie (12 March-3 September 1968)
- Sir Leonard Williams (3 September 1968- 27-December 1972)
- Sir Raman Osman (27 December 1972-31 October 1977)
- Sir Henry Garrioch (31 October 1977-26 April 1979)
- Sir Dayendranath Burrenchobay (26 April 1979-28 December 1983)
- Sir Seewoosagur Ramgoolam (28 December 1983-15 December 1985)
- Sir Cassam Moolan (15 December 1985-17 January 1986 - Acting)
- Sir Veerasamy Ringadoo (17 January 1986-12 March 1972)

Presidents of the Republic of Mauritius:

- Sir Veerasamy Ringadoo 1992 to 1992
- Cassam Uteem 1992 to 2002
- Karl Offman 2002-2003
- Sir Anerood Jugnauth 2003-2012
- Kailash Purryag 2012-2015
- Ameenah Gurib-Fakim 2015-

Left to right, Presidents Sir Veerasamy Ringadoo, Cassam Uteem, Karl Offman, Sir Aneerood Jugnauth, Kailash Purryag, and Ameenah Gurib-Fakim (2015-)

Left to right, former Prime Ministers Sir Seewoosagur Ramgoolam, Sir Anerood Jugnauth, Dr. Navin Ramgoolam, Paul Bérenger, Pravind Jugnauth (20017-)

Chapter 57

2013-2017
The demise of an unpopular Labour/PMSD regime
and a serious democratic deficit yet to be corrected in 2017

"All democracies are systems in which citizens freely make political decisions by majority rule. In the words of American essayist E.B. White: "Democracy is the recurrent suspicion that more than half the people are right more than half the time." But majority rule, by itself, is not automatically democratic. No one, for example, would call a system fair or just that permitted 51 percent of the population to oppress the remaining 49 percent in the name of the majority. In a democratic society, majority rule must be coupled with guarantees of individual human rights that, in turn, serve to protect the rights of minorities and dissenters -- whether ethnic, religious or simply the losers in political debate. The rights of minorities do not depend on the good will of the majority and cannot be eliminated by majority vote. The rights of minorities are protected because democratic laws and institutions protect the rights of all citizens."[1]

Mauritius is a perfect illustration of the half-half national political divide with oppositions getting most of the time over 40% of the national vote and sometimes nearly that in case of a massive victory giving majorities of seats of two thirds or three quarters, while the winning party gets with difficulty 50% of the votes. In recent years, the results have confirmed this observation:

% and no. of seats obtained by winning and runner-up parties 2000-2014					
Election year	Winner	Runner-up	Winner	No. of seats	Runner-up	No. of seats
2000	51.7	36.6	51.7	54	36.6	6
2005	48.8	42.6	48.8	42	42.6	24
2010	49.69	42.01	49.69	45	42.01	20
2014	49.83	38.51	49.83	51	38.51	16
	Average		50.005		39.93	

It is clear that in the 21st century, the normal trend is for five out of ten voters choose a government and four out of ten are behind the constitutional and legal opposition to check the actions of the government and ensure the respect of democratic norms. Yet, governments have tended to use massive majorities of three quarters and two thirds without searching a consensus where the support of and useful amendments accepted from the opposition could be obtained on proposed laws that change the Constitution fundamentally, either before or after the 2014 general election - in reality, this undemocratic practice has occurred since the independence of the country in 1968. In the 21st century, however, nations are increasingly held to account worldwide on their degree of respect for democratic norms and, in this respect, there are numerous challenges to issues as serious in Mauritius like the abuse of ethnic politics, an over-massive male representation to the detriment of women, opaque political funding, unfairness of representation of 40% of the electorate and abuse mainly of the three quarters majority for changing fundamental provisions like the independence of essential conscitutional checks and balances on the executive.[2]

The severe under-representation of women in the Mauritius National Assembly was best summed up following the December 2014 general election as follows:

"Lepep won 47 seats, PTr/MMM Alliance lost all seats in 11 constituencies including the constituency of former Prime Minister, Dr. Navin Ramgoolam, Triolet-Pamplemousses. They won only 13 seats on a total of 60 in the other nine constituencies. Thus all the 12 women candidates fielded by the PTr/MMM Alliance hold no place in Parliament. Eight of the

---

[1] Read more: http://iipdigital.usembassy.gov/st/en

lish/article/2007/11/20071126192634eaifas0.5588953.html#ixzz4abnF5jyv

[2] These are observations by the author of this book based on multiple sources like the several reports for electoral reform already mentioned in this book, particularly since the beginning of the 21st century and organisations like EISA *(Electoral Institute for Sustainable Democracy in Africa)*.

nine female candidates fielded by Lepep Alliance were elected.

Out of 15 SADC countries, Mauritius has regressed in its ranking for the percentage of women in parliament. The country was at 10th place with 19% women parliamentarians, but has now dropped to 12th position with a mere 13% women in parliament (eight women out of 60 parliamentarians) However, on Saturday 13 December the percentage worsened when the seven best losers were announced. Women make up only 12% women in parliament (eight women out of 69 National Assembly seats). Mauritius is now among the five Southern African countries with the lowest percentage of women in parliament-Malawi, Zambia, DRC and Botswana."[3]

Another objective observation needs to be made here: the 21st century in Mauritius has also been dominated by an evil that was considered in the United States in the 19th century as *'government by cliques'*.[4] It was to be the main cause of the downfall of the Navin Ramgoolam government and become again a major issue after he lost the 2014 election, if one takes into account public opinion as expressed massively on the subject in the media, in the streets and on social media platforms.

One of the worst problems of the country and the cause of most major problems and issues, was, from around the year 2005 onward, the installation of a government of cliques that automatically produced undemocratic practices of all sorts including corruption, nepotism, multiple cases of abuse of power like literally domesticating a supposedly independent police force under the Constitution that indulged, at the request of political leaders, in the arbitrary arrest of opponents under *'provisional charges'*, a method common in Mauritius that has been internationally condemned by human rights watch organizations. Significant resistance to such abuses have been put up by the judiciary, rights groups and the Director of Public Prosecution (DPP) and even internationally and by the UK government.

The UK has raised concerns as follows at the UN International Rights Council in its guide updated to 3 June 2016 for British people and businesses seeking to do business in Mauritius:

"You should be aware that Mauritius operates a pre charge system called the 'Provisional Charge'. The police can arrest and imprison an individual on a provisional charge until investigations are completed. It can take over a year for the courts to decide if there is enough evidence for a full charge. The UK government has raised its concerns about the use of the provisional charge including at the UN International Human Rights Council in 2014."[5]

No reform had yet been as of March 2017 undertaken regarding provisional charges despite their still being frequently used against political dissent, foreign investors and local citizens. One would expect radical reform to change this law before the next general election in 2019 as such reform was strongly committed to by the government in power since 2014.

Historically, Mauritius has not invented the wheel. But its system of government, increasingly distancing itself from the Westminster model, has been accompanied over the years and decades, by a nearly complete centralization of government, with regional administrations losing all independence from Government House in Port-Louis.

Another issue is worth noting. There has been a spectacular rise in protests in recent years and in several localities, against public projects that people fear will threaten seriously their environment and even their properties and their lives. Moreover the authorities have been dragging their feet regarding public consultations over such projects and have maintained a system of public notices in the English language that are intelligible to inhabitants especially of the poorest localities.

2013[6]

The year 2013 saw an increase in impopularity of Prime Minister Navin Ramgoolam's Labour-PMSD government. In January, a new *'affair'* started with the revelation concerning the PM's secret sentimental relation with a wom-

---

3 Virahsawmy, Loga, in *Le Mauricien*, 17 December 2014 for the *Gender Link News Service*, http://www.lemauricien.com/article/mauritius-women-and-winds-political-change Accessed 7.3.2017.
4 American historians know that this was the practice in the 19th century in the United States as denounced by the following extract from an editorial piece on 22 May 1861 in *The True New Delta* newspaper: *"If any cause more powerfully than all others contributed to reduce this great country to be the mere apanage of sectional cliques, it was the infamous, prescriptive practice of taking the adherents of one party exclusively to administer national affairs..."*
5 UK Government, *Guidance Doing business in Mauritius: Mauritius trade and export guide* Updated 3 June 2016 https://www.gov.uk/government/publications/exporting-to-mauritius/doing-business-in-mauritius-mauritius-trade-and-export-guide#challenges-to-doing-business-in-mauritius Accessed 7.3.2017
6 Henceforth, unless otherwise stated, most of the events reported can be checked in the media records at the National Library of Mauritius.

an, with the latter seeing a gagging order in the Supreme Court against the press interdicting the media from any mention of the matter. She eventually lost and the media started to make serious allegations regarding business and intimate dealings that allegedly conflicts of interest at the level of government decision-making.

She was found by the media to have benefited from very profitable government contracts at the country's international airport. Ramgoolam blasted the media and the MMM-Opposition, alleging *'mud-slinging'*. The arrest of the leader of the MSM, Pravind Jugnauth, by the police in January for having alleged a cover-up regarding the alleged criminal sexual behaviour of a staff member of a government organization said to be a political agent, caused an uproar in the country, particularly from the MSM-MMM alliance.

However, despite all this, the country was deeply shocked by the news announced by MMM leader Paul Bérenger that he was suffering from throat cancer. He said he had made it his duty to go public as a matter of principle regarding the illness of public figures entrusted by the electorate to represent them in Parliament. Already a legendary historical figure despite the fact that his career was, as seen in this book, a chequered one, marked not just by major achievements, but also a number of mistakes, there was a wave of support for his quick recovery among his supporters and opponents. He entrusted the leadership of the MMM to Alan Ganoo for the time he would fight for his life at a specialised hospital for cancer treatment in Paris.

There was yet another political arrest by the police but the Director of Public Prosecutions Satyajit Boolell had it quashed: it was that of a MSM militant, Yogi Sawminaden, accused of having taken photos of the female friend of the Prime Minister. She later lodged the 'gagging order'case before the Supreme Court. Sawminaden's house had been throroughly searched by the police and two mobile phones seized in connection with the photos he had taken during the municipal election campaign in December when the woman was near a voting centre in Vacoas-Phoenix.

As months went by, the *"Soornack affair"*, until then a secret sentimental venture of the PM, grew in proportion as when it was found out that her business partner Rakesh Gooljaury had obtained a 600-million-rupee loan from the government controlled insurance company, the SICOM, to construct a multi-storeyed building. Gooljaury, a former MSM agent, had joined Labour (he was yet to turn his coat again to get back into the MSM fold when that party seized power in 2014, a common occurrence in politics in Mauritius where such people form clusters or cliques around the head of government). The Soornack/Gooljaury affairs actuelly revealed a lot regarding the nature of relations between political leaders with the business community. In fact both of those persons had grown from rags to riches with a short time after entering the primeministerial inner circle.

From discrete and rare in the past, this type of relationship between money and power became henceforth exposed to the knowledge of the general public. As a result, public opinion turned in favour of inceeased severity in anti-corruption legislation, albeit the fact that governments come and go without implementing various promises regarding political financing. This issue was handed over to the Lepep alliance that won the general elections and came to power in 2014. As of 2017, no radical reform was being implemented and the perception of corruption index by Transparency International increased from 53 in 2015 to 54 points in 2016 and Mauritius ranked 50th worldwide. Mauritius continued to suffer from corruption up to 2017 with the following observation updated to 6 June 2016, recorded in consultation with anti-corruption executives in Mauritius and internationally:

"Corruption in Mauritius is low by regional standards but graft and nepotism nevertheless remain concerns and are a source of public frustration. The arrest of the former prime minister in February 2015 on money-laundering charges has reinforced the perception that corruption exists at the highest political levels. Also in 2015, a senior minister resigned when he was found guilty of conflict of interest in a government procurement contract, and the appeal of that judgment is ongoing. More recently, in March 2016 a minister of the current government stepped down as a result of allegations of bribery." [7]

A fundamental issue raised at the U.N. on ethnicity and politics

Mauritius is faced, year in, year out, with ethnicity matters driven mainly by a political establishment that is heavily reliant on ethnic identity as a driving force for political activism. However, there has been a rising tide of opposition to the exploitation of ethnicity and, particularly, its role as the basis of appointment of 'best losers' following a general election to redress ethnic representation in the National Assembly. A large number of citizens and some political forces argue that the ethnicity issue should be removed from the constitutional procedure for appointing best losers as it hinders the healing process of nation-building following independence which was obtained during

[7] State Department's Office of Investment Affairs, latest published 6 June 2016.

agitated times during where there were ethnic riots. The 1999 racial riots had shown that ethnicity remained an explosive issue.

A relatively small political movement, Resistans ek Alternativ failed to convince the Supreme Court to order the constitutionsl provision that requires mandatorily, under Schedule 1 of the Mauritius Constitution, that candidates at general elections disclose their ethnic identity.

The group, which regards this requirement as damaging the efforts to achieve strong national unity, appealed to the Human Rights Committee of the United Nations arguing that Mauritius was in violation of the International Covenant on Civil and Political Rights. Resistans ek Alternative obtained a favourable judgment on January 13, 2013.[8] Excerpts from the decision of the Committee:

"The Committee observes that in the absence of any classification, a candidate is effectively barred from standing for general elections. It notes the State party's argument that the category General Population is the residual category comprising those who neither are Hindus, Muslims or Sino-Mauritians. According to the First Schedule to the Constitution, the additional eight seats under the Best Loser System are allocated giving regard to the "appropriate community", with reliance on population figures of the 1972 census. However, the Committee notes that community affiliation has not been the subject of a census since 1972.

"The Committee therefore finds, taking into account the State party's failure to provide an adequate justification in this regard and without expressing a view as to the appropriate form of the State party's or any other electoral system, that the continued maintenance of the requirement of mandatory classification of a candidate for general elections without the corresponding updated figures of the community affiliation of the population in general would appear to be arbitrary and therefore violates article 25 (b) of the Covenant... the Committee wishes to receive from the State party, within 180 days, information about the measures taken to give effect to the Committee's Views. The State party is also requested to publish the Committee's Views and to have them widely disseminated in the official languages of the State party."

That was a historic first that forced Mauritius to try reconcile its position to conform with the above decision. The only measure that was taken was a temporary constitutional provision by which candidates were allowed by the outgoing Labour government and the MMM not to decline their ethnic identity based on what the Constitution describes on *'way of life.'* With the inter-ethnic mix continues to be on the rise, it is a fact that it is increasingly difficult to respond to a constitutional provision that arbitrarily divides Mauritians into religious groups considered as racial identities, namely Hindus and Muslims, a third one being an ethnic group of Sino-Mauritians plus afourth group, an identity 'invented' for constitutional purposes that defines a fourth ethnic group as being all people who belong to none of of those two religions and cannot be defined as Sino-Mauritians. In 2017, Mauritius had not yet come up with either an updated census of ethnic identities or a satisfactory solution to its violations of the International Covenant on Civil and Political Rights. However, whatever critics may say, the ethnic identities are derived from the government's Statistics Mauritius figures of the official census regarding religion. The latest figures (2011 census) gave the following as edited and summarized by the author of this book:

2011 Census of resident population of Mauritius: Religions
Source: Statistics Mauritius

Responses collected by census officers	No. of Followers	%
NO RELIGION	8,772	0.71%
TOTAL CHINESE (Buddhist, 'Chinese', 'Other')	5,275	0.43%
TOTAL CHRISTIANS (21 groups, 'Other')	404,553	32.70%
HINDUS	479,812	38.80%
MARATHIS	20,670	1.67%
TAMIL	72,036	5.82%
TELEGU	27809	2.25%
MUSLIMS (3 GROUPS, 'OTHER')	213,969	17.30%
BAHAI	645	0.05%
JEWISH	43	0.00%
OTHER RELIGIONS	1,835	0.15%
NOT STATED	1,398	0.11%
TOTAL RESPONSES	1,236,817	99.99%

---

[8] Human Rights Committee, Communication No. 1744/2007. *"Views adopted by the Committee at its 105th session (9–27 July 2012",* **published on January 13, 2013.**

The deadly floods of 2013

Heavy rainfall spells linked to climate change have become a nightmare Mauritius in the second decade 21st century. Mauritius has always had to grapple with floods since the earliest times of ciolonization. There have always been several regions of the island prone to flooding. However, during the second half of the 20th century, much of the island has been covered with concrete and asphalt and wetlands protecting the coastal regions have disappeared. A report[9] has pinpointed this serious problem as follows:

"The location of Mauritius Island in the Indian Ocean and its small size makes it particularly vulnerable to natural disasters such as tsunamis, flooding and storm surges. Mauritius supports some natural defences in the form of extensive areas of ecologically significant sub-tidal and tidal wetlands, comprising salt marshes, estuaries and mangroves. Two of these coastal wetlands are RAMSAR listed sites, namely Rivulet Terre Rouge Estuary Bird Sanctuary (RTREBS) and Blue Bay Marine Park while a third wetland, Mare Sarcelle, is nationally recognized as a nature reserve park. Coastal wetlands support economic activities such as commercial and recreational fishing and act as buffers against storm surges while protecting the lagoon against sediment and nutrient contamination. These ecosystems and their associated benefits are being threatened by the effects of land-based urbanization, intensive coastal development, storm water and agricultural runoff effluent, and industrial discharges. Marine activities can also have adverse effects (e.g. dredging, oil spills, sea dumping, etc)."

In addition to the receding wetlands, there is a problem of disappearing natural and artificial water courses that drain the island from excessive rainfall, particularly phenomenal amounts of water that runoff the mountains and hills or inland wetland areas, even in towns and villages, that have been blocked off by concrete structures.

Flash floods[10] made of climate change a tragic reality in Mauritius during torrential rains, as had been feared by the meteorological services since the beginning of the 21st century when they also expressed the opinion that several parts of the island's coastal areas would risk being more severely eroded than ever and submerged.[11] One of the worst flash floods to occur was on Wednesday February 13 when heavy rains caused the accumulation of knee-deep water on the Port-Louis Waterfront region, invading that part of the north-south motorway. Authorities ordered all business to stop that day. But that was a first alert and it was already understood, as noted by the media,[12] that the flash flood was caused by choked drains, including a major one, the Ruisseau du Pouce.

On Saturday March 30, another severe occurrence of flash flooding took the lives of eleven people. Six of the victims were caught up by huge amounts of water rushing into two pedestrian tunnels under the motorway and two others in an underground car park. The Mauritius Meteorological Services announced that 152 mm of rain had poured on the capital city in less than one hour. Prime Minister Navin Ramgoolam declared a day of mourning on April 1. The City was literally paralyzed.

In the aftermath of this tragic event, climate change became a major issue and still is. There was much public, media and political furor over the lack of vision in land use and planning that was in fact the root cause of an absence of adequate drainage facilities whereas flash floods had long been predicted official reports submitted by Mauritius over the years to the Earth summits and other international climate chage conferences.

Corruption, a "cultural" trait - dixit lawyer Parvesh Lallah

The government embarked on yet another *'mega-project'* that would, like the white elephants of Jinfei and Neotown projects, mentioned previously in this book, never be achieved and cause public uproar over phenomenal amounts of taxpayers' money wasted or being allegedly involved in widely perceived shady deals over public contracts. The regime even intensified the practice of allocation of public contracts outside the public tendering process. Such behaviour has systematically, over the years, increased, to date, the perception of corruption in Mauritius as already mentioned.

Lawyer Parvesh Lallah wrote in *Le Mauricien* daily newspaper an article on July 9, 2012, entitled, *"ICAC: Ten years on – why we are still the champions of fraud and corruption"* where he observed,

"Research in various African countries underlines the trend that political figures and public officials who have enriched

---

[9] Nigel, Carene and Rughooputh, Soonil, *A National Inventory of Wetlands and their Classification*, Abstract: vcampus.uom.ac.mu/research-week/rw08/abstracts/3sep2008/abstract133.doc Accessed 8.3.2017.
[10] **National Weather Service Weather Forecast Office (USA): Flash flood:** *A flood caused by heavy or excessive rainfall in a short period of time, generally less than 6 hours. Flash floods are usually characterized by raging torrents after heavy rains that rip through river beds, urban streets, or mountain canyons sweeping everything before them. They can occur within minutes or a few hours of excessive rainfall. They can also occur even if no rain has fallen, for instance after a levee or dam has failed, or after a sudden release of water by a debris or ice jam.*
[11] Republic of Mauritius, *A Climate Action Plan*, prepared with the assistance of the United States Country Studies, National Climate Committee, December 1998.
[12] See **Week-End** newspaper, *'Rétrospective 2013: "La leçon de la discrétion"*, December 29, 2013.

themselves then believe that they should return the favour by favouring those who have helped them rise. This sounds viciously familiar to the proximity between business and politicians in Mauritius."

The government was perceived as deeply immersed in corruption and the public itself is generally considered as party to everyday corrupt practices. Lallah, in the same article, observes,

"Should it really be surprising that ten years after the inception of ICAC, the last report from Transparency International indicates that the perception of corruption in Mauritius is gaining ground? When it comes down to it, the everyday Mauritian is the "traceur" or "magouilleur" par excellence – familiar examples being falsifying a home address to get a child into a perceived "star school", bribing whoever it takes to pass a driving test or somehow manage to get more carry-on luggage than the allowed quota at an Air Mauritius counter. Such behaviour has even been exported - Mauritians are notoriously involved in passport scams across Europe. There is an undeniable cultural factor interlinked with the corruption problem in our country."

Other main events of the year were:

LIGHT RAIL:

- More mega-projects apart from the white elephants of Jinfei and Neotown emerged at Government House. There was one for a light rail transport system long overdue but endlessly on and off for several decades, never achieved prior to the advent of the next government in 2014,[13] despite massive preliminary expenses, just like the Jinfei project, truly a costly white elephant. Government even announced that the project would be achieved by 2017, when the railway linking Curepipe and Port-Louis.

SOME SUCCESS, MULTIPLE FAILURES:

- Two mega-projects that did materialise were the completion of the upgrading and refurbishing of the Sir Seewoosagur Ramgoolam Airport at the cost of Rs 13 billion and of the Terre Rouge-Verdun motorway, a welcome addition to the road network that bypassed Port-Louis to alleviate the traffic jams there. Yet, major additional works were ongoing from 2015 due to severe damage to the brand new motorway due to major construction, engineering and administrative oversight, failures and errors that resulted in heavy damages to a part of the road that started to collapse during heavy rains. Remedial works were carried out in 2016 under the new government that came to power in December 2014. Another costly motorway project at Pailles also showed signs of collapsing during the time of the former govvernment and needed major repairs under the new one. Those failures and that of a multi-billion dam that was being constructed at Bagatelle on unstable soil under the former government have cost the country huge sums of wasted public funds. The dame project has been taken up by the new government that came to power in 2014.

CONTROVERSIAL ID CARDS:

- One of the many mega-projects of the Ramgoolam government became highly controversial for various reasons. First, the regime was blasted by the media and the opposition for inserting biometric information of all its citizens into the new cards with considerable risks of leakages of data, misuse, undemocratic use and abuse of power. Then the cost of the project, which had gone from Rs 300 million to about Rs 1.4 billion raised eyebrows even more among the general public. The public outrage was well expressed in an article in *L'Express* newspaper in October 2013.[14] However, the ID card project was ultimately maintained by the new government and was completed in March 2017, with the controversialt detailed biometric information.
- POWER STATIONS: The Central Electricity Board presented an Integrated Energy Plan 2013-2022 with three new coal-fired thermal power stations by the company CT Power, causing protests not just from local communities fearing their environmental impact, but also from within the National Energy Commission chaired by Financial Secretary Dev Manraj.
- INDEPENDENCE: YEAR 45: Indian President Pranab Mukerjee attends as chief guest the national celebration of the 45th year of independence in Mauritius.

---
13 The new government has taken up the rail project with foundation stone in March 2017 and completion anticipated before 2019.
14 *"Biometric National Identity Cards and central data base; Answers please!"*, **by Adi Teelock, L'Express, October 26, 2013.** http://www.lexpress.mu/idee/biometric-national-identity-card-and-central-database-answers-please

- WORST ROAD ACCIDENT OF THE NEW CENTURY: On May 3, 2012, one of the worst road accidents occurred at Sorrèze on the motorway where a bus of the parastatal company, the National Transport Corporation, overturns after the driver lost control of the vehicle as it rushed down a steep slope at a dangerous bend, the brakes having failed: 10 people were killed and 45 wounded. This caused an outburst of anger in the public opinion and the media about the state of maintenance of the vehicle fleet of the government-controlled NTC. The government itself seemed to be running downhill throughout the year as it headed to its demise in the following year.
- PONZI SCHEMES: A wave of illegal financial affairs shocks the nation starting with revelations of ponzi schemes by White Dot International Consultancy Limited and Sunkai Company. Over a thousand Mauritians lose massive sums of money. Popular discontent continues to rise across the country with the multiplication of '*scandals*' that seem never ending year in year out.
- ANTI-DEMOCRATIC MEDIA LAWS: A preliminary report to Prime Minister Navin Ramgoolam by internationally renowned lawyer specialized in the defence of democracy and human rights, Geoffrey Robertson, Q.C., is released. Ramgoolam had wanted at the start to curb press freedom but the report actually found that Mauritius was already curbing press freedom (and still does as of 2017) by making use of old and outdated British and Napoleonic laws, the latter being severely repressive, dating from French occupation in the 19th century, and aiming to maintain and enforce the infamous Code Noir and the abolition of civic rights granted to coloured people in Mauritius during the French Revolution. Those English and French laws, still in force in Mauritius in 2017 at the time this book was written, and similar legislation elsewherem have long been abolished in Europe, the United States and other countries with advanced democratic systems. They are used by the police to arrest and detain political opponents of the government of the day. In brief, those old laws have constituted a political weapon for several decades need to be scrapped and replaced by modern democratic legislation, but the report has been shelved following its submission and nothing have changed as of March 2017.
- LABOUR DAY MEETINGS: The unpopularity of the Labour-PMSD government was such that Ramgoolam opted for not holding the ruling alliance's Labour Day meeting, while the MSM-MMM alliance attracted a sizable crowd in Port-Louis due, in part, to the return of Paul Bérenger from several months of successful treatment for cancer in Paris. Such national political meetings used to attract five to ten times the crowd in 2013 in Port-Louis prior to the 1990s, yet the assistance at that meeting in the capital city dwarfed by far the rallies by the Labour-PMSD alliance in power..
- TROUBLE LOOMS ON THE ECONOMIC AND SOCIAL FRONTS: Inequality increases regarding revenue distribution among Mauritian families according to Statistics Mauritius: *"Income inequality increased between 2006/07 and 2012. The share of total income going to the 20% of households at the lower end of the income range decreased from 6.1% in 2006/07 to 5.4% in 2006/07. On the other hand, the share of the upper 20% of households increased from 45.6% to 47.4%. The rise in income inequality is confirmed by an increase in the Gini coefficient from 0.388 in 2006/07 to 0.413 in 2012.* [15]
- Pessimism sets in the economic front during the first semester of the year with economic and social indicators generally regressing. The Bank of Mauritius revises its estimate of economic growth to 3,3%, largely insufficient to reach the high growth rates that transformed the island in the 1980s. There were over 52,000 unemployed persons in the island. As special guest at the meeting of the Monetary Policy Committee, Financial Secretary Ali Michael Mansoor states, *"The spectre of unemployment is worrisome and the MPC should think very carefully about its responsibility, not only to history, but also right now."*
- A MINISTER RESIGNS: Adding to the woes of the Labour-PMSD government, there was the resignation Justice Minister Yatin Varma. Despite a positive performance as a minister pursuing a reform agenda for the judiciary, he was forced to step down after he was involved in a road accident where he allegedly boxed a young driver whose vehicle had collided with his car in Quatre Bornes. This case contributed to increase the unpopularity of the Labour-PMSD regime. This affair was followed by botched negotiations between the two parties attended by a government MP and a PMSD official.
- NELSON MANDELA DIES: The month of December was marked by the death of the greatest of South African statesmen, Nelson Mandela, aged 95. He passed away on December 5, 2013 after having, during his

---

[15] "Household Budget Survey 2012", Statistics Mauritius.

lifetime achieved fame as one of the most prominent leaders in world history. Mauritius observed a day of mourning on the day of his burial which was attended by the island's top political leaders. Mauritius has a Nelson Mandela Centre for African Culture since 1986. It plays a leading role in promoting *"the advancement of African and Creole Culture in Mauritius."*

- FIRST WOMAN TO BE APPOINTED LORD-MAYOR: Dorine Chuckowry of the MMM was appointed on December 26, 2013, as the first woman in history to be appointed Lord-Mayor of the City of Port-Louis
- Judge Keshoe Parsad Matadeen was appointed Chief Justice at the Mauritius Supreme Court. He is sworn in on the last day of the year in the presence of Prime Minister Navin Ramgoolam.

A year to be remembered as that of the Mauritian 'Game of Thrones' - a year of intrigue, treason, treachery and deceit

The MSM-MMM alliance or Remake 2000, the other name it was given in 2011 when Sir Aneerood Jugnauth had assumed its leadership in the wake of his resignation as President of the Republic, showed, from the beginning of the year, signs of wavering. It became obvious that Prime Minister Navin Ramgoolam had adopted a strategy of winning over the MMM and creating a new Labour-MMM alliance. This becameobvious as he and Paul Bérenger started to meet secretly in Floréal where they live as next-door neighbours.

Reports of this rapprochement soon surfaced in the media.[16] and the MSM did not take much time to react and take counter-measures. A list of candidates for the next general election was already in preparation. Many new adherents had joined the MSM and had been presented to the public. Those new faces in politics were generally qualified professionals for the most part. Surfing on an increasing wave of unpopularity, Ramgoolam believed that the MMM's perceived strength in the urban areas that had systematically ensured to that party nearly half of the national electorate, would give a Labour-MMM alliance a sweeping victory.

However, the alliance with Ramgoolam was to be one of the many major blunders of Bérenger's chequered, yet glorious political career. His party had been the largest one in Mauritius for decades and now, after the Labour-MMM alliance, opposition started to rise among the national electorate and across the media, online and in social media.

Worse was to come. As the year unfolded, Ramgoolam closed parliament for most of the time and he and Bérenger spent their time in discussions as to how to reform the Constitution, as well as make of Ramgoolam the president of a *'second republic',* immune to all prosecution, and Paul Bérenger a 5-year term Prime Minister.

In the proposed *'second republic',* Ramgoolam would be president with a number of executive powers. They also devised an electoral reform that would abolish the post-electoral *'best loser'* system, which consists in the nomination of eight additional MPs to Parliament on the basis of ethnicity/religion to correct inter-ethnic imbalance, and replace it with a degree of proportional representation.

Xavier Duval, who had in the previous year denied any wish to leave the Ramgoolam regime and even multiplied public statements, widely publicised by the local media, that he was and would remain loyal to Ramgoolam, became uneasy as he increasingly became aware that the latter was going to throw him and his PMSD overboard.

Finally there was a revolt within the MMM against the alliance with labour. This revolt saw a well known lawyer, Ivan Collendavelloo, and other members of the party leave Bérenger to join the MSM, while the PMSD, excluded from the Labour-MMM deal, decided in June to resign from government and join the MSM in the opposition. The MMM dissidents formed the Mouvement Liberater and, as the election campaign drew near, they also joined with the MSM. The three parties thus formed the Alliance Lepep and won a landslide victory against Ramgoolam on December 10, 2914.

Prior to the December election, Ramgoolam boasted to the media that he had caught finally a *'big shark',* meaning the MMM. It was obvious that he had used electoral and constitutional reforms as double hooks.

The Ramgoolam regime's success in roping in the MMM and its leader and breaking up the Remake 2000 was a short-lived victory for the year despite his and Bérenger's optimism and their repeated annoncements that they would win all seats in all the 20 constituencies of mainland Mauritius, a total of 60 seats to 0 at the direct election pending nomination of best-losers. Yet, all polls of readers by **L'Express** and **Le Defi Media** group during the year showed a landslide victory for the opposition

---

16 Unless otherwise cited, all events of the 20th century are sourced from the local media as preserved at the National Library of Mauritius, Edith Cavell Street, Port-Louis.

In the second half of the year, the Labour government and the MMM opposition had voted the *Constitution (Declaration of Community) (Temporary Provisions) Bill* providing for candidates to abstain from declaring their ethnic identity to register for the upcoming general election only, pending a Labour-MMM victory following which Ramgoolam and Bérenger promised a more substantial electoral and constitutional reform to meet the requirements of the decision by the Human Rights Committee of the UN.

The electoral campaign lasted from September at the time the Labour-MMM alliance was confirmed by both parties and the Alliance Lepep also was ready to launch a massive campaign that was one of the most efficient in modern Mauritius. Voters massively flocked to Lepep's meetings across the country, changing sides overnight to support the opposition against the Ramgoolam regime. Despite their own polls, the media did not truly believe in a Lepep victory, judging from a cursory reading of editorials published in those days.

In September, MSM leader Pravind Jugnauth was appointed Leader of the Opposition in the National Assembly. The Alliance Lepep made pledges to eradicate extreme poverty by radical measures comprising increased social pensions and a 'Marshall Plan', while creating tens of thousands of new jobs by a 'new economic miracle' as the one that occurred in the 1980s. Its leaders promised also to increase the scope of democracy in the country, to have the labour leaders taken to court to answer charges of shady deals and scandalous conduct as leaders of the country and to have Navin Ramgoolam jailed. Sir Aneerood Jugnauth repeated at several public meetings the following statement he made on Tuesday, August 2012 and which hit the headlines in the media: *"If I become Prime Minister, I will have Ramgoolam jailed."*

For his part, Pravind Jugnauth, son of Sir Aneerood and leader of the MSM, was virulently attacked during the year over the so-called *'Medpoint Clinic Scandal'* where he was denounced by Ramgoolam of having signed, when he was Minister of Finance, a cheque of Rs 145 million for his sister and her husband, owners of that clinic, for its sale to the government. Pravind Jugnauth was even subjected to criminal charges for conflict of interest under the Prevention Of Corruption Act (POCA) from March , at the time he was still in the Remake 2000. The electoral campaign became a battle of 'scandals', the Jugnauths and Ramgoolam trading insults over such matters as Ramgoolam's princely life with expensive cars like his Aston Martin in Mauritius and his Rolls in the UK, and practising nepotism to shower his inner circle of friends, including an intimate female associate, with favours of all sorts at the public expense and with gifts like state lands and profitable contracts.

For his part, the Labour leader blasted the Jugnauths with the Medpoint affair and other issues like allegations of political careers allegedly dedicated to personal enrichment, favours and privileges. Bérenger, who had supported Pravind Jugnauth over the Medpoint Clinic affair, appeared to have forgotten all about his previous stand, and he was attacking the Jugnauths and the Lepep leadership vigorously, despite having been the one who had personally visited President Jugnauth in his mansion of Le Réduit and convinced him to resign and come back in the political arena to head the government again as Prime Minister.

All this illustrated perfectly the fact that politics in Mauritius had literally turned into a replica is what takes place in the *'Game of Thrones'* which depicts a civil-political war between noble families in the ancient land of Westeros.[17] One wonders if politics has actually been always and forever a story of intrigue, that includes *'treason, treachery and deceit'* to quote, all due proportions respected of course, the title of a famous book on alleged murderous political plots in the USA.[18].

Bérenger would comment that this was one of Ramgoolam's major blunders during the electoral campaign during the first MMM press conference held on Saturday, December 13, three days after the general elections.[19] The MMM believed that the comment had been very offensive for his supporters and voters. The thrust of his comment was the electorate had voted more to punish Ramgoolam than for the Alliance Lepep, which, despite his mistaken choice for alliance, actually made sense.

Whatever the arguments used, it escaped nobody that not only Ramgoolam was extremely unpopular to the point of not even getting himself elected in his stronghold constituency of Pamplemousses/Triolet, but that Bérenger had barely escaped the same humiliation, being for the first time elected last on the

---

[17] "Westeros is a continent located in the far west of the known world. It is separated from the continent of Essos by a strip of water known as the Narrow Sea. Most of the action in Game of Thrones takes place in Westeros. Author of the series George R.R. Martin has stated that the continent of Westeros is roughly the same size as the real-life continent of South America." Source: http://gameofthrones.wikia.com/wiki/Westeros

[18] Norvell, D, *"treason, treachery and deceit"*, **paperback, Xlibris,** .

[19] *"Bérenger impute la d;efaite à un 'vote sanction' contre Ramgoolam"*, L'Express Online, December 13.

list, that is, in third position while dissident Collehdavelloo came out first.. The formidable expression of popular anger was directed against him and his party as well because of his alliance with Ramgoolam, to the point that the MMM leader himself barely missed being defeated in his own stronghold in the Stanley/Rose Hill constituency.

The new Cabinet was sworn in on December 17 before President Kailash Purryag at le Réduit. It was composed as follows:

- Sir Anerood JUGNAUTH: Prime Minister, Home Affairs and Rodrigues
- Xavier-Luc DUVAL: Deputy Prime Minister and Tourism
- Showkutally SOODHUN: Vice-Prime Minister, Housing and Lands
- Ivan COLLENDAVELLOO: Vice Prime Minister, Energy et Public utilities
- V. LUTCHMEENARAIDOO: Finance and Economic Development
- Pravind JUGNAUTH: Technology, Communication and Innovation
- Yogida SAWMINADEN: Youth and Sports
- Nando BODHA: Public Infrastructure and Transport
- Leela Devi DOOKUN: Education, Higher Education and Human
- Anil GAYAN: Health and Quality of Life
- Anwar HUSNOO: Local Government
- Pradeep ROOPUN: Social Integration
- Etienne SINATAMBOU: Foreign Affairs, Regional Integration and External Trade
- Ravi YERRIGADOO: Attorney General
- Mahen SEERUTTUN: Agro-Industry
- Dan BABOO: Arts and Culture
- Ashit GUNGAH: Industry and Trade
- Aurore PERRAUD: Gender equality and Child development
- Roshi BHADAIN: Financial services and Good governance
- Sunil BHOLAH: Trade, Entreprises and Cooperatives-
- Fazila DAUREEAWOO: Social security and National Solidarity
- Prem KOONJOO: Oceanic economy, marine resources, Fishing and Outer islands
- Raj DAYAL: Environnement, National emergency centre and Beach Authority
- Alain WONG: Civil serice
- Soodesh CALLICHURN: Labour, Industrial relations, Employment and Training

The first decisions of the new government targeted pensioners and the salaried population who received a raise. This cost the state Rs 4.5 billion in pension increases for around 240,000 social pensioners. For the salaried classes, Minister of Finance Vishnu Lutchmeenaraidoo announced in the week after he assumed office, a Rs 600 salary compensation across the board, while part-time employees earning less than Rs 10,000 obtained a raise of 6%. The salary compensation, said the minister, would cost the state Rs 4.28 billion and the private sector Rs 1.32 billion. Those increases had been one of several electoral promises by the Alliance Lepep, including one to fight poverty, starting from a hike in social pensions.

Chapter 58

2015-2017:

Independence of police, relations money-politics put to test

The euphoria of victory for Alliance Lepep persisted for several months into 2015, whipped by the hikes in pensions and the salary compensation. It was first tempered by a stark reality for the MSM leader, Pravind Jugnauth, whose case before the Intermediary Court where he stood accused under the anti-corruption legislation from the previous year, was called before magistrates Niroshni Ramsoondar and Azam Neerooa on February 2. Three days later, February 5, Labour Party leader and former Prime minister Navin Ramgoolam was arrested and taken to the police headquarters by a strong police squad which had also seized two big safes at his residence. Ramgoolam spent a night in prison and released on bail after being charged with, among other things, having tried to *'pervert the course of justice'* following a robbery at his coastal bungalow in Roche Noires in the night of July 2-3, 2011. The two party leaders were in for a long saga through the justice system. He was also charged for about Rs 220 million rupees in cheques and cash, including dollars found by police during a search in a safe at this residence, a charge later dropped by the Director of Public Prosecutions and re-entered later by the Commissioner of Police and pending Court proceedings due in 2017.

Pravind Jugnauth, for his part, stood charged as follows, according to the judgment by the Independent Commission Against Corruption (ICAC) for having on 23 December 2010,

"...whilst being then a public official whose relative had a personal interest in a decision which a public body had to take .... took part in the proceedings of that public body relating to such decision ..." in breach of section 13(2) &(3) Prevention of

Corruption Act [hereinafter referred to as "POCA" or "the Act"] as amended by section 4(b) of Act No.1/2006... As per Particulars of information, Accused had been acting in his capacity as Vice Prime Minister and Minister of the Ministry of Finance and Economic Development [hereinafter referred to as "MOFED" & MOFED is also referred to as Ministry of Finance and Economic Empowerment ["MOFEE"]] when he " .... approved the re-allocation of funds amounting to Rs.144,701,300.- to pay Medpoint Ltd – in which company Accused's sister, Mrs Malhotra held 86,983 shares out of 368,683."[1]

Magistrates N.Ramsoondar and M.I.A Neerooa convicted the MSM leader and sentenced him to imprisonment for 12 months. Jugnauth appealed to the Supreme Court where the judgment was quashed on 25 May 2016 by K.P. Matadeen, Chief Justice, and A.A. Caunhye, Judge.[2] The latter ruled:

"True it is that the learned Magistrates found that the appellant knew that his sister possessed an interest "in Medpoint Ltd" and also knew that his decision to approve the reallocation of funds related to the payment of Medpoint Ltd... However, it cannot be said that they found the requisite mens rea in respect of all the conduct elements of the offence, in particular the third conduct element, proved beyond reasonable doubt. What they found was that the appellant must have known that his sister was a shareholder. This cannot, de facto, be equated or stretched to a finding that he knew that she had any "personal interest" in the decision to reallocate funds and that he knowingly participated in a decision-making process involving a conflict of interest... it was highly questionable whether the appellant had the requisite guilty intent at the material time that he participated in a decision limited solely to a reallocation of the funds for payment to which Medpoint Ltd was already lawfully entitled, the more so when this was done at a time and in a situation where there was a total absence of any competing interests or conflict of interests."

The Director of Public Prosecutions appealed the above judgment and it was expected that the case could go up to the Privy Council in London if the DPP so wanted.

The cases involving Navin Ramgoolam and Pravind Jugnauth have, above everything else, raised the questions of the relation between money and politics and that of the definition of 'conflict of interest' as per the anti-corruption legislation. Both Ramgoolam and Jugnauth were sons of previous prime ministers and both became PM (Jugnauth in 2017) were awaiting in March 2017 the outcome of their court cases to clear their names and survive politically

---

1 *ICAC v P.K Jugnauth 2015 INT 210 IN THE INTERMEDIATE COURT OF MAURITIUS (Criminal Division) In the matter of :- C.No. 265/2014 Independent Commission Against Corruption ["ICAC"] v Pravind Kumar JUGNAUTH* https://supremecourt.govmu.org/HighlightDoc/J-2015-ICAC%20v%20Jugnauth-FINAL%2030%206%2015.pdf Accessed 9.3.2017

2 *2016 SCJ 187 Record No. 8798 THE SUPREME COURT OF MAURITIUS In the matter of:- P.K. Jugnauth, Appellant v 1. The Independent Commission against Corruption 2. The State of Mauritius 3. The Director of Public Prosecutions, Respondents.* https://supremecourt.govmu.org/HighlightDoc/JUGNAUTH%20P%20K%20%20v%20INDEPENDENT%20COMMISSION%20AGAINST%20CORRUPTION%20and%20ORS%202016%20SCJ%20187.pdf Accessed 9.3.2017

the storm caused nationwide by their arrests and the accusations to which they had to answer, including the Rs 220 rupees found in Ramgoolam's coffers and the Rs 145-million checque in the so called Medpoint Affair involving Sir Aneerood Jugnauth's son and successor at the helm of the country.

Many in the public viewed all this as the continuation of a feud, if not the *'game of thrones'* between two families that had held power alternatively from the time independence in 1968, except for the period 2003-2005, a short interlude during which SAJ had voluntarily offered the *'throne'* to Paul Bérenger while he took up the position of president of the republic. Actually, a long string of allegations, accusations, provisional charges and arrests were effected against members of the former Navin Ramgoolam regime, including ministers, as well as other opponents and critics on social media and elsewhere. Most cases have been either struck out for want of credible evidence by the courts or the Director of Public Prosecutions, if not discontinued as the settling of scores between the new and the former government occupied much of the year. The new government has failed to obtain, as of March 2017, the extradition from Italy of the former friend of Ramgoolam, Mrs. Soornack, who left the country, attempts at such a decision having been foiled by the judiciary in Italy where has sought refuge in the days after the defeat of the Ramgoolam regime at the December 2014 general election.

The new government and DPP Satyajit Boolell were also engaged in a conflict following the discovery that the latter may also have been in a situation of conflict of interest in a land transaction involving his wife and himself that almost landed him in prison, followed by a Bill introduced in Parliament by the government to have decision-making transferred from the DPP to a panel of retired judges appointed by the Executive regarding decisions pertaining to whether appeal can be or not referred to the Privy Council. The Bill was pending in Parliament in March 2017 awaiting government to recovered the required majority of three quarters of members that it had lost as the PMSD decided to leave the ruling coalition for reasons linked to various matters, including PMSD's refusal to vote the Bill.

Another event that hit the headlines during a large part of 2015-2016 was the dismantling of British American Investments, also described by the media as the *'Rawat Empire'*, from the name of the founder-main shareholder, and Chairman Emeritus Dawood Rawat. The latter was one of the most successful entrepreneurs in the history of modern Mauritius. He started out as an insurance agent for British American Insurance and rose to ownership of the New York based conglomerate after brilliantly climbing all the echelons from agent to top management. He was a rare Mauritian of the non Franco-Mauritian communities who had been able to rival the handful of families who control the national economy.[3]

In the BAI affair, the group had made some costly acquisitions over the years on the advice of its top management and showed signs of increasingly urgent fresh capital. Another factor that was used against the group was its close involvement in partisan politics in support of the Navin Ramgoolam government – not that this is a matter of concern for the normal person or country, but in the Mauritian war games in the political arena, it is risky for business to overtly take sides. The sugar oligarchy learned the lesson even before independence and played well its cards with both government and opposition. Aligning himself with Labour drew fire against BAI from the leadership of the MSM, which controlled the new Lepep government led by Sir Aneerood Jugnauth, albeit the fact that the PM described himself, even amidst the tumult of the so-called *'fall of the Rawat empire'*, as a former *'good friend'* of Dawood Rawat.[4]

SAJ and his government have denied political motives behind the dismantlement of BAI, despite media allegations that the closure of the group's Bramer Bank was preceded by ministerial moves that saw the pulling out of government funds and private deposits of some political leaders from that institution. These allegations have created controversy and used as an argument by the Rawat side to blast the government over its approval of the decision to close the bank. The government has argued that the bank had ignored requirements by the Bank of Mauritius of maintaining the mandatory minimum cash reserve radio on deposits and allegedly been carrying out transactions and operations in violation of banking and anti-corruption legislation. Government launched a ferocious attack with a string of allegations against the group, accusing various of its companies of violations of good governance

---

[3] **African Peer Review Mechanism, Country Report No. 13. June 2010, op cit.** The African Peer Review Mechanism observes on the *"control of the economy"* and attempts at economic *'democratisation'* in Mauritius: *"The real meaning of democratisation is to move from an economy controlled by a few Franco-Mauritian families to one in which economic power is shared with other segments of society, particularly those that control the political arena."*

[4] Week-End/Le Mauricien 3 May 2015: *"SAJ à Vacoas, vendredi : « Dawood Rawat : un bon ami ! »* http://www.lemauricien.com/article/lutte-contre-les-crimes-col-blanc-dawood-rawat-ou-l-obstacle-du-passeport-francais Accessed 9.3.2017

requirements and of various laws, including money laundering.

Rawat, for his part, entered a case against the State of Mauritius in Paris claiming USD one billion for what he perceived as illegal actions against the BAI group. He was known already across the country has having been a major financial supporter of the MMM, of which SAJ had been the president for decades, after which he had switched sides to support and finance Labour and even the MSM and the MMM. Supported by the PM, the minister of Fiance and Economic Development, Vishnu Lutchmeenaraidoo led government's operation to dismantle BAI.[5] He stated categorically in Parliament on 4 April 2015,

"...we all know that this is a Ponzi Scheme, a scam that has been set up to steal poor people savings... Let us not play on words!"[6]

It all started with botched negotiations between the group's bank, Bramer Banking Corporation and the Bank of Mauritius over a loan requested from the former by the BAI's top banking executives to help the latter resolve the minimum cash reserve ratio.

The events surrounding the closure of the bank and putting under legal custody of BAI Insurance, on April 3, 2015, are described as follows on April 4, 2015, by the prominent daily *L'Express* (as translated here from French):

Alleged "25-billion Ponzi Scheme" – The Prime Minister, Sir Anerood Jugnauth, has tried to give assurances to the clients of those two entities during a conference yesterday. He explained that he ended a Ponzi scheme amounting to about Rs 25 billion in order to limit its dire consequences, 156,000 policy holders of British American Insurance being at risk.

"The Finance Ministry has been working on this issue for a few weeks already and the rumour of an imminent closure of the Bramer Bank originated directly from Government House. The Ministry of Social Security's decision to withdraw Rs 1.5 billion from that establishment has precipitated its liquidity crisis, even if the government has still an important amount of money there. This has triggered a rush on the bank by holders of clients trying to get back their savings."

Former PM Sir Anerood Jugnauth as well as other ministers who withdrew their money just prior to the closure of the bank were under attack in the media and by the Opposition for having acted in knowledge of the revocation of the licence before the announcement of the decision.[7]

From that time to 2017, the *"BAI affair"* or *"BAI saga"* has appeared endless. Ramgoolam and his friend Mrs. Nandanee Soornack have been linked by government to allegedly irregular transactions with the Bramer Bank. One of the closest friends of the Prime Minister who had been accused by the Alliance Lepep of having played a major role in the alleged '*scandals*' of the past regime beame a turncoat who joined the new regime as an intimate friend of the new ministers. Dawood Rawat and Mrs. Soornack who had left the country before the new government took control remained at large, the first named in Paris and the lady friend of Ramgoolam in Bologna, Italy, while alleging in the courts of law of those countries that they had been victims of political victimization.Government has come forward with an accounting report[8] to support its claims against BAI. Several top officers as well as Rawat's family members, including his three daughters, have been subjected to arrest, detention at police posts and numerous sessions of criminal interrogation by the police. Court cases have been traded with each other by both sides of the controversy. Police have been blamed by defence lawyers and opposition politicians for complacency as was the case also when power was held by the Ramgoolam regime. The independence of the police, a major issue in Mauritius, has been in question since independence under all governments and in 2016 a court in Bologna, Italy, decided in a case lodged by Mrs. Soornack, that Mauritian police was not independent in the matter – to which the Commissioner of Police responded by a denial.[9]

[5] Bhadain resigned from the Cabinet on 24 January, the next day after Pravind Jugnauth was sworn in as Prime Minister, succeeding to his father, Sir Anerood Jugnauth. He said he opposed such a succession from father to son. His statement was made to media as recorded here: http://defimedia.info/roshi-bhadain-explique-pourquoi-il-refuse-un-poste-de-ministre Accessed 9.3.2015.
[6] Mauritius National Assembly, 7 April 2015. http://mauritiusassembly.govmu.org/English/hansard/Documents/2015/hansard1715.pdf Accessed 9.3.2017.
[7] SAJ is heard defending his decision, stating "«*Abe ki mo rann mwa kouyon? Mo less mo kass laba mem? Premie zafer, monn tir mo kass. Enn bato pe koule, mo sov mo la po.*» in a video recording preserved here: https://www.youtube.com/watch?v=8Iv1Jxpyq8g Accessed 9.3.2017 while people threatened to sue him and others who allegedly had privileged inside information prior to the bank closure, see here: https://www.lexpress.mu/article/269113/ex-bramer-bank-saj-sera-poursuivi-pour-complot Accessed 9.3.2017
[8] Mainly the N'tan report used in a long series of articles from 2015 to 2016 by Le Mauricien daily newspaper, which has based itself on that document to accuse Dawood Rawat of illegal transactions. At a press conference on Saturday January 30, the leader of the Opposition Paul Bérenger has maintained that the report *"is full of bias and has been manipulated."* The controversy seemed to persist in 2017, well after the closure of Bramer Bank and the taking control of all BAI assets by the Jugnauth government who has been disposing of them from then on.
[9] Reported in the media in Mauritius where the question was put to a Mauritian lawyer specialised in international law: *"Voilà ce qu'a déclaré Me Parvez Dookhy aux questions de Jean-Luc Émile sur Radio Plus :*

Question : Le juge italien considère que la police mauricienne « n'est pas politiquement indépendante » et que les droits de Nandanee Soornack ne

Overall, all this sound and fury around the BAI saga, appeared to weaken the image of the entire traditional political establishment whether in power or in the opposition. To counter this public perception, government after government have for the last two decades, promised reforms to make those relations more transparent by new legislation, but in 2017, public opinion was still awaiting a positive outcome in the light of numerous reform proposals made over the years. Such reform was still on the new government's agenda in 2017. So was that of an electoral reform to make Schedule 1 of the Constitution meet the requirements of the UN Human Rights Committee on ethnic identification of candidates for general elections.

Other headlines of 2015-2017:

Ramgoolam's coffers:

The controversy, mentioned above, when the police impounded two safes at Ramgoolam's residences in which a total sum of money in banknotes and cheques amounting to Rs 220 million sparked public furor that had not subsided in 2017. Ramgoolam explained that the money represented savings consisting, he said, of legal political donations as received (uncontrolled by the law) by other political parties for the purpose of financing mainly the reconstruction of the party headquarters. He attributed part of the sum to per diem allowances he received as Prime Minister for his overseas missions during multiple mandates as Prime Minister. He has requested the courts to restitute those sums to him as they were still held in custody by the authorities. However in September 2017 he was awaiting a decision announced by the Director of Public Prosecution who announced, as the Court struck off the case for undue delay under the provisional charge that was still pending, that by the end of the same month he would come up with a main case and a new, formal charge against the former PM over his coffers.

The Terre Rouge-Verdun motorway:

Major repairs continued on the Terre Rouge-Verdun motorway to stop landslides caused by heavy rainfall. The issue remained a political one. The new government relentlessly accused the former regime, particularly Anil Baichoo, ex-Minister of Public Infrastructure and Transport Anil Baichoo, and staff members of the ministry of various improprieties in the management and supervision of major works like the new motorway, the airport, the Bagatelle Dam that kept sinking dangerously into unstable ground and a brand new addition to the motorway at Pailles that also showed cracks, all that despite tens of billions of rupees spent on such infrastructure projects. The new government undertook major and costly remedial works on all those projects. But problems persisted in 2017 and works were still not completed.

New president and vice-president

During the electoral campaign, at a press conference, held on September 27, ,[10] the new Lepep Alliance had announced that it intended to appoint '*a Muslim personality*' if it won the general election when the time would come to replace President Kailash Purryag. Following the election, the president resigned and, in June 5, 2015, the new government kept its promise and Dr. Ameenah Gurib-Fakim, a scientist with international reputation, was sworn in to replace him, becoming the first woman president of the country's history. The Prime Ministed, who had promised to appoint '*a Tamil*'[11] to the vice-presidency after the end of the mandate of VP Mrs. Monique Oshan-Bellepeau, refused to appoint a candidate who had been suggested to him and chose another person of the Tamil community to honour his pledge. Mauritian Ambassador to South Africa Paramasivum Pillay Vyapoory was sworn in as vice-president at the State House, Réduit, on April 4, 2016.

Mauritian pilgrims die in Mecca

---

seront pas garantis. En tant qu'expert international, comment voyez-vous tout cela ?

Réponse : C'est l'image de l'île Maurice. Les refus des demandes d'extradition ont souvent eu lieu en Europe, en France et dans d'autres pays comme l'Angleterre. Souvent des juges des pays européens refusent des demandes d'extradition à l'égard des pays comme le Zimbabwe ou le Congo. Je trouve que l'île Maurice entre dans la catégorie de ces pays. Ça fait très mal et c'est très triste.

10 Reported by Le Mauricien/Weekend, published on September 28, . Online edition at: http://www.lemauricien.com/article/lalliance-lepep-prete-challenger-ptrmmm

11 At a function at the Mahatma Gandhi Institute on the silver jubilee for the silver jubilee of the Murutan Foundation on December 6, 2015, Prime Minister Aneerood Jugnauth reminded the audience that he had promised to have a Tamil appointed to the vice-presidency during the electoral campaign. In Le Défi newspaper of December 6, 2015, online edition. http://defimedia.info/vice-presidence-saj-dit-navoir-jamais-promis-la-nomination-de-menon-murday

In one of the worst tragedies occuring in a quarter of a century in Mecca, five Mauritians a stampede as the huge crowd of pilgrims was suddenly seized by collective panic. Over 1,400 people were crushed to death and hundreds were wounded.

New regime wins wins municipal elections

Alliance Lepep wins all municipal seats: The government alliance had remained popular several months after the general elections. In June it campaigned for the municipal elections on virtually the same themes that it had used to blast its opponents at the general elections. The Labour Party, the worst hit by the defeat of the Labour/MMM alliance at the general elections, abstained from taking part in the municipal elections. The MMM went into the contest alone, bogged down by its disastrous alliance with Labour, suffered complete defeat at the hands of the Lepep Alliiance, which won all 120 seats. The MMM leader and his politburo tried to minimise the scope of this defeat by observing that nearly two thirds of the electorate had abstained – yet, it was, for the party, one of its worse defeats in regional politics and a heavy price paid for breaking up the Remake and joining an unpopular Ramgoolam regime at the general elections.

Pravind Jugnauth, MSM leader resigns from Cabinet

The celebration of the municipal victory was shortlived for MSM leader Pravind Jugnauth and his party. He was led to resign from the Cabinet on being found guilty and receiving a 12-month prison sentence under the ***Prevention of Corruption Act,*** as already mentioned. The leader of the MSM was re-appointed as Minister of Finance and Economic Development and by September 2016, Prime Minister Aneroood Jugnauth had announced that he would resign and that his son would succeed him to head the Cabinet. Whereas this is constitutionally possible and legal, the fact that it is a first in Mauritius of a son succeeding his father directly as PM, and doing so without going through an election as candidate for prime ministership was being used by the opposition parties to argue for fresh general elections for Pravind Jugnauth to seek a popular mandate.

On the government side it is being argued that Pravind Jugnauth had already acceded to the leadership of the majority parti in Parliament, the MSM, well before the general election and that the Constitution provides for the party leader who commands a majority in the House to be appointed by the President as Prime Minister. The main thrust of opposition criticism and cases lodged before the Supreme Court by the PMSD and at the individual level to challenge this transfer of power from father to son, while the father was relegated to No. 3 in the government parliamentary front bench as a 'mentor' minister, a post not provided as such in the Constitution, is that it was an 'undemocratic' transition under the Mauritian Constitution. Court cases were pending as of March 2017.

Conflict between government and the DPP

During 2015, ministers of the Lepep government blasted publicly the Director of Publlic Prosecutions, Satyajit Boolell, Senior Counsel, for allegedly having indulged in a transaction for a company, Sun Tan Ltd. where his family has a major interest. Two ministers, Showkatally Soodhun, Vice-Prime Minister, Minister of Housing and Lands and No. 3 of the Jugnauth government, and Minister of Financial Services and Good Governance, made statements to the police on July 15, 2015,[12] asking the latter to open a criminal inquiry against the DPP for having allegedly sworn a false affidavit presented to the Supreme Court containing allegations of undue pressure from them that they both denied. The next day police went to arrest the DPP at his residence in Vacoas to arrest him[13] but were unable to do so upon the intervention of his lawyers Hervé Duval and Anwar Moollan who pointed out that there was a Cour Order by Judge Chui Yew Cheong which was in force interdicting the arrest of the DPP.

The 'Bhadain Laws' controversyMP D. Selvon resigns, bills then amended

The set of three so-called *'Bhadain Laws'* were well-intentioned in the sense that they targeted *'unexplained wealth'* that could not be legally justified. The main one was the ***Good Governance and Integrity Bill***[14] and was accompanied by a constitutional amendment bill, the ***Constitution Amendment Bill***[15] and third one, the ***Asset Recovery (Amend-***

---
12 *Le Mauricien* on July 15, 2015.
13 *L'Express*, on June 17, 2015.
14 Mauritius National Assembly. THE GOOD GOVERNANCE AND INTEGRITY REPORTING BILL (No. XXX of 2015). http://mauritiusassembly.govmu.org/English/bills/Documents/intro/2015/bill3015.pdf Accessed 9.3.2017
15 THE CONSTITUTION (AMENDMENT) BILL (No. XXIX of 2015). http://mauritiusassembly.govmu.org/English/bills/Documents/intro/2015/bill2915.pdf Accessed 9.3.2017

ment Bill).[16] There was a major controversy due to the fact that the bills was perceived as intended to provide wideranging powers to the executive branch of the state, outside of any preliminary judiciary control, for seizure of assets in a summary manner and based on allegations of impropriety. The bills created controversy within the ranks of the MSM where the bill had not been thoroughly debaded prior to its presentation, and was strongly opposed by all the opposition parties in Parliament and various civil society organizations, particularly members of the Bar Association.

Only one of the dissenting MSM parliamentarians, Marie Danielle Selvon, came out and spoke in the defence of, she said, *"the 100,000 or so entrepreneurs of the informal economy who have invested honestly around Rs1 billion and who honestly contribute to the national GDP".*[17] She said those entrepreneurs could be threatened by summary seizure of their wealth legally acquired.

In the days leading to the adoption of the three bills on 2 December 2015, she had pleaded for the minister to amend his proposals and give assurances that there would be thorough judiciary control and preventive clauses that would prevent political and other improper motives to be used for asset seizure that could, she argued, affect the important SME sector in Mauritius. Other lawyers also strongly criticised the *'Bhadain laws',* including Alan Ganoo, Mouvement Patriotique leader and Shakeel Mohamed, leader of the Labour party parliamentary group, while Leader of Opposition Paul Bérenger led the charge against the Bhadain Bills for the entire opposition.

The bill was finally voted after various amendments and assurances given in Parliament and consultations by the minister with a large range of opinion leaders. This finally led to the bills being voted by initial opponents like Selvon and the Mouvement Patriotique, whereas the MMM, which had been opposed to all three legislations, finally voted two of the bills.

During the controversy, MP Danielle Selvon had resigned from the MSM protesting hasty preparation of the bills without proper consultations in the decision-making process which, she said, was not open to debate within that party upon instructions by the party leaders. Yet, she accepted, she said, during her speech, that she did not agree with opposition members and prominent lawyers who had attacked the *'Bhadain laws'* on the basis that they violated the presumption of innocence. She argued that across the world, particularly in the UK, it is now the *"presumption of responsibility"*, not the presumption of innocence, that is being adopted to combat financial crimes, stating, during the debates on December 2, 2015:

"We are introducing a 'presumption of responsibility' on people having unexplained wealth and who may be drug traffickers or criminals of various sorts. There is nothing wrong in that and it is a significant fact that this has been allowed in the very European nation (the UK) where modern democracy was born and from which Mauritius derives its Constitution and democratic and legal traditions."[18]

She quoted the latest case law available in the UK.

---

16 THE CONSTITUTION (AMENDMENT) BILL (No. XXIX of 2015). http://mauritiusassembly.govmu.org/English/bills/Documents/intro/2015/bill3115.pdf Accessed 9.3.2017.
17 Mauritius National Assembly, pages 138 to 142 of the Hansard, downloadable here: http://mauritiusassembly.govmu.org/English/hansard/Documents/2015/hansard4215.pdf Accessed 9.3.2017
18 Hansard, Debates, December 2, 2015. http://mauritiusassembly.govmu.org/English/hansard/Documents/2015/hansard4215.pdf

Chapter 59

2016-2017

21st Century: Quo Vadis Mauritius? [1]

Priorities: the economy, democracy, environment, Chagos, Tromelin and other latest developments

Timeline is not exactly history. The question of where Mauritius is going will refer to some main, current trends of the Mauritian evolution in the 21st century with regard to the most essential priorities of the nation:

- Mauritius needs an econonic revival mainly to provide jobs and decent revenues to everyone.
- We urgently need to re-think and modernise in terms of creating a greater democratic space, with a reasonable degree of devolution of power to civil society and regional administrations as in the world's most democratic societies and of which Mauritius does not form part..'
- We need to face with better chances of survival, together with the global community, the current environmental degradation that threatens the human species of extinction.
- Mauritius needs to complete its independence in getting back the islands of the Chagos and Tromelin.

The sad truth is that we have yet to embark on this journey though, at the time this book was being completed, we were heading to the end of the second decade of a challenging 21st century. The events in 2016-2017 have not been conclusive in this respect,

Economic 'miracle' promise revisited by new Finance Minister

In 2016, a first attempt at an economic revival based on grandiose schemes, called mega-projects, namely 'Smart cities', has been replaced with a more realistic approach. Sophisticated, environmentally friendly smart cities constituted the official centrepiece of the new Lepep government's strategy to achieve an *'economic miracle'* that it undertook to achieve in its electoral manifesto in December 2014. Although the mega-projects have been repeated over and over by former PM Sir Anerood Jugnaugh and former Finance Minister Vishnu Lutchmeenaraidoo from 2014 to 2016, nearly all of this set of undertakings has never materialised. It has been abruptly scrapped and has been replaced in the 2016-2017 budget by new Finance Minister Pravind Jugnauth[2] by a new approach, 38 months ahead of the end of the government's mandate.

The new minister of Finance and Economic Development has been praised, even by the Leader of the Opposition an of the MMM, Paul Bérenger, for this approach, as well as by the Mouvement Patriotique of Alan Ganoo, and the independent MP Danielle Selvon, the latter insisting on econnomic democratization that will give a free hand, in a strictly controlled legal environment respectful of the environment and urban and rural planning rules, to small and medium enterprises (SMEs) starting, as she stated in a series of propositions to the minister, during her comments on the budget, from one-person entrepreneurs, whether professionals or street vendors or other economic operators, without any distinction or discrimination.[3]

The challenge to increase the democratic space

Some of the most important issues in Mauritius comprise arbitrary and politically motivated arrests justified by 'provisional charges' inspired by repressive 19th century legislation imposed to reinforce slavery and its 'Code Noir' and the colour bar. Such laws still exist in 21st century as reported by Geoffrey Robertson, Q.C., who recommended their abrogation to the government of Mauritius in a report to the Prime Minister.[4]

In 2016 Prime minister-in-waiting, Finance Minister Pravind Jugnauth, had a case in Court where he claims damages for having been victim of *'arbitrary arrest'* under the former government. In 2015, independent MP Danielle Selvon, for-

---
[1] Famous latin expression often cited in some modern languages meaning 'Where are you going?'
[2] Budget 2016-2017, "A New Era of Development", http://budget.mof.govmu.org/budget2017/budgetspeech2016-17.pdf **Accessed 9.3.2017.**
[3] **Mauritius National Assembly, Hansard, pages 48 to 56, 3 August 2016:** http://mauritiusassembly.govmu.org/English/hansard/Documents/2016/hansard1916.pdf **Accessed 9.3.2016**
[4] "Media Law and Ethics in Mauritius", Geoffrey Robertson, Q.C. April 2013. http://gis.govmu.org/English/Documents/Media%20Law%20-%20Preliminary%20Report.pdf Accessed 9.3.2017

merly of Pravind Jugnauth's party, MSM, was harassed by police who even entered her room in the intensive care unit at Jeetoo Hospital, Port-Louis. According to *L'Express* newspaper, she was accused by police of having *'incited people to hate the government'*, an incredible accusation in a modern democratic society that boasts of its origin from the Westminster system of government. Eventually, the independent MPs case was referred to the DPP for action and nothing was heard since then of this affair where the government-inspired police as under previous governments, had proceeded with a politically-motivated and discriminatory (other government MPs who also addressed the street vendors on the same day were not questioned by police) police order for questionning under warning (threat of arrest).

Several other persons, including social media commentators were arrested or even jailed in 2015 on the basis of statements by ministers who often use another obsolete law of *'criminal defamation'* which no longer exist in modern democracies. This was a repetition of a practice that was commun under the Ramgoolam regime who had protesters and opponents jailed under various *'provisional charges'*. This system has been vigorously challenged by democratic forces in the country and reform was still pending in 2017.

Many provisional charges were also brought against people who had been close to the former regime. A number of them have been dismissed either by the courts or the DPP.

The other long awaited reform is, as seen earlier in this book, either an update of the 1972 census or legislation that would address the controversial issue of mandatory ethnic identification by candidates at general elections.

One major problem since independence has been the abnormal and suspicious deaths of detainees in police cells. The Lalit party has, over the years compiled and updated a register of such cases. This register indicates that there have been 62 deaths in police cells from 1979 to 2016. Cases had even occurred after the new government took over in December . The issue has been substantially addressed by new legislation creating an *Independent Police Complaints Commission*, proposed by Prime Minister Sir Aneerood Jugnauth and voted by the National Assembly in July 2016. The IPCC is meant to be entirely independent from the police forcewhich until then used to inquire on allegations made against itself. Article 4(a) allows the commission to *"investigate into any complaint made by any person... against any act, conduct or omission of a police officer in the discharge of his functions."* [5]

An environmental threat of phenomenal proportions

Under the new government that came out of the elections of December , environmental awareness reached an unprecedented level across Mauritius. Much of the attribution for the successful awareness campaigns was generated by the appointment of a former commissioner of police and commander of the country's paramilitary force, Raj Dayal. A controversial figure throughout his career, at times excessively restless, but nonetheless very gifted for action and brimful with ideas and inititiatives, Dayal eventually found himself embroiled in an allegedly squalid affair in which he was in the process of defending himself in 2016, and which made him step down as Minister of Environment, Sustainable Development, and Disaster and Beach and Waste and Management. He was at the head of this ministry, one of the most important among all government ministries, from his appointment on December 17, to March 23, 2015, during which time he prepared Mauritius for the global environmental conference and global treaty groundwork at the Conference of Parties in Paris, at the COP 21 event, also known as the Paris Climate Conference. Mauritius participated in COP 22 in 2016

During his time at the ministry, Dayal completed and initiated major projects that received wide publicity. He was involved in regional cooperation particularly in terms of improvements to disaster alarm systems.

The ministry has stepped up works on beaches and flood prone areas, planned and initiated through his ministry the plantation of thousands of trees and other plants and produced plans and projects to provide self-employment in environmentally friendly occupations by individuals, small planters and various local communities. He devised projects for coral planting and coastal tree planting to help rehabilitate and save the beaches and lagoons. Several beach uplifting and protection projects were completed in time during the nearly ten months Dayal spent at the ministry. One of his most notable achievements was the interdiction voted by Parliament of plastic bags, the number of which used by the population had reached 300 million a year. As plastic takes centuries to deteriorate and has been stifling natural forms of life even in the lagoons, and polluting every corner of the towns, villages and coastal areas, the situation was seen to have reached the highest level of gravity and risk for the environmental health of the country and its inhabitants.

Environmental conservation, as the climate has started to change radically and for the worse in our region and across the planet, Mauritius will need men and women of action and not just of words and theories to hold the position of

---
[5] **Mauritius National Assembly, Debates, July 5,**

Minister of Environment. There is no time to waste as everything actually depends on the state of the environment, from human health to chances of survival of all species to healthy economic growth, human happiness and prosperity.

Change of Prime Minister sparks controversies

In December 2016 and January 2017, major events took place that saw a change of Prime Minister from Sir Anerood Jugnauth to his son Pravind Jugnauth, who was awaiting a Privy Council case where he still has to clear his name in the alleged Medpoint corruption as the DPP obtained leave from the Supreme Court to challenge his acquittal. Moreover, a new crisis within government that saw the PMSD and its 11 MPs leave the Alliance Lepep in power - while two PMSD MPs became turncoats within days, in turn leaving the PMSD to join the MSM where they were joined by three MPs elected under the MMM banner in 2014 who transited for some months through the Mouvement Patriotique of Alan Ganoo. In the process, government lost its three quarters majority, yet still hopeful to regain it - even if Financial Services Minister Roshi Bhadain left government to join the opposition - he eventually resigned and was fighting for his re-election against a host of candidates as this book was being completed.

Two major controversies occurred during the same period, first with the opposition contesting the transfer of power from father to son as 'undemocratic' and 'unconstitutional' albeit the fact that Pravind Jugnauth is constitutionally the leader of the majority of MPs constituting what is left of the former Lepep Alliance, a requirement under the Constitution. The Opposition contends that Pravind Jugnauth was never, in the manifesto of the winning alliance in December 2014, presented as Prime Minister for the current mandate of the government and is challenging the legality of the change, absolutely unexpected until its announcement and SAJ ensured the electorate and the country that he was capable of holding his mandate as Prime Minister until the next general election.

The second controversy centered around the President Ameenah Gurib-Fakim and her relations with Planet Earth International and its founder Alvaro Sobrinho, a dual citizen of Angola and Portugal and alleged to have been involved in major corruption scandals that continue to plague Angola. This nation is one of the most corrupt countries of the planet, observe critics of Sobrinho's major influence on high level officials in Mauritius[6]. Opposition parties and worldwide democratic activists also note that president Dos Santos has maintained himself in power for 38 years (since 1979) and that nepotism is rife in Angola.

Nevertheless, the Mauritius government has concluded in March 2017 that Sobrinho's PEI is a laudable organisation in the field of philantrophy and that he has not been convicted in relation to corrupt practices. This is hotly disputed by the Opposition parties.

New leader of Opposition: Xavier Duval (PMSD)

Another major change occurred on December 20, 2016, when MMM leader Paul Bérenger lost, due to the coming of the PMSD on the Opposition benches, his position of Leader of the Opposition. The President of the Republic appointed Xavier Duval, PMSD leader, as the new Leader of the of the Opposition, which boosted his position as one of the contenders, with Bérenger, for the position of Prime Minister. The opposition, according to Erskine May, should be considered «*as a potential alternative Government.*"»

The Chagos Archipelago: completing decolonisation at last?

Mauritius, as already explained in this book, was illegally deprived of the Chagos Archipelago, which is part and parcel of its historical territorial patrimony. This violation of international law as voted by the United Nations to ensure decolonisation of oppressed populations across the planet, was committed by the British government. The Mauritians living there were, from 1965, deported forcefully and all their domestic animals gased to death, their cemeteries left unattend-

---

[6] *"Anti-corruption institutions... are subject to widespread political interference, casting serious doubt on the political will for reform... Major worldwide governance indicators reflect this situation. In 2010, the country ranked 168th of the 178 countries assessed by Transparency International's Corruption Perceptions In... scoring 1,9 on a scale of 0 (highly corrupt) to 10 (highly clean), suggesting widespread and endemic forms of corruption. These findings are consistent with the World Bank's Worldwide Governance Indicators World Bank 2009 Worldwide Governance Indicators which underline Angola's extremely poor performance on all six dimensions of governance assessed…the country… scores very poorly in all other areas of governance, especially in terms of voice and accountability, regulatory quality and rule of law. The situation even seems to be deteriorating in terms of control of corruption (from 6,3 in 2004 compared to 5,2 in 2009). Angola also performs poorly on the 2010 Heritage Foundation's Index of Economic Freedom. The country ranks 161st out of the 179 countries assessed (and 40th out of 46 in the Sub-Saharan Africa region), with an economic freedom score of 46,2 on a 0 to 100 scale (Heritage Foundation, 2010)… the country performed extremely poorly in terms of freedom from corruption, with a score of 19 on a 0 to 100 scale, with corruption perceived to be rampant among government officials at all levels. Similarly, Angola performed poorly on the 2010 Ibrahim Index of African Governance. It was ranked 43 from to 53 in Sub-Saharan African countries assessed, scoring particularly poorly in the areas of Sustainable Economic Opportunity and Human Development (Mo Ibrahim Foundation, 2010)."* http://www.transparency.org/files/content/corruptionqas/257_Corruption_and_anti_corruption_in_Angola.pdf

ed for decades while their humble living quarters have aged to a stage beyond decrepitude.

Over the decades, Mauritius as a nation has suffered a loss in economic earnings that has yet to be calculated. But it must certainly be in hundreds of billions of dollars and innumerable jobs. In 2016, as the British and the Americans signed yet another treaty for the continued use of the illegally acquired territory in 1965, Mauritius appears to be in a quite favourable position to have its sovereignty recognized formally in conformity with severeral resolutions voted by the UN as mentioned in this book and recalled in 2016 with force by the Prime Minister, Sir Anerood Jugnauth, the current Leader of the Opposition, Paul Bérenger, member of the all-party parliamentary committee chaired by SAJ on the Chagos, MP leader Alan and in an intervention at adjournment by independent MP D. Selvon during at adjournment on July 5, 2016.[7] SAJ's speech on Chagos highlighted the following at the United Nations General Assembly on 23 September 2016:[8]

"My delegation comprises the spokesperson of Mauritians of Chagossian origin. He is the symbol of a whole community whose human rights have been baffled. His presence also testifies that the issue of sovereignty and the right of Chagossians to their native lands cannot be dissociated. Mauritius has consistently protested against the illegal excision of the Chagos Archipelago and has unequivocally maintained that the Chagos Archipelago, including Diego Garcia, forms an integral part of its territory, under both Mauritian law and international law. Mauritius has also constantly pressed for the completion of its decolonisation process. For decades, Mauritius has called on the former colonial power to engage with us in order to find a fair and just solution, but our efforts have remained in vain so far. Despite the blatant violation of UN Resolution 1514, the United Kingdom maintains that its continued presence in the Chagos Archipelago is lawful. Yet the United Kingdom also tacitly admits the impropriety of its action in dismembering the territory of Mauritius, as evidenced by the undertaking which it has given on various occasions that the Chagos Archipelago will be returned to Mauritius when no longer required for defence purposes.

This undertaking has been held to be legally binding by the Arbitral Tribunal established in the case brought by Mauritius against the United Kingdom under the United Nations Convention on the Law of the Sea to challenge the legality of the 'marine protected area' purportedly established by the United Kingdom around the Chagos Archipelago. However, the United Kingdom has so far not honoured its undertaking as the criteria on which it relies to contend that the Chagos Archipelago is still required for defence purposes keep changing.

The Arbitral Tribunal ruled that the creation of the purported 'marine protected area' around the Chagos Archipelago by the United Kingdom was in violation of international law. Two of the arbitrators found that the excision of the Chagos Archipelago from

Mauritius in 1965 showed "a complete disregard for the territorial integrity of Mauritius by the United Kingdom", in violation of the right to self-determination and that the United Kingdom is not the 'coastal State' in relation to the Chagos Archipelago. This finding has not been contradicted by the other members of the Arbitral Tribunal.

The General Assembly has a direct institutional interest in this matter given the historic

and central role it has played in the process of decolonisation throughout the world. The General Assembly has a continued responsibility to complete the process of decolonisation, including that of Mauritius. This is why at the request of the Government of Mauritius, the General Assembly has included in the agenda of its 71st Session an item entitled "Request for an Advisory Opinion of the International Court of Justice on the legal consequences of the separation of the Chagos Archipelago from Mauritius in 1965".

An Advisory Opinion would assist the General Assembly in its work on decolonization in general and the decolonisation of Mauritius in particular, pursuant to the requirements of the UN Charter and international law.

I would like to impress on the fact that the decision to have recourse to this action has not been taken in an adversarial mindset. This is not the first time that the Advisory Opinion of the International Court of Justice is being sought on such a subject. In our view, this is a legitimate recourse and it abides by the provisions of the UN Charter and past practice of the United Nations. We have noted that the United Kingdom has now expressed the wish to engage in dialogue with Mauritius in order to sort out the matter by June 2017. Mauritius has always believed in true dialogue. We are acting in good faith and we expect same from our interlocutors.

We believe that this Assembly has the duty to assist in the completion of the decolonisation process. Mauritius shares the view that an Advisory Opinion of the International Court of Justice in respect of the Chagos Archipelago will undoubtedly assist the General Assembly in the discharge of this responsibility.

I wish to heartily thank Member States of the African Union, the ACP, the Non-Aligned Group and the Group of 77 countries plus China, amongst others that have openly expressed their support to my country. I know that when it comes to justice, human dignity and territorial integrity, this Assembly will live up to its mission.

Mr. President, we concur with the UK position of a rule based international system. However, we have to be coherent, not only in what we say but also in what we do. The decolonisation of Mauritius would also not be complete until the issue of Tromelin is resolved. We have had very constructive dialogue with France and we urge France to pursue the dialogue with Mauritius for the early resolution of the dispute over the island in a continued spirit of friendship that characterises the relationship between our two countries.

L'intégrité territoriale est un principe de droit international. Les Nations Unies la reconnaissent ainsi et il est de notre devoir de la faire respecter.

---

7 Selvon, Danielle, MP, Mauritius National Assembly, Debates, Adjournment, Matters raised. July 5, 2016 - pp 93-97: http://mauritiusassembly.govmu.org/English/hansard/Documents/2016/hansard1516.pdf **Accessed 9.3.2017**

8 *The Republic Of Mauritius, Statement By The Rt. Hon. Sir Anerood Jugnauth, Gcsk, Kcmg, Qc, Prime Minister Of The Republic Of Mauritius At The General Debate Of The 71st Session Of The United Nations General Assembly New York, 23 September 2016.* https://gadebate.un.org/sites/default/files/gastatements/71/71_MU_en.pdf **Accessed 9.3.2017**

In concluding, I would like to call on the whole Membership of the United Nations to stand by the right to justice, to show that a better and safer world is only possible if thisis compatible with Rule of law and to show commitment to the principles of the Charter."

As of March 2017, Mauritius and Great Britain were in arduous discussions while the Mauritius parliamentary committee on the Chagos comprising both government and the opposition was also prepared to seek redress in mid-year through an advisory opinion of the United Nations in case the talks were unsuccessful. Government and Opposition were hoping to get back the Chagos to complete decolonisation by the time the country would celebrate its 50th Independence Anniversary on March 12, 2018. In March 2017, talks with the UK reached an impasse and Mauritius was opting for a UN advisory opinion.

Current conomic matters

On the economic front, the latest figures had been given already summed bp by Finance Minister Pravind Jugnauth back in the 2016-2017 budget as follows:

As per the World Bank's classification, Mauritius graduated to the upper middle-income status in 2003. Upper middle-income economies are those with a GNI per capita of between USD 4,036 and USD 12,475. Mauritius was, in 2015, at the level of USD 12, 128. High-income economies are those with a GNI per capita of USD 12,476 or more. GDP at current market prices is estimated at Rs 436.8 billion in 2016. Mauritius continued to grow at a moderate rate of 3.0 per cent in 2015 due to weak external demand and protracted decline in the construction sector. GDP evolved from 3.4% to 3.6% to 3.0% in 2015. The minister predicted that growth would pick up to 3.9% in 2016. In 2016, construction sector is expected to contribute positively to growth with a projected expansion of 1.6 per cent after 5 consecutive years of contraction. Investment rate, defined as the ratio of investment (GDFCF) to GDP, reached a low of 17.5 per cent in 2015. It is expected to increase to 17.9 per cent in 2016 due to higher public investment. The ratio of private investment to GDP was 12.7 per cent in 2015, down one third from its 2008 peak level of 20.5 per cent.[9]

As at budget time each year, facilities for encouraging foreign investment were further improved by the minister in the hope of boosting economic growth to meet the growth rate required to rch its ambitous goal of an *'economic miracle',* accompanied by the creation of enough jobs to drastically reduce unemployment, both objectives being the key undertakings by the government before and after taking office in December 2014. Two major promises, though, were being carried out in addition to the new-style budget and numerous measures to alleviate poverty and the scrapping of the promise of a string of *'smart cities'* across the island. The large projects being implemented under new Prime Minister Pravind Jugnauth were a major education reform introducing nine-year schooling and the re-introduction of rail transport.[10] In the context of the latter project, the PM presided the official launch at Caudan Waterfront on Friday, 10 March 2017, after decades of rail projects, including the 'métro' megaproject of the Navin Ramgoolam government. The government has pledged hawkers to have them working at the train stations along the way.

On 12 March 2017, an editor wrote one of the best assessments of nearly half century of independence in the daily newspaper L'Express.[11] He stressed, from the beginning

"Of course we are proud of our country. But to be proud of integrity implies surely, you will agree, not be, at first, blind!

If we are proud of our sense of welcome, how can we not observe that the country is moving away from its repository of good manners, politeness, restraint, slowly drifting towards the coarsest, most cynical, and more noisy."

The truth is, bluntly put, that Mauritius has achieved enormous economic progress and built a state-of -the-art cybercity in half a century of modern history since independence, and yet, suffers a string of major problems like a port that can process no more than 20-22 containers per hour, a local labour force lacking adequate training forcing employment of foreigners to run economic activities, while despite a 100% schooling rate at pre-primary and primary levels, that of secondary schooling has stagnated at 72%. The quality of education remains poor in contrast with such societies as those of the Scandinavian countries, Australia and other large democracies. School children tell interviewers that the best prime ministers are those who excel at *"giving"*, which quite the contrary of the famous saying by an American president (Kennedy) that young people should first be asking what they can do for their nation. This implies a need to shift priorities among the youth from an early age and thus foster ambition

---

9 *SUPPLEMENT TO BUDGET SPEECH 2016/17 ECONOMIC AND SOCIAL REVIEW,* Available at : *http://budget.mof.govmu.org/budget2017/budgetsupplement2016-17*.pdf Accessed 12.3.2017.

10 Transport Minister Nando Bhoda explained the project in the Mauritius Legislative Assembly in December 2016. http://www.govmu.org/English/News/Pages/Minister-Bodha-Public-transport-system-to-undergo-major-transformation-with-Metro-Express-.aspx Accessed 13.3.2017.

11 This excellent analysis is entitled *"49 ans d'indépendance, 25 ans républicains, LES YEUX OUVERTS!"* https://www.lexpress.mu/idee/302024/49-ans-independants-25-ans-republicains-yeux-ouverts Accessed 13 March 2017.

and the right values expected by society to improve itself.

Problems facing the nation were mind-bending, despite all great achievements made after independence. Some issues remained unresolved like electoral reform, despite Rodrigues having had one that rescued Rodrigues island from a 100% first-past-the-post victory of one party and 100% of all Regional Assembly seats with 56.05% of the votes of the electorate, and an opposition supported by 42.05% of the electorate. The law was changed by former PM Sir Anerood Jugnauth who, surprisingly, expressed considerable uneasiness at the Electoral Commission's decision to appoint PR candidates that reduced, yet maintained, the majority of the OPR party.[12] Yet, in Mauritius, electoral reform and other overdue commitments remained stalled, like those for a Freedom of Information Act as in all true democracies.

At another level, while we have institutions and means to combat corruption, perceptions of partisan interference in police and other institutions persisted in the second decade of the 21st century. The editorial quoted above states,

"Between 1980 and 2015, even though the GINI coefficient fell from 45.7 to 41.3... (...better, with 38.9 in 2006). It is our duty to worry about our economic vulnerabilities and our growing inability to achieve productive investment. A persistent trade deficit of more than Rs 80 billion, a public debt that is still well above 60% of GDP, a poverty problem that is deteriorating (Statistics Mauritius suggests that there are 30,000 more people in poverty " Relative "between 1996 and 2012), a balance of current account deficit of about 5% of GDP for years reminding us of our dependence on (and therefore the importance of our image) abroad are among the main parameters reminding us of the virtues of work, productivity, equality of opportunity, reduction of waste, the elimination of lame para-statal bodies, the madness of being continually removed from the challenges confronting us, often by peripheral considerations... at the end of a day at sea, is it not at least a bad conscience to have, in barely 50 years, destroyed our lagoon of its original wealth, that we are, at least, embarrassed to see our rivers being used as conveyors of " Rubbish and our fields of canes as occasional dumps?...

"If we are proud to be Mauritians, fused together by spoken language, consumed food, mixed genes, we are not blind to the point of not hearing the frantic rap of those who constantly emphasize the parentheses that separate us rather than the hyphens that unite us, those whose raison d'etre, existence itself, depends on division rather than on unity, of those who systematically cross the centripetal forces of Mauritianism lived, assumed, consummated. We are proud of our Cyber Cité, the modern airport of Plaisance, our mandatory elections every 5 years, our free press ... all the more so because the latter prevents us from being blind, being on the alert, in good faith - legitimate questions, highlighting incongruities and coincidences and thus protecting the public interest by helping the authorities (sometimes against their will) to better safeguard the future of this country.

"And you know what ? Like you, I'm proud, but I'm not blind. It is therefore with open eyes that we must judge unfulfilled election promises, incestuous appointments, policy of least effort, doubtful contracts, policies that exclude and lead to social deviance, press conferences that Ostracize rather than illuminate, suspicious connections between "elites" comfortably installed..."

Four major problems remained: a fast deteriorating environment, drugs, criminality and corruption. The public was becoming quite uneasy with them as well as with politics in general.

As Mauritius prepared to celebrate its half century of independence in 2018, there were, infortunately, not just many reasons for Mauritians to be proud of their nation, but as many to be wary of some quite unfortunate trends. Hopefully the future will be better with the changes and reforms already envisaged, yet to be fulfilled.

APPENDICES

1. Appendix 1Housing and Population Census 2011 (latest available in 2016)
2. Appendix 2: The outer islands of Mauritius (Maps, Photos, History): • Rodrigues • Agalega • The Chagos Archipelago • Tromelin
3. Appendix 3: General elections in Mauritius (Results from 1948 to 2014)

APPENDIX 1

2011 (LATEST) HOUSING CENSUS – MAIN RESULTS

1. INTRODUCTION

This issue of the Economic and Social Indicators (ESI) presents the main results of the Housing Census carried out in the Republic of Mauritius from 31 January to 19 June 2011. It also includes a summary of the changes that occurred since the 2000 Census. A list of definitions is given at Section 8.3.

---

[12] View expressed in the media. *http://www.5plus.mu/actualite/elections-rodrigues-proportionnelle-en-attendant-sir-anerood-jugnauth* Accessed 13.3.2017.

2. HIGHLIGHTS

(i) The 2011 Housing Census counted 311,500 buildings, 356,900 housing units and 341,000 households in the Republic of Mauritius as follows:

	Buildings	Housing units	Private households	Population[1]
Republic of Mauritius	**311,500**	**356,900**	**341,000**	**1,257,900**
Island of Mauritius	297,500	344,700	329,950	1,217,175
Island of Rodrigues	13,900	12,115	10,971	40,440
Agalega	100	85	79	285

[1] Population in both private and communal households

- Out of the 311,500 buildings in the Republic of Mauritius in 2011, the majority (264,100 or 84.8%) were wholly residential buildings.
- Between 2000 and 2011, the housing stock grew by 19.9% from 297,700 to 356,900 housing units.
- Out of all housing units enumerated in 2011, 90.5% were used as principal residence, 1.7% as secondary residence and 7.8% were vacant.
- The number of private households increased by 14.5% from 297,900 in 2000 to 341,000 in 2011 while the average household size decreased from 3.9 to 3.6.

(ii) Housing and living conditions improved from 2000 to 2011 with higher proportions of households:
- owning their houses (from 86.5% to 88.9%);
- having access to electricity (from 99.0% to 99.4%);
- with piped water inside their house (from 83.7% to 94.2%).

(ii) In spite of the general improvement in housing and living conditions, some households still lack basic amenities as follows:

APPENDIX 2
OUTER ISLANDS - MAPS, IMAGES, HISTORY

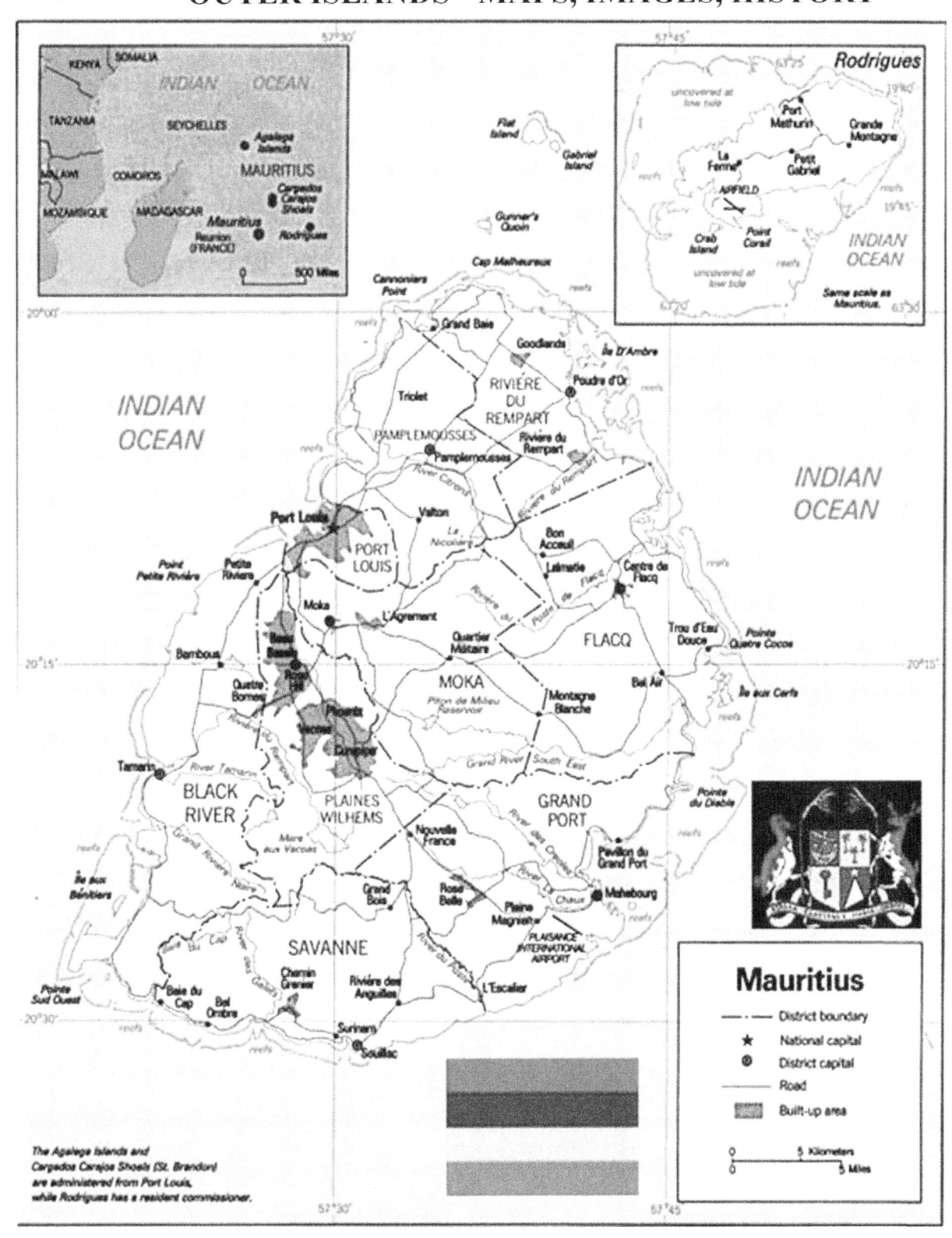

History of the Outer Islands of Mauritius
Rodrigues

The date of the discovery of Rodrigues Island is discussed in Chapter 3 of Volume 1 of this history of Mauritius. The island was not colonised by its first discoverers in ancient times and in the 16th century became part of the Portuguese empire and was still not colonised until the Dutch settled in Mauritius and a group of French protestant refugees from the Netherlands led by François Leguat arrived in 1691. Although there was an abundance of food and the island was considered a tropical paradise by the settlers, all men, they were impossible to realise their dream of a new thriving settlement due to the absence of women and no communication with the rest of the world and they managed to leave the island (see Chapter 11, Vol. 1).

It was during the French colonisation of Mauritius that Rodrigues was colonised on a permanent basis. In 1735, the need for Mauritius, then Isle de France, to get a stable supply of tortoise meat, prompted Governor Mahé de Labourdonnais to set up a colony of French settlers and their slaves in the island.

The hunt for the unique tortoise species, Cylindraspis peltastes, that proliferated all over the island, led to its extinction around 1800.[1] That was a major loss, in addition to a list of other unique species that included various birds, among which the Rodrigues Solitaire, Pezophaps solitaria, which belonged to the same family as the Dodo.

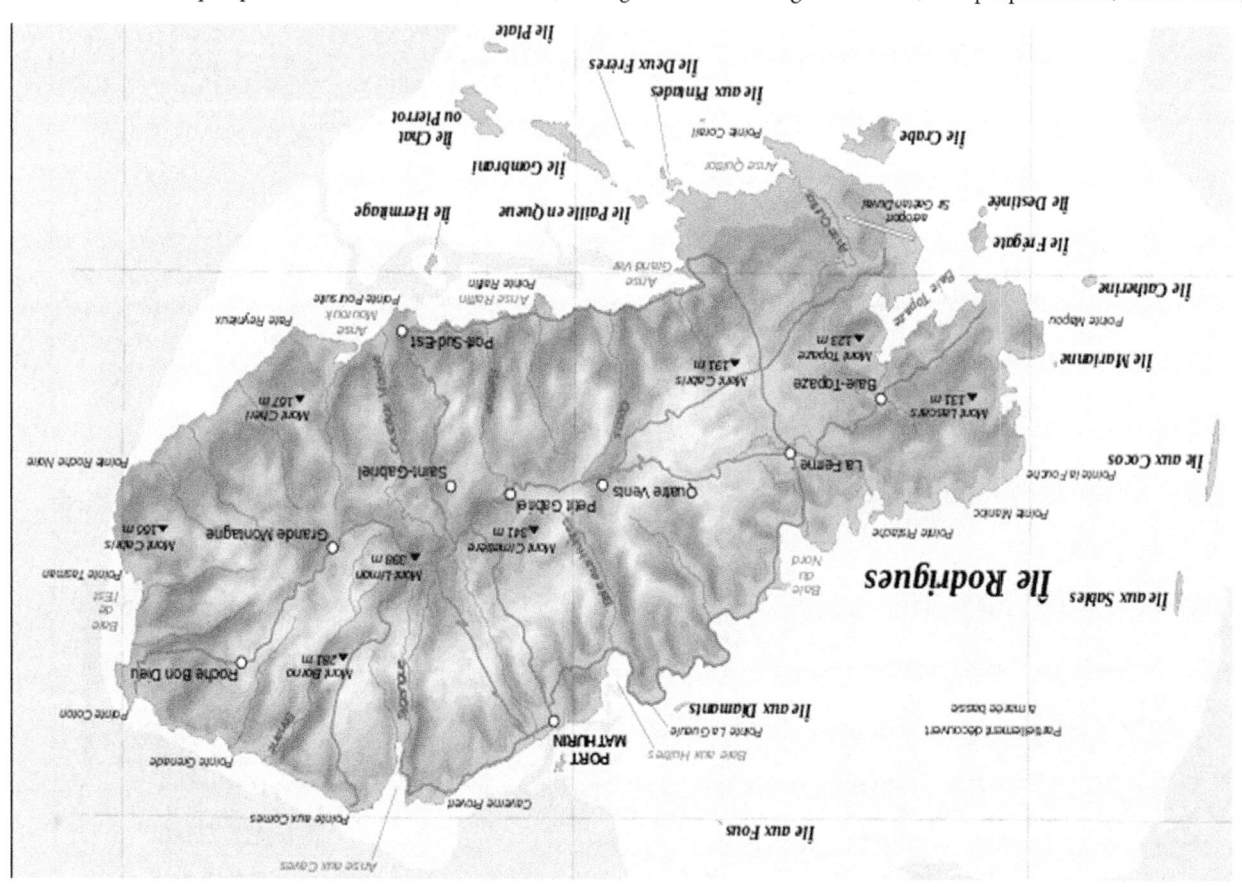

> *"This species was endemic to the island of Rodrigues, Mauritius, but was hunted to extinction in the 18th century. It was reported in 1761, but had become Extinct by 1778... Pezophaps solitaria was endemic to Rodrigues, Mauritius, from where it is known from numerous historical accounts (Cheke 1987), with those of Leguat in 1708 providing particularly rich detail (Hachisuka 1953), and many bones (Cowles 1987). It was very rare by 1761, when Pingré was informed of its presence. Morel reported in 1778 that the birds were certainly extinct."*[2]

---
[1] Cylindraspis peltastes, in: The IUCN list of threatened species, www.iucnredlist.org. Accessed 21 July 2012.
[2] Pezophaps solitaria, IUCN Red List of Threatened Species. IUCN 2006. www.iucnredlist.org. Accessed 21 July 2012.

The island then became known as a vantage point for the observation of the transit of Venus from 1761, when Abbé Pingré, a noted French scientist visited the island for that purpose. To this day, a small hill outside Port-Mathurin, the capital of the island, is called Pointe Vénus in memory of that expedition.

French colonists Philibert Marragon and Gabriel Bégué who settled in Rodrigues in the 1790s are remembered by the Rodriguans as those colonists who, after being granted land concessions, set out to develop farming and fishing. Those two activities are still, in the 21st century, crucial to the island's economy. By 1804, a first census indicated a population of 104 persons, of which 22 French colonists and 82 slaves.

The island was captured by the British in 1809 and it served, in the following year, as the base from which a large fleet carrying British troops, including Indian sepoys from India that sailed to and conquered Mauritius. The British had also conquered the other island of the Mascarenes, Réunion. In 1815, at the end of the Napoleonic Wars, they kept Mauritius and Rodrigues and handed back Réunion to the French. Under British occupation, farming and fishing further developed and Rodrigues became a crucial supplier of the products from those activities to Mauritius, mainly live animals (pigs, poultry), salted fish and octopus, onions, maize, lemons and garlic. Those products, in addition handicraft and honey, are of excellent quality and highly prized by the Mauritian population to this day. Rodrigues became known as the 'grenier de l'île Maurice' (the food loft of Mauritius) due to the importance of Rodriguans exports for Mauritius, helping considerably the latter to save precious foreign currency reserves that would have otherwise gone into food imports.

One of the recorded historical events in Rodrigues related to a natural disaster in 1883[2], when the Indonesian volcano atKrakatoa exploded:

"The August 26 eruptions occurred at 5:30 am, 6:42 am, 8:20 am and 10:02 am local time. The last of these eruptions opened fissures in the walls of the volcano, allowing sea water to pour into the magma chamber. The resulting explosion of superheated steam destroyed most of the island. The sound of the explosion was heard as far away as Australia 3500 km away, and the island of Rodrigues near Mauritius 4800 km away. It is the loudest-ever sound in recorded history."[1]

Another one was the impact of the December 2004 tsunami on the island.

The introduction of the telegraph in Rodrigues in 1901 contributed considerably to improve communications in the island. The lack of a proper landing strip prevented air links until the early 1970s, the only link, until then, being a monthly trip by ship between Port-Louis and Port-Mathurin, where passengers and goods had to be conveyed to shore in smaller boats. Air Mauritius flights in small planes that touched on the first airstrip on the island started in 1972 and today, after several developments, the original airstrip at Plaine Corail is now the Sir Gaëtan Duval Airport, which is served by daily flights. More de- velopments have been announced as Rodrigues has become one of the trendy tourism destinations of the region, with a thriving hotel and bed-and-breakfast activities, and a reputed cuisine and food products.

Rodriguans voted for the first time at the Mauritius legislative general election of 1967, sending two members of PMSD, which opposed independence to the Legislative Assembly in Port-Louis. A challenge was mounted against the PMSD at the 1976 general election by former Catholic priest Serge Clair, who at one time advocated the independence of Rodrigues, but he lost to the PMSD. In 1982, for the first time, the PMSD was defeated at the general elections by the Organisation du Peuple Rodriguais led by Serge Clair, who became minister of Rodrigues. He won in successive general elections in 1983, 1987, 1991, 1995 and 2000. In 2002, he resigned from the assembly to run in the Rodrigues Regional Assembly that was set up by the MMM-MMM government to give the island an autonomous status to run its own internal affairs. He was elected Chief Commissioner of Rodrigues until 2006 and again from 2012.

Apart from the OPR, there are two other important political parties: the Mouvement Rodriguais (MR) led by Nicolas Von Mally (briefly leader of the Op- position in Mauritius in the mid-1990s), and the Front Patriotique Rodriguais (FPR), a dissenting party from MR, led by Johnson Roussety, formerly Chief Commissioner of the MR majority in the Regional Assembly. The MR won 10 of the 18 seats of the Rodrigues regional election in 2006, and acceded to power for the first time in the Rodrigues Regional Assembly, sending Clair into the opposition. The latter defeated the MR in 2012, following which Von Mally resigned as Minister of Rodrigues in the Navin Ramgoolam cabinet. Clair was re-appointed Chief Commissioner.

The results of the February 2012 elections were as follows: OPR 11 seats, MR 8 seats, FPR 2 seats.[2] The Government of Mauritius explains the constitutional *setup of Rodrigues as follows:*

"The Regional Assembly was set up by the Rodrigues Regional Assembly Act (act 39 of 2001) which received the President of the Republic's as

---

[1] The Australian Bureau of Meteorology, The eruption of Krakatoa, August 27, 1883, <http://www.bom.gov.au/tsunami/history/1883.shtml> Accessed 21 July 2012.

[2] Rodrigues Regional Assembly Elections Held On 5 February 2012, Summary Of Results, on the Mauritius Government Portal, < *http://www.gov.mu/portal*> Accessed 21 July 2012. Inaccessible on 27 February 2012 except archived at http://archive.is/QzKo

sent on 20 November, 2001 and came into operation on 18 January, 2002 – The Constitution of Mauritius also provides for the setting up of the Regional Assembly for Rodrigues to be known as "the Rodrigues Regional Assembly". The Assembly met for the first time on 12 October, 2002.

"Thereafter, following the regional election held in 10 December, 2006, the Second Rodrigues Regional Assembly was established on 16 December, 2006... The Assembly normally meets on Tuesdays for all business and other days when this is warranted. However only on Tuesdays may questions be set to Commissioners on matters within their jurisdiction. The Assembly, excluding the Chairperson, consists of eighteen members – twelve Local Region Members

for six Local Regions and six Island Region Members.

"The Rodrigues Regional Assembly is empowered to make Regulations for matters falling within its purview. It may initiate legislation which, however, has to be ushered into the National Assembly to become law for Rodrigues. The Assembly prepares and adopts its annual budgetary estimates. These are then considered by the Cabinet of Ministers before being incorporated in the National Appropriation Bill. The budgetary provision for the Rodrigues Regional

Assembly features as a one line all-comprehensive item in the National budget.

"In view of geographical distance and for the sake of greater efficiency, the law provides for regular interaction between the Rodrigues Regional Assembly, through the Chief Commissioner, and the Prime Minister. Commissioners are also encouraged to consult relevant Ministers on the mainland as often as is necessary."

The area of the island is only 108 km2 in area, measuring 18 km by 6.5 km. The population was estimated at nearly 38,000 in 2011. The island is surrounded by coral reef and some small uninhabited islets. The island is of volcanic origin, having arisen from a ridge along the edge of the Mascarene Plateau. The island is one of the most beautiful among the islands of the south western Indian Ocean, with great beaches, excellent food, an indigenous culture and a variety of the Creole language that has a specific charm. The environment has some unique endemic species. Most of the inhabitants are of the

Catholic faith and descend mainly from the former slaves and free Coloured persons (gens de couleur) who lived there before the British conquest.

Rodrigues is a rich and fascination destination for environmentalists and scientists who indulge in researching its unique indigenous fauna and flora on land and sea. Some forests areas and islets have been decreed nature reserves under the Forest Reserves Act 1983 to afford protection to several quite rare species: 14 hectares at Grande Montagne, 10 hectares at Anse Quitor, and the islets of Ile aux Sables (8 h.) and Ile aux Cocos (14.4 h.). Rodrigues is surrounded by a

well-developed reef system, particularly in the northwest and southwest where it is about 6 km wide, while in the east the width is only 1 km or less.

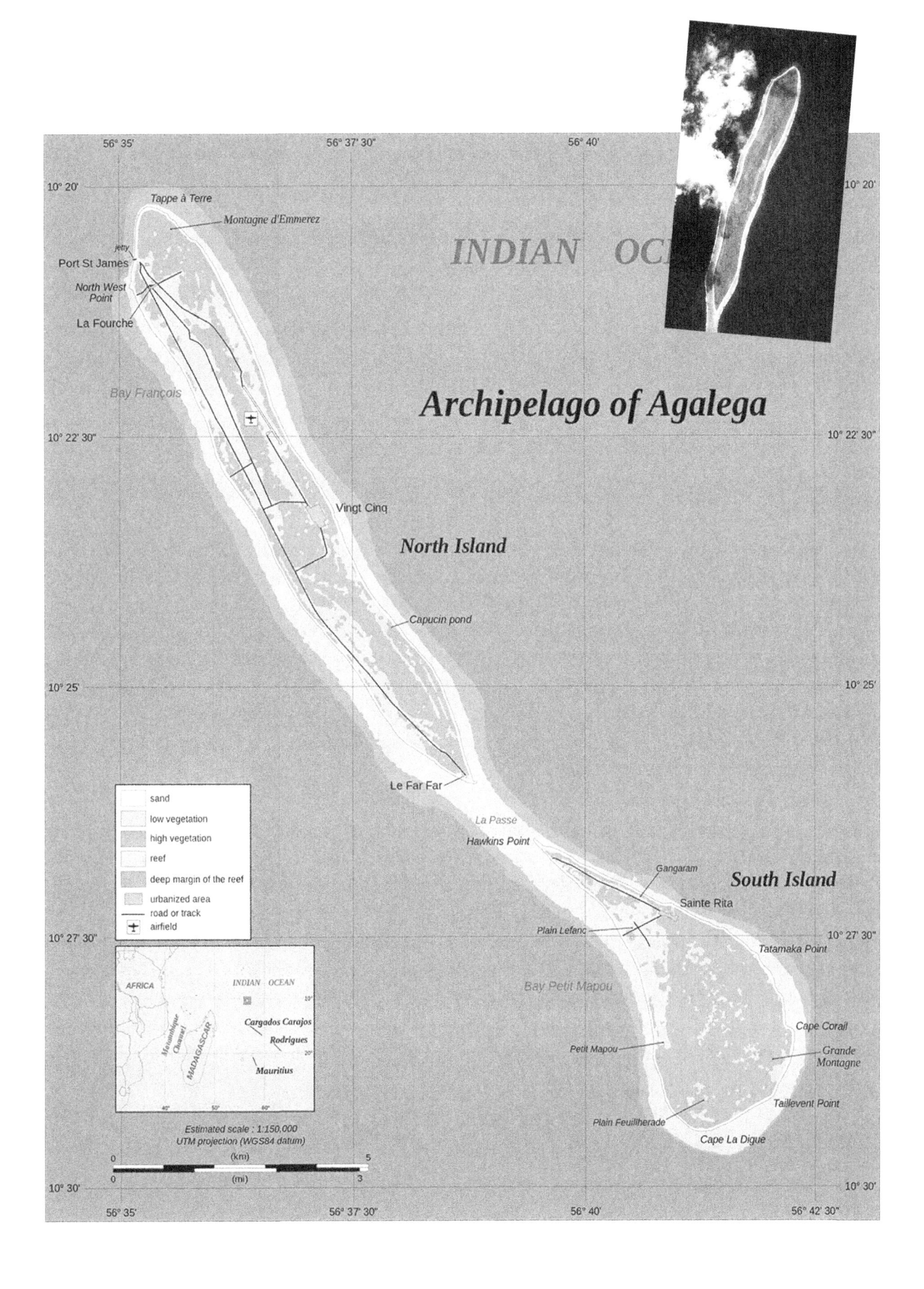

Archipelago of Agalega

INDIAN OCEAN

North Island

- Tappe à Terre
- Montagne d'Emmerez
- Jetty
- Port St James
- North West Point
- La Fourche
- Bay François
- Vingt Cinq
- Capucin pond
- Le Far Far

South Island

- La Passe
- Hawkins Point
- Gangaram
- Sainte Rita
- Plain Lefanc
- Tatamaka Point
- Bay Petit Mapou
- Petit Mapou
- Cape Corail
- Grande Montagne
- Taillevent Point
- Plain Feuillherade
- Cape La Digue

Legend

- sand
- low vegetation
- high vegetation
- reef
- deep margin of the reef
- urbanized area
- road or track
- airfield

AFRICA — INDIAN OCEAN — Mozambique Channel — MADAGASCAR — Cargados Carajos — Rodrigues — Mauritius

Estimated scale: 1:150,000
UTM projection (WGS84 datum)

Agalega

Two very coveted islands of Mauritius are those that constitute the little archipelago of Agalega, 1,100 km north of Mauritius. Their total area is of 24 km² (North Island 14.3 km² and South Island 9.7 km²). Agalega is connected by air thanks to an airstrip in the North Island, where the main inhabited agglomeration, Vingt-Cinq, is located, as well as the village of La Fourche. The village of Rita is in South Island. Agalega's main economic activities are the production of coconuts and fishing.

The island were originally settled from Mauritius for the purpose of producing coprah from coconuts for the production of coconut oil. The Agalega Day Gecko (Phelsuma borbonica agalegae) is a unique diurnal gecko not found anywhere else. The islands and the sea around them are of great interest to scientists of the environment and of the other natural sciences.

The island was probably known to ancient navigators coming from the Arab world and the Far East, including people sailing from the Malaysian and Indonesian islands, especially those who migrated across the Indian Ocean to the South Indian continent, Madagacar and Africa, according to Roger Dussercle, as laureate of the Académie Française and a priest, who visited Agalega in the late 1940s,[1] The name of the islands, though, is Portuguese in origin, probably given by explorer Don Pedro Mascarenhas, one of whose ships, that touched their shores in 1512, was named Galega.

Another hypothesis is that the name's origin is that of a Galician explorer working for the Portuguese, Jean Gallego or Jean the Galician man (real name João de Nova) when he reportedly discovered the island as far back as 1501, 'a galega' meaning the Galician woman. A stopover in the island in 1824 indicated to a ship crew that the northern island was inhabited at some periods because they saw coconuts that had been chopped open. The book that relates this stopover also indicates a pristine natural environment with very large numbers of birds.[2] Yet another hypothesis, made by Sir Robert Scott, is that the islands were discovered in 1509 by Portuguese explorer Dio Lopes de Seqeira who called them Baixas da Gale in relation to the gale force winds in the region.

"The pilots dutifully wrote into their charts Baixas de Gale, or Galeass Bank. It was as Gale, accordingly, that Agalega first appeared on a map: Pedro Reinel's map of 1517."[3]

Two researchers, Cheke and Lawley, quoting various sources, have observed,

"After two centuries of obscurity, Agalega was rediscovered by the French ship Rubis in 1758 (Scott 1961). Fauvel (1909) credited the rediscovery to the Charle and the Elisabeth in 1742, but Scott considered their itinerary very doubtful). The islands became a dependency of the then Ile de France, and remain to this day part of the State of Mauritius. The island was colonised from Mauritius in1808 (Scott 1961)."[4]

According to Scott, the first settlement was founded by Caillou de Rozemont, whose description of the island is still one of the important references regarding the state of the environment in the early 19th century.[5] The name Rosemond is often used, by some writers but that first settler has used Rozemont in his own work on Agaléga.[6]

Dussercle, in his account, has quoted ancien maps where Agalega is called by different names. Apart from Reinel's map quoted above, the word 'Gale' is used in other maps published in 1519 (Lopo Homen) and 1520 (Jorge Reinel). Then

---

1 Dussercle, Roger, Agaléga, Petite île. The General Printing and Stationery Cy. Ltd., Port-Louis 1949.
2 Eyriès, Jean Baptiste Benoît, Les Nouvelles Annales de Voyage, Librairie de Gide Fils, Deuxième série Tome VIII, Paris 1828, pages 88-92.
3 Scott, Robert, *Lemuria. The Lesser Dependencies of Mauritius*, London, 1961.
4 Cheke, A.S., Lawley, J.C. *Biological History Of Agalega, With Special Reference To Birds And Other Land Vertebrates*, [1983]. Cheke. Universidad de Antioquia, Medellin.
5 Caillou (de) Rozemont. *General observations; survey of coconuts and agricultural potential. 1808-09*, as cited by Clarke A.S. and others, op. cit.
6 Clarke A.S. and others, op. cit..

the islands are called Agualega in 1546 and 1569 by other cartographers who also, sometimes, give wrong locations. According to Dussercle, one administrator of Agalega from 1827 to 1846, Auguste Leduc, started in 1838 the construction of a road linking the north and south islands, but it was destroyed because no provision was made for the sea to go through under the structure, and moreover, the waves can be very violent in the vicinity of Agalega. People can move between the two islands on foot at low tide and Dussercle noticed the remains of the old structure built by Leduc.

Caillou de Rozemont arrived in the islands in August 1808 and discovered one day the bodies of two men, those of a privateer, Robert Dufour, and a Mauritian traveller, a young woman named Adélaide d'Emmerez. They had been shipwrecked and had been involuntarily the first inhabitants of the island. Dussercle also stated that Dufour had left a note in a bottle.

Other persons who came to the island include Auguste Le Duc, a Frenchman sent to administer the small colony in 1827. He organised the production of copra, which is the dried flesh of the coconut fruit from which oil is obtained.

Slaves were brought in for this economic activity and the name of the principal agglomeration Vingt-Cinq, that is the Twenty-Five, is one of the legacies of that period because it was the number lashes given to slaves who ran away. The other traces left from those days are two cemeteries, one for the Blacks, one for the Whites.

From 2006 to 2012, Indian newspapers have reported that the Mauritius government of Dr. Navin Ramgoolam was contemplating to hand over the Agalega islands to India for military purposes. Those reports have been denied by the Mauritius government.

The Chagos Archipelago

The history of the Chagos Archipelago prior to its cession in 1965 to the UK for military and strategic purposes (already dealt with in this volume), was known to ancient navigators and had Arab and Indian names given to it. It is a group of over 60 islands that form part of the territory of Mauritius and are currently occupied by Great Britain as already explained in previous chapters of this book (Volume 2).

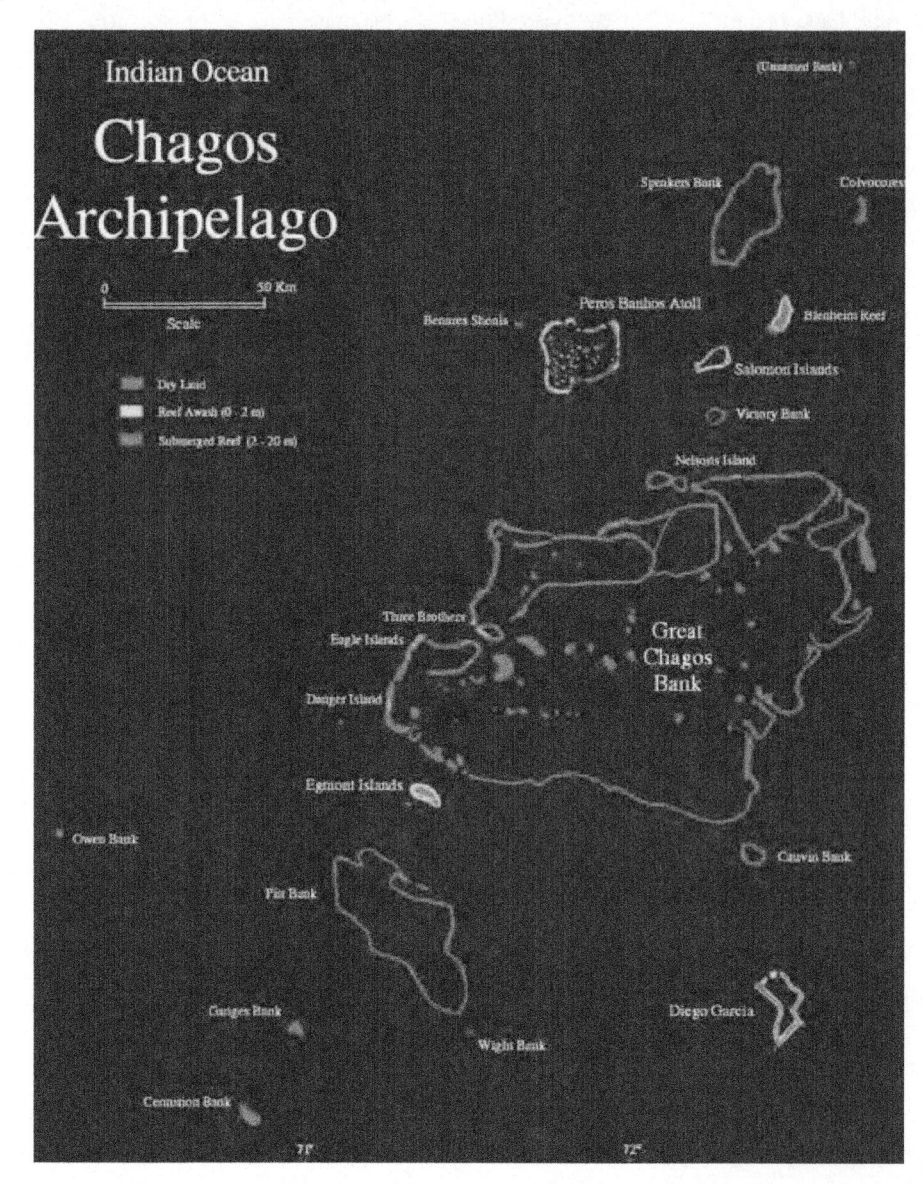

The islands cover only 63.17 km² and the largest one, Diego Garcia, has an area of 27.20 km² of land, but, counting the lagoons inside the atolls, the total area exceeds 15,000 km² and this comprises the Great Chagos Bank, which is second in size after the world's largest, the Saya de Malha Bank, a major fishing site, which also fall in the exclusive economic zone (EEZ) of Mauri- tius and Seychelles. Some other islands are Peros Banhos, Egmont Islands and Salomon Islands.

The largest individual islands are Diego Garcia (27.20 km²), Eagle (Great Chagos Bank, 2.45 km²), Île Pierre (Peros Banhos, 1.50 km²), Eastern Egmont (Egmont Islands, 1.50 km²), Île du Coin (Peros Banhos, 1.28 km²) and Île Boddam (Salomon Islands, 1.08 km²). There are reefs and banks in the archipelago, many of them submerged. Fishing is a lucrative activity in the region. Fishing licences brought revenue that exceeded half a million pounds sterling in 2003-04 according to figures revealed in the UK parliament:

"Jeremy Corbyn: To ask the Secretary of State for Foreign and Commonwealth Affairs what the latest annual income is from fishing licences in the British

Indian Ocean Territories.

"Mr. Rammell: Income from fishing licences in the financial year 2003–04 was £564,431." [1]

Although known to the peoples of the northern, eastern and western rim of the Indian Ocean basin, the Chagos were never colonized in very ancient times, even by the Maldivian people who live 500 kilometres away and who would only find themselves in the Chagos whenever the weather would drive them there. They had two names for the Chagos, Fōlhavahi or Hollhavai, but they still considered the island as being too remote for any durable settlement.[2]

In fact, the Arabs and the Chinese were crossing the Indian Ocean in all directions in the 15th century. That the Arabs were specialist of the northern and western Indian Ocean up to Mauritius and Reunion is a well known fact. Chinese explorations were only discovered in more detail in recent times and a digression is necessary here because of more recent discoveries on the Chinese explorations during the 21st century.

The Chinese explorers travelled in huge ships that dwarfed by several times the later Portuguese discovery ships. Two Portuguese researchers of modern times, Jorge Nascimento and Professor Tessaleno Devezas 13 have noted that the Portuguese were the pioneers of globalization from the 15th century, and Nascimento, in further research, has noted that the Chinese exploration voyages were characterized by *"Religious tolerance, non-ideological* evangelization: it was usual for the Chinese armadas to carry Muslim, Hindu and Buddhist *servants to provide advice and guidance."* Nascimento explains, regarding the great Chinese Admiral Zheng He, an officer of Islamic faith:

"What has been accepted by the Chinese and foreign scientific community so far is that the Chinese would have traveled over much of the Pacific and Indian Ocean, covering more than fifty thousand kilometers (100,000 "li" in the Chinese traditional unit of distance) and visited more than 3000 "barbarian" locations (or 30 countries) in less than 30 years), as reported by the Admiral himself in 1431. One expedition was made up of 62 great junks carrying 17,800 soldiers on

board! It all began with an incipient desire to re-establish the protectorate over the Sunda Islands (now including Borneo, Java, Sumatra, Bali, Flores, as far as Timor), which supplied China with gold and spices, as Fernand Braudel states in his ***Grammaire des Civilisations***.

"Between 1405 and 1433, seven expeditions would have reached Indonesia, Indochina, India (Calicut), Ceylon (now Sri Lanka, where a garrison was erected), Hormuz at the entrance to the Persian Gulf, Jeddah (now the second largest city in Saudi Arabia) in the Red Sea, and finally the Eastern coast of Africa

(Mogadishu, in modern Somalia, and Zanzibar). The Chinese regarded Malacca and Calicut as military bases and strategic commercial "hubs" on[3] these voyages and routes. Much to the surprise of the Chinese at home, the explorers brought back giraffes from Africa (qilin in Chinese) which the Ming Emperor almost immediately transformed into a magical creature."

The Chinese should have been aware, even if they may not have touched there, of the existence of the islands of the Northern and Western Indian Ocean, including the Chagos, because, understandably, they had to have had the proper navigation maps already in the 15th century, before the Europeans.

The first Europeans to arrive in the Chagos Archipelago were the Portuguese, who were crisscrossing the Indian ocean after they reached the Cape of Good Hope for the first time and Vasco da Gama went from there to East Africa and then to India.[4] The names of several Portuguese explorers were or still are associated with several places across the Indian Ocean, and these include Rodrigues, Agalega, the Mascarenes, Saya de Malha, Chagos, Diego Garcia, Peros Banhos and more. Mauritius lost its name of Cirne, which could have been the name of the Portuguese ship Syrne,[5] despite the still current habit of people writing on Mauritius, including Mauritians, still think that Cirne meant 'swan' in Portuguese, while this is not correct because 'swan' is 'cisne' in Portuguese or Spanish and 'Cirne' often appears as a proper and not a common name in Portuguese and it was the name of one of the Portuguese ships that touched Mauritius, commanded by Diogo Fernandes Pereira, believed by many to be the Portuguese discoverer of Mauritius, while others think it was Diogo Dias who made that discovery for Portugal, as discussed in Chapter 3 of Volume 1.

In the case of the Chagos, the original Portuguese name was Bassas de Chagas or Bassas de Chagos, according to ancient navigation

---

[1] House of Commons, Hansard, 21 Jun 2004 : Column 1218W. <https://www.publications.parliament.uk/> Accessed 21 July 2007
[2] Romero-Frias, Xavier, *The Maldive Islanders, A Study of the Popular Culture of an Ancient Ocean Kingdom*, Barcelona. 1999.
[3] Rodrigues, Jorge Nascimento, The two oldest Matrixes of World Discoveries Portuguese and Chinese Historical linkage, at <gurusonline.tv>. Nascimento is co-author a book, Pioneers of Globalization, with Professor Tessaleno Devezas and published January 2008 by Centro Atlântico, Portugal (Available at: www.centroatlantico.pt/globalization).
[4] See Volume 1, Chapter 3.
[5] Ibid.

maps and manuals.[6] 16

In Portuguese, the word 'chaga' means 'wound' and it is believed that the reference is to the wounds of Christ, but this is uncertain as the word 'chagas' refers to a group of plants known as 'nasturbium,' which includes the watercress according to the Portuguese to English translation by the Dicios Dictionary.[7] The words 'bassas'and 'chagos' do not even exist in that dictionary or in another online Portuguese to English dictionary.[8] There is uncertainty also regarding who were the first and also the various Portuguese explorers who named the islands of the Chagos. The closest word seems to be 'baixio' which is used to mean low, and designate low lying things and also shoals and reefs. One island was named Baixio da Judia, later turned into Bassas da India by cartographers and geographers. Similarly, Baixios de Pêro dos Banhos

The earliest recorded account known of the Chagos was in the years following a shipwreck there in 1955. It was made by a survivor and this event has been summed up as follows (the Portuguese words are explained after the excerpt):

"The nau left Belem for India with Captain Francisco Nobre and Pilot Alfonso Pires. They sighted the Cape of Good Hope on the 18th July 1555 and proceeded further off the island of Medagasker in the direction of India when they saw green water indicating the sign of a sand-bank. Soon the vessel dashed against it and got stranded on the bank of the island of Peros dos Banhas. Some people jumped and swam across to the island. 154 persons per- ished in this tragedy. Captain Nobre, Pilot Pires and some other sailors went in a batel. On the island they made a small ship and the newly selected Captain Alvaro de Athiade went in it to India promising to send help. The survivors remained there for about five months with no help. They made another small ship and left for India on 1st

April 1556 withut a Captain or Pilot but with 27 survivors and they reached Cochin in January 1557. It included Manuel Rangel who wrote an account of the tragedy."[9]

(Note: The words 'nau' and 'batel' mean ship and the word Medagasker obviously means Madagascar.)

It would be interesting to obtain, as it forms part of the history of a part of Mauritian territory, the outer islands of the Chagos Archipelago, an English version of Rangel's book "A Tragédia dos Baixos de Pero dos Banhos." Bits and pieces on various internet sites and from books on Portuguese shipwrecks, give some more indications about the event and the number of survivors is not clear. They found thousands of birds and turtles that came from the sea to lay eggs on the beaches. Water was to be found by boring shallow wells.

The next important period in the history of the Chagos was the French settlement that was first established in 1784 by an inhabitant of Isle de France (Mauritius), the Sieur Pierre Marie Le Normand who exploited sugar cane and coconuts in the western district of Black River. As seen in Volume 1, the French adopted a system of land concessions from 1726.[10] Le Normand obtained a large concession on the main island of Diego Garcia in 1783 and sailed to that island in the following year in two ships that transported about 80 slaves. To help him create a permanent settlement and set up the necessary organization, he brought free persons, mainly skilled workers.

It was in this way that Mauritius founded a permanent settlement in its dependent islands in the Chagos Archipelago – an event of major historical significance for the State of Mauritius to this day in its claim of sovereignty. It makes this claim inalienable. The little colony prospered as coconut plantations were expanded by other 'colons' from Isle de France, well before the British conquest of Mauritius. The coconuts were used to produce not only copra, from which oil is extracted, but also numerous objects that have been in everyday use in Mauritius where they have been exported for centuries from the outer islands, including Chagos: brooms made of dried coconut leaf stalks for outside use like cleaning yards, coconut brushes for cleaning floors, dried coconuts used for a large number of purposes in Mauritius, including religious services in the Hindu tradition, handicraft, etc.

Those exports to Mauritius from its outer islands have been flourishing before the advent of the modern era and they were

---

[6] D'Après de Mannevillette, Jean-Baptiste-Nicolas-Denis and Huddart, Joseph, *The Oriental Navigator, Or, New Directions for Sailing to and from the East Indies: Also for the Use of Ships Trading in the Indian and China Seas to New Holland, &c. &c*, James Humphreys, 1801 - 566 pages.
[7] Dicios, language dictionary. http://en.dicios.com/ Accessed 27 February 2017.
[8] <http://www.portuguesedictionary.net/> Accessed 22 July 2012.
[9] Mathew, K.M., *History of the Portuguese Navigation in India, 1497-1600*, Mittal Publications, New Delhi 1988. 352 pages.
[10] Chapter 13, Volume 1.

important for the national Mauritian economy. This contribution by the islanders should not be forgotten today, in the 21st century and it did not prevail among the Mauritian parties present at the 1965 discussions in London during which they ceded the Chagos to Britain without any protest, following which the islanders were sent to exile to live in dire poverty for decades. Those people are an integral part of the Mauritian nation whether they are granted or not British citizenship. In modern times, frozen fish were sent from the Chagos to Mauritius and this potential will certainly be exploited again when Mauritius regains its sovereignty.

During the French period, and the early era of British colonization, slavery prevailed on all those islands that were inhabited and exploited: Diego Garcia, Peros Banhos, Six Iles, Trois Frères, Ile d'Aigles and Iles Salomons. Coconuts were not the only produce as their exports included salted fish and octopus, timber of excellent quality for various uses and guano, which made Mauritian agriculture, especially the sugar plantations, flourish and prosper. Sea turtles were also exported to Mauritius, either live or salted, for their meat, for domestic consumption and also for the treatment of leprosy, so much so that the French sent lepers for their recovery in the Chagos.

Mauritius kept the Chagos after the Seychelles was detached administratively in 1903 to form a separate colony. In 1965 a multi-party delegation from Mauritius accepted to hand over the islands to the UK on the basis that Mauritian sovereignty would resume when the UK and the United States would no longer need the islands. In 1966, the UK government purchased all the assets and real properties of the Chagos Agalega Company of the Seychelles. From 1967 to 1973, the islands were depopulated *manu militari* by the Anglo-Americans and their inhabitants sent to Mauritius and the Seychelles without any measure taken by any of the governments involved, including the Mauritian government, to help them settle down properly.

The Chagos: a rendez-vous for the international yachting community!

The sad story of the cession of the Chagos and of the evolution of Mauritian policy towards a unanimous claim for the return of the islands to Mauritius have been discussed in earlier parts of this book.[11] One of the bones of contention is the refusal of the Anglo-Americans to allow the islanders to return to live in their islands. However, the international yachting community is allowed to enjoy the islands while Mauritians and Chagossians are banned. The following account, from the website of one of the yachting community[12] gives us an interesting view of how well received they are in the so-called BIOT and also a useful and informative snapshot:

"Permanently temporary

"Chagos Archipelago is perhaps the last bastion for would-be Robinson Crusoes. It is a bizarre community of cruising yachts running away from the world, forming a micro-society which is not completely free from the politics of the civilized one.

"From the cruising point of view, Chagos is two atolls; Peros Banhos and Salomon Atoll. Salomon atoll offers a better protection from winds from all directions, though the best shelter requires anchoring on coral or wrapping a chain around a coral boulder for a mooring. Peros Banhos is a much larger atoll (about 12 miles across) and shifting winds force yachts there to move around for protection, particularly during the transition periods of the SW/SE monsoons.

"While the lack of isolated cakes of coral makes navigation easier in Peros the steeply sloping sand bottom forces yachts to anchor in water 20m deep or more. A real pain in the ass for those without a push-button anchor winch. Aliisa never went to Peros, so I can't really tell you much about it. In 2005 the "fleet" of visiting yachts was almost split in half between the two atolls, many yachts spending their time in Peros Banhos and never visiting Salomon Atoll and vice versa. My impression is that Salomon atoll remains generally the more popular one.

"Up to 50 or so yachts visit Chagos each year, though numbers vary from one year to another. The busiest season seems to be around April - May. Chagos is relatively safe at any time of the year, free of cyclones but not stranger to severe weather periods and violent squalls. There are a few remains of wrecked yachts reminding us of the care and common sense needed by all cruisers.

"Administration

"The area is administered by the Brits and officially called the British Indian Ocean Territory or BIOT. (I Hate Those Letter Combinations For Everything, from now on referred as IHTLCFE) The closest paper-pushers and bureaucrats are based in Diego Garcia, 120 miles south of the yachtie community, within a large US military base. (The Yanks are the tenants with practically a perpetual rental agreement.) The Fisheries Patrol travels up from Diego randomly to check up on things and chasing away any illegal fishing vessels in the area. They also carry onboard the British officials. The fee for yachts in 2005 was US 100 for a maximum 3 month stay, longer stays require re-payment only.

---
[11] See Chapter 41 about 'the rape of the Chagos.'
[12] <http://www.laurig.com/voyage_offline/chagos.html> Accessed 22 July 2012. Inaccessible on 27.2.2017 except on http://archive.is/FW7UV

Tromelin Island

The island of Tromelin, also referred to as Ile de Sable, has been made famous by a noted French writer, Irene Frain, who has denounced the way, during French colonization in Mauritius, the Black survivors of a shipwreck were ruthlessly and knowingly abandoned to their fate there in the 18th century.[1] We have also mentioned a major finding by a French archeological mission that has recently discovered the proof of Mauritian sovereignty over the island in the form of the remains of a building used by Mauritian companies on behalf of the Mauritian sugar industry and other agricultural sectors for the extraction of guano, a crucial fertilizer that has historically played a most important role in making Mauritius a prosperous country.[2]

Tromelin is located 470 km east of Cape Masaola in Madagascar and 560 km north of Mauritius. It is a small coral islet measuring 1 km2 this highest point is 6 metres. The island is deprived of fresh water and natural resources save guano, the dejection of sea birds, an excellent fertilizer that was excavated by tons by Mauritian enterprises. Tromelin appears to be a former reef that emerged from the ocean. The reef probably rested on a point where there was volcanic activity.

The island is surrounded by the ocean which is deep by nearly 4,000 metres. Probably, like the other islands of the region, Tromelin was known to ancient navigators who sailed to East Africa and Madagascar. The Portuguese also may have encountered the island. Nevertheless, the island is not hospitable and access and anchorage are very difficult and risky by sea, especially by sail- ing ships and must even have been avoided by ships plying in the region.

Jean Marie Briand de la Feuillée discovered the island on August 11, 1722, bringing it into the French colonial empire. Apart from the shipwreck mentioned in Chapter 41, the island does not have much recorded history, except that the World Meteorological Organization decided to set up a meteorological station there in the 1950s and the British gave France the authority to carry out this mission. From that time, in 1954-55, the French took control of the island and, violating Mauritian sovereignty on an island that was included with Mauritius among the territories of British Mauritius, claimed it as one of their colonial possessions.

The island is important for its bird life and has been proclaimed as an IBA (Important Bird Area) by BirdLife International, which provides the following information: *"Ornithological information - Two seabird species nest, both boobies (Sulidae). During 1993–1996, 200–250 pairs of Sula dactylatra nested (with up to 700 birds present, and increasing), alongside 130–180 pairs of S. sula (up to 500 present, declining). These populations comprise less than 1% of the global populations, but the site is considered to be an Important Bird Area for the following reasons: first, Sulidae populatioin the western Indian Ocean have declined seriously and these are among the healthiest in existence; second, S. dactylatra is represented in the western Indian Ocean by an endemic race (S. d. melanops), of which Tromelin is one of the strongholds; and third, the S. sula population at Tromelin is the only the only polymorphic one in the region, indicating uniqueness and biogeographical isolation. Fregata ariel became extinct before 1968 and F. minor in the early 1980s, but up to 120 Fregata spp. use the island for roosting. Resident landbirds are absent.*

"Other biodiversity - The islet is a nesting site for the sea-turtle Chelonia mydas (EN).

"Management considerations - The islet was made a Nature Reserve in 1975. Classification as a Strict Nature Reserve by Arrêté Ministériel is needed to improve the site's protection (see 'Conservation infra polymorphic one in the region, indicating uniqueness and biogeographical isolation. Fregata ariel became extinct before 1968 and F. minor in the early 1980s, but up to 120 Fregata spp. use the island for roosting. Resident landbirds are absent.

"Other biodiversity - The islet is a nesting site for the sea-turtle Chelonia mydas (EN).

"Management considerations - The islet was made a Nature Reserve in 1975. Classification as a Strict Nature Reserve by Arrêté Ministériel is needed to improve the site's protection (see 'Conservation infrastructure and protected-area system'). Tromelin is an important research site. Human disturbance to the seabird colony is minimal. Rattus norvegicus have been abundant and are a limiting factor to seabird populations, but are controlled periodically (although never eradicated) by poisoning." [3]

The island is now under a comanagement agreement between Mauritius and France, but Mauritius still claims its sovereignty.[4]

---

[1] Chapter 41.
[2] Ibid.
[3] See section on Tromelin. in document downloaded from http://www.lifecapdom.org/IMG/pdf/ibas_reunion_birdlife.pdf **Accessed 27/02/2017,**
[4] Chapter 41.

"MAURITIAN" BUILDING FOUND IN TROMELIN

The 3rd French archaeological mission to Tromelin found in December 2010 the remains of a building *(photo, left)* which they dated after the shipwreck of 1761 and before the sudden occupation of this Mauritian island by France in 1954-55 despite officially acknowledging it as part of British Mauritius and arguing Mauritius never exercised any right on Tromelin. The scientists wrote in their reports that the building was probably built by Mauritian ship crews collecting guano there with a license delivered by Mauritius and were defintely not part of the ruins left by the 1761 castaways.

The other photo has been produced by the French scientist to illustrate the difference between the level of the ruins of 1761, and those of the presumably Mauritian-built building used by Mauitian sorkers operating under licences delivered by the authorities in Port-Louis, Mauritius, prior to the unexpected French occupation. France then decided to offer a co-management arrangement of the island with Mauritius while continuing to affirm its sovereignty. However, Mauritius continues to claim that the island has been illegally occupied by France which had only been assigned by the World Metrorological Organization to set up a weather station when Tromelin was a dependency of Mauritius under British rule and was administered from Port-Louis to license ships collecring guano on Tromelin as fertilizer abundantly used by the Mauritius agricultural sector. Both photos are available in the French online official mission reports at https://www.archeonavale.org If your security settings deny access, you can go to this site where a French official government archeological report even mentions ruins on Tromelin that could be of Mauritian origin here originating from guano exploitation with permits 'delivered by Mauritius': http://www.taaf.fr/Retour-de-la-mission-archeologique-de-Tromelin

Bibliography, references and sources

Hereunder are various books, documents and other sources that have been used in the course of the research for this book:

- Le grand livre de l'histoire du monde. Atlas historique. Paris, 1986; World History, New Jersey. 1995. Much of the information in this chapter is based on those comprehensive histories of the world. How Asteroids Built the Continents. In: The Scientific American. December 28, 2009.) Auber, J, Histoire de l'Océan Indien, (Madagascar, 1955), North-Coombes, A, La découverte des Mascareignes par les
- Arabes et les Portuguais (Port-Louis, 1979), World History (World Almanac, New Jersey, 1995), and Le grand livre de l'histoire du monde (Paris, 1986)
- Pridham, Charles, A Historical, Political and Statistical Account of Mauritius and its Dependencies, T and W Boone. London 1849
- The Voyage of Hanno, translated with Greek text, commentary and map by T. Falconer (London, 1797).
- Pitot, Albert, T'eylandt Mauritius, 1598-1710. Mauritius, Port-Louis. 1906. Precis of the Archives of the Cape of Good Hope (Letters received, Letters dispatched, Journal). Cape Town, 1896, 1898,1905.
- North-Coombes, A. La découverte des Mascareignes par les Arabes et les Portuguais. PortLouis, 1979. His book is one of the most impressively documented on the earlier visits to Mauritius. Volume 2.XML.html[9/30/2016 8:21:06 AM]
- Congresso Internacional de História dos Descobrimentos, Lisboa, 1961. Actas — Vol. III, pp. 163-196.
- The Bull Inter Caetera (Alexander VI), May 4, 1493. Papal Bull. Dias, Bartolomeu (2010). Encyclopædia Britannica. Encyclopaedia Britannica Ultimate Reference Suite.
- Roger Théodora, Candide et l'Ancien Puits, libres considérations sur le passé lointain des îles Mascareignes et de l'Océan Indien, Azalées Editions 2006.
- Hume, Julian P. (2006). The history of the Dodo Raphus cucullatus and the penguin of Mauritius. Historical Biology 18 (2): 65-89 and other works on the Dodo. Internet: http:// julianhume.co.uk/? page_id=14 Retrieved 14 November 2011.
- Vérin, Pierre, Maurice avant l'Isle de France. Anthologie de textes anciens présentés par Pierre Vérin, Professeur à l'Institut des langues et civilisations orientales. Fernand Nathan. Paris, 1983.
- Brébion, Antoine, Bibliographie des voyages dans l'Indochine française du IXe au XIXe siècle, Burt Franklin, New York. 1910.
- Stevenson William,, Historical Sketch of the Progress of Discovery, Navigation and Commerce, In: Kerr, Robert, Collection of Pacific VoyagesA General History And Collection Of Voyages And Travels,
- Forming A Complete History Of The Origin And Progress Of Navigation, Discovery, And Commerce, By Sea And Land, From The Earliest Ages To The Present Time, 18 volumes. W Blackwood, T Cadell. London 1824.
- Linschooten, van Jan Huygen, Itinenari, voyage oste Schipvaert, eClaesz in-fol, Amsterdam 1596.
- A Mauritius government report to the United Nations Forum on Forests www.un.org/esa/ forests/pdf/national_reports/unff2/mauritius.pdf Retrieved 14 November 2011.
- Restoring the Mauritian ecosystem, Natural History Museum, UK. http://www.nhm.ac.uk/ nature-online/science-of-natural-history/researching-the-dodo/restoring-the-mauritianecosystem/ Retrieved 14 November 2011.
- Donald F. Lach, Edwin J. Van Kley, Asia In The Making of Europe, Vol. 3, A century of Advance, The University of Chicago Press. 1993.
- Mundy, Peter, Travels in England, Western India, Achin,Macao, and the Canton..., Richard Carnac Temple (ed.). 1919
- Barnwell, P J and Toussaint A, A Short History of Mauritius Longmans, Green and Co. London, New York, Toronto, 1949.
- Paul KAEPPELJN, Les Escales françaises sur la route de l'Inde, Paris, Challamel, 1908. Barnwell, P J, Visits and Despatches: (Mauritius, 1598 - 1948) Port Louis: StandardPrinting Establishment. 1948
- The Travels of Peter Mundy, Part ii, Second Series, published by the Council Of the Hakluyt Society, 1919
- Tasman, A J, De reizen van Abel Janszoon Tasman en Franchoys Jacobszoon Visscher ter nadere ontdekking van het Zuidland in 1642/3 en 1644, uitg. door R. Posthumus Meyjes, Published 1919 by M. Nijhoff in S-Gravenhage. The book has been translated by the Gutenberg Project: Abel Janszoon Tasman's Journal, Heeres J E (ed.), A Project Gutenberg of Australia eBook. 2006.
- McCall Theal, George, Chronicles of Cape Commanders. An Abstract of Original Manuscripts in the Archives of the Cape Colony dating from 1651 to 1691, Compared with Printed Accounts of the Settlement by Various Visitors during that time. Cape Town, 1832. W A Richards & Sons, Government Printers, Cape Town. 1882; by the same author: History of South Africa Under the Administration of The Dutch East India Company 1652-1795. Swan Sonnenschein, London. 1897.
- The Dodo and ScientificFantasies: Durable Myths Of a Tough Bird, Archives of natural history. Volume 36, Page 136-145 DOI 10.3366/E0260954108000697, ISSN 0260-9541, Available Online April 2009.
- Leguat François, The voyage of François Leguat of Bresse, to Rodriguez, Mauritius, Java, and the Cape of Good Hope, London. Printed for the Hakluyt Society.1891.
- Parmentier, Jean et Raoul, Le discours de la navigation. Voyage à Sumatra en 1529. Description de l'isle de Sainct-Dominigo, Ernest Leroux (ed.). Paris 1883. The introduction to the book of the two explorers states that they did round the Cape of Good Hope based on the information they provided, found Madagascar and the Comoros on their way to the Far East where they touched at Sumatra.
- Lougnon, Albert, L'île Bourbon pendant la régence.Desforges Boucher. Les Débuts Du Café, Editions Larose. Paris 1956.405 Pitot, Albert. L'Ile de France: Esquisses Historiques, E. Pezzani. Port Louis,1899.
- Oberle, Philippe, Provinces malgaches, Antanarivo, Madagascar 1979
- Lettre du Père Brown à Madame La Marquise De Benamont, dated 'towards the end of the 18th century' in: Choix des lettres édifiantes: Missions de l'Amérique, Jean Baptiste de Montmignon - Paris : Maradan, 1808-1809.
- History of the Pyrates, Captain Charles Johnson. London, 1724. D'Unienville, Claude Antoine Marrier (Baron), Statistique de l'Ile Maurice et de ses dépendances, Gustave Barda, Paris, 1838.
- Lagesse, Marcelle, L'Isle de France avant Labourdonnais. 1721-1735. Mauritius Archives, Publication No. 12. Port-Louis, 1973.
- Il y a 300 ans naissait J.-B. Garnier du Fougeray. In : La Gazette des Iles de la Mer des Indes, pp. 8-11, No. 26. Vacoas, Mauritius Jan 1990.
- Prise De Possession de L'Ile De France Par Jean Baptiste Garnier Du Fougeray.(23 Septembre1721), in L'Ile de France, Pitot A, op cit.
- Chelin, A, Une Ile et son passé, 1507-1947, Port-Louis 1972 and a supplement published by the Editions de l'Océan Indien, Rose Hill 1993.
- Le Code Noir ou Edit du Roy, servant de règlement pour le Gouvernement & l'Administration de Justice & la Police des Iles... du mois de mars 1695. A Paris, Au Palais. Chez Claude Girard, dans la Grand'Salle, vis-à-vis la Grande'Chambre: au nom de Jesus. cM. DCC. XXXV. [1735].
- D'Epinay, Adrien, Renseignements pour servir à l'histoire de l'Ile de France, Nouvelle Imprimerie Dupuy. Port-Louis 1890.
- Sen, S N, History of Modern India, New Age International, 2006.
- The Private diary of Ananda Ranga Pillai, Dubash to Joseph François Dupleix, a record of matters political, historical, social, and personal, from 1736 to 1761, translated by Sir J.F. Priceand K. Rangachari. Government Press,

Madras,1904.

- Selvon, S, Vacoas-Phoenix – La genèse d'une ville, Swan Printing. Port-Louis 1984. Pierre CREPIN, Charpentier de Cossigny, fonctionnaire colonial, Paris, Leroux, 1922.
- Falconbridge, A, An Account of the Slave Trade on the Coast of Africa, J Phillips, G Yard. London 1792.
- Guillaume-Thomas-François, abbé Raynal (1713-1796) Histoire philosophique et politique, des établissements et du commerce des européens dans les deux Indes (Didot Le Jeune. Paris 1770).
- Mauritius Archives, Compagnie des Indes. Documents divers concernant la régie de la Compagnie. 1731-1745.
- Voltaire, OEuvres complètes, Tome Quatrième. Paris 1819. Haudrère, Philippe, La Bourdonnais, Marin et aventurier. Edition Desjonquères, Paris, 1992.
- Herpin, E, Mahé de la Bourdonnais et la Compagnie des Indes, René Prud'homme, St. Brieux, France. 1905.
- Peerthum, Satteeanund, Resistance against Slavery, in Slavery in South West Indian Ocean. U. Bissoondoyal, S.B.C.Sevansingh (eds.) Mahatma Gandhi Institute, Moka. Mauitius 1989.
- Chapman. Palmares: The Negro Numantia. Journal of Negro History 3.1, 1918. Diggs, Irene, Zumbi and the Republic of Os Palmares. vol.14 of Phylon (1940–1965).
- Freyres, Gilberto. The Masters and the Slaves: A study in the development of Brazilian civilization. New York: Knopf 1956.
- Gomes. Slavery, Black Peasants and Post-Emancipation Society in Brazil (Nineteenth century Rio de Janeiro). Social Identities 10.6 (2004).
- Saint-Pierre, Bernardin de, Voyage à l'Isle de France, Paris 1773, Editions de l'Océan Indien, Mauritius 1986.
- D'Unienville, Raymond, Histoire politique de l'Isle de France (1789-1803), 3 volumes, Mauritius Archives Publications nos. 13, 14, 15. Port-Louis 1975, 1982, 1989.
- Gerbner, Katharine, Antislavery in Print: The Germantown Protest, the "Exhortation," and the Seventeenth-century Quaker Debate on Slavery, University of Pennsylvania Press, Early American Studies:
- An Interdisciplinary Journal - Volume 9, Number 3, Fall 2011, pp. 552-575. Volume 2.XML.html[9/30/2016 8:21:06 AM]
- La Bourdonnais, Mahé de, Mémoires des îles de France et de Bourbon pendant la régie de Mahé de La Bourdonnais, gouverneur-général des dittes isles et préparé par lui-même, 18th century manuscript consulted by the author in 1984 at the Carnegie Library, Curepipe, Mauritius. Published in Paris by his grandson : B.-F. Mahé de La Bourdonnais: Mémoires historiques de B.-F. Mahé de La Bourdonnais, gouverneur des îles de France et de la Réunion, recueillis et publiés par son petit-fils... (Comte A.-C. Mahé de La Bourdonnais). Paris, 1890 (with a second edition, Paris,1898.
- Rouillard, Guy, Histoire des domaines surciers de l'île Maurice, General Printing & Stationery. Pailles, Mauritius 1980.
- George II. Encyclopædia Britannica. Encyclopædia Britannica Ultimate Reference Suite. Chicago: Encyclopædia Britannica, 2010.
- La Bourdonnais, Bertrand-François Mahé, Count (comte) de . Encyclopædia Britannica. Encyclopædia Britannica Ultimate Reference Suite. Chicago: Encyclopædia Britannica, 2010.
- Newitt, Malynm, A History of Mozambique, C. Hurst & Co. Publishers, 1995. Zbigniew A. Konczacki, Janina M. Konczacki, An Economic History of Tropical Africa, Routledge, Jun 30, 1977.
- José Capela and Eduardo Medeiros, La traite au départ du Mozambique vers les îles françaises de l'Océan Indien – 1720 1904, in: Slavery in the South-West Indian Ocean. Papers presented to the International
- Conference on Slavery held in 1995 at the Mahatma Gandhi Institute (MGI) in Mauritius. U.Bissoondoyal and S.B.C Servansing (eds.). Moka. Mauritius 1989.
- Grant, Charles, The History of Mauritius, or the Isle de France, and the Neighbouring Islands from Their First Discovery to the Present Time., composed principally from the papers and memoirs of
- Baron Grant, who resided twenty years in the island, by his son Charles Grant, Viscount de Vaux, Bulmer & Co.London 1801.
- Milbert, M J, Voyage pittoresque à l'Ile de France, au Cap de Bonne Espérance et à l'Ile de Ténériffe, Tome premier, A Nepveu, Paris 1812.
- Chew, Emrys, Crouching Tiger, Hidden Dragon: The Indian Ocean And The Maritime Balance Of Power In Historical Perspective, S. Rajaratnam School of International Studies. Singapore 25 October 2007.
- The Naval Chronicle Vol. 07, p. 188-189 online: <http://www.archive.org/stream/navalchronicleco07londiala/navalchronicleco07londiala_djvu.txt > Accessed 21 November 2011.
- Mauritius Illustrated, Macmillan, A, ed. London 1915. Rethinking Ancestors and Colonial Power in Madagascar: Jennifer Cole and Karen Middleton in
- Journal of the International African Institute, Vol. 71, No. 1 (2001), pp. 1-37,Cambridge University Press.
- Amicale Ile Maurice-France, Pierre Poivre (1719-1786), Precigraph. Mauritius 1993. Poivre, Pierre Voyages d'un Philosophe, ou Observations sur les Moeurs et les Arts des Peuples de d'Afrique, d'Asie & de l'Amérique, London 1769.
- Astronomical Society of Southern Africa, De la Caille, Louis, Web < http:// assa.saao. ac.za/html/his-astr-lacaille.html> Accessed 21 21 November 2011.
- Rose, John, Holland, Benians, Ernest Alfred, Newton, Arthur Percival, The Cambridge History of the British Empire, Vol I. The Old Empire from the Beginnings to 1783. Cambridge University Press 1929.
- Dull, J R, The French Navy and the Seven Years' War, University of Nebraska Press 2005: "(…) the attack on French shipping, made without a declaration of war, caused terrible losses to France, perhaps as many as 300 ships and their cargoes, worth 30 million livres. Some 7,500 sailors and apprentices, more than half of them trained seamen, were brought to England as prisoners in 1755 (including 1,600 captured on warships)."
- Voltaire, Précis du Siècle de Louis XIV. Berlin 1751. The book was accessed on the web on 22 November 2011 at: http://www.archive.org/stream/lettredescommiss00raim#page/n1/mode/2up
- North-Coombes, Alfred, 1907 – 1998. The Island of Rodrigues. Port-Louis 1971. Napal, D, Les Constitutions de l'ils Maurice: documents réunis, Issue 6 of Mauritius archives publication fund. Mauritius Printing Co. 1962.
- Toussaint, A, Port-Louis. Deux siècles d'histoire (1735-1935), La Typographie Moderne. Port-Louis 1936; an English abridged version exists: Port-Louis, a Tropical City, G Allen & Unwin. London 1973. Also: A.N. Col C/4/28 folio 165, Le 2 septembre 1771 – Desroches au ministre. Revue de détail des méchants et des honnêtes gens. Archives Nationales de France, Available at < http:// www.pierrepoivre.fr/Base-doc-71-72.html> Accessed 26 November 26, 2011.
- Poivre, Pierre, Voyages d'un philosophe ou observations sur les moeurs et les arts des peuples de l'Afrique, de l'Asie et de l'Amérique, Fortuné-Barthélemy de Félice, 1769. Benyowski,Maurice Auguste, comte de, Memoirsand Travels of

- Mauritius Augustus Count de Benyowski, Kegan, Paul, Trench, Trubner. London 1904.
- North-Coombes, A, Histoire des tortues de terre de Rodrigues, 2nd ed. Port-Louis 1994. Daniel Vaxelaire, L'Histoire de La Réunion, Éditions Orphie, coll. « Le Grand Livre », 2005.
- Juan de Lisboa: < http://fr.wikipedia.org/wiki/Juan_de_Lisboa> Accessed 23 November 2011.
- Orian, Alfred, La vie et l'oeuvre de Philibert Commerson, Mauritius Print. Cy. Port-Louis 1973.
- Commerson, Philibert, in: Complete Dictionary of Scientific Biography. 2008. Encyclopedia.com. 23 Nov. 2011.
- Duyker, Edward, An Officer of the Blue, Marc-Joseph Marion Dufresne, South Sea Explorer 1724-1772, Melbourne University Press 1994.
- French Government, Ministère de la Défense (French Defence Ministry), Jean-François de La Pérouse. Biographie. Online <http://www.defense.gouv.fr> Accessed 26 November 2011.
- Jean-François de Galaup, comte de La Pérouse, Larousse.< www.larousse.fr> Accessed 26 November 2011.
- Jean-François de La Pérouse, Voyage autour du monde sur l'Astrolabe et la Boussole, La Découverte / Poche. Paris 2005.
- Charpentier de Cossigny, Joseph François, Mémoire pour la colonie de l'Isle de France, en réponse au précis et au Mémoire des actionnaires de la Compagnie des Indes, P. Fr. Didot le Jeune. Paris 1790.
- Notes sommaires en réponse aux Observations sommaires, sur le Mémoire publié pour la colonie de l'Isle de France, P. Fr. Didot le Jeune. Paris 1790.
- Crépin, Pierre, Charpentier de Cossigny, fonctionnaire colonial: d'après ses écrits et ceux de quelques uns de ses contemporains, E. Leroux. Paris 1922.
- WANQUET, Claude, La France et la première abolition de l'esclavage (1794-1802) [le cas des colonies orientales, île de France (Maurice) et la Réunion, Karthala. Paris 1998. Toussaint, A, Early Printing in the Mascarene Islands. University of London Press 1951. The Spread of Printing: Mauritius, Réunion, Madagascar and the Seychelles, Van Gendt. Amsterdam 1969.
- Napal, Doojenraduth, Les Indiens à l'Ile de France, Editions Nationales. Mauritius 1965. Toussaint, A, La route des îles, S.E.V.P.E.N. Paris 1967.
- Filliot, J-M, La traite des esclaves vers les Mascareignes au XVIIIe siècle, ORSTOM. Paris 1974.
- AM, OC 3, fol. 51, Etat des sommes qui ont été payées (...) à divers employés, lascards et malabards libres et esclaves attachés au service du Roy sur l'isle de Rodrigues à compter du 1er Aoust 1767 jusques et compris le der(nier) avril 1769, Mauritius Archives.
- D'Unienville, baron, op cit, provides detailed population statistics that indicate the presence of Indian slaves and some slaves coming also from Malaysia, and his estimates is that the slaves no more than one seventeenth of the slaves are of Indian extraction. Historians have deducted from those various sources that there were approximately about 3,500 to 5,000 Indian slaves during the period 1773 to 1835, at the time of the abolition of slavery.
- The Hindu: Bill to rename Pondicherry as Puducherry passed. http://www.hindu.com/2006/08/22/stories/2006082207481000.htm Accessed 24 November 2011. Saint-Pierre, de, Bernardin, Paul et Virginie, Hachette. Paris 1863.
- Pingré, Alexandre Guy, Voyage scientifique à l'île Rodrigues. Extracts from an 18th century manuscript by the author. Terres Créoles, Réunion Island, and Editions de l'Océan Indien, Mauritius (eds.) 1993.
- Céré, Jean-Nicolas, Journal de Voyage, original 18th century manuscript by author from a private collection, pubished in La Gazette des Iles de la Mer des Indes, Yvon Martial (ed.). Vacoas, Mauritius January 23 1989. Pp 14-19.
- Revue historique et littéraire de l'Ile Maurice, Lettres inédites de Poivre et de Céré. Published from issue No.13, 4th year, from 24 August 1890, to issue No. 28, 4th year, dated 7 December 1890.
- Pitot, Thomi C, Quelques observations sur l'ouvrage intitulé Voyage à l'Ile de France par un officier du Roi, presented to the Société d'Emulation de l'Ile de France on 3 August 1805.
- Billiard, Auguste, et Montalivet, Jean-Pierre Bachasson, Voyage aux colonies orientales, ou, Lettres écrites des îles de France et de Bourbon pendant les années 1817, 1818, 1819 et 1820, à M. le cte de Volume 2.XML.html[9/30/2016 8:21:06 AM]
- Montalivet, pair de France, ancien ministre de l'intérieur, etc, Librairie française de l'Advocat. Paris 1822.
- On the website of the Université de la Réunion: Débats sur l'esclavage: avant l'abolition, at http://unt.univ-reunion.fr/uoh/idc/co/cours70.html >.
- D'Unienville, Raymond, Hier Suffren, Mauritius Printing Cy. Mauritius 1972. Villiers, Patrick, Les corsaires: des origines au traité de Paris du 16 avril 1856 . Presses universitaires du Septentrion 2002. P. 125.
- Wanquet, Claude, La France et la première abolition de l'esclavage, 1794-1802: le cas des colonies orientales, Ile de France (Maurice) et la Réunion. Karthala 1998. Toussaint, A, Histoire des Iles Mascareignes, Editions Berger Levrault. Paris 1972. Quenette, Louis Rivaltz, La franc-maçonnerie à l'île Maurice. La Vauverdoise. Port-Louis 1988.
- Roux, J S, Le Bailli de Suffren dans l'Inde. Marseille 1862. Digitalised (freely available) by Google Books at: <http://books.google.com/books > Accessed 25 November 2011.
- Hennequin, Essai historique sur la vie et les campagnes du Bailli de Suffren. Paris 1824. Digitalised (freely available) by Google Books at:< http://books.google.com> Accessed 25 November 2011.
- Toussaint, Auguste, Les frères Surcouf, Flammarion. Paris 1979. Guillemin, Robert, Corsaires de la république et de l'Empire, France-Empire 1982.
- Mauritius Archives, Records of the French Occupation of Mauritius, Petite Rivière, Mauritius.
- Tabardin, Jean-Baptiste, La vie ou les aventures de J.B. Tabardin: Imaginé et commencé le premier janvier 1805 dans la Raveline de Bombay, original manuscript consulted by the author of this book at the Carnegie Library, Curepipe. Mauritius. Published by Norbert Benoit at Vivazi, Mauritius, 1993.
- Mauritius Archives: Mauritius Archives: 1808; Gouvernement Républicain. Bureau du Génie. Mémoires et rapports divers. 1790-1801.
- The following digitalized documents (primary sources) of the French Revolution have been made freely available to researchers at <www.openlibrary.org>: Dernières observations des citoyens de couleur des isles et colonies françoises ; du 27 novembre 1789 by Etienne-Louis-Hector de Joly - first published in 1789. Coloured citizens ask for rights and privileges;
- Adresse a l'Assemblée-nationale, pour les citoyens-libres de couleur, des isles & colonies françoises by Etienne-Louis-Hector de Joly - first published in 1789 ;
- Pétition nouvelle des citoyens de couleur des isles francoises, a l'Assemblée nationale by France. Assemblée nationale constituante (1789-1791) - first published in 1791;
- Lettre des commissaires des citoyens de couleur en France, a leurs frères et commettans dans les Isles françoises by Julien Raimond - first published in 1791;
- Lettre aux citoyens de couleur et nègres libres de Saint-Domingue et des autres isles françoises de l'Amérique par M. Grégoire, Député à l'Assemblée Nationale et Evêque de Loir et Cher by Grégoire,
- Henri - first published in 1791. This document supports the granting of rights to the Coloured and Free Blacks;
- Mémoire sur les causes des troubles et des désastres de la colonie de Saint-Domingue by Julien Raimond - first published in 1793 Présenté aux comités de marine et des colonies, dans les premiers jours de juin dernier, par les citoyens de couleurs; d'après l'invitation qui leur en avoit été faite par les comités;
- Constitution française des colonies de Saint-Domingue, en soixante-dix-sept articles by Saint-Domingue - first published in 1801. Abolition de la loi du divorce, qui assure la prospérité des familles.
- La garantie des propriétés individuels des personnes et la liberté des nègres, des gens de couleurs, et de tous genres présenté au premier consul de France, par le citoyen Toussaint-Louverture, général en chef et gouverneur des colonies françaises de Saint-Domingue.411
- Villèle, Joseph, comte de, Mémoires et correspondance du comte de Villèle, 5 vols. Paris 1887-90.
- Original letter from Napoléon, dated 25 July 1802. Web: <http://www.histoire-empire.org/correspondance_de_napoleon/1802/juillet_01.htm> Accessed 27 November 2011.
- Genty Maurice, Yves Bénot et Marcel Dorigny (dir.), Rétablissement de l'esclavage dans les colonies françaises. Aux origines de Haïti, Cahiers d'histoire. Revue d'histoire critique [En ligne] , 96- 97 | 2005, mis en ligne le 23 juin 2009, Consulté le 27 novembre 2011. URL : http://chrhc.revues.org/index1032.html
- Prentout, Henri, L'Ile de France sous Decaen 1803-1810; essai sur la politique coloniale du premier empire, et la rivalité de la France et de l'Angleterre dans les Indes Orientales. Thèse pour le doctorat-es-lettres présentée à la faculté des

- lettres de l'université de Paris, Hachette. 1901.
- Marina Carter & Mark S. Hall, Grand Port: Untold Stories, CRIOS, MPG Books Group. London 2010.
- The Wellesley Papers by The Editor Of "The Windham Papers", Volume Two, Herbert Jenkins Limited. London 1914.
- Avine, Grégoire, Les voyages du chirurgien Avine à l'Ile de France et dans la Mer des Indes au début du XIXesiècle, Mauritius Archives Publications, Publication No. 5 (from original manuscript by the author), Raymond Decary (ed.), G Durassié. Paris.
- Scott, Ernest, The Life of Matthew Flinders, Angus and Robertson. Sydney, Australia 1914. Flinders, Matthew. A Voyage to Terra Australis. London: G. and W. Nicol, 1814: vols 1and 2.
- Flinders, Matthew. Matthew Flinders' private journal from 17 December 1803 at Isle de France to 10 July 1814 at London. Ed. Anthony J. Brown and Gillian Dooley, Adelaide: Friends of the State Library of South Australia, 2005.
- Matthew Flinders - Private letters, vol. 2, 1806-1810 Safe 1/56 Web:<http://acms.sl.nsw.gov.au/_transcript/2007/D00007/a053.html> Accessed 30 November 2011. Bennett, Bruce, Exploration or Espionage? Flinders and the French, in The Journal of the European Association of Studies on Australia, Vol.2. No.1, 2011, ISSN 2013-6897.
- Duyker, Edward. Francois Péron: An Impetuous Life. Melbourne University Press, 2006.
- Estensen, Miriam. The Life of Matthew Flinders. Sydney: Allen & Unwin, 2003.
- Fornaserio, Jean, Peter Monteath and John West-Sooby. Encountering Terra Australis.
- TheAustralian Voyages of Nicolas Baudin and Matthew Flinders. Kent Town: Wakefield Press, 2004.
- Clowes, Laird, Assisted by Sir Clements Markham, K.C.B., P.R.G.S., Captain A. T. Mahan, U.S.N. , Mr. H. W. Wilson, Col. Theodore Roosevelt, President of the United States, etc., The Royal Navy. A
- History From the Earliest Times to the Present, Vol. V (of 6 vols.), Sampson Low, Marston and Company. London 1900.
- Le Trésor de la Sainte-Marie at trésordelasaintemarie.com. Accessed 30 November 2011.) Campbell, John, and Redhead, Henry, Naval history of Great Britain, including the history and lives of the
- British admirals, J. Stockdale, Vol. VIII. London 1813.
- Sermet, Laurent, Une anthropologie juridique des droits de l'homme: Les chemins de l'Océan Indien, Éd. des Archives contemporaines – 2009
- Code Noir 1724, Historical Collections of Louisiana, B. F. French, 1851. LC Rare Book and Special Collections Division. In: Historical journal of the establishment of the French in Louisiana, by
- Bernard de La Harpe. Tr. from the French. Created/Published: New York, 1851. French original published: New Orleans, 1831. Web <http://international.loc.gov/_intldl/fiahtml/fiatheme2c3.html> Accessed 6 December 2011.
- Aïssaoui, Mohammed, L'Affaire de l'esclave Furcy, Prix Renaudot Essai 2010, Prix REF du Livre 2010, Gallimard. Paris 2010.
- Peabody, Susan, La question raciale et le « sol libre de France »: l'affaire Furcy, Annales. Histoire, Sciences Sociales 6/2009 (64e année).
- URL : www.cairn.info/revue-annales-2009-6-page-1305.htm Accessed 1 December 2011.
- House of Commons. Papers (One Volume) Relating to Captured Negroes; also to The Slave Trade; Slave Population at The Seychelles &c. Session From 2 February to 31 May 1826. Volume XXVII. P. 295: Slave Trade at The Mauritius and Bourbon, and The Seychelles, from the time of their capture to the present time (1811-1817).
- Anti-Slavery Reporter, No. 50. For July 1829. No. 2 Vol. iii. The Eiseinhower Library. Web: <http://www.archive.org/stream/antislaveryrepor50soci/antislaveryrepor50soci_djvu.txt> Accessed 4 December 2011.
- Hansard, Commons sitting, Slave Trading and the State of the Slaves in the Mauritius, HC Deb 09 May 1826 vol 15 cc1014-51. Volume 2.XML.html[9/30/2016 8:21:06 AM]
- Thomas Fowell Buxton. Working to End Slavery , in: History's Heroes. East of England Broadband Network: <http://historysheroes.e2bn.org/hero/4259> Accessed 4 December 2011.
- Recollections of Seven Years Residence at the Mauritius, Or Isle of France, by 'A Lady', James Cawthorn (Ed.). London 1830.
- Lebeau, Auguste, De la condition des gens de couleur sous l'Ancien Régime D'après des documents des Archives Coloniales, Guillaumin & Cie (eds.). Paris 1803.
- Hansard 1802-2005, Commons sitting, Administration of Justice in Trinidad, HC Deb 13 June 1811 vol 20 cc610-22.
- Hansard 1802-2005, Commons sitting, Seizure and Imprisonment in Jamaica.Petition of L C Lecesne and J Escoffery. HC Deb 21 May 1824 vol 11 cc796-804.
- Hansard 1802-2005, Commons sitting, Deportation of Messrs. L C Lecesne and J Escofferyfrom Jamaica. HC Deb 16 June 1825 vol 13 cc1173-205.
- Wesley, Charles H, The Emancipation of the Free Colored Population in the British Empire, The Journal of Negro History, Vol. 19, No. 2 (Apr., 1934), pp. 137-170
- Quenette, Rivaltz, La fin d'une légende. Port-Louis, 1980; L'oeuvre du Révérend Jean Lebrun à l'île Maurice, Regent Press, 1982.
- Clarkson T, History of the Rise, Progress and Accomplishment of the Abolition of the African Slave Trade by the British Parliament. London 1808.
- A voice from England: in vindication of the well-earned claims of Remy Ollier, the founder of the "Sentinelle de Maurice" newspaper, to the gratitude of his brethren, members of the Mauritian coloured population, by a coloured gentleman long Hansard 1802-2005, Vote of Thanks, Commons Sitting. HC Deb 07 June 1811 vol 20 cc519-32.
- Hansard 1802-2005, The Lord Commissioners' Speech at the Close of the Session, Lords Sitting, HL Deb 24 July 1811 vol 20 cc1118-20.
- Farquhar, Robert T, Letter to Lord Wellesley, copy of original published by Amédée Nagapen in: La Gazette des Iles de la Mer des Indes, No. 21. Vacoas, Mauritiius. Le Cernéen, 13 février 1822.
- Correspondence of the Governor of the Mauritius with the Colonial office, regarding the State of the Slave Trade, as summed up in: Parliamentary abstracts: containing the substance of all important papers laid before the two Houses of Parliament during the session of 1825, Longman. London 1826.
- Blair, Richard A, Licentious And Unbridled Proceedings: The Illegal Slave Trade To Mauritius And The Seychelles During The Early Nineteenth century, in: Journal of African History, 42 (2001) pp. 91-116. Printed in the United Kingdom. Cambridge University Press 2001.
- La Gazette des Iles, No. 26, p. 48: Nagapen, A: Textes rares de R.T.Farquhar: Lettre à l'Honorable Thomas Clarkson sur le dévelopement de l'île.
- CLARKSON PAPERS Vol. V. Official correspondence of Sir Robert Farquhar, Bart. (1821), Governor of Mauritius, relating to the suppression of the slave trade. Copies. The chief contents are despatches from Farquhar to [Francis, 1st] Marquess of Hastings, Governor-General of Bengal, and correspondence (often in the form of copies transmitted with the despatches) with Capt. Fairfax
- Moresby, CB [GCB 1865; Admiral 1870], Senior Naval Officer at Mauritius, [Pierre Bernard, Baron] Milius al. Mylius, Governor of Bourbon, the Imam of Muscat, the Governor ofZanzibar, the King of Johanna (Comorols) and Radama,

- King of Madagascar. There are two letters from Farquhar to Thomas Clarkson. Paper; ff. 74. Folio. 31 Mar. 1819-18 Feb. 1822.
- Rakotoarisoa, Jean Aimé, La notion d'esclave en Imerina (Madagascar) : ancienne servitude et aspects actuels de la dépendance. TALOHA, numéro 14-15, 29 septembre 2005, http://www.taloha.info/document.php?id=233.
- Campbell, Gwyn, Masagascar and the Slave Trade, 1810-1896, The Journal of African History, Vol. 22, No. 2 (1981), pp. 203-227, Cambridge University Press. http://www.jstor.org/stable/181583 Accessed 30 December 2011.
- Radama's Smile: Domestic Challenges to Royal Ideology in Early Nineteenth-century Imerina,Gerald M. Berg in: History in Africa , Vol. 25, (1998), pp. 69-92. Published by: African Studies Association. Article Stable URL: http://www.jstor.org.virtual.anu.edu.au/ stable/3172181. Accessed 312 December 2011.
- Wieber, Norman, Norbert Wiener, Cybernetics or control and communication in the animal and the machine, MIT Press, 1965, ISBN 978-0-262-73009-9, p27.
- John Oldfield: British Anti-Slavery, 17 February 2011. <http://www.bbc.co.uk/history/ british/empire_seapower/antislavery_01.shtml> Accessed 31 December 2011.
- Hitié, Evenor, Histoire de Maurice (Ancienne île de France), Englebrecht 1897. Cabon, Marcel, Rémy Ollier, Editions Mauriciennes, 1965.
- Peerthum, Satteeanund, Le début de l'immigration indienne, in: Le Mauricien, 26 July 1984.
- Colebrook, W.M.G. and Blair, W. Report of the Commissioners of Inquiry Upon the Slave Trade at Mauritius, London 1829 and Eastern Commission, Mauritius Archives IB 6. Quenette, R, Le grand Beaugeard, Mahatma Gandhi Institute, 1991. House of Lords, Hansard 1803-2005. Condition Of The Slaves In The West Indies. HL Deb 08 February 1830 vol 22 cc180-209.
- Biography of Thomas Fowell Buxton at the British historical educational website: < http://www.spartacus.schoolnet.co.uk/REfowell.htm> Accessed 11 February 2012)
- Jeremie, John, Four Essays on Colonial Slavery, J Hatchard, reproduced and made available on the Internet from Goldsmiths' Library of the University of London. London 1831. <http://www.archive.org/details/fouressaysoncol00jere-goog> Accessed 11 February 2012.
- The National Archives, UK, Power, Politics and Protest. The Growth of Political Rights in Britain in the 19th century. The Great Reform Act. <http://www.nationalarchives.gov.uk/education/politics/g6/> Accessed 11 February 2012.
- Blair, Richard Allen, Slaves, freedmen, and indentured laborers in colonial Mauritius, Cambridge: Cambridge University Press, 1999.
- Adriejn d'Epinay, Réflexions sur la mesure administrative qui autorise la création d'une nouvelle banque et l'émission d'un nouveau papier à Maurice et sur les motifs qui l'ont déterminée, Port-Louis, Imprimerie Deglos, 1838, reproduced by Toussaint A, in : Les missions d'Adrien d'Epinay (1830-1834), The General Printing & Stationery CY. Ltd. Port-Louis, Mauritius 1946.
- Report of the Truth and Justice Commission, Vol 1, Government Printing. Port-Louis, November 2011. 535 pages.
- Selvon, Sydney, Des camps aux villages – le cas de Vacoas-Phoenix, in Slavery in South West Indian Ocean, collection of papers presented at a national seminar on slavery in 1984, edited by U. Bissoondoyal and S. B. C. Servansing. Moka, Mauritius: Mahatma Gandhi Institute Press, 1989.
- Clark, G. A ramble round Mauritius with some excursions into the interior of that island; to which is added a familiar description of its fauna and some subjects of its flora. Pp.i-cxxxii in Palmer & Bradshaw, compilers, The Mauritius Register; Historical, official & commercial, corrected to the 30th June 1959. Post Louis: L. Channell.
- Ryan, Vincent William, Mauritius and Madagascar: Journals of an Eight Years' Residence . Seeley Jackson and Halliday, London 1864.
- Jumeer, Musleem, Les affranchissements et les Indiens libres à l'île de France au 18ème siècle (1721-1803), Faculté des Sciences Humaines, Université de Poitiers, 1984).
- Conditions of antebellum slavery 1830 – 1860 , on a website dedicated to Blacks. Aspects of Slavery during the British Administration, in Slavery in South West Indian Ocean, collection of papers presented at a national seminar, edited by U. Bissoondoyal and S. B. C. Servansing. Moka, Mauritius: Mahatma Gandhi Institute Press, 1989.
- Toussaint A, Histoire des Iles Mascareignes, Berger Levrault. Paris 1972. Allen, J. B., Creoles, Indian Immigrants and the Restructuring of Society and Economy in Mauritius, 1721-1835, Ph.D. thesis, University of Illinois, 1983.
- House of Lords, Sessional papers, Session 1837-38,vol. XIV, Slavery Abolition. Copy of a Despatch by Governor Sir William Nicolay, C.B., to Lord Glenelg, 59, Mauritius 25 July 1836.
- Indian Indentured Labourers , The National Archives UK. < http://www.nationalarchives. gov.uk/records/research-guides/indian-indentured-labour.htm> Accessed 14 February 2012.
- Carter, Marina, in: Founding an Island Society: Inter-Ethnic Relationships in the Isle of France; Colouring the Rainbow: Mauritian Society in the Making , Marina Carter (ed.) Port Louis, Mauritius: Centre for Research on Indian Societies, 1998.
- Ducray, Charles Giblot, Histoire de la ville de Curepipe, The General Printing & Stationery Cy. Ltd. 2nd ed. Port-Louis 1950.
- Benoit, Gaëtan, The Afro-Mauritians. An Essay, MGI, Mauritius 1985.
- Council of Government, Minute by Governor Nicolay, 26 June 1838, in Recueil des lois, ordonnances, proclamations, notes et avis du gouvernement publiés à l'île Maurice pendant l'année 1838. Cited Volume 2.XML.html[9/30/2016 8:21:06 AM] also in Vacoas-Phoenix, op cit.
- Peerthum, Satyendra , Gauging the Pulse of Freedom": A Study of Manumission in Mauritius, the Cape Colony, and Jamaica during the Early Nineteenth century: A Comparative Perspective,
- Proceedings of the Demographic Association of Southern Africa (Demsa), Session 3B, 26 September 2002.
- House of Lords, Sessional Papers, Paper laid before the Honourable the Governor General of India in Council by Mr. J. P. Woodcock of the Bengal Civil Service. Presented to the Council Chamber on 7 June 1837 by H.T. Prinsep, Secretary to the Government.
- Peerthum, Satteeanund, V. Annasamy:un esclavagiste indien à Maurice, in Le Mauricien, 15 July 1984.
- Darwin, Charles, The Voyage of the Beagle, Chapter XXI, Mauritius to England, P.F. Collier 1909.
- Peerthum, Satteeanund, L'immigration indienne : l'échec de 1829, in Le Mauricien, 3 October 1984.
- Peerthum, Satteeanund, Portrait de l'immigrant indien, in Le Mauricien, 3 August 1984. House of Lords, Sessional Papers, op cit, Indian Labourers to the Mauritius.
- Bissoondoyal, U and Servansingh. S.B.C. (eds.) Indian Labour Immigration, MGI 1986. Papers presented at the International Conference on Indian Labour Immigration (23-27 October, 1984) held at the Mahatma Gandhi Institute.
- D'Unienville, Raymond M, Tentative socialiste à l'île Maurice (1846-1851), Société de l'histoire de l'Île Maurice, 2009, 178 pages.
- Nath, Dwarka, A History of Indians in Guyana, published by the author, 1970.
- Tinker, Hugh, A New System of Slavery: The Export of Indian Labour Overseas, 1830-1920(London: Oxford University Press, 1974
- Copies of despatches from Sir William Nicolay on the subject of free labour in the Mauritius . 1840. Annexure No. 1 to the governor's despatch dated 21 May 1839.
- House of Lords, Sessional papers, Lord Glenelg to Sir William Nicolay, 20 January 1836. House of Lords, Sessional Papers, Nicolay to Glenelg, 9 September 1837.
- House of Commons Papers, vol. 16, entitled Accounts and Papers, 19 volumes, Session 26 January – 22 June 1841.
- The Mauritius Almanach, 1913. Arrivals and Departures of Indian Immigrants, 1834 to 1912.
- House of Commons: Copies Of Correspondence Relating To The General Condition Of The Mauritius, letter by J.C. Melvill to the Right Hon. George Stevens Byng, M.P. 3 December 1846.Pages 201-203. In: Account and Papers. Colonies: West Indies and Mauritius, 28 vols. Vol. XLIV. Session 18 November 1847 to 5 September 1848.
- In: Bissoondoyal, U, Indians Overseas. The Mauritius Experience. Mahatma Gandhi Institute 1984.
- Memorial addressed To the Right Honorable Lord JOHN RUSSELL, M.P., Her Majesty's Principal Secretary of State for the Colonies, in: Brief exposure of the deplorable condition of the Hill Coolies, in British Guiana and Mauritius, and

of the nefarious means by which they were induced to resort to these Colonies, Pamphlet, London 1840.
- House of Commons Papers. Vol. 39. Gomm to Gladstone. Page 218. House of Commons Papers. Mr. Secretary Gladstone's Despatch, 14 May, No. 38. Ordered to be printed 26 August 1846, No. 691, Part II. Page 216.
- Colonial Land And Emigration Commission, Ninth General Report, June 1849. London: Printed By William Clowes And Sons, Stamford Street, For Her Majesty's Stationery Office.
- House of Lords, Sessional Papers, Vol. XXXI, Reports from Commissioners, etc.1847.
- Palmer & Bradshaw, A History of Mauritius, in: The Mauritius Register. Historical, officicial & commercial, Published by the Authority of Government, L. Channell, Port-Louis 1859.
- House of Commons papers, vol. 39. Gomm to Gladstone, 30 June 1846. House of Commons Papers, Earl Grey to Sir W.M. Gomm, 29 September 1846.
- MP Bingham Baring in: Hansard's Parliamentary Debates, William IV, Volume LXV, page 645.
- Colonial Office. Despatch No. 32 of Governor Sir W. Anderson to Earl Grey dated 15 February 1850.417 Colonial Office. Sir W. Anderson to Earl Grey, Despatch No. 21, 20 May 1850.
- National Archives, Indian Indentured Labourers, <http://www.nationalarchives.gov.uk/ records/research-guides/indian-indentured-labour.htm> Accessed 20 February 2012. House of Commons,
- Parliamentary Papers, vol. 34, page 272. House of Commons, Accounts and Papers, vol. 21, Session 2, Papers Relating to the Mauritius.
- Peerthum, Satteeanund, Maharaj Singh et la fin de l'immigration indienne and Joseph Thomas Hugon, le premier Mauricien qui dénonca les abus du système d'engagement, in Le Mauricien, 1984.
- Mauritius Archives, Reports of the Immigration Department. Plevitz, Loretta de, Restless Energy. A Biography of Adolphe de Plevitz, MGI Press, Mauritius 1987.
- Governor Sir Henry Barkly The Hurricane in The Mauritius, dispatch from Sir H. Barkly to the Duke of Buckingham, of which a copy can be found at <http://paperspast.natlib. govt.nz> as it was reproduced in New Zealand.
- The Earl of Carnavon: Hansard 1803–2005, Indian Immigration.The Coolie Traffic. Motion For A Paper. HL Deb 19 July 1875 vol 225 cc1630-41.
- Plevitz, Adolphe de, The petition of the old immigrants of Mauritius: Presented on the 6th June, 1871, with observations. E. Drenning, 1871.
- "Hero of Mauritius", an article on de Plevitz in the Anti-Slavery and Aborigines' Protection Society, London, Kraus Reprint, Jan 1, 1874 – History,Vols. 3-8, 3d ser.
- Frere, W.E. & Williamson, V.A. A Report of the Royal Commissioners Appointed to Enquire into the Treatment of Immigrants in Mauritius. Presented to Both Houses of Parliament by Command of Her Majesty, 6th Feb. 1875. London William Clares & Sons 1875.
- Sanderson Committee Report, London 1910.
- Encyclopaedia Britannica's Guide to Black History, <http://www.britannica.com/blackhistory/article-24176> Accessed 23 February 2012.
- Baissac, Charles Basile, Récits creoles, contes et nouvelles, H. Oudin, Paris 1884. 428 pages ; Le folklore de l'île Maurice, Maisonneuve et Larose, Paris 1988.
- Pitot, Albert, Creole Patois and Folklore, in Mauritius Illustrated, London 1915.
- Earl Grey, The Colonial Policy of Lord John Russell's Administration , vol.1, Richard Bentley, Publisher in Ordinary to Her Majesty, London 1853. Page 118. Copy of a Despatch from the Governor of Mauritius.
- The Standard, November 15, 1901.
- Virahsawmy, R, in: Indians Overseas: The Mauritian Experience, op cit. 1984; Morcellement and the Emergence of Villages in Mauritius in: R. Dassyne,J. Benoist et al., Regards sur le monde rural mauricien, Port-Louis 1981.
- Hazareesingh, K., Histoire des Indiens à l'île Maurice, Librairie d'Amérique et d'Orient, Paris 1973.
- Blalock, H.M. Jr, Status Consciousness: A Dimensional Analysis, in: Social Forces 1959, University of North Carolina Press.
- Topics in Sociology: Stratification and Social Mobility, <sparknotes.com>.
- NAGAPEN, Amédée, The Indian Christian Community in Mauritius, in: Indians Overseas, Bissoondoyal, U.,
- Pingré, Alexandre-Guy, Courser Venus : voyage scientifique à l'île Rodrigue » fragments du journal de voyage de l'abbé Pingré, Sainte Clotilde (La Réunion) : ARS Terres créoles and Rose Hill (Maurice) : Ed. de l'océan Indien, 1993.
- Emrith, Moomtaz, History of Muslims in Mauritius, ELP, Mauritius 1994.
- Flemyng, Rev. Francis Patrick, Mauritius, or The Isle of France ,Being an Account of the Island, its History, Geography, Products, and Inhabitants, London 1862.
- Pandit Cashinath Kistoe, pionnier du mouvement Arya Samaj. In Le Mauricien, 5 June 1984.
- The Sessional Papers of the House of Lords, Gomm to Earl Grey, General Report on the State of the Colony, March 6, 1847, page 194.
- Anderson, Daniel Elie, M.D. The Epidemics Of Mauritius With A Descriptive And Historical Account Of The Island, H.K. Lewis & Co. London 1918.
- Nobel Prize Sir Ronald Ross wrote on the deadly malaria disease in The Report on the Prevention of Malaria in Mauritius, Waterlow and Sons, London, 1908. Report of the Committee. Volume 2.XML.html[9/30/2016 8:21:06 AM]
- Government to investigate the history and particular conditions of the cholera epidemic of 1954. Port-Louis 1856.
- Chadwick, Osbert, Report on the general sanitation of Mauritius : with recommendations for the improvement of Port Louis and Curepipe and other villages, Indian camps &c. Port-Louis., 1891.
- Titmuss, Richard M., and Abel-Smith, Brian, Social Policies and Population Growth in Mauritius. Report to the Governor of Mauritius. Frank Cass & Co. Guildford and London 1968. (The Titmuss Report)
- Swettenham, Frank Athelstane, Report of the Mauritius Royal Commission, 1909: presented to both Houses of Parliament by command of His Majesty, H.M.S.O. 1910. (The Swettenham Report).
- Balfour Andrew, Sir, Report on Medical Matters in Mauritius, Acting Government Printer, Mauritius 1921.
- Jadin, Fernand, Vopyage aux Iles Mascareignes (Réunion et Maurice), fait en 1890, Boehm, Montpellier 1890.
- Imsam, Patrick and Minoiu, Camelia, Mauritius, a Competitive Assessment, International Monetary Fund Working Paper, September 2008. 419
- Mauritius Chamber of Agriculture: Rouillard, Guy, Histoire de la Canne à sucre à l'Ile Maurice, 1989, and The Mauritius Chamber of Agriculture (1853-1953).
- Wall Street Journal: England Buys Mauritius Sugar Crop Date: 1920-06-12; Raw Sugar Market Steady Date: 1920-07-28; Sugar Prices Show Marked Decline From 1920 Prices Date: 1921-06-07,
- North-Coombes, A, A History of Sugar Production in Mauritius, 1993; and Rouillard G, op cit.
- Walter, A., The Sugar Industry, Mauritius Illustrated, London 1915. Le Journal de l'Ile, Le premier savant de couleur libre de Bourbon. <http://www.interpc.fr/mapage/fe.hoarau/perso/histoire/gouverneur/geoffroy.htm> Accessed 27 February 2012. British Parliament, Reports from Committees 1847-8. Despatch From Earl Grey to Sir W.M. Gomm.
- Strafford, John, Our Fight For Democracy. A History of Democracy in the United Kingdom. J. Strafford Holdings, London 2009.
- National Archives UK: The Struggle for Democracy. Getting the Vote. <http://www.nationalarchives.gov.uk> Accessed 26 February 2012.
- Le Cernéen, 11 October 1884.
- Will, H.A., 1895, in The English Historical Review, vol. 31, No. 321 (Oct. 1966), pp. 693-716, Oxford University Press.
- Sookdeo Bissoondoyal (1908-1977). L'Express, 26 September 2008. Hansard, HC Deb 19 May 1881 vol 261 cc802-3 802
- Hansard, HC Deb 08 August 1884 vol 292 cc263-4 263 and HC Deb 08 May 1884 vol 287 cc1670-1 1670.
- Matsugi, Takashi & Oberhauser, Alois, Interactions between economy and ecology, Duncker & Humblot, 1994; Grove, Richard H., Green Imperialism: Colonial Expansion, Tropical Island Edens and the Origins of Environmentalism,

1600-1860, Cambridge University Press, Mar 29, 1996.

- Walter, Albert, The sugar industry of Mauritius: a study in correlation. including a scheme of insurance of the cane crop against damage caused by cyclones, A.L. Humphries, 1910.
- Madden, A.F., Fieldhouse, D.K., and Darwin, J., Select Documents on the Constitutional History of the British Empire and Commonwealth, Vol. 7, Greenwood Press (USA 1991), Minute by Andrew Pearson (21st December 1882, CO 167/603)) on Broome to Kimberley (31st October No. 519).
- Government Notice, 18th of January 1832, Port-Louis. Mauritius Archives. Broome to Kimberley, no. 519, 31 Oct. 1882. CO 167/603. Minute by D., 13 Jan. 1883; and Derby to Pope Hennessy, 1 June 1883. Reprinted in c. 4074, p. 60. Also: Madden and others, op cit. Lieut-Governor Sir Frederick Napier Broome to the Earl of Kimberley, 312 October 1882.
- Bruce, Charles, Sir, The broad stone of empire: problems of crown colony administration, with records of personal experience, Macmillan 1910.
- CO documents: Musgrave to Kimberley, Conf., 5 Dec. 1882. CO I 37/507. Minute by R. G. W. H., 28 Dec. 1882; and Broome to Kimberley, no. 408, 4 Sept. 1882. CO 167/602. Minute by K., 2 Nov. 1882.
- Mauritius Council of Government, Debates in the Council of Government on Lord Derby's despatch relative to the reform of the Constitution, 1884-85. Published 1885. Pope-Hennessy, James, Verandah: some episodes in the crown colonies: 1867-1889, G. Allen and Unwin 1964.
- Napal, Doojendraduth, British Mauritius, 1810-1848, ELP 1984. Curieuse victoire des Démocrates en 1886, in L'Express, 20 March 1982.
- Madden, Select Documents on the constitutional history of the British Empire and Commonwealth: Herbert's minutes of: 7 novemenbr 1987 on No. 345: C.O. 137/532; and of 20 June 1895 on No. 186: C.O. 295/363; Wingfield's minute of 20 June 1985, No. 186: C.O. 295/363; and Chamberlain's despatch to Governor Sir Charles Bruce in Mauritius dated 28 February 1900.
- House of Commons: The Mauritius – Constitution Of The Council – And Sir John Pope Hennessy, HC Deb 29 July 1887 vol 318 cc516-8.
- Mauritius Legislative Council. Debate, 4th November 1887. Legislative Council. Debate, 1884.
- Mauritius Legislative Council. Debate 20th September 1887. Laurent, The Hon. Eugène, from Biographical Notes, Mauritius Illustrated, on the leaders of Mauritius in 1914. Page 438.
- Bissoondoyal, U., Gandhi and Mauritius and Other Essays, Mahatma Gandhi Institute, Mauritius 1988.
- The Standard and Le Journal de Maurice, various articles on Gandhi's visit during the period 30 October to 19 November 1901.
- Chazal, Malcolm de, Petrusmok: mythe, Éditions Léo Scheer, Mar 24, 2004 - 501 pages. Ramsurrun, Pahlad, Arya Samaj Movement in Mauritius. Beau Bassin, Mauritius 1970.
- Beejadhur, Anauth, Les Indiens à l'Ile Maurice, La Typographie Mauricienne, Port-Louis 1935.
- Van Der Veer, Peter, Religious Nationalism: Hindus and Muslims in India, University of California Press, 1994.
- Afisi, Oseni Taiwo, Tracing contemporary Africa's conflict situation to colonialism: A breakdown of communication among natives, Philosophical Papers and Reviews Vol. 1 (4), pp. 059-066, October, 2009, Academic Journals, Department of Philosophy, Faculty of Arts, Lagos State University, Ojo, Lagos, Nigeria. Web:< http://www.academicjournals.org/ PPR>
- African Proconsuls. European Governors in Africa . L.H. Gann & Peter Duignan, eds. New York/London/Stanford. The Free PressCollier Macmillan Publishers & Hoover Institution. 548 pages.

Contents

Contents

Introduction to Volume 2   5

From the 19th century to the 20th : The way we were   5

Chapter 35   7

The rise and fall of the Democrats and the Liberals   7

Motion for 'universal suffrage' by Edgar Antelme   7

Dr. Eugène Laurent and Manilal Mangalall Doctor   9

Prominent representatives of the 'Francos'   9

Dr. Eugène Laurent unites the Indo-Creole masses   12

Gandhi, as he was when he visited Mauritius and later in life   13

Governor Chancellor   16

The Mauritius railways in the old days   16

Political and religious matters in the early 20th century 17

Class-based political agitation for democracy on the rise   18

1st decade of the 20th C.: Intense political campaigning   20

Chapter 36   26

More failures for the anti-Oligarchs   26

London worried by retrocession to France and Indian 'terrorists'   28

Anti-Oligarchs 29

The Retrocession Movement   30

Retrocession and the rise of ethnic prejudice   31

The true nature of the retrocession movement   31

First Indo-Mauritians in the Legislative Council   33

Chapter 37   36

Class, community and elections in the 1920's   36

Dr. Edgar Laurent attacks anti-Indian slogans   39

Dr. Maurice Curé: "No great man in this world will (...) make me bend.""   40

The Aapravasi Ghat, World Heritage Site   43

Basdeo Bissoondoyal, a national figure 43

Chapter 38   45

The revolt of the "lambs"   45

United they stood   47

Different political backgrounds for two future Prime Ministers 48

Historical documents: Labour Party alerts the UK and India 49

1930s to 1960s: The pace of History 'accelerates' 50

Dr. Maurice Curé in action 51

The contents of the 1937 Labour Party telegrams 52

The 1937 unrest across Mauritius 54

After the Hooper Commission 58

Bede Clifford severely criticised in Westminster 58

The 1937 disturbances seen by a UK news correspondent in Mauritius 59

Curé and Bissoondoyal blast Dr. Ramgoolam's relations with Governor Clifford 60

The British want a communal system of representation 63

Raoul Rivet, politician and journalist 66

The Old Port-Louis Theatre 66

Chapter 39 67

The end of the status quo 67

The governor's communalistic agenda 69

Jules Koenig: a man of the masses who went astray 70

Ramgoolam's courts the Mauritius Labour Party as franchise is enlarged 72

The British 'worried' by inter-communal cooperation and friendliness in Mauritius 75

New constitution approved for enlarged franchise 75

No Muslim elected, only 1 nominated on 12 appointees 76

Bede Clifford, the Governor who repressed the struggle for freedom 78

Chapter 40 79

The march to Independence (1) 79

The rise of ethnic politics: N.M.U. attacks Ramgoolam and Koenig 79

The NMU 'factor' in Mauritian politics 79

Jules Koenig's mistake: opposing universal suffrage 82

Razack Mohamed's deal with the Labour Party 83

Ramgoolam and the sugar barons 83

Rozemont, the man who paved the way for Ramgoolam 85

Figures of the 1940s and 1950s 87

London worried by retrocession to France and Indian 'terrorists' 88

The Retrocession Movement   89

Retrocession and the rise of ethnic prejudice   90

The true nature of the retrocession movement   90

First Indo-Mauritians in the Legislative Council   92

Makers of history   93

The 1937 disturbances seen by a UK news correspondent in Mauritius   95

Curé and Bissoondoyal blast Dr. Ramgoolam's relations with Governor Clifford   96

Bede Clifford: a highly controversial British Governor   98

The British want a communal system of representation   99

Chapter 41   101

Independence of Mauritius still to be completed   101

In 2015 Mauritius won a case at international level against UK   101

Chagos, Tromelin: Mauritian territory from British Conquest   101

Chagos, a priority in the Mauritius Parliament from 2015   103

The rape of the Chagos: Double responsibility of Mauritian leaders and the Anglo-American alliance   103

The Chagos affair, based on declassified official documents   104

"Intimidated SSR facing Wilson   105

"British policy of continued dismemberment   105

The uphill battle to get back the Chagos   105

The Chagos, integral part of Mauritius   106

The global perspective: the Chagos and the deadly Polaris missiles   107

Chagos deal "outside the process of decolonisation"; population "to be entirely removed"   109

Reactions in the Mauritius Legislative Assembly   110

Mauritian documents on the Chagos excision   111

The establishment of a marine park: 'deceit' used   114

"Je Ne Regrette Rien"   115

BIOT: More Than Just Diego Garcia   115

Angry reactions in Mauritius   116

Chagos and Tromelin: neo-colonial tactics defying international law   116

From 2006 to 2012, more developments in the Chagos affair (see also Chapter 41):   116

How the French seized Tromelin from Mauritius   117

Tromelin, scene of one of the worst tragedies of this part of the Indian Ocean   118

The Franco-Mauritian controversy   119

Tromelin: the Franco-Mauritian compromise: 119

Chapter 42   121

The march to independence resumes amidst controversy   121

MLP, CAM, IFB ask for reserved seats, PMSD for PR 121

A big lie   121

Back home, to ethnic politics   122

Summary of the constitutional proposals after the London talks (sub-titles by author):Human rights, Judicature, Ombudsman   123

All parties agree on Anglo-Mauritian defence agreement   124

The Banwell Report: the demands of the political parties   124

I.F.B.: 'Temporary'reservation of seats for Muslims and Chinese   125

The Banwell Report: main recommendations   125

The Banwell Report: protests from 3 out of the 4 political parties   126

John Stonehouse in Mauritius: Proportional representation scrapped   126

Hindu candidates who stood against independence   127

Supreme Court quashes Legislature's legality; royal intervention prevents crisis   128

Tension rises, date of general elections fixed   128

Victory of the pro-independence coalition Labour/CAM/IFB 129

Foreign observers: elections were not so ethnic in character   129

The January 1968 racial riots   130

Independence Day: intense emotion at the Champ de Mars   131

Chapter 43   133

Priorities: nation building and the economy
St. Guillaume: Duval was for independence, 'deep within himself'   133

PMSD member seconds Independence motion 133

Western geostrategy and the Labour/PMSD coalition 134

France-Nato: secret arrangements that include Mauritius   134

'Terrifying' population explosion, large scale unemployment and poverty   136

Malnutrition, disease, cyclones and housing crises   137

Cyclones Alix & Carol, 1960: in 2 months12% of the population become refugees   137

Economic situation at the time of independence   138

Industrialisation goes hand in hand with a political coalition 139

The 'economic miracle' of the 1970s   140

1936-1968: The long road to Independence   141

14, 000 Mauritians migrate to other countries, including Australia, from 1966-1972   142

Chapter 44   145

A new political force emerges   145

Chapter 45   149

Agitated times - and political assassination   149

MMM's first electoral victory: Triolet-Pamplemousses 149

The wage freeze blasted by the MMM/GWF   150

The coalition government strikes back   151

Chapter 46   153

Successful economic diversification   153

Diplomacy: a key element of the economic revival   153

Highs and lows of a tumultuous decade – the 1970s   154

The social scene remains troubled   156

Government instability sets in, coalition breaks up   158

The PMSD 'hoisted by its own petard'   158

MMM shadow Prime Minister: Bérenger steps down, Jugnauth steps in   159

Chapter 47   161

From May 1975 student revolt to the 1976 general election   161

Former Marxist party turned into a major national electoral force   161

The MMM/PMSD common front   162

1982 election results by main parties   164

The Met's list of the worst cyclones to hit Mauritius from 1832   166

Chapter 48   167

Years of crisis: 1977-1983 (1)   167

Labour splits, the dissidents form a new party, the PSM   167

Alleged 'affairs' that shook the political arena   167

MMM unaffected by setbacks   168

Labour weakened further by dissidence   169

Economic downturn at the end of the 1970s   170

Labour's partner PMSD splits   170

Chapter 49   173

Years of crisis: 1977-1983 (2)   173

Historic first 60-0 and aftermath   174

Cracks in the opposition's ranks   174

Labour hires an American electoral consultant   174

The first 60-0 of political history: an MMM-PSM tsunami   175

Jugnauth and Boodhoo question Bérenger's economic policies   176

First major crisis in the MMM-PSM regime   176

The MMM-PSM government explodes   177

An explosive mix: ideology, ethnic politics, social and economic issues   178

The demise of the MSM-PSM government   180

Fresh elections in August 1983: Jugnauth wins   180

A very tense electoral campaign   181

Positive views on the 1982-83 MMM-PSM government   183

Instability of the new government but economy grows   183

Project of republic dropped   184

The making of the 'Mauritius miracle'   185

Death of SSR   186

The Amsterdam scandal rocks the government   187

The 1987 snap elections   188

More dissent in government   189

The arrest of Sir Gaëtan Duval   190

The MSM-MMM alliance takes the nation by surprise   190

Chapter 51   195

From the 20th to the 21st century – 1991 to 2005 (1)   195

Politics: the issue of electoral fraud and other irregularities   196

The death penalty   196

A singular surprise for everybody   197

The party financing issue   197

Other corruption matters   198

Mauritian citizenship   198

Free radios at last   199

The political scene from 1991 to 2005   199

Court finds 'colourable' device to oust Ramgoolam   199

The MMM splits and joins Labour   200

The PMSD joins Jugnauth   201

Jugnauth has to call elections   201

Chapter 52   205

From the 20th to the 21 century – 1991-2005 (2)   205

Some crucial issues: 1995-2005 205

Law and order   205

Drug offences on the rise   206

The environment with regard to economic imperatives: a snapshot   206

The failure of the Labour/MMM Alliance   210

Local government is not autonomous as they are in greater democracies   210

More transparent voting, judiciary reform   210

Economic Crime Office   211

Racial riots in 1999   211

The demise of a regime 212

The Sabapathee affair   212

A New MSM/MMM Alliance in 2000 212

'Elections claires et nettes': Ramgoolam goes to snap elections 214

The rise and fall of the MSM/MMM: 2000-2005   214

Weakening of MSM/MMM alliance as election looms 217

Ethnic politics: more pronounced than in the 1960s   220

"The FPTP frequently produces results which are grossly disproportionate"   222

Alliance Sociale wins all 5 municipalities   222

Chapter 54   225

The 21st century: serious threats from global warming   225

Maurice, Ile durable: Trying to avert disaster   226

The Mauritius environmental evolution up to 2015   226

Land use, Forestry and Agriculture   226

Forest area is decreasing   226

Area harvested under sugar cane cultivation goes up   227

Energy and Greenhouse gas (GHG)   227

Total primary energy requirement increases   227

Net carbon dioxide emission increases   227

Carbon dioxide (CO2) emission from the energy sector (fuel combustion activities)   227

Energy industries (electricity generation)   227

Transport industries   228

Manufacturing industries   228

Temperature   228

Water   228

Waste   228

Complaints   229

Environmental Impact Assessment Licences and Preliminary Report Approvals   229

Chapter 55   231

2005-2012: Burning local and global issues and challenges   231

Mauritian membership of SADC, COMESA and IOC   232

IOC: Comorian opposition to French 'neo-colonial' action   232

U.S. military cooperation to 'democratise' Africa's governance   233

Highs and lows of the economy: the ministers of finance battle it out   233

Bérenger (Budget Speech 2003-2004):   233

Pravind Jugnauth (Budget Speech 2005-2006)   234

Rama Sithanen (Budget 2010)   235

Xavier-Luc Duval (Budget 2012) – First budget of the PMSD   236

Present day health problems waiting to be solved   237

Chapter 56   241

2005   241

TSUNAMI: THE AFTERMATH   241

'ECONOMIC TSUNAMI' THREATENS   241

CHALLENGE TO ELECTORAL ETHNIC IDENTIFICATION   241

WOMEN AND POLITICS   242

EDUCATION: TWO MORE KEY MEASURES   242

SIDS: SMALL ISLANDS UNITE   242

FERNEY VALLEY CONTROVERSY   242

SURVEY OF CITY'S CHRONIC TRAFFIC JAMS   243

'PLURALISM WORKS'   243

MAURITIUS MOURNS POPE JOHN-PAUL II   243

NEW GOVERNMENT IN ACTION   243

DODO REMAINS DISCOVERED   243

2006   243

CHAGOSSIANS' EMOTIONAL VISIT TO THEIR ISLANDS   243

2007   244

AND NOW AGALEGA?   244

CHIKUNGUNYA: A TERRIBLE EPIDEMIC STRIKES   245

PRICES: CONSUMERS CONCERNED   245

'IDENTITY-BASED POLITICS": "CHALLENGE FOR GOVERNANCE"   245

THE CAMPEMENT TAX ISSUE   245

LE MORNE: HERITAGE SITE   245

POLITICS: SOME MAJOR CONTROVERSIES ERUPT   246

WASTE DISPOSAL NIGHMARE   246

MORE SUGAR FACTORIES CLOSE   246

CONTROVERSY   246

2008   247

CHIKUNGUNYA KILLS   247

WOMEN EMPOWERMENT   247

EQUAL OPPORTUNITIES ACT   247

FATHER GRÉGOIRE'S BIG CROWD   247

PRB REPORT GIVES WAGE HIKE: 36.8% AVERAGE   248

HISTORIC FIRST MAURITIAN OLYMPIC MEDAL   248

BHEENICK, LUTCHMEENARAIDOO: DIFFERENT VIEWS ON GOLD   248

First Mauritian to win the Nobel Prize 248

STIMULUS PACKAGE TO FACE CRISIS   248

2009   249

POLITICS : DEPARTURES   249

TROMELIN: BOOLELL REAFFIRMS MAURITIUS SOVEREIGNTY   249

2010   249

POLITICS: DEBATE OVER A LABOUR/MMM ALLIANCE   249

DIPLOMACY: GORDON BROWN RENEGES ON HIS PROMISE   249

MAURITIANS PERISH IN HAITI EARTHQUAKE   249

AFRICAN PEER MECHANISM REVIEW AND 'COALITION POLITICS'   250

DEATH OF VICE-PRESIDENT CHETTIAR   250

2011-2012   250

The water crisis: one of the worst of national history   251

THE MEDPOINT CLINIC 'AFFAIR'   251

Looming threats for the economy from global crisis   251

2012: Overhauling the Constitution and political system   252

FORMER PRESIDENT JUGNAUTH ENTERS THE POLITICAL ARENA   253

Heads of State of Mauritius from Independence to 2017   255

Heads of State of Mauritius from Independence to 2017   255

Chapter 57   257

The demise of an unpopular Labour/PMSD regime   257

and a serious democratic deficit yet to be corrected in 2017   257

% and no. of seats obtained by winning and runner-up parties 2000-2014   257

2013   258

A fundamental issue raised at the U.N. on ethnicity and politics   259

The deadly floods of 2013   261

Corruption, a "cultural" trait - dixit lawyer Parvesh Lallah   261

LIGHT RAIL: 262

SOME SUCCESS, MULTIPLE FAILURES: 262

CONTROVERSIAL ID CARDS: 262

A year to be remembered as that of the Mauritian 'Game of Thrones' - a year of intrigue, treason, treachery and deceit   264

Chapter 58   267

2015-2017:   267

Independence of police, relations money-politics put to test   267

Other headlines of 2015-2017: 270

Ramgoolam's coffers: 270

The Terre Rouge-Verdun motorway: 270

New president and vice-president		270

Mauritian pilgrims die in Mecca		271

Pravind Jugnauth, MSM leader resigns from Cabinet	271

Conflict between government and the DPP		271

The 'Bhadain Laws' controversyMP D. Selvon resigns, bills then amended		271

Chapter 59		275

2016-2017		275

21st Century: Quo Vadis Mauritius?		275

Priorities: the economy, democracy, environment, Chagos, Tromelin and other latest developments		275

Economic 'miracle' promise revisited by new Finance Minister	275

The challenge to increase the democratic space 275

An environmental threat of phenomenal proportions		276

Change of Prime Minister sparks controversies		277

New leader of Opposition: Xavier Duval (PMSD)		277

The Chagos Archipelago: completing decolonisation at last?		277

Current conomic matters		279

APPENDICES		280

APPENDIX 1		280

2011 (LATEST) HOUSING CENSUS – MAIN RESULTS		280

APPENDIX 2 282

OUTER ISLANDS - MAPS, IMAGES, HISTORY 282

History of the Outer Islands of Mauritius		283

Rodrigues		283

Agalega		287

The Chagos Archipelago		289

Tromelin Island		293

"MAURITIAN" BUILDING FOUND IN TROMELIN		294

Bibliography, references and sources		295

Printed in Great Britain
by Amazon